Varieties of English 4
Africa, South and Southeast Asia

Varieties of English 4

Africa, South and Southeast Asia

Edited by
Rajend Mesthrie

Mouton de Gruyter · Berlin · New York

Mouton de Gruyter (formerly Mouton, The Hague)
is a Division of Walter de Gruyter GmbH & Co. KG, Berlin.

♾ Printed on acid-free paper which falls within the guidelines of the
ANSI to ensure permanence and durability.

Library of Congress Cataloging-in-Publication Data

Africa, South and Southeast Asia / edited by Rajend Mesthrie.
   p. cm. − (Varieties of English ; 4)
   Includes bibliographical references and index.
   ISBN 978-3-11-019638-2 (pbk. : alk. paper)
   1. English language − Variation − Africa.   2. English language −
Dialects − Africa.   3. English language − Variation − South Asia
4. English language − Dialects − South Asia   5. English language −
Variation − Asia, Southeast.   6. English language − Dialects − Asia,
Southeast.   I. Mesthrie, Rajend.
   PE3401.A37 2008
   427'.96−dc22

                2007045287

Bibliographic information published by the Deutsche Nationalbibliothek

The Deutsche Nationalbibliothek lists this publication in the Deutsche Nationalbibliografie;
detailed bibliographic data are available in the Internet at http://dnb.d-nb.de.

ISBN 978-3-11-019638-2

Cover design: Martin Zech, Bremen.
          Imagery provided by Google Earth/TerraMetrics, NASA.
Typesetting: Dörlemann Satz GmbH & Co. KG, Lemförde.
Printing and binding: AZ Druck und Datentechnik GmbH, Kempten (Allgäu).
Printed in Germany.

Contents

Contents of companion volumes viii

Abbreviations xvi

List of features: Phonology and phonetics xix
Edgar W. Schneider

List of features: Morphology and syntax xxv
Bernd Kortmann

General introduction 1
Bernd Kortmann and Edgar W. Schneider

General references 8

Introduction: varieties of English in Africa and South and Southeast
Asia 23
Rajend Mesthrie

Phonology

Nigerian English: phonology 35
Ulrike B. Gut

Nigerian Pidgin English: phonology 55
Ben Elugbe

Ghanaian English: phonology 67
Magnus Huber

Ghanaian Pidgin English: phonology 93
Magnus Huber

Liberian Settler English: phonology 102
John Victor Singler

Cameroon English: phonology 115
Augustin Simo Bobda

Cameroon Pidgin English (Kamtok): phonology
Thaddeus Menang 133

East African English (Kenya, Uganda, Tanzania): phonology 150
Josef Schmied

White South African English: phonology 164
Sean Bowerman

Black South African English: phonology 177
Bertus van Rooy

Indian South African English: phonology 188
Rajend Mesthrie

Cape Flats English: phonology 200
Peter Finn

St. Helena English: phonology 223
Sheila Wilson

Indian English: phonology 231
Ravinder Gargesh

Pakistani English: phonology 244
Ahmar Mahboob and Nadra Huma Ahmar

Singapore English: phonology 259
Lionel Wee

Malaysian English: phonology 278
Loga Baskaran

Philippine English: phonology 292
Ma. Lourdes G. Tayao

Synopsis: the phonology of English in Africa and South and Southeast
Asia 307
Rajend Mesthrie

Morphology and Syntax

Nigerian English: morphology and syntax 323
M.A. Alo and Rajend Mesthrie

Nigerian Pidgin English: morphology and syntax 340
Nicholas Faraclas

Ghanaian English: morphology and syntax 368
Magnus Huber and Kari Dako

Ghanaian Pidgin English: morphology and syntax 381
Magnus Huber

Liberian Settler English: morphology and syntax 385
John Victor Singler

Cameroon English: morphology and syntax 416
Paul Mbangwana

Cameroon Pidgin English (Kamtok): morphology and syntax 428
Miriam Ayafor

East African English (Kenya, Uganda, Tanzania): morphology and
syntax 451
Josef Schmied

White South African English: morphology and syntax 472
Sean Bowerman

Black South African English: morphology and syntax 488
Rajend Mesthrie

Indian South African English: morphology and syntax 501
Rajend Mesthrie

Cape Flats English: morphology and syntax 521
Kay McCormick

St. Helena English: morphology and syntax 535
Sheila Wilson and Rajend Mesthrie

Indian English: syntax 546
Rakesh M. Bhatt

Butler English: morphology and syntax 563
Priya Hosali

Pakistani English: morphology and syntax 578
Ahmar Mahboob

Singapore English: morphology and syntax 593
Lionel Wee

Malaysian English: morphology and syntax 610
Loga Baskaran

Synopsis: morphological and syntactic variation in Africa and South
and Southeast Asia 624
Rajend Mesthrie

Index of subjects 636
Index of varieties and languages 652

Contents of volume 1

Contents of companion volumes vii

Abbreviations xvi

List of features: Phonology and phonetics xix
Edgar W. Schneider

List of features: Morphology and syntax xxv
Bernd Kortmann

General introduction 1
Bernd Kortmann and Edgar W. Schneider

General references 8

Introduction: varieties of English in the British Isles 23
Bernd Kortmann and Clive Upton

Phonology

English spoken in Orkney and Shetland: phonology 35
Gunnel Melchers

Scottish English: phonology 48
Jane Stuart-Smith

Irish English: phonology 71
Raymond Hickey

Welsh English: phonology 105
Robert Penhallurick

English dialects in the North of England: phonology 122
Joan Beal

The English West Midlands: phonology 145
Urszula Clark

The dialect of East Anglia 178
Peter Trudgill

The dialects in the South of England: phonology 194
Ulrike Altendorf and Dominic Watt

Channel Island English: phonology 223
Heinrich Ramisch

Received Pronunciation 237
Clive Upton

British Creole: phonology 253
Peter L. Patrick

Synopsis: phonological variation in the British Isles 269
Clive Upton

Morphology and Syntax

English spoken in Orkney and Shetland: morphology, syntax and
lexicon 285
Gunnel Melchers

Scottish English: morphology and syntax 299
Jim Miller

Irish English: morphology and syntax 328
Markku Filppula

Welsh English: morphology and syntax 360
Robert Penhallurick

English dialects in the North of England: morphology and syntax 373
Joan Beal

The dialect of East Anglia: morphology and syntax 404
Peter Trudgill

English dialects in the Southwest: morphology and syntax 417
Susanne Wagner

The varieties of English spoken in the Southeast of England:
morphology and syntax 440
Lieselotte Anderwald

British Creole: morphology and syntax 463
Mark Sebba

Synopsis: morphological and syntactic variation in the British Isles 478
Bernd Kortmann

Index of subjects 497
Index of varieties and languages 510

Contents of volume 2

Contents of companion volumes viii

Abbreviations xvi

List of features: Phonology and phonetics xix
Edgar W. Schneider

List of features: Morphology and syntax xxv
Bernd Kortmann

General introduction 1
Bernd Kortmann and Edgar W. Schneider

General references 8

Introduction: varieties of English in the Americas and the Caribbean . . . 23
Edgar W. Schneider

Phonology

Standard American English pronunciation 37
William A. Kretzschmar, Jr.

New England: phonology 52
Naomi Nagy and Julie Roberts

New York, Philadelphia, and other northern cities: phonology 67
Matthew J. Gordon

Rural Southern white accents 87
Erik R. Thomas

The urban South: phonology 115
Jan Tillery and Guy Bailey

The West and Midwest: phonology 129
Matthew J. Gordon

English in Canada: phonology 144
Charles Boberg

Newfoundland English: phonology 161
Sandra Clarke

African American Vernacular English: phonology 181
Walter F. Edwards

Gullah: phonology 192
Tracey L. Weldon

Cajun Vernacular English: phonology 208
Sylvie Dubois and Barbara M. Horvath

Chicano English: phonology 219
Otto Santa Ana and Robert Bayley

Bahamian English: phonology 239
Becky Childs and Walt Wolfram

Jamaican Creole and Jamaican English: phonology 256
Hubert Devonish and Otelemate G. Harry

Eastern Caribbean English-derived language varieties: phonology 290
Michael Aceto

Bajan: phonology 312
Renée Blake

The creoles of Trinidad and Tobago: phonology 320
Valerie Youssef and Winford James

Suriname creoles: phonology 339
Norval Smith and Vinije Haabo

Synopsis: phonological variation in the Americas and the Caribbean ... 383
Edgar W. Schneider

Morphology and Syntax

Colloquial American English: grammatical features 401
Thomas E. Murray and Beth Lee Simon

Appalachian English: morphology and syntax 428
Michael B. Montgomery

Rural and ethnic varieties in the Southeast: morphology and syntax 468
Walt Wolfram

Newfoundland English: morphology and syntax 492
Sandra Clarke

Urban African American Vernacular English: morphology and syntax .. 510
Walt Wolfram

Earlier African American English: morphology and syntax 534
Alexander Kautzsch

Gullah: morphology and syntax 551
Salikoko S. Mufwene

Chicano English: morphology and syntax 572
Robert Bayley and Otto Santa Ana

Bahamian English: morphology and syntax 591
Jeffrey Reaser and Benjamin Torbert

Jamaican Creole: morphology and syntax 609
Peter L. Patrick

Eastern Caribbean English-derived language varieties: morphology and
syntax 645
Michael Aceto

The creoles of Trinidad and Tobago: morphology and syntax 661
Winford James and Valerie Youssef

Surinamese creoles: morphology and syntax 693
Donald Winford and Bettina Migge

Belize and other central American varieties: morphology and syntax . . . 732
Geneviève Escure

Synopsis: morphological and syntactic variation in the Americas
and the Caribbean 763
Edgar W. Schneider

Index of subjects 777
Index of varieties and languages 796

Contents of volume 3

Tribute   vii

Contents of companion volumes   xii

Abbreviations   xx

List of features: Phonology and phonetics xxiii
Edgar W. Schneider

List of features: Morphology and syntax   xxix
Bernd Kortmann

General introduction   1
Bernd Kortmann and Edgar W. Schneider

General references   8

Introduction: varieties of English in the Pacific and Australasia   23
Kate Burridge and Bernd Kortmann

Phonology

New Zealand English: phonology   39
Laurie Bauer and Paul Warren

Regional and social differences in New Zealand: phonology   64
Elizabeth Gordon and Margaret Maclagan

Maori English: phonology   77
Paul Warren and Laurie Bauer

Australian English: phonology   89
Barbara M. Horvath

Regional characteristics of Australian English: phonology 111
David Bradley

Australian creoles and Aboriginal English: phonetics and phonology . . . 124
Ian G. Malcolm

Bislama: phonetics and phonology 142
Terry Crowley

Solomon Islands Pijin: phonetics and phonology 164
Christine Jourdan and Rachel Selbach

Tok Pisin in Papua New Guinea: phonology 188
Geoff P. Smith

Hawai'i Creole: phonology 210
Kent Sakoda and Jeff Siegel

Fiji English: phonology 234
Jan Tent and France Mugler

Norfolk Island-Pitcairn English: phonetics and phonology 267
John Ingram and Peter Mühlhäusler

Synopsis: phonetics and phonology of English spoken in the Pacific
and Australasian region 292
Kate Burridge

Morphology and Syntax

New Zealand English: morphosyntax 305
Marianne Hundt, Jennifer Hay and Elizabeth Gordon

Australian English: morphology and syntax 341
Peter Collins and Pam Peters

Australian Vernacular English: some grammatical characteristics 362
Andrew Pawley

Hypocoristics in Australian English 398
Jane Simpson

Australian creoles and Aboriginal English: morphology and syntax 415
Ian G. Malcolm

Bislama: morphology and syntax 444
Terry Crowley

Solomon Islands Pijin: morphology and syntax 467
Christine Jourdan

Tok Pisin: morphology and syntax 488
Geoff Smith

Hawai'i Creole: morphology and syntax 514
Kent Sakoda and Jeff Siegel

Fiji English: morphology and syntax 546
France Mugler and Jan Tent

Norfolk Island-Pitcairn English (Pitkern Norfolk): morphology and
syntax 568
Peter Mühlhäusler

Synopsis: morphological and syntactic variation in the Pacific
and Australasia 583
Kate Burridge

Index of subjects 601
Index of varieties and languages 616

Abbreviations

AAVE	African American Vernacular English
AbE/C/P	(Australian) Aboriginal English / Creole / Pidgin
AfBahE	Afro-Bahamian English
AfkE	Afrikaans English
AmE	American English
AnBahE	Anglo-Bahamian English
AppE	Appalachian English
AusE/VE/C	Australian English/Vernacular English/Creoles
BahE	Bahamian English
Baj	Bajan (Barbadian Creole)
BelC	Belizean Creole
BIE	Bay Islands English (Honduras)
BrC	British Creole
BrE	British English (= EngE + ScE + WelE)
ButlE	Butler English (India)
CajE	Cajun English
CAmC	Central American Creoles (Belize, Miskito, Limón, etc.)
CamP/E	Cameroon Pidgin/English
CanE	Canadian English
CarE	Caribbean English
Car(E)C	Caribbean (English-lexicon) Creoles
CFE	Cape Flats English
ChcE	Chicano English
ChnP	Chinese Pidgin English
CollAmE	Colloquial American English
CollSgE	Colloquial Singapore English
EAfE	East African English
EMarC	Eastern Maroon Creole
EngE	English English
EModE	Early Modern English
ME	Middle English
OE	Old English
ESM	English in Singapore and Malaysia
FijE	Fiji English
GhE/P	Ghanaian English/Pidgin
GuyC	Guyanese Creole
HawC	Hawaii Creole

HKE	Hong Kong English
IndE	Indian English, Anglo-Indian
InlNE	Inland Northern (American) English
IrE	Irish English
JamC/E	Jamaican Creole / English
KenE	Kenyan English
KPE	Kru Pidgin English
LibC/E	Liberian Creole/English
LibSE	Liberian Settler English
LibVE	Liberian Vernacular English
LimC	Limonese Creole (Costa Rica)
LonVE	London Vernacular English
LnkE	Lankan English
MalE	Malaysian English
NEngE	New England English
NfldE	Newfoundland English
NigP/E	Nigerian Pidgin / English
NZE	New Zealand English
NYCE	New York City English
OzE	Ozarks English
PakE	Pakistani English
PanC	Panamanian Creole
PhilE	Philadelphia English
PhlE	Philippines English
RP	Received Pronunciation
SAfE	South African English
BlSAfE	Black South African English
CoSAfE	Coloured South African English
InSAfE	Indian South African English
WhSAfE	White South African English
SAmE	Southern American English
SAsE	South Asian English
SEAmE	South Eastern American English enclave dialects
ScE	Scottish English, Scots
ScStE	Scottish Standard English
SgE	Singapore English
SLVE	St. Lucian Vernacular English
SolP	Solomon Islands Pidgin
StAmE	Standard American English
StAusCE	Standard Australian Colloquial English

StAusFE	Standard Australian Formal English
StBrE	Standard British English
StE	Standard English
StGhE	Standard Ghanaian English
StHE	St. Helena English
StIndE	Standard Indian English
StJamE	Standard Jamaican English
SurC	Suriname Creoles
TanE	Tanzanian English
TobC	Tobagonian Creole
Trad-RP	Traditional Received Pronunciation
TrnC	Trinidadian Creole
T & TC	Trinidadian & mesolectal Tobagonian Creoles
TP	Tok Pisin, New Guinea Pidgin, Neomelanesian
WAfE/P	West African English/Pidgin
WelE	Welsh English
WMwE	Western and Midwestern American English
ZamE	Zambian English

More abbreviations

ESL	English as Second Language
EFL	English as Foreign Language
EIL	English as International Language
ENL	English as Native Language
L1	First Language
L2	Second Language
P/C	Pidgins and Creoles

List of features: Phonology and phonetics

Edgar W. Schneider

Please indicate whether or to what extent the following features / variants occur in the variety that you have discussed by inserting A, B or C in the left-most column as follows:

A occurs normally / is widespread
B occurs sometimes / occasionally, with some speakers / groups, in some environments
C does not normally occur.

If you have covered more than one variety, please give your set of responses for each of them, or give a summary assessment for a group of related varieties as specified.

Elements in parentheses (../..) are optional; ">" suggests a direction of movement.

Please note that the variants suggested for a single item (e.g. lexical set) are meant to be relatively exhaustive but not necessarily mutually exclusive.

Phonetic realization: vowels (lexical sets)

1. KIT [ɪ]
2. KIT raised / fronted, > [i]
3. KIT centralized, > [ə]
4. KIT with offglide, e.g. [ɪə/iə]
5. DRESS half-close [e]
6. DRESS raised, > [i]
7. DRESS half-open [ɛ]
8. DRESS backed, > [ʌ/ɐ]
9. DRESS with centralizing offglide, e.g. [eə]
10. DRESS with rising offglide, e.g. [eɪ]
11. TRAP [æ]
12. TRAP raised, > [ɛ/e]
13. TRAP lowered, > [a]
14. TRAP with offglide, e.g. [æə/æɛ/æɪ/ɛə]
15. LOT rounded, e.g. [ɒ]
16. LOT back unrounded, e.g. [ɑ]

17.   LOT front unrounded, e.g. [a]
18.   LOT with offglide, e.g. [ɒə]
19.   STRUT [ʌ]
20.   STRUT high back, > [ʊ]
21.   STRUT central [ə/ɐ]
22.   STRUT backed, > [ɔ]
23.   FOOT [ʊ]
24.   FOOT tensed [u]
25.   FOOT back, lower, e.g. [ʌ]
26.   BATH half-open front [æ]
27.   BATH low front [a]
28.   BATH low back [ɑ]
29.   BATH long
30.   BATH with offglide, e.g. [æə/æɪ/ɛə]
31.   CLOTH rounded [ɔ/ɒ]
32.   CLOTH back unrounded [ɑ]
33.   CLOTH front unrounded [a]
34.   NURSE central [ɜː/ɚ]
35.   NURSE raised / fronted / rounded, e.g. [ø]
36.   NURSE mid front [ɛ/e(r)]
37.   NURSE [ʌ(r)] (possibly lexically conditioned, e.g. WORD)
38.   NURSE backed, e.g. [o/ɔ]
39.   NURSE diphthongal, e.g. [əɪ/ɔɪ]
40.   FLEECE [iː]
41.   FLEECE with centralizing offglide, e.g. [iə]
42.   FLEECE with mid/central onset and upglide, e.g. [əɪ/ei]
43.   FLEECE with high onset and upglide, e.g. [ɪi]
44.   FLEECE shortened, e.g. [i/ɪ]
45.   FACE upgliding diphthong with half-close onset, e.g. [eɪ]
46.   FACE upgliding diphthong with half-open or lower onset, e.g. [ɛɪ/æɪ]
47.   FACE upgliding diphthong with low / backed onset, e.g. [a(ː)ɪ/ʌɪ]
48.   FACE upgliding diphthong with central onset, e.g. [əɪ]
49.   FACE monophthong, e.g. [eː]
50.   FACE ingliding diphthong, e.g. [ɪə/ɪɛ]
51.   PALM low back [ɑ(ː)]
52.   PALM low front [a(ː)]
53.   PALM with offglide, e.g. [ɑə/ɒə]
54.   THOUGHT [ɔ(ː)]
55.   THOUGHT low [aː/ɑː]
56.   THOUGHT with offglide, e.g. [ɔə/ʊə]

57. GOAT with central onset, e.g. [əʊ/əʉ]
58. GOAT with back rounded onset, e.g. [oʊ/ou]
59. GOAT with low or back unrounded onset, e.g. [a(:)u/aʉ/ʌʊ/ʌʉ]
60. GOAT with relatively high back onset [ʊu]
61. GOAT ingliding, e.g. [ʊə/ʊɔ/ua]
62. GOAT monophthongal, e.g. [o(:)]
63. GOOSE [u:]
64. GOOSE fronted, > [ʉ(:)]
65. GOOSE gliding, e.g. [ʊu/ɪu/ə(:)ʉ]
66. PRICE upgliding diphthong, e.g. [aɪ/ɑɪ/ʌɪ]
67. PRICE monophthong [a:] before voiced C
68. PRICE monophthong [a:] in all environments
69. PRICE with raised / central onset, e.g. [əɪ/ɜɪ]
70. PRICE with backed onset, e.g. [ɔ(:)ɪ/ɒɪ]
71. PRICE with mid-front offglide, e.g. [ae/aɛ]
72. CHOICE [ɔɪ]
73. CHOICE with low onset [ɒɪ]
74. CHOICE with central onset [əɪ/əi]
75. MOUTH [aʊ/aʊ]
76. MOUTH with raised and backed onset, e.g. [ʌu/ɔʊ]
77. MOUTH with raised onset [əʊ] only before voiceless C
78. MOUTH with raised onset [əʊ] in all environments
79. MOUTH with fronted onset, e.g. [æʉ/æʊ/æo/ɛo]
80. MOUTH low monophthong, e.g. [a:]
81. MOUTH mid/high back monophthong, e.g. [o:]
82. NEAR [ɪə(r)]
83. NEAR without offglide, e.g. [ɪr]
84. NEAR with tensed / raised onset, e.g. [i(:)ə]
85. NEAR with half-closed onset [e(:/ə/r)/ea]
86. NEAR with half-open onset [ɛ(:/ə/r)]
87. NEAR high-front to low glide, e.g. [ia]
88. SQUARE with half-open onset [ɛə]
89. SQUARE with half-closed onset [eə/ea]
90. SQUARE with high front onset [ɪə]
91. SQUARE with relatively open onset, possibly rising [æə/æɪ]
92. SQUARE half-closed monophthong, [e(:/r)]
93. SQUARE half-open monophthong, [ɛ(:/r)]
94. START low back unrounded, e.g. [ɑ(:/r)]
95. START central, e.g. [ɐ(:/r)]
96. START low front, e.g. [a(:/r)]

97. START front, raised, e.g. [æ(:/r)]
98. START with offglide, e.g. [ɑə/ɒə)]
99. NORTH half-open monophthong [ɔ(:/r)]
100. NORTH half-closed monophthong [o(:/r)]
101. NORTH [ɒ]
102. NORTH with offglide, e.g. [ɒə/oa]
103. FORCE half-open monophthong [ɔ(:/r)]
104. FORCE half-closed monophthong [o(:/r)]
105. FORCE ingliding, e.g. [ɔə(r)/oə(r)/oa]
106. FORCE with upglide, e.g.[oʊ(r)]
107. CURE [ʊə/ʊr]
108. CURE with tensed / raised onset, e.g. [u(:)ə/ur]
109. CURE lowered monophthong, e.g. [o:/ɔ:]
110. CURE with upglide, e.g. [oʊ(r)]
111. CURE low offglide, e.g. [ua/oa(r)]
112. happY relatively centralized, e.g. [ɪ]
113. happY central, e.g. [ə]
114. happY tensed / relatively high front, e.g. [i(:)]
115. happY mid front, e.g. [e/ɛ]
116. lettER [ə]
117. lettER (relatively) open, e.g. [a/ʌ]
118. horsES central [ə]
119. horsES high front [ɪ]
120. commA [ə]
121. commA (relatively) open, e.g. [a/ʌ]

Distribution: vowels

122. homophony of KIT and FLEECE
123. homophony of TRAP and BATH
124. homophony of *Mary* and *merry*
125. homophony of *Mary*, *merry* and *marry*
126. homophony of TRAP and DRESS before /l/
127. merger of KIT and DRESS before nasals (*pin = pen*)
128. homophony of DRESS and FACE
129. homophony of FOOT and GOOSE
130. homophony of LOT and THOUGHT
131. homophony of LOT and STRUT
132. homophony of NEAR and SQUARE

133. vowels nasalized before nasal consonants
134. vowel harmony / cross-syllable assimilation phenomena in some words
135. vowels short unless before /r/, voiced fricative, or in open syllable (SVLR)
136. commA/lettER (etc.): [ɑ/ɛ/i/ɔ/u], reflecting spelling

Phonetic realization and distribution: consonants

137. P/T/K-: weak or no aspiration of word-initial stops
138. -T-: lenisation / flapping / voicing of intervocalic /t/ (*writer* = *rider*)
139. -T: realization of word-final or intervocalic /t/ as glottal stop
140. K-: palatalization of velar stop word-initially: e.g. kj-/gj-in *can't/ garden*
141. B-: word-initial *bw*- for b-: e.g. *bw*- in *boy*
142. S-/F-: voiceless initial fricatives voiced: [z-/v-]
143. TH-: realization of word-initial voiced TH as stop, e.g. *dis*, 'this'
144. TH-: realization of word-initial voiceless TH as stop, e.g. *ting, 'thing'*
145. TH-: realization of word-initial voiced TH as affricate [dð]
146. TH-: realization of word-initial voiceless TH as affricate [tθ]
147. WH-: velar fricative onset retained, i.e. *which* is not homophonous with *witch*
148. CH: voiceless velar fricative [χ/x] exists
149. h-deletion (word-initial), e.g., *'eart* 'heart'
150. h-insertion (word-initial), e.g. *haxe* 'axe'
151. L-: palatal (clear) variant in syllable onsets
152. L-: velar variant in syllable onsets
153. –L: palatal variant in syllable codas
154. "jod"-dropping: no /j/ after alveolars before /uː/, e.g. in *news, tune*
155. deletion of word-initial /h/ in /hj-/ clusters, e.g. in *human, huge*
156. labialization of word-central voiced -TH-, e.g. [-v-] in *brother*
157. labialization of word-final / word-central voiceless –TH, e.g. [-f] in *mouth, nothing*
158. intervocalic /-v-/ > [b], e.g. in *river*
159. W: substitution of labiodental fricative /v/ for semi-vowel /w/
160. word-final consonant cluster deletion, monomorphemic
161. word-final consonant cluster deletion, bimorphemic
162. deletion of word-final single consonants
163. simplification of word-initial consonant clusters, e.g. in *splash, square*
164. non-rhotic (no postvocalic –r)

165. rhotic (postvocalic –r realized)
166. phonetic realization of /r/ as velar retroflex constriction
167. phonetic realization of /r/ as alveolar flap
168. phonetic realization of /r/ as apical trill
169. /r/ uvular
170. intrusive –r–, e.g. *idea*-r-*is*
171. post-vocalic –l vocalized
172. neutralization / confusion of liquids /l/ and /r/ in some words
173. realization of velar nasals with stop: -NG > [-ŋg]
174. velarization of some word-final nasals, e.g. /-ŋ/ in *down*

Prosodic features and intonation

175. deletion of word-initial unstressed syllables, e.g. '*bout,* '*cept*
176. stress not infrequently shifted from first to later syllable, e.g. *indi*'*cate,* *holi*'*day*
177. (relatively) syllable-timed rather than stress-timed
178. HRT (High-Rising Terminal) contour: rise at end of statement
179. tone distinctions exist

List of features: Morphology and Syntax

Bernd Kortmann

The features in the catalogue are numbered from 1 to 76 (for easy reference in later parts of the chapter) and provided with the short definitions and illustrations. They include all usual suspects known from survey articles on grammatical properties of (individual groups of) non-standard varieties of English, with a slight bias towards features observed in L1 varieties. The 76 features fall into 11 groups corresponding to the following broad areas of morphosyntax: pronouns, noun phrase, tense and aspect, modal verbs, verb morphology, adverbs, negation, agreement, relativization, complementation, discourse organization and word order.

Pronouns, pronoun exchange, pronominal gender

1. *them* instead of demonstrative *those* (e.g. *in them days, one of them things*)
2. *me* instead of possessive *my* (e.g. *He's me brother, I've lost me bike*)
3. special forms or phrases for the second person plural pronoun (e.g. *youse, y'all, aay', yufela, you ... together, all of you, you ones/'uns, you guys, you people*)
4. regularized reflexives-paradigm (e.g. *hisself, theirselves/theirself*)
5. object pronoun forms serving as base for reflexives (e.g. *meself*)
6. lack of number distinction in reflexives (e.g. plural *-self*)
7. *she/her* used for inanimate referents (e.g. *She was burning good* [about a house])
8. generic *he/his* for all genders (e.g. *My car, he's broken*)
9. *myself/meself* in a non-reflexive function (e.g. *my/me husband and myself*)
10. *me* instead of *I* in coordinate subjects (e.g. *Me and my brother/My brother and me were late for school*)
11. non-standard use of *us* (e.g. *Us George was a nice one, We like us town, Show us 'me' them boots, Us kids used to pinch the sweets like hell, Us'll do it*)
12. non-coordinated subject pronoun forms in object function (e.g. *You did get he out of bed in the middle of the night*)
13. non-coordinated object pronoun forms in subject function (e.g. *Us say 'er's dry*)

Noun phrase

14. absence of plural marking after measure nouns (e.g. *four pound, five year*)
15. group plurals (e.g. *That President has two Secretary of States*)
16. group genitives (e.g. *The man I met's girlfriend is a real beauty*)
17. irregular use of articles (e.g. *Take them to market, I had nice garden, about a three fields, I had the toothache*)
18. postnominal *for*-phrases to express possession (e.g. *The house for me*)
19. double comparatives and superlatives (e.g. *That is so much more easier to follow*)
20. regularized comparison strategies (e.g. in *He is the regularest kind a guy I know, in one of the most pretty sunsets*)

Verb phrase: Tense & aspect

21. wider range of uses of the Progressive (e.g. *I'm liking this, What are you wanting?*)
22. habitual *be* (e.g. *He be sick*)
23. habitual *do* (e.g. *He does catch fish pretty*)
24. non-standard habitual markers other than *be* and *do*
25. levelling of difference between Present Perfect and Simple Past (e.g. *Were you ever in London?, Some of us have been to New York years ago*)
26. *be* as perfect auxiliary (e.g. *They're not left school yet*)
27. *do* as a tense and aspect marker (e.g. *This man what do own this*)
28. completive/perfect *done* (e.g. *He done go fishing, You don ate what I has sent you?*)
29. past tense/anterior marker *been* (e.g. *I been cut the bread*)
30. loosening of sequence of tense rule (e.g. *I noticed the van I came in*)
31. *would* in if-clauses (e.g. *If I'd be you, ...*)
32. *was sat/stood* with progressive meaning (e.g. *when you're stood* 'are standing' *there you can see the flames*)
33. *after*-Perfect (e.g. *She's after selling the boat*)

Verb phrase: Modal verbs

34. double modals (e.g. *I tell you what we might should do*)

35.   epistemic *mustn't* ('can't, it is concluded that… not'; e.g. *This mustn't be true*)

Verb phrase: Verb morphology

36.   levelling of preterite and past participle verb forms: regularization of irregular verb paradigms (e.g. *catch-catched-catched*)

37.   levelling of preterite and past participle verb forms: unmarked forms (frequent with e.g. *give* and *run*)

38.   levelling of preterite and past partiple verb forms: past form replacing the participle (e.g. *He had went*)

39.   levelling of preterite and past partiple verb forms: participle replacing the past form (e.g. *He gone to Mary*)

40.   zero past tense forms of regular verbs (e.g. *I walk* for *I walked*)

41.   *a*-prefixing on *ing*-forms (e.g. *They wasn't a-doin' nothin' wrong*)

Adverbs

42.   adverbs (other than degree modifiers) have same form as adjectives (e.g. *Come quick!*)

43.   degree modifier adverbs lack *-ly* (e.g. *That's real good*)

Negation

44.   multiple negation / negative concord (e.g. *He won't do no harm*)

45.   *ain't* as the negated form of *be* (e.g. *They're all in there, ain't they?*)

46.   *ain't* as the negated form of *have* (e.g. *I ain't had a look at them yet*)

47.   *ain't* as generic negator before a main verb (e.g. *Something I ain't know about*)

48.   invariant *don't* for all persons in the present tense (e.g. *He don't like me*)

49.   *never* as preverbal past tense negator (e.g. *He never came* [= he didn't come])

50.   *no* as preverbal negator (e.g. *me no iit brekfus*)

51.   *was–weren't* split (e.g. *The boys was interested, but Mary weren't*)

52.   invariant non-concord tags, (e.g. *innit/in't it/isn't* in *They had them in their hair, innit?)*

Agreement

53. invariantpresenttenseformsduetozeromarkingforthethirdpersonsingular (e.g. *So he show up and say, What's up?*)
54. invariant present tense forms due to generalization of third person *-s* to all persons (e.g. *I sees the house*)
55. existential/presentational *there's, there is, there was* with plural subjects (e.g. *There's two men waiting in the hall*)
56. variant forms of dummy subjects in existential clauses (e.g. *they, it,* or zero for *there*)
57. deletion of *be* (e.g. *She ___ smart*)
58. deletion of auxiliary *have* (e.g. *I ___ eaten my lunch)*
59. *was/were* generalization (e.g. *You were hungry but he were thirsty,* or: *You was hungry but he was thirsty*)
60. Northern Subject Rule (e.g. *I sing* [vs. **I sings*], *Birds sings, I sing and dances*)

Relativization

61. relative particle *what* (e.g. *This is the man what painted my house*)
62. relative particle *that* or *what* in non-restrictive contexts (e.g. *My daughter, that/what lives in London,…*)
63. relative particle *as* (e.g. *He was a chap as got a living anyhow*)
64. relative particle *at* (e.g. *This is the man at painted my house*)
65. use of analytic *that his/that's, what his/what's, at's, as'* instead of *whose* (e.g. *The man what's wife has died*)
66. gapping or zero-relativization in subject position (e.g. *The man ___ lives there is a nice chap*)
67. resumptive / shadow pronouns (e.g. *This is the house which I painted it yesterday*)

Complementation

68. *say*-based complementizers
69. inverted word order in indirect questions (e.g. *I'm wondering what are you gonna do*)

70.   unsplit *for to* in infinitival purpose clauses (e.g. *We always had gutters in the winter time for to drain the water away*)

71.   *as what / than what* in comparative clauses (e.g. *It's harder than what you think it is*)

72.   serial verbs (e.g. *give* meaning 'to, for', as in *Karibuk giv mi*, 'Give the book to me')

Discourse organization and word order

73.   lack of inversion / lack of auxiliaries in *wh*-questions (e.g. *What you doing?*)

74.   lack of inversion in main clause *yes/no* questions (e.g. *You get the point?*)

75.   *like* as a focussing device (e.g. *How did you get away with that like? Like for one round five quid, that was like three quid, like two-fifty each*)

76.   *like* as a quotative particle (e.g. *And she was like "What do you mean?"*)

General introduction

Bernd Kortmann and Edgar W. Schneider

This book, together with its three companion volumes on other world regions, derives from the *Handbook of Varieties of English*, edited by Kortmann, Schneider et al. (2004). To make the material compiled in the *Handbook* more easily accessible and affordable, especially to student pockets, it has been decided to regroup the articles in such a way that all descriptive papers on any of the seven major anglophone world regions distinguished there are put together in a set of four paperback volumes, and accompanied by the CD-ROM which covers data and sources from all around the world. In this brief introduction we are briefly revisiting and summarizing the major design features of the *Handbook* and its contributions, i.e. information which, by implication, also characterizes the articles in the present volume.

The all-important design feature of the *Handbook* and of these offspring paperbacks is its focus on structure and on the solid description and documentation of data. The volumes, together with the CD-ROM, provide comprehensive up-to-date accounts of the salient phonological and grammatical properties of the varieties of English around the world. Reliable structural information in a somewhat standardized format and presented in an accessible way is a necessary prerequisite for any kind of study of language varieties, independent of the theoretical framework used for analysis. It is especially important for comparative studies of the phonological and morphosyntactic patterns across varieties of English, and the inclusion of this kind of data in typological studies (e.g. in the spirit of Kortmann 2004).

Of course, all of this structural information can be and has to be put in perspective by the conditions of uses of these varieties, i.e. their sociohistorical backgrounds, their current sociolinguistic settings (not infrequently in multilingual societies), and their associated political dimensions (like issues of norm-setting, language policies, and pedagogical applications). Ultimately, all of the varieties under discussion here, certainly so the ones spoken outside of England but in a sense, looking way back in time, even the English dialects themselves, are products of colonization processes, predominantly the European colonial expansion in the modern age. A number of highly interesting questions, linguistically and culturally, might be asked in this context, including the central issue of why all of this has happened, whether there is an underlying scheme that has continued to drive and motivate the evolution of new varieties of English (Schneider 2003, 2007). These linguistic and sociohistorical background issues will be briefly addressed in the regional introductions and in some of the individual chapters, but it should be made clear that it is the issue of structural description and comparison which is at the heart of this project.

The chapters in the four paperbacks are geared towards documenting and mapping the structural variation among (spontaneously spoken) non-standard varieties of English. Standard English is of course that variety, or set of closely related varieties, which enjoys the highest social prestige. It serves as a reference system and target norm in formal situations, in the language used by people taking on a public persona (including, for example, anchorpersons in the news media), and as a model in the teaching of English worldwide. Here, however, it is treated as is commonplace in modern descriptive linguistics, i.e. as a variety on a par with all other (regional, social, ethnic, or contact) varieties of English. Clearly, in terms of its structural properties it is not inherently superior to any of the non-standard varieties. Besides, the very notion of "Standard English" itself obviously refers to an abstraction. On the written level, it is under discussion to what extent a "common core" or a putatively homogeneous variety called "International English" actually exists: there is some degree of uniformity across the major national varieties, but once one looks into details of expression and preferences, there are also considerable differences. On the spoken level, there are reference accents like, for example, Received Pronunciation for British English, but their definition also builds upon abstractions from real individuals' performance. Thus, in the present context especially the grammar of (written) Standard English figures as no more than an implicit standard of comparison, in the sense that all chapters focus upon those phenomena in a given variety which are (more or less strikingly) different from this standard (these being perceived as not, note again, in any sense deficient or inferior to it).

The articles in this collection cover all main national standard varieties, distinctive regional, ethnic, and social varieties, major contact varieties (pidgins and creoles), as well as major varieties of English as a Second Language. The inclusion of second-language varieties and, especially, English-based pidgins and creoles may come as a surprise to some readers. Normally these varieties are addressed from different perspectives (such as, for example, language policy, language pedagogy, linguistic attitudes, language and identity (construction), substrate vs. superstrate influence), each standing in its own research tradition. Here they are primarily discussed from the point of view of their structural properties.

This will make possible comparisons with structural properties of, for example, other varieties of English spoken in the same region, or second-language or contact varieties in other parts of the English-speaking world. At the same time the availability of solid structural descriptions may open new perspectives for a fruitful interaction between the different research traditions within which second-language and contact varieties are studied. The boundaries of what is considered and accepted as "varieties of English" has thus been drawn fairly widely. In accepting English-oriented pidgins and creoles in the present context, we adopt a trend of recent research to consider them as contact varieties closely related to, possibly to be categorized as varieties of, their respective superstrate languages (e.g. Mufwene 2001). Creoles, and also some pidgins, in many regions vary along a continuum from acrolectal forms, relatively close to English and used by the higher sociolinguistic strata in formal contexts, to basilects, "deep" varieties maximally different from English. Most of our contributions focus upon the mesolects, the middle ranges which in most creole-speaking societies are used most widely.

For other varieties, too, it may be asked why or why not they have been selected for inclusion in this collection. Among the considerations that led to the present selection, the following figured most prominently: amount and quality of existing data and research documentation for the individual varieties, intensity of ongoing research activities, availability of authors, and space constraints (leading, for example, to the exclusion of strictly local accents and dialects). More information on the selection of varieties will be given in the regional introductions.

While in the *Handbook* there is one volume each for phonology and grammar (i.e. morphology and syntax), this set of paperbacks has been arranged by the major world regions relevant for the discussion of varieties of English: the British Isles; the Americas and the Caribbean; Africa, South and Southeast Asia; and the Pacific and Australasia. Each of the volumes comprises all articles on the respective regions, both on phonology and on grammar, together with the regional introductions, which include accounts of the histories, the cultural and sociolinguistic situations, and the most important data sources for the relevant locations, ethnic groups and varieties, and the regional synopses, in which the editors summarize the most striking properties of the varieties of English spoken in the respective world regions. Global synopses offering the most noteworthy findings and tendencies on phonological and morphosyntactic variation in English from a global perspective are available in the two hardcover Handbooks and in the electronic online version. In addition, there is a list of "General references", all of them exclusively book publications, which are either globally relevant or central for for individual world regions.

What emerges from the synopses is that many of the features described for individual varieties or sets of varieties in this Handbook are not unique to these (sets of) varieties. This is true both for morphology and syntax and for phonology.

As a matter of fact, quite a number of morphosyntactic features described as salient properties of individual varieties may strike the reader as typical of other varieties, too, possibly even of the grammar of spoken English, in general. In a similar vein, it turns out that certain phonological processes (like the monophthongization of certain diphthongs, the fronting, backing or merging of some vowels, and some consonantal substitutions or suprasegmental processes) can be documented in quite a number of fairly disparate language varieties – not surprisingly, perhaps, given shared underlying principles like constraints of articulatory space or tendencies towards simplification and the reduction of contrasts.

The distributions of selected individual features, both morphosyntactic and phonological, across varieties world-wide is visualized by the interactive world maps on the accompanying CD-ROM. The lists of these features, which are also referred to in some contributions, especially the regional synopses, are appended to this introduction. On these maps, each of a set of selected features, for almost all of the varieties under discussion, is categorized as occurring regularly (marked as "A" and colour-coded in red), occasionally or only in certain specified environments (marked as "B" and represented by a yellow circle) or practically not at all ("C", black). These innovative maps, which are accompanied by statistical distribution data on the spread of selected variants, provide the reader with an immediate visual representation of regional distribution and diffusion patterns. Further information on the nature of the multimedia material accompanying these books is available on the CD itself. It includes audio samples of free conversations (some of them transcribed), a standard reading passage, and recordings of the spoken "lexical sets" which define and illustrate vocalic variation (Wells 1982).

The chapters are descriptive survey articles providing state-of-the-art reports on major issues in current research, with a common core in order to make the collection an interesting and useful tool especially from a comparative, i.e. cross-dialectal and cross-linguistic, point of view. All chapters aim primarily at a qualitative rather than quantitative perspective, i.e. whether or not a given feature occurs is more important than its frequency. Of course, for varieties where research has focused upon documenting frequency relationships between variants of variables, some information on relevant quantitative tendencies has been provided. Depending upon the research coverage in a given world region (which varies widely from one continent to another), some contributions build upon existing sociolinguistic, dialectological, or structural research; a small number of other chapters make systematic use of available computerized corpora; and in some cases and for some regions the chapters in this compilation provide the first-ever systematic qualitative survey of the phonological and grammatical properties of English as spoken there.

For almost all varieties of English covered there are companion chapters in the phonology and morphosyntax parts of each paperback volume. In these cases it is in the phonology chapter that the reader will find a concise introductory section on the historical and cultural background as well as the current sociolinguistic situation of the relevant variety or set of varieties spoken at this location.

In order to ensure a certain degree of comparability, the authors were given a set of core issues that they were asked to address (provided something interesting can be said about them in the respective variety). For the phonology chapters, this set included the following items:

- phonological systems
- phonetic realization(s) and (phonotactic) distributions of a selection of phonemes (to be selected according to salience in the variety in question)
- specific phonological processes at work in the relevant variety
- lexical distribution
- prosodic features (stress, rhythm)
- intonation patterns
- observations/generalizations on the basis of lexical sets à la Wells (1982) and Foulkes/Docherty (1999), a standard reading passage and/or samples of free conversation.

It is worth noting that for some of the contributions, notably the chapters on pidgins and creoles, the lexical sets were not sufficient or suitable to describe the variability found. In such cases authors were encouraged to expand the set of target words, or replace one of the items. The reading passage was also adjusted or substituted by some authors, for instance because it was felt to be culturally inappropriate.

This is the corresponding set for the morphology and syntax chapters:

- tense – aspect – modality systems
- auxiliaries
- negation
- relativization
- complementation
- other subordination phenomena (notably adverbial subordination)
- agreement
- noun phrase structure
- pronominal systems
- word order (and information structure: especially focus/topicalizing constructions)

– selected salient features of the morphological paradigms of, for example, auxiliaries and pronouns

Lexical variation was not our primary concern, given that it fails to lend itself to the systematic generalization and comparability that we are interested in in this project. However, authors were offered the opportunity to comment on highly salient features of the vocabulary of any given variety (briefly and within the overall space constraints) if this was considered rewarding. The reader may find such information on distinctive properties of the respective vocabularies in the morphology and syntax chapters. Especially for a student readership, short sets of exercises and study questions have been added at the end of all chapters in the four paperback volumes.

In the interest of combining guidance for readers, efficiency, and space constraints, but also the goal of comprehensiveness, bibliographic references are systematically divided between three different types of reference lists. As was stated above, in each paperback a "General references" list can be found which compiles a relatively large number of books which, taken together, are central to the field of world-wide varieties of English – "classic" publications, collective volumes, particularly important publications, and so on. It is understood that in the individual contributions all authors may refer to titles from this list without these being repeated in their respective source lists. Each of the individual chapters ends with a list of "Selected references" comprising, on average, only 15–20 references – including the most pertinent ones on the respective variety (or closely related varieties) beyond any others possibly included in the General references list, and possibly others cited in the respective article. In other words, the Selected references do not repeat any of the titles cited in the list of General references. Thirdly, a "Comprehensive bibliography", with further publications specifically on the phonology and morphosyntax of each of the varieties covered, for which no space limitations were imposed, is available on the CD-ROM. The idea behind this limitation of the number of references allowed to go with each article was to free the texts of too much technical apparatus and thus to increase their reader-friendliness for a target audience of non-specialists while at the same time combining basic guidance to the most important literature (in the General References list) with the possibility of providing comprehensive coverage of the writings available on any given region (in the Bibliographies on the CD-ROM). It must be noted, however, that at times this rule imposed limitations upon possible source credits allowed in the discussions, because to make the books self-contained authors were allowed to refer to titles from the General and the Select References lists only. In other words, it is possible that articles touch upon material drawn from publications listed in the CD-ROM bibliographies without explicit credit, although every effort has been made to avoid this.

A publication project as huge as this one would have been impossible, indeed impossible even to think of, without the support of a great number of people devoted to their profession and to the subject of this Handbook. The editors would like thank the members of their editorial teams in Freiburg, Regensburg, and Cape Town. We are also much indebted to Elizabeth Traugott, for all the thought, support and feedback she gave to this project right from the very beginning of the planning stage, and to Jürgen Handke, who produced the rich audio-visual multimedia support on the CD. Furthermore, we have always benefitted from the support and interest invested into this project by Anke Beck and the people at Mouton de Gruyter. Finally, and most importantly, of course, the editors would like to thank the contributors and informants for having conformed to the rigid guidelines, deadlines and time frames that we set them for the various stages of (re)writing their chapters and providing the input material for the CD-ROM.

This collection truly represents an impressive product of scholarly collaboration of people from all around the globe. Right until the end it has been an exciting and wonderful experience for the editors (as well as, we would like to think, for the authors) to bring all these scholars and their work together, and we believe that this shows in the quality of the chapters and the material presented on the CD-ROM. We hope that, like the *Handbook*, it will be enjoyed, appreciated and esteemed by its readers, and treasured as the reference work and research tool it was designed as for anyone interested in and fascinated by variation in English!

References

Kortmann, Bernd (ed.)
    2004   *Dialectology meets Typology: Dialect Grammar from a Cross-Linguistic Perspective*. Berlin/New York: Mouton de Gruyter.
Kortmann, Bernd, and Edgar W. Schneider, with Kate Burridge, Rajend Mesthrie, and Clive Upton (eds.)
    2004   *A Handbook of Varieties of English*. Vol. 1: *Phonology*. Vol. 2: *Morphology and Syntax*. Berlin/New York: Mouton de Gruyter.
Schneider, Edgar W.
    2003   "The dynamics of New Englishes: From identity construction to dialect birth." *Language* 79: 233-281.
Schneider, Edgar W.
    2007   *Postcolonial English: Varieties Around the World*. Cambridge: Cambridge University Press.

General references

The following is a list of general reference works relevant across the world regions covered in the Handbook and for individual of these world regions. The list consists exclusively of book publications. Those monographs, dictionaries and collective volumes in the list which are referred to in the chapters of the four paperbacks will not be separately listed in the selected references at the end of the individual chapters.

Aceto, Michael and Jeffrey Williams (eds.)
    2003   *Contact Englishes of the Eastern Caribbean*. (Varieties of English around the World, General Series 30.) Amsterdam/Philadelphia: Benjamins.
Aitken, Jack and Tom McArthur (eds.)
    1979   *The Languages of Scotland*. Edinburgh: Chambers.
Algeo, John
    2006   *British or American English? A Handbook of Word and Grammar Patterns*. Cambridge: Cambridge University Press.
Algeo, John (ed.)
    2001   *The Cambridge History of the English Language, Volume VI: English in North America*. Cambridge: Cambridge University Press.
Allen, Harold B.
    1973
    –1976   *Linguistic Atlas of the Upper Midwest*. 3 Volumes. Minneapolis: University of Minnesota Press.
Allen, Harold B. and Gary Underwood (eds.)
    1971   *Readings in American Dialectology*. New York: Appleton-Century Crofts.
Allen, Harold B. and Michael D. Linn (eds.)
    1997   *Dialects and Language Variation*. New York: Academic Press.
Alleyne, Mervyn C.
    1980   *Comparative Afro-American: An Historical-Comparative Study of English-Based Afro-American Dialects of the New World*. (Linguistica Extranea 11.) Ann Arbor: Karoma.
Allsopp, Richard (ed.)
    1996   *Dictionary of Caribbean English Usage*. Oxford: Oxford University Press.
Anderson, Peter M.
    1987   *A Structural Atlas of the English Dialects*. London: Croom Helm.
Anderwald, Lieselotte
    2002   *Negation in Non-standard British English: Gaps, Regularizations, Asymmetries*. (Routledge Studies in Germanic Linguistics 8.) London/ New York: Routledge.
Atwood, E. Bagby
    1953   *A Survey of Verb Forms in the Eastern United States*. (Studies in American English 2.) Ann Arbor: University of Michigan Press.

Avis, Walter S., Charles Crate, Patrick Drysdale, Douglas Leechman and Matthew H. Scargill
  1967   *A Dictionary of Canadianisms on Historical Principles*. Toronto: Gage.
Bailey, Beryl Loftman
  1966   *Jamaican Creole Syntax*. Cambridge: Cambridge University Press.
Bailey, Richard W. and Jay L. Robinson
  1973   *Varieties of Present-Day English*. New York: Macmillan.
Bailey, Richard W. and Manfred Görlach (eds.)
  1982   *English as a World Language*. Ann Arbor: University of Michigan Press.
Bailey, Guy, Natalie Maynor and Patricia Cukor-Avila (eds.)
  1991   *The Emergence of Black English: Text and Commentary*. (Creole Language Library 8.) Amsterdam/Philadelphia: Benjamins.
Baker, Philip and Adrienne Bruyn (eds.)
  1998   *St. Kitts and the Atlantic Creoles: The Texts of Samuel Augustus Mathews in Perspective*. (Westminster Creolistics Series 4). London: University of Westminster Press.
Bamgbose, Ayo, Ayo Banjo and Andrew Thomas (eds.)
  1997   *New Englishes – A West African Perspective*. Trenton, NJ: Africa World Press.
Baugh, John
  1983   *Black Street Speech: Its History, Structure, and Survival*. Austin: University of Texas Press.
Baumgardner, Robert J.
  1996   *South Asian English: Structure, Use, and Users*. Urbana, IL: University of Illinois Press.
Bell, Allan and Koenrad Kuiper (eds.)
  2000   *New Zealand English*. (Varieties of English around the World, General Series 25.) Amsterdam/Philadelphia: Benjamins and Wellington: Victoria University Press.
Bernstein, Cynthia, Thomas Nunnally and Robin Sabino (eds.)
  1997   *Language Variety in the South Revisited*. Tuscaloosa: University of Alabama Press.
Bickerton, Derek
  1975   *Dynamics of a Creole System*. Cambridge: Cambridge University Press.
  1981   *Roots of Language*. Ann Arbor: Karoma.
Blair, David and Peter Collins (eds.)
  2001   *English in Australia*. (Varieties of English around the World, General Series 26.) Amsterdam/Philadelphia: Benjamins.
Bliss, Alan J.
  1979   *Spoken English in Ireland 1600–1740*. Dublin: Dolmen Press.
Bolton, Kingsley
  2003   *Chinese Englishes. A Sociolinguistic History*. Cambridge: Cambridge Univeristy Press.
Bolton, Kinglsey and Braj B. Kachru (eds.)
  2006   *World Englishes: critical concept in linguistics*. 6 vols. London: Routledge.

Bolton, Kingsley (ed.)
  2002   *Hong Kong English: Autonomy and Creativity*. Hong Kong: Hong Kong
          University Press.
Britain, David (ed.)
  2007   *Language in the British Isles*. Cambridge: Cambridge University Press.
Burchfield, Robert (ed.)
  1994   *The Cambridge History of the English Language, Volume V: English in
          Britain and Overseas: Origins and Development*. Cambridge: Cambridge
          University Press.
Carrington, Lawrence D., Dennis Craig and Ramon Todd Dandare (eds.)
  1983   *Studies in Caribbean Language. Papers Presented at the 3ʳᵈ Biennial
          Conference of the Society for Caribbean Linguistics Held in Aruba,
          Netherlands Antilles from 16–20 Sept 1980*. St. Augustine, Trinidad:
          Society for Caribbean Linguistics.
Carver, Craig M.
  1987   *American Regional Dialects: A Word Geography*. Ann Arbor: University
          of Michigan Press.
Cassidy, Frederic G.
  1961   *Jamaica Talk: 300 Years of the English Language in Jamaica*. London:
          Macmillan.
Cassidy, Frederic G. (ed.)
  1985
  –2002   *Dictionary of American Regional English*. 4 Volumes to date. Cambridge,
          MA/London: The Belknap Press of Harvard University Press.
Cassidy, Frederic G. and Robert B. LePage (eds.)
  1967   *Dictionary of Jamaican English*. Cambridge: Cambridge University
          Press.
Chambers, J.K.
  2003   *Sociolinguistic Theory: Linguistic Variation and its Social Significance*.
          2nd edition. (Language in Society 22.) Oxford: Blackwell.
Chambers, J.K. and Peter Trudgill
  1998   *Dialectology*. 2nd edition. (Cambridge Textbooks in Linguistics.)
          Cambridge: Cambridge University Press.
Chambers, J.K. (ed.)
  1975   *Canadian English: Origins and Structures*. Toronto: Methuen.
Chambers, J.K., Peter Trudgill and Natalie Schilling-Estes (eds.)
  2002   *The Handbook of Language Variation and Change*. (Blackwell Handbooks
          in Linguistics.) Malden, MA: Blackwell.
Cheshire, Jenny L. (ed.)
  1991   *English Around the World: Sociolinguistic Perspectives*. Cambridge:
          Cambridge University Press.
Cheshire, Jenny L. and Dieter Stein (eds.)
  1997   *Taming the Vernacular: From Dialect to Written Standard Language*.
          Harlow: Longman.

Christian, Donna, Nanjo Dube and Walt Wolfram
　1988　*Variation and Change in Geographically Isolated Communities: Appalachian English and Ozark English*. (American Dialect Society 74.) Tuscaloosa: University of Alabama Press.
Christie, Pauline, Lawrence Carrington, Barbara Lalla and Velma Pollard (eds.)
　1998　*Studies in Caribbean Language II. Papers from the Ninth Biennial Conference of the SCL, 1992*. St. Augustine, Trinidad: Society for Caribbean Linguistics.
Clarke, Sandra (ed.)
　1993　*Focus on Canada*. (Varieties of English around the World, General Series 11.) Amsterdam/Philadelphia: Benjamins.
Collins, Peter and David Blair (eds.)
　1989　*Australian English: the Language of a New Society*. St. Lucia: University of Queensland Press.
Corbett, John, J. Derrick McClure and Jane Stuart-Smith (eds.)
　2003　*The Edinburgh Companion to Scots*. Edinburgh: Edinburgh University Press.
Crystal, David
　2003　*The Cambridge Encyclopedia of the English Language*. 2nd edition. Cambridge: Cambridge University Press.
D'Costa, Jean and Barbara Lalla
　1989　*Voices in Exile: Jamaican Texts of the 18th and 19th Centuries*. Tuscaloosa/ London: University of Alabama Press.
Davis, Lawrence M.
　1983　*English Dialectology: An Introduction*. University, Alabama: University of Alabama Press.
Day, Richard R. (ed.)
　1980　*Issues in English Creoles: Papers from the 1975 Hawaii Conference*. (Varieties of English around the World, General Series 2.) Heidelberg: Groos.
De Klerk, Vivian (ed.)
　1996　*Focus on South Africa*. (Varieties of English around the World, General Series 15.) Amsterdam/Philadelphia: Benjamins.
De Wolf, Gaelan Dodds
　1992　*Social and Regional Factors in Canadian English. Study of Phonological Variables and Grammatical Items in Ottawa and Vancouver*. Toronto: Canadian Scholar's Press.
DeCamp, David and Ian F. Hancock (eds.)
　1974　*Pidgins and Creoles: Current Trends and Prospects*. Washington, D.C.: Georgetown University Press.
Devonish, Hubert
　1989　*Talking in Tones: A Study of Tone in Afro-European Creole Languages*. London/Barbados: Karia Press and Caribbean Academic Publications.
Eckert, Penelope (ed.)
　1991　*New Ways of Analyzing Sound Change*. (Qualitative Analyses of Linguistic Structure 5.) New York/San Diego: Academic Press.

Edwards, Viv
    1986   *Language in a Black Community.* (Multilingual Matters 24.) Clevedon: Multilingual Matters.
Edwards, Walter F. and Donald Winford (ed.)
    1991   *Verb Phrase Patterns in Black English and Creole.* Detroit: Wayne State University.
Ellis, Alexander J.
    1869
    –1889   *On Early English Pronunciation.* 5 Volumes. London: Trübner.
Fasold, Ralph W.
    1972   *Tense Marking in Black English: A Linguistic and Social Analysis.* (Urban Language Series 8.) Arlington, VA: Center for Applied Linguistics.
Fasold, Ralph W. and Roger W. Shuy (eds.)
    1970   *Teaching Standard English in the Inner City.* (Urban Language Series 6.) Washington, D.C.: Center for Applied Linguistics.
    1975   *Analyzing Variation in Language. Papers from the Second Colloquium on New Ways of Analyzing Variation.* Washington, D.C.: Georgetown University Press.
Ferguson, Charles and Shirley Brice Heat (eds.)
    1981   *Language in the USA.* Cambridge: Cambridge University Press.
Filppula, Markku
    1999   *The Grammar of Irish English: Language in Hibernian Style.* (Routledge Studies in Germanic Linguistics 5.) London/New York: Routledge.
Foley, Joseph A. (ed.)
    1988   *New Englishes – The Case of Singapore.* Singapore: Singapore University Press.
Foley, Joseph A., Thiru Kandiah, Bao Zhiming, Anthea F. Gupta, Lubna Alasgoff, Ho Chee Lick, Lionel Wee, Ismail S. Talib and Wendy Bokhurst-Heng
    1998   *English in New Cultural Contexts: Reflections from Singapore.* Singapore: Oxford University Press.
Foulkes, Paul and Gerard Docherty (eds.)
    1999   *Urban Voices: Accent Studies in the British Isles.* London: Arnold.
Francis, W. Nelson
    1958   *The Structure of American English.* New York: Ronald Press.
Frazer, Timothy C. (ed.)
    1993   *'Heartland' English: Variation and Transition in the American Midwest.* Tuscaloosa: University of Alabama Press.
García, Ofelia and Ricardo Otheguy (eds.)
    1989   *English across Cultures, Cultures across English: A Reader in Cross-Cultural Communication.* (Contributions to the Sociology of Language 53.) Berlin/New York: Mouton de Gruyter.
Gilbert, Glenn (ed.)
    1987   *Pidgin and Creole Languages: Essays in Memory of John E. Reinecke.* Honolulu: University of Hawaii Press.

Gordon, Elizabeth and Tony Deverson
 1998   *New Zealand English and English in New Zealand.* Auckland: New House
         Publishers.
Gordon, Matthew J.
 2001   *Small-Town Values and Big-City Vowels: A Study of the Northern Cities
         Shift in Michigan.* (Publication of the American Dialect Society 84.)
         Durham: Duke University Press.
Görlach, Manfred (ed.)
 1985   *Focus on Scotland.* (Varieties of English around the World, General
         Series 5.) Amsterdam/Philadelphia: Benjamins.
Görlach, Manfred and John A. Holm (eds.)
 1986   *Focus on the Caribbean.* (Varieties of English around the World, General
         Series 8.) Amsterdam/Philadelphia: Benjamins.
Green, Lisa
 2002   *African American English: A Linguistic Introduction.* Cambridge: Cam-
         bridge University Press.
Guy, Gregory, John Baugh, Crawford Feagin and Deborah Schiffrin (eds.)
 1996   *Towards a Social Science of Language, Volume 1: Variation and Change
         in Language and Society.* Amsterdam/Philadelphia: Benjamins.
 1997   *Towards a Social Science of Language, Volume 2: Social Interaction and
         Discourse Structures.* Amsterdam/Philadelphia: Benjamins.
Hackert, Stephanie
 2004   *Urban Bahamian Creole. System and Variation.* Amsterdam/Philadelphia:
         Benjamins.
Hancock, Ian F., Morris Goodman, Bernd Heine and Edgar Polomé (eds.)
 1979   *Readings in Creole Studies.* Ghent: Story-Scientia.
Hewitt, Roger
 1986   *White Talk, Black Talk: Inter-Racial Friendship and Communication
         amongst Adolescents.* Cambridge: Cambridge University Press.
Hickey, Raymond
 2004   *The Legacy of Colonial English: Transported Dialects.* Cambridge:
         Cambridge University Press.
 2005   *The Sound Atlas of Irish English.* Berlin/New York: Mouton de Gruyter.
Holm, John A.
 1988
 –1989   *Pidgins and Creoles.* 2 Volumes. Cambridge: Cambridge University
         Press.
 2000   *An Introduction to Pidgins and Creoles.* Cambridge: Cambridge University
         Press.
Holm, John A. and Peter Patrick
 forthcoming   *Comparative Creole Syntax: Parallel Outlines of 18 Creole
               Grammars.* London: Battlebridge.
Holm, John A. (ed.)
 1983   *Central American English.* (Varieties of English around the World, Text
         Series 2.) Heidelberg: Groos.

Huber, Magnus and Mikael Parkvall (eds.)
   1999   *Spreading the Word: The Issue of Diffusion among the Atlantic Creoles.*
           London: University of Westminster Press.
Hughes, Arthur and Peter Trudgill
   1996   *English Accents and Dialects: An Introduction to Social and Regional
           Varieties of English in the British Isles.* 3rd edition. London: Arnold.
Hymes, Dell H. (ed.)
   1971   *Pidginization and Creolization of Languages: Proceedings of a Conference,
           Held at the University of the West Indies Mona, Jamaica, April 1968.*
           Cambridge: Cambridge University Press.
James, Winford and Valerie Youssef
   2002   *The Languages of Tobago. Genesis, Structure and Perspectives.* St. Au-
           gustine, Trinidad: University of the West Indies.
Jones, Charles (ed.)
   1997   *The Edinburgh History of the Scots Language.* Edinburgh: Edinburgh
           University Press.
Kachru, Braj B.
   1983   *The Indianization of English: The English Language in India.* Delhi:
           Oxford University Press.
Kachru, Braj B. (ed.)
   1982   *The Other Tongue: English Across Cultures.* Urbana: University of Illinois
           Press.
Kachru, Braj B. (ed.)
   2005   *Asian Englishes. Beyond the Canon:* Hong Kong: Hong Kong University
           Press.
Kachru, Braj B., Yamuna Kachru and Cecil L. Nelson (eds.)
   2006   *The Handbook of World Englishes.* Oxford: Blackwell.
Kachru, Yamuna and Cecil L. Nelson
   2006   *World Englishes in Asian Contexts.* Hong Kong: Hong Kong University
           Press.
Kautzsch, Alexander
   2002   *The Historical Evolution of Earlier African American English. An Em-
           pirical Comparison of Early Sources.* (Topics in English Linguistics 38.)
           Berlin/New York: Mouton de Gruyter.
Keesing, Roger M.
   1988   *Melanesian Pidgin and the Oceanic Substrate.* Stanford: Stanford
           University Press.
Kirk, John M. and Dónall P. Ó Baoill
   2001   *Language Links: The Languages of Scotland and Ireland.* Belfast: Cló
           Olscoill na Banríona [Queen's University Press].
Kirk, John M., Stewart Sanderson and John D.A. Widdowson (eds.)
   1985   *Studies in Linguistic Geography: The Dialects of English in Britain and
           Ireland.* London et al.: Croom Helm.
Kortmann, Bernd, Tanja Herrmann, Lukas Pietsch and Susanne Wagner
   2005   *A Comparative Grammar of British English Dialects: Agreement, Gender,
           Relative Clauses.* Berlin/New York: Mouton de Gruyter.

Kortmann, Bernd (ed.)
  2004   *Dialectology Meets Typology: Dialect Grammar from a Cross-Linguistic Perspective.* Berlin/New York: Mouton de Gruyter.
Krapp, George P.
  1925   *The English Language in America.* 2 Volumes. New York: Century.
Kretzschmar, William A. and Edgar W. Schneider
  1996   *Introduction to Quantitative Analysis of Linguistic Survey Data: An Atlas by the Numbers.* (Empirical Linguistics Series.) Thousand Oaks, CA: Sage.
Kretzschmar, William A., Virginia G. McDavid, Theodore K. Lerud and Ellen Johnson (eds.)
  1993   *Handbook of the Linguistic Atlas of the Middle and South Atlantic States.* Chicago: University of Chicago Press.
Kurath, Hans
  1949   *A Word Geography of the Eastern United States.* Ann Arbor: University of Michigan Press.
Kurath, Hans and Raven I. McDavid, Jr.
  1961   *The Pronunciation of English in the Atlantic States. Based upon the Collections of the Linguistic Atlas.* (Studies in American English 3.) Ann Arbor: University of Michigan Press.
Kurath, Hans (ed.)
  1939
  –1943   *Linguistic Atlas of New England.* Providence: Brown University Press.
Labov, William
  1966   *The Social Stratification of English in New York City.* (Urban Language Series 1.) Washington, D.C.: Center for Applied Linguistics.
  1972a   *Language in the Inner City: Studies in the Black English Vernacular.* (Conduct and Communication 3.) Philadelphia: University of Pennsylvania Press.
  1972b   *Sociolinguistic Patterns.* (Conduct and Communication 4.) Philadelphia: University of Pennsylvania Press.
  1980   *Locating Language in Time and Space.* (Quantitative Analyses of Linguistic Structure.) New York: Academic Press.
  1994   *Principles of Linguistic Change, Volume 1: Internal Factors.* (Language in Society 20.) Oxford/Malden, MA: Blackwell.
  2001   *Principles of Linguistic Change, Volume 2: Social Factors.* (Language in Society 29.) Oxford/Malden, MA: Blackwell.
Labov, William, Richard Steiner and Malcah Yaeger
  1972   *A Quantitative Study of Sound Change in Progress: Report on National Science Foundation Contract NSF-GS-3278 University of Pennsylvania.* Philadelphia: University of Pennsylvania Regional Survey.
Labov, William, Sharon Ash and Charles Boberg
  2006   *Atlas of North American English: Phonetics, Phonology and Sound Change.* (Topics in English Linguistics 41.) Berlin/New York: Mouton de Gruyter.

Lalla, Barbara and Jean D'Costa
1990   *Language in Exile: Three Hundred Years of Jamaican Creole.* Tuscaloosa: University of Alabama Press.
Lanehart, Sonja L. (ed.)
2001   *Sociocultural and Historical Contexts of African American English.* (Varieties of English around the World, General Series 27.) Amsterdam/ Philadelphia: Benjamins.
Leitner, Gerhard
2004a   *Australia's Many Voices. Australian English – The National Language.* Berlin/New York: Mouton de Gruyter.
2004b   *Australia's Many Voices. Ethnic Englishes, Indigenous and Migrant Languages. Policy and Education.* Berlin/New York: Mouton de Gruyter.
LePage, Robert B. and Andrée Tabouret-Keller
1985   *Acts of Identity: Creole-based Approaches to Language and Ethnicity.* Cambridge: Cambridge University Press.
Lim, Lisa (ed.)
2004   *Singapore English. A Grammatical Description.* Amsterdam/Philadelphia: Benjamins.
Lindquist, Hans, Maria Estling, Staffan Klintborg and Magnus Levin (eds.)
1998   *The Major Varieties of English: Papers from MAVEN 97, Växjö 20–22 November 1997.* (Acta Wexionensia: Humaniora; 1.) Växjö: Växjo University.
Matthews, William
1938   *Cockney Past and Present: A Short History of the Dialect of London.* London: Routledge.
McArthur, Tom
1992   *The Oxford Companion to the English Language.* Oxford: Oxford University Press.
2002   *Oxford Guide to World English.* Oxford: Oxford University Press.
McMillan, James B. and Michel B. Montgomery
1989   *Annotated Bibliography of Southern American English.* Tuscaloosa/ London: University of Alabama Press.
McWhorter, John H. (ed.)
2000   *Language Change and Language Contact in Pidgins and Creoles.* (Creole Language Library 21.) Amsterdam/Philadelphia: Benjamins.
Mehrotra, Raja Ram
1998   *Indian English – Text and Interpretation.* (Varieties of English around the World, Text Series 7.) Amsterdam/Philadelphia: Benjamins.
Melchers, Gunnel and Philip Shaw
2003   *World Englishes.* London: Arnold.
Mencken, Henry
1963   *The American Language: An Inquiry into the Development of English in the United States. With the Assistance of David W. Maurer.* New York: Knopf.

Mesthrie, Rajend (ed.)
1995   *Language and Social History: Studies in South African Sociolinguistics.* Cape Town: David Philip.
2002   *Language in South Africa.* Cambridge: Cambridge University Press.
Milroy, James
1981   *Regional Accents of English: Belfast.* Belfast: Blackstaff.
Milroy, James and Lesley Milroy (eds.)
1993   *Real English: The Grammar of English Dialects in the British Isles.* (Real Language Series.) London: Longman.
Montgomery, Michael B. and Guy Bailey (eds.)
1986   *Language Variety in the South: Perspectives in Black and White.* University, AL: University of Alabama Press.
Montgomery, Michael B. and Thomas Nunnally (eds.)
1998   *From the Gulf States and Beyond. The Legacy of Lee Pederson and LAGS.* Tuscaloosa, AL/London: University of Alabama Press.
Mufwene, Salikoko S.
2001   *The Ecology of Language Evolution.* (Cambridge Approaches to Language Contact.) Cambridge: Cambridge University Press.
Mufwene, Salikoko S., Guy Bailey, John Baugh and John R. Rickford (eds.)
1998   *African-American English. Structure, History and Use.* London: Routledge.
Mufwene, Salikoko S. (ed.)
1993   *Africanisms in Afro-American Language Varieties.* Athens: University of Georgia Press.
Mühleisen, Susanne
2002   *Creole Discourse: Exploring Prestige Formation and Change across Caribbean English-Lexicon Creoles.* (Creole Language Library 24.) Amsterdam/Philadelphia: Benjamins.
Mühlhäusler, Peter
1997   *Pidgin and Creole Linguistics.* (Westminster Creolistic Series 3.) London: University of Westminster Press.
Murray, Thomas and Beth Lee Simon (eds.)
2006   *Language Variation and Change in the American Midland: A New Look at "Heartland" English.* Amsterdam/Philadelphia: Benjamins.
Muysken, Pieter and Norval Smith (eds.)
1986   *Substrata versus Universals in Creole Genesis. Papers from the Amsterdam Creole Workshop, April 1985.* (Creole Language Library 1.) Amsterdam/Philadelphia: Benjamins.
Myers-Scotton, Carol
2002   *Contact Linguistics: Bilingual Encounters and Grammatical Outcomes.* (Oxford Linguistics.) Oxford: Oxford University Press.
Nagle, Stephen J. and Sara L. Sanders (eds.)
2003   *English in the Southern United States.* (Studies in English Language.) Cambridge: Cambridge University Press.

Neumann-Holzschuh, Ingrid and Edgar W. Schneider (eds.)
  2000   *Degrees of Restructuring in Creole Languages.* (Creole Language Library 22.) Amsterdam/Philadelphia: Benjamins.
Nihalani, Paroo, Priya Hosali and Ray K. Tongue
  1989   *Indian and British English: A Handbook of Usage and Pronunciation.* (Oxford India Paperbacks.) Delhi: Oxford University Press.
Noss, Richard B. (ed.)
  1984   *An Overview of Language Issues in South-East Asia: 1950–1980.* Singapore: Oxford University Press.
Orton, Harold (ed.)
  1962
  –1971   *Survey of English Dialects: The Basic Material.* 4 Volumes. Leeds: Arnold.
Orton, Harold, Stewart Sanderson and John Widdowson (eds.)
  1978   *The Linguistic Atlas of England.* London: Croom Helm.
Parasher, S.V.
  1991   *Indian English: Functions and Form.* (Sell-series in English Language and Literature 19.) New Delhi: Bahri.
Parkvall, Mikael
  2000   *Out of Africa: African Influences in Atlantic Creoles.* London: Battlebridge.
Patrick, Peter L.
  1999   *Urban Jamaican Creole: Variation in the Mesolect.* (Varieties of English around the World, General Series 17.) Amsterdam/Philadelphia: Benjamins.
Pederson, Lee (ed.)
  1986
  –1992   *The Linguistic Atlas of the Gulf States.* 7 Volumes. Athens, GA: University of Georgia Press.
Plag, Ingo (ed.)
  2003   *Phonology and Morphology of Creole Languages.* (Linguistische Arbeiten 478.) Tübingen: Niemeyer.
Platt, John, Mian Lian Ho and Heidi Weber
  1983   *Singapore and Malaysia.* (Varieties of English around the World, Text Series 4.) Amsterdam/Philadelphia: Benjamins.
  1984   *The New Englishes.* London: Routledge and Kegan Paul.
Poplack, Shana and Sali Tagliamonte
  2001   *African American English in the Diaspora.* (Language in Society 30.) Oxford/Malden, MA: Blackwell.
Poplack, Shana (ed.)
  2000   *The English History of African American English.* (Language in Society 28.) Oxford/Malden, MA: Blackwell.
Preston, Dennis R. (ed.)
  1993   *American Dialect Research: An Anthology Celebrating the 100th Anniversary of the American Dialect Society.* (Centennial Series of the American Dialect Society.) Amsterdam/Philadelphia: Benjamins.

Rampton, Ben
  1995   *Crossing: Language and Ethnicity among Adolescents.* (Real Language Series.) London: Longman.
Rickford, John R.
  1987   *Dimensions of a Creole Continuum: History, Texts, and Linguistics Analysis of Guyanese Creole.* Stanford: Stanford University Press.
  1999   *African American Vernacular English: Features, Evolution, Educational Implications.* (Language in Society 26.) Oxford/Malden, MA: Blackwell.
Rickford, John R. and Suzanne Romaine (eds.)
  1999   *Creole Genesis, Attitudes and Discourse: Studies Celebrating Charlene J. Sato.* (Creole Language Library 20.) Amsterdam/Philadelphia: Benjamins.
Roberts, Peter A.
  1988   *West Indians and their Language.* Cambridge: Cambridge University Press.
Romaine, Suzanne
  1988   *Pidgin and Creole Languages.* (Longman Linguistics Library.) London/ New York: Longman.
Schmied, Josef J.
  1991   *English in Africa: An Introduction.* (Longman Linguistics Library.) London: Longman.
Schneider, Edgar W.
  1989   *American Earlier Black English. Morphological and Syntactical Variables.* Tuscaloosa, AL/London: University of Alabama Press.
Schneider, Edgar W. (ed.)
  1996   *Focus on the USA.* (Varieties of English around the World, General Series 16.) Amsterdam/Philadelphia: Benjamins.
  1997a   *Englishes Around the World, Volume 1: General Studies, British Isles, North America: Studies in Honour of Manfred Görlach.* (Varieties of English around the World, General Series 18.) Amsterdam/Philadelphia: Benjamins.
  1997b   *Englishes Around the World, Volume 2: Caribbean, Africa, Asia, Australasia. Studies in Honour of Manfred Görlach.* (Varieties of English around the World, General Series 19.) Amsterdam/Philadelphia: Benjamins.
  2007   *Postcolonial English.* Cambridge: Cambridge University Press.
Sebba, Mark
  1993   *London Jamaican: Language Systems in Interaction.* (Real Language Series.) London: Longman.
  1997   *Contact Languages – Pidgins and Creoles.* (Modern Linguistics Series.) London: Macmillan.
Singh, Ishtla
  2000   *Pidgins and Creoles – An Introduction.* London: Arnold.
Singler, John V. (ed.)
  1990   *Pidgin and Creole Tense-Mood-Aspect Systems.* (Creole Language Library 6.) Amsterdam/Philadelphia: Benjamins.

Spears, Arthur K. and Donald Winford (eds.)
  1997   *The Structure and Status of Pidgins and Creoles. Including Selected Papers from the Meetings of the Society for Pidgin and Creole Linguistics.* (Creole Language Library 19.) Amsterdam/Philadelphia: Benjamins.
Spencer, John (ed.)
  1971   *The English Language in West Africa.* (English Language Series.) London: Longman.
Thomas, Erik R.
  2001   *An Acoustic Analysis of Vowel Variation in New World English.* (Publication of the American Dialect Society 85.) Durham: Duke University Press.
Thomason, Sarah G.
  2001   *Contact Languages.* Edinburgh: University of Edinburgh Press.
Thomason, Sarah G. and Terrence Kaufman
  1988   *Language Contact, Creolization and Genetic Linguistics.* Berkeley: University of California Press.
Tristram, Hildegard, L.C. (ed.)
  1998   *The Celtic Englishes.* (Anglistische Forschungen 247.) Heidelberg: Winter.
  2000   *The Celtic Englishes II.* (Anglistische Forschungen 286.) Heidelberg: Winter.
  2003   *The Celtic Englishes III.* (Anglistische Forschungen 324.) Heidelberg: Winter.
Trudgill, Peter
  1974   *The Social Differentiation of English in Norwich.* (Cambridge Studies in Linguistics 13.) Cambridge: Cambridge University Press.
  1986   *Dialects in Contact.* (Language in Society 10.) Oxford: Blackwell.
  1999   *The Dialects of England.* 2nd edition. Oxford: Blackwell. also: *The Dialects of England.* 2nd edition. Oxford: Blackwell.
Trudgill, Peter and Jean Hannah
  2002   *International English: A Guide to Varieties of Standard English.* 4th edition. London: Arnold.
  1994   *International English: A Guide to Varieties of Standard English.* 3rd edition. London: Arnold.
  1985   *International English: A Guide to Varieties of Standard English.* 2nd edition. London: Arnold.
  1982   *International English: A Guide to Varieties of Standard English.* London: Arnold.
Trudgill, Peter (ed.)
  1978   *Sociolinguistic Patterns in British English.* London: Arnold.
  1984   *Language in the British Isles.* Cambridge: Cambridge University Press.
Trudgill, Peter and J.K. Chambers (eds.)
  1991   *Dialects of English: Studies in Grammatical Variation.* (Longman Linguistics Library.) London/New York: Longman.
Upton, Clive, David Parry and John D.A. Widdowson
  1994   *Survey of English Dialects: The Dictionary and Grammar.* London: Routledge.

Viereck, Wolfgang (ed.)
    1985   *Focus on England and Wales.* (Varieties of English around the World, General Series 4.) Amsterdam/Philadelphia: Benjamins.

Wakelin, Martyn
    1981   *English Dialects: An Introduction.* London: Athlone Press.

Wakelin, Martyn F. (ed.)
    1972   *Patterns in the Folk Speech of the British Isles. With a Foreword by Harold Orton.* London: Athlone Press.

Watts, Richard and Peter Trudgill (eds.)
    2002   *Alternative Histories of English.* London: Routledge.

Wells, John C.
    1982   *Accents of English.* 3 Volumes. Cambridge: Cambridge University Press.

Williamson, Juanita and Virginia M. Burke (eds.)
    1971   *A Various Language. Perspectives on American Dialects.* New York: Holt, Rinehart and Winston.

Winer, Lise
    1993   *Trinidad and Tobago.* (Varieties of English around the World, Text Series 6.) Amsterdam/Philadelphia: Benjamins.

Winford, Donald
    1993   *Predication in Carribean English Creoles.* (Creole Language Library 10.) Amsterdam/Philadelphia: Benjamins.
    2003   *An Introduction to Contact Linguistics.* (Language in Society 33.) Malden/Oxford/Melbourne: Blackwell.

Wolfram, Walt
    1969   *A Sociolinguistic Description of Detroit Negro Speech.* (Urban Language Series 5.) Washington, D.C.: Center for Applied Linguistics.

Wolfram, Walt and Ralph W. Fasold
    1974   *The Study of Social Dialects in American English.* Englewood Cliffs, NJ: Prentice Hall.

Wolfram, Walt and Donna Christian
    1976   *Appalachian Speech.* Arlington, VA: Center for Applied Linguistics.

Wolfram, Walt and Natalie Schilling-Estes
    2005   *American English: Dialects and Variation.* (Language in Society 25.) 2nd ed. Malden, MA/Oxford: Blackwell.

Wolfram, Walt, Kirk Hazen and Natalie Schilling-Estes
    1999   *Dialect Change and Maintenance on the Outer Banks.* (Publication of the American Dialect Society 81.) Tuscaloosa, AL/London: University of Alabama Press.

Wolfram, Walt and Erik R. Thomas
    2002   *The Development of African American English.* (Language in Society 31.) Oxford/Malden, MA: Blackwell.

Wolfram, Walt and Ben Wards (eds.)
    2006   *American Voices: How Dialects Differ from Coast to Coast.* Oxford: Blackwell

Wright, Joseph
  1898
  –1905   *The English Dialect Dictionary*. Oxford: Clarendon Press.
  1905   *The English Dialect Grammar*. Oxford: Frowde.

Introduction: varieties of English in Africa and South and Southeast Asia

Rajend Mesthrie

1.   Historical spread and geographical coverage

The presence of English (and other European languages) in Africa and South and Southeast Asia (henceforth *Africa-Asia*) is due to several historical events: sporadic and subsequently sustained trade, the introduction of Christianity, slavery, formal British colonisation, and influence from the U.S. (in places like Liberia and the Philippines). Furthermore, after colonisation independent "new nations" were faced with few options but to adopt English as a working language of government, administration and higher education. These contacts have seen the development of several types of English:

> *ENL* (English as a Native language), spoken by British settlers and/or their descendants, as in Zimbabwe, South Africa, Hong Kong etc. (The variety may be adopted by other groups within a territory as well).

> *ESL* (English as a Second Language), spoken in territories like India and Nigeria, where access to English was sufficient to produce a stable second language (L2) used in formal domains like education and government. The ESL is also used for internal communication within the territory, especially as a lingua franca amongst educated speakers who do not share the same mother tongue.

> *Pidgin English*, a variety which arises outside of the educational system and is only partly derived from English, especially in its lexicon; though structurally it cannot really be considered an 'adoption' of English syntax. An example would be Pidgin English in Cameroon. A pidgin shows equally significant influence from both local languages and common or 'universal' processes of simplification and creation of grammatical structure. Some pidgins may turn into a creole (spoken as a first language). In Africa and Asia this is not common, since speakers frequently retain their home and community languages. Some scholars are of the opinion that West African varieties of pidgin have expanded into a creole without necessarily becoming a first language.

These three types are described in this volume. A fourth type *EFL* (English as a Foreign Language) is not considered, since it arises typically for international communication amongst a few bilingual people competent in English in a territory that had not come under the direct influence of British settlement and colonial administration. In such a situation English is learnt in the education system as a "foreign language", but is not used as a medium of instruction. This is truer of some territories than others: China is clearly an EFL country; Eritrea less so, in terms of the greater use of English by fluent bilinguals in the domain of education.

British "Protectorates" like Lesotho and Egypt, which were subject to British influence without being formally colonised, also form an intermediate category somewhere between ESL and EFL. It would not be surprising if the current era of globalisation established English more firmly in EFL territories, producing more focussed varieties which could one day be studied in terms of the concepts and categories emphasised in ESL studies.

Finally, there are what I term "language shift Englishes" – varieties which started as ESLs, but which stabilise as an L1. They then develop casual registers often absent from ESLs (since a local language fulfils 'vernacular' functions). However, they retain a great many L2 features as well. Amongst the varieties of note here are Indian South African English and, elsewhere, Irish English.

Africa-Asia is distinguishable from the remaining regions covered in the companion volumes by the preponderance of ESL varieties, rather than the L1 English which dominates in the U.K., the U.S., Canada, Australia and New Zealand. In other words, indigenous African and Asian languages have survived the impact of colonisation better than their counterparts elsewhere.

Though English is seen as an important resource for international communication as well as for internal "High" functions (in formal domains like education and government), its hegemony in Africa-Asia is not complete. There are other languages of high status which may function as regional lingua francas, for example Swahili in East Africa, Hindi in North India and Malay in Singapore and Malaysia.

At the lower end of the social and educational spectrum it is noteworthy that Pidgin English is spreading rapidly in West Africa. According to Faraclas (this volume), Nigerian Pidgin is now the most widely spoken language in Nigeria, with well over half the population being able to converse in it.

Africa's contacts with English pre-date those of the U.S. and the Caribbean. The earliest contacts were in the 1530s (Spencer 1971: 8), making early Modern English, with accents slightly older than Shakespeare's, the initial (if sporadic) input. In Asia the initial contacts with English go back to 1600 when Queen Elizabeth I granted a charter to the merchants of London who formed the East India Company.

The full force of English in Africa-Asia was not felt until formal colonisation in the nineteenth century (for example Singapore in 1819, India in 1858,

Nigeria 1884, Kenya 1886). A representative selection of the varieties spoken in these territories is given in this volume. The geographical coverage is that of West Africa, East Africa, South Africa, South Asia and South-east Asia. In addition we have taken on board the South Atlantic island of St. Helena, whose nearest mainland port is Cape Town.

2. Second language acquisition

Since the focus in the Africa-Asia section is mainly on ESLs, the dialectological approach has to be supplemented by insights from Second Language Acquisition (SLA) theory. No ESL variety is uniform; rather it exists as a continuum of varying features, styles and abilities. The terms *basilect, mesolect* and *acrolect* are borrowed from Creole studies, where they denote first language varieties on a continuum. The terms *basilang, mesolang* and *acrolang* are sometimes used in connection with interlanguage studies, denoting the individual's level of competence in the L2, rather than a relatively focussed group norm (a newcomer in the L1 English metropolis might learn English as a L2 without being part of a group of L2 learners).

Most writers in *New English* studies adopt the Creole-based terms, without serious misunderstandings. However, in principle, there is a need to distinguish between basilect and basilang, because there is a difference between the fluent norms of a basilect and the rudimentary knowledge of an L2 in a basilang. Since the ESL varieties described in this Handbook are relatively focused and stable the labels basilect, mesolect, acrolect will continue to be used.

At one end of the New English continuum are varieties characteristic of beginning L2 learners or learners who have fossilised at an early stage and evince no need or desire to progress further in their interlanguage variety (basilectal speakers). If they are just beginning an acquaintance with the target language, they are strictly speaking basilang speakers. At the other end are speakers who, by virtue of their education, motivation, life-styles and contacts with L1 and educated L2 speakers of English may well become so fluent as to be near-native (or acrolectal) speakers of English.

Situated between these endpoints is the vast majority of ESL users, who speak fluently but whose norms deviate significantly from those of L1 speakers as well as acrolectal ESL speakers. These are the mesolectal speakers, whose norms are the ones most writers in this section have chosen to focus on, since they represent a kind of average value of the ESL. They are not as strongly denigrated as more basilang varieties might be in terms of intelligibility and fluency. They also pose fewer problems about the reliability of data, since a basilang speaker's command might not be fluent enough to decide what norms underlie his or her speech.

Mesolectal ESL varieties display a degree of levelling of the target language (Standard English) in for example tense forms, prepositions, word order and so on. Moreover, many of these features are carried over into the (unedited) written language of individuals. Finally, mesolectal varieties are more representative of the local ethos than acrolectal varieties. The latter are sometimes stigmatised as being affected or representing outside norms.

Phrases like "speaking through the nose" in Nigeria and Zimbabwe or *been tos* ('people who have been abroad') in India and Nigeria reflect this disaffection on the part of the general populace of the ESL acrolectal elite who might stray too close to the norms of Received Pronunciation (RP). Just as stigmatised is what is described in Ghanaian English terminology as *LAFA* ('Locally Acquired Foreign Accent') – see Huber's article on Ghanaian English Phonology in this volume.

The provisos mentioned by other editors in their introductions regarding the nature of dialectal description also hold for the present area. Where an item is described as a feature, it is not claimed to be unique to the variety concerned. Nor is it necessarily the only variant within the ESL being described. The influence of the standard in formal communication makes it likely that the equivalent standard feature is also in use (especially in syntax), and may even be more commonly employed than the item described as a feature.

Several concepts from Second Language Acquisition Studies are an essential part of New English studies, especially *input, Foreigner Talk* and *Teacher Talk, overgeneralization, analogy* and *transfer*. The robustness of the substrate languages in Africa and Asia makes the likelihood of their influence on ESL very great. Indeed, many researchers take substrate influence to be axiomatic in phonology and only slightly less so in syntax, pragmatics and lexis.

For syntax, however, there is reason to be cautious. In some areas it is possible that what is popularly believed to be interference, might be a survival from a non-standard dialect of British English or even a survival of a form that was once standard but was later jettisoned in the history of Standard English (see for example McCormick's account of Cape Flats English in this volume). This issue will be discussed in more detail in my synopsis at the end of the phonology part.

Many contributors use RP and Standard British English as points of comparison. However, it is important to keep in mind that this is rather a matter of convenience and that RP and Standard British English function as a kind of metalanguage in that respect. RP, especially, would have been, and continues to be, rather remote from the experiences of ESL learners. Especially for the earliest periods in which English was introduced to what were to become the colonies, several non-standard varieties were part of the initial input.

The earliest teachers and providers of input were missionaries (frequently EFL users themselves), sailors, soldiers, hunters, tradesmen, divers and so forth. Teachers with certificates arrived on the scene later. The notion of a target language then should not be construed too literally: more often it was a varied, vexatious and moving target (see Mesthrie 2003).

It is necessary to tackle the prejudice against New Englishes, sometimes evident amongst their own speakers. Although prescriptive-minded critics would prefer to see many of the features identified in this section as errors to be eradicated, their presence must be seen within a broader context. An ESL exists within a local "linguistic ecology". It must therefore become referentially adequate to describe local topography, fauna, customs and so forth. It also has to blend in with the local linguistic ecology by being receptive to favoured turns of phrase, structural possibilities and habits of pronunciation. That is, for English to function "normally" in a country like India, it has to become Indian – a fact that the work of Kachru (e.g. 1983) constantly reminds us of.

3.   Resources

It is only recently that the study of ESLs has come to be seen as a productive sociolinguistic enterprise. Studies of individual varieties have often been based on written sources, both of published writers and of students' writings at school and university. Convenient though this means of accessing data is, for psycholinguistic veracity it is preferable to focus on the spoken word. Most authors in this volume have based their descriptions on speech samples or a combination of written (especially when summarising previous research) and spoken data. Corpus Linguistics is beginning to make its presence felt in this area. The most influential corpora are the ICE Corpora (*International Corpus of English*) originating at the University of London.

The ICE corpora in East Africa under the directorship of Josef Schmied and in South Africa under Chris Jeffery have yielded significant data and analyses. Schmied (this volume) describes the potential of the *World Wide Web* in gathering informal written data in the East African context. In India, the Kolhapur corpus is based on written Indian English. Other smaller-scale corpora are mentioned by individual authors.

4.   The chapters on phonology

Gut's chapter deals with the phonological features of L2 English in Nigeria. In such a vast territory with about 500 languages, it is likely that several Englishes coexist: Gut summarizes her own research as well as that of others according to region and the major regional languages – Hausa, Yoruba and Igbo. She also summarizes her important investigations into suprasegmental phonology, with the analysis of tone being a major challenge for any student of English in Africa. Elugbe's article focuses on Pidgin English in Nigeria, one of the fastest growing languages in West Africa. This study offers the opportunity of examining whether the same features of L2 phonology of Nigerian English co-exist in the pidgin, including features of stress and tone. Huber describes the phonology of Ghanaian English, affording opportunities of comparing features of English in a country which prides itself on its education system and in the teaching of English with that of other West African varieties. Huber contributes a second chapter on Pidgin English in Ghana. This chapter again shows the overlap between pidgin and L2 English phonology in West Africa. Singler's article on Liberian Settler English phonology introduces the sound system of a variety whose origins lie in the speech of slaves who were returned from the American South in the 19th century to found the state of Liberia. Together with Krio, Liberian Settler English is important for its influence on pidgins that developed independently in West Africa. It is also important for historical studies of African American English, since the two varieties are so closely linked. The last two contributions on West Africa are Bobda's comprehensive examination of Cameroon English phonology and Menang's account of the phonology of Kamtok, the name he prefers for Cameroon Pidgin English. His focus is on the reductions to the English vowel system evident in the pidgin.

East Africa is represented by the article by Schmied, which focuses on the similarities between the English varieties spoken in Kenya, Tanzania and Uganda. South Africa presents special challenges to the descriptive linguist, since several types of English are encountered: ENL, ESL and language-shift varieties. The policy of apartheid created relatively rigid boundaries around people, their languages and dialects. It was accordingly felt that a description of the four major varieties according to ethnicity was preferable to any other forms of segmentation.

Bowerman describes White South Africa English, tracing its roots in Southern British dialects and describing subsequent influences arising either spontaneously or out of contact with Afrikaans. He also briefly points to its relation with other Southern Hemisphere Englishes in Australia and New Zealand. Van

Rooy outlines the main phonological features of Black South African English, now a major player in post-apartheid broadcasting, business etc. The article affords significant grounds of comparison with other varieties of English in Africa. Mesthrie provides a description of the phonology of Indian South African English, which had previously been studied mainly for its syntax. Finn provides a detailed description of the phonology of Cape Flats English, the variety spoken by people formerly classified "coloured" in Cape Town and its environs. His paper details the balance between (a) (British and South African) English dialect features, (b) second language interlanguage forms adapted, rather than deriving directly, from English-Afrikaans bilingualism and (c) some spontaneous innovations in the variety.

Wilson provides an overview of the phonology of St Helena English, a variety showing links to British dialects as well as to English-based Creoles.

Gargesh provides an overview of the phonology of Indian English, stressing that it has major regional varieties, especially in the North and South, corresponding to the respective Indic and Dravidian phonological systems. Mahboob and Ahmar describe Pakistani English, which shares many features with the northern varieties of Indian English.

Ahmar's contribution is followed by three articles on South-east Asian varieties. Lionel Wee describes the phonology of Singaporean English, while Baskaran covers Malaysian English, which has previously been linked with Singapore English on the basis of their common socio-political history. Tayo describes the phonology of Philippines English, which is targeted towards American rather than British English, the only such L2 (non-creole) variety in Africa-Asia.

5.   The chapters on morphology and syntax

Each article in the phonology section has a counterpart in the morphology and syntax section, except for the Philippines. In addition there is an article on Butler English morphology and syntax, for which no corresponding account of the phonology exists. It would appear that more research is being done on the morphology and syntax of New Englishes than on the phonology.

Alo and Mesthrie summarise the existing research on Nigerian English, showing how it is fairly typical of African English (or more properly, sub-Saharan English). Faraclas offers a detailed overview of Nigerian Pidgin English, focussing to a large extent on its tense-aspect-modality system.

Huber and Dako examine educated Ghanaian English, which has much in common with other West African varieties, though there are noteworthy differences in the area of the ordering of subordinate clauses of time and related constructions.

In his chapter on Ghanaian Pidgin English morphology and syntax, Huber argues that in some respects this variety appears to be a simplified version of other pidgins in the West African area, for example Nigerian Pidgin. Singler's chapter on Liberian Settler English describes the way in which this variety has retained older features of African American English, and can therefore be used to contribute significantly to the current debate on the origins of African American English. He also details the subsequent influence of local (non-Creole) varieties of English upon Liberian Settler English.

Mbangwana contributes an engaging account of the morphology and syntax of Cameroon English. Whilst a few features (e.g. invariant tags in tag questions) can be considered "garden variety" African English (and New English) structures, a number of the features he describes are not (e.g. an apparent predilection for *wh*- words to be retained in situ in main and subordinate clauses.) The reasons for this innovativeness in the Cameroon have still to be ascertained. Ayafor describes the morphology and syntax of Kamtok, the pidgin English of Cameroon. Unlike its ESL counterpart in Cameroon, as described by Mbagwana, Kamtok does appear to be similar to other varieties of West African Pidgin English. Schmied describes the syntax of East African English (Kenya, Uganda and Tanzania). He outlines several general tendencies towards the modification of the grammar of Standard English, often in the direction of simplification.

With respect to the South African varieties, Bowerman outlines the main grammatical features of White South African English, pointing to ongoing debates about the relative significance of retentions from British dialect grammar over language contact with Afrikaans. Mesthrie's overview of Black South African English shows it to be in most respects similar to the "core" grammar of East and West African Englishes. Mesthrie also contributes a chapter on Indian South African English, showing that whilst the variety has much in common with its antecedent in India, it has innovated a great deal in the process of language shift in the South African environment. McCormick describes Cape Flats English, a variety which shows a fair degree of convergence between the grammars of English and Afrikaans.

Wilson and Mesthrie contribute an overview of St. Helena English, especially of its verb phrase component, which shows a convergence between a pidgin-like system and a more superstratal British English system.

Bhatt provides an overview of the grammar of Indian English, from the viewpoint of modern generative syntax. Hosali gives an overview of Butler English, the minimal pidgin (or fossilised early interlanguage) which originated between domestic servants and their masters in British India. Mahboob covers Pakistani English morphology and syntax, which again has a lot in common with the Northern varieties of Indian English as well as with the New Englishes generally.

Lionel Wee describes the morphology and syntax of Singaporean English, detailing some "positive" innovations, including the addition of new forms of the relative clause and passive. Baskaran describes Malaysian English and focuses on the extent to which substrate languages like Malay and Tamil may have played a role in engendering the typical features of Malayasian English morphology and syntax.

References

Mesthrie, Rajend
    2003   The World Englishes paradigm and contact linguistics – refurbishing the foundations. *World Englishes* 22: 449–62.

Phonology

Nigerian English: phonology

Ulrike B. Gut

1.   Linguistic situation and status of English in Nigeria

In Nigeria, the most populous country in Africa with a surface area of 923,768 km^2 and a population of about 130 million, an estimated 505 languages are spoken (Grimes and Grimes 2000). Of the indigenous Nigerian languages, Igbo (spoken in the South-East), Yoruba (spoken in the South-West) and Hausa (spoken in the North) are the major languages with about 18 million speakers each. Many Nigerians are bilingual or multilingual with a command of several Nigerian and non-indigenous languages. The non-indigenous languages spoken in Nigeria include English, spoken throughout the country; Arabic, mainly spoken in the North in Islamic schools and in inter-ethnic communication; and French. English has often been called "the official language of the country" although there is no government statute or decree specifying this. No reliable numbers being available, estimates of how many Nigerians speak and use English vary from 4% to 20% (Jowitt 1997). It seems realistic to assume that currently about 20% of the population have at least some command of English and use it regularly in at least some aspects of their daily lives and that this number is increasing rapidly. Schaefer and Egbokhare (1999) found for the Emai speaking region of rural southern Nigeria that, especially in the younger generations, the use of English is on the increase. Whereas adults report a multi-language strategy of speaking both Emai and English independent of place (home, market, church…), teenagers report a single-language strategy with Emai spoken at home and English used in all other contexts. This is also true for children, who, in addition, increasingly speak English to their siblings and parents.

In contrast to any of the indigenous languages, which serve as either native language or second language in the different regions of Nigeria, English has a geographical spread throughout the country. One reason why English is often regarded as the official language in Nigeria is probably because it is used in predominantly formal contexts such as government, education, literature, business, commerce and as a *lingua franca* in social interaction among the educated élite. For example, government records, administrative instructions and minutes, legislation, court records and proceedings, most advertisements, business transactions and political manifestos and other documents are all in English. Furthermore, the majority of the national newspapers are published in English, as well as most radio and television programmes. Only a few of the Nigerian languages, mainly the majority languages, are used in official contexts. For example, the 1999 Constitution stipulates that "the business of the National Assembly shall be conducted in English, and in Hausa, Ibo and Yoruba when adequate arrangements have been made therefore". Equally, the language of the business of the House of Assembly in each State is English, "but the House may in addition to English conduct the business [...] in one or more other languages spoken in the State as the House may by resolution approve". Some Nigerian languages, mainly the majority languages, are used in primary education and, to some extent, in official transactions, newspapers, television broadcasts and advertisements. The main role of the Nigerian languages is intra-ethnic and occasionally inter-ethnic communication (mainly Hausa in the North).

Attitudes towards English in Nigeria are mixed: on the one hand, it is seen as ethnopolitically neutral and therefore preferable over any indigenous language in the country's decision-making processes; on the other hand, however, English is considered the language of the élite (Jowitt 1997). Furthermore it is regarded by some as the language of colonialism, which alienates Nigerians from their roots, with only the Nigerian languages being associated with cultural identity. At the same time, English is valued highly by many Nigerians as a potential for material and social gain. It is considered a symbol of modernisation and a means of success and mobility as it is used in international communication and is the language of science and technology, literature and art.

English was introduced in Nigeria with the establishment of trading contacts on the West African coast by the British in the sixteenth century. It served as a language of trade for communication between Englishmen and Nigerians in the various forts along the Nigerian coast. This contact resulted in a form of Nigerian Pidgin, which, in all probability, is the predecessor of present-day Nigerian English Pidgin (Bamgbose 1997), which developed and stabilized in the period between the sixteenth and the nineteenth century. Nigerian Pidgin English is most commonly used for inter-ethnic communication and, to a limited extent, in literature and art, official transactions and international communication.

The English took over power in Southern Nigeria in the middle of the nineteenth century. In 1861, Lagos became a British Crown Colony, and in 1900, the area controlled by the British Niger company was proclaimed a British Protectorate. In 1842 and 1846 the first missionary stations were established in Badagry (near Lagos in the Southwest) and Calabar (in the Southeast) respectively. The missionaries were mainly interested in spreading Christianity but also taught agriculture, crafts and hygiene. In order to easily reach the population, the language of instruction was usually the mother tongue of the natives. English began to be formally studied in Nigeria from the middle of the nineteenth century on. When the British government increasingly felt the need for Africans who were literate in English and would serve British colonial and trade interests (for instance as teachers, interpreters, minor government officials and clerks for local courts and the trading companies), in the 1880s, the missionary stations were ordered to teach English in their schools. Since the missionary schools were increasingly unable to meet the demands for educated Nigerians, the colonial government began to establish state schools. The first state school was in fact founded as a result of pressure from Muslims in Lagos in 1899, who had no access to missionary schools and felt they were at a disadvantage. Equally, in Northern Nigeria, Christian mission schools were not allowed in the Muslim areas, and government schools were established. The first European school opened in the North in Kano in 1909. In 1914, Lagos, the British Protectorate and the Northern parts of today's Nigeria was declared the British "Colony of Nigeria". Nigeria became independent in 1960 and declared herself a Republic in 1963.

In Nigerian education today, English plays a key role. The education system in Nigeria is structured in the 6-3-3-4 model with 6 years primary education, 3 years junior secondary level, 3 years senior secondary level and 4 years tertiary education at Universities. The 1998 National Policy on Education specifies that "the medium of instruction in the primary school shall be the language of the environment for the first three years. During this period, English shall be taught as a subject. From the fourth year, English shall progressively be used as a medium of instruction and the language of immediate environment and French shall be taught as subjects". Only in a few private schools in some urban areas are children taught in English from kindergarten. For the majority of Nigerian pupils, all subjects are taught in English from the fourth year of primary education on. This includes subjects such as English, mathematics, a major Nigerian language, science subjects, arts subjects and vocational subjects. All higher level textbooks, students' written assignments and examinations are in English. A good pass in English is required for transition from primary to Junior Secondary School, to Senior Secondary School and to University.

Received Pronunciation (RP) was for a long time the model held up in Nigerian schools and the model for examinations. The majority of the British who resided in Nigeria for a length of time and who filled the government posts created after the establishment of British rule in 1900 came from the upper or middle classes of British society, speaking RP. Their presence helped to ensure that RP had some predominance and prestige in Nigeria. When, after independence, Nigerians took over the senior civil service posts from the British, Standard British English, spoken by the former rulers, was retained as the prestigious standard dialect. This attitude was shared by many politicians, academics, lawyers, journalists and other members of the élite who had close ties with the British and Britain. Recently, with increasing numbers of Nigerians returning from studies in the United States of America, American English is gaining prestige in Nigeria (Jowitt 1991).

There is no uniform accent of English spoken throughout Nigeria. In fact, the diversity of the different kinds of English in the country is so great that Nigerian English (NigE) is usually divided into several sub-varieties. Based on the observation that the native language of Nigerian speakers of English characteristically influences their accent in English, NigE sub-varieties corresponding to the different ethnic groups have been proposed (e.g. Jibril 1986; Jowitt 1991). The three major Nigerian languages have very different phonological systems: Hausa, for example, has five vowels which all have phonemic length contrast and a number of realizations that include centralized vowels. Igbo has eight vowels and a set of vowel harmony rules, whereas Yoruba has seven vowels with phonemic vowel length contrast. These differences are claimed to become apparent in the Hausa English, Igbo English and Yoruba English varieties of NigE (Jowitt 1991).

Since a continuum of degrees of competence in English is a characteristic of any country where the language functions as a second language, most descriptions of the sub-varieties of English spoken in Nigeria correlate levels of competence with the speaker's educational background. Banjo (1971) proposed four varieties with distinct linguistic features:

– Variety I is used by those Nigerians who picked up English as a result of the requirements of their occupation. They are possibly semi-literate people with only elementary school education. It is characterized by a high transfer-rate of phonological features from the mother tongue and is unacceptable even nationally.
– Variety II speakers are likely to have had at least primary school education. It features some transfer from the mother tongue and does not make 'vital phonemic distinctions'. This variety of English is accepted and understood nationally and internationally.
– Variety III is associated with University education and is recommended as the model for Nigerian Standard English. It is most widely accepted in Nigeria.
– Variety IV is equal to British English and is less accepted in Nigeria than Variety III as it sounds affected.

Udofot (2003) claims that Banjo's Variety IV is not a variety of NigE and that spoken NigE in the 1990s can be divided into at least three sub-varieties. These sub-varieties collectively show phonological differences from British Standard English in both segmental and prosodic terms and, in many cases, the speaker's education is correlated with the degree of proficiency.

- The Non-Standard variety has distinct segmental and non-segmental features such as a lack of fluency, an abundance of pauses, a restricted intonation system, a distinct speech rhythm and accent placement. It is spoken by primary and secondary school leavers, holders of NCE (Nigerian Certificate of Education), OND (Ordinary National Diploma) and some University graduates. It is the variety used by primary school teachers.
- The Standard variety has a distinct phoneme inventory and characteristic prosodic features in terms of speech rhythm, intonation and accent. It is spoken by university graduates and lecturers and other professionals as well as final-year undergraduates of English, secondary school teachers and holders of Higher National Diplomas.
- The Sophisticated variety is spoken by university lecturers in English and Linguistics, by graduates of English, the Humanities and Mass Communication, speakers who had some additional training in English phonology and those who spent some time in English native-speaking areas. It is different from British English in some phonemes and some aspects of speech rhythm, intonation and accentuation.

There is also a small minority of Nigerians who speak English with a (mostly British) native-like accent due to being born in Britain or a long period of residence there or special speech training, which is given to e.g. news readers. The native-like accent, however, does not have a high social prestige in Nigeria and is ridiculed as affected and arrogant. Jibril (1986) claims that the closeness of the various accents to RP is less correlated with social class or education and ethnicity than with speech training, as can be found with some newsreaders and journalists. Equally, Jowitt (1991) points out that education and ethnic background are less reliable indicators of the proficiency of a speaker than his or her opportunity to use the language.

Apart from differences in education, many reasons have been put forward for the varieties of English spoken throughout Nigeria, including historical, geographical and sociolinguistic ones. According to Awonusi (1986), the different paths of Western, Eastern and Northern Nigeria in terms of colonization, administration and education resulted in diverse accents. In Yorubaland in the West, the missionaries first employed Englishmen speaking RP as teachers in their schools. When they left as a result of the World War, Nigerians took over, who had to rely on text books as a guide for English pronunciation. In Igboland in the East, schools recruited missionaries from Scotland and Ireland, and features of these accents can be traced in today's Igbo English. In general, movement between school teachers in the South was great. In the government schools of the North native speakers educated at English public schools were employed as teachers, bringing their RP background to Nigeria. Since there was little interaction between Northern and Southern Nigerians educated in English before the All-Nigeria Legislative Assembly in 1947, two divergent accents of English developed in those parts. However, not only through teachers have Nigerians been exposed to a rich variety of English accents. From the outset, there were traders and businessmen with Cockney, Yorkshire, Birmingham accents and hundreds of American Peace Corps volunteers in the 1960s (Jowitt 1991). Furthermore, various groups of non-native speakers such as German, Danish, Dutch and French missionaries and Indians, Japanese, Greek, Lebanese and Chinese businessmen, technicians and doctors lived in Nigeria for considerable amounts of time.

Jibril (1986: 51) describes NigE as "a cluster of regional and social varieties which interact sufficiently in a sociolinguistic continuum to qualify for a common cover term". It is undisputed now that a process of indigenisation has made NigE a recognizable and highly distinctive variety of English (e.g. Bamgbose 1982, 1997; Jowitt 1997). However, no uniform and universally accepted description of the NigE Standard exists yet.

The lack of a clear-cut policy on the English language in Nigeria has been widely criticized, with some critics arguing that an effective language policy in Nigeria will have as an output the cultivation and use of an endonormative, standard, bilingual-bicultural variety of the English language in Nigeria. This is usually proposed to be the variety broadly associated with a certain level of education and with all "Nigerianisms" most Nigerians conform to (e.g. Bamgbose 1997). The problem of codifying a Standard Nigerian variety of English includes deciding which variations are deviant and which are acceptable. Systematic divergences from British English may result from errors and it is difficult to decide which are accepted usage and which constitute individual mistakes. One of the questions to be solved is: When does an erstwhile error become a legitimate variant? Jowitt (1991) proposes that "Standard NigE" should be the sum of all non-standard English forms occurring in all types of NigE, the stable part which consists of accepted, indigenised errors and variants and calls this standard "Popular NigE".

Due to the lack of a well-defined NigE standard, in the following, the phonological properties of the main accents in NigE will be described. These accents are Hausa English, Yoruba English and Igbo English, which represent the major varieties and the only ones to have been researched in some detail. The description will be restricted to the respective educated varieties as the nationally accepted ones with only occasional reference to less educated varieties.

2.   NigE Phonology

To date, notwithstanding some efforts, no representative corpus of spoken NigE is available. This means that despite a growing number of experimental and instrumental studies on various aspects of NigE phonology, most descriptions of NigE are impressionistic rather than based on empirical findings. Due to this lack of quantitative data and the great variability of NigE as a second language variety as described above, in the following only phonological tendencies can be described. Quantitative corroboration is eagerly awaited.

2.1.   Vowels

Compared to the 23 vowels of Southern British English, NigE has a reduced vowel system, which is especially apparent in the less educated varieties: Basic Hausa English has 15 vowels, Basic Yoruba English and Basic Igbo English have 11 vowels each (Jibril 1986). As in any L2 variety of English, the vowel system of NigE reflects the vowel system of the speaker's native language.

Table 1 lists the vowels of Educated Hausa English and Educated Southern NigE as described in Jibril (1986) and Jowitt (1991). The major differences between the Hausa English and the Southern NigE vowel inventories lie in the lack of phonemic vowel length and the lack of centralized vowels in the latter.

Table 1.   The vowels of Educated Hausa English and Educated Southern NigE (Jibril 1986; Jowitt 1991)

	Educated Hausa English	**Educated Southern NigE**
Monophthongs	/iː/, /ɪ/, /ɛ/, /eː/, /æ/, /ʊ/, /aː/, /a/, /o/, /oː/, /uː/, /ʊ/, /ɜː/, /ə/	/i/, /ɛ/, /e/, /a/, /ɪ/, /o/, /u/
Diphthongs	/ai/, /aɪ/, /oi/, /ɪə/, /ɛə/, /ʊə/	/ai/, /aɪ/, /ɔi/, /ia/, /ea/

The distribution of these vowels in both Hausa English and Southern NigE is illustrated in Table 2.

Table 2. Vowel realizations in Educated Hausa English and Educated Southern NigE

	Hausa English	South. NigE		Hausa English	South. NigE		Hausa English	South. NigE
KIT	ɪ	i	FLEECE	i:	i	NEAR	ia	ia, ija
DRESS	ə, a	ɛ, e	FACE	e	e, a	SQUARE	ea	ia, ea
TRAP	a	a	PALM	a:	a	START	a	a
LOT	a	ɔ	THOUGHT	o:	ɔ	NORTH	ɔ	ɔ
STRUT	ɑ, ʊ	ɔ	GOAT	o:	o, ɔ	FORCE	o, oa	ɔ
FOOT	ʊ	u	GOOSE	u:	u	CURE	ua	ua
BATH	a:	a	PRICE	ai, əi	ai	HappY	i	i
CLOTH	ɔ	ɔ	CHOICE	ɔi	ɔi	LettER	a	a
NURSE	a:	ɛ, ɔ, a	MOUTH	au, əu	au	CommA	a	a

KIT

In Hausa English, /ɪ/ is closely approximated, in Yoruba English and Igbo English realized as [i], which leads to a lack of distinction between word pairs such as *sit* and *seat*. Some Igbo speakers realize this vowel as a pharyngealized [iˤ].

DRESS

In Hausa English, a tendency to realize this vowel as [ə] or [a], in Yoruba English and Igbo English free variation between [e] and [ɛ].

TRAP

In all varieties realized as /a/.

LOT

In Yoruba English and Igbo English realized as [ɔ], in Hausa English sometimes as [a].

STRUT

In Yoruba English and Igbo English realized as [ɔ], in Hausa English an allophone of /a/ close to /ʌ/ is produced, sometimes also [ʊ].

FOOT

In Hausa English very similar to /ʊ/, in Yoruba English it is realized as [u] so that the distinction between *full* and *fool* is neutralized. Some Igbo speakers realize this vowel as a pharyngealized [uˤ].

BATH

In Yoruba English and Igbo English realized as [a] so that word pairs such as *march* and *match* become homophones. In Hausa English the vowel [a:] is produced.

CLOTH

Realized as [ɔ], see LOT.

NURSE

Hausa English realizes this vowel as [a:], in Yoruba English and Igbo English the pronunciation is [ɜ] or, depending on the spelling, with [ɔ] in *work*, [ɛ] in *girl*, [e] in *dirty*, [a] in *perch,* [a] in *Sir*.

FLEECE

In Hausa English [i:], but in Yoruba English and Igbo English the vowel is shorter and the same as in KIT.

FACE

In Hausa English usually realized as [e] so that the distinction between *let* and *late* is neutralized. In Yoruba English the vowel is also realized as [e], whereas in Igbo English it is usually pronounced [a].

PALM

Realized as [a], see BATH.

THOUGHT

In Yoruba English and Igbo English realized as [ɔ] so that *caught* and *cut* become homophones. In Hausa English it tends to be realized as [o:] except for words with the spelling –au- (e.g. *daughter*) where it is pronounced [aʊ] or [əʊ].

GOAT

Usually realized as [o:] in Hausa English and as [o] or [ɔ] in Yoruba English and Igbo English.

GOOSE

In Hausa English it is pronounced [u:], whereas in Yoruba English and Igbo English both /ʊ/ and /u/ are equally long (see FOOT). In Igbo English, the vowel may be realized as a pharyngealized [uˤ].

PRICE

Realized as [ai] in Yoruba English and Igbo English. In Hausa English the first element may be centralized.

CHOICE
Realized as [ɔi] in Hausa English and as [ɔi] in Yoruba English and Igbo English.

MOUTH
In Yoruba English and Igbo English realized as [au], in Hausa English the first element may be centralized [əu].

NEAR
Realized as [ia] or with an epenthetic [j] as [ija].

SQUARE
Like the NEAR vowel realized as [ia], with only very few speakers realizing it as [ea].

START
Realized as [a].

NORTH
Realized as [ɔ].

FORCE
In Yoruba English and Igbo English it is realized as [ɔ], while Hausa English speakers pronounce it [o], [oa] or [owa].

CURE
Realized as [ua] or [uwa].

happY
Realized as [i]. Other /ɪ/ are realized according to spelling with [e] in *greeted*.

lettER
Realized as [a].

horsES
Realized as [e] or [ɛ].

commA
Realized as [a].
In general, in NigE, vowels in unstressed syllables, which are produced as [ə] or [ɪ] or deleted in native varieties of English, can be realized as either [a], [ɛ], [ɪ], [ɔ] or [u], usually depending on the spelling (Simo Bobda 1997):

sofa	[a]
resentment	[ɛ]
visible	[i]
police	[ɔ]
consensus	[u]

Unlike in native varieties of English, in NigE function words do not have strong and weak forms. *But* is always realized as [bɔt] and *the* is realized as [ða] or [da] in Southern NigE and [za] in Hausa English.

In all triphthongs, glide formation processes apply that change the middle vowels into the corresponding semi-vowels (Simo Bobda 1997) as in

fire	[faja]
lion	[lajɔn]
power	[pawa] or [pa:]
our	[awa]

In Yoruba English, nasalization of vowels preceding nasals occurs, and often also a dropping of nasals in word-final position can be observed (Jowitt 1991). For example, *win* will be pronounced [wĩ]. In Hausa English, sometimes a glottal stop is produced before a vowel, which can have an emphasising function (Jowitt 1991).

2.2. Consonants

NigE is non-rhotic. The consonant system of NigE shows a lack of the postalveolar fricative /ʒ/ and the velar nasal /ŋ/, which only exist in the speech of very sophisticated speakers with speech training (Jibril 1986). The consonant phonemes vary in their realisations between Hausa English, Yoruba English and Igbo English as illustrated in Tables 3 to 5 (cf. Jibril 1986; Jowitt 1991).

Table 3. Hausa realisations of some consonants

/p/	[p], [f], [ɸ]
/f/	[f], [p], [ɸ]
/b/	[b], [v]
/v/	[v], [b]
/ð/	[ð], [z]
/θ/	[θ], [s]

Table 4.   Igbo realizations of some consonants

/θ/	[θ], [t], [t̪]
/ð/	[ð], [d], [d̪]
/hj/ (*human*)	[h]
/pj/ (*pupil*)	[p]

Table 5.   Yoruba realizations of some consonants

/v/	[v], [f]
/θ/	[θ], [t], [t̪]
/ð/	[ð], [d], [d̪]
/dʒ/	[dʒ], [ʒ]
/tʃ/	[tʃ], [ʃ]
/h/	[h], deleted
/z/	[z], [s]
/v/	[v], [f]

One general feature of NigE is the (probable) spelling pronunciation of many words. This applies to words ending in orthographic *-mb*, *-ng* and those with *–st* and *–bt* as in

bomb	[bɔmb]
plumber	[plɔmba]
sing	[sɪŋg]
hang	[haŋg]
debt	[dɛbt]

and also (possibly) to a number of loan words such as

élite	[ilait]	
plateau	[platu]	(see Jowitt [1991] for a full list).

Equally, since orthography suggests it, final *–ed* is often realized as [d] as for example in *increased*. This in turn will trigger prevoicing of the consonant preceding the *–ed* so that the pronunciation is [inkrizd]. Voicing of [ks] can be observed in *maximum* [magzimɔm] and *laxity* [lagziti], which has been described as an influence from American English (Görlach [1997]).

On the other hand, devoicing of final consonants is common in NigE (Simo Bobda 1997), as for example in *with*, which is often realized as [wiθ], *robe*, which is realized as [rop] and *leave*, which is realized as [lif]. Similarily, the plural /–z/ and third person singular /-z/ is often replaced by [-s] as in *roads* [rɔds], *doors* [dɔs] and *digs* [dɪgs] (Jibril [1986]).

There are two simplification strategies for consonant clusters in NigE. One is the reduction of word-final consonant clusters by deletion of the last part as in

hand	[han]
post	[pɔs]
cold	[kɔl]

The consonant cluster /kw/ is reduced to [k] as in [ɛkɪpmɛn(t)] for *equipment*. Quantitative support for this comes from an experimental study involving 'reading passage' style (Gut 2003). I found that syllable structures that never occur in NigE speech compared to British English speech are syllables with deleted vowels (C, CC, CCC), syllables with three consonants in the onset position (CCCV, CCCVC, CCCVVC), the syllable type VVC and syllables with three consonants in the coda position (CVCCC). Furthermore, Nigerians produce significantly more open syllables (syllables without a final consonant) than British English speakers reading the same passage, which reflects the high proportion of consonant deletions.

The other consonant cluster simplification strategy is the insertion of the epenthetic vowel [u] or [i] between word-final syllabic consonants and the preceding consonant as e.g. in

bottle	[bɔtʊl]
button	[bɔtun]
cattle	[katul]
silk	[silik]

Epenthetic vowels are especially common in Hausa English.

Other phonological processes occurring in NigE include metathesis as in the pronunciation [aks] for *ask* and, especially in Hausa English, a tendency to gemination as in [gʌmmənt] for *government* (Jowitt 1991).

2.3.   Prosody

2.3.1.   Stress and accent

The terms "stress" and "accent" are used in contradictory ways among researchers. Here, I will define "stress" as an abstract category that is stored as a feature of a syllable in the speaker's mental lexicon and "accent" as its phonetic realization in speech. Word stress in NigE is in many cases different from that in British or American English (e.g. Simo Bobda 1997; Jowitt 1991). No systematic studies being available, a summary of various observations will be presented here.

Simo Bobda (1997) describes a general tendency for stress shifted to the right. This can be seen in realizations of the words *sa'lad*, *ma'ttress* and *pe'trol*. Especially with words whose final syllable contains an [n] or an [i], stress is shifted to the right. Examples are:

plan'tain	bap'tist
hy'giene	ten'nis
jave'lin	bis'cuit

Verbs tend to have stress on the last syllable if

- they have final obstruents (e.g. inter'pret, embar'rass, com'ment, soli'cit)
- or contain the affixes *-ate*, *-ise*, *-ize*, *-fy* or *-ish*

Other affixes that tend to attract stress include

-ative	*-atory/-utory*
-ature	*-cide*
-itive/-utive	*-land*
-man	*-phone*
-day	

Affixes that tend to bring stress to the preceding syllable are:

-able/-ible	*-age*
-al	*-ary*
-ean	*-er*
-ism	*-mony*
-ous	

Equally, strong consonant clusters pull stress to the preceding syllable as in *an'cestor*. In compounds, the second element is stressed as for example in *fire'wood* and *proof'read*. In general, however, it must be noted that word stress patterns are not realized uniformly and that even among educated speakers (and even between productions of one and the same speaker) there is considerable variation in individual words.

Jowitt (1991) suggests that Nigerian speakers of English equate the primary stress in English with a high tone and the tertiary stress with a low tone. In order to avoid three consecutive low tones in e.g. *interestingly*, word stress is shifted to arrive at the pronunciation *interes'tingly*.

In continuous speech, the stressed syllables of words become potential places for sentence stress, i.e. accents realized by the speaker, with the number of accents determined by the speech tempo. In each utterance or sentence the most prominent accent is called the nucleus and tends to fall on the rightmost stressed syllable of an utterance, although pragmatic reasons such as emphasis may cause stress shifts. Sentence stress in NigE is rarely used for emphasis or contrast (Jibril 1986; Jowitt 1991; Gut 2003). Instead of producing "*Mary* did it" Nigerians tend to say "It was Mary who did it".

Given information is rarely deaccented. For example, consider the sequence: *A tiger and a mouse [..] saw a big lump of cheese lying on the ground. The mouse said: "[...] You don't even like cheese"*.

Nigerians produce an accent on the given information *cheese* in the last sentence whereas British speakers accentuate *like*.

An overall preference for "end-stress", i.e. the placement of the nucleus, the most prominent accent, on the last word can been observed in NigE (Eka 1985; Gut 2003). In the dialogue (1) for example

(1)   a. *Come on, who'll volunteer?*
       b. *I will, if you insist.*

British English speakers put a nucleus on *I* in (1b), whereas NigE speakers stress *will* most.

In general, in NigE many lexical items can receive stress that do not usually do so in British English. More stressed syllables are realized as accents in NigE speech than is the case in British English speech. In reading passage style, nearly all verbs, adjectives and nouns are accented in NigE (Udofot 2003; Gut 2003). In spontaneous speech, differences between British English and NigE are most pronounced with a large number of extra accented syllables in NigE (Udofot 2003).

The phonetic realization of accents in NigE seems to be very different from that of other, especially native speaker varieties of English. In the languages of the world, the phonetic realization of accents can have different formats: In languages with "tonal accent" such as Swedish and Norwegian, different types of tones or pitch patterns are used on accented syllables. In languages with "dynamic accent" such as English or German, the phonetic parameters pitch, length and loudness are combined with different relative importance for the phonetic realization of accents. There seems to be an intricate relationship between accents and tone, not only because accents are very often produced with a phonetically high pitch. It has been suggested that in NigE accents are produced primarily by tone. Jowitt (1991) claims that stressed syllables receive a high tone whereas unstressed syllables receive a low tone. Gut (2003) found that tone in NigE is grammatically determined with lexical words receiving high tone on the stressed syllable and non-lexical words receiving low tone. The tonal patterns of some multisyllabic words are illustrated in Table 6 with L symbolising a low tone and H symbolising a high tone.

Table 6.   Intonation/stress pattern of multisyllabic words (Gut 2003)

something	swallow	remove	enough	continued
HH	HH	LH	LH	LHH

The stressed syllable of lexical words is produced with a high tone, which then spreads to the end of the word. Any unstressed syllables preceding the stressed syllable are produced with a low tone.

2.3.2. Speech rhythm

It has been suggested that NigE has a syllable-timed rather than stress-timed rhythm. The languages of the world have traditionally been divided into stress-timed and syllable-timed. Speech rhythm was understood to be a periodic recurrence of events such as syllables in the case of the so-called "syllable-timed" languages and feet in the case of the so-called "stress-timed" languages. In syllable-timed languages such as Yoruba, syllables are assumed to be equal in length. Stress-timed languages such as English, in contrast, are supposed to have regular recurring stress beats. Since the number of syllables between two stress beats varies, their length is adjusted to fit into the stress interval – syllable length, hence is very variable in stress-timed languages. No acoustic basis for either isochrony of feet in stress-timed languages or equal length of syllables in syllable-timed languages has ever been found. Eka (1985) proposes that NigE speech rhythm is 'inelastic' insofar as the durational adjustment of unstressed syllables does not occur.

   Recent approaches of measuring speech rhythm are based on the assumption that speech rhythm is a multidimensional concept which includes various phonological properties of languages. Accordingly, languages are not classified into distinct rhythmic classes anymore but are assumed to be located along a continuum. Dauer (1983: 55), for example, suggested that "rhythmic differences [...] between languages [...] are more a result of phonological, phonetic, lexical, and syntactic facts about that language than any attempt on the part of the speaker to equalize interstress or intersyllable intervals". In Dauer's view, speech rhythm reflects variety of syllable structures, phonological vowel length distinctions, absence/presence of vowel reduction and lexical stress. Whereas languages formerly classified as stress-timed such as English show a variety of different syllable structures, languages formerly classified as syllable-timed have a majority of CV syllables. Equally, differences in rhythm between languages reflect whether a language has vowel reduction or not; those classified as stress-timed usually do. In addition, languages with a tendency to syllable-timing either do not have lexical stress or accent is realized by variations in pitch contour. Conversely, languages with a tendency to stress-timing realize word level stress by a combination of length, pitch, loudness and quality changes, which result in clearly discernible beats.

This approach is reflected in recent measurements of the acoustic correlates of speech rhythm, which are based on phonetic cues such as successive vowel and syllable durations. Experimental studies employing these acoustic measurements of the phonetic correlates of speech rhythm confirmed the impression of a tendency to "syllable-timing" in NigE. Vowel reduction does not occur in NigE, which results in a more equal duration of syllables (Udofot 2003; Gut 2003). Subsequent syllables in NigE are more similar in length than in British English but less similar than in West African languages. Compared to other languages classified with Ramus, Nespor and Mehler's (1999) measurement of rhythm, NigE groups with Spanish, Catalan, Italian and French, all of which are presumed to be syllable-timed, in terms of the vowel percentage, but shows a higher standard deviation of consonantal intervals than those languages.

In general, the overall speech tempo in NigE is slower than in British English, and NigE speakers divide their utterances into more and shorter intonation phrases than British English speakers (Udofot 2003; Gut 2003).

2.3.3. Intonation

Compared to native varieties of English, NigE intonation seems simplified. Most utterances, both in read and spontaneous speech, have a falling tone. Rising tones are relatively rare and occur mostly in *yes-no* questions and tag questions. Complex tones such as fall-rises and rise-falls are even rarer (Eka 1985; Gut 2003).

Gut (2003) investigated the native language influence on NigE intonation. All Nigerian languages are tone languages, where pitch is lexically significant, contrastive and relative. Tone is associated with tone-bearing units such as the syllable or the mora and differences in relative pitch are used to convey lexical and grammatical distinctions. Hausa and Igbo have two tones H (high) and L (low), and Yoruba has three tones: H (high), M (mid) and L (low). Gut (2003) tested the hypothesis that in NigE, like in tone languages, every syllable is associated with a tone and arrived at a first tentative proposal of NigE intonational phonology: two tones are sufficient to describe NigE intonation: H and L. There is initial raising, which causes initial low tones to appear phonetically as a mid tone. Equally, downstep lowers high tones on the second and subsequent lexical words to a phonetic mid tone. NigE has two boundary tones: H% and L%, which may combine with the level tones to form the contour tones HL and LH. A low boundary tone can suppress the H of a lexical word. This proposal now needs to be tested with a wider range of speech types and speakers.

In general, the pitch range in NigE is smaller than in British English (Eka 1985), but Jowitt (1991) reports an exceptionally wide pitch range in Yoruba English in some constructions. For example, a relative pronoun introducing a restrictive clause has a very high tone, as well as a sentence-initial *if*.

Exercises and study questions

1. Describe the variability of the pronunciation of the NURSE vowel in the recorded speech (lexical sets and reading passage).

2. Find evidence for spelling pronunciation in the recordings of the two speakers.

3. Compare the word stress patterns described for NigE with Indian English and Singapore English. In what way are they similar and in what way do they differ? What might be a reason for the similarities?

4. Describe consonant cluster reduction processes in the reading passages.

5. Compare the vowel lists recorded by the two speakers. What are your conclusions regarding their educational background?

6. How many words are accentuated in the reading passages? How does that compare with readings by native speakers of English?

Selected references

Please consult the General references for titles mentioned in the text but not included in the references below. For a full bibliography see the accompanying CD-ROM.

Awonusi, Victor
1986   Regional accents and internal variability in Nigerian English: a historical analysis. *English Studies* 6: 555–560.
Bamgbose, Ayo
1982   Standard Nigerian English: issues of identification. In: Kachru (ed.), 99–111.
1997   English in the Nigerian environment. In: Bamgbose, Banjo and Thomas (eds.), 9–26.
Banjo, Ayo
1971   Towards a definition of standard Nigerian spoken English. Actes du 8ᵗʰ Congress de la Societé Linguiste de l'Afrique Occidentale, 165–175.
Dauer, R.
1983   Stress-timing and syllable-timing reanalysed. *Journal of Phonetics* 11: 51–62.
Eka, David
1985   A phonological study of Standard Nigerian English. Ph.D. dissertation, Ahmadu Bello University, Zaria.
Görlach, Manfred
1997   Nigerian English: Broken, Pidgin, Creole and Regional Standards? In: Uwe Böker and Hans Sauer, *Proceedings of the Anglistentag 1996 Dresden*, 141–152. Trier: Wissenschaftlicher Verlag Trier.
Grimes, Barbara and Grimes, Joseph
2000   *Ethnologue. Languages of the World.* Volume1. Dallas: SIL International
Gut, Ulrike
2003   Nigerian English – a typical West African language? In: Ewald Mengel, Hans-Jörg Schmid and Michael Steppat (eds.), *Proceedings of the Anglistentag 2002 Bayreuth*, 461–471. Trier: Wissenschaftlicher Verlag Trier.
Jibril, Munzali
1986   Sociolinguistic variation in Nigerian English. *English World-Wide* 7: 147–174.
Jowitt, David
1991   *Nigerian English Usage.* Lagos: Bencod Press.
1997   Nigeria's national language question: choices and constraints. In: Bamgbose, Banjo and Thomas (eds.), 34–56.
Ramus, Franck, Marina Nespor and Jaques Mehler
1999   Correlates of linguistic rhythm in the speech signal. *Cognition* 73: 265–292.

Schaefer, Ronald and Francis Egbokhare
   1999   English and the pace of endangerment in Nigeria. *World Englishes* 18:
           381–391.
Simo Bobda, Augustin
   1997   The Phonologies of Nigerian English and Cameroon English. In:
           Bamgbose, Banjo and Thomas (eds.), 248–268.
Udofot, Inyang
   2003   Stress and rhythm in the Nigerian accent of English. *English World Wide*
           24: 201–220.

Nigerian Pidgin English: phonology

Ben Elugbe

1.   Introduction

It is generally agreed that Nigerian Pidgin (NigP) is the product of contact between English and Nigerian languages, especially those of the Niger Delta, and Benin and Calabar. However, as Ryder points out (1969: 24), the first European visitors to the coast of Nigeria were not the English but the Portuguese. The question therefore arises whether there was no Portuguese Pidgin before the arrival of the English. Elugbe and Omamor (1991) suggest that a kind of pidgin Portuguese must indeed have developed between the Portuguese and their Nigerian hosts. They further point out that the presence of a substantial percentage of words of Edoid origin in the Portuguese Creole, Saõ Tomense, of Saõ Tomé Island in the Gulf of Guinea (Hagemeijer 2000), supports the existence of a Portuguese Pidgin in Nigeria before the coming of the English. More direct evidence of the existence of a Portuguese Pidgin, which was presumably supplanted by NigP, would be the existence of relics of Portuguese-origin vocabulary in NigP. These are rare (for example *sabi* 'know' and *cabin* 'a kind of room') – see Elugbe and Omamor (1991) for a detailed examination.

2.   Phonology

2.1.   Some general comments

Mafeni (1971) must be recognised as the first scientific publication on NigP phonology, whose validity remains today. The dialect of NigP described by Mafeni is the Bendelian variety – the same as in Elugbe and Omamor (1991). This variety is spoken in the old Bendel State, now divided into Delta and Edo States. It is spoken very widely throughout Edo State and in the non-Igboid parts of Delta State. In the Igboid parts of Delta State, Igbo competes very strongly with NigP. In the Warri/Sapele parts of the State, NigP has creolised – as Elugbe and Omamor (1991) point out.

Although I address the Bendel variety here, it is necessary to point out that regional varieties often have minor differences in consonant and vowel systems as well as in vocabulary. A very easy and self-evident example is in the area of food. The NigP speaker from Kano may not be familiar with what a speaker from Warri means by /statʃ/ *starch*, a common, cassava-based food in the Delta. On the other hand, the Warri speaker may not know what the Kano speaker means by *tuwo*, a kind of pounded or kneaded food which is mainly rice-based. Nevertheless, there is complete mutual intelligibility between the regional varieties of NigP.

Speakers of NigP are known for the ease with which they use words in an *ad hoc* manner to describe specific concepts. However, a phonology of NigP can and should only describe a sound system based on the core of stable vocabulary that can be established as characterising NigP all over Nigeria. Today several sub-varieties of NigP can be recognised:

(a) Northern variety, heavily influenced by Hausa;
(b) a South-western variety, newly emerged and often very like the Bendel variety;
(c) the Bendel variety, also referred to as Bendelian here, which some regard as standard (for example Elugbe and Omamor 1991);
(d) a Rivers variety with a very noticeable colouration from the Ijoid and other small languages of the Rivers and Bayelsa States;
(e) a South-eastern variety in the geopolitical zone referred to as the Southeast with a heavy Igbo colouration; and, finally,
(f) a Cross River variety which is heavily coloured by the Cross River languages, especially Efik-Ibibio.

In Nigeria, NigP has no official status even though Government and its agents, like the National Orientation Agency (NOA), now use it as a means of reaching a wider audience.

2.2.   The consonants of NigP

Mafeni (1971) presented 24 consonant phonemes for NigP while Elugbe and Omamor (1991: 79) presented 24 systematic phonetic consonants. However, I now recognise about 25 at the systematic phonetic level. It is quite possible that some varieties may have more consonants – especially where local words are drafted in from time to time. However, it is not necessary to account for such transient consonants in a phonology of NigP.

The consonants of the Bendelian variety described here are presented in table 1:

Table 1. The consonants of NigP

	Labial	Alveolar	(Alveo)-Palatal	Velar	Labiovelar	Glottal
Nasal	m	n	ɲ	ŋ	(ŋʷ)	
Plosive	p b	t d		k g	kp gb	
Affricate			(tʃ) dʒ			
Fricative	f v	s z	ʃ (ʒ)			
Lateral		l				
Approximant	w	r [ɹ]	j			h

2.2.1. Exemplification of the consonants

The inventory can easily be exemplified as in table 2 below.

Table 2. NigP consonants exemplified

Nasal:	mat	'mat'	taim	'time'
	nao	'now'	pɔnd	'pond'
	iŋk	'ink'	taŋk	'tank, thank'
Plosive:	pipu/pipo	'people'	tit	'teeth'
	bɔe	'boy'	bɔbi	'breast'
	tɔl	'tall'	bɔtu	'bottle'
	dae	'die'	todee	'today'
	kɔm	'come'	kek	'cake'
	go	'go'	bɛg	'beg'
Affricates:	tʃit/ʃit	'cheat'	titʃ/tiʃ	'teach'
	dʒɔmp	'jump'	dʒulae	'July'
Fricatives:	futubɔl	'football'	tɔf	'tough'
	vã	'van'	faev	'five'
	sit	'sit'	fes	'face'
	zip	'zip'	biźi	'busy'
	ʃip	'ship'	fiʃ	'fish'
	mɛʒɔ/mɛʃɔ	'measure'	plɛʒɔ/plɛʃɔ	'pleasure'

Table 2. (continued)   NigP consonants exemplified

Lateral:	*let*	'late'	*tɛl*	'tell'
Approximant:	*rɛd*	'red'	*tri*	'tree'
	jɛt	'yet'	*ju*	'you'
	wɛt	'wet'	*wund*	'wound'
	hao	'how'	*hɔt*	'hot'

2.2.2. *Consonants and syllable structure*

In NigP, consonants function only at the borders of syllables except that a syllabic nasal consonant exists which functions as the nucleus of a syllable. Consonant clusters are allowed at the beginning and at the end of syllables. At the peak or nucleus of a syllable, vowels and a syllabic nasal are allowed – thus:

Consonants in syllables
sta   'star'
aks   'ask'
ŋ́-kɔ́   'so what?/what if?/what about?, etc.'
krae   'cry'
ples   'place'
flɔg   'flog, beat a younger person'

There are normally no more than two consonants allowed at the beginning of the syllable in NigP. A few words contain three in sophisticated, English-influenced, varieties. Thus the word *street* may be pronounced /strit/ or /srit/. The clusterless form /sitiriti/ is possible in totally uneducated varieties. At the end of a syllable, the maximum number of consonants allowed is two. Again we find, for the English word *help* for example, the two pronunciations /hɛlp/ or /hɛlɛp/.

2.3. Vowels

Across Nigeria, the majority of the dialects of NigP have a simple seven-quality vowel system. However, there are also diphthongs, which are double quality vowels that nonetheless function as single syllable nuclei. A complete inventory of NigP vowels would therefore be as in table 3:

Table 3. The vowels of NigP

Oral vowels		Nasal vowels	
Monophthongs			
ɪ	u	ĩ	ũ
e	o		
ɛ	ɔ	ɛ̃	ɔ̃
a		ã	
Diphthongs			
ae, ao, ɔe			

The three diphthongs listed here correspond to what are normally [aɪ], [aʊ], and [ɔɪ] respectively in Standard British English (StdBrE). In the established numbering of English vowels, these are numbers 15, 16, and 17 respectively, the rising diphthongs. This analysis differs from that of Mafeni (1971), for whom words such as /praod/ *proud* and /smael/ *smile* end in consonant clusters – /prawd/ and /smayl/ respectively. Moreover, in Mafeni's system, the word /bɔe/ *boy* would be /bɔy/, ending in a consonant. Thus Mafeni recognised no vowel sequences and no diphthongs in NigP. By contrast, Elugbe and Omamor (1991) recognised these three diphthongs as /ai/, /au/, and /ɔi/ respectively. In fact, the terminal point never goes as high as /i/ or /u/ – hence /ae/, /ao/, /ɔe/ here.

In NigP as well as in NigE, another pair of rising diphthongs, English vowel number 13, /eɪ/, and number 14, /oʊ/ or /əʊ/ are [e] or [ee] and [o] or [oo] respectively. The double vowel form is found in word-final open syllables while the single vowel pronunciation occurs in closed syllables. At a recent workshop on translating the Bible into NigP, the above rule was found to separate words such as NigP *wet* 'wait' from *wee* 'way'. Thus, 'The way in which it was written by John' is rendered as *di wee we John (tek) raet am*. The relative marker 'which' is *wé* (see below) with a short vowel in NigP, whereas the noun 'way', with an open syllable is *wee*.

The centring diphthongs of StdBrE are numbers 18, /ɪə/, 19, /ɛə/, and 20, /ʊə/. In NigP, these may be analysed as sequences of vowels, (Elugbe and Omamor 1991). Thus we find the following correspondences between StdBrE and NigP:

StdBrE centring diphthongs in NigP:

- /ɪə́/ *ear* is NigP /ia/ with a distinct, albeit weak /j/ between the twin qualities of the diphthong: [ija].
- /ɛə́/ *air* is NigP /ɛa/ or /ɛɛ/ – in each case they are two distinct vowels.
- /ʊə/ *poor* is /puɔ/ with a weak /w/ between the two vowel qualities of the diphthong: /puwɔ/

It should be noted here that the alternative to [ʊə], which in StdBrE is [ɔː], (for example /pʊə/ or /pɔː/ 'poor') does not feature in NigP. The vowels of NigP were clearly based on a variety of English which did not alternate /ʊə/ with /ɔː/. However it did recognise the vowel /ɔː/ which, like /ɔ/ or /ɒ/, corresponds to NigP /ɔ/. For example, the utterances in (1) and (2) are both said without a distinction between *pot* and *Port* (Port Harcourt):

(1)   *i de (insae) pɔt* 'It's in the pot'
(2)   *i de (fɔ) pɔt*   'It's in Port (Harcourt).'

Without the prepositions, the two utterances sound exactly the same.

It can be seen therefore that the simplification of the English vowel system in NigP followed very clear lines as shown in table 4.

Table 4.   Correspondences between English vowels and those of NigP

StdBrE			NigP	
	1.	iː		i
	2.	ɪ		
	3.	ɛ		ɛ
	4.	æ		a
	5.	ɑː		
	6.	ɒ		ɔ
	7.	ɔː		
	8.	ʊ		u
	9.	u		
	10.	ʌ		ɔ
	11.	3ː or əː		ɛ, a
	12.	ə		a, ɔ
	13.	eɪ		e, ee
	14.	əʊ or oʊ		o, oo

Table 4. (continued) Correspondences between English vowels and those of NigP

15.	aɪ	ae
16.	aʊ	ao
17.	ɔɪ	ɔe
18.	ɪə	
19.	ɛə	vowel sequences, see above
20.	ʊə	

Table 5 below exemplifies the vowels of NigP:

Table 5. NigP vowels exemplified

NigP	i	it	*eat*
	ɛ	bɛd	*bed*
	a	bad	*bad*
	ɔ	pɔt	*pot*
		kɔt	*court*
	o	kot	*coat*
	u	ful	*full*
		ful	*fool*
	ae	hae	*high*
	ao	nao	*now*
	ɔe	bɔe	*boy*

2.4.   Nasalisation

Any discussion of the vowels of NigP would be incomplete without reference to nasalisation. Vowels and nasalisation are tied together in NigP; it is with vowels that we find nasalisation without an adjacent nasal consonant to account for it, as we see in ɛ̃ɛ 'yes' and kɔ̃, kɔ̃n 'corn, maize', and in sentence (3):

(3)   *nã ĩ du am*   'he did it'

Examples such as these raise the question of how to account for nasalisation in NigP. We may assume (as did Elugbe and Omamor 1991) that every case of nasalisation arises from the presence of an underlying nasal. Such a position would be amply supported by the forms of 'corn' cited above. Even ĩ in (3) can be traced to an underlying nasal: [*na hĩm du am*] contains a common

alternative for [ĩ], viz. [him]. This analysis also allows us to record nasalisation
as <n> immediately after the nasalised vowel. The orthographic form of (3) is
therefore *na in du am*.

There are cases in which vowel nasalisation affects a preceding consonant:

Consonant nasalisation in NigP

yam	'yam'	becomes	[ɲãm] or [j̃ãm]
yanfuyanfu	'plentiful(ly)'		[ɲãfuɲãfu] or [j̃ãfuj̃ãfu]
wan	'one'		[ŋʷã] or [ŋʷãn] [w̃ã] [w̃ãn]
when	'when'		[ŋʷɛ̃] or [ŋʷɛ̃n] [w̃ɛ̃] [w̃ɛ̃n]
ron	'run'		[ɹ̃ɔ̃] or [ɹ̃ɔ̃n]
hon	'horn'		[h̃ɔ̃] or [h̃ɔ̃n]

These examples suggest that [ɲ] and [ŋʷ] are not phonemic and exist only at the
systematic phonetic level. Their nasalised approximant alternatives show that
there is a general rule by which approximants become nasal (in the case of /j/
and /w/) or nasalised counterparts in the environment of nasalised vowels.

Elugbe and Omamor (1991) claim that /l/ is nasalised before nasalised vowels, but they provide no examples. However, it is a legitimate issue to examine.
In examples such as /lɛnd/, *lend* it is probably the case that the surface form is
[lɛ̃], [lɛ̃n], [lɛ̃nd], with no nasalisation of the [l], or [l̃ɛ̃], [l̃ɛ̃n], or [l̃ɛ̃nd], with
nasalisation of the lateral. In other words, the approximant nasalisation rule
affects both lateral and central approximants except that unlike in Yoruba and
similar languages, the nasalised allophone of /l/ is not [n], but [l̃].

3.   Pitch in NigP

The use to which a language puts pitch determines whether it is a tone language
or a non-tonal one. In Pike's famous definition of a tone language (1948), we
are told that a tone language is one that makes significant use of pitch on every
syllable. By this definition, it is to be expected that pitch differences in individual syllables may be lexically or even grammatically significant. Lexical
use of pitch is seen in Yoruba:

Lexical pitch in Yoruba

ìgbà	(LL)	'time'
ìgbá	(LH)	'garden egg'
īgbá	(MH)	'gourd'
īgbā	(MM)	'800'
ìgbā	(LM)	'fence'

These examples show that a variation on a syllable can cause a change in lexical meaning. In (4) and (5) from Ghotuọ, a North-central Edoid language of the Benue-Congo family in Edo State of Nigeria, we find that a similar change in the pitch of a syllable results in a change of grammatical meaning:

Grammatical pitch in Ghotuọ
(4) *mhā dé róbè* (MHML)   'We bought a book'
(5) *mhà dé róbè* (LHML)   'We did not buy a book'

It should be noted that the case for the significance of pitch on every syllable is still valid even where these minimal pairs or sets do not exist – provided a change of pitch leads to some kind of change, including to an unacceptable (i.e. meaningless) utterance. Mafeni (1971) subjected NigP to this test and concluded that it is a tone language with two tones (low and high) because of lexical examples cited below:

Mafeni's examples of so-called lexical tone in NigP
fádá   'father'
fàdá   'a Roman Catholic father'
sìsí   'young maid'
sísì   'six pence' (= 5 Kobo)
bàbá   'father'
bábà   'a Roman Catholic priest'

Mafeni also suggested what might be called a tone rule by which monosyllabic high-tone words are realized on a falling pitch pre-pausally. Sentences (6) and (7) exemplify such falling pitch:

(6) *ì gò pé mà mòní*   'He will pay my fee'
(7) *ì gò pê*   'He will pay'

However, the way NigP uses pitch does not fit that of a tone language. In languages such as English, pitch variations cover whole phrases, clauses or sentences. Moreover, pitch variations do not alter the basic lexical composition of an utterance. Thus the word 'Yes', said with a variety of pitch variations, remains 'Yes'. This type of language is called an intonation language. English, from which NigP is derived (it is NigP's superstrate), also operates a stress system and there is some evidence that NigP equates stress with high pitch. For example, tense and aspect markers are not normally stressed in English: similarly in NigP, such markers are not said on a high pitch whereas full verbs are (compare 8a and c, as well as 8b and d):

High and low pitch words in NigP

(8) a. *ì gò pé mà mɔ̀ní*   'He will pay my fee'
   b. *ì gò pê*   'He will pay'
   c. *ì gò pé mà mɔ̀ní*   'He went and paid my fee'
   d. *ì gó pê*   'He went and paid'

There seems little doubt that NigP employs pitch for intonation along lines similar to what English does (see Mafeni 1971). For example in sentences 8(a)–(d) above intonation differences can change a statement into a question:

(9) a. *ì gò pé mà mɔ̀ní*   'He will pay my fee'
   b. *ì gò pê*   'He will pay'
   c. *ì gò pé mà mɔ̀ní* ?   'Will he pay my fee?'
   d. *ì gò pé* ?   'Will he pay?'

Note that the high of (9a) is even higher or still rising in (9c) while the falling high of (9b) now lacks a fall and is even higher and rising.

Elugbe and Omamor (1991: 85) suggest that NigP is something of a pitch-accent language in which, given a word there may be only one high tone, or one sequence thereof in opposition to one low sequence:

High pitch accent in NigP (see Elugbe and Omamor 1991)

sísi	'six pence' (now = 5 Kobo)
sisí	'young maid'
hévun	'heaven'
wayó	'trickery'
wakawáká	'layabout'
yangá	'vanity'
kongosá	'gossip'
ɔtɔ́riti	'authority'
míraku	'miracle'

Exceptions to the above pattern are words taken directly from local languages and not adapted into the NigP sound system. Elements of a similar analysis are to be found in Mafeni's suggestion that high-tone syllables in NigP are normally more heavily stressed than low-tone ones. In other words, the high tone may be correlated with (strong) stress while the low tone is correlated with weak stress (or a lack of it?). However, in a word such as *miraku* for example there are three pitch levels of which the first is the highest and the last is the lowest. The same applies to the word *ɔtɔ́riti* in which the pitch descends from the high of *tɔ́* through the mid of *ri* to the low of *ti*. Such examples show that after the accented syllable, a kind of 'downdrift', such as characterises statement intonation in English, occurs also in NigP. That is the reason that Mafeni claimed that the intonation of NigP is very similar to that of English.

Another issue raised by Mafeni is of rhythm. He describes NigP as a "syllable-timed" language in which "The syllables constituting a stretch of utterance occur isochronously and tend to be of equal duration" (1971: 109). In this respect as in Nigerian languages which form the substrate for NigP, every syllable is as prominent as the other and the weakening of syllables as we see in a stress language such as English does not occur.

4.   Conclusion

In sum, then, NigP has a phonology which incorporates elements from English as well as from the local languages of Nigeria. It lacks /θ/and /ð/, it contains labial-velar stops, and it has nasal vowels, and it is syllable-timed – all of which make it look like a typical indigenous Nigerian language. But, unlike a typical Nigerian language, it is not a tone language. It employs pitch lexically as in a pitch-accent language, but employs it for intonation as in English.

Exercises and study questions

1. Compare the consonant inventory of NigP with that of southern NigE (in the preceding chapter).

2. Compare the vowel inventory of NigP with that of southern NigE (in the preceding chapter).

3. Review the evidence against considering NigP as a tone language.

4. In what ways is NigP like a 'typical indigenous Nigerian language', rather than like its lexifier, English?

5. Compare the diphthongs of NigP with those of (a) southern NigE and (b) RP.

Selected references

Please consult the General references for titles mentioned in the text but not included in the references below. For a full bibliography see the accompanying CD-ROM.

Elugbe Ben O. and A. P. Omamor
   1991   *Nigerian Pidgin: Background and Prospects*. Ibadan: Heinemann Educational Books.
Hagemeijer, Tjerk
   2000   *Serial verb constructions in Saõ-Tomense*. MA dissertation, University of Lisbon, Portugal.
Mafeni, Bernard
   1971   Nigerian Pidgin. In: Spencer (ed.), 95–112.
Pike, Kenneth L.
   1948   *Tone Languages*. Ann Arbor: University of Michigan Press.
Ryder, A. F. C.
   1969   *Benin and the Europeans*. London: Longman.

Ghanaian English: phonology

Magnus Huber

1. Historical background

Ghana is a coastal West African country with a population of about 19 million (2000 census). The majority is concentrated in the southern, more fertile and developed part of the country, with Ashanti Region, Greater Accra, and Eastern Region the most populous administrative units. Population density is quite high in the southern urbanized centres, especially around the capital Accra, which is the major focus of Ghana's internal migration.

Direct contact with Europeans goes back to 1471, when the Portuguese made their first landfall on what soon came to be known as the Gold Coast of Africa, at the mouth of the Pra river. In their progress along the West African coast, the primary objective of the Portuguese had been to find a trade route to India, but the availability of gold, ivory and slaves made trade with West Africa very lucrative and soon attracted other European powers as well. Afro-European contact on the Gold Coast can conveniently be divided into three major phases: early trading contacts (1471–1844), colonization (1844–1957), and independence and after (1957–).

The trading phase was characterized by growing European competition. The Portuguese hegemony was broken by the Dutch in the first half of the 17th century, and other European powers followed in their wake: French, English, Swedish, Danish, and Brandenburger merchants all claimed their share of the Guinea trade. English traders had arrived as early as 1553, and their ships regularly visited the Gold Coast up to the 1570s, when they temporarily seemed to have lost interest in that part of West Africa. In 1632, the Company of Merchants Trading on Guinea established the first English trading post on land, at Kormantin. More trading posts, fortified and unfortified, followed in the second half of the century. The biggest among them was Cape Coast Castle, which from 1665 to 1877, that is well into the colonial period, would remain the English headquarters. This early phase of Afro-European contact was characterized by trade between equal partners. No territorial claims were made by the Europeans, who either traded from shipboard or kept to their trading posts. In fact, it was not uncommon for the merchants to pay ground rent and taxes to the local chiefs.

The early phase of British colonization began in 1844, when the chiefs of
the south-western Gold Coast signed an agreement with Governor George
Maclean at Cape Coast Castle. It had long been the custom that legal cases
in the villages surrounding larger European trading posts were tried before

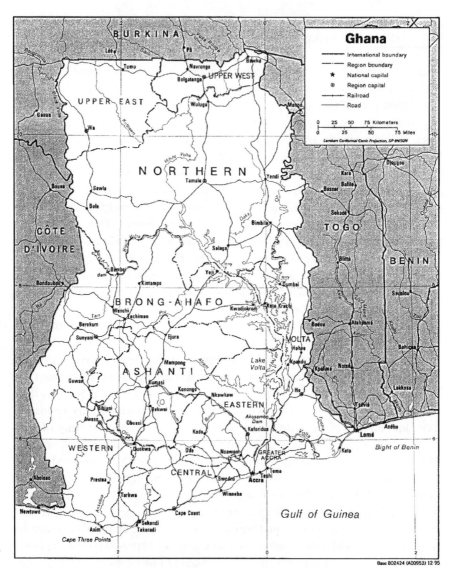

Map 1.   Ghana, political

the commanders of these forts or castles. But in the Bond of 1844, the chiefs for the first time formally yielded some of their juridical power to the British crown. Christian missionary societies had become active on the Gold Coast in the 1830s, so these decades saw an increasing involvement of Europeans in local affairs and a territorial expansion of European influence. After the withdrawal of the Dutch, the only remaining competitors, the British, proclaimed the coastal strip a colony in 1874. Three years later, the capital was moved from Cape Coast to Accra. During the first decades of the Gold Coast Colony, Britain waged several wars against the Ashanti, the powerful Akan state in the hinterland. The British suffered several losses but in 1901 proclaimed Ashantiland and the Northern Territories protectorates, and in 1922 incorporated British Togoland in the colony as a League of Nations mandate. These territories together constitute the modern Republic of Ghana. As the first state in colonial Africa, Ghana achieved independence in 1957.

From as early as the 17th century, Africans received English instruction in schools set up in or around the trading posts, but since the number of pupils was small and schools were often discontinued, the role of English on the coast remained insignificant. Cape Coast advanced to become the main centre of British education early in the 19th century and produced African teachers that staffed schools elsewhere on the Gold Coast. However, the absolute number of literate users of English remained very low. The increasing number of missionary schools did not much change this situation, since many of these schools taught in African languages.

Not before the 1880s did the colonial administration start to set up English medium government schools. The 1882 Education Ordinance encouraged missionary schools to teach in English and a dual language policy was pursued until 1925: the Wesleyan and the government schools used English as a medium of instruction whereas the Basel and Bremen mission schools used the local language, Twi and Ewe respectively. The 1925 Education Ordinance made the use of the local language as the medium of instruction compulsory at the Primary level P1–P3 while English was to be taught as a subject. From P4 to P6, English was the medium of instruction, whereas the local language was taught as a subject. On the whole, Ghanaian language policy has ever since vacillated between the basic tenets of the 1925 Education Ordinance and the wish to push English as a medium of instruction from P1. The 1951 Accelerated Development Plan for Education led to the rapid increase of primary schools throughout the country. The resulting shortage of staff meant that primary school leavers had to be employed as teachers. Coupled with the fact that the Plan provided for an early transition from African languages to English as the medium of instruction, this had serious consequences for the quality of English.

Nevertheless, colonial rule established English as the language of higher-level education, government, administration, and jurisdiction.

Since 1970 the policy has been to use the local languages in the first three years of schooling and to teach in English thereafter. Actual practice varies widely, though, with schools in multilingual urban areas switching to English much earlier than schools in linguistically less complex rural areas. In 2001 the latest language policy was issued. English is now to be the only medium of instruction from P1 and throughout the educational system. The general opinion among linguists and language pedagogues in Ghana is that this does not favour a good standard of English.

Since almost all Ghanaians acquire their English in school, literacy can serve as a rough indicator of the spread and quality of English. It has increased steadily from a mere fifth of Ghanaians aged 15+ in 1962 to two thirds at the turn of the millennium, but its quality varies widely, from native-like fluency to broken varieties.

1.1.   Current sociolinguistic situation

Linguistically, Ghana is highly heterogeneous, with nearly 50 indigenous languages. All of these belong to the Niger-Kordofanian family, in particular two branches of the Central Niger-Congo phylum: Gur languages are spoken in northern Ghana by ca. 24% of the total population, and Kwa languages in the south (ca. 75%). There are also two very small pockets of Mande languages (< 1%). The following table lists the major languages of Ghana and gives a rough estimate of the number and percent of their speakers:

Table 1.   The major Ghanaian languages

Languages	No. of speakers (ca.)	Percent (ca.)
Kwa (south)		
Akan	7.000.000 (1995)	43%
Ewe	1.615.700 (1991)	10%
Ga-Dangme	1.125.900 (1991-93)	7%
Gur (north)		
Dagaari	950.000 (1998)	6%
Dagbani	540.000 (1995)	3%

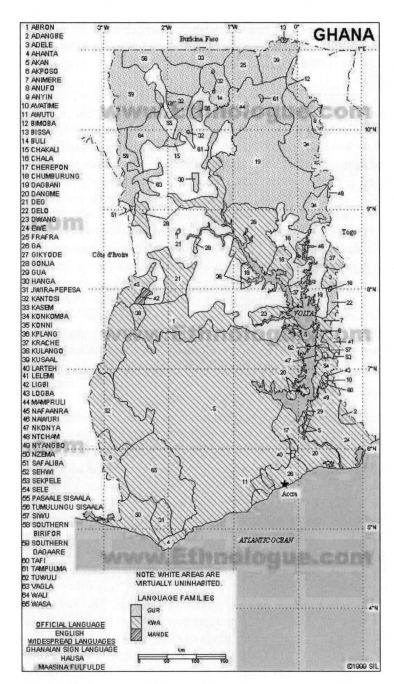

Map 2. The languages of Ghana

Akan (Twi and Fante) is the biggest Ghanaian language. It is the L1 of about 43% of Ghanaians. The latest census figures (2000, but not yet publicly available) show a strong increase in L2 speakers of Akan, which is now spoken by over 70% of the population and thus the most important *lingua franca* in the country. This, together with the fact that in colonial times, but also afterwards, the vast majority of teachers came from the south accounts for the strong Kwa influence (Akan, Ewe, Ga-Dangme) in Ghanaian English (GhE).

There is a sociolinguistic north-south divide in Ghana that roughly coincides with the distribution of Gur and Kwa languages. The former are spoken in the rural and generally poorer north, the latter in the more urbanized and richer south. Originally introduced by Nigerian migrants several generations ago, Hausa, a Chadic language of the Afro-Asiatic family, was used along the so-called Hausa Diagonal, the old trade route through Bawku via Tamale, Kintampo or Salaga to Kumasi. Hausa has thus gained some currency as a *lingua franca* in parts of Ghana's north but is still felt to be a foreign language by the majority of Ghanaians. For about a century, unequal economic opportunities have resulted in massive migration to the southern cities, where many northerners settle in so-called Zongos (Hausa for 'foreigners' quarters', poor and often slummy suburbs of towns and cities, inhabited by migrants from northern Ghana and the Sahel, and generally associated with Islam). Hausa was thus transplanted to the south and is today widely used in the southern Zongos, in some major urban markets, and to some extent in the military and the police.

The Bureau of Ghana Languages officially sponsors nine indigenous languages, which thus have 'national' status and are used for purposes of public information and education: Akan, Ewe, Dangme, Ga, Nzema, Dagaare, Gonja, Kasem, and Dagbani. Although English is universally called the official language of Ghana, it was never so declared on a constitutional level. The first constitution of Ghana (1957) accepted English as a *de facto* official language when stipulating that members of parliament had to be proficient in spoken and written English (Article 24). In the latest constitution (1992) one notices a move away from this implicit endorsement of English to a mere acceptance of its expediency. English is no longer mentioned, and indigenous languages, reference to which was conspicuously absent in the 1957 constitution, are now given prominence: Article 39, for example, states that "The State shall foster the development of Ghanaian languages and pride in Ghanaian culture" (even though the latest language policy gives an alibi for non-implementation of these lofty ideals). This reflects the general feeling among Ghanaians that English is a borrowed, foreign language and a residue of colonialism. Because of this, there has been an ongoing debate on the question of the official language since the earliest days of independence. Akan is the most popular but by no means undisputed alternative to English, which has the advantage of ethnic neutrality and of being an important link to the international community.

In spite of the official sanction of indigenous languages, English continues to function as a sociolinguistic High language. It has a prominent place in the national news media, it is used in parliament and public speeches, and it is the language of secondary and tertiary education. However, in none of these domains is it used to the exclusion of indigenous languages, which perform both High and Low functions, particularly in rural and more traditional areas. English, on the other hand, is more deeply rooted on the formal end of the communicative continuum, in more urban and multilingual settings. However, indigenous languages (especially Akan) are currently encroaching on the domains of English. This is shown e.g. by the success of monolingual African FM stations like *Peace* and *Adom* (Akan), which seem to be more popular than the predominantly anglophone *Joy* and *Choice*.

Since the vast majority of Ghanaians learns English in school, there is as yet no substantial native speaker community, though some middle class children acquire English along with Ghanaian languages or, less frequently, as their sole L1 in the home and English-medium nursery schools and kindergartens. There is also a small group of younger people of the upper-middle-class, the children of the professional elite, often with one foreign parent, who have been raised in homes where only English was spoken and who attended English-medium schools abroad and thus never acquired a Ghanaian language. For the majority of "anglophone" Ghanaians, English, however, coexists with one or more indigenous L1s. The result is a lot of code-switching and borrowing, particularly in the more informal registers of GhE.

Because of Ghana's colonial past, GhE is oriented towards BrE, but the global influence of AmE in the media has also been noticeable in Ghana in recent years. This has not yet affected the news on TV or the radio, but an American or Americanized accent can be heard in less formal broadcasts like host shows and commercials by big companies such as Guinness (this accent has been given the acronym *LAFA* 'locally acquired foreign accent'). A large number of middle-class Ghanaians live in the US and Canada and the accents they acquire while working there are associated with economic success just like the electronic gadgets they bring back on their return. On the other hand, the highly educated Ghanaian who has trained abroad does not acquire this accent – thus none of the senior members of the University of Ghana with PhDs from the US or Canada exhibit this through their accent. This might possibly be associated with an attitude that assumed political significance in the 1950s

– that Nkrumah had studied at a Black College in the US and hence the general perception that Busia and Danquah – both British trained – had enjoyed a superior form of education.

2.   Phonological features of Ghanaian English

It should be kept in mind that on all descriptive levels, GhE is a system of tendencies rather than categorical differences from the British standard, depending on various factors such as the speaker's linguistic competence and L1, the level of L2 command of English (roughly correlating with the level of education), the formality of the situation, the wish of the speaker to project Ghanaianness, etc. There is thus a lot of intra- and interindividual variation in GhE and unless otherwise mentioned, the following sections describe the most "Ghanaian" features in pronunciation, grammar, and the lexicon, i.e. the variety referred to as Conversational GhE in section 3.

2.1. Vowels

Table 2.   GhE vowels – summary

KIT	i > ɪ	FACE	e ~ eⁱ > ei	NEAR	iɛ > ia
DRESS	ɛ		ɛ ~ ɛⁱ > ɛi	SQUARE	ɛ > ɛa
TRAP	a	PALM	a(ː)	START	a
LOT	ɔ	THOUGHT	ɔ > ɔː	NORTH	ɔ
STRUT	a ~ ɔ > ɛ	GOAT, GOAL	o ~ oᵘ > ou	FORCE	ɔ
FOOT	u > ʊ		ɔ ~ ɔ ᵘ > ɔu	CURE	uɛ ~ uɔ ~ ɔ
BATH	a(ː)	GOOSE	u > uː	happY	i ~ ɪ
CLOTH	ɔ	PRICE	ai > aⁱ > a	lettER	a
NURSE	ɛ(ː)	CHOICE	ɔɪ	horsES	i > ɪ ~ ɛ
FLEECE	i > iː	MOUTH	au > aᵘ ~ a	commA	a

2.1.1. Monophthongs

The 12 RP monophthongal vowels are reduced to 5 in the system of the most "Ghanaian" speakers, i.e. those whose English shows all possible mergers or substitutions of the BrE monophthong system. These vowels are /i, ɛ, a, ɔ, u/. To these are added the half-close /e/ and /o/, which result from the monophthongization of the BrE diphthongs /eɪ/ and /ou/, so that in total there are 7 GhE monophthongs, a system shared with the other West African Englishes:

i	u
e	o
ɛ	ɔ
a	

Some of the simplifications of the monophthong system result from the tendency in GhE to neutralize length distinctions present in RP, resulting in homophony of RP minimal pairs. There are three such mergers of RP vowel oppositions:

Table 3. FLEECE-KIT, GOOSE-FOOT and THOUGHT-CLOTH mergers

RP			Example		GhE		
iː	ʃiːp	siːt	*sheep*	*seat*	i	ʃip	sit
ɪ	ʃɪp	sɪt	*ship*	*sit*			
uː	fuːl	puːl	*fool*	*pool*	u	ful	pul
ʊ	fʊl	pʊl	*full*	*pull*			
ɔː	nɔːti	kɔːk	*naughty*	*cork*	ɔ	nɔti	kɔk
ɒ	nɒti	kɒk	*knotty*	*cock*			

This process, a pan-African feature of English (Simo Bobda 2000a: 254), tends to occur in the GhE renderings of the RP pairs /iː-ɪ/, /uː-ʊ/, and /ɔː-ɒ/, i.e. pairs whose second members show a more open (and laxer) realization than the first. That vowel length tends not to be distinctive in such GhE pairs is interesting, since length is a phonological feature in some indigenous languages like the large Akan group or Hausa, which has some currency in the country.

There are two other vowel mergers that often result in GhE homophony. These result from a fusion of RP /ɜː/-/ɛ/ and /ɑː/-/æ/-/ʌ/, vowels not primarily distinguished by degree of openness (laxness). However, RP length differences are more regularly – though not categorically – maintained here:

Table 4.   NURSE-DRESS and BATH-TRAP-STRUT mergers

RP			Example		GhE		
ɜː	tɜːn	bɜːnt	*turn*	*burnt*	ɛ(ː)	tɛ(ː)n	bɛ(ː)nt
ɛ	tɛn	bɛnt	*ten*	*bent*	ɛ	tɛn	bɛnt
ɑː	kɑːt	hɑːt	*cart*	*heart*	a(ː)	ka(ː)t	ha(ː)t
æ	kæt	hæt	*cat*	*hat*	a	kat	hat
ʌ	kʌt	hʌt	*cut*	*hut*	a	kat	hat

Most West African languages do not have central vowel phonemes. Speakers of West African English accordingly replace RP /ə, ɜː, ʌ/ by front or back vowels. On the other hand, /ɑ/ – very close to the English low back vowel – is found in many languages and heard in the names *Ga, Akan, Dagaari, Dagbani*, but does not surface in GhE.

The almost categorical substitution of the front vowel /ɛ/ for RP /ɜː/ in all contexts is one of the main characteristics that sets GhE apart from other West African Englishes. The latter mainly replace the central vowel by /a/ and /ɔ/ and only in a limited and predictable number of cases by /ɛ/ (Simo Bobda 2000b: 190). The cause of the substitution of RP /ɜː/ by GhE /ɛ/ is often attributed to L1 influence. Like the other West African languages, the majority of Ghanaian languages lack the central vowel /ɜː/: in my estimate, based on an examination of the vowel systems of 29 indigenous Ghanaian languages, representing about 87% of Ghana's population, some 14% of Ghanaians are familiar with central vowels. This includes speakers of Ewe, spoken by about 10% of the population – by far the largest Ghanaian language with a central vowel (i.e. [ə]). Note, however, that in all except a couple of very small languages (spoken by a total of about 1% of the population), central vowels are either allophonic variants of front or back vowels, or are heavily restricted in their occurrence. The largest Ghanaian languages, Akan and the Ga-Dangme cluster (the mother tongues of 50% of Ghanaians), do not have central vowels, which may be the reason why RP /ə, ɜː, ʌ/ are largely avoided in GhE. While central vowels are absent from the majority of indigenous languages, most have /ɛ/. Sey (1973: 147) maintains that for the Ghanaian speaker of English "the two vowels [ɛ and ɜː] are sufficiently alike to be confused with each other". Although I cannot at present offer a better explanation for the phenomenon, Sey's scenario does not account for the whole story, since it leaves unanswered the question why in the English of countries like Nigeria, whose indigenous languages similarly lack central vowels but have /ɛ/ (observation based on an analysis of 28 Nigerian languages), /ɜː/ is mostly replaced by /a/ and /ɔ/ – not by /ɛ/. Colonial input varieties of English may have played a role in the establishment of different correspondences of RP /ɜː/ in the various West African Englishes.

The /ɑː-æ-ʌ/ merger seems to be due to L1 transfer, since none of the main Ghanaian languages has all three vowels. Ghana shares the lowering of the TRAP vowel with most other West African Englishes except Liberian English (Simo Bobda 2003: 21). In fact, the replacement of /æ/ by /a/ is a feature found in all African Englishes, east, west, and south (Simo Bobda 2000a: 254). However, it is in the substitution of RP /ʌ/ that contemporary GhE clearly distinguishes itself from other West African Englishes. While the latter render RP /ʌ/ as /ɔ/, today's GhE varies between /ɔ/ and (perhaps more often) /a/. In some cases, /ʌ/ is replaced by /ɛ/.

To start with /ɛ/, Sey (1973: 147) notes that "the /ʌ/ > /ɛ(ː)/ pronunciation is common in the Cape Coast area". This is the region of Ghana that first saw British territorial colonization (territorial expansion going back to the early 19th century), that has had the longest tradition of English-medium schools, and that was the capital until 1877. The indigenous language in and around Cape Coast is Fante (an Akan dialect), and Gyasi (1991: 27) accordingly associates the /ɛ/ pronunciation with Fantes. That RP /ʌ/ > GhE /ɛ/ has long been firmly established in the Cape Coast area is illustrated by a remark by the missionary Dennis Kemp, who worked in Cape Coast from 1887 to 1896:

> A somewhat amusing little accident occurred at the annual school examination. Our scholars, for some inexplicable reason, invariably pronounce the letter "u" as "e," and will insist, for example, in calling "butter" "better." The senior scholars were asked to name the principal seaports of England. One little lad thought of "Hull." But in consequence of the difficulty just mentioned the examiner did not recognise the name, and somewhat absent-mindedly asked in which part of England "Hell" was. (Kemp 1898: 179)

Simo Bobda (2000b: 189) says that today /ʌ/ > /ɛ/ cuts "across all ethnic groups in Ghana" and that its occurrence is lexically or idiolectally conditioned. My own recordings of GhE corroborate this: there is a lot of variation, but /ɛ/ seems indeed to be lexically conditioned. It occurs most regularly in function words like *but, us, just, such*, and *much*, but also in a small number of high-frequency lexical items such as *month*. However, it seems that even in the speech of non-Fantes, /ʌ/ > /ɛ/ replacement is not a particularly new phenomenon: even the oldest speakers, born in the early 1900s and from different ethnic backgrounds, show this characteristic. It must already have been established and widespread in pre-WW I GhE. This does not mean that /ʌ/ > /ɛ/ replacement did not originate with the Fantes: from the earliest colonial days, Cape Coast was the educational centre of the Gold Coast and continues to be an important school and university city today. It was an important teacher training centre and Fante teachers may well have carried the /ɛ/ pronunciation to other parts of the colony in the late 1800s.

As mentioned above, the much more frequent substitution of RP /ʌ/ today is /ɔ/ or /a/, the latter distinguishing GhE from most of the other WafEs. GhE shares /ʌ/ > /a/ with the Hausa English of Northern Nigeria, but the latter appears to be changing towards the dominant Yoruba pronunciation /ɔ/ (Simo Bobda 2000b: 188). Today, /ɔ/ and /a/ are in free variation in GhE. One and the same individual may pronounce the tonic vowels in e.g. *country, culture,* or *much* as [ɔ] or [a]. Personal observation suggests that with some speakers, this variability is simply due to linguistic insecurity since both forms are current in GhE today. Simo Bobda (2000b: 187–188) proposes that /ɔ/ may occur only if certain conditions concerning spelling, assimilation, ethnicity of the speaker, and age are met. However, my data suggests that these factors only partially account for the occurrence of /ɔ/ or /a/. I will illustrate this by speakers A and B in the conversation accompanying this article:

(a)   Spelling

Simo Bobda (2000b: 188) observes that an <o> spelling may trigger /ɔ/ in words like *love, cover, ton,* or *honey*. This is also illustrated by Speakers A and B's /ɔ/ pronunciation of *some* and its compounds – the GhE convention. But at the same time there are also instances where the pronunciation does clearly not follow the spelling, such as *done, nothing,* or *other,* all /a/ in the recording. As such, these do not invalidate Simo Bobda's theory since it allows for /a ~ ɔ/ *variability* when there is an <o> spelling. Note however, that a number of words, such as *come,* are never pronounced with an /a/ in GhE but always with an /a/ even though they are spelt <o>. A psychological factor may explain the /a/ in cases of these high frequency words: it has repeatedly been observed that Ghanaians believe their English to be nearer to the British standard and thus "better" than other West African varieties. In Ghana, /kɔm/ is stereotypically associated with Nigeria and is frequently pointed out as one of the differences between Ghanaian and Nigerian English. The categorical /a/ in words of the *come* type may thus be an attempt by Ghanaian speakers to dissociate themselves from the "bad" Nigerian accent. In addition, Speakers A and B's /ɔ/ in *dr**u**g*, *u**nderstand*, *res**u**lts* cannot be explained by spelling pronunciation. These observations certainly weaken the usefulness of the factor orthography.

(b) Assimilation
According to Simo Bobda (2000b: 188), a following rounded vowel and pos- sibly also a rounded consonant favour /ɔ/ rather than /a/. However, this is dubi- ous for two reasons: first, Simo Bobda's examples of assimilation to a follow- ing rounded vowel, *suppose* and *conduct*, do not really illustrate the phenom- enon since in RP the nucleus of the initial syllables of these words is /ə/, not /ʌ/. These words do not therefore meet the input requirements for the /ʌ > ɔ/ substitution process. Second, Simo Bobda's argument that following "rounded consonants" (/b/ is described as +ROUNDED) tend to trigger /ɔ/ is doubtful, since roundedness is not an intrinsic, distinctive feature of English consonants but is determined by the phonetic context. Possibly, roundedness is confused with labial place of articulation, but even in that case the proposed assimilation rule does not work: cf. *drug* (Speaker B) and *result* (A), which both have /ɔ/ without the following consonant being labial or intrinsically rounded. But note the different vowels in the otherwise phonologically quite similar *drug* /ɔ/ and *blood* /a/ (Speaker B; both voiced throughout, both plosive+liquid+vowel+plo sive), which demonstrates that /a/ and /ɔ/ are used in very similar contexts, in this case before /g/ and /d/, whose roundedness is subphonemic and depends on the preceding vowel and not *vice versa*.

(c) Ga ethnicity
Simo Bobda (2000b: 188) maintains that while a generation ago /ɔ/ was still as- sociated with the Gas, today "the prevalence of /a/ approximates 100% across all ethnic groups". Judging from my data, this somewhat overstates the case. First, even my oldest non-Ga speakers, born in the early years of the 20th cen- tury, show a high rate of /ɔ/ for RP /ʌ/ (cf. also Schachter's 1962: 18 observa- tion on Twi-speakers around 1960 to the same effect). It is doubtful, therefore, whether /ɔ/ had ever been an exclusively Ga characteristic. As to the rate of /ɔ/ in today's GhE, I concur that /a/ has been gaining ground, but it is still far from categorical. This is also exemplified by the recording. Both speakers use 12 tokens each of the STRUT set. Speaker A, whose L1 is Hausa, realizes 10 of these with an /a/ (83%), and Speaker B, whose L1 is Twi, 8 (67%).

(d) Older age
This is the crucial factor accounting for the distribution of /a/ and /ɔ/. Simo Bobda (2000b: 188) observes that /a/ must have started to replace /ɔ/ during the last 40 years or so and is today associated mostly with the older generation. I agree that /a/ is the more modern GhE realization, but apparent time evidence

in my recordings suggests that it must have started to replace /ɔ/ earlier than the 1960s. Apart from the few instances of RP /ʌ/ > GhE /ɛ/ mentioned before, speakers born in the first decades of the 20th century almost exclusively replace RP /ʌ/ by /ɔ/, regardless of their linguistic background and educational attainment. Up to about 1930, this appears to have been the norm, but then /a/ began to replace earlier /ɔ/.

Exactly why and how this /ɔ > a/ replacement has been taking place is unclear, but there are indications that we are dealing with lexical diffusion here: although there is general /a ~ ɔ/ variation today, the occurrence of these phonemes is already strictly lexicalized in some words. The GhE pronunciation of e.g. *some* is always /sɔm/, while *come* is /kam/, across the board and regardless of the sociolinguistic parameters of the speaker. Note that it is not the phonetic/phonological context that determines the occurrence of /ɔ/ in *some* and /a/ in *come*, since both end in a bilabial nasal and assimilation to the place of articulation of the preceding consonant would yield /a/ in *some* (alveolar /s/ imaginably favouring a front vowel) and /ɔ/ in *come* (velar /k/ triggering a back vowel). In fact, the pronunciation /kɔm/ *come* is frequently pointed out by Ghanaians as one of the characteristics of Nigerian English and one of the most salient differences between GhE and NigE. It therefore seems that, at least with some high-frequency words, the replacement of RP /ʌ/ appears to be primarily lexically conditioned.

RP /ə/ in unstressed syllables is generally substituted by front and back vowels, depending mainly on orthography and the phonological context:

(a) in post-tonic syllables involving <er, re, or, ur, ure> spellings, RP /ə/ is rendered as /a/ in open syllables and as /ɛ/ in closed syllables. Compare *paper* /pepa/ but *papers* /pepɛs/, and in the accompanying conversation *torture* /tɔtʃa/ but *tortured* /tɔtʃɛd/, *doctor* /dokta/ (both in speakers A and B) but *investigators* /ĩnvɛstigetɛs/ (speaker B). Post-tonic syllables of the type <our, ous, um, us> favour /ɔ/, as in *honour*, *dangerous*, *column*, or *focus* (contra Simo Bobda 2000b: 191–192, who predicts /a/ for <our>, and /ɛ/ for <ous, um, us>), though sometimes /a/ can also be heard. /ɔ/ in open post-tonic syllables, e.g. *rumour* /rumɔ/ (speaker A), has been associated with the older generation (Simo Bobda 2000b: 191), but my recordings show that younger speakers use it just as often.

(b) RP /-ən/, tends to be realized as /-in/ rather than /-ən/. This affects -*ed* and -*en* participle forms, for example *taken* /tekin/ or *spoken* /spokin/, but also other words, like e.g. *even* /ivin/ (speaker B).

(c) in other non-tonic syllables, RP /ə/ usually triggers spelling pronunciation. This is illustrated by speakers A and B's *about* /abaut/, *official* /ɔfiçia/ and speaker C's *submit* /sabmit/. There are a few exceptions to this, though, such as *alone* /ɛlon/.

(d) weak forms: Simo Bobda (2000b: 193) reports GhE /a/ for the indefinite article *a*, but this is decidedly a minority form in my recordings, /ɛ/ being by far the more common realization. The prevocalic form *an* is pronounced /an/. The distribution of the variants of the definite article *the*, /ðɛ ~ d̪ɛ ~ dɛ/ and /ði ~ d̪i ~ di/, usually follows that in BrE: /dɛ/ is preconsonantal and /di/ precedes a vowel. There is some degree of variation, though, with the occasional preconsonantal /di/ (*the forty women* /di fɔti wumɛn/) and /dɛ/ before vowels (*the eight women* /dɛ eⁱt wumɛn/) – both speaker A. Vowels in other function words are generally modelled on the RP citation form, that is the RP schwa is replaced by spelling pronunciations, except in *and*, which is usually /ɛn(d)/ and only sometimes /an(d)/.

2.1.2. Diphthongs

(a) RP closing diphthongs

GhE tends to monophthongize most of the RP closing diphthongs. This is not categorical, however: one and the same speaker may vary between a monophthong, slight diphthongization (marked by a superscript ⁱ or ᵘ in the table below), or may retain the RP diphthong. In the case of diphthongization, the RP offglides /-ɪ/ and /-ʊ/ are usually replaced by /-i/ and /-u/.

Table 5.   RP closing diphthongs and their GhE equivalents

RP	GhE
eɪ	e ~ eⁱ > ei or ɛ ~ ɛⁱ > ɛi
aɪ	ai > aⁱ > a
ɔɪ	ɔi
aʊ	au > aᵘ ~ a
əʊ	o ~ oᵘ > ou or ɔ ~ ɔᵘ > ɔu

As the table shows, all RP closing diphthongs except /ɔɪ/ can be monophthongized in GhE, /eɪ/ and /aɪ/ more frequently than /aɪ/ and /aʊ/. The realization of the first segment of RP /eɪ/ and /əʊ/ varies between /e ~ ɛ/ and /o ~ ɔ/, respectively. The RP diphthong+monophthong /aɪə/ (e.g. *desire*) and /aʊə/ (*our*) are often smoothed to [a] in acrolectal GhE, often with a falling tone, [â]. Smoothing can often be observed in Ghanaian news speakers (*the news on the hour* [dɛ nius ɔn di â]) but is not restricted to this group. Since this phenomenon is also observable in advanced RP, including the spoken media, it is not unlikely that British news language serves as a model here.

(b)   RP centring diphthongs
Like RP, GhE pronunciation is non-rhotic (see below, consonants). In words containing a final orthographic *r* GhE retains the diphthongization of RP word-final /ɪə/ and /ʊə/, while /eə/ is mostly monophthongized to [ɛ]. The latter is often realized with a falling tone [ɛ̂], which to ears not accustomed to tone languages makes it sound like a diphthong.

Table 6.   RP centring diphthongs and their GhE equivalents

RP	GhE
ɪə	iɛ > ia
eə	ɛ > ɛa
ʊə	uɛ ~ uɔ ~ ɔ

One particularity of GhE is that RP /uː/ is rendered as [iu] rather than [u] in words with orthographic *u*, *ue*, *eu*, or *ew*, e.g. *blew* [bliu] (hypercorrect forms such as *two* /tiu/ and *do* /diu/ are also heard). This cuts across all age groups and ethnicities, but there is also intra-speaker variability. Roughly, /iu/ occurs about twice as often as /u/. There are a number of possible sources of GhE [iu]: it may result from an analogy to other *ew* spellings such as in *new*, or *sewage*, whose RP /juː/ is rendered as /iu/ in GhE and/or an attempt to approximate the slightly centralized and diphthongized realization of /uː/ in advanced RP, in the region of [ʊʉ]. Another not unlikely source of GhE /iu/ is the historical Scottish influence through missionaries or the good number of Scotsmen in the Colonial Service.

2.1.3. *Factors contributing to variation*

As mentioned above, the GhE vowel system is characterized by a lot of inter- and intra-individual variation. One source of the latter may be advanced tongue root (ATR) vowel harmony, which is found in a number of Ghanaian languages including Ahanta and the Akan group in the south, and Dagaare and Kasem in the north. The vowels of these languages can be grouped in two sets, advanced and unadvanced, as illustrated here for Akan:

– advanced vowels	i	e	ạ	o	u
– unadvanced vowels	ẹ	ɛ	a	ɔ	ọ

As a general rule, only vowels of one set occur in polysyllabic words. Some speakers carry ATR vowel harmony over to English, so that the advanced and unadvanced members of the two sets become free variants in GhE: [i-ẹ], [e-ɛ], [ạ -a], etc. This accounts for a lot of the vowel height variation observable in GhE and explains pronunciations like *agencies* [ɛdʒɛnsẹs] instead of the expected [edʒɛnsis]. It may also account for some unexpected vowels: it was said above that RP /iː/ and /ɪ/ merge to /i/ in GhE, so that we would expect *three* [tri] and *six* [siks]. Instead, many Ghanaians realize these words as [tre] and [sɛks], respectively, thereby maintaining the /i – ɪ/ opposition in RP by replacing the tense-lax opposition by an advanced-unadvanced vowel pair. RP /ɪ/ > GhE /ɛ/ is the more frequent substitution, found in the pronunciation of e.g. *it*, *killed*, *people*, or *things*.

Another area of variability is vowel nasalization. Nasalization is distinctive in many Ghanaian languages and there is a strong tendency for GhE speakers to nasalize vowels before /n/ (much less so before the other nasals). In many cases this is accompanied by the reduction (indicated by a superscript ^{n}) or complete loss of /n/, so that we find the following pronunciations of *twenty* and *nine*:

twenty   [twɛnti ~ twɛ̃ⁿti ~ twɛ̃ti]
nine   [nain ~ naĩ̃ⁿ ~ naĩ]

In some cases, the loss of final /-n/ leads to near-homophony of pairs like *can – car*, *been – bee*, *coffin – coffee*, etc. These words are then only distinguished by the presence or absence of nasalization in the final vowel: [kã - ka], [bĩ - bi], [kɔfĩ - kɔfi]. As far as such pairs are concerned, nasalization could be said to be distinctive in GhE. However, since individual speakers use full, reduced, and elided forms side by side (e.g. kɔfin - kɔfĩⁿ - kɔfĩ), it appears that the nasal is part of the underlying phonological representation of such words and that its reduction or loss are surface co-articulation effects.

Vowel ellipsis in polysyllabic words is rather common in Ghanaian Radio and TV English, even more so than in BrE: forms like *police* [plis], *necessary* [nɛsɛsri], *operational* [ɔpreiʃnal], etc. have some currency in the spoken media but also among very acrolectal or language-aware speakers.

On the phonetic level, GhE syllable-initial vowels, especially those at the beginning of words, are characterized by glottal reinforcement [ˀV], e.g. *hour* [ˀaua], *all* [ˀɔl], *auditorium* [ˀɔditɔriɔm], *office* [ˀɔfis], *east* [ˀist]. Other than in BrE, glottal reinforcement does not signal special emphasis but is an intrinsic, sub-phonemic property of vowels in initial positions.

2.2.   Consonants

As with vowels, there is a lot of variation in the realization of consonants in GhE. In the following, I will discuss GhE consonants grouped according to their manner of articulation in RP under the headings of plosives, nasals, fricatives, affricates, and approximants.

(a)   Plosives

Like in colloquial BrE, т-glottalization and т-deletion have some currency in GhE. Syllable-final /t/ can be replaced by a fully or only weakly realized glottal stop (ʔ or ˀ) or it may be dropped altogether in word-final position. The following examples illustrate instances of т-glottalization and т-deletion:

– *go_t_*   [gɔt ~ gɔʔ ~ gɔˀ ~ gɔ]
– *wha_t_ever*   [watɛva ~ waʔɛva ~ waˀɛva]

Glottalization and deletion sometimes also affect /d/, as in *shoul_d_* [ʃuˀ], but this is possibly due to the fact that word-final obstruents are frequently devoiced in GhE, so that /-d/ becomes [-t] and is then glottalized (see also below, fricatives).

In the Fante dialect of Akan, /t/ has two allophones: [t] before back vowels and affricated [ts] before front vowels. Speakers of the dialect sometimes transfer this allophony to English and, for example, pronounce the name *Martin* [matsin].

RP word-initial /kw-/ is reduced to [k] in a number of words, like *_qu_ota*, *_qu_ote*, *_qu_arter*. However, other words, like *_qu_ality*, remain largely unaffected by this, so it seems that we are dealing with a lexicalized rather than productive phenomenon here.

(b)   Nasals

The loss of syllable-final /n/ and compensatory nasalization of the preceding vowel has been discussed in the section on vowels, above.

RP /-ɪŋ/ in progressives or deverbal nouns is more often than not replaced by [-ɪn], cf. *morn_ing_* [mɔnin], *lead_ing_* [lidin], *the meet_ing_* [dɛ mitin]. However, since [-ɪŋ] forms are current too, the GhE underlying representations seem to be /-ɪŋ/.

RP does not allow [mb] or [ŋg] sequences in the coda, but GhE has almost regular spelling pronunciations like *bo_mb_* [bɔmb], *thu_mb_* [tamb], *cli_mb_* [klaimb] or *si_ng_ a so_ng_* [siŋ ɛ sɔŋg], *amo_ng_* [amɔŋg], and *bri_ng_* [briŋg]. Spelling pronunciations are not restricted to the colloquial level but are common even in very formal and conservative GhE. Concerning [ŋg]-sequences: even if certain speakers tend to pronounce specific words without the final [-g], they may insert a kind of linking *g* before a vowel, e.g. *do I have to hang it?* [du ai haf tu haŋg it].

(c)   Fricatives
As in many other varieties of English, RP /θ, ð/ are often replaced by the dental or alveolar plosives [t̪, t, d̪, d] or they are dropped altogether in word-final position. Some speakers also produce affricated versions, [tθ, dð] as in *nothing* [natθiŋ] or *they* [dðei]. Replacement or deletion of the dental fricatives are especially frequent in more informal and mesolectal/basilectal varieties, but they are not altogether unknown even in very formal GhE, particularly the affricated variants. Again, one and the same speaker may vary between [θ, ð] and the corresponding GhE plosives or affricates, so that at least for acrolectal speakers an underlying /θ, ð/ can be assumed in words like *thousand* [θausɛn ~ tθausɛn ~ tausɛn] or *gathering* [gaðɛrin ~ gadðɛrin ~ gadɛrin]. In her study of the use of dental fricatives among students at the University of Ghana, Dako (forthcoming) found that women are more likely than men to retain RP dental fricatives (87% of the women were classed as /θ/-retainers and 65% as retainers of /ð/, as opposed to 53% and 37%, respectively, of the men).

Word-final /-θ/ is sometimes replaced by [-f] in words like *bath*, *cloth*, *mouth*, *with*, *eighth*. Again, Dako (forthcoming) showed that women prefer the standard form: only 16% of the female informants used word-final [-f], in contrast to 54% of the males.

Akan does not have the postalveolar fricatives /ʃ/ and /ʒ/, but the rather similar voiceless palato-alveolar fricative [ç] occurs as an allophone of /h/ before front vowels. Furthermore, speakers of Akan are familiar with its voiced counterpart [ʑ] from its occurrence in an allophone of /g/ (see below, affricates). Ghanaians regularly use [ç, ʑ] as substitutes for BrE /ʃ, ʒ/, e.g. in *official* [ɔfiçia], *issue* [içiu], *sure* [çiuɛ]. Note that in contrast to the RP version of these words – /əfɪʃl, ɪʃjuː, ʃʊə/ – GhE inserts an epenthetic [i] between [ç] and a following back vowel, in keeping with the allophonic distribution of this fricative in Akan (which occurs only before front vowels).

Interestingly, the substitution of [ç, ʑ] for /ʃ, ʒ/ is not only restricted to speakers whose L1 is Akan but can also be observed in the English of speakers of other Ghanaian languages, the majority of which does not have /ʃ, ʒ/ or phonetically near-identical substitutes (although in some languages these sounds have allophonic status). Therefore, a good number of non-Akans have adopted [ç, ʑ] as substitutes for RP [ʃ, ʒ]. It seems that this phonetic detail has become a truly national, if subconscious, feature of GhE, transcending mother tongue boundaries. However, it has to be pointed out that educated speakers vary between [ç, ʑ] and [ʃ, ʒ], depending on their level of education and phonetic competence.

Still others replace RP /ʃ/ by [s], for example in *machine* [masin]. These are predominantly speakers whose L1 does not have /ʃ/ (like Frafra) and who have had little schooling and/or little exposure to educated GhE. Probably as a reaction to this stigmatized /ʃ/ > [s] variant, hypercorrect forms like *nursery* [nɛçri] or *bursary* [bɛʃri] are not uncommon, even among educated Ghanaians.

As indicated in the section on plosives, there is a tendency in GhE to devoice final obstruents: *end* [ɛnt], *Lord* [lɔt], *news* [nius], *world* [wɛlt], etc. On the other hand, obstruents often get voiced in voiced environments – in intervocalic position (*pieces* [piziz], *taxable* [taᵍzabu]), but also if voiced consonants are involved (*bursary* [bɛzri], *pencils* [pɛnzils]). Such voicing can also be observed across word boundaries, cf. *what about* [hwad abaut] or *first degree* [fɛz digri] or *if Ghanaians* [iv ganɛɛns]. As these examples show, it seems that the sibilants /s/ and /ʃ/ are particularly, though not exclusively, affected by this process.

At the same time, hypercorrection with regard to final devoicing can lead to pronunciations like *dance* [dãz] or *process* [prosɛz]. Such voicing is possibly supported by the fact that final obstruents may become voiced when the following word starts with a voiced sound. Similarly, overgeneralized reversal of voicing leads to hypercorrect *vision* [viʃin] etc.

(d)   Affricates
Of the major Ghanaian Kwa languages Akan, Ga-Dangme, and Ewe (all located in the southern half of Ghana) only Dangme (spoken by ca. 4.5% of Ghana's population) has the affricates /tʃ, dʒ/. These sounds have greater currency in the Gur and Mande languages of Ghana's north, but population density is much lower there. Thus, at least half of Ghana's population is not familiar with /tʃ, dʒ/ from their mother tongues, but since English is much more widespread in the urbanized south, the proportion of GhE speakers whose L1 lacks these phonemes is probably in the region of three quarters.

Before high front vowels, Akan /k/ and /g/ are realized by the allophones [tç] and [dʑ] (orthographically *ky* and *gy*), as in *kyi* 'dislike', *kye* 'catch', *kyɛ* 'share out'. These are sufficiently similar to RP's more fronted /tʃ, dʒ/ to be employed by GhE speakers as substitutes for these phonemes. Examples are *church* [tçɛtç] or *larger* [ladʒa]. The plosives in these affricates are often reduced, so that forms like *major* [meᵈʑa] are widely used. Similarly to what has been said with regard to the fricatives /ʃ, ʒ/ above, Akan [tç] and [dʑ] have been adopted by other Ghanaians, so that they are used widely among speakers with a Kwa language background, but also by others. Again, there is [tʃ ~ tç, dʒ ~ dʑ] variability.

(e)   Approximants

GhE is non-rhotic (i.e. non-prevocalic R is usually not pronounced) since its historical model is the British standard. However, in contrast to RP, GhE does not have linking or intrusive R's.

The phonetic quality of GhE /r/ is usually [ɻ] (retroflex approximant as in RP), with which Ghanaians are familiar from some dialects of Akan. A large number of Ghanaians lives and works abroad, in Europe but especially in the United States and Canada. During their absence from Africa, a good number acquires some measure of an American accent and such a pronunciation is regarded by many Ghanaians as a sign of material success, characterizing someone who has made a small fortune abroad. Thus, some features of American English, like rhoticity or intervocalic flapping of /t/, are present in the speech of some *been-tos* 'returnees from overseas'. Americanisms in pronunciation are also strongly present in radio and TV advertizing and in the speech of radio moderators hosting music programs or other informal broadcasts. It seems, however, that Americanisms are largely restricted to the informal sector in the media; the news, for example, is always read by speakers with a non-rhotic accent.

L-reduction and/or vocalization can be observed especially where RP has a syllabic L: *available* [avelabuˡ], *circle* [sɛkɔˡ], *apple* [apɔ], *example* [ɛgzampu]. In these reduction processes, the vowel preceding L is velarized to [ɔ ~ u]. These processes also occur in environments where colloquial BrE does not show L-vocalization: *will* [wɔˡ ~ wuˡ], *fiscal* [fiska], *shall* [ʃa]. Ghanaian languages differ as to the phonological status of /l, r/: in the majority of the Kwa languages, including most of the Akan dialects, Ewe, and Ga-Dangme, [l, r] are in allophonic distribution. Some northern languages like Dagaare, Dagbani, and Kasem have /l/, but [r] occurs only as an allophone of /d/. Other Gur languages, including Frafra and Kusal, have two separate phonemes /l/ and /r/, as does the Kwa language Gonja. Because of this [l ~ r] alternation, especially in the south of Ghana but to some extent also in the north, pronunciations like *bless* [brɛs], *block* [brɔk], *play* [pre], or *properly* [prɔpɛrɪ] can be heard particularly among less educated, older speakers. The reverse, i.e. [l] for /r/, appears to be less frequent, but one example is *problem* [plɔblɛm].

GhE pronunciation differs from RP in that orthographic *wh-* is often rendered as [hw], so that the question words *what, where, which,* or *why* are pronounced [hwɔt], [hwɛ], [hwitɕ], and [hwai], respectively. This is another feature that could have its historical origin in Scottish influence in the Gold Coast, reinforced by spelling pronunciation. As with many other features, there is again variability, with speakers alternating between [hw-] and [w-].

Another difference from RP is that in GhE we find variable yod-dropping (RP /juː/ > GhE /u/), e.g. in *annual* [anual], *continuing* [kɔntinuiŋ], *duress* [durɛs] or *during* [durin].

2.2.1. Consonant cluster reduction

Cluster reduction is a phenomenon that GhE shares with other West African Englishes. It will therefore only be mentioned briefly here. There are two basic strategies to reduce consonant clusters. The first, elision of one or more consonants, is the most common strategy in acrolectal speech. It is illustrated in words like *hundreds* [handrɛs] (/dz/ > [z] + final devoicing), *artists* [atis] (/sts/ > [s]), or *texts* [tɛks] (/ksts/ > [ks]). It also operates across syllable boundaries, e.g. in *elec.tricity* [elɛtrisiti]. It frequently happens that consonants are not elided but only weakened in their realization, cf. *access* [aᵏsɛs] or *sleeps* [sliᵖs]. The second strategy is the insertion of epenthetic vowels in the consonant cluster. This is more common with less educated speakers. The principle here is that the tone-bearing vowel of the syllable containing the cluster is copied and inserted between the consonants, resulting in forms like *strange* [sᵉtᵉrendʐ] and *skin* [sⁱkin].

2.2.2. Spelling pronunciations

Spelling pronunciations of the NASAL + HOMORGANIC PLOSIVE (*lamb*, *tong*) and the *wh-* type (*where*, *which*) have already been mentioned in the sections on nasals and approximants, above. Consider also *Wednesday* /wɛdnɛsdɛ/, with a PLOSIVE + HOMORGANIC NASAL sequence. Other near-regular spelling pronunciations are based on *st* letter sequences, as in *castle* /kastɛl/. In the area of vowels, we find *ia* pronounced in e.g. *Parliament* [paliamɛn] or *official* [ɔfiçia](but see also 2.2.[c]), and the unsystematic occasional *women* [wumɛn]. Another example is *country* /kauntri/, which can be traced to ex-president Rawlings – he speaks LAFA (see above, 1.1) and established this pronunciation of the word, which is only used by younger speakers.

2.3.   Suprasegmentals

Like other West African Englishes, GhE is syllable-timed, resulting in the characteristic up and down of sentence intonation. A corollary of syllable-timing is that, unlike BrE, GhE does not show vowel reduction in unaccented syllables. Thus, unaccented vowels generally retain their full quality and schwa is hardly ever heard (see also the section on monophthongs in the phonology chapter).

The majority of Ghanaians speak a tone language as their L1. In contrast to accent languages like English, these languages show prominence of an individual syllable by realizing it at a higher pitch than neighbouring, non-prominent, syllables. They are also characterized by downdrift, a general lowering of absolute pitch as the utterance proceeds. At the end of a sentence, the tonal register is usually reset (upstepped) and the downdrift starts again. There is a tendency, especially with less educated speakers, to carry these features over to GhE.

Accent (or tone) shift can be observed in a number of polysyllabic words. Many Ghanaians move the main word stress forward in words like *facili'tate*, *investi'gate*, *ca'tegory*, or *te'lecommunication*. Backward shift can also be observed, as in *Eu'ropeans*, *a'ssociation*, and *'exchange*.

Vowel lengthening for emphasis is much more common than in BrE and seems to mirror usage in Ghanaian languages, as in the ubiquitous *at aaaaall* 'not at all'. Another common paralinguistic expression of emphasis is the use of creaky voice, often accompanied by voicing of voiceless consonants, cf. speaker B's *did hi se hwat hi did?*

In *that*-subordination, informal GhE often places a noticeable pause after, not before, the conjunction: *I saw that ‖ they had stolen it*. This is possibly a carry-over from Akan, whose complementizer *sɛ* derives from the verb *se* 'say' and has retained some of the verb's quotative characteristics (cf. *I said ‖ "They had stolen it"*).

3.   Conclusion: Major issues in current GhE research

Descriptive accounts of GhE are comparatively few and not always easily available outside Ghana. Since the first studies from around 1950, Ghanaian scholarship has often taken a more practical, pedagogical approach to GhE, discussing its quality and intelligibility to Ghanaians and non-Ghanaians alike and proposing ways in which language teaching can be improved. A good number of these studies show a decidedly prescriptive attitude and deplore deteriorating standards of English in Ghana, echoing public opinion that things "used to be much better" a couple of decades ago. However, to put such claims into perspective it should be noted that concerns about falling standards are not a recent phenomenon – they go way back to the colonial period, as the title of Brown and Scragg's 1948 *Common Errors in Gold Coast English* shows, and probably have always been around. Adherents of this prescriptive-pedagogical camp feel that Ghana as a developing country has more immediate needs than identifying (or conjuring up, as they see it) and promoting a local standard of English, as is made poignantly clear by Gyasi (1990: 26):

What we need in Ghana to rescue English from atrophy and death is not algebra masquerading as grammar, or the linguistic anarchism preaching the 'nasty little orthodoxy' (…) that any variety of English is as good as the other. We need the scholarly but humane and relevant approaches of those distinguished standard-bearers of Standard English, Professor Sir Randolph Quirk and his colleagues, Professors Sidney Greenbaum, Geoffrey Leech and Jan Svartvik.

Whether or not the existence of a distinct GhE is acknowledged very much depends on one's theoretical standpoint in this debate. The prescriptivists deny the reality of GhE as an autonomous variety and maintain that it essentially is (or ought to be) BrE. Anything else is simply labelled wrong English. In his seminal *Ghanaian English* Sey lists phonological, grammatical, and lexical "deviances" of GhE but says that "the educated Ghanaian would not 'accept' anything other than educated British Standard English" (1973: 7). This is also confirmed by the results of a language-attitude study of 30 educated Ghanaians (Dako 1991), which shows that to this group (a) GhE is an accent but has also some distinct lexical features; (b) British Standard English is considered the target language and therefore the norm in Ghana; (c) anything short of this target is felt to be substandard; but crucially also (d) that RP or any other native accent is not the target in spoken English. That is, it is in pronunciation more than any other area that speakers express their Ghanaianness, and an accent that sounds too British is usually frowned upon or even ridiculed. There is thus a double target of GhE: except maybe for the use of some lexical Ghanaianisms, standard written GhE in newspapers, magazines, etc. approximates to an exocentric norm, standard British written English. This is the professed (though not always attained) target in the educational sector and the variety modelled on it is spoken in formal settings by a small number of highly educated Ghanaians and is here tentatively called Cultivated GhE. The target of pronunciation, by contrast, is certainly endocentric, even for most speakers of Cultivated GhE. Many anglophone Ghanaians, however, speak a variety that is further removed from British standard grammar than Cultivated GhE and which could be called Conversational GhE, to emphasize its more informal character.

What is urgently needed are (preferably corpus-based, quantitative) descriptive studies of Conversational GhE and of informal and formal writing. These should be complemented by a study of the cline between broken and native-like varieties of GhE, as well as the various and complex interfaces between indigenous languages, Ghanaian Pidgin English and GhE.

Though a number of investigations have been based on privately compiled corpora, no text collections documenting GhE are currently publicly available. Ghana is listed as one of the West Africa components of the *International Cor-*

pus of English, but compilation and computerization of the texts has not neared completion at the time of writing.

Exercises and study questions

1. In what ways is the monophthong inventory of GhE similar to other varieties of English in West Africa?

2. In what details does the monophthong inventory differ between them?

3. Compare the diphthongs of GhE with those of any other West African variety of English.

4. What is ATR vowel harmony, and how does it operate in the Akan sub-variety of GhE?

5. From the information in 2.2 compile an inventory of the consonants of GhE.

Selected references

Please consult the General references for titles mentioned in the text but not included in the references below. For a full bibliography see the accompanying CD-ROM.

Brown, P. P. and J. Scragg
    1948   *Common Errors in Gold Coast English*. 3rd edition. London: Macmillan.
Dako, Kari
    1991   Some reflections on English in Ghana. Terminology and Classification. In: Emmanuel Quarcoo (ed.), *Proceedings of the Ghana English Studies Association. September 1991*, 42-56. Legon: (no publisher).
    forthcoming   Some thoughts about the use of dental fricatives by students at the University of Ghana. *Exploration: Journal of the University of Ghana* 1(2).
Gyasi, Ibrahim K.
    1990   The state of English in Ghana. *English Today* 23: 24–26.
    1991   Aspects of English in Ghana. *English Today* 26: 26–31.
Kemp, Dennis
    1898   *Nine years at the Gold Coast*. London: Macmillan and Co.

Schachter, Paul
   1962   Teaching English pronunciation to the Twi-speaking student. Legon: Ghana University Press.
Sey, Kofi A.
   1973   *Ghanaian English. An Exploratory Survey*. London: Macmillan.
Simo Bobda, Augustin
   2000a   Comparing some phonological features across African accents of English. *English Studies* 81: 249–266.
   2000b   The uniqueness of Ghanaian English pronunciation in West Africa. *Studies in the Linguistic Sciences* 30: 185–198.
   2003   The formation of regional and national features in African English pronunciation. An exploration of some non-interference factors. *English World-Wide* 24: 17–42.

Ghanaian Pidgin English: phonology

Magnus Huber

1. Introduction

Ghanaian Pidgin English (henceforth GhP) is part of a wider West African Pidgin English (WAP), and accordingly needs to be studied in close comparison with similar varieties in Nigeria and Cameroon. As shown in the history section of the article on Ghanaian English, Afro-European contacts on the Gold Coast evolved in three stages: early trading contacts (1471–1844), colonization (1844–1957), and independence and after (1957–).

During the phase of early trading contacts, several Pidgins lexified by the languages of the European merchants developed. Pidginized Portuguese was the earliest, falling out of use only in the second half of the 18th century, some 150 years after the Portuguese lost their supremacy on the Gold Coast. A Pidgin English came into being with the establishment of English traders on the coast from the middle of the 17th century onwards. Structurally, this was considerably simpler and more variable than today's GhP.

The origin of GhP as current today took place in the colonization period. From the 1840s onwards, Africans liberated from slave ships and freed on the Sierra Leone peninsula went back to their respective places of origin, thus spreading an early form of Krio along the West African coast, Nigeria in particular. Historical and linguistic evidence indicates that in the 1920s the Nigerian variety of Krio was introduced to Ghana by migrant workers. This decade can therefore be seen as the birthdate of GhP. For more detailed information on the history of GhP see Huber (1999a, 1999b).

1.1. Current sociolinguistic situation and varieties of GhP

The multilingual setting in Ghana is outlined in the article on English in Ghana. Huber (1995, 1999a) describes in detail the current sociolinguistic situation with special emphasis on GhP. The following is a summary of the most important facts.

GhP, locally known as 'Pidgin (English)', 'Broken (English)', and formerly as 'Kru English', or 'kroo brofo' (the Akan term), is a predominantly urban phenomenon. It is spoken in the southern towns, especially in the capital Accra. As will become apparent in the following sections, GhP is confined to a smaller (though growing) section of society than Pidgin in other anglophone West African countries. Also, its functional domain is more restricted and the language is more stigmatized.

There are two varieties of GhP that form a continuum. Basilectal varieties are associated with the less educated sections of society and more mesolectal/ acrolectal forms are usually spoken by speakers who have at least progressed to the upper forms of secondary school. I call these the 'uneducated' and the 'educated/student' varieties of GhP.

The difference between the two GhP varieties lies not so much in their linguistic structure (there are some differences but the two are mutually intelligible) as in the *functions* they serve: uneducated GhP is used as a lingua franca in highly multilingual contexts, whereas the more educated, or acrolectal, varieties are better characterized as in-group languages whose main function is to express group solidarity. There is a high rate of illiteracy in the linguistically heterogeneous immigrant quarters in southern Ghanaian cities where the uneducated variety has some currency. It is for this reason that Ghanaians usually equate Pidgin with a low level of education. On the other hand, GhP is also used by speakers with a high educational attainment, as among students at the Ghanaian universities. In these contexts, GhP does not fulfil basic communication needs – English is available to all parties in these settings and could be resorted to if no common indigenous language were at hand. Rather, Pidgin is used as a group-binder, to signal group identity and solidarity. Of course, interference from StGhE is much stronger with this last group than it is with uneducated speakers. However, the main differences between the two GhP varieties are lexical, not structural: by its very nature the variety used by the students is characterized by a high number of short-lived slang words, which may only be current on one campus or among one sub-group of students.

1.2.   Uneducated Pidgin

The traditional indigenous language in the capital Accra area is Ga, but there is a high number of immigrants from both inside and outside Ghana. In 1970, over 50% of the population in the Greater Accra Region were immigrants, and the percentage in immigrant quarters (called *zongos*, from Hausa *zango* 'camp, caravanserai') of Accra, like Nima, Kanda, or Mamobi, was and is much higher. These quarters are characterized by linguistic heterogeneity, overpopulation, slum conditions, and a high level of unemployment. Personal observation suggests that the rate of illiteracy is far higher than the Ghanaian average. There are no reliable data on the ethnic composition of the *zongos* but one inhabitant enumerated no less than 15 tribes that form distinct communities in Nima, many of them immigrants from northern Ghana, Togo, Mali, Burkina Faso, and Niger, besides speakers of Akan, Ewe, and Ga-Dangme. While Hausa, spoken in various forms from pidginized to Standard Nigerian Hausa, is the dominant lingua franca in Accra's multilingual immigrant quarters, Pidgin English also fulfils this function. Hausa seems to derive its ethnic neutrality from the fact that many do not consider it a genuinely Ghanaian language. It also carries some prestige through its association with Islam, the dominant religion in the *zongos*. Pidgin English draws its neutrality from the fact that it has no native speakers.

The label 'uneducated Pidgin' does not imply that its speakers necessarily had no or little formal education, but rather that this variety is transmitted and used in non-educational contexts. This is why Ghanaians most readily associate it with unskilled labourers, lorry and taxi drivers, watchmen, household servants, and the like. This type of Pidgin is typically used in multilingual settings characterized by low educational attainment of the speakers – in other words, settings which diminish (but do not necessarily exclude) the usefulness of an areal Ghanaian lingua franca such as Twi (or Hausa) and at the same time preclude StGhE as a language of interethnic communication. Places where this uneducated Pidgin can be heard are *lorry stations* (taxi or bus ranks), places of trans-shipment where the so-called *truck boys* load or unload lorries, or workers' bars.

1.3.   Educated Pidgin: secondary schools and universities

Speakers of the educated variety of GhP had at least some years of secondary education. One variety of educated GhP is spoken in secondary schools, especially by boys in the upper three forms (Senior Secondary School). Schools strongly discourage the use of Pidgin, but boys freely resort to it when unobserved by teachers. This variety of GhP serves as a social register, as an in-group language, being used not so much out of communicative necessity but as a means of expressing solidarity and intimacy with peers. Girls use Pidgin English more seldom than boys, possibly because they are much more susceptible to social norms. Education is an highly esteemed asset and Pidgin is still very much associated with the uneducated section of society. In this context it is understandable that girls should choose to speak StGhE rather than a non-standard variety that bears the stigma of illiteracy. Many of the female pupils do, however, have a passive command of Pidgin.

From the schools, Pidgin has been carried into the homes, where it is now used among brothers with secondary education, often to the exclusion of the vernacular. Although it used to be considered offensive to speak Pidgin to girls, I happened to observe a schoolboy courting a girl in Pidgin, which indicates that its function to signal intimacy is apparently being extended to inter-gender relationships.

The rise and spread of Pidgin in Ghanaian secondary schools started in the mid-1960s. From the secondary schools Pidgin was soon carried into the universities, where it established itself as the main informal code of male students. It is today heard on campus, in students' bars, and in the halls of residence. As in the schools, female students rarely speak Pidgin, although independent women may be observed to use it.

From the schools and universities Pidgin has also been carried into non-educational domains and is frequently heard among male peers in informal situations. Today, educated urban males under 45 years of age can be expected to switch to Pidgin in informal settings. The educated variety is currently spreading fast and is being used in more and more contexts. For one thing, secondary schoolboys or male students increasingly resort to Pidgin rather than StGhE or another Ghanaian language when female peers are present. Moreover, schoolgirls and female students are starting to use Pidgin actively more frequently than just a couple of years ago. In addition, pre-school children of middle class families appear to pick up GhP from their fathers.

1.4.   Pidgin in the police and army

Today, Pidgin has wide currency in the armed forces. Amoako (1992: 44) was informed by a police officer at a training depot that police recruits are taught Pidgin. Ghanaians readily associate Pidgin English with the police and army.

1.5.   Uses, function, and stigmatization of Pidgin in Ghana

The function of GhP is rather restricted in comparison with other WAPs. For example, in contrast to e.g. Nigeria and Cameroon, Pidgin is rarely used in the media. Ghanaian newspapers are almost exclusively in StGhE or Ghanaian languages and even their cartoons, where (quasi-)Pidgin often features in other West African newspapers, are surprisingly standard-like. A kind of mock pidgin is used in satire in some of the political magazines. In these publications Pidgin is attributed to uneducated speakers, policemen, or soldiers. Films are usually in StGhE. There are a few productions in which uneducated characters use Pidgin, but its use on screen is the exception rather than the rule. Pidgin used to be rarely heard on the radio, although Pidgin commercials seem to have come into fashion in recent times. Again it is uneducated characters who speak GhP. The function of Pidgin here is more to amuse and to create an authentic atmosphere than to reach a wider public.

Pidgin in Ghana is more stigmatized and less widespread in terms of area and number of speakers than it is in other anglophone West African countries. Especially among the educated section of Ghanaian society (but this is also true for less educated Ghanaians) Pidgin is still frowned upon as a mark of illiteracy and unpolished manners. GhP does, however, enjoy covert prestige: it is one of the preferred codes that a growing number of educated adult males use in an urban, informal, and unmonitored setting: in 'drinking spots', discos, among friends, etc. But in formal and traditional situations Pidgin is felt to be inadequate, rude, or disrespectful and a Ghanaian language or Standard English is preferred.

As new generations of scholars enter teaching positions at the universities, it is only a matter of time before Pidgin English will be heard in informal conversations between university lecturers. This is because unlike their senior and linguistically more conservative colleagues, young male Ghanaian lecturers did speak Pidgin at the time they were students.

The considerable stigmatization of GhP in some sections of Ghanaian society contributes to the widespread conviction that there is no true *Ghanaian* Pidgin and the belief that Pidgin is not a home-grown phenomenon but was introduced from other West African countries, especially Liberia and Nigeria.

2. Phonology

The sound system of GhP is similar to that of GhE, with a tendency of GhP speakers to use the more basilectal variants. For an overview of GhP phonetics and phonology, the reader is therefore referred to the respective section in the article on GhE. In the following, I will mainly point out those features where GhP differs from GhE.

2.1. Vowels

As an overview of the GhP vowels, table 1 reproduces the summary table from the article on GhE, which should be consulted for further comments.

Table 1.   GhP vowels – summary

KIT	i > ɪ	FACE	e ~ eⁱ > ei	NEAR	iɛ > ia
DRESS	ɛ		ɛ ~ ɛⁱ > ɛi	SQUARE	ɛ > ɛa
TRAP	a	PALM	a(ː)	START	a
LOT	ɔ	THOUGHT	ɔ > ɔː	NORTH	ɔ
STRUT	a ~ ɔ > ɛ	GOAT, GOAL	o ~ oᵘ > ou	FORCE	ɔ
FOOT	u > ʊ		ɔ ~ ɔᵘ > ɔu	CURE	uɛ ~ uɔ ~ ɔ
BATH	a(ː)	GOOSE	u > uː	happY	i ~ ɪ
CLOTH	ɔ	PRICE	ai > aⁱ > a	lettER	a
NURSE	ɛ(ː)	CHOICE	ɔi	horsES	i > ɪ ~ ɛ
FLEECE	i > iː	MOUTH	au > aᵘ ~ a	commA	a

2.2.   Consonants

Plosives

ᴛ-glottalization (e.g. *got* [gɔʔ]) is less frequent in GhP than in GhE. The reason for this may be that even in its colloquial registers GhE is still very much oriented towards the exocentric norm of BrE (whose informal varieties show glottalization). By contrast, in terms of its target GhP is a truly endocentric phenomenon and is therefore less likely to adopt such mechanisms from outside. The notion of degree of endocentricity also explains why ᴛ-glottalization is more common in educated than in uneducated GhP. The good command of StGhE of educated GhP speakers frequently results in the carry-over into their GhP of characteristics of the standard variety.

Fricatives

/θ/ and /ð/ are virtually absent from uneducated GhP, where they are replaced by /t/ and /d/. As with T-glottalization, educated GhP shows a higher rate of /θ, ð/, caused by StGhE interference.

   GhP, especially in its more basilectal, uneducated variety, shows some measure of replacement of /v/ by /b/ or /f/: *seven* /sɛbɛn/ and *shovel* /sɔful/. This is most frequent with speakers whose L1 is Akan or Hausa, since the phoneme inventories of these languages do not include /v/.

Approximants

Whether or not the lexifier [ɹ] is realized as an approximant or a trill depends on the quality of the *r*-sound in the speaker's first language and his phonetic competence. Most of the Akan dialects have an *r*-sound similar to English [ɹ], while other languages spoken in Ghana, e.g. Hausa, have trills or fricatives instead. The trills and the approximant may be used interchangeably or in stylistically different registers (e.g. [r] = basilectal and [ɹ] = more mesolectal/acrolectal), but they are not phonologically distinctive. Uneducated GhP, especially the variety spoken by northern immigrants in the *zongos*, prefers the trill, while the educated variety prefers the more BrE realization. Intervocalic flapping of /t/, acquired by some GhE speakers in the US and Canada, is uncommon in GhP.

There is allophonic distribution or free variation of [l] and [r] in the major Ghanaian substrate languages, e.g. in Akan, Dangme, Ewe, Ga, but also in Gur languages like Dagbani and Dagarti. As a consequence, the two sounds may be used interchangeably on the lower end of the GhP continuum. This phenomenon is most common with older speakers who had little formal education, but it is at times also found in other speakers. Examples of /l ~ r/ alternation are *broke* /blok/ and *bottle* /bɔtru/.

2.3. Syllable complexity

Consonant cluster reduction, as described in the contribution on GhE, also operates in GhP. However, it has to be pointed out here that GhP – contrary to what is often said about other WAPs – allows complex onsets and codas, mirroring the phonological structure of the words in BrE. Examples of such clusters can be found in *plant* /plant/ (CCVCC), *struggle* /strɔ.gɔl/ (CCCV), *street* /strit/ (CCCVC), and *strange* /stendʒ/ (CCCVCC). Again, complex clusters are less frequent in the uneducated variety.

2.4. Major issues in current research on GhP

So far, little has been published on GhP. Up until very recently, studies on Ghanaian English only mentioned the existence of Pidgin in passing. In his investigation of "Education and the role of English in Ghana" Boadi (1971: 51-2) says that Pidgin is widely used in the larger towns, but is not current among educated Ghanaians. Sey (1973: 3) states that apart from a continuum of more or less educated English there is Broken English and Pidgin, the latter usually associated with uneducated labourers from Northern Ghana or other West African countries. Criper's (1971: 13-4) "Classification of types of English in Ghana" similarly acknowledges the existence of Pidgin.

Since at least the 1980s, there has been an ongoing debate in Ghanaian universities about the supposedly harmful effects that the students' use of Pidgin has on their academic performance, but most of the articles relating to this question have remained unpublished. The two positions in this controversy are (a) that Pidgin presents a serious threat to literacy and the standard of education in a country that has traditionally prided itself on the high quality of its educational system; and (b) that Pidgin is just one code in the linguistic repertoire of young educated Ghanaians and that it is a useful means of horizontal communication with other anglophone West African countries and of vertical communication (literates-illiterates) in Ghana.

The debate about the spread of Pidgin in secondary schools and universities has mainly centred on the measures to be taken to prevent its supposedly harmful effects on the standard of education. The only studies known to me that also seriously investigate the structure of the student variety are Hyde (1995), who describes some lexical aspects and word-formation processes, whereas Ahulu (1995) provides a short sketch of the lexicon and grammar of what he calls "hybridized English". Kari Dako of the Department of English at the University of Ghana has been researching the variety used on Ghanaian campuses.

The stigma Pidgin carries in educated circles may also explain why so few structural or sociolinguistic descriptions of the variety have been published. For some linguists, describing GhE would declare it an object worth serious study and would be tantamount to giving official sanction. Only in recent years has Pidgin started to attract the interest of Ghanaian scholars, who now begin to study the variety spoken on campus.

Descriptions of the off-campus ('uneducated') variety of GhP are even fewer and again mostly unpublished – see the longer reference list on the CD-ROM accompanying this text.

Exercises and study questions

1. Compare the consonant inventory of GhP with that of southern GhE (in the preceding chapter).

2. Compare the consonant inventory of GhP with that of RP.

3. Compare the vowels of GhP with those of GhE (in the preceding chapter).

4. In what ways is the syllable structure of GhP different from that of other West African pidgins?

Selected references

Please consult the General references for titles mentioned in the text but not included in the references below. For a full bibliography see the accompanying CD-ROM.

Ahulu, Samuel
    1995   Hybridized English in Ghana. *English Today* 11: 31–36.
Amoako, Joe K. Y. B.
    1992   Ghanaian Pidgin English: in search of synchronic, diachronic, and sociolinguistic evidence. Ph.D. dissertation, University of Florida at Gainsville.
Boadi, Lorence A.
    1971   Education and the role of English in Ghana. In: Spencer (ed.), 49–65.
Criper, Lindsay
    1971   A classification of types of English in Ghana. *Journal of West African Languages* 10: 6–17.
Huber, Magnus
    1995   Ghanaian Pidgin English: An overview. *English World-Wide* 16: 215–249.
    1999a   *Ghanaian Pidgin English in its West African Context. A Sociohistorical and Structural Analysis.* Amsterdam/Philadelphia: Benjamins.
    1999b   Atlantic English Creoles and the Lower Guinea Coast: a case against Afrogenesis. In: Huber and Parkvall (eds.), 81–110.
Hyde, Faustina
    1995   On pidginization of English in Ghana. Unpublished typescript.
Sey, Kofi A.
    1973   *Ghanaian English. An Exploratory Survey.* London: Macmillan.

Liberian Settler English: phonology

John Victor Singler*

1.   Introduction

English is Liberia's official language. There is a Liberian variety of International English; it is the language of Liberia's media and institutions of higher learning, and it is the target of language instruction in Liberian schools.

The focus of the present article is Liberian Settler English (LibSE), the language of the Settler ethnic group. The Settlers are the descendants of the 16,000 African Americans who immigrated to Liberia in the nineteenth century. The modern Liberian state began with their arrival. In Liberia, formal education has performed an integrative function. The more education a Liberian has had, the more her/his English will correspond to the English of other Liberians of comparable educational achievement, regardless of one's ancestry and upbringing. Conversely, within the Settler group, those with the least extensive formal education are the ones who speak in the most distinctly Settler way.

Even as the Settlers have reclaimed their African heritage, it can be argued that their language – at least the language of the Settlers who have lived in the greatest isolation and who have had the least amount of formal education – has remained North American. Accordingly, the article that follows, while it acknowledges local influence on Settler speech, will be North American in orientation.

1.1.   Other varieties of English in Liberia: Pidgins

The earliest references to "English" along the coast of what is now Liberia date from the very beginning of the eighteenth century. Over the next century the use of "English" grew so much that, in the 1820's when the Settlers landed and founded their city of Monrovia, the missionary Jehudi Ashmun reported that "very many in all the maritime tribes, speak a corruption of the English language" (*African Repository*, Nov. 1827: 263). The "corruption" was undoubtedly pidgin English, the ancestor of today's Vernacular Liberian English (VLibE). (This term, with a slightly different reference, comes from Hancock 1971.) The following quotation illustrates this early pidgin. Attributed to King

Jo Harris, a Bassa chief, it appeared in an 1834 article in the Monrovia newspaper, the *Liberia Herald*:

> I savey: you man for governor, tell governor, him send one punch rum for dash we (meaning kings)[;] top, tell him send two punch, one for me King Jo Harris, me one, and tother for dash all country gentleman. (*Liberia Herald*, quoted in the *African Repository* 1834, 10:123–124; parenthetical assistance in the original)

The Settlers quickly came to dominate the region and established the independent nation of Liberia in 1847. While the new Liberian government claimed large areas of the interior, it initially took no steps to enforce the claim, and the Settlers themselves remained near the coast. Only at the beginning of the twentieth century did the government send its troops – the Liberian Frontier Force – into the interior to establish control. VLE was the language of the Frontier Force and of the labourers at the Firestone rubber plantation (begun in 1926); the alternative terms 'Soldier English' and 'Firestone English' for the VLE of the interior reflect the role that these two groups of men played in the pidgin's dissemination.

As noted, the Settlers themselves remained on the coast. The linguistic consequences of the interaction that took place between them and the indigenous people on the coast were overwhelmingly unidirectional, with the language of the powerful – LibSE – influencing the language of the dominated – VLE – but not itself being profoundly influenced in turn. Thus, while the pidgin had at first been a local variety of the pidginized English that developed along the West African coast more generally, the influence of LibSE upon it caused it to diverge sharply from pidgin English in the rest of West Africa.

Today VLE is the language of most English-speaking Liberians. It is unique among West African Englishes in that it fits the creole continuum model (De-Camp 1971; Singler 1984, 1997). The massive displacement of Liberians from 1989 onward as a consequence of civil war has thrown together people with no Niger-Congo language in common; the circumstances have promoted the use of VLE not only inside Liberia but also outside it, in refugee camps and communities.

In addition to VLE, there is or, more accurately, *was* a second pidgin English. Kru Pidgin English (KPE) was the language of "Kru sailors," the Klao and Grebo men who worked on board European vessels along the African coast from at least the beginning of the nineteenth century onward. By the latter part of the nineteenth century, "Krumen" also held low-status jobs in British colonies, most numerously on the Gold Coast (modern Ghana) but also Nigeria and Sierra Leone. The pattern quickly emerged whereby males who had grown up in monolingual villages would, at the age of fifteen or so, join a work group headed by an older individual from the village. The group would then travel to its working place and remain for a growing season (in the case of cocoa plantations in the Gold Coast), a year, or a few years before returning home, where they would remain for a comparable period of time. An individual would repeat this pattern on a regular basis until he was 45 or so, at which time he would cease making such trips. Research carried out in a Klao village shows that, for the most part, the Krumen had had little contact with Settlers, and there is little evidence of Settler influence upon KPE, or vice versa (cf. Singler 1990). Changes in maritime practice and, especially, the removal of the British colonial presence have eliminated a role for Krumen in Ghana and elsewhere. As a result, as old Krumen die, their pidgin is dying out. VLE has made inroads into the Klao and Grebo villages that had provided the British with Krumen; thus, if the children and grandchildren of the old Krumen are acquiring a pidgin, it is VLE, not KPE.

1.2.   The history of LibSE

LibSE is a direct descendant of the nineteenth-century African American English (AAE) that the immigrants brought with them. While the existence of features in LibSE has been used to show that putative innovations in modern African American Vernacular English (AAVE) have in fact been around for a long time (cf. the chapter on LibSE syntax and Singler 1998), LibSE is not itself nineteenth-century AAE; it has had 175 years in which to undergo change from that "starting point."

The political state of Liberia represents the legacy of an early nineteenth-century American attempt to solve an American problem by, quite literally, getting the problem to go away. The "problem" involved the status of free African Americans. They were American citizens, yet the discrimination against them everywhere in the US was so pervasive that many people held that they would always be subject to an inferior status. In 1816 white clergymen founded the American Colonization Society (ACS) in Washington, DC, and in 1822 the Society placed its first group of African American colonists in what was to become Liberia. The ACS had as its goal the founding of a colony in Africa where free people of color could enjoy the full privileges of freedom. Setting up such a colony – Liberia – proved extremely costly, and most of the funding actually came from Southern slaveholders who saw the presence in the US of free African Americans as a threat to the status quo. The connection between slaveholders and the ACS served to discredit the ACS among the free African Americans whom it most sought to recruit. The mortality rate among colonists during the Liberian scheme's first two decades was "shockingly high" (Shick 1980: 27);

news of this further dissuaded those with a choice from immigrating there. In the decades prior to the American Civil war, a majority of those who immigrated to Liberia had been slaves emancipated on condition that they immigrate.

Over the first 25 years of immigration to Liberia, the largest number of African Americans came from Virginia followed by Maryland and North Carolina. Subsequently, Georgia sent large numbers of immigrants and South Carolina as well (cf. Singler 1989). While the Settlers established communities along a 250-mile stretch of the Atlantic Ocean, from Robertsport in the northwest to Harper in the southeast, most of the colonists settled in Monrovia or in nearby communities along the banks of the St. Paul River. From the outset Settler politics and society were dominated by those who had emigrated from Virginia and states north of it.

A second population also arrived in Liberia in the nineteenth century, Recaptured Africans. They were individuals who had been on slave ships headed to the Western Hemisphere when these ships were intercepted by the US Navy. Almost all of them came from the Congo River; the Liberian term for Recaptured Africans is "Congo." (This is the Liberian spelling, as illustrated by the name of a Monrovia neighborhood, "Oldest Congotown," but the pronunciation is [kɔŋgɔ].) In all, more than 5700 Recaptured Africans were delivered to Monrovia, 4700 of them in or around 1860. The one numerically significant group of Recaptured Africans not from the Congo River region was a boatload of Yorùbá people from the Nigerian coast; upon arrival in Liberia, they were placed in Sinoe County.

Like the Settlers, the Recaptured Africans had no pre-existing ties to the indigenous population. They entered into the lower echelons of Settler society and became part of that group. Ultimately the term "Congo" came to be used to refer to the Settlers as a whole. While it carries a somewhat pejorative connotation, it is also by far the most common term used today to refer to the Settlers. In the same way, "Congo English" is the most common designation for what I term "Liberian Settler English." As for specific Bantu elements or, representing a smaller presence, Yorùbá elements, I have never been able to identify any in Settler speech. That is not to say they don't exist, only that my search has not uncovered them. In the discussion that follows of Settlers today and their language, the term "Settler" is meant to encompass Recaptured Africans as well.

The fundamental demographic divide in Liberia from 1822 onward has been that between Settlers and indigenous people. The Settlers perceived themselves as superior. They held that their westernness, with its Christianity and English literacy, endowed them with the right to rule.

In an 1860 Liberian Independence Day oration, the Cambridge-educated Episcopal priest the Rev. Alexander Crummell proclaimed:

> Here, on this coast ... is an organized community, republican in form and name; a people possessed of Christian institutions and civilized habits, with this one marked peculiarity, that is, that in color, race, and origin, they are identical with the masses around them; and yet speak the refined and cultivated English language (1862: 9).

In his speech Crummell recalled that in an oration two years earlier he had

> ... pointed out among other providential events the fact, that the exile of our fathers from their African homes to America, had given us, their children, at least one item of compensation, namely, the possession of the Anglo-Saxon tongue; that this language put us in a position which none other on the globe could give us; and that it was impossible to estimate too highly, the prerogatives and the elevation the Almighty has bestowed upon us, in our having as our own, the speech of Chaucer and Shakespeare, of Milton and Wordsworth, or [sic] Bacon and Burke, of Franklin and Webster ... (1862: 9)

Crummell's rhetoric embodies the Settlers' assertion that their literacy in English endowed them with the right to dominate the non-English-speaking population. In modern times members of indigenous ethnic groups have asserted their right to participate in Liberian government, but they have never challenged the primacy of English.

From the arrival of the earlier Settlers to the present day, a discrepancy has endured between the Settlers' language about language, specifically about written standard English, and their own command of English literacy and standard English. For, even by the most rudimentary criteria, only a minority of the early Settlers were actually literate. Not one of the colonists who arrived in the first few years of settlement had had even a "plain English education" (*Family Visitory*, quoted in the *African Repository* 1825: 236). A remark a generation later showed that there had been little change over the years: a Settler complained that among those who were newly arrived "[m]en of means ... [are] exceptions ... to the common rule, that is the no money, no A.B.C. men, that come directly from the plantation &c.&c." (*Liberia Herald* August 2, 1854). Certainly Liberia in its early days featured a Settler intelligentsia, a handful of highly educated immigrants (cf. Singler 1976–1977). They were, however, so few in number that from the outset the Settlers found it difficult to establish and maintain schools for their children. Because their own children were not being well-educated, Settler leaders objected to missionary efforts to educate indigenous children. Nonetheless, the Settlers' limited literacy and their difficulties in maintaining schools do not gainsay the central role of the book in such key Settler institutions as government, religion, formal schooling, and the Masonic lodge.

The Settlers, occasionally with the timely support of a US gunboat, established their hegemony along the coast. As noted, they extended their control into the interior early in the twentieth century. Never more than 3% of Liberia's population, the Settlers ruled Liberia until a military coup in 1980 placed Samuel Kanyon Doe, an indigenous Liberian, in power. Even though the 1989–1997 civil war and subsequent rebellions have not been simply or even primarily about the Settler-indigenous divide, that division remains a defining feature of Liberian politics and society.

The discussion of LibSE phonetics and phonology below, like most of my research on LibSE, focuses on the LibSE of Sinoe County, 150 miles down the coast from Monrovia. Founded by the Mississippi Colonization Society to be Mississippi in Africa, the Sinoe Settlers differed from other Settlers both in their provenance and in their post-immigration history. Far more than was true of other Settler communities, a significant number of people who immigrated to Sinoe came from large plantations (rather than small agricultural holdings or cities), and a far greater proportion came from the Deep South, particularly Mississippi and Georgia. Abandoned by the Mississippi Colonization Society almost immediately, the Sinoe settlements received far less support from the central government in Monrovia than did the other Settler communities. Moreover, Sinoe was the one cluster of Settler communities without a significant missionary presence in the nineteenth century. Taken together, the lack of government resources and the absence of missionaries mean that standardizing forces would have been weaker in Sinoe than elsewhere. Finally, except possibly for Maryland-in-Africa, nowhere else was Settler-indigene hostility so intense and so protracted. All of these factors appear to make Sinoe the likeliest stronghold in Liberia and possibly in the entire African American diaspora for the ongoing retention and transmission of the vernacular features that African American émigres had brought with them from the US.

In evaluating the speech of Sinoe Settlers, the impact of formal education upon an individual's speech must be considered. In Sinoe as elsewhere in Liberia, the more schooling someone has, the less distinctively Settler the person's speech will be, particularly in a formal setting such as a recorded interview. (Among the elders whose interviews form the Sinoe Settler corpus, five had at least begun secondary school, six had completed fourth, fifth, or sixth grade, and three had had no formal education to speak of.) Strictly speaking, within the Sinoe corpus, a speaker's occupation was a more consistent indicator of a speaker's style in an interview, with teachers least likely to use distinctively vernacular Settler features, that is, even less likely than non-teachers who had had more extensive formal education. For all speakers, but for teachers most of all, the question arises as to the extent to which they controlled and used two varieties, one the in-group Settler English, the other a variety that was less distinctively Settler.

Within Sinoe, there is a political – and linguistic – distinction between the county seat, Greenville, and settlements up the Sinoe River. In modern times Greenville is perceived as everyone's county capital, but upriver settlements like Lexington, Louisiana, and Bluntsville are recognized as "belonging" to the Settlers. Thus, the speech of the upriver Settlers shows much less accommodation to the speech of non-Settler Liberians. A further point in considering the LibSE of Sinoe County is its relationship to the LibSE of the rest of the coast. The rest of Liberia's Settler English has been studied very little; however, what seems to show up is that the difference between Sinoenians and non-Sinoenians is more quantitative than qualitative. On limited evidence, then, it is usually the case not that Sinoe Settlers use a greater number of distinctive features (here, distinctively American, and, usually, distinctively African American) than other Settlers, but rather that they use them more often. At the same time, there may be some instances in which non-Sinoe Settlers use standard-like features that Sinoe Settlers do not. For example, because Sinoe Settler speech shows a strong preference for CV syllables, the grammar blocks contracted forms of *will*, e.g. *I'll*; non-Sinoe Settlers, on the other hand, do use *I'll* and the other *'ll* contractions.

2.   Phonetics and phonology

2.1.   Phonemic inventory

2.1.1.   Vowels

Table 1.   The vowels of LibSE according to Wells's lexical set

KIT	ɪ > e	FLEECE	i	NEAR	iə, ɪə > eə
DRESS	ɛ	FACE	e		i, ɪ > e
TRAP	æ	PALM	ɑ > æ	SQUARE	ɛ > e, æ
LOT	ɑ	THOUGHT	ɔ	START	ɑ
STRUT	ʌ	GOAT	o	NORTH	o, ɔ
FOOT	u > ʊ	GOOSE	u	FORCE	o, ɔ
BATH	æ	PRICE	a > aⁱ, aⁱ	CURE	o
CLOTH	ɑ	CHOICE	ʌⁱ, ʌⁱ > ʌ	happY	i
NURSE	ʌ > ʌⁱ	MOUTH	ʌᵘ, aᵘ	lettER	ə
DANCE	æ̣			horSES	ə > ɛ
BED	e			commA	ə > ʌ

(DANCE and BED are not part of the lexical set, but they have been included here to distinguish their vowels from those in TRAP and DRESS, respectively.)

LibSE can be said to have ten or eleven monophthongs, depending on whether /ʌ/ and /ə/ are considered to be distinct. While there is a contrast between high front vowels between /i/ and /ɪ/, there is no consistent corresponding contrast in the back. Instead, a word like *foot* is ordinarily realized as [fu] or [fut].

LibSE has five front vowels, illustrated by the minimal quintuple *beat*, *bit*, *bait*, *bet*, and *bat*. When occurring before a nasal consonant, the /æ/ and /ɛ/ are raised, but the contrast with other vowels is preserved. Before voiced stops, what was historically /ɛ/ has undergone raising to [e]. Thus, *head* is pronounced [he] or [hed]. The infrequency with which the following voiced stop is realized on the surface in such words has led to the re-analysis of American English *bed* when it has the meaning 'an area of ground where flowers or plants are grown' as LibSE *bay*.

Further acoustic work is needed to determine the basis of the following contrasts: /i/ vs. /ɪ/, /e/ vs. /ɛ/, and /o/ vs. /ɔ/. The question is the extent to which the contrasts are based on differences in length, height, and/or peripherality. It is also possible that a tense/lax distinction forms the basis for the contrasts; if that is so, it would be necessary to address the relationship of the tense/lax distinction to the other distinctions, an ongoing issue in the study of English vowels. The American English generalization that lax vowels other than /ə/ can only occur in closed syllables does not hold on the surface in LibSE: [tɛ] is a common pronunciation of *tell*, and [sɪ] of *sit*. In the case of /e/ vs. /ɛ/ and /o/ vs. /ɔ/, there seems to be a clear height difference, with the first of the two vowels the higher of the two.

Diphthongs are frequently monophthongized, particularly the diphthong in PRICE. The diphthongs in PRICE and CHOICE are nearly homophonous, with the nucleus of the vowel in PRICE slightly lower than the nucleus of the vowel in CHOICE.

The greatest range of variation among speakers involves the vowels in NURSE, NEAR and SQUARE. In the case of NURSE, the nucleus tends to be mid and central, but there is variation both in height (from mid-low to mid-high) and backness (from central to somewhat front). For some speakers at least, the vowel sometimes ends with a high, central upglide. The vowel in NEAR is always front, but speakers vary not only in their realization of the vowel (i, ɪ, or e) but also as to whether it is followed by /ə/. Thus, /i/, /iə/, /ɪ/, /ɪə/, /e/, and /eə/ are all possible realizations.

The range and number of vowels in LibSE place it in contrast with VLE and with other Liberian languages. For most speakers of VLE, there is an eight-vowel system, a basic seven-vowel system plus /ə/. Most of Liberia's Niger-Congo languages have the basic seven-vowel system, though Klao and Grebo have nine owing to an ATR contrast.

2.1.2. Consonants

(a) Obstruents

The consonant inventory in LibSE is the same as that for American dialects of English except that LibSE does not have the voiced interdental fricative /ð/; /d/ shows up instead, as in *they* [de]. Its voiceless counterpart, /θ/, does occur, but only in syllable-initial position and only variably. Thus, *thatch* is pronounced both [θæʃ] and [tæʃ]. In syllable-final position, /t/ or /f/ is used, e.g. *both* [bof], *teeth* [tit]. Loanwords from Niger-Congo languages and VLE with labiovelar consonants are extremely rare in LibSE, and many speakers convert the labiovelar to a bilabial, so that *Kpanyan*, a district in Sinoe County, is realized as [pãỹã] rather than [kpãỹã].

The affricates /tʃ/ and /dʒ/ occur in syllable-initial position, as in *child* and *jail*. In other environments, the corresponding fricative occurs, e.g. *teach* [tiʃ], *age* [eʒ].

Obstruents in LibSE are sometimes subject to syllable-final devoicing .

(b) Sonorants

In LibSE, the sequence VN syllable-internally is frequently realized as Ṽ i.e. with the nasality transferred to the preceding vowel and the nasal consonant not realized, e.g. /time/ [tã]; however, when the sequence is VNV, the consonant is resyllabified rather than deleted, e.g. *timer*, [ta.mə]. Also, /l/ is often not present in coda position. Thus, *small* is realized as [smɑ], *tell* as [tɛ]. That /l/ is present underlyingly is readily demonstrated by the addition of a vowel-initial suffix, which triggers resyllabification of the lateral, i.e. *telling* [tɛ.lẽ]. The other liquid, /r/, has disappeared entirely from final and preconsonantal environments. In a few cases where /r/ occurs after a stressed vowel, /r/ and the unstressed vowel that follows it have dropped out. Accordingly, *carry* is realized as [kɛ], *Merican* 'Settler' as [mɛkẽ]. Despite its absence in these environments, /r/ usually does show up in onset clusters, e.g. *tree* [tri], *priest* [pris]. However, in words where the syllable preceding the onset cluster is stressed, then the /r/ often goes unrealized on the surface, e.g. *secretary* [sɛkətɛri], *cartridge* [kɑtɪʒ].

One of the speakers whose interview forms part of the Sinoe corpus had a distinctive velar /r/ like that found in Sierra Leonean Krio. It is not clear whether the speaker's velar /r/ was idiosyncratic or was instead a relic of a pattern that was more common in the past. In the Sinoe Settler speech community as a whole, the word *shrimp* has changed to *swimp* [swɪm], a sound change consistent with a velar /r/. An elderly Settler teacher in an upriver settlement in Sinoe, asked if there was any other name for "crawfish," answered, "Yes, swimp [swɪm], s-w-i-m-p."

2.2.   Suprasegmentals

2.2.1.   Syllable structure: the status of the coda

LibSE's treatment of coda consonants distinguishes it from North American varieties of English. Specifically, it is the frequency with which coda consonants are absent on the surface that sets LibSE apart from its North American cohort. The difference is not absolute: all dialects of English are given to dropping the /d/ and /t/ in phrases like *sand castle* and *fast car*. However, the surface absence of coda consonants is far more frequent in LibSE than in North American dialects. Moreover, this statement applies not only to the simplification of coda clusters as in *sand castle* and *fast car* (simplification by the omission of one of the consonants in the cluster) but also to the absence of single coda consonants, e.g. *what* [wɑ], *place* [ple].

There are no morphemes in LibSE that contain coda clusters. When the first element of a cluster is a nasal consonant, the nasalization shifts to the preceding vowel, and the nasal consonant drops out, e.g. *think* [tẽk], *camp* [kæ̃p]. In all other cases, i.e. in all the instances where the consonants in the coda cluster are both oral, a segment simply drops out. Thus, *lC* clusters have lost the *l*, e.g. *false* [fɑs]. When a cluster consists of a fricative plus a stop, the stop has dropped out, e.g. *desk* [dɛs] and *raft* [ræf]. When the cluster consists of two stops, the second one (which is always alveolar) drops out, e.g. *act* [æk], *except* [ɛsɛp]. The only time when a word (as opposed to a morpheme) displays a coda cluster on the surface is when the plural is added, e.g. *jobs* [dʒɑbz], *face caps* [feskæps] 'baseball caps'. Surface clusters like this are relatively rare; usually, when a plural marker is added, the preceding consonant drops out, e.g. *jobs* [dʒɑz], *face caps* [feskæs].

As indicated, individual coda consonants are variably absent on the surface, e.g. *God bless* [gɑ blɛ]. Stops are more likely to be absent on the surface than fricatives (and /l/ more likely than stops). A third alternative, arguably intermediate between presence and absence of a coda consonant, is the consonant's replacement by a glottal stop, e.g. *all right* [ɔraʔ]. While a glottal stop is most likely to stand in for a voiceless stop, it can take the place of any obstruent.

At the same time that LibSE speakers show far fewer individual coda consonants than do speakers of AAVE or other dialects in North America, they show vastly more individual coda consonants than do speakers of VLE, the latter having transferred to VLE the prohibition in Liberia's Niger-Congo languages against coda consonants (categorical in Kru and Mande languages, widespread but not categorical in the Atlantic languages Gola and Kisi).

2.2.2. *Prosody*

(a)   Stress-timing
The prosody of LibSE sets it apart from all other Liberian varieties of English and, indeed, all other Liberian languages. All of the languages other than Lib-SE - including VLE at its most acrolectal – are strict syllable-timed languages. Essentially, every syllable gets equal weight and, consequently, vowel reduction rarely occurs. In contrast, LibSE is far less syllable-timed, hence more stress-timed. It seems appropriate to position the syllable-timed languages of Liberia at one pole, white northern American dialects of English at the opposite pole, and LibSE somewhere in between (cf. Thomas and Carter 2003). Certainly, there is far less vowel reduction in LibSE than in the white dialects of American English.

(b)   Rate of speech
A characteristic of some Settler men is an extremely rapid rate of speech. In the Sinoe corpus, some men speak very, very fast; no women do. My awareness of a sex difference in this regard was brought to my attention in a Settler community in Grand Bassa County. I commented to a Settler friend that I had sometimes been unable to understand his uncle because of the uncle's rapidity of speech. My friend's answer was that this was how some men talked. My friend's uncle and also the fastest talker among the Sinoe Settlers were both members of the clergy. It is possible that fast speech is intended to signal erudition and formal education, but only among men.

3.   Conclusion

The phonology of LibSE is an understudied topic. I have tried to show that it is, nevertheless, an important one in its own right and in the comparative study of AAE in the diaspora.

* A National Science Foundation grant and a National Endowment for the Humanities summer stipend made possible my research on the Liberian Settler English of Sinoe. I am grateful to the Rev. D. Hosea Ellis for his assistance throughout. I wish to thank the older heads of the Settler community in Sinoe County for allowing Hosea and me to carry out sociolinguistic interviews with them. Peter Roberts Toe and Comfort Swen Toe facilitated my research in Sinoe. I thank Paul DeDecker for his assistance in mapping Settler vowels.

Exercises and study questions

1. Compare the vowel inventory of LibSE with that of any other West African variety of English.

2. Compare the obstruents of LibSE with those of a standard variety of English (e.g. RP or U.S. English).

3. Review the properties of liquids in LibSE.

4. Compare the LibSE treatment of coda consonanats with that of a variety of English you are familiar with.

5. How is LibSE different form other West African varieties of English in terms of prosody?

Selected references

Please consult the General references for titles mentioned in the text but not included in the references below. For a full bibliography see the accompanying CD-ROM.

Ashmun, Jehudi
    1827   in: *African Repository* 1: 261.
Crummell, Alexander
    1862   *The Future of Africa, Being Addresses, Sermons, etc., Delivered in Liberia*. New York: Scribner.
DeCamp, David
    1971   Toward a generative analysis of a post-creole speech community. In: Hymes (ed.), 349–370.
Hancock, Ian F.
    1971   Some aspects of English in Liberia. *Liberian Studies Journal* 3: 207–213.
Shick, Tom W.
    1980   *Behold the Promised Land: A History of Afro-American Settler Society in Nineteenth-century Liberia*. Baltimore: Johns Hopkins University Press.
Singler, John Victor
    1976–77 Language in Liberia in the nineteenth century: The Settlers' perspective. *Liberian Studies Journal* 7: 73–85.
    1984   Variation in tense-aspect-modality in Liberian English. Ph.D. dissertation, UCLA.
    1989   Plural marking in Liberian Settler English, 1820–1980. *American Speech* 64: 40–64.
    1990   The impact of decreolization upon TMA: Tenselessness, mood, and aspect in Kru Pidgin English. In: Singler (ed.), 203–230.

1997   The configuration of Liberia's Englishes. *World Englishes* 16: 205–231.
1998   What's not new in AAVE. *American Speech* 73: 227–256.
Thomas, Erik R., and Philip M. Carter
2003   A first look at rhythm in Southern African American and European American
            English. Paper presented at NWAVE 33, University of Pennsylvania.

Cameroon English: phonology

Augustin Simo Bobda

1.   Introduction

Cameroon English (CamE) will be understood in the present study as the English of the educated Anglophone Cameroonian. Although the notion of education is vague and elusive, the data for the analyses are generally taken from the speech production of university graduates and professionals of all walks of life. CamE is meant to be clearly distinct from Cameroon Pidgin English, and from the speech of the typical Francophone which can be considered a performance variety, even though it is largely influenced by the English of the Anglophone compatriots. By the turn of the century, CamE has been shown by various authors, starting with Todd (1982), to have a high degree of stability (see also Simo Bobda 1994). Despite some predictable ethnic and educational variations, CamE is fairly homogeneous, due partly to the relatively small size of the Anglophone population on which it is basically modelled; the two Anglophone provinces cover 9% of the national territory with 42,210 square km, and have about three million inhabitants, which represents about 20% of the country's population.

2.   The sounds of CamE

2.1.   The vowels

Seen through the realisation of the standard lexical sets (Wells 1982), the vowels of CamE appear as follows:

KIT

The most common realisation of the KIT vowel in CamE is a tense and relatively short /i/ as in *sit, bit, pity, myth, English* [sit, bit, piti, mit, ɪŋgliʃ]. The KIT vowel thus clearly merges with the FLEECE vowel. When the KIT vowel in Wells' paradigm results from vowel reduction, its realisation in CamE is generally suggested by the underlying strong vowel, usually reflecting the spelling. Thus, words with post-tonic <-ace, -age, -ain, -ate> have /e/ (the restructured form of the FACE vowel), as in *popul[e]ce, vill[e]ge, mount[e]n, liter[e]te; women* and words in <-ed, -less, -ness> have /ɛ/: *wom[ɛ]n, paint[ɛ]d, usel[ɛ]ss, happin[ɛ]s*. Note the particular behaviour of the vowels of *horsES* words and words with past tense *-ed*. There is no special provision for them in Wells' (1982: 128) list. But Foulkes and Docherty (1999) set them apart as showing variations in the Sheffield accent different from the other KIT vowels. CamE also presents a different picture: while *horsES* words have /i/ (*hors[i]s, clash[i]s, judg[i]s, -ed* words have /ɛ/, as shown above.

The other realisations are suggested by the spelling (e.g. [sɛkuit, sekuit] *circuit*, [bjuzi] *busy*), or analogy with some existing pattern. Thus *coward[ai]ce* and *jaund[ai]ce* are induced by the analogy with *dice, d[ai]vorce*, and *b[ai]gamy* by the analogy with the pronunciation of the prefixes *di-*, and *bi-*, respectively, in many words; *imp[ai]ous* by the analogy with *pious; [ai]dio-syncracy, -atic* by the analogy with *idea* and its derivatives; *h[ai]deous* by the analogy with *hide; h[ai]biscus, h[ai]pocritical* by the analogy with other words with [hai-] (*hibernate, hypertension, hypercritical*); *v[ai]neyard* by the analogy with *vine; Cather[ai]ne, femin[ai]ne, mascul[ai]ne, favour[ai]te, gran[ai]te, infin[ai]te, later[ai]te,* (less commonly *fam[ai]ne, genu[ai]ne, defin[ai]te*) by the analogy with the many English words in *–ine* and *–ite* which have /ai/.

Note finally the dropping of the KIT vowel represented by final *e* in some words of foreign origin, like [apɔkɔp, fɔt, haipɛbɔl, siŋkɔp] i.e. *apocope, forte, hyperbole, syncope.*

DRESS

The main splits in the KIT set, as seen above, warrant the establishment of at least two other sets which I will call the *paintEd* and *villAge* sets. The *paintEd* set would comprise words in *-ess* (*actress, princess*), *-less, -ness, -men*. The *villAge* set would comprise words in *–ace, -ain, -ate, -ein.*

RP has only one mid-front vowel, which many authors situate slightly above cardinal vowel No 3. It is represented in many systems of transcription, including the one used by Wells' UCL Department of Phonetics, with the symbol /e/ which, in strict phonetic terms, is the symbol for cardinal vowel No 2 which does not represent the exact quality of the DRESS vowel. Since RP has only one mid-front vowel, the use of /e/ poses no major problem. But the situation is different in CamE, which offers an interesting split of the DRESS vowel. The regular realisations of the DRESS vowel are /ɛ/ and /e/, which are in complementary distribution in some cases: /ɛ/ occurs in final syllables as in *pen, rest, breast,* while /e/ occurs before one and only one medial consonant, and before Cj, Cw and Cr sequences as in *element, medical, special, educate, equity, equalize, metric, retrograde.* The tensing of /ɛ/ to /e/ in this context is known in the literature (Simo Bobda 1994: 181f) as the E-Tensing Rule. /e/ further occurs frequently before the sequences *mC* and *nC* as in *embassy, emperor, member, centre, mention*. /e/ finally occurs with the common word *says*, as a result of the local restructuring of the FACE vowel induced by the analogy with *say* and other words in orthographic *ay*.

Other realisations of the DRESS vowel are induced by some analogy with an existing pattern. *S[i]nate* is thus due presumably to the influence of *seen, scene; Gr[i]nwich* is induced by the pronunciation of *green; m[i]dow, p[i]sant, z[i]lous, cleanly* (adjective) are induced by the majority of the words in *ea* pronounced with /i/; and /i/ in *de-, pre-,* and *re-* words like *d[i]claration, pr[i]paration, r[i]servation* is induced by the pronunciation of *declare, prepare, reserve*, etc. Loose resemblance with words beginning with *–in, -inter,* etc. can be held responsible for *[i]nter, [i]ntrance*, while *English, England* can be seen as the source of confusion for CamE *[i]ngine, [i]ngineer.*

Finally, the non-application of the RP rule of Trisyllabic Tensing is responsible for /i/ in *ser[i]nity, supr[i]macy, obsc[i]nity,* and /iɛ, iə/, the CamE version of the NEAR vowel as shown below, in *aust[iɛ, iə]rity, sinc[iɛ, iə]rity, sever[iɛ, iə]rity*, which correspond to the pronunciation of the bases *austere, sincere, severe,* respectively.

TRAP
The TRAP vowel is generally realised as /a/, the primary cardinal vowel No 4 (e.g. in *man, tap, hand, thank, arrow, saddle*). The other realisations are due to the analogy with some existing pattern. For example, [plet] *plait* is due to the analogy with other words with *ai* (*maid, plain, trail*) where the FACE vowel is locally restructured to /e/. /e/ further occurs in a sizable number of words where the RP Trisyllabic Laxing rule does not apply, and the vowel of the base is maintained; e.g. *s[e]nity, prof[e]nity,* (quite often) *n[e]tional* and *decl[e]rative.* The occurrence of /e/ in [rieliti] *reality* is difficult to account for. Finally, the /ɔ/ of *[ɔ]lgiers,[ɔ]lgeria* is presumably due to the analogy with other words with *al* like *chalk, salt, talk.*

LOT
The LOT vowel is generally realised as /ɔ/, roughly in the position for cardinal vowel No 6, and merges with the THOUGHT and FORCE vowels. A spelling-derived /a/ occurs in a number of words, after *w(h)* and *qu* as in *wander* [wanda], *want, warrant, watch, swallow, swamp, swan, what, squad, squalid, squash, swallow.*

STRUT
The STRUT vowel is characteristically rendered as /ɔ/ (e.g. in *number, son, tough, blood, does*), and thus merges with the LOT, THOUGHT and FORCE vow-

els. One often hears [wan, kam] *one, come* which can historically be ascribed
to the influence of the pronunciation of the Cameroon Pidgin English of these
words, which indeed have /a/. /ɛ/ is further heard for *but* and, by some speech-
conscious speakers, in words like *cut* and *discuss*. The influence of spelling
yields /u/ in words like *Brussels, buffalo, buttock, buttress, lumbago, culprit*,
and occasionally *supplement* and its derivatives. Finally, many Cameroonians
have /au/ in *southern* (under the influence of *south*) and in *country* under the
influence of other words with <oun> like *count, county, round, sound*, and for
pronunciation whose spelling is often changed to **pronounciation*.

FOOT

The FOOT vowel is almost systematically realised as a tense and relatively
short /u/ (e.g. in *good, cook, put, full, pudding*). Miscellaneous realisations include /ɛ/ in acrolectal speech in the unique word *pus*, and the spelling-derived
/ɔ/ in *bosom*.

BATH

The BATH vowel is systematically realised as /a/, like the TRAP vowel.

CLOTH

The CLOTH vowel is almost systematically rendered as /ɔ/. A spelling-derived
/a/ occurs after *w* and *qu* in words like *warrant, warren, quarry*.

NURSE

In CamE, there is a radical split of the NURSE lexical set, a split mostly conditioned by the spelling. /ɔ/ occurs for orthographic *or, our, ur* as in *work, journey,
purpose;* in acrolectal speech, /ɔ/ alternates with /ɛ/ in words like *work, burn,
turn, church;* interestingly, the word *nurse* itself seems to be realised more often as /ɛ/ than as /ɔ/; it is therefore not a good representative of the set, in terms
of CamE. The second syllable of *incur* rhymes with *cure* and is pronounced
like CURE vowel ([inkjɔ]), a pronunciation that changes the spelling of the
word to **incure*. /ɛ/ is the common realisation of the NURSE vowel for words
with orthographic *er, ear, ir, yr* like *term, learn, thirty, myrrh*. /a/ occurs in mesolectal and basilectal speech in *Sir*. /a/ is even more common in *her*. Finally,
the occurrence of /a/ in *maternity*, (verb) *transfer*, and often in *servant* [mataniti,
transfa, savant] is presumably due to the influence of /a/ in the neighbouring
syllable, and can be considered as a case of vowel assimilation or harmony.

Given the major splits observed above with clear orthographic conditioning,
it seems more convenient in CamE to establish another set, which I will call the
TERM set. Leaving the NURSE set for words with <ur, or, our>, the TERM set
will comprise words with <er, ere> as in *were*, and words with <ear, ir, yr>.

FLEECE
The FLEECE vowel is realised as /i/, tense like Wells' FLEECE, but definitely much shorter. A spelling-derived /ɛ/, which may be converted by the E-Tensing rule to [e] (see the discussion under the DRESS vowel), occurs in a large number of words including *cohesion, comedian, Egypt, intervene, legal, mete* (mete out a sanction), *amnesia, Armenia, encyclopaedia, collegial, Cornelius, media, Nicodemus, penal, recent, Slovenia, species, strategic, trapezium, vehicle.* Note that the occurrence of /e/ in words like *cohesion, comedian, Slovenia, trapezium* and many others is due to the non-application of the rule of CiV Tensing (see Simo Bobda 1994: 179-182) which applies in many mother-tongue accents, including RP. Analogical realisations include the pronunciation of *quay* as [kwe] where /e/ is due to the analogy with other words in *ay,* and the pronunciations of *elite* and *trio* as *el[ai]te* and *tr[ai]o* where /ai/ is due to the analogy with other words in *iCe,* and *tri-,* respectively.

FACE
The FACE vowel is generally monophthongised to /e/, and is occasionally rendered as a more open /ɛ/ in words like *labour, later on.* The spelling-derived /a/ occurs in a large number of cases, including *adjacent, Barbados, blatant, Donatus, fatal, Graham, nasal, naval, papal, radar, Romanus, sadism* and its derivatives, *Satan, savour.* The non-application of the RP CiV Tensing rule in some words further yields /a/ in words like *Arabian, Athanasius, aviation, gymnasium, Ignatius, inter alia, radiation, spatial, salient.* /ai/ occurs as a spelling pronunciation in *Haiti* and *Jamaica.*

When the FACE vowel is followed by a vocalic segment, the underlying /i/ is converted to [j], in keeping with a Gliding Rule which, in CamE, changes the intervocalic high vowels /i, u/ into the corresponding glides [j, w] (Simo Bobda 1994: 201-206). The phenomenon produces data like [leja, pleja, pɔtreja] *layer, player, portrayer.*

PALM
The PALM vowel is systematically realised as /a/, merging with TRAP and START.

THOUGHT
The THOUGHT vowel is rendered as /ɔ/, merging with LOT, CLOTH and FORCE. A spelling-derived /a/ occurs in *bald, Balkan, malt, Malta* and /au/, another spelling pronunciation, is very common in some words with orthographic *au* like *laud* and its derivatives, *gaunt* and *haunt.*

GOAT

The GOAT vowel is rendered as /o/ (primary cardinal vowel No 7) typically in word-final position (e.g. *go, no, so, know),* before final consonants (e.g. *coat, comb, don't, mould, control, joke, note*). It generally becomes a more open /ɔ/ in the environment ____CV, as in *f[ɔ]cus, m[ɔ]ment, n[ɔ]tice.* A notable dialectal variation, /u/, for both of the above environments, is worth noting here: it is characteristic of Banso speakers in the North West Province; it is very well known and much talked about.

When the GOAT vowel is followed by a vowel, the underlying /u/ may be converted to the corresponding glide [w] by the Glide Formation rule (see under FACE), yielding pronunciations like [lowa, mowa, towa] *lower, mower, tower* (from the verb *tow),* which alternate with [loa, moa, toa].

Foulkes and Docherty's (1999) GOAL set behaves like the GOAT vowel discussed here.

GOOSE

The GOOSE vowel is generally rendered as /u/, like FOOT. Spelling-derived realizations include the /ɔ/ of *tomb* and less often *movement* and *manoeuvre,* and the /ui/ of *juice, juicy, nuisance.* Note the unique occurrence of /ɔ/ in *pseudo-:* [sɔdɔ-].

PRICE

The common realisation of the PRICE vowel is /ai/. A spelling-induced /i/ occurs in a number of words including *Elias* [eli'as], *indict* [indikt], *hybrid, Mathias* [ma'tias], *primordial, siren,* (less often) *prior.* When the PRICE vowel is followed by a vowel, /i/ is converted to /j/ by the Glide Formation rule, which yields [trajal] *trial,* [baja] *buyer,* [admaja] *admire,* [pajɔs] *Pius,* [lajɔn] *lion,* [ba'jas] *biased.*

CHOICE

The CHOICE vowel is generally rendered as /ɔi/. When it is followed by another vowel, the Glide Formation rule converts /i/ to /j/, yielding pronunciations like [lɔjal] *loyal,* [anɔjans] *annoyance,* [dʒɔjɔs] *joyous.*

MOUTH

The MOUTH vowel is generally rendered as /au/, and less often /aɔ/. /o/ occurs in some MOUTH words like *shower, towel, vowel* [ʃoa, toɛl, voɛl], having merged with the GOAT set. *Devour* merges with the FORCE set and is pronounced [di'vɔ] by a large number of educated speakers. When the MOUTH vowel is followed by another vowel, /u/ is converted to [w] by the Glide Formation rule, yielding pronunciations like [alawans] *allowance,* [kawat] *coward,* [pawa] *power.*

NEAR

The realisation of the NEAR vowel alternates between /iɛ/ and /iə/; [fiɛ, fiə] *fear,* [giɛ, giə] *gear,* [spiɛ, spiə] *spear;* /iə/ seems to be more characteristic of acrolectal speakers. A spelling-derived /ɛ/ is common in *interfere, atmosphere, sphere, mere* which thus merge with the SQUARE set. *Clear* [kliɛ] also merges with SQUARE.

/i/ is very common in the sequence *erV* as in *Algeria, hero, Liberia, Nigeria, period, series, serious, serum, zero.* A spelling-derived /e/, which may be seen as the tensing of an underlying /ɛ/ through the E-Tensing rule, occurs in other *erV* words like *cafet[e]ria, crit[e]ria, [e]ra, imp[e]rial, minist[e]rial, Presbyt[e]rian.* Another spelling-derived realization, /ea/, occurs in words like [erea] *area,* [kɔrea] *Korea.*

When the second member of the NEAR diphthong is the agentive or comparative *-er,* the diphthong is rendered in CamE as /ia/. We thus have [kaʃia, karia] *cashier, carrier,* and [elia, pritia, silia] *earlier, prettier, sillier.* And when the second member in Wells' set results from Vowel Reduction, it is restructured in CamE to a vowel suggested by the strong form or the spelling; e.g. *gymnas[iu]m, nutr[iɛ]nt, per[iɔ]d, illustr[iɔ]s, mater[ia]l.*

The above realizations of the NEAR vowel in CamE warrant the re-arrangement of Wells' set into several sets. The label NEAR will be maintained for words in orthographic *ear* and *eer,* pronounced /iɛ, iə/ in CamE. The label SPHERE will be used for words with orthographic *ere,* pronounced /ɛ, iɛ, iə/. zERo will be adopted for words in *erV,* pronounced /i, e/. carrIER will be chosen for agentives and comparatives in *ier,* pronounced /ia/. And cordIAl will be chosen for words where the second member of Wells' NEAR diphthong results from vowel reduction, and the sequence may be pronounced /ia, iɛ, iɔ, iu/ depending on the spelling.

SQUARE

The most common realisation of the SQUARE vowel is /ɛ/; [dɛ, fɛ, kɛ] *dare/ there, fair/fare, care.* /ɛ/ often tenses to [e] by the E-Tensing rule, yielding pronunciations like *[e]ria, mal[e]ria, p[e]rent, parliament[e]rian, S[e]rah, secret[e]riat;* interestingly, this pattern of restructuring has caused in CamE some fossilized spellings like **maleria* (malaria) and, more systematically, **Serah* (Sarah). A spelling-derived /a/ occurs in words like *Aaron, fanfare, Hilarious, Hungarian, nefarious, precarious, vary* and its derivatives. The following words of Wells' SQUARE set merge with NEAR to be pronounced with /iɛ, iə/: *chair, share* and borrowings in *-aire* like *millionaire, questionnaire. Their* (but not *there* which maintains the regular pronunciation) has as many as four diphthongal realizations: [iɛ, ia, eɛ, ea].

Finally, note the pronunciation of *mayor* and *prayer* (request made to God) as [mejɔ] and [preja], respectively, which results from the merging of these words with FACE, and the gliding of the underlying /i/ to [j].

START

The START vowel is almost systematically realised as /a/, thus merging with the TRAP vowel. The few words in *er* where RP has the START vowel merge with the NURSE vowel: we thus have *D[ɛ]rby / d[ɛ]rby, H[ɛ]rtford, s[ɛ]rgeant.*

NORTH

The common realisation of the NORTH vowel is /ɔ/, like LOT and THOUGHT. A spelling-derived /a/ occurs after *w* and *qu,* as in *swarm, warp, quarter, quartz.*

FORCE

The FORCE vowel is almost systematically rendered as /ɔ/, like LOT, THOUGHT and NORTH. A spelling-derived /ɔa/ occurs in the unique word *roar,* pronounced [rɔa]. Finally, note that *pour* merges with CURE and becomes homophonous with *poor.*

CURE

When orthographically represented by *ure* and *our,* the CURE vowel is realised as /(j)ɔ/, as in [kjɔ, pjɔ, lɔ, ʃɔ, maˈtʃɔ, tɔ, gɔd/gɔt] *cure, pure, lure, sure, mature, tour, gourd.* There is an interesting split with words having the orthographic sequence *urV*: /ɔ/ occurs when V is preceded by a free base as in [aʃɔrans] *assurance* (assure + ance), *surety, security, maturity;* and a spelling-derived /u/ occurs when V is followed by a bound base, as in *curious* [kjuriɔs], *jury* [dʒuri], *mural, plural, rural.* When the second member of the CURE diphthong is the agentive or comparative *er,* the diphthong is rendered in CamE as /ua/; e.g. [njua, trua, skrua, sua] *newer, truer, screwer, suer.* Finally, when the second member results from Vowel Reduction, the pronunciation of this second member in CamE corresponds to the underlying strong form, or to the vowel suggested by the spelling; e.g. [anual, fluɛnt, kɔntinuɔs] *annual, fluent, continuous.*

Note the following miscellaneous realisations: *your* [jua, ja]; *yours* [juɔs], *poor* [puɔ], *Europe* [jũ̃ɔrɔp].

As with NEAR above, the splits observed above warrant the re-arrangement of the CURE set altogether into several sets. CURE will be maintained for words in *ure, our,* and *urV* when V is preceded by a free base, pronounced /ɔ/. *cUrious* will be the convention for words in *urV* where V is preceded by a bound base, pronounced /u/. TRUER will be the label for agentives and comparatives in *uer,* pronounced /ua/. And TRUANT will be adopted for cases where the second member of RP /ʊə/ results from vowel reduction; TRUANT words in CamE are pronounced /ua, uɛ, uɔ/ depending on the spelling.

HappY
The *happY* vowel is rendered as /i/. Note that words in *-day* (*holiday, Monday, Tuesday, Wednesday*), which fluctuate between /eɪ/ and /ɪ/ in British English, systematically have /e/ in CamE, merging with FACE.

LettER
The lettER vowel is very often conditioned orthographically in CamE. When it is represented by *er/re,* it is systematically represented by /a/; e.g. *memb[a], teach[a], cent[a].* When it is represented by *ure* and *o(u)r,* it is rendered as /ɔ/; e.g. [figɔ, meʒɔ, tɛkstʃɔ, stupɔ, kandɔ, lebɔ] *figure, measure, texture, stupor, candour, labour.* Miscellaneous pronunciations include *martyr* and *satyr* which, under the influence of *tire* (CamE [taja], are pronounced [mataja] and [sataja]).

CommA
The spelling-induced /a/ is the most common realisation of the *commA* vowel in CamE. When the vowel is represented by *o,* it is realised as /ɔ/; e.g. *abb[ɔ]t, big[ɔ]t, Lenn[ɔ]n.* CamE has a predilection for /i/ before final /n/ irrespective of the grapheme, as in *Samps[i]n, Wils[i]n.* /i/ is even more systematic in words which have an /i/ in the preceding syllable, as in *hidd[i]n, Hilt[i]n, kitch[i]n, pris[i]n.* This can be considered as a case of vowel assimilation or harmony. This phenomenon yields other vowels in other contexts, like [ɔ] in *Rob[ɔ]rt* and *Thom[ɔ]s.*

Seen through Wells' lexical sets, and accommodating both Foulkes and Docherty's (1999) addition as well as the modifications suggested by the split observed in CamE phonology, the vowels of CamE can be summarized as in Table 1.

Table 1. The vowels of CamE, seen through the standard lexical sets

Key word	Pronunciation	Key word	Pronunciation
CHOICE	ɔi > ɔj	KIT	i > ai
MOUTH	au > aw > aɔ	paintEd	ɛ
NEAR	iɛ ~ iɛ	villAge	e
SPHERE	ɛ > iɛ ~ iə	DRESS	ɛ > e > i > iɛ ~ iə
Zero	e > i > ɛ	TRAP	a > e
CarrIER	ia	LOT	ɔ > a

Table 1. (continued)   The vowels of CamE, seen through the standard lexical sets

Key word	Pronunciation	Key word	Pronunciation
CordIAL	ia ~ iɛ ~ iɔ ~ iu	STRUT	ɔ > u ~ a
SQUARE	ɛ > e > iɛ ~ iə	FOOT	u
START	a > ɛ	BATH	a
NORTH	ɔ > a	CLOTH	ɔ
FORCE	ɔ	NURSE	ɔ > ɛ > e
CURE	ɔ > ua	TERM	ɛ > e > a
cUrious	u	FLEECE	i > ɛ > e
TruER	ua	FACE	e > a > ej
TRUANT	ua ~ uɛ ~ uɔ	PALM	a
officEs	i	THOUGHT	ɔ > au
happY	i > e	GOAT	o > ɔ > u
LettER	a ~ ɛ ~ ɔ	GOAL	o > ɔ > u
CommA	a ~ ɛ ~ ɔ > u	GOOSE	u
		PRICE	a > i > aj

From the above picture, a seven-vowel system ([i, e, ɛ, a, ɔ, o, u]), plus a marginal schwa, appears. The marginal nature of the schwa is due to its extremely low frequency. It normally occurs only as the second member of the NEAR diphthong in acrolectal speech, and in epenthetic environments like [ebəl, riðəm, kapitalizəm] *able, rhythm, capitalism*. The low frequency of the schwa is mostly due to the fact that CamE generally does not apply the Vowel Reduction rule.

Of particular interest in the discussion of the patterns of realisation of the standard lexical sets has been the phenomenon of splits (e.g. of the NURSE and CURE vowels) and mergers (e.g. of the LOT, THOUGHT, NORTH, FORCE and STRUT vowels). The splits are responsible for the splitting of some pairs which are homophonous in RP, like *dollar/dolour* [dɔla, dɔlɔ], *fisher/fissure* [fiʃa, fiʃɔ], *word/whirred* [wɔd/wɔt, wɛd/wɛt], *swab/swob* [swab/swap, swɔb/swɔp], *kernel/colonel* [kɛnɛl, kɔlɔnɛl]. The mergers create new homophones in CamE, like *match, march* [matʃ], *talk, thug* [tɔk], *circular/secular* [sekula], *fodder, further* [fɔda], *hod, hud, hoard* [hɔd/hɔt]. A more comprehensive list of such splits and mergers can be found in Simo Bobda (1994: 157–161).

The discussion has also highlighted, beyond mere cases of segment restructuring, some vocalic processes like E-Tensing, Glide Formation, i-Assimila-

tion, as well as the behaviour of CamE with regard to some RP rules like Vowel
Reduction, CiV Tensing and Trisyllabic Laxing.

2.2. The consonants

In terms of the mere inventory of the consonant system, CamE exhibits very
few differences from RP, for example. The marked peculiarity resides in the
TH sounds, which are generally pronounced /t/ and /d/, /θ/ and /ð/ in fact not
being uncommon in educated speech. But consonant substitution is only the
tip of the iceberg. Although RP and CamE have basically the same consonant
system, there are tremendous differences in the environments in which these
consonants occur in the two accents. The consonantal peculiarities of CamE
are best examined in terms of phonological processes. Using RP as a point of
reference, the analysis below will highlight some rules which do not apply in
CamE, those which apply differently or partially, and those which can be considered specific, that is, do not apply in RP.

There is a large common core of features which CamE shares with RP and
other accents, and that is what ensures and guarantees resemblance and intelligibility, to a large extent. But some RP rules do not apply in CamE. These rules
include several linking processes. CamE keeps orthographic words separate
in connected speech, leaving clear junctures between them. This picture radi-
cally contrasts with what obtains in all native accents of English, where speech
appears in chunks of units linked with each other. The radical separation of
words, predictably, does not create a propitious environment for assimilation
and other linking processes to apply. Examples of features illustrating the
non-application of assimilation can be found in Simo Bobda (1994: 254–255).
But the conspicuous absence of linking /r/ can be considered more important,
as seen in the following data from Simo Bobda (1994: 255): [diɛ ˈɔpɔnɛnts]
their opponents, [awa anˈsɛstɔs] *our ancestors,* [fɔda amaunt] *further amount,*
[jua ˈadvais] *your advice,* [fɔ e piriɔt] *for a period.* The absence of linking
/r/ in these data leaves two adjacent vowels across the word boundary, which
breaks the requirement of euphony in RP.

The RP rules which apply differently or partially include the voicing or devoicing of the alveolar fricative in word-medial position, Ks-Voicing, Yod Deletion, Non-coronal Deletion, and Spirantisation in *-stion* words. Concerning
the voicing and devoicing of the alveolar fricative the first peculiarity of CamE
is found in intervocalic position, where CamE has /s/ for RP /z/ as in words like
acqui[s]ition, compo[s]ition, phy[s]ical, po[s]ition, vi[s]ible and /z/ for RP /s/ in
words like *di[z]agree, di[z]appear, ba[z]ic, ba[z]in, compari[z]on, garri[z]on,
pro[z]ody, uni[z]on.* There is even the interesting case of *De[z]ember* and

de[z]eased where CamE has /z/ for orthographic *c*, an unknown phenomenon in RP; CamE equally has /z/ in the environment /r/_____V as in *nur[z]ery* and /l/_____V as in *compul[z]ory*, another oddity in terms of RP. Even more frequently, /z/ occurs in the environment *con#____*V, as in *con[z]ume*, and *con[z]erve* and its derivatives.

In RP, Ks-voicing applies mostly before stressed vowels, as in *exam, executive, exhaust, exonerate.* But in CamE it tends to apply before all vowels, as in *e[gz]ecute, fle[gz]ible, ma[gz]imum, e[gz]odus.*

In RP yod is absent mostly after palatals (e.g. *sugar, chew, jew*), /r/ (e.g. *rumour, rural, drew*) and /Cl/ (e.g. *clue, flu, glue)*; but CamE speakers also delete it in many other words (e.g. *dubious, duplicate, education, numerous, Portugal, situation, student*) and more systematically before /ul/ (e.g. ambulance, modulate, population), and before /uV/ (e.g. *annual, conspicuous, genuine).*

The two non-coronals involved in Non-coronal Deletion are /b/ and /g/. RP speakers delete /b/ after nasals as in *bomb, comb, lamb, hand* and between /m/ and a following neutral suffix as in *bombing, singer, hanger*, but CamE does not apply this rule, since it has *bom[b]ing, sin[g]er, han[g]er.*

The occurrence of [tʃ] (rather than [ʃ] as for other words in *-ion*) is due to the non-application of spirantisation blocked before /s/ (which converts the underlying /t/ to [s] which in turn interacts with gliding and palatalisation (Rubach 1984) in *-tion* words. But in CamE, spirantisation applies also after /s/, yielding *combus[ʃ]ion, ques[ʃ]ion, exhaus[ʃ]ion, sugges[ʃ]ion* (instead of RP [tʃ].)

Phonological processes specific to CamE include several cases of consonant cluster simplification, Pre-*ion* Devoicing, Final Devoicing and Pre-Yod Deletion.

Although cluster simplification occurs in onset position, the most frequent cases of simplification are found in coda position. Cluster simplification in coda position, according to Simo Bobda (1994: 249–253), is subject to a number of variables including the following:

(i)   with the exception of data like [fit] *fifth*, [hɛp] *help*, [fim] *film*, it is generally the final member of the cluster that is deleted and not an earlier segment;

(ii) plosives, like /t, d, p, k/, are particularly prone to deletion, as in *past, missed, cold, end, grasp, jump, task, dust*;

(iii) deletion is more prevalent in the environment of a following consonant than in that of a following vowel, as in *past#C* vs *past#V*, and *passed#C* vs *passed#V*;

(iv) a final stop which agrees in voicing with the preceding segment is more prone to deletion than one which does not; e.g. *cold* vs *colt, hand* vs *grant, send* vs *sent, veld* vs *belt*;

(v) a final stop which agrees in place of articulation with the preceding segment lends itself to deletion more readily than one which does not; e.g.
planned vs *programmed, stump* vs *grasp, sunk* vs *sulk*;

(vi) a final stop **not** preceded by a morpheme boundary is more resistant to deletion than one which is; e.g. *find* vs *fined, mind* vs *mined, left* vs *laughed,
lost* vs *tossed, act* vs *cracked*.

Pre-*ion* Devoicing devoices the underlying /d/ and /z/, respectively, in words
like *conclude+ion* and *revise+ion* to /t/ and /s/; /t/ and /s/ then interact with the
other rules (spirantisation for /t/, which yields /s/ and palatalisation for both
cases) to yield [ʃ] instead of RP [ʒ] (see Simo Bobda 1994: 226–228, and Simo
Bobda and Chumbow 1999 for details).

Final Devoicing devoices final obstruents and obstruents before consonantal
inflectional suffixes, as in [lap, bat, dʒɔtʃ, stif] *lab, bad, George, Steve;* [staps,
lifs, rɔpt, lɔft] *stabs, leaves, robbed, loved*.

Pre-yod Deletion deleted /h/ before /j/ as in [juman, jumit, jutʃ] *human, hu-
mid, huge*.

2.3. Word stress

Word stress is clearly the aspect of suprasegmental phonology of CamE
which has received the greatest scholarly attention, and about which we know
most. Research shows that CamE has truly revolutionised the stress pattern of
English. Indeed, thousands of words are stressed differently from the patterns
in native Englishes, and the frequency of occurrence of new (local) forms very
often reach 100% (see, for example Simo Bobda 1994). In fact, studies have
shown that even teachers and university professors of English, in the most
careful speaking style, find it almost impossible to change to *im 'possible,
pro 'fessor, a 'cute, suc 'cess, dis 'tribute, lieu 'tenant, pre 'paratory,
se 'mester* (from their usual *'impossible, 'professor, 'acute, 'success,
distri 'bute, 'lieutenant, prepa 'ratory, 'semester*).

Taking the RP pattern as the point of reference, the following data show
some stress peculiarities in CamE, illustrating the movement of stress to a later
syllable, and to an earlier syllable.

(a)   Movement of stress to a later syllable:

From the first to the second syllable in dissyllabic words:
chal 'lenge, col 'league, hi 'jack, mat 'tress, pe 'trol, spe 'cies, ty 'pist.

From the penultimate syllable to the ultimate syllable in trisyllabic
words:

attri '*bute, contri* '*bute, embar* '*rass, inter* '*pret, prohi* '*bit, tar* '*paulin.*

From the initial syllable to the penultimate syllable in trisyllabic words:
A '*gatha, a* '*morous, A* '*rabic, ca* '*lendar, co* '*vetous, Do* '*rothy, Jo* '*nathan, main* '*tenance, ma* '*rital, moun* '*tainous, pas* '*toral, spi* '*ritual, ten* '*tative.*

From the antepenult to the penultimate syllable in words of four syllables:
infor '*mative, mono* '*gamous, peri* '*pheral, pheno* '*menal, poly* '*gamist, steno* '*grapher.*

From the antepenult to the penultimate syllable in words of five syllables:
argumen '*tative, represen* '*tative.*

From the first to the ultimate syllable in words of three syllables:
Cathe '*rine, cele* '*brate, classi* '*fy, Emi* '*ly, gentle* '*man, mara* '*thon, recog* '*nise.*

From the antepenult to the ultimate syllable in words of four syllables:
articu '*late, compute* '*rise, diversi* '*fy, insinu* '*ate, negoti* '*ate.*

From the initial syllable to the antepenult in words of four syllables:
a '*limony, jour* '*nalism, ma* '*gistracy, ne* '*gligible, pe* '*dagogy, sta* '*tutory, tri* '*balism.*

From the pre-antepenultimate syllable to the antepenultimate syllable in words of five syllables:
admo '*nitory, empi* '*ricism, expla* '*natory, fana* '*ticism, prepa* '*ratory.*

From the first to the penultimate syllable in words of four syllables:
cumu '*lative, gene* '*rative, quanti* '*tative, specu* '*lative.*

From the pre-antepenultimate to the penultimate syllable in words of five syllables:
adminis '*trative, authori* '*tative, coope* '*rative.*

From the initial to the antepenultimate syllable in words of five syllables:
capi '*talism, natio* '*nalism, regio* '*nalism.*

Other patterns can be found in Simo Bobda (1994: 266–269).

(b)   Movement of stress to an earlier syllable:

From the ultimate syllable to the initial syllable in words of two syllables:
ˈ*acute,* ˈ*despite,* ˈ*extent,* ˈ*July,* ˈ*record* (verb), ˈ*success,* ˈ*suspense,* ˈ*towards,* ˈ*unlike.*

From the ultimate syllable to the penultimate syllable in words of three syllables:
Ca ˈ*ribbean, Eu* ˈ*ropean, Tan* ˈ*zania.*

From the penultimate syllable to the initial syllable in words of three syllables:
ˈ*agenda,* ˈ*agreement,* ˈ*associate* (adj/noun), ˈ*attorney,* ˈ*deposit* (noun), ˈ*diploma,* ˈ*insurance,* ˈ*opponent,* ˈ*phonetics,* ˈ*umbrella.*

From the penultimate syllable to the antepenultimate syllable in words of four syllables:
a ˈ*dolesence, a* ˈ*postolic, con* ˈ*valescence, con* ˈ*valescent, scientific* [sa ˈjantifik].

From the last syllable to the initial syllable in words of three syllables:
ˈ*expertise,* ˈ*cigarette,* ˈ*referee.*

From the antepenultimate syllable to the pre-antepenultimate (initial) syllable in words of four syllables:
ˈ*appropriate* (adj), ˈ*impossible,* ˈ*incredible,* ˈ*irrelevant,* ˈ*irregular.*

For more patterns, see Simo Bobda (1994: 269ff).

Stress placement in CamE is not random: it is predictable from a number of parameters which include the phonetic factor, the morphological factor, the word class, whether a noun is a common noun or a forename; several factors can also combine to generate a stress pattern.

One illustration of the phonetic factor is that words ending with rhyme /i (C)/ tend to be stressed on the final syllable as in *aun* ˈ*tie, cur* ˈ*ry, Ira* ˈ*qui, Israe* ˈ*li, Pakista* ˈ*ni, pet* ˈ*ty, se* ˈ*mi -* (semi-final), *Soma* ˈ*li, sure* ˈ*ty; Bap* ˈ*tist, bis* ˈ*cuit, spe* ˈ*cies, ten* ˈ*nis, ty* ˈ*pist.* Words ending with a final /n/ also tend to be stressed finally, as in *cara* ˈ*van, harmat* ˈ*tan, plan* ˈ*tain, cello* ˈ*phane, hurri* ˈ*cane, Ama* ˈ*zon, car* ˈ*ton, cou* ˈ*pon, mara* ˈ*thon, mo* ˈ*ron, cy* ˈ*clone, hor* ˈ*mone, o* ˈ*zone, bari* ˈ*tone;* and there is an even greater predilection for final stress in words ending in /in/, e.g. *aspi* ˈ*rin, bulle* ˈ*tin, gan* ˈ*grene, hy* ˈ*giene, jave* ˈ*lin, para* ˈ*fin, penicil* ˈ*lin, tarpau* ˈ*lin.* A further illustration of the phonetic factor in stress placement is that consonant clusters tend to attract stress to a later syllable, as in *ancestor, calendar, comment* (verb), *cy ˈlinder, or ˈchestra, Pro ˈtestant.*

The morphological factor refers to the fact that a large number of affixes have predictable and stable stress patterns. For example, the negative prefix is almost systematically self-stressed; e.g. *ˈillegal, ˈimpossible, ˈimmature, ˈirrelevant*. The following suffixes are self-stressed **-ative**, (e.g. *cumu ˈlative, ten ˈtative*), **-atory** (*expla ˈnatory, prepa ˈratory*), **-ature** (*candi ˈdature, legis ˈlature*), **-cide** (*homi ˈcide, pesti ˈcide*), **-itive** (*compe ˈtitive, repe ˈtitive*), **-land** (*Nether ˈlands, New-Zea ˈland, Switzer ˈland*), **-man** (*fire ˈman, gentle ˈman*), **-oir(e)** (*me ˈmoire, reser ˈvoir*), **-phone** (*Anglo ˈphone, tele ˈphone*). The following suffixes attract stress to the preceding syllable (they are referred to in Simo Bobda (1994, 1997) as *pre-stressed One* (PS1) suffixes): **-age** (*pa ˈrentage, vaga ˈbondage*), **-an** (*cosmopo ˈlitan, dio ˈcesan*), **-ary** (*le ˈgendary, pla ˈnetary*), **-al** (*elec ˈtrical, pas ˈtoral*), **-ism** (*bilingu ˈalism, tri ˈbalism*), **-ist** (*dra ˈmatist, poly ˈgamist*), **-ous** (*moun ˈtainous, volu ˈminous*). A more comprehensive analysis of the stress property of affixes can be found in Simo Bobda (1994).

The word class factor can be illustrated by the fact that in nouns, rather than in verbs for example, stress tends to be established earlier in the word, as in *ˈadvice* (contrast *ad ˈvise*), *ˈapplause* (contrast *ap ˈplaud*), *ˈexchange* (n) (contrast *ex ˈchange* (verb)), *ˈconstraint* (noun) (contrast *cons ˈtraint* (verb)); further examples of backward nominal stress are *ˈabyss, ˈcanoe*([ˈkenu]), *ˈacumen, ˈarena, ˈassassin, ˈdiploma ˈlumbago, ˈumbrella.*

English forenames have a greater predilection for forward stress than common nouns. The multitude of forenames with forward stress in CamE include *A ˈgatha, Chris ˈtopher, Jes ˈsica, Jo ˈnathan, Pa ˈmela, Fer ˈdinand.* Further evidence for the predilection of forenames to have forward stress is provided by the fact that words like *comfort* and *prudence* which can be both a common noun and a forename have backward stress (as in RP) in their common noun form (*ˈcomfort, ˈprudence*) and forward stress in their forename form (*Com ˈfort, Pru ˈdence*).

Illustrations of the combination of factors for stress placement include the fact that verbs ending in obstruents are almost systematically stressed on the final syllable, as in *chal ˈlenge, eli ˈcit, embar ˈrass, exhi ˈbit, hi ˈjack, inter ˈpret, kid ˈnap, ran ˈsack* (combination of the phonetic and word class factors). Another illustration is the fact that the final rhyme /i (C)/ and the fact that the following items are forenames both combine to yield final stress: *Be ˈcky, Jes ˈsie, Lu ˈcy, Nel ˈly, Sam ˈmy; A ˈlice, Do ˈris, Sal ˈly*. Final stress is even more systematic when /C/ is a nasal, as in *Cathe ˈrine, Jacque ˈline, Jose ˈphine.*

2.4.   The autonomy of CamE phonology and the concept of Trilateral
        Process

The CamE accent, though still intelligible to mother tongue accents to a large
extent, is markedly different from several points of views. In fact it has reached
a very high degree of autonomy. This autonomy, as amply demonstrated and
exemplified notably in Simo Bobda (1994), is seen in the restructuring of the
sound system of mother tongue English. This restructuring results in the numerous and major splits and mergers of Wells' (1982) lexical sets. Autonomy
is also seen in the way CamE applies existing phonological rules and, above all,
in the application of its own *sui generis* rules.

    The concept of "Trilateral Process", proposed by Simo Bobda (1994) and
discussed further by Simo Bobda and Chumbow (1999), best illustrates the
autonomy of Cameroon English. According to this concept, the underlying
representations of mother tongue segments A are restructured to new CamE
underlying representations B; while the underlying representations A undergo mother tongue English phonological rules to yield the surface representation A', the CamE underlying representations B may undergo their own independent phonological rules or surface unchanged as B'. For example, RP
s[ʌ]cceed is restructured to CamE underlying representation *s[ɔ]cceed*. While
RP *s[ʌ]cceed* undergoes Vowel Reduction to become *s[ə]cceed,* the CamE underlying representation surfaces unchanged as *s[ɔ]cceed.* A second example
is RP underlying representation *veg[ɛ]tate,* restructured to CamE underlying
representation *veg[ɛ]tate*; while RP *veg[ɛ]tate* undergoes Vowel Reduction to
surface as *veg[ɪ]tate,* the CamE underlying representation *veg[ɛ]tate* does not
undergo Vowel Reduction; in contrast, it undergoes E-Tensing and surfaces as
veg[e]tate.

    One example with consonants is the occurrence of [ʃ] (for RP [ʒ]) in words
like *conclu[ʃ]ion, divi[ʃ]ion, inva[ʃ]ion, revi[ʃ]ion,* as seen above. Seen
through the Trilateral Process, [ʃ] can be traced from an underlying /d/ or /z/
changing to /s/ through autonomous CamE rules, before becoming [ʃ] through
the application of existing rules of English phonology.

    Tracing thus the peculiarities of CamE phonology to their underlying repre-
sentations seems more rewarding than previous analyses based solely on surface forms; indeed, in the above examples, surface analysis would have limited
itself to showing that RP /ə/, /ɪ/ and /ʒ/ are replaced in *s[ə]cceed, veg[ɪ]tate* and
conclu[ʒ]ion by [ɔ], [e] and [ʃ], respectively.

3. Conclusion

The particular phonology of CamE is an exciting topic. At the same time I have tried to give an overview of the constructs (like trilateral process) which I believe are useful for the comparative phonologies of sub-Saharan varieties of English. I have undertaken some comparisons in my own research, but there is ample scope for further work in the area.

Exercises and study questions

1. Compare the CamE vowel inventory with that of southern Nigerian English.

2. Discuss the 'marginal nature of schwa' in CamE.

3. 'CamE exhibits surprisingly few segmental differences from RP' – discuss.

4. Discuss some properties of CamE stress placement that differentiate it form RP or another L1 variety of English you are familiar with.

5. Outline the notion of 'trilateral process' (2.4) with an example.

Selected references

Please consult the General references for titles mentioned in the text but not included in the references below. For a full bibliography see the accompanying CD-ROM.

Rubach, J.
    1984   Segmental rules of English and Cyclic phonology. *Language* 60: 21–54.
Simo Bobda, Augustin
    1994   *Aspects of Cameroon English Phonology*. Bern: Peter Lang.
    1997   Further demystifying word stress. *English Today* 52: October 1997: 48–55.
    2000   Explicating the features of African English Pronunciation: Some steps further. *Zeitschrift für Anglistik und Afrikanistik (ZAA)* 2: 123–136.
Simo Bobda, A. and B. S. Chumbow
    1999   The trilateral process in Cameroon English phonology: underlying representations and phonological processes in non-native English. *English World-Wide* 20: 35–65.
Todd, Loreto
    1982   The English language in West Africa. In: Bailey and Görlach (eds.), 281–305.

Cameroon Pidgin English (Kamtok): phonology

Thaddeus Menang

1. Introduction

"Kamtok" is one of the labels used to refer to a pidginized variety of English
used in parts of Cameroon. It is also referred to as "Cameroon Pidgin English"
or simply as "Pidgin English". Earlier studies (Dwyer, 1966; Schneider, 1966)
have used the label "West African Pidgin English" to include other pidginized
varieties of English spoken along the west coast of Africa, particularly in Nigeria, Sierra Leone and Liberia. "Kamtok" is mutually intelligible with these
other varieties to a large extent but has developed its own characteristic features over the years.

The history of Kamtok is closely linked to that of contacts between Europe
and the coasts of West and Central Africa. Contact between Europe and West
and Central Africa was first made in the fifteenth century when the Portuguese,
under Henry the Navigator, decided to explore this part of the African continent. Contact with the coast of Cameroon was made shortly after 1472 when
a Portuguese expedition, led by a certain Fernando Gomes, reached Fernando
Pô, an island off the coast of Cameroon which is part of Equatorial Guinea
today. It is reported (Schneider 1966) that this contact with the coastal regions
of West and Central Africa first gave rise to various Portuguese-based pidgins
and creoles that spread from Sâo Tomê, off the coast of Central Africa, to the
Cape Verde islands in the west. Bouchaud (1952) confirms the use, along the
coast of Cameroon in the sixteenth century, of a Portuguese-based language for
commercial transactions between Portuguese traders and natives of the area.

The exact manner in which an English-based Pidgin first came about in this
region remains uncertain. What is known is that Portuguese influence in the
region started dwindling by the end of the sixteenth century. The Dutch began
to replace the Portuguese at the beginning of the seventeenth century. Dutch
influence was relatively short-lived, however, and made no real impact on the
linguistic situation left behind by the Portuguese. The Dutch were soon replaced by the British, whose influence in the region began to be felt as early
as 1618 when a trade monopoly was granted to a British firm 'the Governor
and Company of Adventures of London Trading to Gynney and Binney'. Later,
in 1672, the Royal African Company succeeded to the monopoly and traded

till 1712 (Mbassi-Manga 1973). British influence is thus seen to have spread to many locations along the coast of West and Central Africa in the eighteenth century. Closer contact between the British and inhabitants of the area was enhanced by the introduction of the "factory" and "trust" systems of trade and by the active part taken by the British in the slave trade (Dike 1956).

The spread of British influence and the establishment of closer contact between the British and the inhabitants of these coastal regions led to the formation of an English-based pidgin, which eventually replaced the Pidgin Portuguese that had been used in the area for over two centuries. The exact manner in which the shift from Pidgin Portuguese to Pidgin English took place is a matter of debate. Relexification has been suggested, but it is more likely that Pidgin Portuguese existed side by side with a more recently formed Pidgin English until the latter gradually replaced the former. In support of the second hypothesis, Schneider (1966), citing early Dutch accounts and other scattered pieces of historical information, places the beginning of the development of an English–based pidgin in the seventeenth century.

One thing seems fairly certain: by the end of the eighteenth century, Pidgin English was firmly established throughout the West African coast. Schneider (1966) cites sources which confirm that an Efik slave-trading chief of the coastal region of what is today Nigeria kept a diary in Pidgin English which was described as "a jargon which was mainly English in vocabulary although the constructions were often modelled on those of Ibibio" (a local language). A series of historical events led to the further development of what has come to be known today in Cameroon as Pidgin English or Kamtok. First, the abolition of the slave trade led to the resettlement, early in the nineteenth century, of freed slaves in three communities along the coast of West Africa: in Liberia, Sierra Leone and Fernando Pô. Within each of these communities, Pidgin English was the principal medium of communication, as this was the only language the slaves had in common. Meanwhile, contacts between British explorers and merchants and inhabitants of the coastal region of Cameroon continued to intensify. Bouchaud (1952) mentions regular visits to the area in 1800 by vessels of the Congo District Association, a British explorers' association. He also mentions an earlier individual initiative by a British merchant, Henry King, whose boats also visited Cameroon regularly. His sons, Richard and William King, were later to found a firm that continues to prosper today and bears the name R. and W. King. Missionaries soon followed the explorers and merchants and helped to spread the new language further.

Missionaries from the Baptist Missionary Society of London and the Jericho Baptist Mission in Jamaica arrived and settled in Clarence, Fernando Pô in 1841 (Keller, Schnellback and Brütsch 1961). After making contacts with the Cameroon mainland, they succeeded in founding Christian communities at Bimbia in 1844 and Douala in 1854. In 1845, meanwhile, Alfred Saker arrived in Fernando Pô and when, in 1858, the Spanish authorities there declared the Protestant religion illegal on the island, Saker and his group moved to the Cameroon mainland and founded a mission station in Victoria. Freed slaves were among the first lay members of these early Christian communities. They spoke Pidgin English. From Victoria, today renamed "Limbe", and Douala, the new language was going to spread gradually to parts of the Cameroon hinterland, aided by commerce, missionary activity and colonial rule.

Taking advantage of British procrastination, the Germans annexed Cameroon in 1884. But German rule over Cameroon was quite short-lived. It ended by the end of World War I when under the terms of the Treaty of Versailles signed in 1919, Cameroon was placed by the League of Nations under the trusteeship of France and Britain. Under German rule, Pidgin English continued to thrive in spite of German hostility. The creation of plantations along the coastal area by the Germans drew workers from various parts of the territory where different languages were spoken. Brought together in these plantations, the workers who did not share an indigenous language quickly learned Pidgin English, which they used while on the plantations and eventually took back to their areas of origin in the hinterland. Thus the language continued to develop and spread.

After World War II, Cameroon was maintained as a trust territory under the French and the British. Each colonial power set up a system of administration and opened schools in which the colonial language was the medium of communication and instruction. But Pidgin English was already so firmly implanted that it continued to be used even in parts of the territory that had come under French colonial rule. In the part of the country under British trusteeship, Pidgin English developed rapidly alongside English with which it shared close ties which, over the years, have come to influence its phonology and vocabulary. Where French was the colonial language, Pidgin English spread was slowed down, but the language largely survived, borrowing occasionally from French to complement its vocabulary and cope with new situations. This historical and linguistic divide at the level of the colonial language has today given rise to two broad varieties of Kamtok: one that clearly leans towards English and borrows freely from it and one that is more conservative and borrows rather cautiously from French. These two broad varieties have been otherwise referred to as "Anglophone Pidgin English" and "Francophone Pidgin English" (Mbassi-Manga 1973).

Since the two territories re-unified in 1961 to form the Federal Republic of Cameroon, the situation of Kamtok has not changed very much as far as the influence of English or French is concerned. But there are clear indications that the language continues to spread in spite of occasional hostility from people who think that it stands in the way of a rapid mastery of 'standard' English by school pupils and other learners. As one of Cameroon's languages of wider communication, Kamtok today bridges the linguistic gap among an estimated one quarter to one third of the country's rural and particularly urban populations. The language is used intensively among the inhabitants of the so-called English-speaking provinces of the North West and South West which account for at least one fifth of Cameroon's total population of about 15 million inhabitants. It is also fairly frequently used in most parts of the French-speaking Littoral and the West Provinces which are adjacent to the two English-speaking provinces. Outside these four (out of ten) provinces, Kamtok is found in varying extents in urban centres.

A survey conducted in the early 1980s by the Department of English at the University of Yaounde sought to describe the linguistic profile of Cameroon's urban centres. The survey revealed the spread of Kamtok in the country. According to its findings (published in Koenig, Chia and Povey [1983]), Kamtok has spread throughout the southern half of the country. In the urban centres surveyed in the southern half of Francophone Cameroon, 30% to 60% of the people consulted claimed they knew and used the language. The number of people who claimed to know and use Kamtok in the six urban areas studied in the English-speaking provinces of the country hardly dropped below 80%.

From a fairly marginal language that grew out of contacts between European explorers, merchants and missionaries and the coastal inhabitants of Cameroon some three hundred years ago or so, Kamtok has grown to become a fully-fledged language that is put to a wide range of uses. It remains the language of buying and selling in most local markets of the regions where it is used. The sociolinguistic survey of Cameroon's urban centres revealed for example that in Douala, Cameroon's economic capital that is located in the French-speaking part of the country, 83% of the people interviewed used Kamtok in buying or selling in the local markets.

Kamtok also continues to be used by Christian missionaries in evangelisation and liturgical services. It occurs in numerous translations of biblical texts, catechisms and Christian liturgies which constitute most of the written texts available in the language so far. These texts come in varying orthographies but each one clearly serves the purpose of its author. Kamtok occupies a prominent place in many homes in Cameroon where it shares functions with the mother tongue. The survey of urban centres revealed that in the English-speaking part of the country, up to 97% of school-age children already use Kamtok at the time they enter school. It is also the preferred language among these children when they communicate among themselves. Because it happens to be the shared language that is best mastered by school-age children, nursery school teachers tend to use it as a medium of communication and instruction until such a time that the children have acquired some mastery of English.

Kamtok's role as a medium of interethnic communication has already been emphasized. On the basis of the linguistic survey data, it was found that Cameroon could be divided into four *lingua franca* zones: a Kamtok zone, a French zone, a Fulfude zone and possibly a Fang-Beti zone. The Kamtok zone was found to be matched only by the French zone in the size of its population.

Kamtok is also a language of science and technology. It is widely used by local craftsmen and technicians such as mechanics, masons, carpenters, hairdressers, seamstresses and tailors, all of whom acquire their skills thanks to the language. It is widely used for technology transfer in domains such as health, agriculture, animal husbandry and conservation. This explains why many Western volunteers who offer to serve in Cameroon have to spend time learning some rudiments of Kamtok before proceeding to meet the people among whom they intend to work. Further, Kamtok is the language of an urban mass or popular culture in Cameroon. It is widely used in popular music, theatre shows, special radio broadcasts and newspaper columns, for socialisation in general and for in-group identification and differentiation in particular. The latter function is giving rise to interesting varieties of the language which remain largely unexplored.

Apart from French and English which are Cameroon's official languages, Kamtok enters into frequent contact with several of Cameroon's more than two hundred indigenous languages. Users bring into their Kamtok idiolects various features that derive from both the official and indigenous languages that they use in different circumstances. This has given rise to an impressive number of Kamtok accents that challenge the researcher. These horizontal forms of variation have resulted in slightly differing varieties of Kamtok that are being described after analyses conducted mostly at the phonological and lexical levels. The distinction between "Anglophone" and " Francophone" Kamtok has been established on this basis. Other regionally more restricted varieties have been identified within these two broad varieties.

The nature and extent of variation in Kamtok is also determined by the extent of the speakers' formal education in English and exposure to situations in which English is used. Such considerations have led to the identification of so-called "educated" and "uneducated" varieties of Kamtok. The "educated" variety is said to be more elaborate in its form and richer in its choice of words many of which are borrowed directly from English in both their form, meaning and pronunciation. The "uneducated" variety is less elaborate in form and contains fewer occasional borrowings from English.

Contextual variation arises mostly from the uses to which Kamtok is put. Various uses of Kamtok have been discussed earlier but the nature and frequency of forms of variation arising from function still have to be thoroughly investigated. Some functional varieties of Kamtok have however been suggested: ecclesiastical, commercial, technical, and in-group. One such variety with an in-group function that has caught recent scholarly attention is "Camfranglais". It is popular among school-age youth and school leavers, and, as the name suggests, comprises an intricately woven combination of expressions from indigenous languages, from French and from English. It is an evolving linguistic phenomenon that deserves to be carefully studied.

What makes variation in Kamtok so difficult to track is the fact that it remains largely unstandardized. There have been attempts to describe it by various researchers, who have focused on its grammatical and lexical features. No formal grammar or dictionary has yet come to be accepted by users as a guide that lays out norms that are worth respecting. Kamtok thus remains everybody's language and each person uses it to the best of his/her ability and almost at leisure. This makes the task of description quite onerous. The present descriptive survey focuses on those features that are found in the speech of a cross-section of Kamtok users. As most of these users are found within or near the English-speaking provinces of Cameroon, examples will be drawn from the broad variety that tilts towards what has been termed "Anglophone" Kamtok. Care has been taken however to rid the description of features that are considered random borrowings from English, particularly those that may pose problems of intelligibility to less 'educated' users. Nevertheless the survey points to features that augur new trends in the development of the language.

2.   Phonology

The present survey of Kamtok phonological features is far from exhaustive. It focuses particularly on Kamtok sounds, the distribution of these sounds in speech and on certain prosodic features such as stress and tone.

Although the language is treated here as an autonomous system, the description nevertheless relates its distinctive sound features to those of English and its other source languages, whenever possible, in an effort to show how Kamtok has come to achieve its autonomy.

2.1.   Kamtok sounds

Initial studies of Kamtok phonology reveal that the language has 6 vowel sounds and 21 consonant phonemes. Kamtok thus makes use of almost as many consonants as English, although Kamtok and English consonants are quite not the same. As for vowels sounds, Kamtok has barely half the number used in English. This apparent economy of vowel sounds at the phonemic level hides a certain complexity that becomes visible when one examines their concrete realizations. Cases of sounds in complementary distribution will require more careful study. Kamtok's phonemes are presented in tables 1 and 2 and figures 1 and 2.

The first column contains the symbol used to represent the sound. The second contains a brief description of the sound, while the third provides an example of a Kamtok word or form in which the sound is found. This word is also presented in contrast with another word with which it constitutes a minimal pair.

2.1.1.   Kamtok vowels

Table 1.   Description of the vowel phonemes of Kamtok

Sound symbol	Description	Examples
ɪ	High unrounded front vowel	Compare /si/ 'see' and /so/ 'so'
e	Mid unrounded front vowel	Compare /tek/ 'take' and /tɔk/ 'talk'
a	Central low unrounded vowel	Compare /man/ 'man' and /mun/ 'moon'
u	High rounded back vowel	Compare /put/ 'put' and /pɔt/ 'pot'
o	Mid-high rounded back vowel	Compare /lo/ 'low' and /lɔ/ 'law'
ɔ	Mid-low rounded back vowel	Compare /lɔk/ 'lock' and /luk/ 'look'

Although the vowels presented in the preceding section are generally said to be the only clearly distinctive ones in Kamtok, recent usage includes certain vowel combinations that resemble some English diphthongs in a manner that suggests that they may have a phonemic status. Four such vowel combinations have been identified:

/ai/ as in /bai/ 'buy', as opposed to /ba/ 'bar';
/au/ as in /kau/ 'cow', as opposed to /ka/ 'car';
/ɔi/ as in /nɔis/ 'noise', as opposed to /nɔs/ 'nurse';
/ia/ as in /bia/ 'beer', as opposed to /bi/ 'bee'.

Further research is needed on such vowel combinations.

2.1.2. *Kamtok consonants*

Table 2.   Description of the consonant phonemes of Kamtok

Sound symbol	Description	Examples
p	Voiceless bilabial stop	Compare /put/ 'put' and /fut/ 'foot'
b	Voiced bilabial stop	Compare /big/ 'big' and /dig/ 'dig'
t	Voiceless alveolar stop	Compare /ti/ 'tea' and /bi/ 'bee'
d	Voiced alveolar stop	Compare /dig/ 'dig' and /big/ 'big'
k	Voiceless velar stop	Compare /kuk/ 'cook' and /buk/ 'book'
g	Voiced velar stop	Compare /gɔn/ 'gun' and /sɔn/ 'sun'
m	Bilabial nasal	Compare /man/ 'man' and /pan/ 'pan'
n	Alveolar nasal	Compare /nek/ 'neck' and /tek/ 'take '
ŋ	Velar nasal	Compare /tiŋ/ 'thing' and /tin/ 'tin'
ñ	Palatal nasal	Compare /ñus/ 'news' and /tʃus/ 'choose'
f	Voiceless labiodental fricative	Compare /fam/ 'farm' and /lam/ 'lamp'
v	Voiced labiodental fricative	Compare /vot/ 'vote' and /got/ 'goat'

Table 2. (continued) Description of the consonant phonemes of Kamtok

Sound symbol	Description	Examples
s	Voiceless alveolar fricative	Compare /si/ 'see' and /ti/ 'tea'
z	Voiced alveolar fricative	Compare /zip/ 'zip' and /kip/ 'keep'
ʃ	Voiceless pre-palatal affricate	Compare /ʃem/ 'shame' and /sem/ 'same'
h	Voiceless glottal fricative	Compare /hama/ 'hammer' and /fama/ 'farmer'
tʃ	Voiceless pre-palatal affricate	Compare /tʃuk/ 'pierce' and /buk/ 'book'
dʒ	Voiced pre-palatal affricate	Compare /dʒam/ 'scarcity' and /fam/ 'farm'
r	Alveolar trill	Compare /riva/ 'river' and /liva/ 'liver'
l	Dental alveolar liquid	Compare /lɔŋ/ 'long' and /rɔŋ/ 'wrong'
j	Palatal glide	Compare /jam/ 'yam' and /lam/ 'lamp'
w	Bilabial glide	Compare /wan/ 'one' and /man/ 'man'

Table 3 provides a classification of these consonants.

Table 3. Classification of Kamtok consonants

	Bilabial	Labio-dental	Alveolar	Palato-alveolar	Palatal	Velar	Glottal
PLOSIVE	p b		t d			k g	
AFFRICATE				tʃ dʒ			
FRICATIVE		f v	s z	ʃ			h
NASAL	m		n		ñ	ŋ	
LATERAL			l				
GLIDE/ APPROXIMANT	w			r	j		

2.2.   Consonant clusters

Consonant clusters do exist in Kamtok. Dwyer and Smith (1966) report that in some forms of Kamtok speech, /s/ can precede /p, k, t, m, n, l/ in words such as: /spun/ 'spoon', /skul/ 'school', /stik/ 'stick', /smɔl/ 'small', /snek/ 'snake' and /slak/ 'weak'.

Consonant clusters are also formed by /p, b, f, k, g, d, s/ preceding /l/ and /r/. Here are some examples:

/pleja/ 'player'   /preja/ 'prayer'
/bred/ 'bread'   /blak/ 'black'
/flai/ 'fly'   /frai/ 'fry'
/klin/ 'clean'   /krai/ 'cry'
/glad/ 'glad'   /gras/ 'grass'
/draiva/ 'driver'   /slip/ 'sleep'

Dwyer and Smith (1966) note that, in addition to occurring by themselves in Kamtok, nasals are often homorganic with other consonants. But they do not seem to consider such *nasal + consonant* combinations as forming clusters because the preceding vowels are nasalised. Some examples, however, appear to involve genuine clusters:

/mb/, /ŋg/ in /mbaŋga/ 'palm-kernel'
/ŋg/, /nd/ in /ŋgɔndere/ 'young woman'
/nj/, /mb/ in /njumba/ 'girl or boy friend'
/ns/ in /nsɔ/ 'Nso' (place name)
/nc/, /nd/ in /ncinda/ 'attendant'
/ŋk/, /nd/ in /ŋkanda/ 'skin'

Such *nasal + consonant* combinations are not limited to words taken from Cameroonian languages, as the /nj/ in /jinja/ 'ginger' shows.

2.3.   Realization and distribution of some Kamtok vowels.

A number of processes have contributed to the building of an autonomous sound system in Kamtok. Similar processes have been discussed by Simo Bobda in his study of aspects of Cameroon English phonology (see his article in this volume). As far as Kamtok vowel sounds are concerned, these processes entail the following: (a) the restructuring of the vowel system; (b) the non-reduction of vowels in unstressed position; (c) restrictions in the distribution of certain vowel sounds.

2.3.1. Restructuring of the vowel system.

In the process of building a new system, Kamtok has drastically reduced the number of vowels it uses. Whereas English makes use of a dozen vowels, Kamtok vowels stand at six. This reduction in the number of vowels has been achieved partly through "mergers".

A merger can occur within a language when, over the years, several sounds gradually become one. A number of similar or closely related English sounds are merged in Kamtok as one sound with which users are more familiar. Such a sound is usually one that is found in both English and most Cameroonian languages or only in the local languages. Some mergers are listed below:

English /æ, ɑː, ə/ merge to form Kamtok /a/:
English /mæn/ > Kamtok /man/ 'man'
English /fɑːðə/ > Kamtok /fada/ 'priest'
English /əgriː/ > Kamtok /agri/ 'agree'

English /ɛ, ɜː/ merge to form Kamtok /e/:
English /hɛd/ > Kamtok /het/ 'head'
English /bɜːd/ > Kamtok /bet/ 'bird'

English /iː, ɪ/ merge to form Kamtok /i/:
English /fɪʃ/ > Kamtok /fiʃ/ 'fish'
English /shːp/ > Kamtok /slip/ 'sleep'

English /ɔː, ʌ/ merge to form Kamtok /ɔ/:
English /gɔːd/ > Kamtok /gɔd/ 'god'
English /kʌt/ > Kamtok /kɔt/ 'cut'

English /uː, ʊ/ merge to form Kamtok /u/:
English /pʊt/ > Kamtok /put/ 'put'
English /muːn/ > Kamtok /mun/ 'moon'

A second aspect of vowel restructuring is a strong tendency to produce simple vowels in the place of certain English diphthongs, with the second element of the diphthong usually being dropped:

English /eɪ/ becomes Kamtok /e/:
English /meɪk/ > Kamtok /mek/ 'make'

English /əʊ/ becomes Kamtok /o/:
English /gəʊ/ > Kamtok /go/ 'go'
English /səʊ/ > Kamtok /so/ 'so'

English /ɛə/ becomes Kamtok /e/ or /ɛ/:
English /ɛə/ > Kamtok /de/ 'there'
English /ɛə/ > Kamtok /ke/ or / kɛ/ 'care'

The pronoun 'I' /aɪ/ is usually produced in Kamtok as /a/.

Other centring diphthongs of English are restructured to produce new sound combinations, which accord with Kamtok phonology:

English /ɪə/ becomes Kamtok /ia/, /iɔ/ or /i/:
English /fɪə/ > Kamtok /fia/ 'fear'
English /sɪərɪəs/ > Kamtok /siriɔs/ 'serious'

English /ʊə/ becomes Kamtok /ua/, /uɔ/ or /ɔ/:
English /jʊə/ > Kamtok /jua/ 'your'
English /pʊə/ > Kamtok /puɔ/ 'poor'
English /ʃʊə/ > Kamtok /ʃɔ/ 'sure'

English triphthongs are restructured through glide formation. This process involves the transformation of the central element of the triphthong: /ɪ/ becomes /j/ and /ʊ/ becomes /w/. This splits the vowel sequence into two syllables as in the following examples:

English /aɪə/ becomes Kamtok /aja/:
English /faɪə/ > Kamtok /faja/ 'fire'

English /aʊə/ becomes Kamtok /awa/:
English /paʊə/ > Kamtok /pawa/ 'power'

2.3.2. Non-reduction of Kamtok vowels

Although Kamtok makes use of many words of English origin and continues to borrow heavily from that source, it hardly makes use of stress such as is found in English. All the syllables in Kamtok words tend to be stressed to some degree. This feature has considerably affected the manner in which words of English origin are produced in Kamtok. Thus the vowel sounds which would normally be reduced in English whenever they occur in unstressed position do not undergo reduction. The presence of unreduced vowels in every syllable often completely modifies the pronunciation of English words when these are used in Kamtok. Some examples follow:

English /aftə/ > Kamtok /afta/ 'after'
English /kəmpleɪn/ > Kamtok /kɔmplen/ 'complain'
English /fiːvə/ > Kamtok /fiva/ 'fever'
English /gɪnɪs/ >Kamtok /ginis/ 'Guinness'
English /ɔːdə/ > Kamtok /ɔda/ 'order'
English /teɪbl̩/ > Kamtok /tebul/ 'table'

2.3.3. Vowel sounds with restricted distribution.

Some of the mergers and restructuring of vowels and diphthongs reported above are not generally found in the Kamtok of English-Kamtok bilinguals. The resurfacing of these sounds in regular Kamtok speech arises from the very close contact that exists between the two languages in the English-speaking provinces of Cameroon which are home to mainstream Kamtok. The presence of such sounds in Kamtok speech constitute a kind of linguistic interference, though some of the sounds have also been found in the Kamtok of those whose knowledge and use of English are not confirmed. Thus, the close contact that exists between English and Kamtok may be leaving more permanent marks on the latter. On the one hand, diphthong-like combinations of vowels such as /ai/, /ɔi/, /au/ and /ia/ are seen to occur in the same word positions as the English diphthongs /aɪ/, /ɔɪ/, /aʊ/ and /iə/ respectively:

English /bɔɪ/ > Kamtok /bɔi/ 'boy'
English /kraɪ/ > Kamtok /krai/ 'cry'
English /haʊs/ > Kamtok /haus/ 'house'
English /fiə/ > Kamtok /fia/ 'fear'

On the other hand, the Kamtok vowel /e/ is being "split" to produce /ɛ/ and /ə/ which had earlier been merged to produce it. Hence, instead of having a word like /bet/ stand for both English *bed* and *bird*, some Kamtok users regularly distinguish between /bɛd/ and /bəd/, leaving the vowel /e/ to occur mostly in place of English /eɪ/. These trends certainly deserve more attention from future researchers.

2.4.   Some phonological processes

2.4.1. Consonant devoicing

Words of English origin undergo certain changes when they are adopted into Kamtok. One of these changes is the devoicing of final consonants such as /d, g, v, z/ to produce [t, k, f, s]. When pronounced in isolation, words like /gud/ 'good', /big/ 'big', /bad/ 'bad' and /bed/ 'bed' sometimes retain voice on the final consonant, but when they are followed by a word with a voiceless consonant at initial position, the devoicing is obligatory. Consider these examples:

/het pan/	'headpan'
/gut tɔk/	'good talk'
/bik cɔp/	'big chop'
/bat tiŋ/	'bad thing'
/bet pan/	'bed pan'

Final consonant devoicing has also been observed to occur systematically in words such as:

/muf/ from English /muːv/ 'move'
/tʃus/ from English /ɛkskjuːz/ 'excuse'
/twef/ from English /twɛlv/ 'twelve'

2.4.2. Cluster simplification

Consonant clusters in English can occur at the initial position, in the middle or at the end of the word. Kamtok words hardly have consonant clusters at final position. As a result, when Kamtok adopts English words, their final consonant clusters are usually simplified through the deletion of one or more consonants. The following examples illustrate final consonant deletion:

English /graʊnd/ > Kamtok /graun/ 'ground'
English /hænd/ > Kamtok /han/ 'hand'
English /læmp/ > Kamtok /lam/ 'lamp'
English /sɛnd/ > Kamtok /sen/ 'send'
English /fɜːst/ > Kamtok /fes/ 'first'
English /mʌst/ > Kamtok /mɔs/ 'must'
English /ænd/ > Kamtok /an/ 'and'
English /kɒrəkt/ > Kamtok /kɔrek/ 'correct'

One rare example of consonant deletion at initial position is seen in the Kamtok word /trɔŋ/ from English /strɔːŋ/ 'strong'. A more common process in Kamtok is to reduce clusters at initial, and sometimes at final, position through vowel epenthesis, i.e. the insertion of a vowel between the two consonants forming the cluster as shown in the following examples:

English /sliːp/ > Kamtok /silip/ 'sleep'
English /spiə/ > Kamtok /sipia/ 'spear'
English /teɪbl̩/ > Kamtok /tebul/ 'table'
English /sneɪk/ > Kamtok /sinek/ 'snake'

2.4.3. Resurfacing of /ð/ and /θ/

These are two English consonants which are usually replaced in Kamtok by /d/ and /t/ respectively. Like some diphthong-like sounds discussed above, these sounds are increasingly resurfacing in the speech of English-Kamtok bilinguals, particularly in recent loans from English. If the trend persists, /ð/ and /d/

and /θ/ and /t/ will come to be considered as being in free variation in words such as /ðis/ and /dis/ "this" and /bɜːθ/ and /bɜːt/ "birth".

2.5. Prosodic features in Kamtok

Most discussions of prosodic features in Kamtok tend to focus on whether Kamtok is a tone language or not. There is indeed an on-going debate on this issue, one that has been going on for decades. Research findings at this stage unfortunately do not permit one to provide a conclusive answer to the question. The aim of this section is thus to simply provide a summary of the characteristic prosodic features that existing studies have identified.

2.5.1. Tone as a significant feature in Kamtok

Most studies – e.g. Dwyer and Smith (1966), Mbassi-Manga (1976), Bellama, Nkwelle and Yudom (1983) – agree that tone is a feature of Kamtok speech, in that it distinguishes differences in meaning between words and utterances. Hence tone is used in Kamtok to bring out differences in meaning between the following:

> /bábà/ 'barber' and /bàbá/ 'father'
> /póp̀ɔ̀/ 'proper' or 'real' and /pɔ̀pɔ́/ 'pawpaw'
> /gó/ 'go' and /gò/ future tense marker
> /nàsò/ 'It is so' and /nàsó/ 'Is it so?'

Most studies acknowledge at least two tones: a rising or high (´) and a falling or low (` ) tone. Dwyer and Smith (1966) talk of three tones: a strong high tone ( ´ ), a weak high tone (unmarked) and a low tone ( `). Because the weak high tone is generally unmarked some researchers tend to ignore it.

Dwyer and Smith (1966) also suggest that the high and low pitches of tone in Kamtok operate in registers. Within the register, all high pitches are at the same level just as are all low pitches. The strong high pitch usually terminates the register of which it is a member, as in /dát nà búk/ 'that is a book'. Mbassi-Manga (1976) considers the minimal tone unit in Kamtok to correspond to a syllable or word, the maximal unit being the polysyllabic sense group.

2.5.2. The link between pitch and stress.

Most discussions of tone in Kamtok suggest an obvious link between pitch and stress. Dwyer (1966) state that Kamtok tone involves two separate but related features that are pitch and stress. The high pitch is usually accompanied by stress while the low pitch is usually unstressed. Mbassi-Manga (1976) goes further to point out that Kamtok does not have unstressed syllables as one finds in English. Except for emphatic stress, each syllable is uttered with the same amount of strength, except the last syllable which receives slightly more energy. Thus instead of talking about stressed and unstressed syllables, he suggests the notions of primary and secondary stress. Consider the following examples:

/ˌkɔ̀ ˈmɔ́t/ (secondary + primary stress)
/ˌà sà ˈlút/ (secondary + secondary + primary)

Mbassi-Manga (1976) argues that in casual speech stress occurs on the final syllable of each word taken in isolation and of the sense group in connected speech. Thus pitch and stress combine in Kamtok to give its speech a characteristic melody that distinguishes it very clearly from English. Most researchers agree on the significance of tone in Kamtok and on the fact that although it exhibits stress, the language is syllable-timed. Those who accept the significance of tone in Kamtok but hesitate to conclude that it is a tone language argue that similar tone differentiations exist in the local variety of (standard) English, without leading to the conclusion that English is a tone language. Clearly developments in the area of tone are worthy of longitudinal studies.

Exercises and study questions

1. Compare the consonant inventory of Kamtok with that of Cam E.

2. Do the same for the vowel inventory.

3. Now compare the consonant inventory of Kamtok with that of NigP.

4. Do the same for the vowel inventory.

5. Discuss the treatment of diphthongs of RP in Kamtok.

Selected references

Please consult the General references for titles mentioned in the text but not included in the references below. For a full bibliography see the accompanying CD-ROM.

Bellama, David, Solomon Nkwelle and Joseph Yudom
    1983   *An Introduction to Cameroonian Pidgin*. Revised Edition, Peace Corps. Cameroon.

Bouchaud, Joseph
   1952   *La côte du Cameroun dans l'histoire et la cartographie: des origins à l'annexion allemande.*
Dike, K. Onwuka
   1956   *Trade and Politics in the Niger Delta, 1830–1885.* Oxford: Clarendon.
Dwyer, David
   1966   An Introduction to West African Pidgin English, African Studies Center, Michigan State University.
Keller, Werner, J. Schnellback and J.R. Brütsch
   1969   *The History of the Presbyterian Church in West Cameroon.* Victoria: Press Books.
Koenig, Edna, Emmanuel Chia and John Povey (eds.)
   1983   *A Sociolinguistic Profile of Urban Centers in Cameroon.* Los Angeles: Crossroads Press.
Mbassi-Manga, Francis
   1973   English in Cameroon: a study of historical contacts, patterns of usage and common trends. Unpublished Ph.D. dissertation, Leeds.
   1976   Pidgin English is not a Tone Language. *Annals of the Faculty of Arts and Social Science (Yaounde)*, 6: 5–16.
Schneider, Gilbert
   1974   Masa Troki Tok Sey: A Compilation of Pidgin English Materials, Ohio University
   1966   West African Pidgin English: A Descriptive Linguistic Analysis with Texts and Glossary form the Cameroon Area. Ohio University Center for International Studies, Ohio.
Simo Bobda, Augustin
   1992   Aspects of Cameroon English Phonology. Ph.D. disseration, University of Yaounde.

East African English (Kenya, Uganda, Tanzania): phonology

Josef Schmied

1.   Introduction

The geographical limits of East Africa are not always clearly defined. Sometimes it ranges from the Red Sea down to the end of the Rift Valley somewhere in Mozambique. More usually the northern part (Ethiopia, Eritrea, Somalia, Djibouti and occasionally Sudan) is treated separately as North East Africa and the southern part with Zambia, Malawi and Zimbabwe is referred to as Central Africa, or with Mozambique, Namibia, Swaziland, Lesotho and the Republic of South Africa as Southern Africa (cf. also Schmied 1991). This contribution will concentrate on the "heartland" of Kenya, Uganda and Tanzania since they share a common "anglophone" background, despite some interesting differences in colonial heritage. These three countries are also characterised by a complex pattern of African first languages (mainly from the Bantu and Nilosaharan language families), a common lingua franca (Kiswahili) and an equally complex mixture of Christian, Islamic and native African religious and cultural beliefs. The revived East African Community (1967–1976 and from 1997) is a sociopolitical expression of this common heritage.

Although many sociolinguistic (like code-switching and borrowing) and linguistic features (like vowel mergers and syllable-timed rhythm in pronunciation or overgeneralization in grammar and a formal tendency in style) can also be found in other parts of Africa, East African English (EAfE) can be distinguished clearly enough from other varieties to justify a coherent descriptive entity. Today such a description can only be based on authentic data from three types of empirical sources: exemplary quotations from individual recorded utterances, a quantified and stratified pattern retrieved from a corpus of EAfE, like ICE-East Africa (described in the part on morphology and syntax), or quantitative results from internet search engines or tools using the www as a corpus.

The following description tries to give a coherent picture by emphasising reasons and patterns, rules or rather tendencies, since no reason is unique and no rule applies to 100%. These patterns are illustrated by short examples and finally set into a larger co- and context by examples from real English. As in most dialectal and sociolinguistic research one isolated marker may indicate a characteristic usage clearly, but usually only a cluster of features gives us the authentic flavour of EAfE. In this sense it is a descriptive abstraction, not necessarily an established, recognised norm, which should become clear from the following survey.

1.1. Historical background

English came late to East Africa, since for a long time the colonialists were not really interested in Africa. Instead the Swahili towns on the coast (Kilwa, Zanzibar, Mombasa, Malindi, etc.) were used as stepping stones to the jewel of the imperial crown, India. The last decades of the 19th century saw the establishment of British and German colonial power, mainly through Zanzibar. The most famous East African explorers Livingstone and Stanley (who met at Ujiji in 1871) were accompanied by other explorers and missionaries. The German missionaries Krapf, who founded Rabai near Mombasa in 1846, and Rebmann were the first Europeans to see the snows of Mount Kilimanjaro and Mount Kenya – but were not believed in Europe. Methodists opened a mission near Mombasa in 1862, Anglicans in Zanzibar in 1863 and Catholics in Bagamoyo in 1868. Ten years later they moved along the traditional trading route inland through Morogoro and Tabora to Ujiji on Lake Tanganyika. This shows that European intrusion followed the established Swahili trade routes – and used their language, Kiswahili, as a lingua franca.

The brief German interlude (from Carl Peter's first "treaties" in 1884 to World War I) established not German but Kiswahili in the colony, and laid the foundation for its success as a truly national language in Tanzania later.

After the war some differences in colonial administration between Kenya, Uganda and Tanganyika/Zanzibar can be attributed to the role of the white settlers in Kenya, but a lot of similarities remain, although Tanganyika was only held by the British as a Mandate from the League of Nations. The system of "indirect rule" through African leaders (developed by Lord Luggard in Nigeria) was introduced everywhere. In contrast to Rhodesia (esp. present-day Zimbabwe), where the settlers were given self-governance, the primacy of "African interests" was decided in 1923. This is documented in the Land Ordinance Act, which secured land rights for Africans and not only Europeans, over 2000 of whom had spread particularly in the "White Highlands" north of Mount Kenya and east of Mount Elgon. In reality, British rule established a three-class system with the white colonial officers and settlers at the top, the Indian in the middle and the Black Africans at the bottom.

The system of communication developed along the railway and highway lines with a few ethnic nuclei in fertile areas like Buganda, Kikuyuland/Mount

Kenya or Chaggaland/Mount Kilimanjaro. The Indians had come to East Africa partly via the Swahili trade in Zanzibar, but mainly for the construction of the railways. They stayed not only in the (railway) administration but also as traders with their small dukas in the centres, often as "middleman", who could be accused of exploitation by the European settlers and even more by the Africans. This made them easy targets for dictator Idi Amin, who caused their exodus from Uganda in 1972, and also for Africanisation policies in the other new nations.

1.2.   Colonial language policies

Despite British colonial rule, colonial language policy was not simply pro-English and more complex than is often assumed (cf. Spencer 1971). Of course, the various colonial administrations tried to regulate official language use in their territories. But this involved usually three types of language, the local "tribal" mother tongues and the African lingua franca (usually Kiswahili, only occasionally Luganda) besides English, for local, "intraterritorial" and international communication respectively. Other agents played a role as well, like the churches, who had enormous influence not only on church language but also on school language. Even the three British mission societies (the Universities Mission to Central African, the Church Mission Society and the London Mission Society) did not use English for evangelisation. The German missionary Krapf (in the services of the Church Mission Society) propagated a Latin spelling system for Kiswahili, which had been written in Arabic traditionally and maintained many Islamic connections, since he saw Kiswahili as "the most cultivated of dialects" and as a key to the inland languages. Protestant missions in general favoured (in Martin Luther's tradition) "the language of the people", i.e. the ethnic languages, but also the African lingua franca, Kiswahili. The Catholic church was usually more orthodox, supporting not only Latin in its services but also Kiswahili in their preaching.

Even the British administration in Tanzania did not introduce English wholesale after taking over the former German colony. Rather, they admired the efficient German system, which according to a report from 1921 "made it possible to communicate in writing with every akida and village headman, and in turn to receive from him reports written in Kiswahili".

Thus English was established only in élitist circles when the colonial powers tried to regulate communication within the administrative, legal and education system. The considerations summarised in a report by the Phelps-Stokes Fund (cf. Schmied 1991: 15) led to a basically trilingual language policy with the ethnic "vernacular" for local communication and basic education, Kiswahili in ethnically mixed centres and English for the highest functions in administration, law and education. This led to the foundation of the Interterritorial Language Committee in 1929, which developed into the East African Swahili Committee later, responsible for standardisation, orthography reform and expansion on the basis of the Zanzibar variety KiUnguja (and not the KiMvita of Mombasa). English was the language of instruction mainly in the few prestigious secondary schools, e.g. in King's College, Budo, Uganda, the school for chiefs' sons in Tabora or Alliance High in Nairobi, and of course in the first East African university, Makerere (founded as a Technical School in 1922 and as a University College in 1949).

It is important to remember that colonial language policies did not favour English, or other European languages, wholesale, but established a "trifocal" or trilingual system with (a) English as the elite and international language, (b) the regional lingua franca and (c) the "tribal" languages or "vernaculars" for local communication. The expansion of English down the social hierarchy began mainly at the end of colonial rule with the democratisation and expansion of education that was to prepare Africans for independence (cf. Schmied 1991: 18). After independence, surprisingly few changes occurred; although lip-service was usually paid to African languages. Only Tanzania made great progress towards expanding the functions of Kiswahili at the expense of English and local African languages.

1.3.   Sociolinguistic background

1.3.1.   The range of variation in English in Africa

One of the broadest categorisations of the English used in Africa is suggested by Angogo and Hancock (1980: 71), who distinguish the following types according to speakers:

(a) native English of African-born whites and expatriates;
(b) native English of locally-born Africans;
(c) non-native English spoken fluently as a second language (...);
(d) non-native English spoken imperfectly as a foreign language (...).

The first category, White African English, is relatively insignificant in East Africa today, although the influence of the early British and South African settlers may have been considerable. The other three categories of (Black) African English constitute a continuum of English forms, which ranges from 'native' to 'second-language' to 'international' varieties. It is worth noting, however, that these categories were used to illustrate differences between entire nations, especially in the process of developing (hypothetical) national varieties of English. When it comes to analysing language forms which are actually used in Africa, intranational and intrapersonal variation, the individual speaker's sociolinguistic background and the actual speech-act situation must be taken into consideration. At the individual level, the type of English spoken by Africans depends largely (i.e. if we ignore special exposure to English either through personal acquaintances or the modern mass media) on two factors: (a) their education, i.e. the length and degree of formal education in English, and (b) their occupation, i.e. the necessity for and amount of English used in everyday life.

The second category is also less important than in Southern or West Africa, although English may be used as the primary language even in the home in mixed marriages of highly educated partners.

The last category reflects, of course, less the colonial heritage than the role of English as the international language of science and technology, international development and communication today. But "broken" English, "school" English or "bad" English is usually looked down upon as a sign of little education and ridiculed, especially in Kenya, in literature or political campaigns (e.g. in cartoons in the daily newspapers).

Thus the varieties of EAfE show the characteristic features of New Englishes (cf. Platt, Weber and Ho 1984 or Hickey 2004), background, genesis and function. In particular they are not transmitted directly through native-speaker settlers; usage is formed mainly through its use as media of instruction in school and reinforced outside school; and they are used in public functions in the national educational, legal and administration system. Interestingly enough, the term New English is rarely used in East Africa, probably because Standard English even with EAfE pronunciation or as an (hypothetical) independent East African Standard is considered more appropriate.

1.3.2. The sociolinguistic situation today

The common cultural background of the three countries makes the sociolinguistic situation rather similar. The major difference is the status of Kiswahili: in Tanzania, it is the true national language, since it is spoken nation-wide as a lingua franca, learnt in a relatively homogeneous form (sometimes called "Government Swahili") in all primary schools and used in most national functions including education in most secondary schools; in Kenya it is just losing its associations with the coast or with lower social positions; in Uganda it is unfortunately still associated with the military and the "troubled" times in the 1970s and 1980s. This leaves more room for English and the other East African languages in Uganda and Kenya.

The official status of English in government, parliament or jurisdiction is not always easy to establish, as conflicting laws, regulations and proclamations since independence 40 years ago may contradict each other. Whereas it is clearly the language of nation-wide politics in Uganda, it is rarely used in those functions in Tanzania. Kenya occupies a middle position in this regard.

English is not really associated with white settlers any more. Although distinct accents can still be heard in this group, they range outside the general national norm. The multilingual educated African elite invests large sums of money in "good education", which is usually based on "good English". The Asians in East Africa are usually equally multilingual, speaking not only their native languages, mainly Gujarati or Panjabi, but also their own versions of Kiswahili and English.

Knowledge and actual use of English are based on very rough estimates, since no nation-wide census data are available and the last language survey was sponsored by the Ford Foundation more than 30 years ago. Thus to say, for instance, that English is "spoken" by 30% in Uganda, 20% in Kenya and only 5% in Tanzania may give an indication of the (historical) differences in education, urbanisation, modernisation or internationalisation. However, this must be taken with great caution. Since English gives prestige, informants' self-evaluations are unreliable, and nation-wide proficiency tests for national certificates of education often disappointing. The fact that even universities have started extensive course programmes in "Communication Skills" or even explicitly "Remedial English" reveals some of the problems at the highest level. The discussions can be followed even on the internet today in various contributions including numerous letters-to-the-editor to major national newspapers (e.g. "MUK enforces English for all" in The New Vision, Uganda's leading daily 13/01/02). The key problem is that English is used as the language of instruction from upper primary school onward (in Uganda) and is thus the basis for all further education. The discussion is less about teaching English properly than teaching (other subjects) in English properly.

In all countries English is still (in Tanzania again?) a result and a symbol of good education and, directly or indirectly, a prerequisite for well-paid jobs with international links in trade and tourism. This is often reflected in popular debates on language attitudes in East Africa.

1.3.3.   Language attitudes today

Attitudes towards languages in Africa can be heard in many debates, but systematic studies are rare and difficult. At least three types of attitudes have to be distinguished as far as English in East Africa are concerned.

The stereotyped notions on English are usually extremely positive. It is seen as "sophisticated" and "superior" (but also as "difficult" and "formal"). Such notions may however have little effect on attitudes towards practical language use and usage in East Africa. Usually East Africans do not really subscribe to language-inherent properties (like English is "cool and impersonal", "colonial" or "European"), although it may be considered more appropriate for formal and official use than other African languages.

Language is mainly viewed in extremely practical terms, since it is too obvious that English is the international language of science and technology and world-wide communication. Thus international arguments in favour of English are also uncontroversial. Even the great supporter and translator of Kiswahili, President Nyerere of Tanzania, emphasised the importance of English calling it "the Kiswahili of the world". The real issue is the use (and usage) of English in intranational communication, especially in African schools. Although the first-language principle (based on UNESCO recommendations since the 1950s) is normally accepted by African educationalists, nationally minded Tanzanians support the use of Kiswahili from the first day at school, whereas internationally minded parents in Uganda advocate a "fast track" to English, which had been common at independence. The stage of switching to English is usually after lower primary (four school years) in Uganda and after secondary school in Tanzania, whereas in Kenya it is at the beginning of the four years of secondary school at the latest. The debate is most heated in Tanzania, where on the one hand in recent years many new private secondary schools have advertised English as a medium of instruction, while on the other hand even some universities have proposed teaching in Kiswahili. The same arguments pro and con have been used for decades (cf. Schmied 1991: chap. 7) and they can be detected again in most recent newspaper debates (e.g. in www.ippmedia.com).

In contrast to these debates on practical language issues, attitudes towards African varieties of English are rarely discussed outside scholarly circles. Accepting African forms is hardly openly admitted except in pronunciation, where "aping the British" is seen as highly unnatural. Grammar and syntax in particular are considered the glue that holds the diverging varieties of English together; and international intelligibility is deemed absolutely essential as the major asset of the international language cannot be jeopardised. Thus Standard English with African pronunciation may be accepted as an intranational norm, but Ugandan, Kenyan or Tanzanian English will not be tolerated at least in the near future. On the other hand the theoretical British norm is only upheld in books and rarely experienced in use in present-day Africa.

1.4.   Reasons for East African forms of English

The reasons for the occurrence of African forms different from Standard English are manifold and can basically be attributed to at least four factors as far as their origin is concerned. For EAfE today the role of distinctly different native speaker English (e.g. Scottish English or even Scots) may be neglected, hence the importance of three major factor groups or reasons.

(a)   Influence of the learners' mother tongue and other African languages
Since English is learnt as a second language in East Africa, it is likely that features and strategies from first language acquisition are transferred; negative transfer is usually called interference. This has long been seen as the basic cause for African variation in English, because it obviously influences the pronunciation, often distinctly. Since non-African mother-tongue speakers as role-models are rare nowadays, common deviations become institutionalised and give a specific stamp to African English in its various forms. The great fear in Africa is that when one generation of poorly-trained African teachers passes on their English to the next generation, mother-tongue interference could be cumulative so that, with time, English could deviate more and more from accepted norms (like the minimal five-vowel system in EAfE below).
    From today's perspective, mother-tongue influence on African English seems to have been overestimated. Because English is for many Africans only one possible choice in their verbal repertoire, which will include more than one African language, it may be safer to assume the influence of a common substratum of the African languages known by the English user. Interestingly enough, some speakers of African English exhibit "interference features" although they do not derive from their mother tongues but from other languages used in the area. Furthermore, often several factors may converge

(b)   General language learning strategies
The influence of general psycholinguistic processes on a second language is very difficult to assess; it is only possible to compare input and output of the human brain and draw conclusions on cognitive processing. There is some evidence that language learners in general use simplification strategies at an early stage (*it seem_ that* ..., where morphological simplification may be supported by pronunciation simplification of an alveolar in front of a dental fricative). Later they try to reproduce memorised phrases from the target language, irrespective of the linguistic and pragmatic context (his/her level best seems to occur more often in African than in European English). From a certain stage onwards learners enjoy complicating their language and even tend to exaggerate typically English features (*he is living in Eldoret* is an overgeneralization

when temporary meaning is not implied; *she ran fastly* is a hypercorrect form, as unmarked adverbs are associated with broken English). When the learning process does not progress normally, certain developmental errors, which occur regularly in first and second language acquisition, become fossilised, i.e. they become permanent features (like the plural of non-count nouns like *informations* or *discontents*). This includes overgeneralisations like neglecting restrictions or differences between gerunds and infinitives in complementation (such as *I wouldn't mind to give* instead of *giving*). All these creative strategies of language learners must have played a certain role in the development of African varieties of English.

(c)   Exposure to the written language

The fact that in many societies, including African ones, the written word has an authority exceeding that of the spoken form has far-reaching consequences for English language learners, particularly in a situation where languages other than English dominate in oral communication. Thus African speakers of English tend to reproduce characteristics of written English even in the spoken form. Grammatical constructions and lexical items from relatively formal registers or spelling pronunciations, like [saɪd] or [dʒuɪs] for *said* and *juice*, will often be used. This explains the articulations of /h/ in *heir* or of /b/ in *debt* and generally the tendency of the central NURSE vowel to assume the sound value "suggested" by the orthographic symbol that represents it (e.g. [adʒ] for *urge* vs. [heːd] for *heard*). As Shakespeare and the Bible have until recently – when they were replaced by modern African classics like Achebe and Meja Mwangi – been most commonly used for teaching the target language, African varieties have tended to have an archaic flavour.

2.   Phonology

The phonology of EAfE is of particular importance because (non-standard) pronunciation features seem to be the most persistent in African varieties, i.e. they are retained even in the speech of the most educated speakers. This may be because in many languages pronunciation seems to be the most flexible element, which can be used (subconsciously) to express subtle sociolinguistic messages of speaker identity and of distance from or solidarity with the listener. English appears to be particularly fluid at this level. Even the supposed norms in Britain have moved so far away from the institutionalised written form that the graphemic system cannot symbolise the diverging phonemic systems any more. Mistakes in the form of phonetic spellings do, however, allow conclusions on the pronunciation even from written texts. The features characterising

African pronunciations of English can be found at subphonemic, phonemic and supraphonemic levels.

Differences at the phonemic level are important because here differences of lexical meaning are maintained. This can be illustrated (and elicited) in minimal pairs like *ram* and *lamb*; *beat* and *bit*; or *show* and *so*. Many Africans would not distinguish clearly in pronunciation between the elements of such pairs tending towards the same pronunciation (homophony).

2.1.   Consonants

Among the consonants, /r/ and /l/ are a particularly infamous pair for many Bantu speakers, both rendered as one and the same, often intermediate sound between /loli/ and /rori/ instead of /lori/, for instance. In Kenya, the pair is a clear subnational identifier, since even educated Gikuyu clearly tend towards /r/ and the neighbouring Embu towards /l/. Occasionally the sets /tʃ/, /ʃ/ and /s/, and /dʒ/, /ʒ/ and /z/ are not distinguished clearly either. Other problematic consonants are /θ/ and /ð/, which often deviate in the direction of /d/ and /t/ or, sometimes, /z/ and /s/, rarely /v/ and /f/. Most of these deviations are registered by East Africans as subnational peculiarities. However, even though phoneme mergers are clearly noticeable, they do not endanger the consonant system as a whole. These examples show three general tendencies for consonants:

(a) The merger of /r/ and /l/ is wide-spread, but still stigmatized.
(b) Intrusive or deleted (as a hypercorrect tendency) nasals, especially /n/ in front of plosives, are common, since some languages like Gikuyu have homorganic nasal consonants.
(c) English fricatives are generally difficult but particular deviations are often restricted to certain ethnic groups

At the subphonemic level, which is not important for differences in meaning but gives the English spoken a particular colouring, an interesting consonant is /r/. As in most English varieties, /r/ is usually only articulated in pre-vocalic positions (i.e. EAfE is non-rhotic) and its pronunciation varies considerably (whether it is rolled or flapped).

2.2.   Vowels

A comparison of the English phoneme system with that of most African languages shows that the major difference are not the consonants but the few vowel contrasts compared to the extensive English vowel system. Thus the vowel system of EAfE deviates systematically, vowels tend to merge, because the extreme range of the English vowel continuum is not covered by the under-lying African systems of, for instance, the Bantu languages. On the whole three basic generalisations may be made for English vowels:

(a) Length differences in vowels are levelled and not used phonemically; thus FLEECE and KIT, GOOSE and FOOT, THOUGHT and NORTH, and BATH, STRUT and TRAP tend to merge. This is not only a quantitative, but also a qualitative shift, as usually short vowels in EAfE are longer and more peripheral than in RP, especially /ɪ/ tends towards /iˑ/, /ʊ/ towards /uˑ/, /ɔ/ towards /oˑ/ and /ʌ/ and /æ/ towards /aˑ/.

(b) The central vowels of STRUT, NURSE and lettER, are avoided and tend to-wards half-open or open positions of BATH and, less often, DRESS. This conforms to the tendency towards more extreme articulatory positions of the tongue in general. It leads (together with the syllable-timing, cf. 2.2.3. below) to the phenomenon that, whereas vowels in full syllables tend to be underdifferentiated, those in unstressed ones may be overdifferentiated. Hence the difference between *policeman* and *policemen* or between the suffixes *-ance* and *-ence* may be clearer than in Standard English.

(c) Diphthongs tend to have only marginal status and to be monophthongized. In the short closing diphthongs MOUTH and particularly FACE the second element is hardly heard in many African varieties (as in Scotland; thus coinciding almost with the DRESS vowel). Diphthongs with a longer glide are preserved, but they are not really pronounced as falling diphthongs, i.e. with less emphasis on the second element than on the first, but rather as double monophthongs (e.g. [ɔɪ], [aʊ]). All the centring diphthongs (NEAR, SQUARE, CURE) tend to be pronounced as opening diphthongs or double monophthongs ([ɪa, ea, ua]; cf. tendency (b) above).

These general observations on vowel pronunciation seem to hold for so many African varieties that this cannot be interpreted merely as a product of mother-tongue interference. In fact, some of these features of "Africanization" have already been predicted by Gimson (1980: 306) in very general terms, i.e. with-out any reference to Africa, because of the particularly complex structure of the English vowel system:

> … the full systems [20 vowels and 24 consonants] must be regarded as complex compared with the systems of many other languages. In particular, the opposition of the close vowels /iː/-/ɪ/, /uː/-/u/, the existence of a central long vowel /ɜː/ and the delicately differentiated front vowel set of /iː/-/ɪ/-/e/-/æ/ + /ʌ/, together with the significant or conditioned variations of vowel length, will pose problems to many foreign learners.

Finally, it is worth considering the vowel system as a whole (in terms of Wells 1982). In contrast to West African varieties, which tend towards a basic seven-vowel system, East African varieties tend towards a basic five-vowel system (Table 1).

Table 1. The vowels of East African English (mesolectal tendencies)

KIT	i	FLEECE	i	PRICE	aɪ
FOOT	u	GOOSE	u	CHOICE	oɪ
TRAP	a	DRESS	e	SQUARE	ea
NURSE	a	THOUGHT	o	NEAR	ɪa
LOT	o	FORCE	o	GOAT	o
CLOTH	o	NORTH	o	CURE	ʊa
STRUT	a	START	a	FACE	e
COMMA	a	BATH	a	MOUTH	aʊ
lettER	a	PALM	a	ABOUT	a
happY	ɪ	horsES	ɪ		

An interesting single parameter in this respect is the deviation of the RP long central NURSE vowel: it tends toward a back vowel /ɔ/ in West African varieties, towards a front vowel /a/ in Eastern and towards /e/ Southern African varieties, but these tendencies are not uniform in a region, neither across all ethnic groups, nor across the lexicon, as in Tanzania *girl* tends towards front (DRESS) and *turn* towards back pronunciation (START) because of spelling pronunciation – cf. 1.4 (c) above.

2.3.   Suprasegmental patterns

Other important features of African English are supraphonemic, i.e. related to phoneme sequences, word stress, intonation and general rhythmic patterns. Many of these phenomena are difficult to describe, so that some examples from three particularly striking aspects may suffice: the avoidance of consonant clusters, the more regular word stress and the special rhythm.

2.3.1. Phonotactic patterns

Consonant clusters are a major phonotactic problem in EAfE, as many African languages have a relatively strict consonant-vowel syllable structure (often CV-CV-CV). This explains African English tendencies with regard to consonant clusters and final consonants. Consonant clusters tend to be dissolved, either by dropping one/some of the consonants involved or by splitting them through the insertion of vowels.

Final consonants are dropped when there are two or more in a sequence, e.g. in [neks] for *next* and [hen] or [han] for *hand*. But this tendency also occurs in native-speaker English and its frequency seems to vary a lot. The general rule appears to be that if plosives are preceded by fricatives, they are dropped in word-final position; if they are preceded by other plosives or occur in non-final position they are split by vowels inserted between the consonants. A similar phenomenon occurs when final vowels are added to closed syllables, i.e. syllables ending in consonants. The vowels inserted or added are normally [ɪ] or [ʊ], depending on the occurrence of palatal or velar consonants in the environment (e.g. [hosɪpɪtalɪ] for *hospital* or [spɪrɪnɪ] for *spring*) or on vowel harmony (e.g. in [bʊkʊ] for *book*).

2.3.2.   *Word stress*

A particularly striking feature is the African tendency towards more regular stress rhythms. Again, the problem lies often within the English tendencies to maintain partly the Romance principle of word stress on the penultimate syllable in contrast to the general Germanic principle of stressing the stem. This leads to differences in word stress between etymologically obviously related words when prefixes and suffixes are added, thus ad'mire is not stressed on the same syllable as *admi'ration* and *'admirable*; here East Africans are tempted to stress [ad'maɪrabl] and sometimes even [ad'maɪre'ʃen] just like [ad'maɪa]. Of course, the problem of a whole series of unstressed syllables is intrinsic to British Standard English; even American English has secondary stress regularly in words like secretary. Thus the final word stress on suffixes like -'ize and particu. larly -'ate may not be that surprising in theory, but it may be in practice. The tendency is not systematic, since in most cases the frequency and familiarity of words supports the "correct" British English pronunciation. In other cases better known, etymologically related or similar words may serve as models. This tendency faces the problem that Standard English uses stress to indicate word class. In EAfE the distinction between the verbs *pro'test, alter'nate, at'tribute* and the nouns *'protest, 'alternate, 'attribute* through stress is not always maintained.

2.3.3. Syllable-timed rhythm

The most striking feature of African Englishes is the tendency towards a syllable-timed rather than a stress-timed rhythm. Thus an EAfE speaker tends to give all syllables more or less equal stress and does not "cram" up to three unstressed syllables together into one stress unit to form so-called "weak" forms as speakers of British English do. This underlying pattern accounts for most suprasegmental patterns in EAfE mentioned above (e.g. to give too much weight to unstressed syllables), and its sometimes unfamiliar rhythm. It may also cause misunderstandings in intercultural communication, when EAfE may be misjudged as "unfriendly machine-gun fire" or "childish song-song". The interesting question is whether this helps communication with francophone Africans, whose speech is also syllable-timed.

Exercises and study questions

1. 'Whereas vowels of EAFrE in full syllables tend to be underdifferentiated, those in unstressed ones tend to be overdifferentiated' – discuss.

2. 'Diphthongs of EAfrE tend to have only marginal status and to be monophthongized' – discuss.

3. Compare the vowel inventory of EAfrE with that of a West African variety like GhE.

4. Compare the vowel inventory of EAfrE with that of BlSAfE.

5. Compare the treatment of consonants in EAfrE with that of a West African variety like GhE.

Selected references

Please consult the General references for titles mentioned in the text but not included in the references below. For a full bibliography see the accompanying CD-ROM.

Angogo, Rachel and Hancock, Ian
    1980   English in Africa: emerging standards or diverging regionalisms? *English World-Wide* 1: 67–96.
Gimson, Alfred Charles
    1980   *An Introduction to the Pronunciation of English.* London: Arnold. (3rd ed.)

White South African English: phonology

Sean Bowerman

1. Introduction

The term 'White South African English' is applied to the first language varieties of English spoken by White South Africans, with the L1 English variety spoken by Zimbabweans and Namibians, mainly of British descent, being
recognised as offshoots. There is some social and regional variation within
the variety. Social variation within White South African English (henceforth
WSAfE) has been classified into three groupings (termed 'The Great Trichotomy' by Lass (2002: 109ff)): **Cultivated**, closely approximating RP and associated with upper class; **General**, a social indicator of the middle class, and
Broad, associated with the working class and/or Afrikaans descent, and closely
approximating the second-language Afrikaans English variety.

An historical overview of the origins of English in South Africa will place
these variations into perspective.

1.1. The origins and propagation of English in South Africa

1.1.1. The Cape Colony

British ships en route to the East in the 18th century were frequent visitors to
the Cape, which was then an invaluable trading and refreshment station under
Dutch control. After the French Revolution of 1789–1791, republican France
overran the territories of the royalist Netherlands and laid claim to all its colonies and territories, including the strategically positioned Cape colony. Britain
perceived this as a threat to (their interests at) the Cape, and in 1795 a British
fleet landed at the Cape, having driven back the Dutch defenders, and laid claim
to the territory. The Netherlands briefly re-established sovereignty as the Bata-
vian Republic, upon which the Cape was returned; but in 1806 the Napoleonic
Wars again saw the Netherlands subjugated to France, and Britain once more
launched a successful assault on the Cape, this time proclaiming a colony and
installing a governor. The Cape was formally surrendered to Britain in 1814.

Seeking to establish the Cape as a viable colony, Britain launched a settlement programme in which approximately 4500 Britons were landed at Algoa

Bay in the eastern Cape in 1820 and 1821. The 1820 Settlers, as they came to be known, were mainly working class people drawn from all over Britain. While their speech was homogenously L1 English, they spoke a large variety of regional dialects, rather than RP. The Settlers were given land for farming, and came to live in close contact with their Dutch neighbours. Within two generations, the regional dialect distinctions had been levelled (Lanham 1982: 325).

In 1822, English was proclaimed as the sole official language of the Cape Colony, supplanting Dutch in almost all public spheres. The British colony expanded rapidly, and Settlers were dogged by conflict with indigenous peoples, into whose territory the colony was now intruding. Moreover, political tensions between Dutch and English settlers continued to mount, leading to the Great Trek of 1834–1836, in which Dutch settlers left the Cape Colony in large numbers to escape British rule and seek autonomy elsewhere. The 'Trekkers' pushed northwards and eastwards, establishing three territories: the 'South African Republic', which later became known as Transvaal; the Orange River Sovereignty, later Orange Free State, and Natalia. While Dutch became the official language of these territories, a competency in English remained a hallmark of good education (Lanham 1982: 325).

1.1.2. Natal

The autonomy of Natalia (which occupies most of present-day KwaZulu-Natal) was short-lived. After a brief period of war, Britain annexed Natalia to the Cape Colony, and shortly thereafter proclaimed it a crown colony (Natal) in its own right. This led to an influx of English speaking settlers, and large numbers of English settlers arrived in Natal under an organised British settlement programme between 1848 and 1862. Lanham (1982: 325) reports that a higher proportion of settlers to Natal were middle or higher class, and that there was very little contact with Dutch settlers, and no conflicts with indigenous peoples in which civilian colonists were involved. While social distinctions based on position and rank were levelled in the Cape Colony, they tended to be maintained in Natal. Moreover, the origins of the settlers to Natal were less diverse than those to the Cape, and the population more urbanised. Thus, the English of the first generation settlers in Natal differed from that of the Cape settlers in that there was much less social and regional differentiation, but also much less social levelling (Lanham 1982 : 325f).

1.1.3.   South African Republic (Transvaal) and Orange Free State

Until the 1870s, South Africa (as it is currently known) comprised four major territories: the British-administered and English speaking Cape and Natal colonies, and the independent, Dutch-speaking Voortrekker (or 'Boer') republics: the South African Republic/Transvaal and the Orange Free State.

The discovery of gold and diamonds in the Voortrekker republics in the 1870s brought a rush of fortune seekers from all over the world, as well as from the British colonies. This significantly swelled the English-speaking population of the Voortrekker republics, and led to increased contact between the two groups. The 'mineral revolution' (Lanham 1982: 327) in southern Africa coincided with the Industrial Revolution in Europe and the United States, and industrialisation began in South Africa. Meanwhile, all four of the (main) settler territories battled continuously with the indigenous peoples for land, and the indigenous peoples were finding themselves overrun as settler populations expanded.

The pursuit of fortune in the mining centres led to social stratification (Lanham 1982: 327), as some were successful and others weren't. The relatively sophisticated, urbanite Natalians were better-placed, being used to this lifestyle; but the more rural frontiersmen, both English and Dutch-speaking, from the Cape, and the Dutch settlers of the Voortrekker republics found themselves at the lower end of the social strata. Lanham (1982: 328) reports on the fortunate position of the Natalian, whose better education, slightly dubious higher-class status and speech in the colonies could not be faulted by the lower-placed colonials from the Cape ('whose sensitivities to the fine detail of British behaviour had faded') and others, who had had no contact with Britain and things British.

1.1.4.   English in 'unitary' South Africa: 1870s to 1994

By the late 1800s, social stratification in the White communities could be categorised as follows: British (immigrant), colonial, Dutch and European Jew (Lanham 1982: 327). British immigrants and Natal colonials occupied the upper ends of the hierarchy, with British and Natal accents being perceived as having the highest status. Cape colonial English and second language varieties had much lower status; indeed, the first language Cape colonial variety and the Afrikaans English variety were 'not differentiated ... in the ears of the majority in the mining city' (Lanham 1982: 327).

British interests in the mineral and other industries in Southern Africa, and the desire to expand the British empire, saw the occupation of the Boer republics from the late 1870s. This culminated in the South African War of 1899–1902, in which the British prevailed. The Boer republics were annexed to the British crown, and given the status of Crown Colonies. This led to a further influx of English first language speakers to the former Boer republics, and increased status for English. The four crown colonies—the Cape, Natal, Orange Free State and Transvaal—formed the Union of South Africa, under British rule, in 1910. British colonials, and English, dominated the political scene until after World War II. Mining, a chiefly British interest, was the dominant industry, with the home-born, successful, upper-class Englishman setting the standard to aspire to (Lanham 1982: 329). Locally, the prestigious Natal variety of English set the standard for South African English, while Cape colonial English and the second language Afrikaans-English variety remained stigmatised, relatively low status varieties.

South African Dutch, which became known as Afrikaans in 1924, retained official language status and remained a significant home language, but was dominated in the cities and in all public spheres by English (Watermeyer 1996: 103). Resistance to British rule and English increased, giving rise to Afrikaner nationalism, which openly promoted loyalty to Afrikaans and hostility to English. In White society, English and Afrikaans speakers became more and more divided, and during World War II the Afrikaner Nationalist Party aligned itself with Nazi Germany, making the rift even deeper (Lanham 1996: 25).

In 1948, the Afrikaner Nationalist Party triumphed over the English United Party in national ('Whites only') elections, and set about increasing the status of Afrikaans in public spheres. The Nationalist Party dominated South African politics until 1994, imposing Afrikaans as the *de facto* first official language of the country, and limiting the influence of English, particularly in African education (Lanham 1996: 26). However, the English first language community remained significant, English remained legally equal to Afrikaans, and continued to dominate in commerce, higher education and industry (Mesthrie 2002: 22). All White pupils had to learn both official languages as school subjects: the usual pattern was for the home language to be learnt as 'first language', and the 'other official language' was to be learnt as second language. This meant that most Afrikaans L1 speakers gained some competency in English.

The apartheid policies of the National Party government had disastrous consequences in all areas of life. It was the attempted imposition of Afrikaans as a joint medium of instruction with English in Black secondary schools that led to the tragic Soweto riots of 1976, and resistance to Afrikaans was greatly increased. In terms of language status, English benefited from this. English was the *lingua franca* of the struggle (strengthening its position for the role it was later to play in the country), and became the sole medium of instruction in nearly all Black secondary schools. Thus, English played a dominant role in the education sector, with each province setting its own standards for the teaching of English – the variety associated with middle to upper class in each region was accepted as the provincial standard.

1.1.5.   English in post-apartheid South Africa

In 1994, the National Party was ousted by the African National Congress in the country's first democratic elections, and Afrikaans was deposed from its role as first official language. Along with English, Afrikaans was given legal status as one of eleven official languages. In reality, the decline of Afrikaans in public roles has been drastic, while the dominance of English is almost total, particularly in education, where it is by far the dominant medium of instruction of secondary and higher education. English is the language to aspire to in the New South Africa, even though it is the L1 of only 8.2% of the population (Census 2001 results). It is likely to retain this role for the foreseeable future.

Since 1994, English has only marginally increased as a home language among Black people, though an increase in this statistic among middle-class Black people residing in formerly 'whites only' suburbs is likely in the near future.

It is important to note that labels such as 'White South African English', 'Black South African English', etc. are not intended to reflect the apartheid classifications; however, owing to South Africa's legacy, the correlations between ethnic affiliation and dialect of English remains significant. The old label, 'South African English', used to refer only to WSAfE as the source variety, and L2 varieties were given an additional descriptor: Black SAfE, Indian SAfE, etc. As these varieties become or show the potential of becoming first language varieties, SAfE is held over as a cover term (following de Klerk 1996), and all varieties of South African English are given a descriptor. WSAfE continues to be the standard, and, following the collapse of apartheid, children from 'non-white' communities who attend (prestigious) schools which uphold WSAfE norms are increasingly adopting these norms into their own speech. At the less prestigious end of the spectrum, WSAfE varieties tend to merge with the second language Afrikaans English (generally the norm of White Afrikaans – English bilinguals, or, in the Cape, so-called Cape Flats English, mainly associated with 'Coloured' people. These labels reflect generalities, though, and are not in fact confined to apartheid-style ethnic groupings.

Regional variation in WSAfE is naturally associated with the strongest concentrations of White English speaking communities. These can broadly be divided into (Western) Cape, Natal and Transvaal (Gauteng) English, and recognisable Namibian and Zimbabwean varieties.

2.   Phonology

2.1.   Overview

The two main phonological indicators of White South African English are the behaviour of the vowels in KIT and BATH. The KIT vowel tends to 'split', so that there is a clear allophonic variation between the close, front [ɪ] and a somewhat more central [ï]. The BATH vowel is characteristically open and back in the General and Broad varieties of WSAfE. The tendency to monophthongise both MOUTH and PRICE to [aː] are also typical features of General and Broad WSAfE.

Consonantal indicators include the tendency for voiceless plosives to be unaspirated in stressed word-initial environments; [tj] *tune* and [dj] *dune* tend to be realised as [tʃ] and [dʒ] respectively; and I have noticed a strong tendency for /h/ to be voiced initially.

2.2.   The vowel system

Table 1. The Wells' lexical sets for WSAfE

KIT	[ɪ] ~ [ï], [ə]; [i]
TRAP	[æ] > [ɛ]
DRESS	[e]
LOT	[ö] > [ɔ], [ʌ]
STRUT	[ä] > [ɐ]
FOOT	[ʊ] > [ʉ]
FLEECE	[iː]
NURSE	[ɜː], [œː]
GOOSE	[uː], [ʉː] > [yː]
THOUGHT	[ɔː], [œː]
BATH	[äː], [ɑː]
FACE	[eɪ] > [æɪ], [ʌɪ]
PRICE	[aɪ], [aː]
MOUTH	[aʊ], [aː]
CHOICE	[ɔi]
	[ɛʊ] > [ˌʊ] ,
GOAT	[œʉ] > [œÿ]
SQUARE	[ɛː], [eː]
NEAR	[ɪə]
CURE	[uə]
HAPPY	[ɪ], [i]
LETTER	[ə]
COMMA	[ɐ], [ə]

2.2.1. The short monophthongs

KIT

KIT is 'split' (see Lass 2002: 113f) between the realisations [ɪ] and [i] in General, and [i] and [ï] to [ə] in Broad. The split is an allophonic variation, with the fronter realisation occurring in velar and palatal environments, and the more central one occurring elsewhere. Cultivated WSAfE lacks this split, but KIT is a reliable sociolinguistic marker for White South African English in general. Before [ɫ], the vowel may be as far back as [üï].

DRESS

This vowel is usually realised as [e], though it is lowered to [ɛ] in Broad, sometimes approaching [æ], especially before [ɫ]. Some varieties of Broad and General WSAfE place this vowel higher, around raised [e] or lowered [ɪ].

TRAP

A slightly raised [æ] is the usual realisation for this vowel in Cultivated and General. In Broad varieties, it is often raised to [ɛ], so that TRAP encroaches on DRESS for some speakers. (Lanham 1967: 9)

LOT

The range of this vowel is between [ɒ̈] and [ɔ]. Lass (2002: 115) noted a tendency towards [ʌ] in younger Cape Town and Natal speakers of General WSAfE.

STRUT

This is typically a low to mid, centralised vowel ([ä] to [ɐ]) in WSAfE.

FOOT

Generally realised as high, back centralised [ʊ]. There is little variation, except that there is very little lip rounding relative to other L1 varieties of English worldwide. The pronunciation [ʉ] (with added lip-rounding) is associated with Broad, but is more a feature of Afrikaans English.

2.2.2. The long monophthongs

FLEECE

In all varieties, a long close front unround vowel, [iː].

NURSE

In Cultivated varieties, a somewhat central vowel approximating the RP [ɜː]. In General and Broad, it is more rounded, and fronter: [øː] – [ø̈ː], as in French *peu*.

GOOSE

This vowel is usually high central [ʉ:] or fronter, significantly more forward than its RP equivalent [u:]. Cultivated speakers, however, produce a vowel closer to [u:]. Lass (2002: 116) notes a tendency towards [y:] in younger, and especially female, General speakers.

BATH

Except in the Cultivated variety, this vowel is low and fully back, [ɑ:]. In Broad varieties, there is a tendency to shorten, round and raise the vowel, so that it becomes [ɒ] – [ɔ] (Lass 2002: 117; Lanham 1967: 14). Cultivated speakers realise a more central version, [ɑ̈:].

THOUGHT

In Cultivated speech, the vowel is quite open, like RP [ɔ:]. In General and Broad, it is higher, [o:]. Broad varieties also have THOUGHT in words like *cloth* and *loss*, where LOT is more typical (Lass 2002: 116).

2.2.3. The diphthongs

FACE

The norm for Cultivated and General WSAfE varieties is [eɪ]. Lass notes a tendency for the onset to be opener the further one deviates from the standard (2002: 117), even to [æɪ]. Broad White South African English is characterised by the onset being both open and back, [ʌɪ].

PRICE

The Cultivated WSAfE realisation is close to RP [aɪ]. In General and Broad, the articulation of the first element is often monophthongised to [a:]. In Broad, the first element is somewhat back, but more forward and higher than in BATH, and the offglide is often retained: [ɑ̈ɪ]. See also MOUTH, below.

MOUTH

Cultivated usually has [ɑ̈ʊ], while General again follows the tendency to monophthongise diphthongs, and often has [ɑ:]. Broad has a much fronter on-set, and retains the offglide: [æʊ].

CHOICE

In all varieties, the realisation is usually [ɔɪ]; the onset can be as low as LOT in older Cultivated WSAfE speakers (Lass 2002: 118).

GOAT
There is a tendency among some Cultivated speakers not to round the onset of this diphthong, so that a Cultivated realisation ranges around [ɛʊ] or [œʊ]. The onset is always rounded in General varieties, usually mid-low; but the offglide is more central, sometimes unrounded, and there is once again a tendency to monophthongise. Thus, 'normal' General pronunciations of GOAT would be [œʉ], [œÿ] or [œː]. In Broad, the onset is much further back, and unrounded: [ʌʊ].

SQUARE
In Cultivated, square is pronounced [ɛə], as it is in RP. General speakers follow the tendency to monophthongise, and usually realise the long vowel [ɛː]. Broad speakers monophthongise and raise, to [eː].

NEAR
This is usually [ɪə] in all varieties, with a tendency to monophthongisation in Broad, particularly after [j]. E.g. [njɪː] *'near'*.

CURE
This is usually realised as diphthongal [ʊə] in Cultivated and General; but there is a growing trend, especially when the vowel does not occur after /j/ (*sure*), in General toward Broad's monophthongal [oː], perhaps slightly lower than THOUGHT. This probably accounts for the spelling of *you're* as *your* in everything from student essays to newspaper advertisements.

HAPPY
The unstressed (or secondarily stressed – see Lass 2002: 119) vowel is usually /iː/, but half-long [iˑ]. Lanham marks this as an indicator of White South African English (1968: 8).

LETT*ER*
[ə] in all varieties; very often omitted before another consonant: [kɪtn̩] *kitten*.

COMM*A*
Usually [ə], but may be as open as [ɐ] in Cultivated WSAfE; and also in Broad varieties close to Afrikaans English.

2.3.   The Consonant System

2.3.1. Plosives

/p, b, t, d, k, g/
The 'voiced' and 'voiceless' plosives are distinctive in White South African English, and voiceless plosives are generally unaspirated in all positions in

Broad White South African English, serving as a marker for this subvariety (Lass 2002: 120). Other varieties aspirate a voiceless plosive before a stressed syllable. The contrast is neutralised in Broad.

Broad speakers tend to pronounce /t, d/ with some dentition.

2.3.2. Fricatives and affricates

/f, v, θ, ð, s, z, ʃ, ʒ, x, h/

White South African English is one of very few varieties to have a velar frica-tive phoneme /x/, (see Lass 2002: 120) but this is only in words borrowed from Afrikaans (e.g. *gogga* [xoxə] = *bug, insect*) and Khoisan [x]*amtoos* (the name of a river). Many speakers use the Afrikaans uvular fricative [χ] rather than the velar.

The tendency for [θ] to be realised as [f] is a stereotypical Broad feature, but is more accurately associated with Afrikaans English (AfkE).

As in many varieties of English, word-final /v, ð, z, ʒ/ are usually voiceless, and are distinguished only by the length of the preceding vowel.

In Broad varieties close to AfkE, /h/ is realised as voiced [ɦ] before a stressed vowel.

2.3.3. Nasals

/m, n, ŋ/

The nasals are not distinctive markers for any variety of White South African English; though /n/ may be dental [n̪] before dental consonants.

2.3.4. Liquids

/j, w, r, l/

In Broad and some General WSAfE varieties, /j/ strengthens to /ɣ/ before a high front vowel: *yield* [ɣɪːɫd].

/r/ is usually postalveolar or retroflex [ɹ] in Cultivated and General WSAfE, while Broad varieties have [r] or sometimes even trilled [r]. The latter is more associated with the L2 Afrikaans English variety, though it is sometimes stig-matised as a marker of Broad (Lass 2002: 121). WSAfE is non-rhotic, los-ing postvocalic /r/, except (in some speakers) as a liaison between two words, when the /r/ is underlying in the first (*for a while, here and there* etc.) However, intrusive /r/ is not represented in other contexts: (*law and order*) [lɔːnɔːdə]. The intervocalic hiatus that is created by the absence of linking /r/ can be broken by vowel deletion, as in the example just given; by a corresponding glide [loːʷənoːdə], or by the insertion of a glottal stop: [loːʔənoːdə]. The latter is typical of Broad WSAfE. There is some evidence of postvocalic /r/ in some Broad Cape varieties, typically in *–er* suffixes (e.g. *writer*). This could be under the influence of Afrikaans (and it is a feature of Afrikaans English); or perhaps a remnant of (non-RP) British English from the Settlers. Postvocalic /r/ appears to be entering younger people's speech under the influence of American dialects. This is a development to be monitored; as yet it is not vernacular.

/l/ is clear [l] syllable initially, and dark (velarised) [ɫ] syllable finally. When /l/ occurs at the end of a word, but before another word beginning with a vowel, it tends to be realised as clear in Cultivated WSAfE (Lass 2002: 121).

Some (particularly older) Cultivated speakers retain the [w] ~ [w̥] distinction (as in *witch* ~ *which*, but this distinction is absent from General and Broad, which have only [w]).

3.   Conclusion

The most salient feature of WSAfE is perhaps the behaviour of KIT, DRESS, TRAP: TRAP and DRESS are raised (relative to RP and most other L1 varieties of English), and KIT is centralised. This has often been attributed to the influence of the Afrikaans vowel system (see e.g. Lanham 1968: 7ff). Lass and Wright proposed an alternative and more feasible alternative: that these three vowels are in fact involved in a chain shift. Raising of British/RP TRAP in (early) WSAfE encroached on DRESS, which itself raised (to keep the distinction), encroaching on KIT, which was pushed across towards [ɪ]. This can be illustrated as follows: the RP or input vowel is shown in miniscules, and the WSAfE innovation in capitals:

Figure 1.   The short front vowel chain shift in WSAfE

The diagram is taken from Lass (2002: 113); for a full elucidation of the chain shift, see Lass and Wright (1986: 207ff).

This identifies WSAfE as a Southern Hemisphere English, as Australian English and New Zealand English also show raising in the high front vowels; though neither have yet achieved the push from [ɪ] to more centralised [i], realising lowered [i] instead. AusE and NZE also share /i/ in happy with WSAfE. WSAfE and NZE share /ɑː/ in *dance, glass*, etc. (Trudgill and Hannah 1994:30). Some marked distinctions between WSAfE and AusE and NZE are:

- the behaviour of FLEECE, which is diphthongal [ɪi] ~ [ɪi] in the latter varieties (Lass 2002: 116)
- the backness of BATH: fully back [ɑː] in WSAfE, contrasting with the fully frontal [a] in AusE and NZE (Trudgill and Hannah 1994: 30).

The expansion of WSAfE to younger middle class members of other ethnic groups who have been exposed to different varieties of SAfE is a recent development, which is bound to have an impact on the variety in the future. The changes and conservations evoked by this development will be monitored with keen interest.

Exercises and study questions

1. Discuss the 'KIT-split' in WSAfE.

2. Outline the short front vowel chain shift in WSAfE.

3. Which diphthongs of WSAfE are subject to glide weakening?

4. What are the distinguishing characteristics of fricatives in WSAfE?

5. In what ways is WSAfE similar to other 'Southern Hemisphere Englishes' like those of Australia and New Zealand? In what vowel details does it differ?

Selected references

Please consult the General references for titles mentioned in the text but not included in the references below. For a full bibliography see the accompanying CD-ROM.

Lanham, Leonard W.
    1967   *The Way We Speak.* Pretoria, Van Schaik.
    1982   English in South Africa. In: Bailey and Görlach (eds.), 324–352.
    1996   A history of English in South Africa. In: de Klerk (ed.), 19–34.
Lass, Roger
    2002   South African English. In: Mesthrie (ed.), 104–126.
Lass, Roger and Susan Wright
    1986   Endogeny vs contact: "Afrikaans influence" on South African English. *English World-Wide* 7: 201–223.
Trudgill, Peter and Jean Hannah
    1994   *International English: A Guide to the Varieties of Standard English.* London: Edward Arnold. (3ʳᵈ ed.)
Watermeyer, Susan
    1996   Afrikaans English. In: de Klerk (ed.), 99–124.

Black South African English: phonology*

Bertus van Rooy

1. Introduction

There is little doubt that an African variety of English is very much part of the communicative economy of the new South Africa (for which I shall use the label Black South African English, in short BlSAfE). Since 1994, the year that ushered in a new democratic order, this variety has become prominent in parliament, administration, the media and so forth. Whereas the segregative and oppressive practices of apartheid had led to the development of a relatively homogenous second language variety, BlSAfE is today becoming slightly more diffuse. This reflects a new diversity of lifestyles, educational and cultural mixing, which sees English not only as the main language of a multilingual Black elite, but even making inroads into some homes. For some children English has become the first language. The hope persists in some quarters of South Africa that Black students should ideally have command over their first language and a variety of English that was more-or-less standard in grammar and not too deviant in accent/intonation from the southern British norms that have hitherto prevailed in broadcasting. Where the ideal fails (and it does for almost all but those educated in latter-day multi-racial or private schools in which Black pupils are in a minority), the educational system is held to blame (rightly in some instances). From studies of English elsewhere, however, we are also aware that even where the educational system is reasonably sound and on the side of the pupil (which was seldom the case in the Bantu education system of apartheid South Africa) an indigenised (or nativised) form of English is likely to develop. Whilst such a variety may not have a fully acknowledged status in its country of origin, it is more or less acceptable even in informal educational contexts.

Research on BlSAfE has understandably had a predominantly pedagogical bias. One approach involves an older prescriptivism which sought to pinpoint the distortions that English teachers 'suffered' in their L2 pupils, often attributing it to 'interference' from the mother tongues. Another trend which was motivated by developmental perspectives aimed at producing educational materials for different levels of schooling, focused more on written discourse than an already existing grammar of Black English. A third trend that has become prominent is one that aims at describing the grammar of Black English, partly by presenting its departures from standard English and by exploring the historical and cultural influences on the development of this new variety.

With the exception of work by Hundleby (1963) in the Eastern Cape, the phonology of BlSAfE has not been studied in any depth until recently. There have been a few publications examining aspects of BlSAfE pronunciation in the 1980s and 1990s (see bibliography on CD). A systematic attempt to study this variety has been initiated by Daan Wissing with a workshop on BlSAfE in January 2000 (proceedings circulated among the about 70 participants at the workshop), and subsequent publication of a volume of articles in Supplement 38 of the *South African Journal of Linguistics*, with five papers examining aspects of the pronunciation of BlSAfE (including Van Rooy 2000; Van Rooy and Van Huyssteen 2000; Van der Pas, Wissing and Zonneveld 2000). Subsequent work includes Van Rooy (2002) on stress placement, and Wissing (2002) who examined vowel perception and evaluated claims about differences in the pronunciation of speakers with different native languages.

The research on BlSAfE offers a picture that is very similar to work done on varieties of African English elsewhere on the continent. Vowel contrasts characteristic of the native varieties of English are reduced by neutralisation of the tense/lax contrast and the avoidance of central vowels, particularly schwa. Consonants are realised largely similar to native varieties, although consonant cluster simplification is observed in some cases. Stress placement is different from native varieties, the speech is syllable-timed rather than stress-timed and other prosodic aspects are also different, particularly in the more frequent occurrence of pragmatic emphasis, leading to a different intonation structure of spoken BlSAfE.

One important caveat must be stated before examining the phonology of BlSAfE. In work within the World/New Englishes paradigm, it is customary to distinguish different varieties of outer circle Englishes. These different varieties are often labelled as basilect, mesolect and acrolect, although these constitute a continuum. In previous work, I have already adopted this classification system and will continue to use it here, focussing on the mesolectal form of BlSAfE, but contrasting it where possible with the acrolectal variety. The basilectal variety has not been researched sufficiently to allow any claims made about it. The mesolectal variety described in this article is spoken fluently by educated speakers, but because of salient features of pronunciation (like vowel mergers) and certain features of grammar it would not be judged as overtly prestigious by speakers of the variety or other South Africans.

This chapter offers a survey of the phonological features of BlSAfE that have been established with some degree of certainty. In addition, to the extent that it is possible to distinguish between a mesolectal and acrolectal variety of BlSAfE, the different features of these two lects are outlined. Vowels are considered first, followed by consonants and selected suprasegmental features. I draw largely on my own previous research and that of my colleague Daan Wissing. In addition, I rely in a few cases on on-going, as yet unpublished data analyses of the speech of about forty speakers from the African Speech Technology database (*www.ast.sun.ac.za*) and detailed phonetic transcriptions, based on acoustic criteria, of informal spoken conversation of seven speakers from diverse mother tongue backgrounds, age groups and on different positions on the lectal continuum. The contribution of other researchers is reflected in the extended bibliography on the CD.

2.   Vowels

Like most other African varieties of English, BlSAfE is characterised by the absence of the tense/lax contrast and central vowels in the mesolectal variety. The typical realisations of vowels are represented in Table 1 below. The basis for the presentation in this table is the work of Van Rooy and Van Huyssteen (2000), but subsequent analyses were undertaken of data within the African Speech Technology project, particularly to refine the transcriptions of diphthongs.

Table 1.   The vowels of Black South African English (mesolect) – summary

KIT	i	FLEECE	i	PRICE	ʌɪ
FOOT	u	GOOSE	u	CHOICE	ɔɪ
TRAP	ε	DRESS	ε	SQUARE	ε
NURSE	ε	THOUGHT	ɔ	NEAR	e
LOT	ɔ	FORCE	ɔ	GOAT	ɔ > ɔʊ
CLOTH	ɔ	NORTH	ɔ	CURE	o
STRUT	ä	START	ä	FACE	εɪ ~ eɪ > ε
commA	ä	BATH	ä	MOUTH	ɔʊ > o
lettER	ä	PALM	ä		
happY	ɪ	horsES	i	About	ε ~ ə

The phonetic quality of the monophthongs, transcribed as tense vowels throughout, is in actual fact somewhat variable, and often a realisation that is intermediate between a tense and lax vowel is found. For instance, it is not uncommon to find that the vowel in both FLEECE and KIT are realised with a first formant value of 350Hz and second formant of just below 2000Hz by male speakers. Vowel length is variable. In terms of our current understanding, there is no systematic use of vowel length to distinguish between pairs like FLEECE and KIT, but lengthening may take place as cue for stress placement. Thus, length may perform a suprasegmental function, but it is not distinctive at phonemic level.

Central vowels are realised as mid front vowels or as central low vowels. Typically, the tense vowel in NURSE is realised as [ɛ]. A schwa in the final syllable of native varieties of SAfE, particularly if the syllable is open, is usually realised as a low vowel in BlSAfE, transcribed as [ä] in Table 1 above, but its phonetic quality ranges from slightly backed to slightly fronted. In the majority of all cases, the second formant value of this vowel is below 1500Hz for male voices, but seldom below 1300Hz.

More variability is observed with the realisation of the vowel in the first syllable of *About*, and other unstressed vowels that do not occur in final syllables. Previous research (particularly Van Rooy and Van Huyssteen 2000, also see references there) suggests that in syllables other than open final syllables, the dominant allophone for native varieties' schwa is [ɛ], while the allophone [ə] is also observed but with less frequency. An analysis of further data from the African Speech Technology databases suggests that the frequency of schwa might actually be higher, although distributed slightly differently than in native varieties of English, because of differences in stress placement between mesolect BlSAfE and other varieties, but the main finding remains that the forms [ɛ] and [ə] are the two variants in perhaps roughly equal distribution and by far the two most frequent forms in unstressed syllables. There also appears to be a preference for letter pronunciation, selecting the allophone [ɔ], in the case of items spelled with the letter 'o' in unstressed syllables, such as the second syllable of the word 'opportunity'. Finally, while the examples analysed are not sufficient to allow a definite statement, there appears to be a tendency (80% or more of the analysed cases, but type frequency low in the corpus) to pronounce a lax [ʊ] in final closed syllables between a labial obstruent in onset position and a final lateral [l], for example in the words 'double' or 'careful'.

In summary, there are essentially five contrastive vowel phonemes in mesolectal BlSAfE: /i/, /ɛ/, /a/, /ɔ/ and /u/. Perception studies by Wissing (2002) confirm this phonemic structure of mesolect BlSAfE, and also indicate that there is very little difference between BlSAfE speakers with different native languages.

The diphthongs are very often realised as monophthongs. Van Rooy and Van Huyssteen (2000) claim that more centralised acoustic values are used, but maintain that too little tongue movement (as judged by an analysis of movement in the first and second formant values) takes place to warrant transcription of these phones as diphthongs. Subsequent analysis of diphthongs in the African Speech Technology speech corpus reveals that a number of diphthongs are found, particularly in PRICE, CHOICE, FACE and MOUTH, and sometimes also in GOAT. These diphthongs are all rising diphthongs, and are realised as diphthongs in most varieties of English. The remainder of the diphthongs of SAfE, the centring diphthongs that occur in the words SQUARE, NEAR and CURE, are almost always realised as monophthongs in BlSAfE, but this happens in other varieties of English as well, notably many American English varieties. Since mesolectal forms of BlSAfE avoid central vowels otherwise, it is not surprising that these diphthong phonemes that have a central vowel as their offset target are realised by monophthong phones. One can conclude that there are six contrastive phonemes, additional to the five used for monophthongs, which are mainly used for the diphthongs of native varieties of SAfE: /ʌɪ/, /ɔɪ/, /aʊ/, /eɪ/, /e/ and /o/. Hundleby (1963) and others after him have claimed to observe the occurrence of vowel-glide-vowel sequences as realisations of the diphthongs in the speech of BlSAfE. While a small number of such cases were observed in the data, they account for less than 1% of the realisations of all the vowel types represented by diphthongs in SAfE, and less than 10% for any one of the separate vowel types. Also, there is no indication of a systematic use of vowel length to realise the diphthong phonemes, with no single diphthong having a long vowel allophone in more than 20% of all observed cases.

As pointed out earlier, it is important to consider differences between the pronunciation of the acrolect and mesolect varieties of BlSAfE. Apart from Hundleby (1963), such differences have not received serious consideration. In the discussion to follow, I rely on results of my own on-going research into this variety.

Table 2. The vowels of Black South African English (acrolect) – summary

KIT	ɪ > i	FLEECE	i > ɪ	PRICE	ʌɪ > ʌ
FOOT	ʊ > u	GOOSE	ʊ > u	CHOICE	ɔɪ
TRAP	ɛ ~ æ	DRESS	ɛ	SQUARE	ɛ ~ e
NURSE	ɜ ~ ə > ɛ	THOUGHT	ɔ	NEAR	e
LOT	ɔ ~ ɒ	FORCE	ɔ	GOAT	o ~ ɔ > əʊ
CLOTH	ɔ ~ ɒ	NORTH	ɔ	CURE	ʔ

Table 2. (Continued)   The vowels of Black South African English (acrolect) –
summary

STRUT	ʌ > ä	START	ä ~ ʌ	FACE	e ~ ɛɪ
commA	ə	BATH	ä ~ ʌ	MOUTH	aʊ > ɔ
lettER	ə	PALM	ä ~ ʌ		
happY	ɪ > i	horsES	ɪ ~ ə	About	ə

A comparison between the mesolect and acrolect data suggests that the acrolect
is closer to native varieties of SAfE in many respects, but at the same time, it
is characterised by more variability rather than less. A particularly noteworthy
property of the acrolect is the use of both tense and lax monophthong phonemes. In some cases, there is a degree of contrast between pairs such as KIT x
FLEECE, LOT x NORTH and STRUT x START, but many exceptions are also
observed. In the case of the pair FOOT x GOOSE, the lax allophone occurs far
more frequently than the tense allophone, but no consistent contrast/opposition
is maintained.

Related to the use of lax vowels in the acrolect form is the use of central
vowels, and most significantly, the schwa. Reduced vowels occur in the
acrolect form of BlSAfE in ways very similar to native varieties of SAfE, and
the low vowel phone as realisation of a native schwa has disappeared almost
completely.

In comparison to the five phonemes of the mesolect, /i/, /ɛ/, /a/, /ɔ/ and /u/,
the acrolect also uses /ɪ/, /ɜ/ and /ʌ/ as phonemes, with /æ/ and /ɒ/ emerging as
phonemes, although not with enough consistency to regard them as established
phonemes yet.

The diphthongs are perhaps the area where the acrolect and mesolect are
more similar than other aspects of the vowel system. Lots of variation is observed in the speakers' rendition of the phonemes represented by the words in
Table 2. In general, variants of the same five diphthongs, the rising diphthongs,
occur that also occur in the mesolect, while the centring diphthongs are realised as monophthongs in the acrolect as well. At the time of writing, I have
insufficient evidence about the realisation of the vowel in cure to make any
strong claims, but suspect that it will be realised as monophthong [o], similar
to the mesolect. There are no further diphthong phonemes in the speech of the
acrolect speakers, as compared to the mesolect speakers.

One last comment must be made about the vowel pronunciation of BlSAfE.
In white native varieties of SAfE, there is a unique vowel contrast, usually represented by the pair KIT *vs.* SIT. KIT is pronounced similar to major British varieties, but SIT is realised with a vowel quality closer to schwa, or at least a much

more centralised variant of [ɪ]. In the mesolectal variety of BlSAfE, both these words are realised by a high front vowel, but in the acrolect form, the contrast is sometimes maintained, with the allophones [ɪ] and [ə] both observed with roughly equal frequency. Thus, while not with the same consistency of native varieties of SAfE, acrolect BlSAfE has an emerging contrast between KIT and SIT too.

3.　Consonants

Hundleby (1963: 101) already claimed that the consonants of BlSAfE are more similar to native varieties of SAfE than the vowels, a claimed confirmed by most subsequent publications. The most important phonemes and allophones of mesolect and acrolect BlSAfE are presented in Table 3.

Table 3. The consonants of Black South African English

Phoneme	Mesolect allophones	Acrolect allophones
/p/	[p, ph]	[p, ph]
/t/	[t, th]	[t, th]
/k/	[k, kh]	[k, kh]
/b/	[b, ɓ]	[b, ɓ]
/d/	[d, ɗ]	[d, ɗ]
/g/	[g,ɠ]	[g, ɠ]
/f/	[f]	[f]
/θ/	[t] > [θ]	[θ]
/s/	[s]	[s]
/ʃ/	[ʃ] ~ [s]	[ʃ]
/v/	[v]	[v]
/ð/	[d]	[ð] > [d]
/z/	[z]	[z]
/ʒ/	[s] > [z]	[ʒ]
/tʃ/	[ʃ]	[ʃ] ~ [tʃ]
/dʒ/	[dʒ] ~ [ʒ]	[dʒ] > [ʃ] ~ [ʒ]
/m/	[m]	[m]
/n/	[n]	[n]

Table 3. (continued)   The consonants of Black South African English

Phoneme	Mesolect allophones	Acrolect allophones
/ŋ/	[ŋ]	[ŋ]
/l/	[l]	[l]
/r/	[r]	[r] ~ [ɹ]
/h/	[ɦ]	[h] > [ɦ]
/w/	[w]	[w]
/j/	[j]	[j]

Plosives in BlSAfE are similar to native varieties of SAfE in respect of manner and place of articulation. Final devoicing takes place very consistently, while regressive voicing assimilation is observed in the speech of Tswana speakers, but it is not certain if this is true for all BlSAfE speakers and has not been researched yet. A slightly more widespread distribution of word initial devoicing of [g] has been reported and observed in some of my data, but it is not a consistent phenomenon, and there is no suggestion of the neutralisation of the voicing contrast between the phonemes /k/ and /g/. In the acrolect form, most of these features are maintained, so there is little difference between the two varieties of BlSAfE in this respect.

Aspiration occurs regularly, and is phonemic in all the Southern Bantu languages. In the mesolect, aspiration is present in slightly more than half of the syllable-initial plosive onsets (excluding those followed by sonorants before the nucleus vowel), while this increases to about three quarters in the acrolect. Some aspiration is also observed in other positions, but usually in less than a quarter of all cases (see Van Rooy 2000 on the mesolect).

The dental fricatives /θ, ð/ in mesolectal BlSAfE are usually realised as plosives, with both dental and alveolar articulations observed, but nothing further back towards the post-alveolar place of articulation, whereas in the acrolect two thirds or more of these phonemes are realised as fricatives, with some inter-speaker variation. The palatal fricatives /ʃ, ʒ/ tend to become alveolar [s, z], particularly in the case of the voiced /ʒ/, while the acrolectal speakers again approximate the phonetic quality of the native varieties of SAfE more closely. In the case of all these fricatives, the voiceless /θ/ and /ʃ/ are more likely to be realised as fricatives, while the voiced /ð/ and /ʒ/ are more likely realised as plosives. Final devoicing also affects fricatives consistently in the acrolect and mesolect.

The affricates /tʃ, dʒ/ show lots of variation in the mesolect and the acrolect. In the mesolect, the voiceless /tʃ/ is realised as fricative [ʃ] in most cases, while /dʒ/ is realised by at least five different allophones, including [dʒ] and [ʃ] each occurring in about one third of the observed cases. In the acrolect, the allophones [tʃ] and [dʒ] occur in about half of all cases, with the fricative variants [ʃ] and [ʒ] being observed in most other cases.

The sonorants are generally very similar to native varieties of SAfE. The nasals show little if any difference, while the liquid /l/ has some co-articulatory velarisation in the environment of back vowels, but perhaps less so than in native varieties of SAfE. The rhotic /r/ is generally realised by a trilled [r] in the mesolect, and this remains the case in just more than half of all observed cases in the acrolect, although the approximant [ɹ] is observed in the remainder of the cases. The glottal sound /h/ is usually realised as a voiced [ɦ] in the mesolect, but the acrolect is characterised by a voiceless [h] in the majority of cases. The other two glides, /j/ and /w/ are very similar in BlSAfE and native varieties of SAfE (cf. Van Rooy 2000).

4.   Suprasegmental structure

Two aspects of suprasegmental structure have been examined in some detail. Van Rooy (2000) presents an analysis of syllable structure restrictions in the mesolect, and Van der Pas, Wissing and Zonneveld (2000), and Van Rooy (2002) analyse stress placement in the mesolect. Very little is known about the acrolect, and it will therefore not be discussed here.

The Bantu languages generally do not allow consonant clusters in the onsets of syllables, and do not allow syllable codas. BlSAfE is clearly not bound by the syllable structure constraints of the Bantu languages. Van Rooy (2000) indicates that onset clusters in BlSAfE are generally no different from other varieties of SAfE. More recent data analysis suggests that the rhotic phoneme /r/ is under pressure to delete in onset clusters, particularly in spontaneous speech as opposed to read speech. Some simplification occurs in the codas, particularly where more than one obstruent is present in the same coda. In cases such as *perfect* or *eats*, a plosive is likely to be deleted. Faithful realisation of two underlying obstruents in syllable codas occurs in less than a third of all observed cases, but it is uncertain if other varieties of English in South Africa are not perhaps subject to similar simplification – the relevant comparative data have not been examined to the best of my knowledge.

Previous work on stress in BlSAfE offers very little conclusive analysis or interpretation. Generally, researchers claim that stress in BlSAfE is different from native varieties of SAfE and present examples of such differences. Interpretation is often restricted to the claim that the penultimate lengthening phenomenon of the Bantu languages is transferred to BlSAfE. Van Rooy (2002) examines a small corpus of data from mesolect speakers and concludes that there is indeed a highly systematic system for stress placement in the mesolect BlSAfE. A very salient property is the syllable-timed rhythm of BlSAfE, as opposed to the stress-timed rhythm of most native varieties (Wissing, Gustafson and Coetzee 2000). Consequently, Van Rooy (2002) argues that there is no organisation of syllables into metrical feet in BlSAfE. Stress assignment is on the second last syllable, e.g. *sevénty*, except when the final syllable is superheavy, i.e. it has a tensed vowel (usually a diphthong) and coda consonant, e.g. *campáign* or any vowel and a consonant cluster in the coda, e.g. *contrást*. In such cases, stress is assigned to the final syllable.

In older research, a few relevant observations are made about other aspects of prosodic structure in BlSAfE. Gennrich-de Lisle (1985) claims that tone/information units in BlSAfE are shorter than in native varieties of SAfE; there are consequently more syllables and words that receive semantic stress than in native varieties of SAfE. Furthermore, they identify a general lowering of pitch through the course of a sentence, combined with a weakening of the intensity. No recent work has been done on these properties, and too little is known about the acrolect to judge whether this is also true for the acrolect.

* Part of the introduction was originally prepared by R. Mesthrie in connection with the companion piece on BlSAfE syntax. I wish to acknowledge my colleague Daan Wissing for his contribution to my research and this article.

Exercises and study questions

1. Compare the vowels of BlSAfE with those of EAfrE.

2. Compare the consonants of BlSAfE with those of EAfrE

3. Compare the vowels of BlSAfE with those of CamE or any other variety of West African English.

4. Compare the consonants of BlSAfE with those of CamE or any other variety of West African English.

5. Discuss the treatment of diphthongs in BlSAfE.

Selected references

Please consult the General references for titles mentioned in the text but not included in the references below. For a full bibliography see the accompanying CD-ROM.

Gennrich-de Lisle, Daniela
   1985   Theme in conversational discourse: Problems experienced by speakers of Black South African English, with particular reference to the role of prosody in conversational synchrony. M.A. thesis, Department of Linguistics, Rhodes University.
Hundleby, C. E.
   1963   Xhosa-English pronunciation in the south-east Cape. Ph.D. thesis, Rhodes University.
Van der Pas, Brigit, Daan Wissing and Wim Zonneveld
   2000   Parameter resetting in metrical phonology: the case of Setswana and English. *South African Journal of Linguistics* Supplement 38: 55–87.
Van Rooy, Bertus
   2000   The consonants of BSAE: current knowledge and future prospects. *South African Journal of Linguistics* Supplement 38: 35–54.
   2002   Stress placement in Tswana English: the makings of a coherent system. *World Englishes* 21: 145–160.
Van Rooy, Bertus and Gerhard B. van Huyssteen
   2000   The vowels of BSAE: current knowledge and future prospects. *South African Journal of Linguistics* Supplement 38: 15–33.
Wissing, Daan
   2002   Black South African English: a new English? Observations from a phonetic viewpoint. *World Englishes* 21: 129–144.
Wissing, Daan, Kjell Gustafson and Andries Coetzee
   2000   Temporal organisation in some varieties of South African English: Syllable compression effects in different types of foot structures. In: Daan Wissing (ed.), Proceedings *of the Workshop on Black South African English*, 59–68. Linguistics Society of Southern Africa Conference, Cape Town, 12–14 January 2000.

Indian South African English: phonology

Rajend Mesthrie

1.   Introduction

South African Indian English (henceforth InSAfE) is worthy of the attention of sociolinguists for a variety of reasons. It offers the opportunity of exam-ining in a relatively fossilised form (on account of former rigid segregative tendencies in South Africa) the evolution of a dialect of English under less than perfect conditions concerning educational and social contact with target-language speakers. It provides, again in a relatively fossilised form, the oppor-tunity of studying the changes a language undergoes as it shifts from L2 to L1. Indian languages have existed in large numbers in South Africa, chiefly in the province of Natal (now KwaZulu-Natal), since 1860. Their existence in this country is ultimately a consequence of the abolition of slavery in the European colonies. Colonial planters in many parts of the world looked to migrant labour from Asian countries to fill the gap caused by the understandable reluctance of slaves to remain on the plantations once they were legally free. The British-ad-ministered Indian government permitted the recruiting of labourers to a variety of colonial territories. This resulted in a great movement of hundreds of thou-sands of Indian labourers first to Mauritius (1834), then British Guyana (1838), Jamaica and Trinidad (1844), and subsequently to various other West Indian islands, Natal, Suriname and Fiji. Although Natal was a new colony that had not employed slave labour, the policy of consigning the indigenous, mainly Zulu-speaking population into `reserves' created a demand for Indian labour on the sugar, tea and coffee plantations. Just over 150 000 workers came to Natal on indentured contracts between 1860 and 1911. A large majority chose to stay on in South Africa on expiry of their five or ten year contracts.

The languages spoken by the indentured workers were as follows:

(a) From the South of India chiefly Tamil and Telugu, and in small numbers – Malayalam and Kannada. The latter two languages did not have suffi-ciently large numbers of speakers to survive beyond a generation in South Africa.
(b) From the north of India a variety of Indo-European languages including Bhojpuri, Awadhi, Magahi, Kanauji, Bengali, Rajasthani, Braj, etc. These

dialects coalesced to form one South African vernacular, usually termed 'Hindi'.

(c) A small number of Muslims amongst the indentured labourers (about 10% among North Indians and slightly fewer amongst South Indians) would have spoken the village language of their area as well as varieties of Urdu.

From 1875 onwards smaller numbers of Indians of trading background arrived in Natal, establishing languages like Gujarati, Konkani and Meman which are still spoken today in South Africa. In addition to these spoken languages people of Hindu background used Sanskrit as their prestige religious language, while Muslims looked to Arabic for this purpose.

The sociolinguistic milieu in which Indians found themselves was a particularly complex one. Not only did they lack a knowledge of English and Zulu, but they would not always have been able to converse amongst themselves. In particular people from the north, speaking Indo-European languages, would not have been able to understand people from the south who spoke Dravidian languages. Furthermore only about 2% of incoming Indians had a knowledge of English (these would have been Christian Indians, some of whom had been recruited as teachers or a small proportion of the trading-class Indians). Under these circumstances a pidgin English might have arisen, but for the prior existence of a Zulu-based pidgin, Fanakalo. The learning of English was a relatively gradual process (see Mesthrie 1992: 11-33), though Gandhi mentions the use of English by some urban youths amongst themselves, in a newspaper article of 1909 – i.e. before the end of the period of indenture. Multilingualism and the lack of a lingua franca of Indian origin resulted in a shift to English (not without regrets and resistance) by the 1960s, when English started to be introduced as a language of the home. The period of language shift can be thought of as gradual or rapid, depending on one's defining criteria. As 1960 was exactly one hundred years since the first immigrations, the period of shift might seem a gradual one; but as 1960 was also less than fifty years since the last shipload, the period is perhaps not all that gradual.

The kind of English that stabilised was, as I have already indicated, a very special one, given that the policy of apartheid (1948-1991) kept Indian children away from first-language speakers of English descent, in hospitals, homes, neighbourhoods, public facilities, schools, and even universities. The result is that whilst being quite South African in some respects (aspects of lexis and phonology), it is a recognisably different variety of South African English. The peculiarities of apartheid society have ensured that there is continuity between IndE and InSAfE (in aspects of pronunciation, lexis and syntax). The relationship between the two varieties is not straightforward, however. Some of the early input into InSAfE was indeed directly from India, but of a diverse nature. This included: (a) the first generation of clerks, interpreters and teachers brought over in small numbers, (b) indentured workers of Christian background, mainly from South India, (c) some traders from India with a previous knowledge of English and (d) political leaders from India (e.g. Gandhi, Sastri, Gokhale). But given the fact that most first generation immigrants did not learn English we should be careful not to overestimate the links between IndE and InSAfE. Although the second and third generations learnt English without direct contact with India, conditions of acquisition and teaching were such that there was considerable transfer from the Indian languages. This was a factor that ensured further continuity between InSAfE and IndE. However, in South Africa the substrate comprised of both Indic and Dravidian languages, causing a blend of Indic and Dravidian influence in InSAfE that I suspect is not found in India. And, of course, the features of L1 English of Natal as well as contact with Zulu and (to a small extent) Afrikaans made InSAfE further diverge from IndE.

InSAfE uses a great many words of Indian origin and a great many neologisms from other sources (see Mesthrie 1992b, a lexicon comprising about 1400 of such items). Only a few of these have passed into the wider society. These tend to be terms pertaining to vegetables (e.g. *dhania* 'coriander') and culinary terms (e.g. *masala* 'ground spices', *roti* 'flat, round unleavened bread', *bunny chow* 'half a loaf of bread stuffed with curry').

2.   Segmental phonology

InSAfE has been studied mostly as a contact variety that involves a great deal of syntactic variation. If less attention has been paid to its phonetics, it has to do with the paucity of researchers working on the accents of varieties of South African English (SAfE) rather than any intrinsic qualities of InSAfE phonetics. On the contrary, InSAfE holds the promise of subtle variations along the following dimensions:

(a) Five substrate languages belonging to two distinct language families: Dravidian (Tamil, Telugu) and Indo-European (Bhojpuri-Hindi, Gujarati, Urdu, Konkani and Sindhi/Meman dialect);
(b) Links with IndE (the English of India);
(c) Links with South African varieties of English, especially varieties spoken in KwaZulu-Natal;
(d) Emergence of a core InSAfE phonology as younger speakers lose contact with the languages of their grandparents' generation;

(e) Ongoing acculturation amongst middle-class speakers to "General" and "Cultivated" varieties of SAfE as the rigid barriers between young people of different backgrounds weaken, especially in the post-apartheid school-grounds;

(f) Regional variation within InSAfE, involving the main dialect in KwaZulu-Natal and smaller pockets in other provinces – Gauteng, Eastern Cape and Western Cape.

The description below is based on my analysis of a cross section of tape recordings carried out in the mid-1980s, reported in Mesthrie (1992: 34-43) for fieldwork, (1992:136-141) for phonetics. These have been supplemented by more recent recordings in the late 1990s and early 2000s. In addition I rely on earlier discussions by Bailey (c 1985, unpublished notes), Naidoo (1971) and Bughwan (1970).

Table 1. The vowels of Indian South African English (mesolect) – summary

KIT	ï>ɪ>ɣ̈	FLEECE	i:	PRICE	aɪ
FOOT	ʊ>ɣ	GOOSE	u:>ʉ:	CHOICE	ɔɪ
TRAP	ɛ>æ	DRESS	e>ë>ɛ̈	SQUARE	e:
NURSE	ɜ:>e:	THOUGHT	ɔ:>ɒ	NEAR	ijɛ>ɪə
LOT	ɒ>ɔ:	FORCE	ɔ:>ɒ	GOAT	oʊ
CLOTH	ɒ	NORTH	ɔ:>ɒ	CURE	jɔ:
STRUT	ʌ	START	ɑ:	FACE	eɪ
*comm*A	ɑ:	BATH	ɑ:	MOUTH	aʊ
*lett*ER	ɛ	PALM	ɑ:		
*happ*Y	i:	*hors*ES	ə	*About*	ɛ>a

2.1. The short monophthongs

1. KIT: As with general SAfE, InSAfE shows a 'KIT-split'. That is, the value before or after velar and glottal consonants is [ɪ] (as in *kit, big, sing, hit, sick, give*). The most common realisation in other contexts is a centralised vowel [ï] (as in *bit, fit, sit, bin*, etc.). Further retraction before /l/ as in *bill, kill, will* to [ɪ] or [ɣ̈] is possible.

2. DRESS: The usual realisation of this vowel is [e] or a slightly centralised [ë], which differs from raised equivalents in general SAfE and [ɛ] in varieties of British and American English. Before /l/ the latter ([ɛ]) does occur with some centralising, as in *bell, sell*, etc.

3. TRAP: The usual realisation of this vowel is a lowered [ɛ] or raised [æ]. In this regard it differs from raised equivalents like [e] in broad SAfE or fully lowered equivalents like [æ] in RP and general American English.

4. FOOT: The usual realisation in InSAfE is a weakly-rounded back [ʊ]. An unrounded, lowered variant [ɤ] may also occur. Centralising of the vowel, which is an increasing feature of varieties of L1 English world-wide, is not associated with core InSAfE. However, younger speakers in contact with general SAfE may show this feature in certain non-vernacular styles.

5. STRUT: The usual realisation is [ʌ], which is a low back vowel. Although some centralisation is possible within the InSAfE spectrum it is never as fronted as younger, general SAfE centralised [ɜ̈]. Allophones are more re-tracted before velars, as in *duck* and *rug*, which have [ʌ].

6. LOT: The usual realisation is [ɒ], a weakly-rounded back vowel. The un-rounding and centralising that one finds among younger, general SAfE speakers, is not an option in InSAfE. There is some sharing between el-ements of the LOT and CAUGHT sets among older InSAfE speakers. In vernacular styles the following may be lengthened to [ɔː]: *lot, coffee, pond, pod, boss, salt.*
    Before nasals there is an age-graded difference in the treatment of the LOT vowel. Some older speakers have [ʌ] in words like *comment, condemn, non-whites.* This is probably an inheritance from IndE, as speakers at-tempted an approximation of schwa. Younger InSAfE speakers generally produce [ɒ] here, though *non-* allows [ɒ] or [ɔː]. Related words like *tomato* and *connect* are discussed under schwa (section 2.4).

2.2.   The long monophthongs

7. NURSE: The most usual variant is [ɜː], a mid-central, unrounded vowel, slightly closer than RP [ɜː]. A variant amongst middle-class, and mostly female speakers, is similar to RP [ɜː], but possibly overshooting this target to a slightly fronted and lowered equivalent. Older speakers of an Indo-European background (chiefly Bhojpuri-Hindi and Urdu) use [ɛː] or [eː] here. The rounding of the NURSE vowel that one finds in some varieties of SAfE does not occur in InSAfE.

8. FLEECE: The FLEECE vowel is uniformly [iː] as in all L1 varieties of SAfE.

9. GOOSE: This vowel tends to retain a back, rounded quality [uː]; the cen-tralised and weakly-rounded quality [üː] spreading in young peoples' L1

English worldwide is not generally part of InSAfE. Younger InSAfE speakers may well have the latter [uː] as a stylistic option. After palatalised consonants as in *few*, *news* the centralised [uː] is the norm.

10. PALM: [ɑː] is a low back, unrounded vowel. It is neither as back as its equivalent in broad SAfE nor subject to raising or rounding.

11. THOUGHT: The usual vowel in InSAfE is [ɔː], a half-open, weakly-rounded, back vowel. For some speakers raising to [oː] occurs in formal styles, under influence of general SAfE. A less prestigious variant involves shortening to [ɒ] in words like *taught* (vernacular form [t̪ɒt], *shorts* [ʃɒts], *caught* [kɒt], *north* [n̪ɒt̪]). There is thus a fair amount of overlap in the membership of the sets LOT and THOUGHT (see 6 above in section 2.1). After /w/ in words like *war, warm, water* the usual vowel is [ɑː], not the raised and rounded [ɔː] of general SAfE, RP, and other varieties.

12. START: Postvocalic /r/ is not pronounced in InSAfE, the only exception being the letter *r* itself, which is pronounced [ɑːr] with a weak trill. The usual vowel here is [ɑː].

13. NORTH: The usual vowel here is [ɔː], which is a half-open, weakly-rounded, back vowel. Raising to [oː] does not occur, except as a prestige variant for some speakers in formal styles. A less prestigious variant involves shortening to [ɒ] in words like *taught, shorts, caught, north* (see 11 above).

14. FORCE: FORCE behaves the same as NORTH. That is the usual vowel is [ɔː], with [oː] a prestige variant in formal styles. A less prestigious variant involves shortening to [ɒ] in words like *sports, horse, orphan*.

2.3.   The diphthongs

15. FACE: The only realisation is [eɪ]. The first element tends to be short, as is the [ɪ] glide. In this regard InSAfE differs from varieties of SAfE which involve varying degrees of lowering, with centralising of the [e].

16. GOAT: The usual diphthong here is [oʊ] with a weakly-rounded first element. For some speakers the glide [ʊ] is short, resulting in [oᵘ] as a variant. However, monophthongal [oː], as in varieties of northern British English, is rare. The range of the initial element /o/ ranges from back to central-back, but does not approach fully-central or fronted or lowered variants found in other varieties of SAfE.

17. PRICE: The usual variant here is [aɪ], with degrees of centralising of the [a]. The glide element [ɪ] is not weakened in contrast to other varieties

of SAfE, including local prestige 'white' varieties in KwaZulu-Natal, in which a tendency towards monophthongisation exists.

18. CHOICE: The usual variant here is [ɔɪ], with half-open [ɔ]. Closer variants involving [o] may be used by some speakers in formal public styles, in response to the greater prestige of this variant within general SAfE.

19. MOUTH: The usual variant is [ɑʊ], with fronter pronunciations of the first element in the direction of [a] also possible. The gliding element [ʊ] is not weakened, unlike general SAfE, where a tendency towards monophthongisation is present.

20. NEAR: The usual pronunciation of this diphthong is [iːjɛ], that is a long [iː] and a fairly open [ɛ] are spread over two syllables with an intervening glide [j]; thus [fiːjɛ] 'fear', [t∫iːjɛ] 'cheer', etc. However, [ɪə] surfaces in polysyllabic words like *fea*rsome [frəsm̩], and ch*ee*rful [t∫ɪəfl̩].

21. SQUARE: This diphthong is usually reduced to the long monophthong [eː] as in general SAfE. The [eː] is slightly retracted in InSAfE. The RP equivalent [ɛə] is associated with 'Speech and Drama' accents, and is not aimed at by InSAfE speakers outside the acting world.

Some speakers exhibit considerable overlap between the NURSE and SQUARE vowels, i.e. between [ɜː] and [eː]. A cross-over is sometimes heard between pairs like *fur-fair*, with [eː] – [ɜː] respectively, rather than the expected reverse pattern of other varieties. Likewise *hair* and *parents* may each waver between centralised [eː] and [ɜː].

2.4.   Other vowels

22. CURE: This is a mixed bag in InSAfE, as in SAfE generally. *Cure* and *pure* have [jɔː]; *sure* has [ɔː]; *poor* and *tour* have [ʊə]; while *plural* and *jury* have [uː].

23. happY: This class takes a half-lengthened /i/ i.e. [iˑ]

24. lettER: The norm for final schwa in InSAfE is /ɛ/, a half-open to open vowel. It is subject to style-shifting, with middle-class speakers producing [ə] in formal styles.

25. horsES: The usual vowel here is [ə].

26. commA: Words spelt with final *a* - *sofa, zebra, comma* – typically take a half-lengthened /ɑ/, i.e. [ɑː]. Bailey notes a minimal pair *mynah–miner* having [ɑː] and [ɛ] respectively in InSAfE.

28. About: The usual vowel here is /æ/ ranging from [ɛ] to [a]. Schwa occurs in non-vernacular contexts. Schwa is absent in some words like *tomato* and *connect*. The first vowel in *tomato* is [ʌ] for older speakers. ([tʌˈmaːtou]); and [ʌ] or [ɒ] for younger speakers. For *connect* the first vowel is generally unreduced [kɒˈnekt].

2.5. Stops

P, T, K have aspiration patterns that differ from the prototypical English patterns of aspiration. As this is a complex issue, it is discussed under 'current research' below.

There is not much to be said about B, D, G as a set. T, D however, are subject to variation. The usual variants are alveolar [t] and [d]. However, retroflex variants are still heard, though this feature is recessive in InSAfE, and not the prominent characteristic it is in IndE. Furthermore, the degree of retroflexion (curling of the tongue tip to strike the palate) is not as strong in InSAfE. Retroflex /ʈ/ and /ɖ/ are far outnumbered by their alveolar equivalents and there are no contrasts made between [t] and [ʈ] or between [d] and [ɖ]. They are stylistic variants: the more 'public' or 'formal' the speech, the less retroflexion; the more vernacular the context and emphatic the utterance, the greater the likelihood of some retroflexion. Thus *die* might ordinarily have alveolar [d] but in emphatic (vernacular) utterance, G*o and die!*, the chances of a retroflex [ɖ] increase.

2.6. Nasals

M, N, and /ŋ/ are unremarkable, except for the occasional retroflexion of N, under the same conditions as for T and D. It is more likely to be retroflexed homorganically with /ʈ/ and /ɖ/, rather than on its own. Thus *send* may appear as [seɳɖ] and *aunty* as [ɑːɳʈiː] in certain styles, but *sin* and *sun* do not have retroflex [ɳ].

2.7. Fricatives

F and V are realised more as approximants [ʋ] and [ʋ̥], rather than as fricatives; i.e. contact between the lower lip and upper teeth is made without the audible friction that one finds in RP or SAfE. The *v/w* overlap that one finds in IndE is rare and recessive in InSAfE; only some older speakers say things like *wamit* [ˈwʌmɪt] for *vomit*.

/θ/ and /ð/ are regularly realised as dental stops /t̪/ and /d̪/, thus *theme* = [t̪iːm], *weather* = [wed̪ɛ] and *then* = [d̪en]. An interesting set of substitution of dental [t̪] for the alveolar stop [t] concerns words dealing with the mouth cavity: *tooth, teeth, tongue, tonsil* all have an initial dental stop, making a set with *throat*. Likewise, though *teach* has initial [t], *taught* has initial dental [t̪], possibly a dissimilation from the final [t] or based on an analogy with *thought*.

/s/ and /z/ are regular alveolar fricatives. Likewise there is little significant difference between /ʃ/, /ʒ/, /tʃ/ and /dʒ/ in InSAfE and general SAfE. Combinations of /t/ or /d/ with /j/ may be realised as [tʃ] and [dʒ], thus *tune* = [tʃuːn] and *deuce* = [dʒuːs] for some speakers.

/h/ has several realisations, depending on speakers' language and social class backgrounds. People of North Indian origin usually produce a voiced fricative [ɦ] or a murmured (breathy-voiced) fricative [ɦ̤]. People of South Indian background, especially Tamil, tend to produce what is popularly seen as H-dropping. That is H is realised as either a glottal construction (with discernible rise in pitch of a following vowel), or as a weak murmur on a following vowel. Within the InSAfE community H-dropping is a stereotype associated mainly with Tamil speakers. Some speakers of this group may even produce hypercorrections like *hant* for 'ant' and *hout-'ouse* for 'out-house'. Occasionally speakers substitute a 'euphonic' [j] and [w] in place of *h* (*yill, yad, liveliwood*, for 'hill', 'had', 'livelihood'). More generally some 'euphonic' [j] and [w] occurs amongst older speakers of Dravidian background as in *yevery* for 'every', but this is recessive in InSAfE.

/l/ is reported to have 'light' (= non-velarised) allophones in place of dark (velarised) ones in words like *ball*. (Bughwan 1970). This feature has not been studied to ascertain if there have been more recent changes. As far as /r/ is concerned, InSAfE is non-rhotic (in strong contrast to IndE); the only exception being the pronunciation of the letter *r* itself as [ɑːr], as in all SAfE varieties. /r/ varies between an approximant or obstruent [r], depending on linguistic context and speaker variables. In clusters it is usually a rolled *r* as in *trap, drake, break*. In initial position it is either an approximant or a roll. Linking and intrusive /r/ are uncommon, since [ʔ] is used instead. Thus *far out* is likely to be pronounced as [fɑː ʔaut] rather than [fɑːr aut]. This is generally true of SAfE.

3.   Suprasegmentals

It is still easy to deduce the linguistic background of older InSAfE speakers on the basis of an 'articulatory setting' that involves murmur or 'breathy voice' for people of North Indian descent and its absence amongst people of South Indian descent (especially Tamil speakers). This difference is slowly being levelled out amongst younger speakers. It is claimed that InSAfE is syllable- rather stress-timed, though this has yet to be researched objectively. Subjectively, the speech rate is deemed fast and the stress patterns fairly different from those of general SAfE. Furthermore sentence rhythm results in shortening of long vowels and even of short vowels.

Although word stress approximates to that of SAfE there are instances of stress being postponed to a medial or final syllable, where SAfE (like RP) has word-initial stress. The InSAfE pattern is, accordingly, closer to that of Hiberno-English (Ó Sé 1986). Furthermore, it is a feature of all informal InSAfE speech. The following representative list of InSAfE words follows the IPA convention that the stress mark precedes the main-stressed syllable:

accommo'date	immi'grate
corp(o)'ration	immi'grating
criti'cise	imi'tate
exagge'rate	in'dustry
re'gister	or'chestra

For further examples see Bughwan (1970: 256).

4. Current research issues

The phonology of InSAfE is still open research territory. I shall concentrate on the possibilities offered by the study of aspiration. P, T, K have aspiration patterns that are different from the prototypical English patterns of aspiration in all initial positions. Detailed research has still to be undertaken, and a preliminary analysis suggests the following in vernacular mesolectal speech:

P is always unaspirated before /ɑː/, /ɔː/, /ʊ/, /ɒ/, /eɪ/, /oʊ/ and /ɛə/. Thus *park, pork, put, pot, pay, poke, pair* all have unaspirated initial P. Likewise P is always unaspirated before /r/ and /l/, e.g. in *pray* and *play*. This means that /r/ and /l/ are voiced in InSAfE in contrast to many varieties of English in which the aspiration on initial consonants causes /r/ and /l/ to become voiceless. In all other contexts whether P is aspirated or not, depends on the particular word. Taking P before /e/ as an example, the following words always have aspiration – *pen, pebble, pet*; whereas *penny, pepper, petal, peck* are always unaspirated. It has still to be researched whether there is intra-speaker variability (i.e. pronouncing the same word differently) or variation across speakers. Speakers who produce aspiration invariantly with initial P, T, K would be judged as putting on a 'Speech and Drama' accent. The dialect has minimal pairs like *pʰea* and *pee; pʰiece* and *piss* (pronounced [piːs]). It also has near-minimal pairs like *pʰet* and *petal, pʰen* and *pencil*.

Similar principles apply to T and K. The reason for this unusual system is twofold. Firstly it represents a shift from languages with differential patterns of aspiration towards the general English norm. The Indic languages have phonemic distinction between aspirated and unaspirated P, T, K. Speakers appear to be comfortable with the categorical absence of aspiration in some words and its categorical presence in others. On the other hand, as the Dravidian language, Tamil, does not have aspiration, its speakers have to adopt this feature afresh in their English. The InSAfE mesolect seems a happy compromise between the two systems: no aspiration before certain back vowels, certain diphthongs and both liquids; and in all other contexts aspiration is word-dependent. The actual minimal pairs are marginal: both *pee* and *piss* cited above are, in fact, taboo words, and therefore do not occur in the same register as p^hea and p^hiece. The second reason for this unusual system is that it is probably a stage in the language acquisition-cum-lexical diffusion process. It is not hard to envisage a gradual shift to a system with aspiration for all initial P, T, K.

Exercises and study questions

1. The vowels of InSAfE are closer to those of RP than to typical WhSAfE values. Discuss.

2. The diphthongs of InSAfE are closer to those of RP than to typical WhSAfE values. Discuss.

3. The consonants of InSAfE are not closer to RP than are the consonants of WhSAfE. Discuss.

4. What similarities does InSAfE share with IndE regarding vowels and consonants?

5. What differences in segmental phonology are there between InSAfE and IndE?

Selected references

Please consult the General references for titles mentioned in the text but not included in the references below. For a full bibliography see the accompanying CD-ROM.

Bailey, R.
  c1985   South African Indian English Phonology. Unpublished notes. Department
           of Speech and Hearing Therapy, University of Durban-Westville.
Bughwan, D.
  1970   An investigation into the use of English by the Indians in South Africa,
           with special reference to Natal. PhD thesis, University of South Africa.
Mesthrie, R.
  1992   *English in Language Shift.* Cambridge: Cambridge University Press.
Naidoo, K.
  1971   Some aspects of the phonetic deviations in the speech of Tamilians in
           Durban. Unpublished MA thesis, University of Natal.
Ó Sé, D.
  1986   Word-stress in Hiberno-English. In: J. Harris, D. Little and D. Singleton
           (eds.) *Perspectives on the English Language in Iceland: Proceedings of
           the First Symposium on Hiberno-English.* Dublin: Centre for Language
           and Communication Studies, Trinity College, pp. 97-107.

Cape Flats English: phonology*

Peter Finn

1. Introduction

Cape Flats English (CFE) originated in working class neighbourhoods in inner-city Cape Town. However, as a result of Apartheid social engineering, most of its speakers now live far from the city centre in a number of adjoining areas collectively known as 'The Cape Flats'. (The name refers to a large, flat, sandy expanse bordered by mountain ranges and the sea.)

This variety of English is also sometimes called 'Coloured English' but that term is problematic for two reasons. Firstly, it is an over-generalisation: not all people who were classified as 'Coloured' during the Apartheid era speak this dialect since they are not homogenous with regard to region and social class. Secondly, the term 'Coloured' as a descriptor is not universally accepted by those to whom it has been applied. From the mid 19th century, it was used to refer to people of mixed Asian, African, and European ancestry. A hundred years later, it was assigned by the Apartheid government to people who did not fit its two major population categories: 'European' or 'white', and 'Bantu' or 'black'. It was thus a catch-all category for people who did not constitute a group on any intrinsic grounds of shared ethnicity, culture or region. For this reason 'coloured identity' is still a hotly debated concept. However, segregation did create some common ground which is of sociolinguistic significance because it minimised the possibility of intensive contact with speakers of other varieties of English. Members of each official population group were forced to spend most of their lives together in segregated residential areas, educational, leisure and other institutions.

1.1. Historical and cultural background

Settlement in South Africa by English-speaking people started in the closing decade of the 18th century, when British forces occupied the Cape. In 1815, at the end of the Napoleonic Wars, the Cape was allocated to Britain by the Congress of Vienna. This put an end to one and a half centuries of control by the Dutch East India Company. By this time Cape Town was very cosmopolitan. Indigenous people did not constitute a large proportion of its inhabitants, having been decimated by smallpox or driven out of the area, or – as was the case for many hunter-gatherers – killed by settlers. Prior to the arrival of the British, the settlers were mainly of Dutch origin, but included people from other European countries. The large slave population was the most heterogeneous in the world, having been brought from Dahomey, Angola, Madagascar, Mozambique, Zanzibar, Oibo, various parts of India, Ceylon, the Malayan Peninusula and the Indonesian Archipelago (particularly Java, Sumatra, the Celebes, Macassar, Ternate and Timor). Most of the slaves' languages did not survive beyond the first generation, Malay being a notable exception. Portuguese Creole and a Cape Dutch pidgin acted as *lingua francas* for slaves, but they all had to learn Dutch. In doing so, they contributed to the development of what is now known as Afrikaans, a language that has significant structural differences from Dutch. Slavery was abolished in 1834, almost two decades after the establishment of British colonial rule.

In 1822 a policy of anglicization was instituted by Governor Charles Somerset. It was aimed at weakening the independence of those who had previously been dominant, namely the Dutch/Afrikaans-speaking slave-owning group, but obviously the policy also affected the rest of the people in the colony. Of the three domains subjected to anglicization – law, religion and education – it was in education that the policy had the greatest success. English was entrenched as a medium of instruction by the simple expedient of refusing state funding to schools that taught through the medium of any other language. A few private schools were established to provide education in Dutch, but they were unable to survive financially for more than two decades. Aided by grants from the state, Christian religious institutions took a major share of responsibility for primary and secondary education in the Cape Colony during the nineteenth century. In Cape Town most of the church schools and all the state schools taught through the medium of English, regardless of the fact that the home language of many learners was Afrikaans.

The phasing out of socio-economic structures based on slavery did not result in an egalitarian society. There was stratification based on class and, increasingly, on colour though legally entrenched segregation started only in the 20th century. As is common, working-class areas were more multicultural and multilingual than middle-class areas. They were home to freed slaves and their descendants, to indigenous people (both local and from territories further north), and also to immigrants. In the early years of the colony, the majority of the immigrants were English-speaking. Later in the century, economic opportunities in South Africa created by the discovery of mineral wealth, coupled with events in Europe prompted the immigration of thousands of people from Eastern and Western Europe. Many of them started their South African life in the boarding houses and rented accommodation of inner-city neighbourhoods. One of these, District Six, included among its residents East European Jewish immigrants who spoke Yiddish, Russian and Polish, and read Hebrew; Muslim descendants of slaves and political exiles who understood Malay, read Arabic, but spoke Afrikaans as their home language; Christians – descendants of settlers and of slaves, and newer immigrants, whose languages included Afrikaans, English, Zulu, Xhosa, Sotho. Cape Flats English has its roots in these old, mixed residential areas where language contact was the order of the day, and where everyone needed to acquire some command of English if they had any dealings in the adjacent city centre or the middle-class suburbs to the south. The dialect spread to the Cape Flats as residents of the older suburbs moved to that area voluntarily or through the massive forced removals of the 1960s and 70s.

Information on the areas of origin of 19th century English-speaking immigrants to Cape Town is sparse. Most of them did not come in the kind of organised immigration schemes used by settlers in the Eastern Cape or Natal, which provided documentation about background. Because British subjects could travel relatively freely in the Empire, if they came as individuals or in small privately organised groups, they did not have to fill in their particulars on immigration forms when they arrived in Cape Town. Thus there are no consolidated documentation bases to draw on in working out which dialects of English these immigrants would have spoken. Church and secular registers of marriages and births provide some clues, as do ships' passenger lists, but as yet these have not been systematically followed up. Studies of the English of nineteenth century immigrants who settled in other parts of South Africa show non-standard British English dialect features which are also found in Cape Flats English (see Mesthrie and West 1995). Whatever their provenance, non-standard dialects of English spoken in Cape Town would have had an important role shaping the early form of what is now known as 'Cape Flats English.'

Since the dominant language of the central business district was English, residents of the adjacent working-class neighbourhoods who wanted to engage with its resources had to learn some English, if it was not their home language. Adults mostly did this informally, picking it up from their neighbours who, if they were not also speakers of an L2 English, were more likely to speak a regional dialect of British or Irish English, than standard English. Children had more exposure to standard English from their teachers and text books. However, in the playgrounds they would have been more likely to have heard L2 English or regional dialects than standard English. This is because working-class children tended to go to what were called 'mission schools', which offered a practical curriculum and were for poorer children, while middle-class children attended 'church schools', which had an academic curriculum. Christian schools offered both secular and religious education. Madressahs and cheders offered only religious and related cultural Islamic and Jewish education, respectively. The former had taught through the medium of Malay until about the 1830s, when they started to use Afrikaans. They taught pupils to read Arabic. The latter used Yiddish and, later, English, and taught the reading of classical Hebrew.

In 1905 racially-based segregation was introduced in Cape schools. This obviously affected the range of English varieties to which children were exposed in the classroom and the playground. In 1915 Afrikaans was recognised nationally as a viable medium of instruction, and a 'mother-tongue' policy was put on the statute books shortly thereafter. However, it was not strictly enforced, and in Cape Town most schools for coloured children continued to teach through the medium of English, regardless of the children's home language. In the 1950s, when apartheid education policies forced the implementation of mother-tongue education, many of these schools had to change to Afrikaans as medium of instruction or at least add an Afrikaans stream.

Being forced to use Afrikaans in this way was bitterly resented by coloured parents and teachers, some of whom circumvented the law by placing Afrikaans-speaking children into the English stream or into English schools. A very widespread belief developed among parents and children that children got a better education in English schools and classes than in the Afrikaans counterparts, and therefore would have better opportunities for further study and for employment. Separation by language was seen as contributing to the construction of social class division. (In neighbourhoods which wished to counter such division, one of the markers of solidarity was the use of a bilingual vernacular – see McCormick 2002.) A common thread in oral history interviews is the memory of playground division, with children from the Afrikaans and English classes not mixing with one another at all while at school because 'the English children are snobbish' or 'the Afrikaans children are rough and wild'. Thus, the combination of government policy and social divisions meant that the generation who had their education through the medium of Afrikaans after 1950 had far less exposure to English than previous generations had had. As a result, by the nineteen seventies there were clear intergenerational differences with regard to proficiency in English in those working-class coloured families who spoke mainly a local dialect of Afrikaans at home and in the neighbourhood. The grandparents and great-grandparents had had all their schooling in English and were comfortable speaking it. Some had L1 proficiency. The parent generation had had little opportunity to use English outside the classroom and were less confident in the use of their L2 variety. As they did not want their children to have the same experience of what they saw as second-rate education, they raised their children in English so that they could go into English classes. Thus it was common that the input for the children's L1 was an L2 variety of English.

1.2.   Previous research on CFE phonology

CFE is an under-researched variety overall, but especially in terms of phonology. The main earlier studies are referenced in the CD Rom accompanying this text.

In terms of the phonological system as a whole, CFE (like SAfE) differs little from the reference variety, RP. As with mainstream South African English (SAfE, more specifically WSAfE), probably the only case where a difference in the overall system can be argued for is in the 'KIT-Split' (see below).

As a type of South African English, CFE most closely resembles the lect of (typically) white SAfE most closely associated with the lowest socio-economic class (that is, the English of white working-class native speakers). This is the lect termed 'Extreme SAfE' by Lanham (1982), which in turn closely resembles the L2 English accent of white native speakers of Afrikaans (Afrikaans English, or AfkE).

Wood (1987) argues that a similar dichotomy of lects can be set up for CFE itself, with 'Extreme' and 'Respectable' sub-lects characteristic of working-class and middle-class speakers respectively. I would argue (Finn [2003]) that this dichotomy tends to correlate with whether or not speakers could be said to have CFE or CVA (Cape Vernacular Afrikaans) as L1, since L2 CFE speakers tend to be working-class and L1 speakers middle-class.

2.   Phonetic description – segmental features

2.1.   Vowels

Table 1.   The vowels of CFE according to Wells' Lexical Sets

KIT	*IT*	ɪ ~ i
	SIT	ï
DRESS		e > ɛ ~ æ
TRAP		ɛ > æ > æᵉ
LOT		ɔ ~ ɒ > ɒ(ː)ᵉ
STRUT		a ~ ɐ > ʌ > ɒ
	ONE	a ~ ɐ > ɒ

Table 1. (continued)   The vowels of CFE according to Wells' Lexical Sets

FOOT		u > ʉ > ʏ
BATH		a ~ ɑ > aː(ə) ɑː(ə) > ɒː(ː)ə
	DANCE	æː(ə) > aː(ə) ~ ɑː(ə)
CLOTH		ɔ ~ ɒ
NURSE		ɜː > ø (ə) > ɐ ~ ɒːə ~ ə > oː
FLEECE		iː~ i > i (ː) ə ~ iʊ
FACE		ɛi ~ e > əi ~ ɐi ~ ʌi > ɛ
	LAYER	eij
PALM		a ~ ɑ > aː(ə) ~ ɑ(ə) > ɒ(ː)ə
THOUGHT		ɔ ~ oː > oːə
GOAT		ɐu ~ ʌu > [əu] > [uʊ] ~ [ɒu] > [ou] ~ [au]
	GOAL	ɔʊ ~ oʊ > ɒˑ
	GOING	ɐuw
GOOSE		uː > ʉ > u > ʉ
PRICE	*BITE*	ɐi > ʌi ~ əi > ɛi ~ æi ~ əi
	BIDE	ai > ɑi ~ ɒi > aˑə >aː
	BYRE	aij
	BILE	aˑə >aː
CHOICE		ɔi ~ oi
MOUTH	*BOUT*	ɐu > æu > ʌu ~ əu
	BOWED	au > ɑu ɒu
	BOWER	auw
	BOWEL	aːə
NEAR		iː ~ ɛː ~ əː eː ~ ɜː> iɐ > iɜ ~ iə
SQUARE		eː > eːə > ɛː
START		aːə > ɒː ~ aːɜ
NORTH/FORCE		oː ~ ɔː > oː(ə) > ɒ
CURE		uə ~ oː ~ ɔː
happY		iˑ ~ iː > i
lettER		ə ~ ɜ ~ ɐ > əɾ
horsES		ə
commA		ɐ > ə
uncLE		θ ~ ɔ ~ o

Vowel retraction before /l/

This process is noted here in advance because it is a general, pervasive feature. Wood (1987: 127–128) maintains that such retraction occurs across the social scale, as in WSAfE, so it probably also has prestige value. However, an 'iota-cised' sub-variant (e.g. *self* [sjælf]), occurring in Wood's and my own data, is stigmatised.

KIT

CFE, like SAfE, evidences the (ongoing) 'KIT-split' (Lass 1995: 97; Wood 1987: 122–123), whereby KIT is realised as (a) [ɪ] ~ [i] initially, after /h/, in velar environments, and often before /ʃ/ (the *IT* subset), while (b) and as centralised [ɨ] elsewhere (the *SIT* subset). Lass notes that while 'Respectable' (= Educated) SAfE usually has IT = [ɪ] vs. SIT = [ɨ]; Extreme SAfE (and AfkE) usually has IT = [ə] vs SIT = [ɨ]. My data indicate that this general pattern is also true of CFE, except that the patterning IT = [i], SIT = [ɨ] extends higher up the social scale than it does for SAfE – as confirmed by Wood (1987: 122), who notes that the 'low schwa' realisation of KIT occurs in the speech of both Extreme and Respectable CFE speakers (see also Hastings 1979, quoted in Wood 1987: 111). Also as with SAfE, before /l/ (= [ɫ]) KIT is typically realised as [ɤ] (also [ɤ(ᵊ)], [ɔ]).

DRESS

Predominantly 'raised' to [e] (as also Wood 1987: 122; Hastings 1979, quoted in Wood 1987: 111), but with some tendency for lowering towards [ɛ]. Wood (1987: 123) also notes a tendency for [ə(ː)] in certain contexts, e.g. *yes*. As with SAfE, realisations are affected by following /l/ (= [ɫ]), typically towards [æ ~ ɛ] (e.g. *self* [sælf], often also with iotacisation).

TRAP

As in Extreme SAfE and AfrikaansE (the English of White Afrikaans speakers), there is a marked tendency towards [ɛ] (as Wood 1987: 122, Hastings 1979, quoted in Wood 1987: 111), though [æ] and [æᵊ] do also occur. TRAP retains this value before /l/ in CFE and SAfE generally, this time in contrast to RP, where [ɔː] is usual.

LOT

For L2 (and Extreme CFE) speakers typically [ɔ] ~ [ɒ], for L1 speakers more consistently [ɒ] (as Wood 1987: 122, Hastings 1979, quoted in Wood 1987: 111), although [ɒ(ː)ᵊ] also occurs. Wood (1987: 133) also notes the apparently consistent pronunciations *want* [wʌnt] and *non-* [nʌn]. LOT is not apparently affected by following /l/.

STRUT

According to my own and Wood's data (1987: 122), for L2 speakers typically [a] ~ [ɐ], for L1 speakers more consistently [ɐ] (sporadically also [ʌ]). According to Wood, STRUT-lowering is not obviously stigmatised. STRUT is typically realised as [ɒ] before /l/ (as also Wood 1987: 128). In the subset ONE (comprising (-)*one*, *once*), realisations vary between L2 [a] and L1 [ɐ, ɒ].

FOOT

Very typically in the region of [u], i.e. with a marked degree of backing and rounding (though perhaps somewhat less so for L1 than L2 speakers). Also [ʉ], [ɤ]. Not apparently affected by following /l/.

BATH/PALM

Typically [a] ~ [ɑ] (often [aː(ə) ~ ɒː(ə)]), with some instances of [ɒ(ː)ə]-type realisations. However, in the subset DANCE realisations are typically in the region of [æː(ə)] (as Wood 1987: 123); also [ɑː(ə)] ~ [ɑː(ə)]. Wood (1987: 137) claims DANCE Raising is typical of Extreme CFE speakers.

CLOTH

See LOT. For L2 (and Extreme CFE) speakers typically [ɔ], for L1 speakers more consistently [ɒ].

NURSE

There is a high degree of variability. Wood (1987) records mainly [ɜː], with some instances of [ə(ː)]. My data (especially from L1 speakers) showed especially [øː(ə)], with some instances of [ɐː], [ɒːə] and [ə]. Before /l/, NURSE seems to be realised especially as [oː].

FLEECE

Typically [iː] in stressed position, [i] in unstressed position, for all speakers. Before /l/, FLEECE generally remains as [iː] , but there is some tendency to 'breaking' (e.g. [i(ː)ə], [i(ː)ʊ], as also Wood 1987: 128).

FACE

According to my own and Wood's (1987: 123) data, typically [ɛi] for L2 speakers, [ei] for L1 speakers, though for all speakers there is also some tendency towards centralisation of the onset (nucleus), e.g. [əi], [ɐi], [ʌi]. There is also some evidence for a Canadian Raising-type distribution, with front onsets tending to occur in pre-fortis environments and non-front onsets elsewhere (see GOAT). Wood (1987: 123) and Hastings (1979, quoted in Wood 1987: 111) also note (sporadic?) instances of glide weakening, e.g. *take* [tɛk]; Hastings claims diphthong offset weakening is typical of CFE. However, note also the typically markedly peripheral (i.e. strongly high front) offset; this is particularly noticeable in word-final position. According to Lanham (1982: 343), this 'high diphthongal glide' is characteristic of Afrikaans-influenced English generally, and used even by well-educated speakers – as confirmed in Wood's (1987: 137–138) and my own data. In hiatus (as in the subset LAYER), this offset is typically realised as [j], e.g. ['ɫeijɐ']. Realisations are not apparently affected by following /l/.

THOUGHT
According to Wood (1987: 122), Extreme CFE speakers typically have [ɔ]. My data indicates realisations typically in the region of [oː] for all speakers; [oːᵊ] is also frequent. Not apparently affected by following /l/.

GOAT
Although there is a high degree of variability here, analysis of Wood's (1987: 125ff) and my own data reveals that realisations are typically in the region of [ɐu] and [ʌu], for all speakers; other realisations observed include [əu], [ɔu], [ɒu] fairly frequently, and less often [ou], [au]. There is also some evidence for a Canadian Raising-type distribution, with back onsets tending to occur in pre-fortis environments and non-back onsets elsewhere (see FACE). Despite the fact that Wood records some cases of offset weakening, e.g. [ɔᵘ], [oᵘ], and Hastings (1979, quoted in Wood 1987: 111) maintains that diphthong weakening is typical of CFE, the available data would suggest that in fact such weakening occurs especially (a) before /l/ – where, in common with SAfE, onset quality is also affected, typically yielding [ɒˈ] (e.g. ['kɒˈɫdɐ']) – and (b) in unstressed position (though see Non-Reduction, below). In fact, as with MOUTH, offsets of GOAT are typically markedly peripheral (i.e. strongly backed and rounded) rather than weakened (see also Wood 1987: 128). Yet again, Lanham (1982: 343) maintains that this 'high diphthongal glide' is characteristic of Afrikaans-influenced English generally, and used even by well-educated speakers – as confirmed in Wood's (1987: 137–138) and my own data. It is particularly noticeable in word-final position. In hiatus (as in the subset GOING), the offset is typically realised as [w] (e.g. ['gɐuwiŋ]). Wood (1987: 137–138) observes that both onset lowering and markedly backed and rounded offsets, are typical across the social scale.

GOOSE
Several commentators (Hastings 1979, quoted in Wood 1987: 111; Wood 1987: 128; Lass 1995: 98–99) note that CFE (as well as South African Indian English; see Mesthrie 1995: 253) is to be distinguished from SAfE by typically having 'old-fashioned' (in SAfE terms) realisations for GOOSE, in the area of [uː] – that is, with a marked degree of backing and rounding (as also for FOOT). This

is especially noticeable in word-final position. Wood maintains that marked rounding (but not backing) is typical across the social scale, and Lass similarly claims that there is a strong tendency to avoid fronter values even in very standard registers. However, my data revealed that some (mainly L1) speakers do approximate to the more centralised SAfE norm, with [ʉː]. Both types of realisation are typically shortened when unstressed, sometimes making them indistinguishable from FOOT. Realisations are not apparently affected by following /l/.

PRICE
Wood (1987: 123–125, 135) notes two typical realisations of PRICE: (a) with raised onsets (e.g. [ɛɪ], [æɪ], [əɪ]), and with low onsets and offset weakening (e.g. [aː], [aɪ]). He maintains that raised-onset variants are associated with Extreme CFE speakers, although also occurring further up the social scale, and are only found in CFE (since Extreme SAfE typically has low back onsets), while the low, glide-weakened variants are a defining variable of Respectable SAfE, and are associated with Respectable CFE also. Detailed research by Finn (in progress) has revealed that in fact, PRICE (along with MOUTH) is subject to a sub-phonemic Canadian Raising rule, whereby non-low onsets occur in pre-fortis environments and low ones elsewhere. Thus, typical realisations are BITE as [bɐit] compared to BIDE and BUY as [baid̥] and [bai] respectively (see full discussion below). Other pre-fortis realisations include [ʌi] and [əi], while non-pre-fortis realisations include [ɑi] and [ɒi]. Note also that in fact, PRICE offsets are typically markedly peripheral rather than weakened (i.e. strongly fronted and raised); when reduction does occur it is typically in unstressed position, and especially for the high-frequency pronoun *I*. As in the case of FACE above, Lanham (1982: 343) maintains that 'high diphthongal glides' are characteristic of Afrikaans-influenced English generally, and used even by well-educated speakers – as confirmed in Wood's (1987: 137–138) and my own data. It is particularly noticeable in word-final position. In hiatus (as in the subset FIRE), this offset is typically realised as [j], e.g. [faijɐˑ]. Realisations are affected by a following /l/, with the offset being reduced (e.g. [aˑə], as in [tʃaˑə l̴d̥] *child*) or – less commonly – backed (e.g. [aʊ], as in [tʃaˑʊl̴d̥] *child*; see Wood 1987: 128).

CHOICE
Realisations are typically in the region of [ɔi], [oi]. The observations made above regarding markedly peripheral offsets as in PRICE and FACE generally apply to CHOICE also, although it is not apparently affected by following /l/.

MOUTH

Wood (1987: 124–125) maintains that 'raised' (and often glide-weakened) onsets in MOUTH are typical of Extreme CFE speakers and are very common among L1 speakers, but would be avoided by those higher up the social scale, who usually use [aʊ]. Hastings (1979, quoted in Wood 1987: 111) maintains that diphthong weakening is typical of CFE. However, detailed research by Finn (2003) has revealed that in fact, MOUTH (like PRICE) is subject to a subphonemic Canadian Raising rule, whereby onsets are non-low in pre-fortis environments but low elsewhere. Thus, typical realisations are BOUT as [bɐut], [bæut] compared to BOWED and BOUGH as [bau̯d] and [bau] respectively (see full discussion below). Other non-low pre-fortis realisations include [ʌu] and [əu], while other non-pre-fortis realisations include [ɑu] and [ɒu]. Also similarly to PRICE, offsets of MOUTH are in fact typically markedly peripheral (i.e. strongly backed and rounded) rather than weakened. Once again, Lanham (1982: 343) maintains that 'high diphthongal glides' are characteristic of Afrikaans-influenced English generally, and used even by well-educated speakers – as confirmed in Wood's (1987: 137–138) and my own data. It is particularly noticeable in word-final position. When reduction does occur it is typically in unstressed position or before /l/ (e.g. [ʔaˑəɫ] *owl*). In hiatus (as in the subset POWER), the offset is typically realised as [w] (e.g. [ˈpauwɐˑ]).

NEAR

My data reveals a usual realisation in the region of [iɐ], with [iɜ] and [iə] also occurring. Wood (1987: 126), whose data reveals monophthongised variants, [iː], [ɛː], [əː], [eː] and [ɜː], maintains that such monophthongal realisations occur across the social scale.

SQUARE

My data revealed a usual realisation of [eː], with some cases of [eːə]. Wood (1987: 126) also notes [ɛː] and again maintains that such monophthongal realisations occur across the social scale.

START

In my data START was typically realised as [aːə], with [ɑː] and [aːᶾ] also occurring. Wood (1987) notes only [ɑː].

NORTH/FORCE

According to Wood (1987: 122), Extreme CFE speakers typically have [ɔ]. My data indicated realisations typically in the region of [oː] ~ [ɔ], with some instances of [oː(ə)], as well as [ɒ]. Shortening typically occurs when unstressed.

CURE

Realisations typically vary between [əu] and [oː] ~ [ɔː]. Wood (1987: 126) maintains that monophthongal realisations (especially in word-final position, e.g. in *poor* [pɔː]) occur across the social scale.

happY

Although Wood (1987) records only [i], my data revealed a tendency toward happY-lengthening, with [iˑ] or [iː].

lettER

Typical realisations in my data were [ə], [ɜ] (also in Wood 1987: 127), [ɐ]. Wood also notes rhotic realisations for some L2 speakers, e.g. [əR].

horsES

Typically [ə].

commA

Typically [ɐ], [ə]; however, realisations may be affected by following /l/, yielding [ɵ], [ɔ], [o] (as also Wood 1987: 128).

2.2. Consonants

Saffery (1986, apparently following Hastings 1979) notes the occurrence of 'unreleased consonants'. However, Wood (1987: 112) notes that frequencies for these would appear to be low.

2.2.1. Obstruents

(a)   Variability

According to Hastings (1979, quoted in Wood 1987: 111), in CFE there is typically sporadic "confusion" between /d/ ~ /ð/, /s/ ~ /z/, /n/ ~ /ŋ/, /ɦ/ ~ /h/ and / /β/~ /b/ (some of the latter occurred intervocalically in my own data, e.g. *about* [ɐ'βʌt], *available* [ɐ'βeiləbɤɫ]).

(b)   Final devoicing

Wood (1987: 132) maintains that a typical feature of Extreme CFE is devoicing of final /d/ and /z/ (e.g. *eight hundred* [ɛitʌndrəd̥], *seconds* [sekəndz̥]). I would claim, on the basis of my own data, that CFE generally has a (variable) rule of final-obstruent devoicing (terminal devoicing), whereby *all* obstruents will tend to be voiceless (lenis) in syllable-final position (that is, final /b d g v ð z ʒ/ will typically be realised as [b̥ d̥ g̥ v̥ ð̥ z̥ ʒ̥]); see the discussion on Canadian Raising below. Additionally, in my data /g/ and /dʒ/ – phonemes not occurring in CVA –

were often devoiced also in initial position. On devoicing in CFE see also Lanham (1982: 343).

2.2.2. Plosives

According to Hastings (1979, quoted in Wood 1987: 111), in CFE there is 'typically some extra pressure on plosive release'; there is also 'slow release' on some plosives.

P, T, K

According to Hastings (1979, quoted in Wood 1987: 111) de-aspiration of voiceless initial stops is typical of CFE; according to Saffery (1986, cited in Wood 1987: 112) there is variation between aspirated and de-aspirated initial stops. Deaspiration is also noted separately by Lanham (1982), and Wood (1987: 129, 137–138), who claims its use is more typical of Extreme CFE than Respectable CFE speakers. My own data evidenced both aspiration and de-aspiration, although L1 (= primarily more middle-class speakers) tended to aspirate in line with RP norms.

T, D

My own data indicate that /t/, /d/ are very typically realised as dental, i.e. [t̪], [d̪].

Consonant lengthening

Wood (1987: 133) observes that continuants occurring before word-final voiced alveolar consonants may be lengthened, e.g. *things* [θiŋŋz].

2.2.3. Nasals

According to Wood (1987: 131), final nasals may be elided in CFE; see discussion of elision, below.

2.2.4. Fricatives and affricates

F

Wood (1987: 123) notes the occurrence, especially among Extreme CFE speakers, of antedental /f/, (that is, with the lower lip in front of rather than below the top teeth).

TH

Wood (1987: 130–131) notes the presence of TH-Stopping, with /θ/ and /ð/ variably realised as (dental) [t̪] and [d̪]. He maintains that this is typical of Extreme CFE speakers.

SH, ZH, CH, J

Wood (1987: 129–130) notes that the hushing fricatives and affricates have, as well as /ʃ ʒ tʃ dʒ/, two major distinctive realisations, involving hushing segments realised as (a) hissing fricatives (thus, /ʃ ʒ tʃ dʒ/ realised as [s z ts dz]), or as (b) backed hushing fricatives (thus, /ʃ ʒ tʃ dʒ/ realised as [ʃ ʒ tʃ dʒ]). The former set of realisations is typical of L2 (= mainly working-class, Extreme CFE) speakers, the latter of L1 (= mainly middle-class speakers); in my data (mainly from middle-class, L1 speakers), there was considerable use of backed variants. Wood suggests these are hypercorrect forms. Lanham (1982: 343) also notes the tendency (probably among L2 speakers) for /dʒ/ to be realised as [j] (e.g. *judge* [jɐtʃ]), as may occur also in White Afrikaans English. Wood also notes an L2-speaker tendency to substitute /s/ for /ʃ/ and vice-versa when in close proximity to following /ʃ/ or /ʒ/ , e.g. *social* ['ʃɒusəl].

2.2.5. *Approximants*

R

Wood points out that although CFE has a characteristically 'obstruent' /r/, as a variety of English CFE is generally non-rhotic; that is, unlike Afrikaans English (AfkE), /r/ is not pronounced in pre-consonantal or word-final contexts, probably because CVA itself generally has no pronounced /r/ in similar contexts, such as *kerk* 'church', *ver* 'far' (see Wood 1987: 114, 129). Steenkamp's study (1980, cited in Wood 1987: 112–114; see also Hastings 1979, cited in Wood 1987: 111), which focussed on /r/, found at least four types in use – resonant [ɹ], fricative [ɾ̞], tap [ɾ] and trill [r] – with social differentiation correlating with linguistic variation. Thus, [ɹ] and [ɾ̞] were most typical of middle-class speakers and [r] was most typical of working-class speakers, but [ɾ] was most typical overall. Wood confirms that tapped or flapped /r/ is typical of Extreme CFE speakers and that with [ɾ] is the most usual realisation, but notes a further variant – uvular [ʀ], which is probably an L2 feature associated with speakers originating in the Western Cape interior. The impression gained from my own data is that the predominant realisation is [ɾ], supporting Wood's and Steenkamp's findings. Additionally, Saffery (1986, also cited in Wood 1987: 112) notes the presence of intervocalic linking /r/.

L

According to Saffery (1986, cited in Wood 1987: 112), there is variation between [l] and [ɫ], although [ɫ] occurs especially word-finally. In my own data, /l/ was almost exclusively realised as 'dark', i.e. [ɫ].

J (and hiatus)
Wood (1987: 132) notes the presence of /h/-insertion (hiatus or glide replacement by /h/), which apparently occurs in all Afrikaans-influenced varieties of English (see also Lass 1996) and which he claims occurs across the social scale. The favoured context seems to be intervocalically after an unstressed syllable, e.g. *piano* [pi'fiænɐu] – a typical realisation in my data also. Other hiatus-fillers in my data included [j], [ʔ] and [ʍ].

H
Typically, /h/ = [ɦ]. According to Wood (1987: 132), /h/ is often realised as [j] in word-initial position, e.g. *hell* /'hɛl/ = [jæɫ]. This occurred frequently in my data.

Glottal onset
CFE, like SAfE generally (see Lass 1996), tends very strongly to have a glottal onset ('hard attack') in vowel-initial syllables.

3.   Suprasegmental Features

3.1.   Phonotactics

Wood (1987: 131) notes several types of elision, occurring frequently in Extreme CFE and paralleled in CVA. Predictably, relatively few cases occurred in my data.

3.1.1.   *Consonant cluster reduction*

In common with reduction in other varieties of English, this especially applies to clusters involving final stops, e.g. *ask* [ɑːs], *addicts* [ɛdiks], *underground* [ənəgræən]. Again, predictably, relatively few cases occurred in my data.

3.1.2.   *Elision of final nasals*

Wood notes that final nasals may be elided, leaving behind nasalisation of the preceding vowel, e.g. *plan* [plæ̃], *exciting* [eksæɪfi]. His data indicate that a further change may occur involving loss of nasalisation, producing a purely oral vowel. These processes, combined with cluster reduction, are seen in Wood's example *don't* [dəu]. Nasalisation with loss of nasal is characteristic of Afrikaans, with further denasalisation characteristic of CVA.

3.2.   Stress

3.2.1.   Non-reduction of unstressed vowels

Wood (1987: 126–127) notes as a very salient characteristic of CFE the marked tendency not to reduce vowels in unstressed syllables as consistently as is done in RP (e.g. in CFE *possess* is typically [pəuˈzes]). He maintains that this is typical across the social scale, and indeed such phenomena were noted across my own data (mainly from middle-class and L1 speakers). While the issue is too complex to analyse in detail here, it most likely relates to innovative changes in RP at the 'core' of the English-language speech community, with more conservative varieties like CFE, SAfE, and American, Caribbean and Northern English Englishes being at the periphery.

3.2.2.   'Stress shift'

Wood (1987: 132) notes that in more Extreme CFE, the stress in polysyllabic verbs (actually, certain Latinate verb *stems*) occurs on the ultimate instead of the penultimate syllable, e.g. *realíse, participáte, intoxicáted*. He also notes that other, less systematic shifts occur. Such patterns also occurred very widely in my data (mainly from middle-class speakers); there were also many involving marked secondary stress (e.g. *gráduàted*). Such patternings also occur in other non-RP varieties (e.g. South African Indian English, Caribbean Englishes, Southern Hiberno-English, Scottish English), and would seem to reflect patterns of stress in earlier and/or regional British English. However, the issue is too complex to analyse in detail here.

3.3.   Intonation

According to Lanham (1982: 343), CFE has especially distinctive intonation contours, with little use of falling pitch in statements and a tendency for rising pitch in final accented syllables. Douglas (1984, cited in Wood 1987: 116) found that, compared to RP, tone-units were shorter, and there were more cases of nuclear tones (implying greater nuclear pitch movement) and of rising tones, especially with rising tails. According to Wood, the latter observation correlates with the impression that CFE tends to have more rising intonations, especially noticeable in the case of statements.

4.   Phonological features

It may be argued that only certain features serve to distinguish CFE as a variety, being shared with no other South African variety. Some features are shared with other local varieties than L1 'white' SAfE, while the majority are shared with at least some lects of the latter.

Thus, features shared with varieties of L1 white SAfE include:

(a)   vowel retraction before /l/;
(b)   the South African Short Front Vowel Shift (KIT-, DRESS-, TRAP-Raising; see Lass 1995: 96–98);
(c)   the KIT-Split;
(d)   *ONE*-Rounding;
(e)   *DANCE*-Fronting (although this is not usual for Respectable SAfE);
(f)   STRUT-Lowering;
(g)   BATH/PALM/START-Fronting;
(h)   NURSE realised as [ɜ:], [ø:];
(i)   FLEECE realised as [i:];
(j)   Onset Centralisation of FACE, GOAT;
(k)   Onset Raising in CHOICE;
(l)   THOUGHT/NORTH/FORCE-Raising;
(m)   Monophthongisation of NEAR, SQUARE, CURE;
(n)   happY-Lengthening;
(o)   Initial Stop De-aspiration;
(p)   /h/ as [ɦ];
(q)   Obstruent-/r/;
(r)   Dark /l/;
(s)   Non-Reduction;
(t)   (probably) Consonant Cluster Reduction

Features shared with other SAfE varieties than L1 white SAfE include

(a)   those shared with White Afrikaans English:
    (i)   LOT-Raising;
    (ii)   Markedly Peripheral Offglides (PRICE, MOUTH, FACE, GOAT CHOICE);
    (iii)   Final-Obstruent Devoicing;
    (iv)   B-Fricativisation;
    (v)   Dental T, D;
    (vi)   Sibilant Confusion;

(vii)   Hushing/Hissing Substitution;
(viii) Initial /g/, /dʒ/ Devoicing;
(ix)   'Hard Attack'/Hiatus Filling with [ʔ];
(b)   those shared with South African Indian English:
(i)   Markedly Peripheral FOOT, GOOSE;
(ii)   TH-Stopping;
(iii)   Stress-Shift.

Unique features within the South African context – that is, the defining features of CFE – would therefore comprise:
(a)   Antedental /f/;
(b)   Final-Nasal Elision;
(c)   Canadian Raising in PRICE, MOUTH (and FACE, GOAT?);
(d)   NURSE realised as [ə(ː)], [ɐː], [ɒːᵊ];
(e)   Hushing Fricative Backing.

5.   Research issues

5.1.   Afrikaans influence: The argument

Since L1 CFE may be described as a "language-shift variety", the issue arises of the potential influence on it of (Cape Vernacular) Afrikaans. However, demonstrating such influence is not always straightforward.

Lass and Wright (1986) argue that most of the features of L1 'white' SAfE phonology commonly believed to stem from the influence of Afrikaans can be shown to have a probable or at least possible origin in the varieties of British English brought to South Africa in the 19ᵗʰ century – although it could still be argued that the influence of Afrikaans in these cases is likely to have been a reinforcing one. Since most of the features occurring in CFE are also found in white L1 varieties of SAfE – especially Extreme SAfE – it is difficult to argue unambiguously for Afrikaans influence. Nevertheless, some cases remain where a very clear case for such influence can be made.

Thus, the features mentioned in Section 3 above may be categorised in terms of probable origin, as follows:

(a)   Probable primarily input feature from varieties of British English (including BrE archaisms/regionalisms):
(i)   ONE-Rounding; DANCE-Fronting
(ii)   NURSE realised as [ɜː] [øː]
(iii)   FLEECE [iː]
(iv)   THOUGHT/NORTH/FORCE-Raising

       (v)   CHOICE Onset Raising
       (vi)   NEAR-Monophthongisation (some cases)
       (vii)   SQUARE-Monophthongisation
       (viii) CURE-Monophthongisation
       (ix)   happY-lengthening
       (x)   lettER realised as [ə], [ɜ], [ɐ]
       (xi)   Stress-Shift

(b)   Probable or possible BrE input feature reinforced by CVA:
       (i)   At least some cases of vowel retraction before /l/ (especially with iotacisation)
       (ii)   STRUT-Lowering
       (iii)   Markedly peripheral FOOT, GOOSE
       (iv)   BATH/PALM/START-Fronting
       (v)   LOT-, CLOTH-Raising
       (vi)   FACE, GOAT Onset Centralisation
       (vii)   NEAR-monophthongisation (some cases)
       (viii) B-Fricativisation
       (ix)   Final-Obstruent Devoicing
       (x)   Initial Stop De-aspiration
       (xi)   Dental T, D; Obstruent-/r/
       (xii)   Dark /l/
       (xiii) Non-Reduction

(c)   Probable internal development/BrE input feature reinforced by CVA:
       (i)   South African Short Front Vowel Shift, involving KIT/DRESS/TRAP-Raising
       (ii)   KIT-Split; Consonant Cluster Reduction

(d)   Probable internal development: Antedental /f/

(e)   Probable (near-)direct transfer from CVA:
       (i)   LOT-Raising
       (ii)   Markedly peripheral offglides in rising diphthongs (PRICE, MOUTH, FACE, GOAT, CHOICE)
       (iii)   TH-Stopping
       (iv)   Sibilant Confusion
       (v)   Hushing/Hissing Substitution
       (vi)   /h/ as [ɦ]
       (vii)   Initial /g/, /dʒ/ Devoicing
       (viii) Final-Nasal Elision
       (ix)   'Hard Attack'/Hiatus-Filling based on [ʔ]

(f)   Probable interlanguage feature (new intermediate form):
   (i)   Canadian Raising in PRICE, MOUTH, and possible similar
          phenomena in FACE and GOAT
   (ii)   NURSE as [ə(ː)], [ɐː], [ɒːˤ]
   (iii) Hushing Fricative Backing

5.2.   Afrikaans influence: Investigation

Research on CFE carried out by Finn (forthcoming) attempts to gain a better appreciation of how substratum effects can lead to language change in a situation of language shift, by taking better cognisance of the complex role of second-language acquisition processes – embodied in the concept of interlanguage that such a scenario implies.

   Auditory analysis of audiotaped data collected in Cape Town indicates the existence in CFE of a type of 'Canadian Raising' (CR), whereby the onsets of closing diphthongs of the PRICE and MOUTH classes are centralised in pre-fortis environments but low elsewhere:

Table 2.   The CFE major closing-diphthong system

Pre-fortis:			*Elsewhere:*			
PRICE:	BITE	[bɐit]	BIDE	[baˑid̥]	BUY	[baːi]
MOUTH:	BOUT	[bɐut]	BOWED	[baˑud]	BOUGH	[baːu]
FACE:	BAIT	[beit]	BADE	[beˑid]	BAY	[beːi]
GOAT:	BOAT	[bʌut]	BODE	[bʌˑud]	BEAU	[bʌːu]

Trudgill (1986: 153–161) plausibly attributes the rise of CR in Canadian and other varieties of English to the reallocation, according to the phonetic principle of pre-fortis clipping, of low- and centralised-onset PRICE and MOUTH variants originating in different dialects of English. My claim is that the development of Canadian Raising in CFE similarly involved the interaction of variants originating in different varieties – but in this case the varieties were different distinct *languages* (English and Afrikaans), instead of varieties of the same language (English). It is proposed that the direct substitution of Afrikaans for English closing diphthongs in the early Afrikaans-English interlanguage adversely affected intelligibility, since quality and quantity contrasts required in the target language were not made, as the following tables make clear:

Table 3. Proposed development of early L2 CFE

	Cape English	**Closest CVA phoneme**	**Early L2 CFE**
PRICE:	*/ɑɪ/	/əi/ (*[ɑːj])	*/əi/ (*[ɑːj])
MOUTH:	*/ɑʊ/	/əu/	*/əu/
FACE:	*/eɪ/	/əi/	*/əi/
GOAT:	*/ʌʊ/	/əu/	*/əu/

Table 4. Early L2 CFE mergers

bide ~ bite ~ bade ~ baiT	*/bəit/
bowed ~ bout ~ bode ~ boat	*/bəut/
buy ~ bay	*/bəi/
beau ~ bough	*/bəu/

It is argued that the CR pattern arose after learners utilised L1 length distinctions between 'pure' diphthongs and vowel-glide clusters – a process necessarily involving reanalysis of L1 phonotactic restrictions. CVA word-final /ɑːj/ more closely resembles Cape English word-final [ɒːɪ] than does /əi/, in terms of onset quality and quantity. Preferential substitution distinguishing BUY ~ BAY will provide the key to the wider merger problem – *as long as* learners violate their L1's phonotactic rules by extending /ɑːj/ substitution to cover not just word-final environments, but also pre-lenis ones (as in BIDE). Once this is achieved, BITE with [əi] will be clearly distinguished from BIDE with [ɑːj] in terms not only of actual onset duration, but also of a CR-type difference in onset quality. It is proposed that the durational differential principle is then extended in turn to the MOUTH set, where a CR distinction is similarly set up, and then to the FACE and GOAT sets.

The evidence suggests CR in CFE is indeed an interlanguage feature – since no superior alternative explanations, such as local interaction of purely British English dialects, or of universal language principles, could be found. The presence of CR in all forms of CFE, as well as its continued salience at the latest stage of entrenchment as an L1 in cases of longer-term intergenerational shift from CVA, provides at least some support for the hypothesis that IL features can be shown to play a role in shift-induced language change.

* Most of the introduction to this chapter was originally written by K. McCormick as part of her contribution on the Morphology and Syntax of CFE in this volume.

Exercises and study questions

1. Does the short front vowel shift of WhSAfE occur in CFE?
2. Discuss other similarities between the vowels and diphthongs of CFE and WhSAfE.
3. What vowel and diphthong characteristics of CFE are not generally found in WhSAfE.
4. What are the main differences between the consonants of CFE and those of WhSAfE?
5. What is 'Canadian Raising'? What similarities to this rule can be found in CFE? What is the likely impetus for this similarity?

Selected references

Please consult the General references for titles mentioned in the text but not included in the references below. For a full bibliography see the accompanying CD-ROM.

Douglas, Christine
  1984   A preliminary investigation into the intonation patterns of a small socio-
           linguistically definable group of South African speakers. Research report,
           University of Cape Town.
Finn, Peter A.
  2003   Interlanguage, language shift and phonological change in the development
           of Cape Flats English. Ph.D. dissertation, University of Leeds/College of
           York St John.
Hastings, J.
  1979   The phonetic system of Coloured English. Honours dissertation,
           Department of Logopaedics, University of Cape Town.
Lanham, Leonard W.
  1982   English in South Africa. In: Bailey and Görlach (eds.), 324–352.
Lass, Roger
  1995   South African English. In: Mesthrie (ed.), 89-106.
  1996   Glottal stop and linking [h] in South African English: with a note on two
           antique connections. In: Juhani Klemola, Merja Kytö and Matti Rissanen
           (eds.), *Speech Past and Present: Studies in English Dialectology in
           Memory of Ossi Ihalainen*, 130-151. [Bamberger Beiträge zur Englischen
           Sprachwissenschaft 38.] Frankfurt: Lang.

Lass, Roger and Susan Wright
  1986   Endogeny vs. contact: "Afrikaans influence" on South African English. *English World-Wide* 7: 201–224.
Malan, Karen C.
  1996   Cape Flats English. In: de Klerk (ed.), 125–148.
Mesthrie, Rajend
  1995   South African Indian English: from L2 to L1. In: Mesthrie (ed.), 251–264.
Mesthrie, Rajend and Paula West
  1995   Towards a grammar of proto-South African English. *English World-Wide* 16: 105-133.
Saffery, Sandra M.
  1986   A sociolinguistic study of the consonant system of "Coloured English". Unpublished B.Sc. thesis, Logopaedics Department, Universoty of Cape Town.
Steenkamp, Jennifer
  1980   A comparison in Coloured English-speaking children of pronunciation of /r/ as a function of socio-economic status. Dissertation, Department of Logopaedics, University of Cape Town.
Wood, Tahir M.
  1987   Perceptions of, and attitudes towards varieties of English in the Cape Peninsula, with particular reference to the "Coloured Community". MA thesis, Rhodes University, Grahamstown.

St. Helena English: phonology

Sheila Wilson

1. Introduction

The volcanic island of St Helena is situated in the South Atlantic Ocean, 1 930 km west of Angola. Its nearest neighbour is Acension Island, approximately 1 100 kilometres to the northwest. St Helena covers 122 sq km, a large proportion of which consists of steep, relatively barren and rocky territory, unsuitable for cultivation. The island's capital and only town is Jamestown, although there are other smaller settlements such as Blue Downs, Sandy Bay and Longwood (home to Napoleon Bonaparte during his exile on the island from 1815 to his death in 1821). St Helena's population of approximately 5 000 (1998 census) is almost without exception of mixed European, African and Asian origin. English is the only language spoken on the island.

1.1. A brief history

Originally uninhabited, St Helena was discovered by the Portuguese in 1502, and was used by them and many other European seafaring nations as a refreshment station on their journeys to and from the East. Until claimed by the British East India Company in 1658, the island was never permanently or formally settled. From this date, a concerted policy of settlement was implemented, and Company employees (soldiers and servants) and 'planters' were recruited to St Helena, along with slaves supplied on request by EIC ships.

Of the European population, little is recorded of their precise origins, except that most probably hailed from the southern parts of England. Various records and correspondence detailed requests for, and the arrival of, slaves from the Guinea Coast, the Indian sub-continent and Madagascar, as well as some mentions of slaves coming from the Cape, the West Indies, the Malay Peninsula and the Maldives. In 1789, the importation of slaves ended. The first consignment of Chinese indentured labourers arrived on the island in 1810, followed by more in 1816. It appears that very few, if any, stayed on permanently.

In 1815 the total population was 2 871, comprising 776 whites, 1 353 slaves, 447 free blacks, 280 Chinese and 15 lascars (Barnes 1817). When slavery was finally abolished on the island in 1832, only 614 people were classed as 'slaves'. In 1834, St Helena's administration was transferred from the East India Company to the British government. By 1837, the population figures were noted as "2 113 whites and 2 864 coloureds", implying that miscegenation had already occurred to a large degree. In 1875, Melliss notes that about one-sixth of the population constitutes "pure West Coast Africans", who were introduced after 1840 when St Helena was used as a base for rehabilitating slaves from captured slave ships. Some chose to stay while the majority were sent on to the West Indies or repatriated to the African mainland.

St Helena was host to 500 Afrikaans-speaking Boer War prisoners in 1902. Upon their release, negligibly few stayed and left little influence of their culture or language.

The advent of steam-driven ships and the opening of the Suez Canal voided the island's *raison d'etre* as a refreshment station for shipping and a strategic British possession. Left 'stranded' in mid-Atlantic, St Helena relies heavily on financial support from the British government. With the exception of a short-lived flax industry (which ended in 1965 when the British postal service switched to cheaper synthetic fibre for tying mail bags), no industry has provided a viable means of sustaining the island. There is no airport, and a single government-subsidized ship plies between the United Kingdom, Ascencion, St Helena and Cape Town (with an annual run to Tristan da Cunha). Many St Helenians (or 'Saints') undertake contract work on the military bases on Ascencion and the Falkland Islands, and up until 1999, when the British Government conceded full citizenship rights to islanders, had limited access to work in the UK.

Given the historical demographics and socio-economic conditions of the island, it is unlikely that a full-blown creole language ever developed on St Helena. The relatively small and impoverished European population and paucity of arable land meant that slave ownership was on a small scale, with tiny communities living in relative isolation from each other due to the volcanic geography of the island – deep valleys and steep hillsides which could only be traversed by narrow, winding donkey-paths. Slaves initially lived in a close – if socially stratified – relationship with their settler masters. By the 19th century, the population was further integrated by the practice of garrisoned soldiers marrying or entering into common-law relationships with free blacks. Such circumstances made the development of a creole unnecessary, as access to English was generally always close at hand. What is fairly probable is that the non-European population exerted an influence on the English dialect which developed in the mid-Atlantic, in a similar vein to the Cayman Islands and Bay Islands in the Caribbean – Holms' "creole-influenced non-creole Englishes" (1988/89).

There is still evidence of phonological variation between the various settlements on St Helena, particularly among the older population who are not as mobile as the younger people who all attend a centrally located high school, or who may travel across the island to work in Jamestown. While some St Helenians have access to a more or less standard variety of English, particularly if they have undergone tertiary education on the British mainland, the speech community could be considered as spread over a continuum, from the basilectal 'broad' variety of St. Helena English (StHE) (commonly referred to on the island as 'Saintspeak') to a fairly Standard British English at the acrolectal end. There is no evidence that there is any one-way movement towards standard English, as young speakers, if anything, have a more marked tendency to use non-standard features.

2.   Phonology

2.1.   The vowels of StHE

Table 1.   The vowels of StHE

KIT	ɪ > i > i.	FLEECE	i:
FOOT	ʊ	GOOSE	u: > ü:
TRAP	æ > ɛə	DRESS	e > ɛ
NURSE	a:	THOUGHT	ɔ:
LOT	a > ʌ	DOOR	ʉə > ɔː
CLOTH	ɒ > a	START	ɑ:
STRUT	ʌ	BATH	ɑ:
COMMA	ə	PALM	ɑ:
LETTER	ə > ɛ	HAPPY	i
PRICE	ɑɪ > aɪ > ɔɪ >ʌɪ	HORSES	ə
CHOICE	oɪ > ɔɪ	SQUARE	eə
NEAR	iə > ɪː > iːjɛ	GOAT	oʊ > əʊ
CURE	juə	FACE	eɪ
MOUTH	ɑʊ > aʊ > aə		

The short monophthongs

KIT
StHE does exhibit a 'KIT-split', [ɪ] being the common realisation in velar and glottal contexts, as in *kit, big, sing, hit* and *give*; and a more centralised vowel

[ɪ] elsewhere, as in *bit, fit, sin, bin* etc. Particularly in older speakers the split is not as widespread, with the vowel in *tin, mill, spin* etc. often realised as high front [i]. There is some variation even in individual speakers, who might, for example, pronounce a high front [i] in *tin* and a rather central to back [ɪ] in *mill*. There is another notable anomaly to the split, in the realisation of segments that are preceded by [s] and end in [k], such as *sick* and *sixty* where the /i/ vowel is articulated much further back and laxer, approximating [ÿ]. To a lesser extent, before /k/ the vowel is realised as central or even slightly back of central as in *cricket* and *pick* [ɪ].

DRESS
The usual realisation of this vowel is mid-front [e], approximating to slightly lowered [ɛ] in many environments e.g. before the nasal /n/ in *second* for some speakers. For some words ending in [g], such as *leg*, there are occasional realisations of the vowel as a diphthong – [leɪg] (see discussion below under LOT).

TRAP
The vowel here is generally equivalent to RP [æ]. However some speakers have [ɛə] in *bed, that*, etc.

FOOT
Generally a weakly-rounded back [ʊ]. In some speakers this vowel is slightly centralised and unrounded.

STRUT
This is generally articulated as a low back vowel [ʌ], with occcasional tendency towards centring.

LOT
There is some variation, with RP standard [ɒ] used by some speakers on occasion, but the general tendency is towards unrounding to [a]. In monosyllabic words ending in [g], such as *fog* and *dog*, a certain number of speakers articulate a lengthened diphthong [oʊ], analagous to the pronunciation of *vogue*. This doesn't appear widespread, and is generally considered by the speakers themselves as amusingly parochial, and is probably an archaism that was much more prominent in the past. A diphthong quality also appears with [e] before /g/. Evidence that this is a related archaism could be taken from the fact that one of the common, and therefore historical, family names on St Helena is *Legg*, pronounced by the local radio station interviewer as [leɪg], whereas in his everyday speech he would not use such a realisation.

The long monophthongs

NURSE
Although some older speakers use the vowel similar to RP [ɜ:], there is a prominent 'island variant' here, which is unrounded, lax and more open than RP [ɜ:]. It is difficult to transcribe and I tentatively use [a:] for it. It has a fronter value approximating [æ:] in *church* and a backer value approximating [ʌ:] in *work*.

FLEECE
This vowel is uniformly [i:].

GOOSE
Generally a back rounded vowel, approximating [u:].

PALM
The usual vowel here is [ɑ:].

THOUGHT
Generally [ɔ:], but tendency in some speakers to articulate vowel as diphthong [ɔə].

NORTH
StHE is a non-rhotic variety. Hence this vowel is often realised as a diphthong [ɔə] or less commonly [ʊə] in words like *before* and *door*.

START
The vowel quality here is normally [ɑ:], sometimes raised and/or rounded.

The diphthongs

FACE
This diphthong is generally realised as [eɪ].

GOAT
Realised as [oʊ] with first element weakly rounded; in some speakers, the onset is more centralised with even less rounding – [əʊ] or even [aʊ] occasionally.

PRICE
Although there are some realisations of this diphthong that approach an equivalent of RP [aɪ], there is a certain amount of variation. There is evidence (from occasional visitors' parodies) that at least in the 19th and early 20th century a broad tendency to approximate [ɔɪ] was usual for this diphthong. An interesting split is evident, taking the much-used word *island*. In some speakers the vowel element has become monophthong [a:], while others retain a diphthong with rounding in the first element. *Why* is enunciated with rounding, as is *size*

228   *Sheila Wilson*

and *kind. Time,* has a rounded diphthong but also is enunciated as a monophthong [ɑ:], varying even in the same speaker. There is also a tendency among younger speakers towards 'Canadian' raising in words such as *like* and *right* – where the vowel quality is [əɪ]. This is also apparent in the speech of some elderly speakers.

CHOICE
This diphthong is generally [ɔɪ] ~ [oɪ].

MOUTH
Generally [aʊ], but some realisations of [oʊ], in *about* etc. In this class *town* is exceptional since for many certain StHE speakers the diphthong in *town* has the realisation [aə].

NEAR
Usually [iə] or [ɪə]; occasionally the second element glide is not enunciated, resulting in a monothong [i:].

SQUARE
For the most part, this diphthong is realised as [iə], thus pairs like *hear/hair*, *steers/stairs* are homophones. The vowels in *here, there* and *bread* are noticeably [iə].

Schwa

In some multisyllabic words, such as *expensive,* the unstressed vowel in the first segment results in a weak initial [ə]. This would also be influenced by the glottal consonant following the initial vowel. With certain other words such as *animal* and *hospital,* where the second vowel would be schwa in most dialects of English, StHE speakers use a high front vowel [i].

Consonants and processes affecting consonants

V and W

In most speakers, /w/ is variable occurring as [w] or more commonly, especially word-initially as a labiodental approximant [ʋ] - e.g. *ven the vether is vet* ('when the weather is wet')*; tin vistles* ('...whistles'), *the Prince of Vales ('...* Wales')*,* and *veel* (wheel). The opposite change – [w] for /v/ also occurs, but this is rare – e.g. *ower* for 'over'. Hancock (1991:20) comments as follows:

> The most evident feature is the transposition of [v] and [w], which is widespread in the island and coastal dialects (e.g in Pitcairn, Norfolk, Gullah, some varieties of Nova Scotian, & c.), and which have sometimes fallen together as [v] or [β]. This feature was common in some 19th Century British dialects, but has largely disappeared in Britain.

D and T
In most cases, especially word initially, the interdental fricatives are replaced by other sounds, most commonly [ð] > [d] and [θ] > [t]; e.g. *dat* (that); *tings* (things). Sometimes there are dental stop realisations rather than alveolar stops; and less commonly an aspirated alveolar [tʰ], thus some speakers produced [tʰænks] for *thanks*.

Consonant cluster simplification
Consonant clusters are often simplified, especially at word endings; e.g. [fa:s] for 'fast', [pɒʊn] for 'pound', and [kəlɛk] for 'collect'. Consonant cluster simplification, although not as common, has also been noted e.g. [tʃɪrn̩] for 'children', [tʃaɪd] for 'child' and [spɪdl] for 'spindle'.

–ING
This suffix is almost unexceptionally reduced to [ən], with the vowel occasionally dropped in fast, connected speech to produce a syllabic /n̩/.

Devoicing
Final devoicing occurs in StHE. It is particularly common in the plural morpheme /s/ e.g. in *beans, peas, days, houses, stairs* and *things*.

Glottalisation and flaps
In casual StHE speech, secondary or unstressed segments, particularly word endings, are accorded even less stress than in standard varieties like RP. This affects the pronunication of intervocalic [t] in words like 'sitting', which is realised as a glottal stop with the last syllable reduced, approximating [sɪʔn]. In words like 'letter', [t] is flapped, resulting in [lɛɾə].

/v/ > [b] and /b/ > [β]
In intervocalic position [b] occasionally turns up as a realisation of /v/ and [β] for /b/. Slight evidence that this may have been more common historical process is suggested by two examples. One informant identified a breed of duck as a *scoby* (from *Muscovy*). Conversely, two other elderly informants, talking of their work in the now defunct flax mills, enunciated the /b/ in 'fibre' as a bilabial fricative [β]. It appears that this articulation of /b/ is not productive, and is limited to particular words.

3. Conclusion

It is evident that that StHE is a fascinating variety in terms of its historical retentions of certain sounds and processes common to the input British dialects.

It also shows common processes like final devoicing that might be motivated by language and dialect contact on the island. As a variety whose history involves BrE dialects, languages of slaves from West Africa (and other parts) and their versions of English, StHE invites comparisons with African American English, Caribbean Englishes and so forth. At the same time in some features, like rounded realisations of the PRICE vowel and the KIT split, it invites comparisons with other Southern Hemisphere Englishes. There is clearly much work to be done.

Exercises and study questions

1. Discuss the 'KIT-split' in StHE.

2. What archaisms in consonant realisation can be found in StHE?

3. What archaisms in vowel realisation can be found in StHE?

4. What are the main similarities that StHE shares with other Southern Hemisphere Englishes?

5. List three salient differences between StHE phonology and that of other Southern Hemisphere Englishes.

Selected references

Please consult the General references for titles mentioned in the text but not included in the references below. For a full bibliography see the accompanying CD-ROM.

Hancock, Ian
    1991   St. Helena English. In: Francis Byrne and Thom Huebner (eds.), *Development and Structures of Creole Languages. Essays in Honor of Derek Bickerton*, 16-28.Amsterdam/Philadelphia: Benjamins.
Barnes, John
    1817   *A Tour through the Island of St Helena.* London: JM Richardson.
Mellis, John Charles
    1875   *St Helena. A Physical, Historical and Topographical Description of the Island: Its Geology, Fauna, Flora, and Meteorology.* London: L Reeve

Indian English: phonology

Ravinder Gargesh

1.   Introduction

Indian English (IndE) is a cover term for a number of varieties of English used as a second language in India. These varieties exhibit significant phonological variations, stemming from regional linguistic differences. However many of these features converge into what can be considered a 'general' phonology of IndE. English is widely used in India - it is the 'associate official' language of the country and it also serves as a link language between the educated. It is the most potent medium of higher education, perhaps the sole medium of science and technology. Most books, newspapers, reports, seminars and so forth directed to a nationwide audience are brought out in this language.

Work on IndE phonology has so far been largely sketchy or tilted towards the use of English in a particular region. Because of an earlier focus on language teaching, IndE has often been characterized as a 'deviant' variety, with researchers focusing on its phonetic differences from RP. It is nonetheless surprising that no full-length description of IndE is available, despite its widespread use. English is spoken in India by a very large section ranging from the semi-literate to the highly educated. For the purposes of this paper a random selection has been made of educated speakers who use English as a second language. An effort has been made to broadly cover all the major areas of the country in order to make phonological generalizations and show the range of variation in IndE.

2.   Phonology of IndE

The present study is based on the phonological description of the variety used by educated speakers in the areas of education, administration, science and business etc.

2.1.   Overview of previous studies

Work on the phonetics and phonology of Indian English can be divided into five broad categories, which are more fully referenced in the CD accompanying this Handbook. The first category consists of works describing the phonetic aspects of IndE (e.g. Bansal 1978). The second category comprises studies that compare the sound system of RP with an Indian language and in the process involve a variety of IndE (e.g. with Tamil - Balasubramanian 1972). In the third category occur works which contrast RP with a regional variety of IndE (Marathi English – Kelkar 1957). The fourth category consists of works that study the perception and intelligibility of IndE (e.g. Bansal 1978). The fifth category consists of scholars who focus on the study of IndE in sociolinguistic contexts (e.g. Agnihotri 1991). In this process significant phonological patterns have been highlighted by Nihalani, Tongue and Hosali (1979), Kachru (1982: 359), Trudgill and Hannah (1982: 105) and others. The view emerging from most of these studies is that IndE is largely shaped by the phonological patterns of the respective mother tongues and that this process needs to be studied in depth. The description of IndE in the present work is based on tape recordings carried out in 2003 and 2004. The elicited data consists of word lists of Wells (1982) and Foulkes and Docherty (1999), a reading passage and a stretch of free conversation by speakers of IndE from various parts of the country. Since there is a large transferring or migrating population in Delhi, the entire recording was done in this capital city. For the analysis this work will first enumerate the distinctive sounds of IndE and then go on to look at the major phonological processes, and the principles of word accentuation and intonation.

2.2.   Distinctive sounds of Indian English

The distinctive sounds of Indian English have been identified by Bansal (1978: 101–111) and Nihalani, Tongue and Hosali (1979: 209–212) by viewing IndE as a uniform variety of an educated group. However, much regional variation is found in the utterance of many vowels and consonants across the length and breadth of the country. The variations are mainly due to the following factors:

(i)   The influence of the phonology of Indian languages which consist of over 200 mainstream languages belonging to four distinct language families: Indo-Aryan, Dravidian, Austro-Asiatic and Tibeto-Burman.

(ii) Within the languages of the respective language families there is much regional variation.

(iii) Since English is taught to Indians by Indians the local influence of sounds can be easily perceived.

(iv) Sociologically, the IndE speech community consists broadly of three kinds of speakers: (a) a small number of people whose command over English is near-native, (b) a significant number of administrators, teachers, scientists, journalists, businessmen etc., at the middle level, whose variety is considered to be the educated variety and a benchmark for English Language teaching (ELT) and (c) at the lower level there are many others whose competence is severely limited and who can use English only in their restricted domains, e.g. shopkeepers, waiters etc.

2.3   The vowels of IndE

Table 1.   The vowels of IndE according to Wells' lexical sets.

KIT	ɪ > iː
DRESS	e > ɛ > ə
TRAP	æ > ɛ
LOT	ɔ > ɒ > a
STRUT	ʌ > ə > ʊ
FOOT	ʊ > uː
BATH	ɑː
CLOTH	ɔ > o > aː
NURSE	ɜː > ʌ > ə > aː
FLEECE	iː > ɪ
FACE	eː
PALM	ɑː
THOUGHT	ɔː > oː > aː
GOAT	oː > ɔː
GOOSE	uː
PRICE	aɪ
CHOICE	ɔɪ > oɪ > oe
MOUTH	aʊ
NEAR	ɪə > iːjə > ɪjəː > eə
SQUARE	æ > eː > eə > ɛː

Table 1.   The vowels of IndE according to Wells' lexical sets.

START	ɑː
NORTH	ɔː > aː > ɒ
FORCE	ɔː > oː
CURE	ɪjoː > ɪjɔː > ɪjuː > ɪjuə
happY	ɪ > iː
lettER	ə
horsES	ə > ɨ
commA	a

The short monophthongs

KIT

This short, stressed, high vowel is generally articulated all over India, except for the Bengal-Orissa region in Eastern India where the languages of this region do not have the long-short vowel distinctions. Hence, this vowel freely alternates with the long, stressed, high vowel [iː] in the category of FLEECE.

DRESS

The major realizations of this vowel are [e] and [ɛ]. In regions of Uttar Pradesh, Haryana, Rajasthan, Gujarat, Tamil Nadu and Karnataka, it is realized as [e]. However, in Maharashtra, Kashmir, Punjab, Bihar, and Orissa and in the North-eastern region of India it is realized as [ɛ]. At times it is also realized as [ə].

TRAP

By and large the vowel is realized as [æ], however in Haryana, Rajasthan and Gujarat it is often heard as the lowered [ɛ].

LOT

The usual vowel realization is [ɔ]. In some regions like Gujarat, Maharashtra and Kashmir it is realized as [ɒ]. Its variation [aː] can also be heard in most parts of India.

STRUT

While it is usually realised as [ʌ], some informants from Kashmir, Harayana and Uttar Pradesh (UP) articulate it as the non-stressed [ə]. Some follow the written convention to realize it as [ʊ].

FOOT

Mostly it is realized as a weakly-rounded [ʊ]. However, there are regions like Bengal, Orissa, and parts of Bihar, UP and Rajasthan where the long back vowel [u:] can often be heard.

The long monophthongs

BATH

It is realized as long low back vowel [ɑ:].

CLOTH

It is mostly articulated as [ɔ:] and is also realized as [o:] in Haryana, UP, Rajasthan and Bengal. However, in most parts of the country it is also realized as [a:].

NURSE

It is mostly realized as [ɛ:]. It occurs as [ʌ] in Gujarat, Rajasthan, Haryana, Punjab and in North-East India. In Maharashtra, UP, Tamil Nadu, Karnataka, Andhra Pradesh (AP), and Kerala it realized as [ə]. In areas of Orissa and Bengal it is also articulated as [a:].

FLEECE

It is by and large articulated as [i:] with [ɪ] being in variation amongst speakers of Orissa and Bengal.

PALM

It is realized as the low-back, long, unrounded vowel [ɑ:] as in BATH.

THOUGHT

The usual realization is [ɔ], a half-open weakly rounded back vowel. It is also realized by some speakers as [o:] and by still others as [a:].

GOOSE

It is usually realized as the high, back rounded [u:].

START

Mostly realized as [ɑ:], at times with a postvocalic trilled /r/.

NORTH

Largely it is realized as [ɔ]. However, extensive variation exists in the form [a:] and [ɒ:].

FORCE

Mostly it is realized as [o]. Some variation is available in the form [ɔ].

The diphthongs

FACE
It is invariably realized as the monophthong [e:].

GOAT
It is usually realized as a monophthong [o:]. Some speakers articulate it as [ɔ:] due to, probably, spelling convention in words like *broad*.

PRICE
It is realized as a diphthong [aɪ]. The glide element of [ɪ] is quite distinct.

CHOICE
This diphthong has three variations: [ɔɪ], [oe], and [oɪ].

MOUTH
It is uniformly realized as the diphthong [aʊ]. The latter sound of the diphthong is relatively stronger than the one in RP.

NEAR
The most widespread realization is the diphthong [ɪə]. The other significant variations are [i:jə], [ɪjə:] and [eə].

SQUARE
Mostly it is realized as [ɛ:]. Other variations are [e:], [æ] and [eə].

CURE
Generally the diphthong is realized as [ɪjo:]. But it has variations such as [ɪjɔ:], [ɪju:], and [ɪjuə].

TUEsday
Generally it is realized as [ɪju:].

FIRE
The triphthong is realized as [aɪə] mainly in South India, Bengal and Orissa. The variant form [aeə] is realized in UP, Haryana, Punjab, and Rajasthan.

EITHER
The initial diphthong is realized as [aɪ] most of the time. Its variant form [eɪ] is heard more in South India, particularly in Tamil Nadu and Kerala. Some speakers also realize it as [i:], and in the northeast some even as [e:].

Other vowels

happY
Generally it is articulated as the short front high vowel [ɪ], but its variant form
[i:] can be heard in parts of the country.

lettER
This is realized as [ər] although in the highly educated variety it tends to be
the non-rhotic [ə]. Generally, the trilled /r/ is highly pronounced whenever it
occurs in the graphic script in all varieties of IndE as second language.

horsES
It is realized as the mid high vowel [ɨ] and at times as the low mid-vowel [ə].

commA
It is realized as the half-lengthened [a.].

The opposition between /ʌ/ and /ə/, /ɒ/ and /ɔ/ and /ɛ/ and /æ/ is not clear-cut in
IndE varieties. There is recognizable alternation between /ɒ/, /ɔ/ and /ɑ:/ (LOT
vs THOUGHT vs PALM).

2.4.   The consonants of IndE

Stops
Out of the stops P, T, K, B, D, G, it is only the former three that show different
realizations. Firstly, the voiceless stops are not aspirated in the syllable-initial
position in IndE. This may be because aspirated voiceless stops are phonemic
in North Indian languages, and the relatively weakly aspirated allophones of P,
T, K in BrE are either not noticed or not associated with the phonemic aspirates
of North Indian languages. Secondly, T, and D tend to be retroflexed as in the
words *certificate* [sərʈifike:ʈ] and *London* [ləndən].

Nasals
In syllable-initial position only /m/ and /n/ occur; the velar nasal /ŋ/ occurs
as a homorganic variant of /n/ before velars. The velar nasal is realized as a
combination of the nasal and the voiced velar consonant as in the words *sing*
and *rung* - [sɪŋg], [rʌŋg]. The retroflexed nasal /ɳ/ can also be heard when the
alveolar nasal is articulated before a retroflexed stop as in the words *aunty* and
band – [a:ɳʈi:], [bæɳɖ]

Affricates

The affricates [tʃ] and [dʒ] are distinct as in the words *chin* and *gin* and not generally subject to variation.

Fricatives

F and V are not realized as labiodentals in some varieties of IndE. For most speakers of Oriya and Bangla and those in the Hindi speaking belt, F is realized as [pʰ] and V often overlaps with W as in the realizations of the word *power* - [pa:vər] ~ [pa: wər]. In Orissa and Bengal the V is also realized as [bʰ] as in the word *never* - [nebʰ ər].

The dental fricatives /θ/ and /ð/ are non-existent in IndE. The aspirated voiceless stop [t̪ʰ] is realized for /θ/; the voiced stop [d̪] is realized for /ð/ - as in *thin* = [t̪ʰɪn] and *then* = [den]. In South India the alveolar stop /t/ is often used instead of /θ/ as in *thought* - [tɔt].

/s/ and /z/ do occur in IndE. However, regional variations are often heard. E.g., in Bengal /s/ is replaced by /ʃ/ as in [ʃem] for *same*. The [z] is also often realized as [dʒ] as in [pʰri:dʒ] or [fri:dʒ] for *freeze* and [praɪdʒ] for *prize*.

The palato-alveolars /ʃ/, /ʒ/ also have their variant forms. While /ʃ/ is realized in most places as in RP, in Orissa it is often replaced by a /s/ as in [si:] for *she*, and [si:p] or [sɪp] for *ship*. The /ʒ/ sound is mostly non-existent in IndE. It is realized as /dʒ/, /z/ or /j/ as in [ple:dʒər], [ple:zər] or [plaɪjər] for *pleasure*.

The glottal fricative /h/ is generally realized in North India. There is, however, a tendency towards H-dropping, substituted by a low tone amongst some Punjabi speakers; e.g., *house* is realized as [àus] and *heat* as [ìːt]. In South India a 'euphonic' /j/ and /w/ are sometimes realized in place of the /h/ as in [jill] for *hill*, [jæd] for *had* and [laɪvliwud] for *livelihood* .

IndE has two liquids, /l/ and /r/. The /l/ is generally `clear' (i.e. alveolar), even after contexts that induce a dark /l/ in other dialects of English (e.g. after back vowels). The liquid /r/ is generally trilled; in consonant clusters in words like *trap*, *drain*, *cry* etc it has a trilled rather than approximant realization. This is true of postvocalic /r/ as well: e.g., [ka:r] and [ka:rt̪] for *car* and *cart* respectively. Although postvocalic realizations of /r/ might be an instance of spelling pronunciation, it must be conceded that the English brought to India from the earliest times is likely to have its postvocalic *r*'s intact.

Amongst the semivowels /j/ is only realized as [j]; while /w/ has an overlap with the labiodental fricative /v / as in [pa:vər] or [pa:wər] for *power*. It has already been pointed out that the 'euphonic' /j/ and /w/ exist in most South Indian speech as can be seen in [jevery] for *every* and [won] and [wonly] for *own* and *only* respectively.

3. Some specific phonological processes of IndE

As a formally-learnt variety IndE shows greater correlation between writing and speech sounds than one encounters in informally learnt L1 English. In North India vowel-initial consonant clusters of the type #sp- ; #st-, # sk- and #sl- are generally broken up. In eastern Uttar Pradesh and Bihar a short high prothetic vowel /ɪ/ is inserted in the word-initial position: hence [ɪspi:tʃ] for *speech* and [isku:l] for *school*. In Punjab and Haryana, on the other hand, the low-back, untensed, svarabhakti (or anaptyctic) vowel /ə/ is inserted between the clusters: hence [səpi:tʃ] for *speech* and [səku:l] for *school*. Both these processes convert the initial monosyllable into a disyllable.

In the north-east, particularly in Nagaland and Manipur, a word-final consonant cluster is simplified by dropping the last consonant, e.g., *act* is realized as [ɛk] and *fruits* as [fru:ʈ].

In South India svarabhakti operates in word final –nst # clusters. Thus, *against* is realized as [age:nəst].

IndE also reveals at times /ə/ deletion in relatively light positions, in keeping with BrE norms: *dispensary* = /dɪs'pɛnsəri:/ = [dɪs'pɛnsri:]; *allegory* = /ə'lɛgəri:/ = [ə'lɛgri:]; *confederation* = /kənfɛdə're:ʃən/ = [kənfɛd're:ʃən].

Wh- words are often articulated with the /wh/ sequence, as in [wha:i] and [wheyər] for *why* and *where* respectively. That is, /w/ is aspirated, not pre-aspirated as in RP and a few other English dialects.

Geminates frequently occur within and across morpheme boundaries in words like the following:

| *innate* | [ɪnneʈ] | *fully* | [fulli:] |
| *cannot* | [kɛnnoʈ] | *oppressive* | [oppressiv] |

IndE shows greater usage of [d] rather than of [t] for *–ed* inflections after voiceless consonants. Thus *traced* = [tre:sd], *advanced* = [ɛdva:nsd] and *packed* = [pækd]. Words like *trust* and *trussed* are homophones in RP but are distinguished in IndE by the realization of [t] and [d] in the respective words.

Some speakers omit the semivowels /j/ and /w/ when following a mid or close vowel agreeing in backness. Thus *yet* is realized as [ɛʈ] and *won't* as [o:nʈ]. Conversely, it has already been mentioned that some other speakers add a semivowel before an initial vowel in exactly the same conditions, thus *every* = [jevri], *about* = [je'bauʈ] and *old* = [wo:ld], *own* = [wo:n] etc.

It should also be noted that the rule of syllabic consonant formation (which converts [ə] plus a sonorant into a syllabic sonorant) does not apply in IndE. Thus *metal* = [meʈəl], *button* = [bʌʈən] etc.

4.   Prosodic features

One of the markers of IndE as a distinct variety is its peculiar word-stress and intonation patterns. These make IndE less comprehensible to speakers from outside South Asia than to its own speakers and those of South Asian English generally. This is because the rules of accentuation of IndE are closer to those of Indian languages than to those of RP.

4.1.   Word stress/accentuation

Word accentuation in IndE shows a heavy influence of the filter language(s). It is observed that in IndE a syllable of a word is more prominent than in RP. A careful examination shows that there is significant correlation between the weight and position of syllables within a word and their prominence. The problem can be explained by accepting the tripartite division of syllable types in terms of their weight: (a) Light = (C)V, (b) Heavy = (C)V: /VC, and (c) Extra–heavy = (C)V:C/(C)VCC (see Singh and Gargesh 1995).

The following rules of accentuation broadly appear to apply in IndE:

(a) All monosyllabic words are accented irrespective of the quantity of the syllable.
(b) In bisyllabic words the primary accent falls on the penultimate syllable if it is not followed by an extra–heavy syllable, otherwise the primary stress would full on the ultimate syllable.
(c) In trisyllabic words the primary accent falls on the penultimate syllable if it is heavy by nature or position, otherwise it falls on the antepenultimate syllable.

The above rules can account for the placement of primary accent in a word of IndE. The first of these rules leads to the tendency of providing relatively strong stress to weak syllables such as in auxiliary verb forms, articles etc. Rules (b) and (c) go on to provide primary stress to a syllable in a polysyllabic word. Thus, for the application of rules (b) and (c) the following examples can be viewed:

Rule (b):

taboo	['tæbu:]	*degree*	['dɪgri:]
mistake	['mɪsʈek]	*bamboo*	['bæmbʊ]
defy	[dɪf'aɪ]	*impact*	[ɪm'pækʈ]
record	[rɪ'kɑːrɖ]	*servile*	[sər'vaːɪl]

gymnast	[dʒɪmˈnɑːst]	*cartoon*	[ˈkɑːrʈuːn]
monsoon	[ˈmɔːnsuːn]	*concrete*	[ˈkɔːnkriːʈ]
abstract	[ˈæbsʈrækʈ]		

Rule (c):

tendency	[tɛnˈdɛnsɪ]	*modesty*	[moˈdɛsʈɪ]
minster	[mɪˈnɪsʈər],	*character*	[kæˈræktər]
curvature	[kərˈveːtʃər]	*literature*	[lɪʈˈreːtʃər]
necessary	[nɛˈsɛssərɪ]	*terrific*	[ˈtɛrrɪfik]
diminish	[ˈɖɪmɪnɪʃ]	*category*	[kəˈʈægorɪ]
attestation	[əˈʈɛsʈeʃən].		

In the case of compounds the leftmost primary stress is generally retained. Thus:

animation	[ˈænɪmeʃən]	*relaxation*	[rɪˈlækseʃən]
Chinese	[ˈtʃaɪjniːz]	*Japanese*	[ˈdʒæpəniːz]
meditative	[ˈmædɪteʈɪv]	*dramatic*	[ˈdræmətɪk],
photography	[ˈfoʈogrɑːfɪ].		

As a result of the rules of accentuation many times the shift of accent due to grammatical factors is not observable. Thus the noun and verb form often remain the same: *permit* [ˈpərmɪʈ]; *transfer* [ˈʈrɑːnsfər]; *impact* [ɪmˈpækʈ]; *protest* [proˈʈɛsʈ].

4.2.   Rhythm and intonation

IndE has its own syllable-timed rhythmic patterns. Here syllables are uttered with an almost equal prominence. This also means that often IndE does not use weak forms of vowels in unstressed positions. Thus a sentence like *I'm thinking of you* can be heard as: [ˈaːɪ ˈæm ˈt̪ʰɪŋkiŋ ˈɔf ˈjuː]. Here the first person singular pronoun, the auxiliary and the preposition too have a relative stress and hence they are not realized in their shortened forms like [aːɪm] or [əv] etc. Since the syllables are articulated more fully, IndE takes relatively more time in articulating similar stretches of the English language than, say, RP.

IndE reveals a falling intonation in statements, such as in: *The boy is running on the road* = [də bɔe ɪz ↗ ˈrʌnnɪŋ ɔn ↘ də roːɖ]. A falling intonation can be perceived in commands and exclamations.

Rising intonation is visible in *yes-no* questions, tag questions, some *wh*-questions, and in dependent clauses:

Yes-No question
Are you coming? = [aːr juː ↗ kʌmɪŋg?]

Tag question
He has done the work, hasn't he? = [hiː hæz dʌn də vərk, ↗ hæznt̪ hiː?].

Wh- question
What is the financial benefit? = [wʌt̪ɪz də faɪnænʃəl ↗ bɛnɛfɪt?].

Dependent clause
The boy who is walking will come here soon. = [də bɔe ↗ huː ɪz vaː kɪŋg ↘ wɪl kʌm heər suːn].

5.   Current research issues

The phonology of IndE requires more work on the sound patterns of the many regional varieties of IndE. Intonation has been a more or less neglected field that offers many challenges to researchers. Given the expanse of the country and its immense linguistic variation there is scope for research in almost every branch of the phonology of IndE.

Exercises and study questions

1. Of the vowels and diphthongs of IndE, which are most different from their equivalents in RP?

2. What differences are there in the realisation of PTK in IndE and RP? Listen for these differences in the IndE phonetic sample on the CD.

3. What different tendencies in the realisation of H are there in sub-varieties of IndE?

4. What different tendencies in the realisation of F and V are there in sub-varieties of IndE?

5. Use the word stress rules described in 4.1 to predict the stress of the following words in IndE:
literature
cartoon
diminish
modesty

Selected references

Please consult the General references for titles mentioned in the text but not included in the references below. For a full bibliography see the accompanying CD-ROM.

Agnihotri, Rama Kant
    1991   Soundpatternsoflndian English: Asociolinguistic perspective. In: R.S. Gupta and K. Kapoor (eds.) *English in India: Issues and problems,* 175 – 88. Delhi: Academic Foundation.
Balasubramanian, T.
    1972   The vowels of Tamil and English. *CIEFL Bulletin* 9: 27–34.
Bansal, R.K.
    1978   The phonology of Indian English. In: R. Mohan (ed.), *Indian Writings in English.* Madras: Orient Longman.
Nihalani, Paroo, R.K. Tongue, and Priya Hosali
    2004   *Indian and British English: A Handbook of Usage and Pronunciation.* Delhi: Oxford University Press. 2nd ed.
Singh, A. and Ravinder Gargesh
    1996   Some aspects of syllable structure and word- accent in Hindi. In: S.K. Verma and A. Singh (eds.), *Perspectives on Language and Society. Papers in Memory of Prof. R.N. Srivastava,* Volume II. Delhi: Kalinga Publications.

Pakistani English: phonology

Ahmar Mahboob and Nadra Huma Ahmar

1.   Introduction

A study of Pakistani English (PakE) must begin with an understanding of its
historical and social roots in an undifferentiated, pre-partition 'British India'.
English was first introduced in the Indo-Pak subcontinent by the British in the
16th century. It received official recognition with the passing of Macaulay's
minutes of 1835. Throughout the British era, English kept gaining political
and social status. By 1947, when Pakistan and India gained their independence
from the British, the English language had become so entrenched in the socio-
political fabric of the region that it was retained as an official language in both
countries (see Ali 1993).

English in British India initially spread because of economic and social mobility associated with the language. People learned English either by contact or
through formal schooling. However, since there were not enough native English-speaking teachers to meet the demand, most English teachers were Indians.
Thus, the input that English language learners received in South Asia was non-
native and local. There was relatively little contact with native varieties of English in India, and after independence, this contact was further reduced. These
factors have contributed to the institutionalization and evolution of South Asian
English as a distinct variety.

During the British era, as various nationalist and ethnic movements in South
Asia used language as a symbol of their identity, linguistic issues complexified.
An example of such symbolism is the division leading to linguistic changes
between Hindi and Urdu which strengthened (and is strengthening) as a result
of religious affiliation of these languages with Hinduism and Islam, respectively. In a regional setting, the status of Hindi vs. Dravidian languages of
South India in post-colonial India, or the role of Urdu vs. Sindhi in Pakistan,
has been a cause of strife within each country. As a result of this politicization
of local languages, English, because of its 'foreignness', has been preferred as
a neutral language and gained political acceptance in the new countries. These
local needs and uses of English, and the limited contact with native speakers
of English has resulted in what has been called 'nativization' of English in the
Indian sub-continent.

With the political partition of the sub-continent, the fate of English fell into the hands of the respective political leaders in India and Pakistan. In Pakistan, English was to go on a roller-coaster ride. While it was initially maintained by the Pakistani leadership, it soon became a symbol of resentment amongst the religious parties, who felt that maintaining the status of English symbolized a new form of colonization. There was intense opposition to English by these groups. However, there were three reasons why these demands were not taken into consideration by the government: (1) there was insufficient material in local languages to use in education and other domains (lack of corpus planning), (2) there was no other politically neutral language that could replace English, and (3) the religious parties did not have sufficient political power. As a result, English maintained its supremacy in Pakistan and little was done to change this. However, this status quo changed with General Zia-ul-Haq's capture of power through a military coup in 1977. General Haq justified his coup by implementing rapid Islamization and Urduization policies and decentralizing the role of English. His was the first serious effort by a Pakistani government to decrease the role of English. This change in the government's attitude towards English was manifest in the 1978 language in education policy which advised all English medium schools (schools where all classes were taught in English) to switch to Urdu. However, elite English medium schools, where children of the people in power studied, were waived from the need to make these changes. Although these changes were supported by leaders of certain political parties and religious organizations, they did not find favour among the populace. By 1983, there was recognition within General Haq's government that the language in education policy had been hurriedly passed without the required planning, and, by 1987, it was retracted. Although the Urdu-only policies have been revised, the impact of non-English education for approximately a decade and its dismissal from official use (especially in government) is still evident. Today, the government realizes the value of English in a global economy and is implementing policies to teach it at primary level in all schools. This change in policy is supported by most of the people who prefer learning English to other languages and see it as a means of economic development

1.1. Pakistani languages and PakE

While work on South Asian English suggests that there is a need for a description of a pan-South Asian model of English, it also recognizes differences between various sub-varieties of South Asian English (Kachru 1983). These sub-varieties are defined in terms of local languages. Thus, PakE and Indian English have unique features based on the differences in the vernaculars of the population of each country (and on the different political, educational and economic policies of each country). Similarly, PakE itself is heterogeneous not only because of the socio-economic, geographic, and educational background of the people who speak it, but also because of the various first languages of its speakers. An example of this is the difference in the placement and quality of the epenthetic vowel in English spoken by native speakers of Urdu and Panjabi.

- Native speakers of Urdu: [ɪstɑːrt] 'start'
- Native speakers of Panjabi: [sətɑːrt] 'start'

Another example of variable influence of first language on PakE concerns the realization of [ʒ]:

- Native speakers of Urdu: [meʒʌr] 'measure'
- Native speakers of Panjabi: [mejʌr] or [medʒʌr] 'measure'

In this example, the [ʒ] is either realized as a [j] or a [dʒ] by Panjabi speakers of PakE. The exact distribution of this variation has not been studied.

These examples of differences in PakE suggest that there may be considerable variation within PakE based on speakers' first language. Pakistan is a multilingual country with at least 69 living languages (*Ethnologue* 2002), and speakers of these different languages may be predicted to speak English differently. Unfortunately, at present, there is no research that explores the extent of influence of various mother tongues on PakE(es). A review of the small number of studies that focus on PakE is presented in the companion paper on PakE in the syntax part of this volume.

The dominant (numerically and politically) languages of Pakistan include (in alphabetical order), Balochi, English, Pashtu, Panjabi, Sindhi, Siraiki, and Urdu. The percentage of native speakers of these languages is given in Table 1 below. The numbers (except for English) provided in Table 1 are based on the CIA World Fact Book (2002). The estimated percentage for English is based on the literacy rate of 42.7%, and the ratio of English medium schools. In interpreting the numbers provided in Table 1, the total estimated population of Pakistan, of approximately 150 million, should be kept in mind. Thus a seemingly tiny 3% of Baluchi speakers corresponds to about 4.5 million people. Similarly, if English is spoken with some proficiency by 4% of the Pakistani population, the number represented is approximately 6 million people, more than the total population of New Zealand.

Table 1.   Major languages of Pakistan

Language	Percentage of native speakers (except English)
Panjabi	40%
Sindhi	12%
Siraiki (a variant of Panjabi)	10%
Pashtu	8%
Urdu (official and national language)	8%
Balochi	3%
Other	19%
English (official language; used as a second language with a focus on writing rather than oral communication)	4% (not verified)

Although this information has not been fully utilized in research on PakE at present, it is hoped that future research will explore the relationship between PakE(es) and various indigenous languages. It might be useful to begin a comprehensive study of PakE with a focus on English as used by native speakers of the major languages listed here. The present study focuses on native speakers of Urdu because it is the national language of Pakistan and one of the two official languages of Pakistan (the other official language being English). Reference to speakers of other languages is made where information is available.

2.   Sounds of PakE

At present, there are no detailed studies of the phonology of PakE. This paper therefore attempts to present a preliminary description of PakE phonology based on data collected in Karachi in the summer of 2002. Language samples presented and analyzed in this paper (unless otherwise stated) were collected from six educated Pakistanis between the ages of 22 and 37. Four of these participants were female and two were male. All of the participants were native speakers of Urdu. Language samples were first elicited using the Sheffield word-list (Foulkes and Docherty 1999) and then the 'North Wind' reading passage.

Table 2.   Vowel realization in PakE using Wells' lexical sets

KIT	ɪ	DRESS	e
TRAP	æ	LOT	ɔː
STRUT	ʌ	FOOT	ʊ ~ uː
BATH	æ ~ ɑː	CLOTH	ɔː ~ɔ ~ oː
NURSE	ʌ	FLEECE	iː
FACE	eɪ ~ eː	PALM	ɑː
THOUGHT	ɔː	GOAT	əʊ ~ oː ~ ʊ
GOAL	əʊ ~ oː	GOOSE	uː
PRICE	aɪ	CHOICE	ɔɪ
MOUTH	aʊ	NEAR	ɪə ~ eə
SQUARE	eə ~ əɪ ~ ɑɪ	START	ɑː
NORTH	ɔː	FORCE	ɔː ~ əʊ
CURE	jʊə ~ eɔː ~ jeɔ	HAPP*Y*	ɪ
LETT*ER*	ʌ	HORS*ES*	ɪ
COMM*A*	ʌ		

2.1.   Vowels

Vowels collected using the Sheffield set as listed in Table 2 can be sorted into two main groups. The first group contains vowels which were spoken without variation by the Pakistani speakers. The second group consists of vowels that varied in their realization as spoken by different speakers.

2.1.1.   Group 1: invariant vowel realisations

Pakistani speakers did not exhibit any variation in their realization of vowels in this group. Vowels within this group can be further categorized into two sub-groups *vis-à-vis* RP. The first sub-group (Group 1A) contains vowels that are similar to RP and the second sub-group (Group 1B) includes vowels which are different.

Group 1A
Table 3 provides a list of words that fall in this category. This list itself has two sections. The first section lists monophthongs and the second section lists diphthongs.

Table 3. List of vowels with no variation among Pakistani speakers and similar to RP

Lexical item	PakE	RP (based on Oxford Dictionary)
Monophthongs		
KIT	ɪ	ɪ
HAPPY	ɪ	ɪ
THOUGHT	ɔː	ɔː
NORTH	ɔː	ɔː
FORCE	ɔː	ɔː
PALM	ɑː	ɑː
START	ɑː	ɑː
DRESS	e	e
TRAP	æ	æ
STRUT	ʌ	ʌ
FLEECE	iː	iː
GOOSE	uː	uː
Diphthongs		
PRICE	aɪ	aɪ
CHOICE	ɔɪ	ɔɪ
MOUTH	aʊ	aʊ

This group is the largest containing 15 of the 29 words in the Sheffield set. These vowels did not vary among the six Pakistani speakers studied and were also similar to RP.

Group 1B
This group consists of vowels which showed no variation within Pakistani speakers, but differed from RP. Table 4 is a list of these vowels.

Table 4.   List of vowels with no variation among Pakistani speakers but different from RP

Lexical item	PakE	RP
horsES	ɪ	ə
lettER	ʌ	ə
commA	ʌ	ə
NURSE	ʌ	ɜː
LOT	ɔː	ɔ

The first three words in this group are bi-syllabic. In RP, the second syllable is unstressed and, as a result of unstressing, the vowel is frequently reduced to [ə]. For example, RP speakers stress the first vowel and reduce the second to a lax mid-central vowel, schwa, in [letə] *letter* or [kɔmə] *comma*. Pakistani speakers did not reduce the vowel but rather used a full vowel, e.g., [lettʌr] *letter* or [kɔːmmʌ] *comma*. Thus, there were no observed instances of schwa in the data collected using the Sheffield set (however, instances of /ə/ were observed in connected speech and will be discussed later).

The NURSE vowel is [ʌ] and the LOT vowel [ɔː]. Their RP equivalents, [ɜː] and [ɔ], are not attested in the samples of PakE collected for this study. The tense mid-high central vowel [ɜː] is not attested in Rahman (1990) – see section on rhoticity for a discussion of Rahman's work on PakE. Nihalani, Hosali and Tongue (1989) also do not list this vowel in their table of 'Educated Indian English' monophthongs. However, they do list the lax low back vowel [ɔ] in words such as *cot* and *caught*. Pakistani speakers in this study substitute [ɔ] with either a tense mid back vowel, [ɔː], as in LOT or a tense mid-high back vowel, [oː], as in CLOTH (see group 2 below). It is possible to explain the absence of the vowels [ɜː] and [ɔ] by looking at the Urdu vowel system. Urdu does not use either of these vowels and thus it may be the case that PakE speaker replace these with Urdu vowels.

2.1.2.   Group 2: vowels exhibiting variation

There was some variation in the vowels in this group as realized by Pakistani speakers. These vowels are again grouped within the chart as monophthongs and diphthongs and are listed in Table 5 below. While this paper documents variation in the realization of these vowels in PakE (of native speakers of

Urdu), the range and distribution of these variations within the community has not been examined.

Table 5. List of vowels with variation among Pakistani speakers

Lexical item	PakE	RP
Monophthongs		
FOOT	ʊ ~ uː	ʊ
BATH	ɑː ~ æ	ɑː
CLOTH	ɔ ~ ɔː ~ oː	ɔ
Diphthongs		
FACE	eː ~ eɪ	eɪ
GOAT	oː ~ əʊ ~ ʊ	əʊ
GOAL	oː ~ əʊ	əʊ
NEAR	ɪə ~ eə	ɪə
SQUARE	eə ~ əɪ ~ ɑɪ	eə
CURE	jʊə ~ jeɔː ~ eɔː	jʊəː

The vowel in FOOT varies between a lax mid-high rounded back vowel, [ʊ], and a tense high rounded back vowel, [uː]. The vowel in BATH varies between a tense low back vowel, [ɑː], and a lax low front vowel, [æ]. The vowel in CLOTH is realized as a tense mid back vowel, [ɔː], a tense mid-high back vowel, [oː], or a lax mid back vowel [ɔ]. In all the three cases here, it appears that the vowels vary between a tense and a lax form. In addition, another commonality between the pronunciations of these three words is that, while some speakers of PakE use the same vowel as in RP, others have a slightly raised variant.

The diphthongs in FACE, GOAT, and GOAL in PakE vary between a diphthong and a monophthong. Whereas Rahman (1990: 25–26 and 90) suggests that monophthongisation is a general characteristic (especially in case of [eɪ] → [eː]) of PakE, data here shows that there is variation across speakers. In all three cases, two speakers (the same ones) use a diphthong while the other four use a monophthong.

The diphthongs and triphthongs in SQUARE and CURE respectively vary between being centring and closing. The centring diphthong in NEAR varies in its point of origin. One of them starts from a mid-high vowel, [ɪ], and the other from a mid-low vowel, [e].

2.2.   Consonants

2.2.1. Rhoticity

PakE, based on the language samples collected, may be labeled a rhotic variety of English. [r] is pronounced in all contexts, including after a vowel, by most speakers. Examples of this were found in both the Sheffield set and in the passage: [fɔːrs] 'force' and [wɑːrm] 'warm'.

Postvocalic [r] is produced variably – individual speakers did not pronounce it all the time. However, the presence or absence of [r] was not categorical for any given speaker. For example, the same speaker was observed to use [r] in *start, cure* and *letter*, but to drop it in *force*. The rules and distribution for such variation need to be explored.

Rahman (1990) states that the degree of rhoticity in PakE varies based on sociolinguistic factors. He claims that speakers of an acrolectal variety of PakE may or may not pronounce instances of postvocalic [r]. However, the exact distribution of rhoticity within acrolectal speakers of PakE is not discussed. He further states that mesolectal and basilectal varieties of PakE are rhotic and speakers of these varieties pronounce [r] in all contexts. While it may be possible to identify sub-varieties of PakE using this terminology (as has been done for other varieties of English, e.g. Singaporean), we have avoided doing so. To date, there is very limited documentation of the linguistic features of PakE (in any social context) and therefore we feel that it is too early to sub-categorize PakE and attempt descriptions of possible sub-categories. Rahman's work is based on only 10 speakers (from various L1 backgrounds), and his data was collected (rather anomalously) from Pakistanis living in the United Kingdom. His study has accordingly been severely criticized for a number of reasons.

2.2.2. Retroflexion of [ṭ] and [ḍ]

PakE uses retroflex stops. The alveolar stops of other English dialects are realized as [ṭ] and [ḍ]. This use of retroflex stops instead of RP alveolar stops is listed as an example of 'series substitution' by Kachru (1992: 62) and is a feature of South Asian English. Examples of use of retroflex stops [ṭ] and [ḍ] in PakE are: [ɪsṭrʌṭ] 'strut' and [ḍres] 'dress'.

2.2.3. [ṯ] and [ḏ] (dentalization)

Pakistani speakers used dental stops instead of the RP dental fricatives. This change in the manner of articulation is also cited as a feature of South Asian

English (Kachru 1992: 62). Examples of [t̪] and [d̪] in PakE are [nɔːrt̪] 'north' and [d̪en] 'then'.

2.2.4.   /v/ and /w/

Urdu does not have a phonemic distinction between /v/ and /w/. A phonemic distinction between [v] and [w] was not evident in PakE either. The two sounds were realized as allophones of /w/. An example of variation between these sounds was observed in the pronunciation of the word *wind* which was either realized as [vɪnd] or as [wɪnd]. Examples of the variation in use of [v] and [w] are also found in Rahman (1990). The use of [v] for [w] appears to be a feature of South Asian English and is also discussed by Bhatt (1995) and Sahgal and Agnihotri (1988) among others.

Rahman (1990: 33) also discusses this feature in reference to Pushto speakers. He states that Pushto speakers do not articulate [v] in word final positions and gives the example of [luo] 'love'.

Rahman states that this is an influence of Pushto, which also deletes [v] in these contexts. The realization of [v] and [w] in other contexts is not discussed.

2.2.5.   Clear [l]

All realizations of /l/ were 'clear'. Kachru (1992: 62) lists this as a feature of South Asian English as well. In RP there is an allophonic distribution between a clear and a dark [l]. /l/ is realized as 'dark' or velarised [ɫ] when it is in a word final position or when it is followed by a consonant. It is realized as [l], a 'clear' or alveolar [l], in all other contexts. The following examples show that Pakistani speakers do not exhibit this allophonic variation: [goːl] 'goal' and [lɔːt̪] 'lot'.

The absence of this allophonic variation in PakE may be explained by looking at Urdu, which does not make a distinction between a dark and clear /l/.

3.   Phonological features

A number of phonological features were observed in the data collected. While we have described some of the key features below, these should be considered preliminary findings and generalizations should be avoided. The exact distribution of these features in PakE and the contexts in which they operate need to be studied.

3.1.   Spelling pronunciation/gemination

PakE tends to use spelling as a guide to pronunciation. One manifestation of this is in the gemination of consonants based on spelling. For example, all the speakers geminated the [p] and the [t] in [hæppɪ] *happy* and [lettʌr] *letter*. Gemination was also noticed in connected speech. For example, all speakers geminated the [m] consonant in *immediately* [ɪmmɪdʒɛtli]. However, exceptions to gemination were also observed in the language samples. For example, one regular exception was the word *wrapped*.

3.2.   Vowel reduction

The only instances of /ə/ observed were in connected speech. In our analysis of the passage, as read by the six speakers, there were certain words in which an unstressed vowel was systematically reduced to a schwa. Examples of these words include: (a) the indefinite article *a*; (b) the definite article *the*; (c) the past singular BE form *was*; and (d) words with initial *a* like *attempt*. These words were predictably pronounced as [ə], [d̪ə], [wəz] and [əttemp(t)] respectively. Based on the language samples, it appears that vowel reduction in PakE is limited to certain (grammatical) words and environments in fast speech, rather than being a correlate of unstressed syllables.

It is possible to explain this non-reduction of unstressed vowels in terms of spelling pronunciation of PakE. A good example of this is the pronunciation of *of*. RP speakers realize this word as [əv] by reducing the vowel in this word to a schwa and voicing the labiodental fricative. However, in PakE this word is realized as [ɔf], based on the way it is spelt.

3.3.   Epenthesis

One of the most predictable contexts where epenthesis was observed was in a consonant cluster where the first consonant was a voiceless sibilant and the second consonant was a stop. Thus, *stronger* was pronounced [ɪstrɔːŋgʌr] and *start* was realized as [ɪstɑːrt]. A less predictable context for epenthesis was between a voiced bilabial stop and an alveolar lateral approximant. Thus, *blue* was pronounced [bɪljʊ] by some of the speakers. Both these cases of epenthesis may be explained by looking at Urdu, which does not permit these consonant clusters.

Rahman (1990: 31) gives examples from speakers of PakE who speak Panjabi as a first language. Such speakers break the consonant cluster by inserting a short vowel, /ə/, between the sibilant and the stop. He gives the examples of [səpiːk] 'speak', [səkuːl] 'school', [sətɑːl] 'stall'.

In contrast, Pushto speakers of English do not have any problems with this consonant cluster because Pushto permits these clusters (Rahman 1990: 33).

3.4. Aspiration

Pakistani speakers do not aspirate stops in word initial position when they occur before a vowel. Thus, the word *kit* was realized as [kɪt], without an aspiration on [k] unlike RP [kʰɪt]. This non-realization of an allophonic distribution of voiceless stops in PakE can be explained by looking at Urdu. Urdu, like many other South Asian languages, has a four-way phonemic contrast between voiced and voiceless stops, and aspirated and unaspirated stops. This phonemic contrast is represented in the orthography of the language. There is therefore a good cause for L1 influence in English, with speakers treating stops in all positions as unaspirated. For further discussion see Kachru (1983: 29).

4. Prosodic features

Kachru (1983) states that it is the non-segmental features of South Asian English (SAsE) such as stress and rhythm, rather than segmental features, that mark its uniqueness. He argues that while the segmental features of SAsE are heavily influenced by mother tongues and may therefore be different between various speakers, non-segmental features are shared. One of the primary examples given by him and other linguists working on SAsE is its stress pattern. Variation in stress between RP and SAsE (and a lack of vowel reduction in SAsE) also causes differences in the rhythm of the two varieties.

Research shows that the stress patterns of various sub-varieties of SAsE are comparable and that they do not seem to be influenced by the various first languages of its speakers (Pickering and Wiltshire 2000). In their study, Pickering and Wiltshire looked at SAsE spoken by native speakers of Hindi/Urdu, Bengali, and Tamil and found that there was no significant difference in the lexical stress pattern in the English spoken by speakers of these three languages. This supports Kachru's claim that SAsE shares non-segmental features. Thus, the following description of stress, based on studies of other South Asian dialects of English, may be used to describe PakE as well, since no independent reliable studies of stress of the latter are currently available.

Four dimensions of stress in SAsE have been studied: syllable-time, frequency, pitch, and amplitude.

4.1.   Syllable timing vs. stress timing

SAsE, including PakE, is described as a syllable-timed variety (Nelson 1982; Kachru 1983). Syllables in PakE occur at regular intervals. This is different from RP which is stress-timed with variation in the length of syllables. The traditional explanation for this difference between RP and PakE is given in terms of the first language. Most South Asian languages, including Urdu, are syllable-timed and therefore it is concluded that this pattern is adopted by Urdu speakers of English. The syllable-timed rhythm of PakE goes hand-in-hand with a lack of reduction.

4.2.   Frequency, pitch and amplitude

Pickering and Wiltshire (2000) found that accented syllables were marked by a lower frequency as compared to unaccented syllables in speakers of Indian English, including those of Hindi/Urdu. They find this in contrast with American English and state (2000: 177), "compared to A[merican] E[nglish], in which accented syllables have increased frequency in these contexts, I[ndian] E[nglish] shows a distinct use of a decrease in frequency in accented syllables in similar contexts. This use of low frequency on accented syllables can also be found in Indian languages, suggesting a possible source". Based on the use of frequency to mark stress, Pickering and Wiltshire label South Asian English as a 'pitch-accent' language. They use the distinction between a pitch-accent and a stress-accent language and state that the major marker of accent in South Asian English is pitch. Pickering and Wiltshire also find that unlike speakers of American English, South Asian speakers do not use amplitude to mark stress.

In conclusion, they state (2000: 181) that "there are two differences between IndE and AmE in the phonetic realization of word accent. First, AmE is a stress-accent language, and uses cues such as amplitude and duration as well as frequency, while IndE uses pitch-accent, and relies primarily on the frequency to indicate an accented syllable. Second, AmE indicates an accented syllable with a high frequency, while IndE marks it with a low".

5.   Conclusion

In this paper we have attempted to provide a brief overview of the history and phonology of PakE. However, the description of PakE phonology is far from being thorough. This is partly because no detailed studies of PakE phonology are currently available. In order to compensate for this gap, this paper provides a phonological analysis based on a small language sample. Research in World Englishes in general and Indian and Singaporean English in particular has shown a richness of sociological markings within varieties of English. PakE, as a living language, displays such variations as well. However, these variations have not yet been investigated. We hope that this paper will motivate linguists to explore these variations and study PakE in more detail.

Exercises and study questions

1. Compare the vowels of PakE and IndE.

2. Do the same for the diphthongs.

3. Are there any differences between PakE and IndE regarding consonants?

4. It is not the PakE vowels but the consonants which differ most from RP. Discuss.

5. How is PakE different from RP prosodically?

Selected references

Please consult the General references for titles mentioned in the text but not included in the references below. For a full bibliography see the accompanying CD-ROM.

Ali, Ahmed
    1993   English in South Asia: A Historical perspective. In: Robert J. Baumgardner (ed.), *The English Language in Pakistan*, 3–12. Karachi: Oxford University Press.

Baumgardner, Robert J. (ed)
    1993   *The English Language in Pakistan*. Karachi, Oxford: Oxford University Press.

Baumgardner, Robert J.
    1993a   The indigenization of English in Pakistan. In: Robert J. Baumgardner (ed.), *The English Language in Pakistan*, 41–54. Karachi: Oxford University Press.
    1993b   Utilizing Pakistani newspaper English to teach grammar. In: Baumgardner (ed.), 255-273.

Bhatt, Rakesh
    1995   Prescriptivism, Creativity, and World Englishes. *World Englishes* 14: 247–259.

CIA.
    2002   *CIA: The world factbook*. CIA. Retrieved December 10, 2002, from the
            World Wide Web: http://www.cia.gov/cia/publications/factbook/

Ethnologue.
    2002   *Ethnologue: Languages of the world*. SIL Bibliography. Retrieved
            December 15, 2002, from the World Wide Web: http://www.ethnologue.
            com/web.asp

Kachru, Braj B.
    1992   *The Other Tongue: English Across Cultures*. Urbana: University of Illinois
            Press.

Nelson, Cecil
    1982   Intelligibility and non-native varieties of English. In: Kachru (ed.), 58–
            73.

Pickering, Lucy and Caroline Wiltshire
    2000   Pitch accent in Indian-English teaching discourse. *World Englishes* 19:
            173–183.

Rahman, T.
    1990   *Pakistani English: The Linguistic Description of a Non-native Variety of
            English*. Islamabad: National Institute of Pakistan Studies Quaid-i-Azam
            University.

Sahgal, Anju and R.K. Agnihotri
    1988   Indian English phonology: A sociolinguistic perspective. *English World-
            Wide* 9: 51–64.

Singapore English: phonology

Lionel Wee

1. Introduction

To understand the English language in Singapore, it is useful to make a distinction between two different varieties, Standard Singapore English and Colloquial Singapore English (CollSgE) (popularly known as Singlish). Though it is generally acknowledged that the variation within Singapore English is in actuality a continuum, language policies and attitudes, as well as academic perspectives, are often based on the polarization of this continuum into the two varieties just mentioned.

In this overview, I begin first with a brief historical sketch of the 'arrival' of English in Singapore under British colonial rule, followed by a discussion of modern Singapore society and its language policy of "English-knowing bilingualism". I then continue with a description of attitudes towards the colloquial variety, Singlish, before concluding with academic debates on whether Singapore English is better described in terms of a lectal continuum or a framework of diglossia.

1.1. A brief history of the English language in Singapore

English came to Singapore when in 1819 Sir Stamford Raffles set up the first major British trade settlement there. Prior to that, English speakers had visited the island for purposes of trading and reconnoitering, but it was the arrival of Raffles that "began a formal connection with Britain which was responsible for the prominence that English has in Singapore today" (Gupta 1998: 106). Upon its arrival, the British administration encountered a 'capitan' system, which divided the society into three groups: Malays, Chinese, Indians, plus a capitanless group of 'others', and each ethnic community had in effect its own legal system under the jurisdiction of its own 'capitan' (Bloom 1986: 352). This ethnically-based division was preserved by the British and till today, can be seen in Singapore's policy of 'multiracialism' that underpins its current language policy (see below).

The British were keen to cultivate a group of English-educated elites, and in 1870, produced young men "competent to earn a livelihood in Government and mercantile offices, but the majority of these clerks know only how to read, write and speak English imperfectly" (cited in Bloom 1986: 358). Crucially, however, English had been established as the language by which socio-economic mobility was to be attained, and by 1900, this group of elites had come to enjoy a much greater degree of English language proficiency and to also cover a much wider occupational range.

Alongside the more standardized variety of English taught in the schools, there also developed a colloquial variety, one which showed a high degree of influence from other local languages such as Hokkien, Cantonese, Malay and Tamil (Platt and Weber 1980: 18). The varieties of Malay most important to the development of the colloquial variety were Bazaar Malay (a simplified form of Malay then used predominantly as an inter-ethnic lingua franca) and Baba Malay, spoken primarily by the Straits Chinese. The Straits Chinese or Peranakans are of mixed (Chinese and Malay) ancestry. While they tend to see themselves as culturally and ethnically Chinese, they often use a variety of Malay as the home language.

As Gupta (1998: 109) points out,

> These two contact varieties of Malay had themselves been influenced by the southern variety of Chinese, Hokkien. The lexical items in CollSgE which are not from English are overwhelmingly from Malay and Hokkien – contributed from these two varieties of Malay.

This colloquial variety also developed in the English-medium schools, though more in the playgrounds than in the classrooms. According to Platt and Weber (1980: 19):

> The English-medium schools of Malaya and the Straits Settlements used English as the medium of instruction for all lessons and children were expected to speak English in the classroom. It is well known that children at many schools were expected to pay a small fine if caught speaking anything else. Furthermore, English was regarded as a prestige language, the way to better employment, the language which opened up knowledge of the Western way of life. In a situation like this, children often acquired some English from elder siblings even before commencing school, used it with other children at school and later on extensively in the Employment and Friendship domains …

This developing colloquial variety spread from the school playgrounds to the homes where

> it became a more prestigious variety than the local colloquial ethnic variety spoken by servants, parents (especially mothers) and younger siblings. Younger siblings were impressed by the new language and, as mentioned before, they often picked it up well before entering school in the version transmitted to them by their elder brothers and sisters, and used it together at home and when playing with neighbouring children.

(Platt and Weber 1980: 20-21)

A number of things from this brief historical sketch will be relevant in the rest of this overview: the classification of modern Singapore society along ethnic lines, the view of English as a language serving instrumental functions, and the status relation between the standard and colloquial varieties.

1.2. English and the official mother tongues

Singapore's language policy today treats Malay, Mandarin, Tamil and English as the four official languages. Malay is also the national language, having a primarily ceremonial function: the National Anthem is sung in Malay, and military commands are given in Malay. Malay's national language status is primarily due to Singapore's past when it was briefly a member of the Malaysian Federation until it achieved full independence in 1965. A reason for retaining Malay as the national language is essentially diplomatic: Singapore is surrounded by Malay-Muslim countries such as Malaysia, Indonesia and Brunei. Keeping Malay as the national language is intended to reassure these countries that Singapore will not go the way of becoming a Chinese state.

The other point to note is that, aside from English, there is a very specific reason why Mandarin, Malay, and Tamil are the three official languages. This is because the Singapore government groups the population into four main categories: Chinese, Malay, Indian, and 'Others'. Here we see a modern-day version of the 'capitan' system, a policy of multiracialism, where equal status is accorded to the cultures and ethnic identities of the various races that comprise the population, and which, crucially, serves to maintain the compartmentalization and distinctiveness amongst the races.

Singapore has a population of about 3.2 million, and its racial composition is as follows (2000 Census of Population):

Chinese	76.8%
Malays	13.9%
Indians	7.9%
Others	1.4%

'Others' is a miscellaneous category comprising mainly Eurasians and Europeans. The first three are specific ethnic communities, and these three official languages are their official mother tongues: Mandarin for the Chinese, Malay for the Malays, and Tamil for the Indians. There is no official mother tongue for 'Others' since this does not constitute a specific ethnic community. Thus, English is the only one of the four official languages that does not have a specific ethnic affiliation. This point is important to bear in mind because English is intended by the government to be a 'neutral' language, serving as the lingua franca for international and inter-ethnic communication. It allows access to Western science and technology, and is the medium of education so that success in the school system depends to a great extent on proficiency in the language. As Gupta (1998: 120) points out, citing data from the 1990 census, this means that "(w)hatever measure of social class is taken, it is still the case that the higher the social class, the more likely it is that English is an important domestic language."

The government clearly acknowledges the gatekeeping role that English plays in Singapore, but is also committed to the view that Singapore society is meritocratic. This notion of meritocracy is intimately tied up with the government's commitment to multiracialism, which calls for the equal treatment for all ethnic groups. Where English is concerned, this means that the government does not want it to be seen as being tied to any particular ethnic community. That is, the role of English in the unequal allocation of social and economic capital is acceptable precisely because English is officially no one's mother tongue. Thus, to accept English as a mother tongue for any ethnic community would undermine its officially neutral status.

Having encouraged the learning of English as a means of facilitating economic prosperity, the government is also concerned that English could act as the vehicle for unacceptable Western values. Here, the mother tongues are important because they are supposed to act as 'cultural anchors' that prevent Singaporeans from losing their Asian identities. This dichotomy between English and the mother tongues was underscored by Lee Kuan Yew (former Prime Minister and currently Senior Minister) in his 1984 Speak Mandarin Campaign speech, when he stressed that English is not "emotionally acceptable" as a mother tongue for the Chinese (the same rationale applies to the other communities):

> One abiding reason why we have to persist in bilingualism is that English will not be emotionally acceptable as our mother tongue. To have no emotionally acceptable language as our mother tongue is to be emotionally crippled... Mandarin is emotionally acceptable as our mother tongue...It reminds us that we are part of an ancient civilisation with an unbroken history of over 5,000 years. This is a deep and strong psychic force, one that gives confidence to a people to face up to and overcome great changes and challenges.

This bilingual policy of learning English and the mother tongue, known as "English-knowing bilingualism", is a fundamental aspect of Singapore's education system. Passage from one level to the next, including entry into the local universities, depends not only on academic excellence, but also on relative proficiency in one's mother tongue. In 1986, Dr Tony Tan, then Minister for Education, underlined the importance of the bilingual policy:

> Our policy of bilingualism that each child should learn English and his mother tongue, I regard as a fundamental feature of our education system... Children must learn English so that they will have a window to the knowledge, technology and expertise of the modern world. They must know their mother tongues to enable them to know what makes us what we are.

Together, this statement and the one by Lee Kuan Yew clearly lay out the government's position on the relationship between English and the mother tongues. There is a division of labor where English functions as the language of modernity allowing access to Western scientific and technological knowledge while the mother tongues are cultural anchors that ground individuals to traditional values. By contrasting English with a mother tongue, the policy makes clear that English is not acceptable as a mother tongue.

1.3.   Attitudes towards Colloquial Singapore English/Singlish

The official unacceptability of English as a mother tongue creates an arena of conflict since there is evidence that English is growing rapidly as a home language. The data below, based on the 2000 Census of Population, show that, except for the Malays, the officially assigned mother tongue is often not necessarily the home language.

Language most frequently spoken at home (figures in %):

Chinese homes:	English (23.9),
	Mandarin (45.1),
	Chinese dialects (30.7)
Malay homes:	English (7.9), Malay (91.6)
Indian homes:	English (35.6), Tamil (42.9)
Others (i.e. mainly Eurasians and Europeans):	English (68.5)

This has led to occasional calls for English to be officially recognized as a mother tongue. But it has also created a tension between the standard variety of English and its more colloquial counterpart (better known as Singlish). This is because the government insists that English must continue to serve a purely instrumental role if Singapore is to maintain its economic competitiveness. The existence of the colloquial variety is felt by the state to undermine the development of proficiency in the standard, and hence, to threaten that economic competitiveness. Thus, in his 1999 National Day Rally Speech, Prime Minister Goh Chok Tong stated that:

The fact that we use English gives us a big advantage over our competitors. If we carry on using Singlish, the logical final outcome is that we, too, will develop our own type of pidgin English, spoken only by 3m Singaporeans, which the rest of the world will find quaint but incomprehensible. We are already half way there. Do we want to go all the way?

The Prime Minister thus expressed the hope that in time to come, Singaporeans will no longer speak Singlish:

Singlish is not English. It is English corrupted by Singaporeans and has become a Singapore dialect... Singlish is broken, ungrammatical English sprinkled with words and phrases from local dialects and Malay which English speakers outside Singapore have difficulties in understanding... Let me emphasise that my message that we must speak Standard English is targeted primarily at the younger generation... we should ensure that the next generation does not speak Singlish.

(*The Straits Times* 29 August 1999)

This led the government to launch the Speak Good English Movement (SGEM) on 29 April 2000, and according to the chairman of SGEM, Col. David Wong (*The Straits Times*, 31 March 2000):

We are trying to build a sense of pride, that as Singaporeans, we can speak good English as opposed to pride that we can speak Singlish. We are trying to check a trend in which younger Singaporeans are beginning to feel that it is perhaps a way of identifying themselves as Singaporeans if they speak Singlish.

The view that Singlish should be eliminated or at the very least, discouraged, has met with resistance from some Singaporeans who see it as "a key ingredient in the unique melting pot that is Singapore" (Hwee Hwee Tan, *Time* magazine, 29 July 2002).

As Bloom (1986: 402) puts it,

We now come to the crux of our problem. We seem at times to be talking about two different languages. On the one hand, English is this marvellous instrument of nation-building, the language of the "true" Singaporean; on the other hand it is a language learned strictly for the purpose of getting rich, divorced from the traditional values of Singapore's component peoples, the language of, in the terms of S. Rajaratnam, the Second Deputy Prime Minister (Foreign Affairs), the religion of "moneytheism".

This tension between, on the one hand, accepting Singlish as a legitimate part of Singapore's linguistic ecology, and on the other, rejecting it in favor of a more standard variety is a continuing and important aspect of understanding English in Singapore. A similar preoccupation with the relationship between the colloquial and standard varieties can be seen in more academically-oriented discourses, to which we now turn.

1.4. Approaches to Singapore English

There have been two main approaches to the study of Singapore English: in terms of a lectal continuum, and in terms of diglossia. The lectal approach is primarily associated with the work of Platt and Weber (1980), and treats Singapore English as a range extending from a basilect (which is supposed to show features associated with creoles) to an acrolect, which approximates a superstrate standard, with the two mediated by a transitional mesolect:

> Unlike other varieties of English such as British English… and the English spoken in the U.S.A., Canada, Australia and New Zealand, where there are two dimensions, one on a scale of regional variation and one of social variation, the variation in SE can be observed along one axis which is related to the educational level and the socio-economic background of the speaker. There is considerable variation within spoken, and to some extent written, English from the more prestigious variety of SE, the acrolect, through mesolects down to the basilectal sub-variety, and speakers of SE can be placed along a scale according to a range of linguistic features.
> (Platt and Weber 1980: 46-7)

This approach has been criticized (e.g. Kandiah 1998: 95) for, one, assuming that concepts developed in the study of pidgins/creoles can be straightforwardly applied to Singapore English; two, for treating the superstrate as the standard that is aspired to by speakers of Singapore English; and three, for assuming that the continuum is mainly a cline of proficiency.

The diglossia approach (Gupta 1994), in contrast, treats the continuum in terms of communicative choice rather than proficiency. It also treats Singapore English as a native variety which can and should be described autonomously. Thus, Gupta (1994: 7-9) suggests that the Low differs from the High mainly in syntax and morphology, and that the use of the Low "is not the result of error in using a language which may or may not be native, but a matter of choice based on context and affective messsage." However, the diglossia approach is not without problems of its own. The fact that the Low and High are not strictly compartmentalized and 'leak' into each other suggests that the concept of diglossia is being used here in a non-traditional manner. Either that or we are simply looking at cases of code-switching without any society-wide functional organization of codes. Also, a large number of Singaporeans do share the government's negative attitude towards the colloquial variety, pointing to a degree of linguistic self-flagellation and suggesting that this continuing anxiety over issues of standards and intelligibility may well encourage an attitude of exonormativity. As such, we need to recognize that while some Singaporeans easily code-switch between the standard and colloquial varieties, the very pervasive negative attitude towards the colloquial variety suggests that rather than simply assuming the correctness of one approach over the other, it may be more pertinent to combine insights from both if we are to achieve a better understanding of the grammatical and sociological issues surrounding English in Singapore. The dichotomy between the lectal and diglossia approaches, at this point, is thus best viewed as an unresolved debate.

2.   Phonology

Because the focus of this volume is on features that are different from the standard varieties, this discussion of the phonology of Singapore English, as well as the later discussion of its morphology/syntax, is restricted mainly to features of CollSgE. Lim (forthcoming) is a major treatment of various aspects of Singapore English and the discussion of reduplication and discourse particles draws on Wee's contribution to this source. In the case of CollSgE phonology, most of the discussion is based on Bao (1998), which provides a comprehensive survey of the relevant works.

In some of these works, the authors refer to the variety they are concerned with as 'Singapore English'; in others, the reference is to 'English in Malaysia and Singapore'. In order to better bring out the distinctive properties of CollSgE, these authors also often provide descriptive contrasts with RP (Received Pronunciation). This decision, it must be stressed, is purely intended to facilitate the description of CollSgE; it is conceptually a separate issue from the more controversial one of whether CollSgE can in fact be analyzed as an autonomous linguistic system.

In what follows, I shall simply use 'CollSgE'. I also continue the contrast with RP when describing the various properties of CollSgE.

2.1.   Phonemic inventory

The following set of keywords illustrates the lexical incidence of the vowels.

Table 1.   The vowels of CollSgE according to Wells' lexical sets

KIT	i	FLEECE	i	NEAR	iə
DRESS	æ	FACE	e	SQUARE	æ
TRAP	ɛ	PALM	ɑ	START	ɑ
LOT	ɔ	THOUGHT	ɔ	NORTH	ɔ
STRUT	ɑ	GOAT	o	FORCE	ɔ
FOOT	u	GOOSE	u	CURE	ɔ

Table 1. (continued)   The vowels of CollSgE according to Wells' lexical sets

BATH	ɑ	PRICE	ai	happY	i
CLOTH	ɔ	CHOICE	ɔi	lettER	ə
NURSE	ə	MOUTH	au	commA	ə
horsES	ə	POOR	uə		

(POOR is not part of the standard lexical set, but has been included here because the CollSgE diphthong /uə/ appears in words such as *poor*, *sure* and *tour*.)

Table 2.   The vowel chart for CollSgE

	Front	**Central**	**Back**
Close	i		u
Close-mid	e	ə	o
Open-mid	ɛ		ɔ
Open	æ		ɑ

The following table provides a summary of the consonant inventory of CollSgE. It has been noted that accents of English do not differ very much in their consonant inventories, and in this respect, the consonant inventory of CollSgE is similar to that of a variety such as RP.

Table 3.   Consonants of CollSgE

	Labial	**Inter-dental**	**Alveolar**	**Post-alveolar**	**Palatal**	**Velar**	**Glottal**
Plosive	p b		t d			k g	
Affricate				tʃ dʒ			
Fricative	f v	θ ð	s z	ʃ ʒ			h
Nasal	m		n			ŋ	
Liquid			l r				
Glide	w				j		

Two points are particularly worth noting. One, there is no aspiration of voiceless plosives or affricates in CollSgE. This means that /p/, for example, is realized the same way in words like *pin* and *spin*. Two, the interdental fricatives tend to be realized as [t, d] when pre-vocalic and [f] when at the end of a word. For example, *thin* is realized as [tin] and *then* as [den], but in word-final position, we get [brɛf] and [brif] for *breath* and *breathe* respectively. This gives an alternation between [f] and [t] in *filth* [filf] and *filthy* [filti] since in the second word, the consonant is in pre-vocalic position. Words ending in /t/ do not display this alternation, as seen with a pair such as *guilt* [gilt] and *guilty* [gilti]. It is this alternation which leads Hung (1995: 32) to tentatively posit the interdental fricatives as CollSgE phonemes even though they are, in fact, never phonetically realized as such:

> It is therefore quite possible that there is a separate phoneme in SE (represented in other accents as /θ/) which is distinct from /t/ and /f/, and which is phonetically realised as [t] in the onset and [f] in the coda of a syllable. Obviously, further data and analysis are required before any such conclusion can be drawn.

Hung's caution is understandable since this, of course, bears on the theoretical question of just how abstract phonological representations ought to be. This is a controversial issue, and perhaps particularly so in the study of new varieties of English since there are often ideological as well as more 'purely' linguistic ones for wanting to treat each variety as a self-contained system. Whether this is in fact possible is a matter of some contention.

Where the vowels are concerned, CollSgE contains nine monophthongs and five diphthongs. Table 2 provides a list of the monophthongs. The five CollSgE diphthongs are /ai, ɔi, au, iə, uə/.

Two features of the CollSgE vowels bear mentioning, both relating to the neutralization of vowel distinctions. The first is that there is no length contrast so that any length difference tends to be sporadic. Hung (1995: 29) points out that while Singaporean speakers may be able to detect and even mimic vowel length differences in other varieties of English, "in their own spontaneous, natural speech, no distinction is normally made...". Thus, the distinction found in RP, for example, in pairs like *pool/pull* or *beat/bit* is absent in CollSgE; the pairs are essentially homophonous instead. The other is that there is also no contrast between tense and lax vowels so that all vowels tend to be 'equally tense'. However, given that the tense-lax distinction has been criticized for being too vague, and that tense vowels are more likely to be longer, it might be possible to reduce the two features to one, and simply note the absence of contrastive vowel length in CollSgE.

2.2.   Phonotactics

The phonotactic distribution of sound segments in CollSgE is best understood in terms of the syllable structure. In the onset, CollSgE allows a maximum of three consonants, much as in RP. Examples include *string* and *spray*.

Where the coda is concerned, CollSgE is much more restrictive. Hung (1995: 33) notes that for most speakers the upper limit seems to be either two or three consonants in the coda as shown in words like *texts* or *glimpsed* below.

	RP	CollSgE
texts	[teksts]	[teks]
glimpsed	[glimpst]	[glims]/[glimst]

Hung (1995: 33) goes on to suggest that "(p)erhaps as a result of these syllable-structure constraints, final consonant clusters are regularly simplified in SE, by the deletion of some of the word-final consonants." The deletion of final consonants is discussed below.

Regarding the nucleus of the syllable, unlike a variety of English such as RP, where the lateral /l/ and the nasals can be syllabic, that is, occupy the nucleus position of a syllable, in CollSgE this is simply not possible. Instead, a process of schwa insertion takes place, leading this vowel to occupy the nucleus position, and thus relegating the lateral or nasal to the coda. The following examples, from RP and from CollSgE, provide the relevant contrasts.

	RP	CollSgE
button	[bʌtn̩]	[batən]
bottle	[bɔtl̩]	[bɔtəl]
whistle	[wɪsl̩]	[wɪsəl]

In a word like *button*, the schwa intervenes between the /t/ and the /n/. In *bottle*, it is inserted between /t/ and /l/. And, similarly, in *whistle*, it appears between /s/ and /l/. In all such cases, the effect is that syllabic laterals and nasals are avoided.

3. Phonological processes

There are four phonological processes that should be mentioned in connection with CollSgE: consonant devoicing, consonant deletion, glottalization, and metathesis. These are discussed in turn.

3.1. Consonant devoicing

In CollSgE, voiced obstruents commonly become devoiced when in word-final position, as the following examples indicate.

	RP	CollSgE
leg	[lɛg]	[lɛk]
news	[njuːz]	[njus]
tab	[tæb]	[tɛp]
believe	[bɪliːv]	[bilif]
judge	[dʒʌdʒ]	[dʒatʃ]

Emphasizing the extent to which devoicing takes place in CollSgE, Hung (1995: 34) points out that

> [i]n other varieties of English, word-final obstruents are also partially devoiced, but not as completely as in SE. The 'dg' in *judge* is in fact as voiceless as the 'ch' in *batch*.

The contrast between voiced and voiceless obstruents, however, is maintained in non-final position, as can be seen from the pronunciations of *to* [tu] and *do* [du].

3.2.   Consonant deletion

In discussing consonant deletion in CollSgE, it is useful to distinguish two factors which together serve to delimit the conditions under which the process occurs. These are (i) the kinds of consonants that get deleted – only stops get deleted, and (ii) the contexts in which such deletions take place – the stops are deleted only if they are in word-final position, and if they are preceded by a continuant.

We first begin with examples indicating that only stops get deleted. As the following examples illustrate, in words like *limp* or *cent* where the final stops /p, t/ are preceded by the nasal consonants /m, n/, the stops are deleted.

	RP	CollSgE
limp	[lɪmp]	[lim]
cent	[sɛnt]	[sɛn]
stink	[stɪŋk]	[stiŋ]

This deletion process does not occur with other kinds of consonants such as fricatives or affricates so that in words like *nymph* or *laps*, the word-final /f/ and /s/ are retained in the phonetic realization.

	RP	CollSgE
nymph	[nɪmf]	[nimf]
laps	[læps]	[lɛps]
lunch	[lʌntʃ]	[lantʃ]

As for the contexts in which the deletion occurs, notice that once these stops are no longer in final position, as when they are suffixed with –*ing*, there is no deletion.

Thus, being in final position is crucial. Examples are given below.

limping   [limpiŋ]
standing   [stɛndiŋ]

This deletion process also takes place with words derived by the addition of the past tense suffix –*ed*, so that the final [t] or [d] is not pronounced.

	RP	CollSgE
helped	[hɛlpt]	[hɛlp]
stabbed	[stæbd]	[stɛp]
backed	[bækt]	[bɛk]

Two points are worth noting. One, though the deletion of [t] in *helped* follows from the fact that the consonant is in final position and preceded by another consonant, the fact that [p] is retained (despite being preceded by [l]) suggests that consonant deletion does not take place if the preceding consonant is a continuant. Thus, in words like *milk*, *silk*, and *bolt*, the final stop is not deleted. Two, the realization of *stabbed* as [stɛp] follows if we take into account the process of consonant devoicing (mentioned in the previous section). Thus, the addition of the past tense suffix gives us /stɛb +d/. Consonant deletion leads to the removal of the final consonant, and devoicing results in [p], giving us [stɛp] for *stabbed*.

3.3.   Glottalization

In CollSgE, stops in final position are often unreleased (represented by the ˺ diacritic), causing the vowels that precede them to become glottalized.

	RP	CollSgE
tap	[tæp]	[tɛp˺]
tab	[tæb]	[tɛp˺]
leak	[liːk]	[lik˺]
league	[liːg]	[lik˺]

Admittedly a variable phenomenon, the stops may on occasion themselves get deleted so that the word then ends in a glottal stop, as in *like* [laiʔ] and *hit* [hiʔ]. Bao (1998: 164) suggests that this is an influence from the phonology of the substrate languages, in particular, Malay and the Chinese dialects. In these languages also, the word-final stops are unreleased, and the vowels that precede them glottalized.

Glottalization also takes place in words beginning with vowels, as indicated in words like *a* [ʔə], *of* [ʔɔf], *eat* [ʔit] and *apple* [ʔɛpəl]. Brown (1988: 119) points out that there is no phenomenon of liaison (the linking of the final sound of one syllable or word directly onto the initial sound of the following) in CollSgE, and suggests a relationship between the absence of liaison and the predominance of glottal stops. He hypothesizes that because CollSgE words tend to be separated by glottal stops, this has prevented features associated with liaison (such as linking and intrusive /r/) from arising.

3.4.   Metathesis

Metathesis in CollSgE seems to be highly specific, being limited to the cluster *sp*, which is realized as [ps]. Exactly why the *sp* cluster should be prone to metathesis remains unclear.

	RP	CollSgE
lisp	[lɪsp]	[lips]
grasp	[graːsp]	[graps]
crisp	[krɪsp]	[krips]
wasps	[waːsp]	[waps]

Other clusters such as *st* or *sk* do not seem to undergo metathesis (examples below); instead, they undergo the process of consonant deletion mentioned earlier.

	RP	CollSgE
last	[last]	[las]
mask	[mask]	[mas]

4.   Prosodic features

Three prosodic features of CollSgE are of particular interest. One is its syllable-timed rhythm, which has been claimed to give CollSgE its 'Singaporean' characteristic. The other is its pattern of stress assignment, which can be rather complex. The third is its lack of pitch contrasts to express various kinds of speaker meaning.

4.1.   Syllable-timed rhythm

In a stress-timed variety (such as RP), the stressed syllables occur at regular intervals. For this to happen, the unstressed ones have to be 'squeezed in between'
the stressed syllables. This can often lead these unstressed syllables to undergo
further reduction so that speakers not familiar with the stress-timed variety
may often have difficulty hearing the unstressed/reduced syllables.

In contrast, the syllable-timed rhythm of CollSgE essentially means that all
syllables take up the same amount of time, regardless of whether the syllables
are stressed or not. According to Platt and Weber (1980: 57), this gives Singapore English "an even, somewhat staccato rhythm" and Tay (1993: 27) has
been quoted as saying that "(t)his 'machine-gun rhythm' is one of the most
prominent features of Singaporean English."

However, Brown (1988: 116), while agreeing that CollSgE does lack a stress-
timed rhythm, disputes the sharp dichotomy being made between stress-timed
and syllable-timed rhythms. He suggests (1988: 117) instead that it is prema-
ture to treat CollSgE as syllable-timed "merely because it lacks the relatively
strong stress-based rhythm of native accents." Thus, Brown prefers a negative
characterization of timing in CollSgE, speaking in terms of the *absence* of a
strongly stress-timed rhythm rather than the *presence* of an unambiguously
syllable-timed rhythm.

4.2.   Stress patterns

Patterns of stress assignment are difficult to detect in CollSgE because of its
syllable-timed rhythm. Since all syllables are given equal time, it is not always
easy to detect relative differences in prominence among the syllables. This is
unlike a stress-timed variety, where stressed syllables are typically realized
with higher pitch, loudness and length.

Tay (1993: 27-28) suggests a number of ways in which CollSgE stress patterns are distinctive. One is the use of equal stress in words which otherwise
receive primary and secondary stress. Thus, in RP, a word like *celebration*
receives primary stress on the syllable *bra*. In CollSgE, however, all four syllables receive equal stress.

RP	CollSgE
cele'bration	'ce'le'bra'tion
anni'versary	'an'ni'ver'sa'ry

Another source of distinctiveness arises from the absence of differential stress
patterns to mark changes in parts of speech. Thus, whether as a verb or a noun,

the word *increase* is stressed in the same way; there is no difference in stress pattern corresponding to the change in grammatical category. This contrasts with RP, where in the case of *increase*, for example, stress is mainly on the second syllable (if meant as a verb) and on the first syllable (if meant as a noun).

RP	CollSgE
in'crease (verb)	'in'crease (verb and noun)
'increase (noun)	
com'ment (verb)	
'comment (noun)	'com'ment (verb and noun)

Similarly, in RP, stress placement systematically distinguishes compounds from phrases. Thus if *white house* is a phrase, stress falls on *house*, while if it is a compound, stress falls on *white*. In CollSgE, however, regardless of whether it is a phrase or a compound, stress is consistently placed on the second word *house*. Thus stress in CollSgE does not distinguish nouns from verbs, nor compounds from phrases.

And finally, there is also the fact that in a number of words, the placement of stress simply occurs on a different syllable.

RP	CollSgE
'faculty	fa'culty
'character	cha'racter
eco'nomic	e'conomic

Trying to formulate a set of general rules that would predict how stress assignment works in CollSgE is not easy. However, there is a general opinion that stress in CollSgE tends to be oriented towards the end of a word. More specific attempts to describe the rules of CollSgE stress assignment run into difficulties. For example, Bao (1998: 169) suggests three possible rules: heavy syllables are stressed, stress occurs on alternative syllables, and if a word has more than one stressed syllable, the last stressed syllable carries the main stress. The distinction between heavy and non-heavy (light) syllables is based on the length of the vowel, which is assumed to be phonemically distinctive even though there is no phonetic evidence for this assumption. Bao thus acknowledges that for the rules to work, he has to assume that vowel length is phonemic in CollSgE. But this is a highly controversial assumption since there is no real evidence internal to CollSgE for treating vowel length as phonemic; the only justification is to argue, as Bao himself does, that RP (where vowel length is indeed phonemic) acts as the input to CollSgE. This is a position that other researchers may find untenable since it undermines claims that CollSgE can or should be analyzed as an autonomous variety without reference to more established varieties (e.g. Hung, 1995: 30).

4.3.   Intonation

A number of authors have observed that CollSgE makes use of a much smaller number of pitch contrasts than a variety such as RP. Thus, Platt and Weber (1980: 58) note that CollSgE speakers "do not use variations in pitch to express certain differences which may be expressed partly by such variations in RP". For example, in RP, in a sentence like *Sam likes coffee*, a high falling pitch on *Sam* could be interpreted as contradicting the assumption that nobody likes coffee. And similarly, a high pitch on the first syllable of *coffee* could be interpreted as contradicting the assumption that Sam doesn't like caffeine-based beverages. In CollSgE, speakers do not generally use such forms of pitch variations to express contrastive meaning.

However, CollSgE speakers do often lengthen the final syllable as a form of emphasis. For example, when *Reading!* is uttered in reply to a question such as *What are you doing?* the final syllable of *Reading!* can be clearly lengthened as part of the assertion. Thus, coming back to a sentence like *Sam likes coffee*, a CollSgE speaker might, for emphasis, simply lengthen the final syllable of *coffee* regardless of whether he/she is challenging the assumption that nobody likes coffee or that Sam doesn't like caffeine-based beverages.

Exercises and study questions

1. Consider the Singapore government's position that the presence of Singlish will undermine Singapore's economic competitiveness (see the section Attitudes Towards Colloquial Singapore English/Singlish). Supporters of Singlish, on the other hand, tend to emphasize its value as a reflection of a Singaporean identity. In your opinion, how important is it to pay attention to the economic value of a language variety, as opposed to its value as an identity marker? If you had to make a judgement about the Singapore situation, who would you agree with more?

2. Listen to the conversation recordings of all speakers, paying close attention to any indication of glottalization. All speakers regularly glottalize stops in final position. List a number of such examples, and compare them with your own pronunciation.

3. Given the discussion of stop deletion, metathesis and plural formation in Singapore English, how do you think Singaporeans might pronounce the following pairs of words?
   a. list   lists
   b. hiss   hisses
   c. ask   asks
   d. ass   asses
   e. grasp   grasps
   f. grass   grasses

4. What salient differences do you notice between the vowels of SgE and those of a South Asian variety like IndE?

5. Review the rules for the assignment of stress in SgE.

Selected references

Please consult the General references for titles mentioned in the text but not included in the references below. For a full bibliography see the accompanying CD-ROM.

Bao, Zhiming
   1998   Theories of language genesis. In: Joseph A. Foley, Thiru Kandiah, Bao Zhiming, Anthea F. Gupta, Lubna Alsagoff, Ho Chee Lick, Lionel Wee, Ismail S. Talib, and Wendy Bokhorst-Heng, *English in New Cultural Contexts: Reflections from Singapore*, 41–72. Singapore: Oxford University Press.
   1998   The sounds of Singapore English. In: Joseph A. Foley, Thiru Kandiah, Bao Zhiming, Anthea F. Gupta, Lubna Alsagoff, Ho Chee Lick, Lionel Wee, Ismail S. Talib, and Wendy Bokhorst-Heng, *English in New Cultural Contexts: Reflections from Singapore*, 152–174. Singapore: Oxford University Press.
Bloom, David
   1986   The English language and Singapore: A critical survey. In: Basant K. Kapur (ed.), *Singapore Studies: Critical Surveys of the Humanities and Social Sciences*, 337–458. Singapore: Singapore University Press.
Brown, Adam
   1988   The staccato effect in the pronunciation of English in Malaysia and Singapore. In: Joseph Foley (ed.), *New Englishes: The Case of Singapore*. Singapore: Singapore University Press.
Foley, Joseph A., Thiru Kandiah, Bao Zhiming, Anthea F. Gupta, Lubna Alsagoff, Ho Chee Lick, Lionel Wee, Ismail S. Talib, and Wendy Bokhorst-Heng
   1998   *English in New Cultural Contexts: Reflections from Singapore*. Singapore: Oxford University Press.

Gupta, Anthea F.
  1992   The pragmatic particles of Singapore Colloquial English. *Journal of Pragmatics* 18: 31–57.
  1994   *The Step-Tongue: Children's English in Singapore.* Clevedon: Multilingual Matters.
  1998   The situation of English in Singapore. In: Joseph A. Foley, Thiru Kandiah, Bao Zhiming, Anthea F. Gupta, Lubna Alsagoff, Ho Chee Lick, Lionel Wee, Ismail S. Talib, and Wendy Bokhorst-Heng, *English in New Cultural Contexts: Reflections from Singapore*, 106-126. Singapore: Oxford University Press.

Hung, Tony
  1995   Some aspects of the segmental phonology of Singapore English. In: Teng Su Ching and Ho Mian Lian (eds.), *The English Language in Singapore: Implications for Teaching*, 29–41. Singapore: Singapore Association for Applied Linguistics.

Kandiah, Thiru
  1998   The emergence of New Englishes. In: Joseph A. Foley, Thiru Kandiah, Bao Zhiming, Anthea F. Gupta, Lubna Alsagoff, Ho Chee Lick, Lionel Wee, Ismail S. Talib, and Wendy Bokhorst-Heng (eds.), *English in New Cultural Contexts: Reflections from Singapore*, 73–105. Singapore: Oxford University Press.

Lim, Lisa (ed.)
  2004   *Singapore English: A Grammatical Description.* Amsterdam/Philadelphia: Benjamins.

Platt, John and Heidi Weber
  1980   *English in Singapore and Malaysia: Status, Features, Functions.* Kuala Lumpur: Oxford University Press.

Tay, Mary W. J.
  1993   *The English Language in Singapore: Issues and Development.* Singapore: Unipress.

Malaysian English: phonology

Loga Baskaran

1.   Introduction

In considering the sociolinguistic profile of Malaysia it is important to study the ethnic diversity so characteristic of this nation. This diversity is a consequence of several phases and aspects of conquest or colonization and settlement (see Baskaran 1987). Thus we have the indigenous Malay speakers (Austronesian speakers) with their Austroasiatic counterparts (the aboriginal tribes) and the settler populace – by way of the Chinese, Indians, Arabs and Eurasians.

The Austronesian speakers are the Malays in West Malaysia (with Bahasa Malaysia as their language) whilst the Kadazans of Sabah and the Dayaks of Sarawak are the major Malay groups in East Malaysia (with Kadazan and Iban as their languages respectively). The Austroasiatic speakers are the Malays in West Malaysia (the majority of whom are Negritos). There are many smaller groups of speakers speaking among themselves a host of languages of the Austroasiatic group. The language most commonly spoken among these groups is Temiar. However, all the languages spoken amongst these people have now been categorically classified as *aslian* – from the term *asli* 'aborigine' originally assigned to them. For purposes of conciseness, the umbrella term *Malays* would be used to include both the Austronesian and Austroasiatic speakers who form altogether about 55% of the total population of Malaysia.

The settler population of Malaysia is mainly found in the Chinese, Indians, Arabs and Eurasians, with a sprinkling of Thais and Europeans. Of these, the Chinese and the Indians are the majority groups who are represented constitu-tionally on a *pro rata* basis. The Chinese form the second biggest portion of the population. They constitute about 30% of the total population of Malaysia. Just as the Malays have a kaleidoscope of minority racial groups with their equally diverse language groups, the Chinese also have a variety of dialectal groups. The main dialectal groups are the Hokkien, Cantonese, Hakka, Teochew and Hainanese peoples. The official Chinese language is Mandarin (also known as Kuo-Yu), which is used for all official purposes and in the media.

The third largest group in the composite population of Malaysia is the Indian community. It forms about 10% of the Malaysian population and is just as heterogeneous as its Malay and Chinese counterparts. The majority of the Indians are Tamil-speaking followed by the Malayalis, Telugus, Punjabis, Bengalis, Gujaratis and Singhalese.

The minority groups like the Thais, Eurasians (a blend of Europeans and Asians) and Arabs are all designated under the term *others* in the Constitution, their proportion totalling about 5% only. The Thais and Arabs use their own language; whilst the Eurasians and those who inter-marry use mainly English or Malay.

Education has been significant in determining the importance of the various languages of the nation. With the National Education Policy as well as the New Economic Policy (of equal rights and opportunities for all the constituent ethnic groups) there has emerged an attempt to unify the various races of the nation by an official and national language. The official national language – that used as the medium of instruction in education at all levels and that used in oral and written communication in the various channels of officialdom – is Bahasa Malaysia. Previous to 1967, both English and Bahasa Malaysia were official languages. But since 1967, English has been accorded the status of a *strong second language*, whilst Bahasa Malaysia remains the official national language.

The languages accorded *vernacular* status are the Chinese language (Mandarin) and Tamil, with Iban in Sarawak and Kadazan in Sabah. These languages represent the majority languages of the major ethnic groups (Chinese, Indians, Dayaks and Kadazans). Thus Mandarin is used as an overall representative language of the Chinese via the media, for religion and for purposes of vernacular education in national schools where provision is made for pupils to have instruction in their *own languages* – if there is a substantial enough number of pupils requesting such instruction (these are termed *pupils' own languages* – P.O.L.).

The situation is similar where the Indians are concerned. The official representative language of this subgroup is Tamil. Thus the media mostly caters for Indians in this language – through films, radio broadcasts via a special network, certain allotted television programmes and the dailies. In matters of religion too, Tamil is the predominant and official language used – both in the temples of the Hindus (where some of the verses are, however, in Sanskrit) and the churches of the Indian Christians. There are, however, small, rather insignificant deviations from this norm in the other Hindu temples (Punjabi or Bengali Hindu temples) using Punjabi/Urdu and Bengali/Gujarati respectively, and Malayali Christian churches (termed *Syrian Christian* or *Orthodox Christian*) using Malayalam as their language of worship. There are some Indians who are Muslim by religion and these are almost entirely Malay in their way of life. Thus Malay is their language both in the official and unofficial domains of life.

The status of English as a *strong second language* means that meetings, conferences and any such liaison with an international audience would warrant the use of English as the official language. The Government, therefore, deems it important to use English as a language of international communication whilst maintaining Bahasa Malaysia as the official language within the country. This tolerant and rational policy is further extended to the other major languages as well, in that there are provisions in the media for both Bahasa Malaysia and English as well as Chinese and Tamil – on a *pro rata* basis.

In the field of education, as outlined earlier, the official medium of instruction is now Bahasa Malaysia at all levels – primary, secondary and tertiary, whilst English is used as second language in all schools. In the universities, some courses are given in English, with other *designated* courses being given in their respective languages.

With the various official statuses accorded to the four basic languages in the country (Bahasa Malaysia, English, Chinese-Mandarin and Tamil) along with the diverse range of languages in actual currency amongst the people of Malaysia, it is unsurprising then that the average Malaysian is at least bilingual, if not conversant in three or more languages.

1.1.   Malaysian English – a preamble

In Malaysia, the variety known as Malaysian English (MalE) owes much to its co-existence with other local languages. Several indigenised sub-varieties of MalE can be identified at the informal level, depending on the L_1. These sub-varieties co-exist with a more codified and standardised *model* variety. In some aspects, however, (on the lexical level particularly) this tendency is slowly being changed, with some of the informal features also appearing in rhetorical and official discourse. Some lexical items occur in the Malaysian print and broadcast media not only in headlinese style but in full reporting style. Some headline examples are *Anti-**dadah*** ('drug') *operations in **kampong*** ('village'); ***Ganja*** ('marijuana') *victim gets six years and **rotan*** ('caning'); ***Sawi*** ('spinach') *glut hits farmers; Eight get **Datukship*** ('lordship') *for Ruler's Birthday;* ***Toddy*** ('fermented coconut water') *to be bottled and canned for export* and ***Penghulus*** ('village-chiefs') *get ultimatum.*

Apart from such influx of lexis into the MalE speaker's repertoire, the phonological and syntactic features too have elements of nativisation. The extent or degree to which each of these levels have been indigenised varies, however, from one non-native variety to the other. Furthermore, within each of these *new* Englishes there is also differentiation between the standardised norm (the model acceptable for official purposes like teaching in schools, official functions etc.) and the more communicative style used in the speech of most users. The terms used to distinguish these two levels are the acrolect and the mesolect respectively. In Malaysia, the acrolect tends towards StdBrE although some local influence at the lexical and phonological levels is tolerated. The mesolect is very much the Malaysian variety – the informal style used among Malaysians. Speakers often weave into and out of this mesolect, using an almost International English at one instance (perhaps when speaking to a superior or with a non-Malaysian) and then switching into the mesolectal MalE when speaking to a friend.

There is a *third* lect so to speak – the basilect – which most often signifies the uneducated style of speech communication which can be considered the *patois* form of the new Englishes – be they Malaysian, Indian or African English. In Malaysia, this is often termed *broken English* or *half-past six English* (*half-past six* being a local adjective referring to something below expectation or standard).

With almost two centuries of nurturing and over three decades of nursing, English in Malaysia has developed into a typical progeny of the *New Englishes*. Two centuries indicate the period of English language currency in Malaysia. Three decades represent, firstly, the time span during which English in Malaysia was officially ascribed secondary status (1965 to 2003) and when its official role has changed. Secondly, it represents the approximate period of time during which most recent issues in the identification and recognition of the *New Englishes* have been vehemently debated.

Although its basic features of phonology, syntax and lexis are not totally different from the original British English, MalE shows sufficient influence from local languages as well as modifications by way of over-generalisation, simplification, omission etc. that have become fossilised enough to be recognisably Malaysian. This is attested to by captions like the following which appear frequently in articles and editorials in the local English dailies: '*Our special way of talking; The Malaysian 'lah' is here to stay; We all talk like machine-gun aa?; Our own lingo-lah and Malaysian English dictionary on the way'*.

1.2.   MalE – global change

Although previous studies of MalE closely linked it to Singapore English (SgE), it is now appropriate to divorce them from each other at least on two historical considerations. Firstly, since 1965 Singapore is no longer in any way politically connected to Malaya or Malaysia; the case for sociolinguistic differentiation over 40 years is therefore reasonably strong. Secondly, the language policies in both nations have been different for the past 40 years. This will have varied implications on the role and long-term effects of English on the local populace of each nation. Tongue (1974), who describes the English of Singapore and Malaysia (ESM) in his book, predicted that within a hundred years the idea of one 'ESM' would become inapplicable. In linguistic terms, there are significant differences in substrate too. Chinese varieties predominate in Singapore, but are a minority in Malaysia. The implications of this difference have yet to be researched.

Many researchers have described 'ESM' in terms of a standard and colloquial form with various terms like 'standard', 'informal', 'uneducated', 'low' and 'communicative forms'. Platt and Weber (1980), along with Mary Tay (1993), see a three-tiered lectal continuum. I, too, prefer to take a three-tiered approach to describing MalE although I prefer to use the terms official MalE (standard MalE), Unofficial MalE (dialectal MalE) and Broken MalE (patois MalE). Thus the basic subdivision in my description of MalE would be as tabulated below:

Table 1.   Characteristics of the three sub-varieties of MalE

	Official MalE	**Unofficial MalE**	**Broken MalE**
General character- istics	**Standard MalE:** Spoken and written; Formal use; International intelligi- bility.	**Dialectal MalE:** Spoken and written; Informal use; National intelligi- bility.	**Patois MalE:** Spoken only; Colloquial use; Patois intelligibility and currency.
Phonology	Slight variation preva- lent and internationally intelligible.	More variation is prevalent – includ- ing prosodic features, especially stress and intonation.	Severe variation – both segmental and prosodic, with intonation so stig- matised – almost unin- telligible internationally.
Syntax	No deviation.	Some deviation present.	Substantial variation/ deviation – national in- telligibility.
Lexis	Variation acceptable es- pecially for words not substitutable in an international context (or to give a more localised context).	Lexicalisations quite prevalent even for words having in- ternational English substitutes.	Major lexicalisation – heavily infused with local language items.

2.   Vowels

2.1.   Phonemic inventory of the vowels

Close phonetic analysis of the vowels of MalE remains a desideratum. The following account is a preliminary one that, it is hoped, will form the basis of future work and of refinements.

Table 2.   The vowels of MalE according to Wells's lexical sets

KIT	i	FLEECE	i > iː	NEAR	iə > iː
DRESS	æ > ɛ > e	FACE	e > e	SQUARE	æ > ɛ
TRAP	æ > ɛ	PALM	ɑ > ä	START	ɑ > ä
LOT	ɔ	THOUGHT	ɔ	NORTH	ɔ
STRUT	ɑ	GOAT	o > oː	FORCE	ɔ
FOOT	u	GOOSE	u > uː	CURE	ɔ
BATH	ɑ > ä	PRICE	ai	happY	i
CLOTH	ɔ	CHOICE	ɔi	lettER	ə
NURSE	ə	MOUTH	au	commA	ə > ʌ
horSES	ə	POOR	uə		

2.2.   Vowel qualities

There are some differences in vowel quality, especially that of back vowels. The THOUGHT vowel is somewhat raised and centralised. The same applies to the BATH vowel.

2.3.   Vowel length

There is a general tendency to shorten long vowels in MalE – no doubt under the influence of Bahasa Malaysia, which lacks long vowels. This shortening occurs mainly in medial position. Some examples follow:

/iː/ realised as [i]   e.g.   [fild] 'field'
                               [pil] 'peel'

/ɑː/ realised as [ʌ]   e.g.   [haf] or [hʌf] 'half'
                               [pak] or [pʌk] 'park'

/ɔː/ realised as [ɔ]   e.g.   [wɔtə] 'water'
                               [bɔn] 'born'

/uː/ realised as [u]   e.g.   [fud] 'food'
                               [muv] 'move'

/ɜː/ realised as [ə]   e.g.   [gəl] 'girl'
                               [wəd] 'word'

Conversely short vowels may be lengthened in MalE, especially before /n, l, r, s, ʃ/, though the example of *would* shows that this might be lexically governed and not just phonological:

/i/ realised as [iː]   e.g.   [fiːʃ] 'fish'
                              [piːn] 'pin'

/ʌ/ realised as [aː]   e.g.   [raːn] 'run'
                              [daːs(t)] 'dust'

/ɒ/ realised as [ɔː]   e.g.   [sɔːri] 'sorry'
                              [gɔːn] 'gone'

/u/ realised as [uː]   e.g.   [wuːd] 'would'
                              [fuːl] 'full'

/ə/ realised as [əː]   e.g.   [sæləːd] 'salad'
                              [brekfəːs(t)] 'breakfast'

2.4.   Use of unreduced vowels

As reported for several 'New Englishes', vowel reduction is not as common as in RP. In the following MalE words schwa of RP is replaced by a full vowel:

[ʌ'raʊn(d)]   '<u>a</u>round'
[æ'ses]   '<u>a</u>ssess'
[ʌpɔn]   '<u>u</u>pon'
[kɔnsiːl]   'c<u>o</u>nceal'

In the above set the vowel that is reduced to schwa in RP is underlined.

2.5.   Diphthongs

Some diphthongs of RP have a reduced quality in MalE, with glide weakening to the extent that they can be considered as monophthongs:

/eɪ/ realised as [e]   e.g.   [mel] 'mail'
                              [relwe] 'railway'

/əu/ realised as [o] e.g. [foːto] 'photo'
                             [sloː] 'slow'

/ɛə/ realised as [ɛ] e.g. [ðɛ] 'there'
                             [hɛ] 'hair'

The RP diphthong /ʊə/ is realised as [ɔ] in MalE. This represents a different quality to the lexical set CURE, rather than monophthongisation *per se*. Thus [kjɔ] 'cure', [pjɔ] 'pure' are the usual realisations in MalE. Similarly whereas the <er> sequence in words like 'mat<u>er</u>ial', 's<u>er</u>ious' and 'exp<u>er</u>ience' is realised as [ie] in RP, the usual rule in MalE is not to diphthongise /i/ before /r/ [siːriəs] 'serious', [matiːriəl] 'material' and [ekspiːriəns] 'experience'.

3. Consonants

3.1. Consonant cluster reduction

Although consonant cluster reduction is normal in fast speech in many L_1 dialects of English, the process appears to be particularly characteristic of MalE. Clusters of three consonants may be reduced medially to two as in the following examples:

> [hʌnsmən] 'huntsman'   (nts > ns)
> [ʌmridʒ] 'umbrage'   (mbr > mr)

The reduction of tri-consonantal clusters is even more common in final position:

> [glims] 'glimpse'   (mps > ms)
> [mids] 'midst'   (dst > ds)

In clusters of two consonants, /l/ is frequently deleted if it is the first consonant:

> [rizʌt] or [rizʌl] 'result' [ebəu] 'elbow'
> [sef] or [sel] 'self' [ɔːsəu] 'also'

Loss of final /t/, /d/ or /θ/ in clusters can be seen in the following:

> [iksep] 'except' [stæn] 'stand'
> [daidʒes] 'digest' [fif] 'fifth'
> [indʒek] 'inject'

3.2.   Fricatives

(a)   Devoicing
There is a tendency for the devoicing of /v, z, ð, dʒ/ in final position. Some examples follow:

[gif] 'give'   [is] 'is'
[muːf] 'move'   [dʌs] 'does'
[weif] 'wave'   [nɔis] 'noise'
[wiθ] 'with'   [ruːʃ] 'rouge'
[beiθ] 'bathe'   [beiʃ] 'beige'
[smuːθ] 'smooth'

There is also evidence of occasional devoicing of /z, ʒ/ in medial position:

[iːsi] 'easy'   [juʃuəl] 'usual'
[hʌsbən] 'husband'   [pleʃə] 'pleasure'
[θausn̩d] 'thousand'   [riviʃən] 'revision'

(b)   Voicing
Contrary to the tendencies in (a) above, there is also a tendency to voicing of /s/ and /ʃ/ in certain lexical items. Once again the phenomenon is restricted to final and medial position. The examples below illustrate final voicing:

[naɪz] 'nice'   [puʒ] 'push'
[fiəz] 'fierce'   [wɔʒ] 'wash'
[inkriːz] 'increase'   [fiʒ] 'fish'

In medial position voicing is restricted to /ʃ/:

[speʒl̩]   'special'
[preʒə]   'pressure'
[neiʒn̩]   'nation'

(c)   Avoidance of dental fricatives:
The dental fricatives /θ/ and /ð/ are often realised as the corresponding alveolar stops [t] and [d] respectively:

[tik] 'thick'   [æntəm] 'anthem'
[triː] 'three'   [metəd] 'method'
[θɔːt] 'thought'
[də] 'the'   [fɑːdə] 'father'
[dis] 'this'   [eidə] 'either'
[dəm] 'them'   [rɑːdə] 'rather'

In final position /ð/ is not really substituted by [d], but is devoiced to [θ]. /θ/ itself is frequently realised as [t] word-finally:

[bret]	'breath'
[wət]	'worth'
[fɔːt]	'fourth'

3.3. Glottalisation

Final stops are frequently replaced by glottal stops, especially in lower sociolects (sometimes referred to as *patois* or broken English):

[həuʔ] 'hope'	[mʌʔ] 'mud'
[rʌʔ] 'rub'	[Σɔʔ] 'shock'
[kʌʔ] 'cut'	[frɔʔ] 'frog'

3.4.   Consonant substitution according to substrate

In lower sociolects, characteristic of speakers with low educational levels and social status, the influence of the mother tongue is particularly felt in the differential treatment of consonants. MalE speakers of Malay background frequently produce [p, b, dʒ] for /f, v, z/:

[pæn] 'fan'	[bitəmin] 'vitamin'
[pilm] 'film'	[dʒibrʌ] 'zebra'
[beri] 'very'	[dʒiːrɔ] 'zero'

Speakers of Chinese background frequently turn /r/ into [l], and /z/ into [dʒ]:

[flaɪd] 'friend'	[dʒirɔ] or [dʒilɔ] 'zero'
[læn] 'ran'	[dʒibra] or [dʒiblaː] 'zebra'

Speakers of Tamil background are recognisable by the substitution of [w] for /v/ and the deletion of /h/:

[wæn] 'van'	[aus] 'house'
[new] 'never'	[ʌŋgri] 'hungry'

4.   Suprasegmental features

4.1.   Stress

Generally speaking, the stress-patterns of educated MalE speakers are similar to those in RP but there is still a certain degree of variation in both word- and sentence-stress patterns. This is true of all informal speech and especially of lower sociolects.

(a)   Stress-position

Where RP has ascribed stress-position in disyllabic and polysyllabic words that have only single stress, MalE differs where such stress-position is concerned:

[eksə'saiz]	'exercise'
['leftenən(t)]	'lieutenant'
['intəlektuəl]	'intellectual'
['misʌndəsten(d)]	'misunderstand'

In the same vein, the MalE speaker often tends not to produce differential stress on pairs of words derived from the same root like RP '*import* (n) versus *im*'*port* (v). Such noun-verb derivatives are homophonous in MalE, as can be seen in an example like *Malaysia produces a lot of rubber which is the import of many industrialised countries.* In MalE the realisations of *produces* and *import* are ['prɔdjusiz] and [im'pɔːt] respectively.

(b)   Stress-quantity

MalE does not necessarily have the same number of stresses in polysyllabic words as does RP. MalE may reduce or increase the number of stresses in the word:

['mænju'fæktʃə]	'manufacture'
['dʒenrə'laizeiʃn]	'generalisation'

In some cases (as in '*misunder*'*stand,* '*question*'*naire,* '*inter*'*rupt,* and '*fare*'*well*) secondary stress is given equal prominence as primary stress so that the MalE version has two equal stresses.

An extension of this feature of stress-quality would be word- and sentence-stress for emphasis or contrast. MalE speakers may emphasise or contrast a statement by lengthening and stressing particular syllables:

Speaker 1: "How many years are you going away for?"
Speaker 2: "Three years!" /'θriː 'jiːəz/

4.2.   Rhythm

Rhythm in MalE is more often one of a syllable-timed nature – where all syllables (stressed as well as unstressed) recur at equal intervals of time. RP has a stress-timed rhythm instead, which MalE speakers do use, though only in formal declamatory style or reading style. Even educated MalE speakers use a syllable-timed rhythm in casual style.

4.3.   Intonation and pitch

In RP connected speech (as well as within the word), intonation has a range of functions, the main ones being to cue in the primary accented words and to differentiate the various sentence-types along with indicating the various speaker attitudes (and emotions) involved within the context of discourse. The various types of nucleus (falling \, rising /, fall-rise \ /, and rise-fall / \) that are operant in RP are used to signify the differences in a speech situation, depending on the position and type of nucleus involved. In MalE however, there are not so many patterns of intonation and they do not perform so many functions. Thus if any syllable is to be stressed within the word or any word is to be stressed within the sentence, loudness is the differentiating factor (i.e. greater breath effort and muscular energy is effected by the MalE speaker). Change in pitch direction, both within the word as well as within the sentence, is not common in MalE as it is considered affected.

In other words pitch direction does not change within the accented (stressed) word (say as a fall \ or a rise / etc.). Intonation within the word is most often level intonation, except in a few particles that are used in informal speech as indicators of intimacy, emotion, acceptance, excitement and the like.

For signifying various sentence-types or for showing the speaker's attitude or emotion, MalE does not have as wide a range of intonation as RP. In MalE, there are such markers of questions and attitudes or emotions as particles – examples of which are the *lah*, *man*, and *ah*(*uh*) particles. These are substitutes for intonation especially in indicating emotions and attitudes.

As for range of pitch in the MalE speakers, it certainly is not as wide as that in the RP speaker (except for extremely excitable situations).

4.4.   Phonotactic features

(a)   Gradation
In RP unaccented words show reductions of length of sounds and obscurations of vowels – e.g. *do* has the strong form [duː] and the weak equivalent [də]; *but* has [bʌt] and [bət]. In MalE such gradation is not common. The definite and indefinite articles *the* and *a,* as well as the preposition *of* and the conjunction *and,* are sometimes reduced in connected informal speech, although the frequency of such gradation is considerably low.

(b)   Liaison

While liaison is a prominent feature of RP connected speech, it is seldom observed in MalE – except in the official speech of the educated MalE speaker. 'Linking *r*' is more frequently used than 'intrusive *r*' in MalE. This may be because there is an <r> in the orthography:

here and there	/hiər æn(d) ðɛə/
far and near	/faːr æn(d) niə/
rare opportunity	/rɛər ɔpətʃunəti/

(c)   Syllabicity

The use of syllabic nasals and laterals in MalE is rare: thus we have [bʌtən] 'button', [litəl] 'little' and [botəl] 'bottle'. Here schwa takes prominence in syllable structure, making MalE consistent with the CVC syllable orientation of Bahasa Malaysia.

5.   Conclusion

The degree of phonological variation – be it segmental, suprasegmental or phonotactic – depends on variables like the education and socio-economic background of the MalE speaker – along with register and the style of discourse. Certain features are definite enough to be considered diagnostic of MalE – yet it is difficult to decide to which level of MalE they belong. The MalE speaker, on the whole, has a competence that is near-native, if not, even native. This competence includes an ability to 'switch levels' and perform in a lect well below one's highest level. For example: the same speaker may use a style which enunciates all three consonants of a consonant cluster in public speaking, but will use a style that reduces the same cluster to just one consonant when speaking to, say, his colleague in the office or a parking attendant at the car park. There are, in addition, the 'patois' MalE speakers who can be placed rigidly at a single level, as they are unable to switch lects. However, the actual phonological variations between the educated speaker's official and unofficial speech have yet to be studied carefully. Patois MalE features, on the other hand, are predictable and identifiable.

Exercises and study questions

1. Compare the vowels of MalE and SgE, tow varieties with very close historical and geographical ties.

2. Do the same for the diphthongs.

3. List the phonological processes affecting consonants that are shared between the two varieties.

4. What differences in consonant phonology occur between SgE and MalE?

5. Discuss the substrate influences that result in consonant variation in MalE.

Selected references

Please consult the General references for titles mentioned in the text but not included in the references below. For a full bibliography see the accompanying CD-ROM.

Baskaran, Loga
  1987   Aspects of Malaysian English Syntax. Unpublished Ph.D. thesis, University of London, London.
Platt, John and Heidi Weber
  1980   *English in Singapore and Malaysia: Status, Features, Functions.* Kuala Lumpur: Oxford University Press.
Tay, Mary W. J.
  1993   *The English Language in Singapore: Issues and Development.* Singapore: Unipress.
Tongue, R.
  1974   *The English of Singapore and Malaysia.* Singapore: Eastern Universities Press.

Philippine English: phonology

Ma. Lourdes G. Tayao

1.   Introduction

The Philippines is a multilingual country, with no less than 87 ethnic languages, eight of which are considered major in terms of the number of native speakers. After its annexation from Spain by the United States in the early 1900s, the Philippines made English its official language to be taught and used as medium of instruction in Philippine schools and to serve, together with Spanish for some time, as official medium of communication in other government domains such as the legislature, the courts, etc. It was likewise used in business transactions and in religious services and even gave rise to a body of Philippine literature in English. The language policy then was prompted by a desire to have a common language for negotiation in a multilingual society since at that time there was no single lingua franca for the entire nation.

However, with the wave of nationalism that resulted ultimately in the gaining of independence, a clamour arose for a national language based on one of the major Philippine languages, but drawing from the other Philippine languages as well. Named *Pilipino* (now respelled *Filipino*) the national language shares with English the status of official languages of the country. Initially, the Philippine Bilingual Education Policy sought to develop bilinguals competent in English and *Filipino*, the national language, with specific domains allocated to the two languages. Science, mathematics and English were to be taught using English as medium of instruction while the other subjects were to be taught in Filipino.

The 1987 Revised Philippine Bilingual Education Policy however saw some modifications made to the policy. It endorsed the use of the regional languages as auxiliary languages of instruction for beginning literacy. In this it was motivated by Cummins' Interdependence Hypothesis (see Cummins and Swain, 1986) as the rationale for using the child's native language in teaching cognitively demanding concepts and thus avoiding cognitive deficit and possible semilingualism on the part of the learner. A close examination of the policy reveals its goal to be that of transitional bilingualism with the non-exclusive use of English in the domains that were previously allocated solely to it.

Subsequent factors have influenced the language policy of the country. On the one hand, deterioration in English proficiency has been noted even among educated Filipinos. This phenomenon is attributed in part to the reduced time in the use of English in school and to the increased exposure and use of Filipino in the mass media. Other contributing factors cited by Gonzalez, Jambalos and Romero (2003) are "the inadequacy of learning resources, and the absence of good models in English since the teachers are not themselves good models".

On the other hand, globalisation and the widespread use of English in the global village and the growing Filipino workforce seeking employment outside the country necessitate proficiency in English. But with the widening circle of English users and the rise of different varieties of English, an old issue has resurfaced. What variety of English should be taught in schools? Should it be Philippine English (henceforth PhlE) as an evolving local Asian variety, or General American English (henceforth gAmE) as the influential western medium from which it sprung?

1.1. Philippine English

PhlE is used extensively in different domains by educated Filipinos throughout the Philippines. As early as 1969, studies were conducted describing Philippine English as a variety of General American English and recommending that it be taught instead of gAmE in Philippine schools. T. Llamzon (1997: 43), a pioneer in establishing the existence of Standard Filipino English and describing it, pointed out in one of his more recent studies that Filipinos are willing to copy American English, but only up to a point especially where spoken English is concerned:

> … an *approximation* of the English formal style is what they want. They retain something of their identity – in their lack of the nasal twang, in the careful articulation of individual syllables, and in their refusal to use the "reduced signals" of the informal conversational style of American English. … when educated Filipinos speak to their fellow Filipinos, they speak English the Filipino way.

The status of Standard Philippine English was also taken up by McKaughan (1993: 52), who pointed out that "Philippine English has emerged as an autonomous variety of English with its own self-contained system. It has its own distinct accent. The differences in form in Philippine English are not deficiencies but distinct forms belonging to the Philippine English speech fellowship … As to accent, any of the varieties, so long as they are from educated Filipino speakers can model good Philippine English."

Socio-political developments resulting from changes in language attitudes characterised by objections to a monolithic or single standard of language performance in English, along with the current emphasis on varieties of English, have brought to the fore renewed interest in Philippine English which has been evolving through the years.

In this chapter I describe the phonological features of Philippine English citing whenever possible, reasons to explain differences between PhlE and its 'matrilect' gAmE.

1.2.   Previous studies on the phonetics of Philippine English

Among the earliest studies is Llamzon's (1969) *Standard Filipino English*, which attempts to establish English spoken in the Philippines as a distinct variety. His term covers the English spoken by educated Filipinos and considered intelligible and acceptable not only in educated Filipino circles, but also among native speakers of Canadian English and American English. Where phonology is concerned, initial objections were raised stipulating that there can be no Standard Philippine English pronunciation because of regionalisms. Bautista (2000), however, points out that the existence of regionalisms need not prevent the development and recognition of a standard variety.

Other synchronic studies of PhlE focused on its phonology, lexicon and syntax (Casambre 1986) and its use in the mass media (Gonzalez and Alberca 1978). Llamzon's (1997) study initiated a shift in focus from research on a single standard used by Filipinos in educated circles to the different varieties of PhlE across the levels identified as acrolect, basilect, and mesolect.

Among the diachronic studies were the generational studies of Sta. Ana (1983) which sought to determine the problem sounds and grammatical features of Philippine English spoken across eight generations and that of Gonzalez, Jambalos and Romero (2003) which described Philippine English spoken across generations in line with historical landmarks on developments in English language teaching in the country. The generational studies showed "perduring" features of Philippine English phonology which have remained stable through the years as well as developments that took place in the course of time.

1.3.   A "lectal" description of the phonetic features of Philippine English

Considering that the Philippines is a multilingual country, different regions with different indigenous native languages would necessarily have their own distinct pronunciations of English words resulting from interference from the phonological structure of the native tongue. This is the reason for earlier claims made that there can be no Standard Philippine English pronunciation because of regionalisms. However, the studies on Philippine English phonology have shown sociolectal rather than geographical variables to provide a better account for differences in pronunciation among the different varieties of PhlE. While differences in the phonological structure of one's native language and the target language usually affect a speaker's L_2 phonology, the three sociolectal varieties of PhlE cut across the different linguistic regions of the country. Thus, the features of each variety would be true to all speakers of that variety irrespective of the region from which they come.

Llamzon's (1997) study of the phonetic features of Philippine English describes three distinct sociolinguistic varieties of PhlE as far as pronunciation is concerned. One is the acrolect, which closely approximates the formal style of gAmE and is acceptable to educated Filipinos. Llamzon refers to this approximation of gAmE formal style as the "Filipino English formal style" and he cites well-known figures in the media and education as speakers of that style. The second is the *mesolect,* which exhibits more differences from the phonological structure of gAmE but is also used by educated Filipinos – notable personages in government, higher education and in the mass media. The last variety, referred to by Llamzon as the *basilect* variety, is one where "the speaker's ethnic tongue forms the substratum," hence more substitutions are evident in it than in the other two varieties

Although the acrolect variety of PhlE closely resembles gAmE, varied studies of the former (Llamzon 1969, 1997; Gonzalez 1985; Casambre 1986) have noted that some of its phonetic features which serve to distinguish it from the latter have remained stable through the years. More differences are notable in the mesolect variety and are even more pronounced in the basilect.

2. The phonetic features of PhlE

2.1. Vowels

Table 1 summarises the vowels of PhlE in terms of Wells' lexical sets.

Table 1. The vowels of PhlE in terms of Wells' lexical sets

KIT	i:> i > ɪ	FLEECE	i: > i > ɪ	NEAR	ir
DRESS	ɛ	FACE	eɪ	SQUARE	er
TRAP	ɑ	PALM	ɑ	START	ɑr
LOT	ɑ	THOUGHT	o	NORTH	or
STRUT	ʌ	GOAT	o	FORCE	or

Table 1. (continued)   The vowels of PhlE in terms of Wells' lexical sets

FOOT	u: > u > ʊ	GOOSE	u: > u > ʊ	CURE	ur
BATH	ɑ	PRICE	ɑɪ	happY	ɪ
CLOTH	o	CHOICE	ɔɪ	lettER	ɛr
NURSE	ɛr	MOUTH	ɑʊ	commA	ɑ
horSES	ɛ	POOR	ur		

Since there is considerable lectal variation further details are provided in Table 2, of the three PhlE varieties alongside those of gAmE. In table 2 a minus sign (-) represents a set present in gAmE but absent in the PhlE variety. Substitutions made for those absent phonemes are enclosed in parenthesis in the last column of the tables. As the U.S. phonological tradition generally classes /eɪ/ and /oʊ/ with the monophthongs, I have left them in table 2, whilst excluding the other diphthongs.

Table 2.   Vowel phonemes in the different varieties of PhlE vis-à-vis gAmE

gAmE Phonemes	PhlE *Acrolect*	PhlE *Mesolect*	PhlE *Basilect*	Substitutions
High				
Front				
/iː/ 'fleece, near, feel'				
/ɪ/ 'kit, pin, fill, *happY*'		free variation with [iː] –		(i)
Back				
/uː/ 'foot, cure, goose, pool'				
/ʊ/ 'pull'		free variation with [uː]–		(u)
Mid				
Front				
/eɪ/ 'face, fail, square'			–	(i)
/ɛ/ 'dress, fell, pen, merry'			–	(i)
Central				
/ə/ '*comm*A'		free variation with [ɑ] –		(ɑ)
/ʌ/ 'strut'			–	(ɑ)
Back				
/oʊ/ 'goat, goal'		free variation with [o] –		(u)
/o/'cloth, thought'			–	(u)

Table 2. (continued)   Vowel phonemes in the different varieties of PhlE vis-à-vis gAmE

gAmE Phonemes	PhlE *Acrolect*	PhlE *Mesolect*	PhlE *Basilect*	Substitutions
Low				
Front				
/æ/ 'trap, bath, dance, hand, marry'		[ɑ] in 'bath' versus [ɛ] in 'cat'	–	(ɑ)
Central				
/a/ 'lot, palm, start, power'	[ɑ] is low back			

The vowels of the acrolect group resemble those of gAmE except for PALM which is low back in the former but low central in the latter. The de-stressing of vowels rendering them [ə] or [ɪ] in rapid speech also occurs in this group. The generation study of Gonzalez, Jambalos and Romero (2003) shows the increased use of schwa in unstressed syllables.

The mesolect group has six stressed vowels plus schwa. [i] (or [ɪ]) is used for both KIT and FLEECE. These short vowels are in free variation with [i:]; no words are distinguished purely by length. Similarly [u] (or [ʊ]) is used for both FOOT and PULL; with once again some free variation with the long vowel [u:]. [o] is used for both CLOTH and THOUGHT; [ɑ] for PALM; and schwa in free variation with [ɑ] for *commA*. The other vowels in the inventory of the mesolect variety are [ɛ] in DRESS; [e] and 'stressed schwa' /ʌ/ in STRUT. Some differences from gAmE pronunciations occur as in [o] in *model* rather than [ɑ]; and [ɑ] in *bag* instead of [æ]. The vowels of the mesolect group are given full value even in unstressed syllables, in contrast to acrolectal norms.

The basilect, on the other hand, has three vowels. [i] is used for KIT and FLEECE as well as DRESS vowels. [ɑ] is used for TRAP, NURSE and *A*bout. [u] is used for FOOT and GOOSE as well as for CLOTH and FORCE. Thus, in this variety, *trap* is pronounced [tɑrɑp], *north* is rendered [nurt] and *nurse*, [nɑrs]. Like those of the mesolect group, vowels in polysyllabic words are not de-stressed in the basilect.

In spontaneous speech, vowel length differences between monophthongs and diphthongs are not evident in the mesolect and basilect varieties of PhlE. As far as vowel length in contrastive pairs like *feel/fill* and *pool/pull* is concerned, mesolectal speakers do produce them distinctly in focused, deliberate speech. However, in other styles [i] and [i:] and [u] and [u:] do not contrast; there is a slight tendency for the long vowels to be preferred under the influence of Philippine languages.

2.2.   Diphthongs

The diphthongs /au/ in MOUTH and /aɪ/ in PRICE are present in all three varieties of PhlE. On the other hand, whereas the diphthongs /oɪ/ in CHOICE and /eɪ/ in FACE are present in the phonetic inventory of the acrolect and mesolect groups, the former is rendered /uj/ and /ij/ by the basilect group. Likewise the GOAT vowel occurs as [oʊ] in the acrolect; in free variation with [o] in the mesolect; and as [u] in the basilect.

PhlE is rhotic, that is /r/ is preserved after the vowels. Hence, the vowel in NEAR is pronounced [ir]; in SQUARE [er]; in START [ɑr]; in NORTH and FORCE [or]; in LETTER and NURSE [ɛr] and in CURE and POOR [ur].

2.3.   Consonants

Given in Table 3 are the consonant phonemes of the three varieties of PhlE presented also alongside those of gAmE. As in the vowel chart, categories present in gAmE, but absent in the PhlE variety, are marked by a minus sign (-) as indicated in the table and substitutions made for those absent phonemes are enclosed in parenthesis in the last column of the table.

Table 3.   *Consonant* phonemes in the different varieties of PhlE vis-à-vis gAmE

gAmE Phonemes	PhlE *Acrolect*	PhlE *Mesolect*	PhlE *Basilect*	Substitutions
Stops [p t k]				
[b d g]				
Fricatives [f v]			–	[p b]
[θ ð]	[θ ~ t; ð ~ d]	[θ ~ t; ð ~ d]	–	[t d]
[s z]			–	[s]
[ʃ ʒ]			–	[sij] in initial, [s] in final position
[h]				

Table 3. (continued)   *Consonant* phonemes in the different varieties of PhlE vis-à-vis gAmE

gAmE Phonemes	PhlE *Acrolect*	PhlE *Mesolect*	PhlE *Basilect*	Substitutions
Affricates				
[t ʃ]			–	(ts)
[dʒ]			–	(dj) in initial, (ds) in final position
Nasals [m n ŋ]				
Lateral [l]				
Retroflex liquid [r]		rolled/one-tap	rolled/one-tap	
Glides [w j]				

Stops

P, T, K and B, D, G resemble gAmE articulation. However, though aspiration of voiceless stops in syllable-initial, stressed position is present, it is rare among the acrolect group and not evident in the mesolect and basilect varieties. Some linguists believe that the Philippine languages' tendency to avoid syllables having just a vowel is carried over into L₂ English. A glottal stop is therefore used to create a CV syllable; hence [ʔɑbaʊt] 'about'.

Fricatives

F and V are present in the acrolect and mesolect but absent in the basilect, except among speakers of Philippine languages like Ibanag, which has these two fricatives in its phonetic inventory. Amongst basilectal speakers the voiceless [p] and [b] are substituted for [f] and [v] respectively. In the mesolectal group the substitution of [p] for [f] is not as frequent as of [b] for [v]. Some inconsistencies from the point of view of gAmE occur – for example, there is no distinction in the pronunciation of the prepositions *of* and *off* in PhlE, although the former calls for the use of [v] and the latter [f] in many varieties of AmE.

The interdental fricatives [θ] and [ð] are likewise absent in the basilect (and in most Philippine languages). They are substituted with the alveolar stops [t] for [θ] and [d] for [ð] in the basilect; but, as Table 3 indicates, are in free variation in the other two varieties. Acrolect and mesolect speakers produce /θ/ and /ð/ sounds in focused and deliberate speech.

Of the sibilants [z], [ʃ] and [ʒ], are absent in the basilect variety (as in most Philippine languages). This is an example of a split category where one phoneme in the native language, /s/, has several different distinct phoneme equivalents in the target language. Hence, among speakers of the basilect, /z/ is rendered [s], /ʃ/ and /ʒ/ are pronounced [sij] in initial position and [ts] and [ds] in final position. Examples of the former are [sijur] for *sure,* and [sijor] for *shore.* Examples of the latter are [garads] for *garage* and [bus] for *bush.*

All of the sibilants are present in the acrolect. Among the mesolect group of speakers, [z], [ʃ], or [ʒ] are pronounced as in gAmE in word-initial, but not in word-medial or word-final position. Thus, initial /z/ in *zoo* is pronounced as [z] but is rendered [s] in final position as in *buzz.* The phoneme /ʃ/ in word-medial and word-final positions occur as [sj] and [s] respectively; thus [lisjur] for *leisure* and [bɑs] for *bash.*

There is final devoicing of [ʒ] in all three varieties of PhlE. This applies even to the noun plural and 3rd singular verb morphemes. Thus *plays, birds* and *runs* all have [s], rather than the voicing assimilation rule of gAmE, which would result in [z]. The same applies to the /ɪz/ allophone of noun plurals, which occurs as [is] or [ɛs] – thus [bɑsɛs] for *buses*, rather than [bʌsɪz] in the target language.

Affricates

/tʃ/ and /dʒ/ are to be found in the mesolect and acrolect, but not in the basilect. Basilectal speakers produce [ts] in initial and final positions for [tʃ] – for example [tsip] for *cheap* and [wɑts] for *watch.* /dʒ/ is pronounced [dij] in initial position and [ds] in final position – thus [dijɑnitor] for *janitor* and [wɛds] for *wedge.*

Other consonants

All three varieties of PhlE have the nasals M, N, /ŋ/, the glides W, /j/ and the lateral L. R is a retroflex liquid in the acrolect, as in gAmE. In the other lects it has a different quality. Whereas earlier studies describe it as trilled, it is more accurate to say that it is rolled, or occurs as a single tap.

3.   Syllable structure and stress

3.1.   Syllables

Consonant clusters are rare in PhlE because of the influence of speakers L₁s which favour V, CV, VC and CVC syllables. Consonant clusters of the target language are dealt with in various ways. For initial clusters beginning with /s/ the basilect group adds a vowel before /s/: [is-tɑrt] for *start*; [is-tɑ-rɑt] for *strut*; and [is-ku-wir] for *square*. With final clusters of /s/ + consonant all groups drop the final consonant – thus [lɑs] for *last*. An alternate rule of breaking up clusters in the basilect is via vowel epenthesis: [ku-lut] for *cloth*; [di-ris] for *dress* and [tɑ-rɑp] for *trap*. The vowel harmony evident in the choice of epenthetic vowel follows a rule from Philippine languages.

The syllable structure of most Philippine languages also accounts in part for the non-existence of syllabic consonants in the mesolect and basilect varieties of PhlE and for its rare occurrence in the acrolect. Moreover, the absence of the vowel reduction rule in those two varieties likewise precludes the production of syllabic consonants. With the first two groups, vowels are given full value even if they occur in unstressed syllables. This contrasts with the acrolect group, which observes de-stressing of vowels rendering them [ɪ] or [ə] in unstressed syllables. The absence of vowel reduction has been a stable feature of PhlE. It may be attributed to the fact that on the whole Philippine languages are syllable-timed and not stress-timed like gAmE. The basilect and mesolect groups do not produce syllabic consonants. Instead, full forms are observed [mɑunten] for *mountain*; [gɑrden] for *garden*; [litɛl] for *little*; and [bɑndɛl] for *bundle*.

Since Philippine languages are syllable-timed, the individual syllables of words are generally pronounced distinctly in PhlE and the de-stressing of function words is usually not observed. This syllable-timed rhythm has in fact been found to be stable in the basilect and mesolect varieties. Moreover, the stress-timed rhythm of gAmE is one reason cited for the difficulty of Filipinos to make out what native speakers of gAmE say.

3.2.   Stress

Word, sentence, and emphatic stress in PhlE were also examined to note deviations from gAmE. The findings of the studies reveal that there are words like baptism, hazardous, pedestal, utensil, dioxide, and percentage, whose word stress in all three varieties of PhlE differs from that of gAmE. Table 4 gives polysyllabic words found to be stressed differently from gAmE by all three groups.

Table 4.   Sample lexical items stressed differently in PhlE compared to gAmE

gAmE stress pattern	PhlE – Acrolect				PhlE – Mesolect				PhlE – Basilect			
	1st	2nd	3rd	4th	1st	2nd	3rd	4th	1st	2nd	3rd	4th
1st Syllable:												
colleague		*				*				*		
govern		*				*				*		
menu		*				*				*		
precinct		*				*				*		
ancestors	*					*				*		
baptism		*				*				*		
hazardous		*				*				*	*	
pedestal		*				*				*		
subsequent	*					*				*		
formidable		*				*				*		
2nd Syllable:												
bamboo		*			*				*			
throughout		*			*				*			
centennial		*				*			*			
committee	*				*				*			
dioxide	*				*				*			
lieutenant		*				*			*			
percentage	*				*				*			
semester		*			*				*			
utensil	*				*				*			
1st and 3rd Syllables:												
adolescence		*				*				*		
antecedent		*				*				*		
rehabilitate		*				*				*		
commentary	*				*				*			
complimentary	*		*			*					*	
documentary	*		*			*					*	
2nd and 4th Syllables:												
hereditary	*			*	*				*			
interpretative		*		*	*		*	*				*
itinerary		*		*	*		*	*				*
pronunciation	*			*	*			*		*	*	

The table shows that of the ten words (*colleague, govern, menu, precinct, an-cestors, baptism, hazardous, pedestal, subsequent*, and *formidable*) stressed on the 1st syllable in gAmE, only *ancestors* and *subsequent* were stressed by the acrolect group on the 1st syllable. The others were stressed by all three groups on the second syllable.

On the other hand, nine words stressed on the second syllable in gAmE *(bamboo, throughout, centennial, committee, dioxide, lieutenant, percentage, semester,* and *utensil)* were stressed by the basilect group on the first syllable with the other two groups likewise stressing the last four words on the same syllable. The first five were stressed by the acrolect group on the second syllable while the mesolect group did so only with the words *lieutenant* and *centennial*.

Regarding the six words stressed on the first and third syllables in gAmE, with main stress on the third, *(adolescence, antecedent, rehabilitate, commentary, complimentary,* and *documentary),* the first four were stressed on only one syllable by all three groups in PhlE, the second syllable for the first three words and the first syllable for the fourth. With the acrolect group, the last two words in the set – *complimentary* and *documentary* – were stressed on the first and third syllables following gAmE pronunciation but the other two groups stressed them only on the third.

Concerning the final set of words, *hereditary, interpretative, itinerary* and *pronunciation*, which are stressed on the second and fourth syllables in gAmE, all three groups stressed the first word on the first syllable. The acrolect group stressed the next two words following gAmE pronunciation and so did the mesolect group with the word *interpretative,* which the basilect group stressed on the first syllable. The word *hereditary* was also stressed by the mesolect and basilect groups on the first syllable. Whereas the basilect group stressed the last word, *pronunciation* as per gAmE pronunciation, the other two groups stressed the first and fourth syllables instead.

Other gAmE word stress patterns not found in PhlE are contrasts made between number words ending in *–teen* and those ending in *–ty* (e.g. ˈthirty vs. thirˈteen); between words that may be used as nouns or as verbs (a ˈrebel vs. to reˈbel); noun compounds in contrast to phrasal or compound verbs (a ˈdrop-out vs. to drop ˈout) noun compounds as contrasted with adjective + noun combinations (ˈsewing machine vs. sweet-smelling ˈflowers).

Some trends concerning word stress in PhlE among the mesolect and basilect groups may be pointed out, but these will warrant further investigation and verification. With the addition of affixes to form 4- or 5-syllable words (e.g. *commentary* and *centenary),* the mesolect and basilect tend to put the stress on the penultimate syllable. The two varieties tend to favour stressing the 2nd syllable in 4- or 5-syllable words (e.g. *formidable* and *rehabilitate).* For some words that have both a primary and secondary stress (e.g. *cemetery, commentary),* there is a tendency in the two groups to interchange the two, placing the primary stress where the secondary should be and vice versa, an observation also noted in previous studies (e.g. Llamzon 1969).

Where sentence stress is concerned, the acrolect and mesolect more often than not stress the last content word in breath groups, but this is not apparent in the basilect group who would stress function words or even two words instead of just one in a breath group. Also absent from the basilect variety, but present in the acrolect and mesolect groups is the use of contrastive and emphatic stress.

4.   Intonation

The use of three intonation patterns was scrutinised in studies of Philippine phonology. These were the final and non-final 2-3-3 rising intonation, the non-final 2-3-2 rising-falling (back-to-normal) intonation, and the final 2-3-1 rising-falling (down-to-fade out) intonation. In keeping with the final intonation patterns in most Philippine languages, one of the stable features noted in PhIE is the use of the final rising-falling intonation in statements and the final rising intonation in questions. No distinction is made in the final intonation of *wh-* questions and *yes-no* questions in PhIE, although Gonzalez and Alberca (1978) noted the use of the rising intonation in the former and the rising-falling in the latter. This stands in direct contrast to the final intonation patterns of gAmE. In the latter final rising intonation is generally used in *yes-no* questions while final rising-falling intonation is used in *wh-* questions, in *yes-no* tag questions seeking confirmation, and in statements. However, it must be conceded that even gAmE norms are in flux here, with the increase of 'high rise terminals' in ordinary statements.

Concerning non-final intonation, three uses of the non-final 2-3-3 rising intonation were examined. These were the obligatory use of the non-final rising intonation on nominatives of address and on the non-final options in alternatives, and the optional use at the end of subordinate clauses appearing in sentence-initial position. Gonzalez, Jambalos and Romero's generational study (2003) noted an increase in the use of non-final rising intonation in alternatives and in a series, in line with expectations of Target Language speakers. This, however, has yet to be established as a stable phonetic feature of PhIE. My own data show the use of non-final rising intonation in nominatives of address to be non-existent in the basilect variety, rare in the mesolect and occasional in the acrolect.

5. Conclusion

The study of PhlE phonology is an important one, since its 'target' is AmE, rather than BrE, in contrast to most other 'New English' varieties in Africa and Asia. Furthermore, the substrate languages form an important counter-influence. The generational studies of Gonzalez, Jambalos and Romero (2003) forms a solid basis for charting out future developments in PhlE.

Exercises and study questions

1. Discuss some of the major influences of American English on PhlE.

2. Compare the vowels of PhlE and SgE.

3. Review the discussion of vowel length in PhlE.

4. Review the treatment of sibilants in PhlE.

5. Review the 3 ways in which consonant clusters are broken up in PhlE.

Selected references

Please consult the General references for titles mentioned in the text but not included in the references below. For a full bibliography see the accompanying CD-ROM.

Alberca, Wilfredo L.
    1978   The distinctive features of Philippine English in the mass media. Unpublished Ph.D. dissertation, University of Santo Tomas, Manila.
Bautista, Ma. Lourdes S.
    2000   Studies of Philippine English in the Philippines. *Philippine Journal of Linguistics* 31: 39–65.
Casambre, Nelia G.
    1986   What is Filipino English? *Philippine Journal for Language Teaching* 14: 34–49.
Cummins, Jim and Merril Swain
    1986   *Bilingualism in Education: Aspects of Theory, Research and Practice.* London: Longman
Gonzalez, Andrew
    1985   *Studies on Philippine English.* Singapore: SEAMEO Regional Language Centre.

1997   The history of English in the Philippines. In: Ma. Lourdes S. Bautista (ed.)
            English is an Asian Language: The Philippine Context, 25–40. Sydney:
            The Macquarie Library.

Gonzalez, Andrew and Alberca, Wilfredo L.
1978   *Philippine English of the Mass Media* (preliminary edition). Manila: De
            La Salle University Research Council.

Gonzalez, Andrew, Thelma V. Jambalos and Ma. Corona S. Romero
2003   *Three Studies on Philippine English across Generations: Towards an
            Integration and Some Implications*, Manila: Linguistic Society of the
            Philippines.

Llamzon, Teodoro A.
1969   *Standard Filipino English*. Quezon City: Ateneo de Manila University
            Press.
1997   The Phonology of Philippine English. In: Ma. Lourdes S. Bautista (ed.)
            English is an Asian Language: The Philippine Context, 41–48. Sydney:
            The Macquarie Library.

McKaughan, Howard P.
1993.   Towards a Standard Philippine English. *Philippine Journal of Linguistics*
            24: 41–55.

Sta. Ana, Alan
1983   English in the Philippines across generations: A pilot study. Unpublished
            masters' thesis, Ateneo de Manila University, Quezon City.

Synopsis: the phonology of English in Africa and South and Southeast Asia

Rajend Mesthrie

1. Introduction

This synopsis will provide a very general overview of the phonological characteristics of varieties of English in Africa and south and Southeast Asia (henceforth *Africa-Asia*). The focus will inevitably fall on those characteristics that
differ from varieties that are more or less accepted as a norm in international
English: RP and 'General American' (however hard the latter may be to define).
These two somewhat idealised varieties are chosen as a convenient means of
comparison, as well as for the fact that they do have some prestige in the former colonies, especially via the media and in newsreading styles (rather than in
colloquial speech). RP is the model promulgated by the British in all territories,
but two, covered in this volume. The exception is the Philippines, which, after
Spanish domination, came under the sway of the U.S. and *ergo* U.S. English.
The second is LibSE, an offshoot of AAVE. As with the synopsis of morphological and syntactic characteristics, the features identified are unlikely to be
used by all L2 speakers in a given territory at all times. Rather, the principles
of variationist sociolinguistics apply: there is a degree of intra-speaker, inter-
speaker and stylistic variation. In addition the features cited are mainly found
in mesolectal and basilectal speech; acrolectal speakers usually evince accents
that are closer to prestige TL norms.

2. Vowels

2.1. The short monophthongs

Varieties in Africa-Asia either retain the 6-vowel system for short monophthongs or transform it into a 5-vowel system. The latter is exemplified by almost all African L2 varieties (except educated varieties of NigE). A 6-vowel
system for short vowels is found among all the L1 varieties (WSAfE, StHE,
CFE, InSAfE, LibSE), the Asian varieties (IndE, PakE, SgE and MalE; PhlE
mesolect) and (with several structural changes) in southern NigE. The 5-vowel

short monophthong system is in fact the core vowel system in its entirety for African varieties (except NigE), since (a) schwa is marginal in these varieties and (b) length distinction between vowels is not a general feature. There are two subtypes of the 5-vowel system for short vowels, depending on particular mergers:

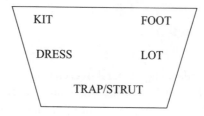

Figure 1.   5-vowel system – Type 1

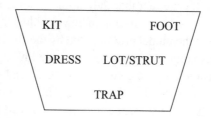

Figure 2.   5-vowel system – Type 2

Type 1, with merger of TRAP and STRUT is found in BlSAfE, EAfrE, GhE, GhP. Type 2 with merger of LOT and STRUT is found in CamE, Kamtok and NigP.

In WSAfE and CFE though there is a 6-way distinction amongst the short monophthongs, there is a chain shift amongst the front vowels, with each vowel moving one step higher and /ɪ/ becoming centralised (as ï). I now turn to the specific characteristics of each lexical set in Africa-Asia varieties. In SgE the DRESS and TRAP classes appear to have merged (to [ɛ]) (Brown 1988: 134) or in Wee's formulation (in this volume) there may well be a crossover effect in terms of vowel height, with [ɛ] for TRAP and [æ] for DRESS. Further research is needed to confirm this crossover of a whole class rather than of individual and isolated words as sometimes happens in other varieties.

KIT

In several varieties (WSAfE, StHE, CFE, InSAfE) KIT is 'split' into a subclass with [ɪ] (in velar and glottal contexts) and a subclass with a centralised vowel [ï] (in all other contexts). KIT may variably be realised as [i] in StHE, CFE, all L₂ African and south-east Asian varieties. In all L₂ African and south-east Asian varieties it may also be lengthened in certain contexts (as with all potential long-short pairs, since length is non-contrastive).

DRESS

[e] is the main variant in WSAfE, StHE, CFE, InSAfE, EAfrE, CamE, Kamtok, IndE and PakE. [ɛ] is the main variant in BlSAfE, GhE, LibSE, NigP, GhP and PhlE. In southern NigE there is free variation between [e] and [ɛ]. [æ] occurs in SgE and MalE; [a] is the usual variant in northern NigE.

TRAP

A raised variant [ɛ̝] is usual in WSAfE, CFE, BlSAfE, SgE and to some extent InSAfE. The usual variant is [æ] in StHE, LibSE, IndE, PakE and MalE. [a] is the usual realisation in LibSE, NigE, NigP, GhE, GhP, CamE and Kamtok. [ɑ] is reported in PhlE. In SgE TRAP and DRESS appear to cross over, as discussed above.

LOT

[ɒ] is a major variant in WSAfE, StHE, CFE, InSAfE and southern NigE. [ɔ] is found in WSAfE, BlSAfE, GhE, CamE, Kamtok, GhP, NigP, IndE, SgE and MalE. [ɔː] is reported as a major variant in IndE, PakE and InSAfE. [a] is the usual realisation in northern NigE; [ɑ] in LibSE and PhlE.

STRUT

[ɔ] occurs in CamE, NigP, southern NigE and Kamtok. [ʌ] occurs in StHE, InSAfE, LibSE, IndE, PakE and PhlE. [a] occurs in CFE, EAfrE, GhE and GhP. [ɑ] is the usual variant in northern NigE, SgE and MalE.

FOOT

A weakly rounded [ʊ] occurs in WSAfE and StHE. A rounded [u] occurs in CFE, InSAfE, NigE, IndE, PakE, and as a variant in GhE, LibSE and GhP. A short [u] is the usual realisation in BlSAfE, EAfrE, GhE, CamE, LibSE, Kamtok, GhP, NigP, SgE, MalE, PhlE, and as a variant in PakE.

2.2   The long monophthongs

In most L2s in Africa and south-east Asia vowel length is not distinctive. In the sets KIT – FLEECE; FOOT – GOOSE; LOT – THOUGHT the usual realisations are [i u ɔ]. There is some variation within these sets (described below), and even more variation in BATH and NURSE.

FLEECE
[iː] occurs in WSAfE, StHE, CFE, InSAfE, northern NigE, IndE, PakE and occasionally in GhE, GhP and MalE. [i] is reported in BlSAfE, EAfrE, southern NigE, GhE, CamE, LibSE, NigP, Kamtok, GhP, SgE and MalE. [ɪ] is reported as a lesser variant in IndE. In PhlE there is no distinction between KIT and FLEECE, though under the influence of Philippine languages there appears to be free variation, with a tendency towards [iː] rather than [i] or [ɪ].

GOOSE
There is symmetry with the FLEECE vowel in all varieties. Thus [uː] occurs in all the varieties that use [iː]; and [u] in all the varieties that use [i]. In WSAfE a noticeably centralised equivalent [ʉː] occurs. In PhlE there appears to be free variation between [uː] and [u] or [ʊ], with a tendency towards [uː].

THOUGHT
[ɔː] occurs in WSAfE, InSAfE, PakE and as lesser alternatives in GhE, GhP and IndE. [oː] is used in WSAfE, StHE, CFE and northern NigE. In StHE a diphthongal variant [ɔə] also occurs. Unlengthened [ɔ] or [o] occurs in BlSAfE, EAfrE, southern NigE, GhE, CamE, LibSE, NigP, GhP, Kamtok, IndE, SgE, MalE and PhlE.

NURSE
There is immense variation in the realisation of the NURSE vowel:

- [ɜː]   in the non-rhotic varieties, WSAfE, StHE (occasionally), CFE, In-SAfE and in the rhotic IndE, and as an occasional variant in GhE and GhP;
- [aː]   in northern NigE and StHE and as a lesser alternative in IndE;
- [ɛ]   in BlSAfE, southern NigE, GhE, GhP, NigP, in the rhotic PhlE;and as a lesser alternative in CamE;
- [a]   in EAfrE and as a lesser alternative in NigE;
- [ʌ]   in LibSE, and PakE (rhotic) and as a lesser alternative in IndE;
- [ɔ]   in CamE;
- [ə]   in SgE, MalE and as a lesser alternative in IndE;

[e]   in Kamtok;
[ø:]   in WSAfE.

BATH

The usual values are as follows:

[ɑ:]   in WSAfE, StHE, InSAfE, IndE, PakE, and as an alternative in CFE;
[a]   in CFE, EAfrE, southern NigE, GhE, CamE, NigP, Kamtok and GhP;
[ɑ]   in SgE, MalE, PhlE and as an alternative in CFE;
[ɒ:]   in BlSAfE;
[aː]   in northern NigE and as a lesser alternative in GhE and GhP;
[æ]   in LibSE;
[ɔ:] or [ɒ:] in WSAfE and [ɒ:] in CFE.

2.3.   Diphthongs

FACE

[eɪ]   occurs in WSAfE, StHE, InSAfE, PakE, and as a lesser alternative in
       BlSAfE, GhE, GhP and MalE;
[ɛɪ]   or slightly lower or backed equivalents of the nucleus occurs in WSAfE,
       CFE and BlSAfE;
[e]   occurs in EAfrE, NigE, GhE, CamE, LibSE, NigP, Kamtok, GhP, SgE,
       MalE and PhlE;
[e:]   occurs as a lesser alternative in PakE and NigP;
[eⁱ]   occurs as a lesser variant in GhE and GhP.

PRICE

[aɪ]   occurs in WSAfE, StHE (occasionally), InSAfE, NigE, IndE and
       PakE;
[ɑɪ]   occurs in EAfrE and PhlE;
[ʌɪ]   occurs in BlSAfE;
[ɑ̈ɪ]   occurs as an alternative form in WSAfE;
[ai]   occurs in GhE, CamE, Kamtok, GhP, SgE, MalE and as an alternative
       form in NigE, LibSE and CFE;
[ɐi]   occurs in CFE;
[ɔi]   occurs in StHE;
[a:]   occurs in LibSE;
[a]   occurs as a lesser alternative in Kamtok, GhE and GhP;
[ae]   a diphthong, occurs in NigP;
[ɑ:]   occurs in WSAfE and StHE.

MOUTH

[aʊ] occurs in CFE (before voiced segments), StHE, EAfrE, NigE, GhE, CamE, GhP, IndE and PakE. Nuclei with [ä] or [ɑ] are reported in WSAfE, InSAfE and PhlE. The glide element [u], rather than [ʊ], is reported in LibSE (as a lesser alternative), Kamtok, SgE and MalE. [æʊ] is reported in WSAfE; [aʊ] in CFE (before voiceless segments); [ɔʊ] in BlSAfE; [ʌᵘ] in LibSE; and [ao] in NigP.

Monophthongal qualities also occur: [ä:] in WSAfE; [o] in BlSAfE; and [a] as a lesser alternative in GhE and GhP.

CHOICE

- [ɔɪ] occurs in WSAfE, StHE, CFE, InSAfE, BlSAfE, IndE and PakE, NigE;
- [ɔi] occurs in GhE, CamE, Kamtok, GhP, IndE, SgE and MalE;
- [oɪ] occurs in WSAfE, StHE, EAfrE, and PhlE;
- [ɔe] occurs in NigP and as a lesser alternative in IndE;
- [ʌ], [ʌᶦ] or [ʌⁱ] occur in LibSE.

GOAT

- [o] occurs in EAfrE, southern NigE, GhE, CamE, LibSE, NigP, Kamtok, GhP, SgE, MalE and PhlE;
- [ɔ] is reported for BlSAfE;
- [o:] occurs in northern NigE, IndE, PakE, and as lesser alternatives in NigP and MalE;
- [oʊ] occurs in StHE, InSAfE and as lesser alternatives in GhE and GhP;
- [ɔʊ] occurs in BlSAfE;
- [əʊ] is reported in PakE;

Lowered and fronted nuclei also occur:

[ɛʊ] or [œʊ] or [ʌʊ] in WSAfE;
[ɐʊ] or [ʌʊ] in CFE.

SQUARE

- [e:] occurs in WSAfE, CFE, InSAfE and IndE;
- [ɛ:] occurs in WSAfE and IndE;
- [ɛ] occurs in BlSAfE, GhE, CamE, LibSE, Kamtok, GhP and as a lesser alternative in MalE;
- [æ] occurs in SgE, MalE and as a lesser alternative in LibSE;
- [e] occurs in Kamtok, PhlE and as a lesser alternative in LibSE;
- [ea] or [ɛa] occur in GhE, NigE, NigP and GhP;
- [iə] occurs in StHE; [ia] in southern NigE and [eə] or [əɪ] in PakE.

NEAR
The diphthongal realisations are as follows:

- [ɪə] in WSAfE, IndE, PakE and (as a lesser alternative) in StHE;
- [iə] in StHE, LibSE, SgE and MalE;
- [iɛ] in GhE, GhP and CamE, and as [ijɛ] in InSAfE;
- [iɐ] in CFE;
- [ɪa] in EAfrE;
- [ia] in Kamtok and as a lesser alternative in GhE and GhP, and as [ija] in NigP.

Monophthongal [e] is reported in BlSAfE, and as lesser alternatives, [jɪː] in WSAfE and [iː] in MalE.

CURE
There is a great array of variation here. Among the diphthongal realisations are the following:

- [ʊə] in WSAfE and PakE;
- [əʊ] in CFE;
- [ʊa] in EAfrE;
- [ua] in NigE and Kamtok;
- [ua] or [uɔ] in GhE and GhP;
- [uwɔ] in NigP.

Monophthongal values are reported in the following:

- [ɔː] in SAfE;
- [o] in BlSAfE and LibSE;
- [ɔ] in CamE, SgE, MalE and as lesser alternatives in GhE, Kamtok and GhP;
- [u] in PhlE (with postvocalic /r/).

2.4.   Other vowels

happY
The variants are as follows:

- [iː] in InSAfE, and as lesser alternatives in CFE and IndE;
- [iˑ] in WSAfE and CFE;
- [i] in GhE, CamE, LibSE, NigP, Kamtok, GhP, SgE and MalE;
- [ɪ] in BlSAfE, EAfrE, IndE, PakE, PhlE and as lesser alternatives in GhE and GhP;
- [iɪ] in NigE.

lettER

The variants are as follows:

[ə]   in WSAfE, CFE, LibSE, IndE (plus postvocalic /r/), SgE and MalE;
[ɛ]   in PhlE (plus postvocalic /r/) and in InSAfE;
[a]   in EAfrE, NigE, GhE, CamE, NigP, Kamtok, GhP;
[ä]   in BlSAfE;
[ʌ]   in PakE.

commA

The variants are as follows:

[ə]   in WSAfE, CFE, LibSE, SgE and MalE;
[ɐ]   in WSAfE and CFE;
[a]   in NigE, GhE, CamE, NigP, Kamtok, GhP and IndE;
[ɑ]   in InSAfE and PhlE;
[ä]   in BlSAfE;
[ʌ]   in PakE and as lesser alternatives in LibSE and MalE.

horsES

The variants are as follows:

[ə]   in InSAfE, LibSE, IndE, SgE, MalE and as lesser alternative in CFE;
[ɐ]   in CFE;
[iˑ]   in BlSAfE;
[ɨ]   as an alternative in IndE;
[ɪ]   in PakE;
[ɛ]   in PhlE.

3.   Consonants

3.1.   Stops

P, T, K may be unaspirated in WSAfE (in some subvarieties), CFE and In-
SAfE (variably) and very commonly in IndE, PakE, SgE and PhlE. No such
deaspiration is reported in StHE and the African varieties researched. T, D are
retroflexed in IndE and PakE, and occasionally in InSAfE. Glottalising of syllable-final T is reported for GhE and to a lesser extent GhP. Final stops have
glottalised variants in MalE. P is realised as [p], [f] or [Φ] and B as [b] or [v] in
northern NigE. T is realised as [ts] in some GhE varieties. St Helena B occurs
as [ß] occasionally, in intervocalic position.

3.2. Fricatives

The most striking feature among fricatives is that ALL varieties (except WSAfE) treat /θ/ and /ð/ as something other than an interdental fricative. /θ ð/ are realised similarly as a pair as follows:

> [t̪ d̪] in CFE, InSAfE, IndE, PakE;
>
> [t d] in EAfrE, GhE, LibSE (here [t] occurs variably with [θ]), Kamtok, SgE, MalE, PhlE;
>
> Variably as [t t̪] for /θ/ and [d d̪] for /ð/ in StHE, BlSAfE, GhE and GhP;
>
> Affricate realisations [tθ] and [dð] are reported as lesser variants in GhE and GhP.

/θ/ is realised as [f] word-finally in some words in EAfrE, GhE, LibSE, GhP and SgE.

In EAfrE /θ/ and /ð/ may be realised as [t s f] and [d z v] respectively.
Other changes to fricatives are less widespread:

> Velar fricatives [x] and [ɣ] occur in WSAfE and CFE, mainly in borrowings, place names, proper names etc.

H may be voiced in WSAfE, CFE, BlSAfE, InSAfE, IndE, PakE; it may also be murmured in the last three varieties. H may also be dropped in InSAfE, IndE and MalE, especially by Tamil speakers. In IndE it may be dropped in initial position with tonal adjustments, amongst Panjabi speakers. H may be substituted by [j] in CFE or by [j] or [w] amongst Tamil speakers of InSAfE, IndE and MalE. It may be dropped before [j] in CamE (e.g. in *human*). Hyper-correction may also occur in those varieties that drop H.

F occurs as an approximant ('antedental') in CFE, InSAfE and IndE. In northern NigE F is realised as [f], [p] or [Φ]; for many speakers of IndE as [pʰ]; and in basilectal PhlE as [p].

V has the following realisations:

> an approximant [ʋ] in InSAfE and IndE;
>
> [v] or [f] in northern NigE;
>
> [b] or [f] in GhP, especially intervocalically;
>
> [bh] amongst Bengali speakers of IndE;
>
> [b] in basilectal PhlE;
>
> [v] or [w] in StHE, IndE and amongst Tamil speakers of MalE.

/ʃ ʒ/ have the following realisations:

[s z] variably in CFE, BlSAfE, EAfrE and IndE;
[ɕ ʑ] in GhE.

In addition /ʃ/ may occur as [z] occasionally in CFE, CamE and (in final position) in MalE. It may occur as [s] occasionally in CFE and GhE.

Z occurs as [dʒ] occasionally in IndE and amongst Malay and Chinese speakers of MalE.

3.3.   Affricates

/tʃ dʒ/ have the following realisations:

[s z] in EAfrE;
[tɕ dɕ] in GhE;
[ts ds] in PhlE;

In addition /tʃ/ is realised as [ʃ] in BlSAfE, EAfrE, occasionally in CamE and word-finally in LibSE. /dʒ/ is realised as [ʒ] in CFE, BlSAfE, EAfrE, among Yoruba speakers of NigE and word-finally in LibSE. It is realised as [z] amongst Malay speakers of MalE.

3.4.   Nasals

N is retroflex before [ʈ] and [ɖ] in InSAfE, IndE and PakE. Epenthetic [n] occurs before consonants in EAfrE. Vowels are nasalised before final nasals, with subsequent loss of the nasal consonant in CFE, GhE and LibSE. The suffix –ING is realised as [n̩] in StHE and GhE.

3.5.   Liquids

The rhotic varieties are IndE, PakE and PhlE. There is occasional rhoticity in some varieties of WSAfE, especially with –*er* suffixes. There is *r* ~ *l* alternation in EAfrE, GhE and GhP, depending on speakers' home languages. R is regularly realised as [l] amongst Chinese speakers of MalE. Linking [r] is absent in GhE, CamE and LibSE, and is rare to non-existent in varieties of South African English. L-vocalisation is reported in GhE and LibSE. Dark [ɫ] is very common in CFE; whereas light [l] prevails in IndE and amongst older speakers of InSAfE.

3.6. Glides and approximants

[h] occurs in place of [j] or [w] in CFE (and other varieties of Afrikaans-influenced English in South Africa). W is replaced by [hw] in wh- words in GhE. /j/ occurs occasionally as [ɤ] in WSAfE. Clusters of /t/ plus /j/ and /d/ plus /j/ occur as [tʃ dʒ] occasionally in InSAfE and other varieties of South African English. There is dropping of /j/ (yod-dropping) in NigE, GhE and CamE. W and V occur interchangeably in StHE (frequently), occasionally in IndE and rarely in InSAfE.

4. Common phonological processes

Two processes are very commonly reported. Final devoicing of obstruents occurs in StHE, CFE, BlSAfE, NigE, GhE, CamE, Kamtok, SgE and MalE. Consonant-cluster reduction is reported to varying degrees in CFE, BlSAfE, GhE, LibSE, NigP, GhP, IndE, PakE, SgE, MalE and PhlE.

5. Stress, tone and intonation

Assuming a continuum between syllable timing and stress timing, the number of varieties which exhibit tendencies towards syllable timing is impressive: InSAfE, BlSAfE, EAfrE, NigE, GhE, NigP, GhP, IndE, PakE, SgE, MalE and PhlE. For these varieties vowel reduction is not as common as in RP and in some of them [ə] is rare, or more a feature of fast and connected speech, rather than of citation forms. On the other hand some of these varieties are reported to avoid syllabic consonants, in favour of schwa plus consonant: IndE, SgE, MalE and PhlE. All varieties that were cited in connection with syllable timing also display stress shifts in individual words or sets of words, in relation to RP norms. These are often shifts to the right (e.g. *real'ise* rather than RP *'realise*); though some words in some varieties exhibit shifts to the left (e.g. from penultimate to antepenultimate syllables as in CamE a *'dolescence*, rather than RP ado*'lescence*). Most of these varieties do not use stress to differentiate between pairs like *'absent* (adj.) versus *ab'sent* (verb).

As far as intonation is concerned most varieties report a smaller range of intonational contours compared to RP. Whilst this area is one that needs closer attention, statements like the following will illustrate this general claim:

CFE: great use of rising intonation in statements;
BlSAfE: tone and information units are shorter than in RP;

NigE: Sentence stress is rarely used for contrast. Given information is rarely de-accented;
MalE: less change of intonation (or pitch direction) occurs in sentences compared to RP.

A number of African varieties of English make use of lexical and (sometimes) grammatical tone, and report an interaction between stress and tone: NigE, GhE, NigP and Kamtok.

6.   Conclusion

It is clear from this synopsis that varieties of English in Africa-Asia, especially the L2 varieties, share a great deal of phonological similarities. Particularly striking are the use of a 5-vowel system, plus diphthongs in many varieties; the tendency towards syllable timing; the non-fricative realisation of /θ/ and /ð/. In the interests of fidelity to the original transcriptions minute differences between vowels were retained in this summary, rather than attempting to 'normalise' some transcriptions (e.g. [a] versus [ä] versus [ɐ]), in the hope of uncovering further broad phonological similarities. This synopsis must therefore be taken as a starting rather than end point of the challenging but stimulating study of the systemic phonological similarities, as well as of the phonetic differences within those overall similarities amongst the Englishes of Africa-Asia.

Exercises and study questions

1. Review the two types of 5-vowel systems, labelled 'type 1' and 'type 2' respectively, which are common in L2 varieties of English in Africa and Asia. Which varieties exhibit type 1 characteristics and which are of 'type 2'. Are there any difficulties in this formulation?

2. How is the NURSE vowel redistributed in L2 varieties in Africa?

3. How is the NURSE vowel redistributed in L2 varieties in Asia?

4. What are the variants of schwa in the varieties of English in Africa and Asia? Listen to the audio material on CD and consult the interactive maps for these variants.

5. How is the SQUARE vowel treated in English varieties in Africa and Asia? Listen to the audio material and consult the interactive maps for its variants.

6. How strong is the tendency towards monophthongisation in L2 varieties in Africa and Asia?

7. Which is the most striking feature of fricative realisation in all the L2 varieties of English in Africa-Asia? What are the differential realisations of this feature? Why do you think these changes occur?

8. Discuss patterns of stress and intonation that differentiate the L2 varieties of Africa and Asia from L1 varieties of English.

References

Brown, Adam
    1988   Vowel differences between Received Pronunciation and the English of Malaysia and Singapore: which ones really matter? In Joseph Foley (ed.), *New Englishes – the Case of Singapore*, 129–147. Singapore: Singapore University Press.

Morphology and Syntax

Nigerian English: morphology and syntax[*]

M.A. Alo and Rajend Mesthrie

1.   Introduction

Nigerian English (NigE) is a term used to designate the variety of English
spoken (and sometimes written) in Nigeria. NigE is an indigenised variety
of English, functioning as a second language within the Nigerian linguistic
and socio-cultural setting. It therefore has a distinctive local Nigerian flavour,
which can be seen at all levels of linguistic organisation. Among the factors
that have contributed to this distinctness are the following:

(a) mode of acquisition primarily via the classroom
(b) transfer ("interference") from many of Nigeria's indigenous languages
(c) culture contact (including bilingualism and biculturalism)
(d) sociolinguistic functions (including the high status accorded to English)
(e) influence of dialectal features from non-Standard British English (StBrE)
      sources (e.g. recent influence from AmE)

The details of the initial introduction of English in West Africa and its subsequent growth and stabilisation is given in the chapter on Nigerian English
phonology (this volume). Certain aspects of that overview pertaining to the
sub-varieties of English in Nigeria are worth reiterating in deciding which sub-
variety's features count as part of a "core" syntax of NigE.

Brosnahan (1958) identified four levels of proficiency in the use of English,
together with their corresponding levels of education, of typical speakers:

Level 1 (pidgin)	:	no formal education
Level 2	:	only primary education completed
Level 3	:	only secondary education completed
Level 4	:	university education completed

According to this scheme, the level of proficiency progresses with educational
attainments of users. This assumption is, of course, not infallible. Furthermore,
the placement of pidgin in this classification is problematic. Nigerian scholars
do not recognise pidgin as a variety of English alone, but rather as an independent code.

Banjo's (1971) classification, in contrast, is based on the extent of transfer from speakers' mother-tongues and of approximation to a standard variety of English. In his scale, Variety 1 (V_1) exhibits the greatest density of mother-tongue transfer, whilst Variety 4 (V_4) exhibits the least. Varieties 2 (V_2) and 3 (V_3) are intermediate. See the companion chapter on NigE phonology by Ulrike Gut (this volume) for details. Banjo (1995: 205) remarks that V_3 is a home-grown variety and is accordingly more appropriate as an endonormative standard model than V_4. The latter is an exonormative variety inculcated by speakers with direct experience of living in Britain. For the purposes of this essay, the features described will be that of V_2 and V_3 rather than V_4. In this we echo Banjo's (1995) concern for

> an appropriate model [...] based on the twin criteria of social acceptability and international intelligibility, on the assumption that such a model, given the second-language situation, should possess a high prestige at home and reasonably easy intelligibility abroad. (Banjo 1995: 209)

One problem with this typology, as pointed out by Bamgbose (1992: 152), is that not all features of Nigerian lexis, semantics and syntax can be accounted for in terms of substrate interference. Many features result from the normal process of language development, including narrowing or extension of meaning and the creation of new idioms.

The last categorisation of relevance is that of Jowitt (1991: vii), who posits two broad poles – Standard English (StE) and popular NigE, and claims that "usage of every Nigerian user is a mixture of standard forms and popular Nigerian English forms, which are in turn composed of errors and variants." There are critics who deny the existence of Nigerian English, seeing it as a mixed bag of errors, especially in the case of prepositions, articles, concord and the like. As in cases elsewhere, we confine ourselves to identifying recurrent features of syntax in NigE, without prescriptive bias. However, it is necessary to factor out the efforts of "learner language" and focus on the speech characteristics of fluent (and usually educated) speakers, identified by previous researchers – our chief sources being Bamgbose (1992 [1982]), Banjo (1971) and Jowitt (1991). Our examples are also based on data from speech and (where specified) writing drawn from the senior author M.A. Alo. On the whole we concur with Bamgbose's (1992: 154) insistence that "the natural and spontaneous usage of the locally educated Nigerian user of English is a more reliable guide to the identification of typical Nigerian usage."

2. Tense – aspect – modality systems

2.1. Tense

There is little to be said about tense categories used by educated speakers. Jowitt (1991: 116) notes that errors of inflection are common amongst V_1 and V_2 speakers but are stigmatised by educated speakers. Such stigmatised forms include the occasional use of unmarked verb forms for both present and simple past as in (1), the occasional double marking of the simple past in negatives and interrogatives as in (2) and (3).

(1)   *Yesterday they **go** to your office.* (Jowitt 1991: 117)

(2)   *He **did** not **went**.*

(3)   ***Did** she **wanted** him*? (Jowitt 1991: 117)

Other features include the occasional regularisation of past endings like *grinded* for *ground* and *hitted* for *hit* and the occasional lack of third person sg. present tense -s. Further facets of tense formation are given under section 3. on auxiliaries.

2.2. Aspect

As in many varieties of English as a Second Language (ESL), the distinction between stative and non-stative verbs is overridden. This applies particularly to verbs of perception like *see, hear, smell, taste, feel* and *recognise*:

(4)   *I am **smelling** something burning.*
       '…smell…'

(5)   *I am **hearing** you.*
       '…hear/can hear…'

(6)   *It is **tasting** terrible.*
       '…tastes…'

In Nigerian languages, these examples would be unremarkable since verbs of perception freely take the progressive.

The use of *be* + *-ing* also applies to other stative verbs:

(7)   *We **are having** something to do.*
       '…have…'

2.3.   Modality

The modal auxiliaries show several differences from StE usage. Jowitt (1991: 122) notes the phrase *can be able*, which, as in other varieties of English in Africa, is an equivalent of *can* or *am/is/are able*. In the expression of politeness the present form of modals is preferred to the standard, (indirect) past forms: thus *will* for 'would', *can* for 'could', *shall* for 'should' and *may* for 'might':

(8)   *I **will** be happy, if you can come, please.*
       '…would…'

(9)   *I **will** like to see you, sir.*
       '…would…'

Jowitt (1991: 120) points to the use of *might have* in a rather complex manner in NigE:

(10)   *After the referee **might have** arrived the match will begin.*

This use of modal + perfect is not a direct equivalent of BrE 'After the referee arrives/will arrive the match will begin'. Sentence (10) does not presuppose the arrival of the referee, rather, it expresses some uncertainty about the matter. Sentence (10) thus does not have a direct equivalent in StE, but would have to be unscrambled and rephrased as (11):

(11)   *It is not certain that the referee will arrive, but if he does the match will begin.*

Jowitt (1991: 122) mentions a similar semantics for *must have to*, which corresponds to StE 'must' 'shall have to' or 'will have to'.

   Jowitt (1991: 124) describes patterns of cliticisation of modals and *be* with pronouns. Forms like *isn't*, *I'm* and *she's* are common. However, forms like *I've* and *you're*, involving cliticisation of *'ve* and *'re*, are rarer. Forms like *I'll* and *I'd* are very rare, even in colloquial speech.

3.   Auxiliaries

Jowitt (1991: 123) notes that complex auxiliary forms with *have* and *be* tend to be avoided in popular NigE. Thus forms like the future perfect (*will have* V), perfect infinitive (*to have* V+ *-en*) and the continuous forms of perfect tenses (*to have been* V+ *-ing*) are rare in lower sociolects, but make an appearance in V_3 speech. Jowitt also notes that the use of present and past continuous tenses for future reference appears to be avoided, as simple future tenses seem to suffice. He links this one-to-one mapping to the needs of learners, who hypothesise that future time always requires a future tense. As far as other auxiliaries are concerned, Jowitt (1991: 123) notes that in popular NigE "*might* seems to have less currency than *must* or *should,* and *needn't, dare* and *be to* in all forms are avoided."

The use of auxiliaries in response to *yes/no,* tag and echo questions differs from StE. *Yes/no* questions with auxiliary *have* frequently meet with a response that uses some form of *do*:

(12) Q: *Have you been to university of Ibadan, today?*
      A: *I **didn't** go.*

(13) Q: *Have you seen John?*
      A: *No, I **didn't**.*

In (12) and (13) the expected response in StE would involve either a simple affirmative or negative (*yes/no*) and/or the repetition of the auxiliary *have* (*I have/I haven't*).

As in other parts of Africa and Asia, the invariant tag *isn't it* is favoured by NigE speakers:

(14) *You like that, **isn't it**?*

The invariant form avoids the complexities of StE tag formation, which requires copying the pronoun form, copying the auxiliary (or adding *do* if no auxiliary exists in the main clause) and reversing the polarity of the main verb (positive to negative or vice versa).

Jowitt (1991: 123) points out that invariant *isn't it* occurs with echo questions too:

(15) a. A.   *He didn't greet his father.*
          B.   (echo question) *Didn't he?* (StE)

      b. A.   *He didn't greet his father.*
          B.   (echo question) *Isn't it?* (NigE)

As invariant all-purpose tags and verification questions occur in Nigerian languages like Hausa and Igbo, it is possible that there is a convergent effect between second-language learning strategies and transfer from the mother-tongue.

A related phenomenon – responses to *yes/no* questions couched in the negative – is discussed in the next section.

M.A. Alo and Rajend Mesthrie

4. Negatives

Jowitt (1991: 124) notes that contracted negatives, as in (16a), are preferred to contracted verb forms (16b), even when the need for emphasis might make the latter preferable in StE:

(16)   a. *She **won't** come.*
       b. ***She'll** not come.*

Jowitt (1991: 121) also notes that double negatives are not found in popular NigE. This generalisation holds for educated NigE as well. NigE shows similarities to other varieties of African English in its response to *yes/no* questions couched in the negative. A detailed analysis of the dynamics of this construction occurs in Mesthrie's analysis of Black South African English (this volume). NigE appears to be quite similar. That is, *yes/no* questions posed positively show no differences between NigE and StE:

(17)   Q: *Did Ayo receive his award?*
       A: *Yes (he did)* or *No (he didn't).* (NigE and StE)

On the other hand, the same question posed negatively evokes a different response pattern in NigE:

(18)   Q: *Didn't Ayo receive his award?*
       A: *Yes (he didn't)* or *No (he did).* (NigE)
(19)   Q: *You don't want this, do you?*
       A: [*Yes (I don't)* or *No (I do).* (NigE)

In (19) NigE speakers appear to respond to the proposition, rather than the operator in the tag. The proposition itself would appear to carry a different presupposition from StE: that is it is biased towards a negative reading ('Ayo didn't receive his award/I don't want this') which is confirmed by the *yes* in the response (or contradicted by the *no*).

5. Relativisation

NigE allows resumptive pronouns in non-subject relativisation:

(20)   *The guests whom I invited **them** have arrived.* (Bokamba 1992: 131–132)

(21)   *I know the person who **his** father has died.* (Jowitt 1991: 122)

As Bokamba notes, relative clauses with resumptive pronouns are a typological characteristic of many African languages. It is not surprising that this feature should be reported in L2 English of West Africa, East Africa and southern Africa.

Jowitt (1991: 120) notes that in popular NigE (V_1 and V_2) *what* is used as a relative pronoun after *all*:

(22)   *All **what** he said was false.*

In non-restrictive (or appositional) relatives some speakers use *of which* rather than *which* (Jowitt 1991: 122):

(23)   *It was a very horrible experience, **of which** I hope it will not happen again.*

6.   Complementation

6.1.   Infinitive without *to*

Bamgbose (1992: 155) cites as a feature of NigE the dropping of *to* from the infinitive after certain verbs:

(24)   *...enable him Ø do it.*
        '...enable him to do it.'

Jowitt (1991: 115) observes that this phenomenon also applies to *allow*. Conversely, *make*, which doesn't allow *to* in StE active sentences, often co-occurs with *to* in NigE:

(25)   *Make her **to** do her work.*

6.2.   *To*-infinitives in place of *-ing*

Jowitt (1991: 115) notes that in lower sociolects *to* + infinitive may replace *-ing* in constructions starting with *instead of* + NP:

(26)   *Instead of him **to travel** home for the vacation, he was one of those who travelled to Sokoto for the sports competition.*
        'Instead of him travelling home...'

Jowitt supplies an example from a written source, which implies that the construction may well be more widespread than he claims:

(27)   *He asserted that instead of the press **to highlight** that, it resorted to capitalising on his arrest.* (*The Triumph*, 1/11/1986)

A related usage avoids the gerund form in -*ing* after *to* in construction with *be used to*, *look forward to* and *object to*. Forms like *is used to go*, *looks forward to go* and *object to go* are common in NigE.

6.3.   Comparatives

Bokamba (1992: 133–134) analyses sentences involving the comparison of inequality (StE 'taller than Mary'), in which the comparative form may be marked singly, either by *than* or (less commonly) by the comparative form of the adjective. Example (28) is from Chinebuah (1976, cited by Bokamba 1992: 134):

(28)   *It is the youths who are Ø skilful in performing tasks **than** the adults.*
        '…more skilful…'

(29)   *He has Ø money **than** his brother.*
        '…more money than…'

7.   Other subordination and co-ordination phenomena

7.1.   Double conjunctions

Jowitt (1991: 123) mentions the double use of *although* or *though* in a subordinate clause accompanied by *but* or *yet* in the main clause.

(30)   ***Although** he is rich **but** he is stingy.*

7.2.   Innovations in the form of conjunctions

In addition to double conjunctions, one per clause, NigE occasionally combines two related conjunctions of StE. Thus *should in case* is sometimes used in place of *should* + S or *in case* + S. Likewise *on my way going* may replace *on my way* [*to* NP] or *going* [*to* NP].

(31)   *He has been in this school for five years, still yet he is not tired.*
        '…still/yet…'

8.   Agreement

Jowitt (1991: 116) observes that inflectional suffixes give trouble to learners, often when their mother-tongues lack inflections. Errors of inflection, he notes, are common among V_1 speakers, not uncommon among V_2 speakers and stig- matised by V_3 speakers. This applies especially to verb endings of tense and agreement, with V_1 and V_2 speakers using the unmarked verb form in place of past -*ed* and third person singular present -*s*. Further aspects of agreement are discussed in section 10.

9.   Noun phrase structure

9.1.   Articles

There is a noticeable tendency towards the omission of articles where StE re- quires them:

(32) $\emptyset_1$ *Depreciating value of the naira and $\emptyset_2$ increase in $\emptyset_3$ cost of wheat in the international market have been identified.*

Variability in article usage shows up well in (32). Although the sentence does contain two standard definite articles and one correct zero form (*of wheat*), it contains three non-standard zero forms, with $\emptyset_1$ = 'the', $\emptyset_2$ = 'an/the' and $\emptyset_3$ = 'the' in StE.

Sentence (33) shows other types of variability in article usage – the occur- rence of unstressed *one* as an equivalent of indefinite *a* and occasional substitu- tion of *the* for *a*:

(33)   *Gani is **one** man who does not tell lies, he calls **the** spade a spade.*

Jowitt (1991: 114) notes a tendency, even among educated speakers, to drop the indefinite article before a singular countable noun functioning as the object of certain high-frequency and semantically full verbs. Thus *get $\emptyset$ contract, give $\emptyset$ chance, have $\emptyset$ bath, make $\emptyset$ effort, make $\emptyset$ mistake, take $\emptyset$ bribe, take $\emptyset$ excuse, tell $\emptyset$ lie, tie $\emptyset$ wrapper* etc. Whether these are due to analogy to StE expressions like *give notice, make mischief* etc. or whether the nouns concerned are reclassified as uncountable still needs to be researched.

9.2.   Adjectives

Jowitt (1991: 111–112) reports on some novel forms of adjectives and some adjectives involved in class (or category) shift. Certain adjectives denoting nationality of a person are made to function as singular nouns. Thus:

(34)   *He is a British/English/Irish/French/Dutch/Swiss etc.*

Certain adjectives which function as generic nouns in StE (e.g. *the poor, the blind*) take plural forms in NigE (*the poors, the blinds*). Jowitt (1991: 118) also notes that the StE distinction between comparative and superlative, like *worse – worst,* is frequently ignored:

(35)   *His condition is now getting **worst**.*

The innovations discussed in this section are mostly characteristic of lower sociolects, which also contain neologisms like *insultive* 'insulting (adj.)', as well as class shifts from adjective to verb (e.g. *naked*$_v$, *pregnant*$_v$, *jealous*$_v$):

(36)   *He **naked** himself.*

(37)   *He **pregnanted** her.*

(38)   *She **jealoused** her elder sister.*

Ordinal adjectives beyond *third* are avoided even by educated speakers, notably when they feature dates. Jowitt (1991: 124) provides the example of *on the five* for 'on the fifth'. He suggests that the avoidance may be motivated by phonological considerations notably avoidance of consonant + /θ/ clusters.

9.3.   Nouns

Bamgbose (1992: 155) considers one of the four main features of educated NigE morphology and syntax to be the fact that "peculiar word formation may occur with plurals". He supplies the examples *equipments, aircrafts* and *deadwoods*. Jowitt (1991: 112–113) adds further examples from popular NigE of pluralisation of what are non-count nouns in StE: *accommodation, advice, behaviour, blame, chalk, cutlery, damage, evidence, furniture, gossip, grass, information, jargon, junk, machinery, money, permission, personnel, stationery, underwear* and *wire*. There is thus a general tendency in NigE to treat mass and abstract nouns as count nouns. As Jowitt (1991: 113) notes, the impulse for this regularisation may come from special contexts or usage within StE that allow these nouns to be pluralised (X + -s) if they denote 'types of X'. Thus, in StE *grasses* may be used to mean 'different types of grass'. Idiomatic differences also account for this regularisation in NigE – e.g. the distinction in StE between *damage*$_n$ (mass noun) and *damages*$_n$ (in its legal/insurance/business context). Jowitt notes a reversal of this tendency with the noun *fund* in NigE not generally admitting a plural form, contrary to StE *funds*.

10.   Pronouns

10.1.   Reflexives

There is a tendency to use plural pronoun + *selves*, not just as a plural reflexive, but as reciprocal too, in place of StE 'each other, one another':

(39)   *Adebanjo and Suliat love **themselves**.*
        '…each other'

(40)   *After greeting **ourselves**, Tolu and I started work*
        '...each other'

(41)   *James and Lanre like quarrelling with **themselves**.*
        '...one another'

A sentence like (42) could be ambiguous even in educated NigE:

(42)   *The couple bought **themselves** a nice car.*

Either interpretation 'for themselves' (reflexive) or 'for each other' (reciprocal) is permissible here.

10.2.   Indefinite or honorific *they*

NigE favours the use of third person indefinite *they* often with a singular refer-ent, meaning 'he, she, person(s) unknown':

(43)   ***They** gave me some money.*

(44)   ***They** are calling you.*

They in (43) refers to a singular, definite referent, uttered by a child in response to his mother's query about the source of his money. Since *they* refers to an elder family member, it can be construed as a polite use of the plural for the sin-gular. In (44) a similarly respectful use of *they* occurs to draw the addressee's attention to a call by an elderly woman in a market.

They also functions as an indefinite pronoun used when the referent is un-known, indefinite or generic (i.e. the specific identity of the individual does not matter). Jowitt (1991: 123) links this usage to the rarity of passives in Nigerian languages and popular NigE: "MTs [mother-tongues] lack inflected passive forms but make use of a third person singular indefinite pronoun in combination with the active forms.", as in (45):

(45)   *There was a security light outside my house, but **they have stolen it***.
       '...but it has been stolen.'

However, the passive is used in educated NigE.

11.   Word order

11.1.   Demonstratives with possessive pronouns

Bokamba (1992: 133) follows Kirk-Greene (1971) in drawing attention to the Bantu rule that when a possessive and demonstrative pronoun occur in the same NP, they follow the noun in the order (Demonstrative + N + Possessive). This rule has an indirect influence on NigE and West African English generally:

(46)   *I met the **teacher our new***.
       '...our new teacher.' (Bokamba 1992: 133)

However, it appears to be just as common to have the order Demonstrative + Possessive + N):

(47)   ***That your brother**, will he come*?
       'Will your brother come?'

(48)   *Saying Amen to **those his prayers**...*
       'saying Amen to prayers/those prayers of his...' (Kirk-Green 1971:136)

This construction is avoided by some educated speakers.

11.2.   Left dislocation

As in colloquial varieties of English world-wide and especially other "new Englishes", left dislocation is commonly used in NigE. Bamgbose (1992: 155) characterises it as a focus construction, involving the subject of the sentence as focus, with an anaphoric pronoun subject:

(49)   ***The politicians and their supporters***, *they don't often listen to advice.*

(50)   ***A person who has no experience***, *can he be a good leader?*

Bamgbose's examples, reproduced here as (49) and (50), both involve complex NP subjects – a co-ordinated NP in (49) and NP + Rel in (50). In addition, the construction occurs with simple NPs too, as in (51):

(51)   ***The students*** *they are demonstrating again.*

12.   Selected salient verb forms

12.1.   HAVE

Jowitt (1991: 125) notes the rarity of causative *have* constructions as in (52):

(52)   *I want to have my hair cut.*

He argues that this is a result of the similarity of such constructions to perfect tenses and the apparent (to second language learners) risk therefore involved in using them.

Jowitt notes the neologism *haven* for *having* which may even occur in writing:

(53)   ***Haven*** *waged a serious legal battle against Gomwalk ... people felt that Mr Aper Aku will be mindful of whatever policy direction his administration was bound to initiate.* (*The Triumph*, 2/4/1986; Jowitt 1991: 117)

The converse process is more common in lower sociolects, with *-ing* replacing *-en* in forms like *giving* and *taking* for 'given' and 'taken'.

12.2.   Phrasal and prepositional verbs

These admit of considerable variation from the StE idioms. One set involves the addition of a preposition: *cope up* for 'cope', *discuss about* for 'discuss', *voice out* for 'voice$_v$', *advocate for* for 'advocate'. Another set, conversely, involves the absence of a preposition where StE requires one: *dispose* for 'dispose of', *operate* for 'operate on', *reply* for 'reply to'. A third set uses a different preposition from that of StE, e.g. *congratulate for* for 'congratulate on'. Perhaps this can be related to a general fluidity of preposition use in NigE, where a number of non-standard usages prevail – e.g. *at* for *in* in expressions like *at my old age* or *at London* (see further Jowitt [1991: 119]).

12.3.   Other salient verb forms

Enjoy and *disappoint* may be used elliptically as intransitive verbs:

(54)   *She promised to come, but I don't really expect to see her – she always likes to* **disappoint** ∅. (Jowitt 1991: 115)

A further kind of ellipsis can be observed with certain reciprocals (see *borrow/lend* [55]), passives (see *drop/be dropped/alight* [54]) and causatives (see *back/carry on one's back* [57]):

(55)   *Please borrow me your pen.*

(56)   *Please, I would like to drop at the next bus stop.*

(57)   *Ronke backs her baby to work.*

A final class of verb neologism involves derivation from other parts of speech, especially in lower sociolects. Thus *horn* 'to hoot', *jealous* 'make jealous', *naked* 'make naked'. Examples (58)–(60) are taken from Jowitt (1991: 112):

(58)   **Horn** *before overtaking.*

(59)   *She* **jealoused** *her elder sister.*

(60)   *He* **naked** *himself.*

13.   Reduplication

Under the influence of indigenous languages like Yoruba, NigE makes extensive use of reduplication in generating new lexis or creating a particular nuance or emphasis. The main elements reduplicated are adjectives and adverbs:

(61)   *He likes to talk about* **small-small** *things.*
       '…insignificant things.'

(62)   *My friend* **before-before**…
       '…former friend…'

(63)   *Tell Mr Bello to come* **now-now**.
       '…at once.'

(64)   *Labake does her work* **half-half**.
       '…in halves/incompletely.'

14. Lexis

This is an area of considerable richness in NigE, showing a full indigenisation of English to the Nigerian cultural setting. For reasons of space, only the briefest of expositions is given here.

14.1. Verbs of bribery and corruption

In the context of bribery and corruption (usually involving politicians, civil servants or the police) certain verbs are used circumspectly.

(65) *The man **ate** our money.*
      '…embezzled…'

(66) *Chief Lagbaje can **deliver**.*
      '…fix/rig an election…'

(67) *He **understands**.*
      '…is ready to offer a bribe…'

Other verbs used euphemistically in this context are *co-operate, enter, talk, settle, perform* and *play.*

14.2. Other lexical innovations

Semantic extension
A number of everyday English terms have a widened meaning in Nigeria. These include a range of kinship terms (e.g. *father* could refer to one's male parent or any of his brothers) expressions of sympathy or politeness (e.g. *sorry* denotes sympathy for someone's misfortune or discomfort without a sense blame on the part of the speaker) and anatomical terms used in association with the human spirit, life and destiny (e.g. *head* for 'one's essence, destiny, luck').

Borrowings
Not surprisingly, a number of words from Igbo, Hausa and Yoruba make an appearance in NigE, either in noun switching or as borrowings, for example *akara* 'beancake', *akwete* 'type of cloth' and *bolekaja* 'bus with tightly packed seats'.

Idioms, neologisms and semantic shifts
A small selection of these items which give NigE its lively flavour is given here:

been-to	'one who has been abroad on an extended stay'
cash madam	'wealthy woman'
bottom power	'undue influence of females using sex'
chase	'to woo'
move with	'to associate with'
to take in	'to be pregnant'
not on seat	'not available in one's office'
long leg	'use of undue influence to reach a goal'
national cake	'the common wealth belonging to all Nigerians'

15.   Conclusion

This chapter has attempted to give an overview of the main lexical and (especially) syntactic features of NigE. It is obvious that further work has to be done in terms of relating the different sub-varieties to each other and in comparing NigE to other West African varieties of English. We do not wish to impose a static view of NigE, which like all varieties of English is subject to growth and change. One change that has become prominent over recent years is the influence of American English, due to American broadcasts (*CNN* and *Voice of America*), American music, cinema and contact with American-trained professionals.

This influence shows up in many ways, for example in the pronunciation of words like *schedule* (now pronounced with initial /sk/), in idioms like *what's up*, in business terms like *Monday through Friday* (versus *Monday to Friday*), in lexical choices and doublets (e.g. *nursery* and *day-care*, *flashlight* and *torch*) and in verb sub-categorisations like *to protest* + direct object, rather than *to protest against*. Nevertheless, Jowitt's (1991: 109) remark about the overall structure of NigE seems appropriate: "it is important to realize that while (popular NigE) syntactic errors are numerous and often glaring, the gap between NigE syntax and BrE syntax, when each is considered in its entirety, is narrow, not wide."

*   Our debt to previous writers on this topic, especially David Jowitt, is immense.

Exercises and study questions

1. Review the semantics of sentence (10) *After the referee might have arrived the match will begin*. Supply another paraphrase for this sentence beginning with the modal *should*. Try and make up another NigE sentence with similar semantics.

2. What would the typical echo question response to a statement like *He doesn't like cabbage* be in NigE?

3. Supply an example of a Standard English appositional (non-restrictive) relative clause with *which*, and give its possible NigE equivalent.

4. Review the difference between a resumptive pronoun and a copy pronoun (appositional pronoun) in left dislocation.

5. Discuss the pragmatics of *yes/no* questions and their responses in NigE.

Selected references

Please consult the General references for titles mentioned in the text but not included in the references below. For a full bibliography see the accompanying CD-ROM.

Bamgbose, Ayo
    1992 [1982]   Standard Nigerian English: issues of identification. In: Kachru (ed.), 148–161.
Banjo, Ayo
    1971   Towards a definition of standard Nigerian English. In: *Actes du 8th Congress de la Societé Linguiste de l'Afrique Occidentale,* 165–75. Abidjan: University of Abidjan.
    1995   On codifying Nigerian English: research so far. In: Ayo Bamgbose, Ayo Banjo and Andrew Thomas (eds.), *New Englishes: A West African Perspective,* 203–231. Ibadan, Nigeria: Mosuro.
Bokamba, Eyamba
    1992 [1982]   The Africanization of English. In: Kachru (ed.), 125–147.
Brosnahan, Leonard F.
    1958   English in southern Nigeria. *English Studies* 39: 97–110.
Jowitt, David
    1991   *Nigerian Usage – an Introduction.* Ikeja, Lagos: Longman Nigeria.
Chinebuah, Isaac K.
    1976   Grammatical deviance and first language interference. *West African Journal of Modern Languages* 1: 67–78.
Kirk-Greene, Anthony
    1971   The influence of West African languages on English. In: Spencer (ed.), 123–144.

Nigerian Pidgin English: morphology and syntax

Nicholas Faraclas

1. Introduction

Nigerian Pidgin (NigP) is the dialect of Afro-Caribbean English Lexifier Creole which is spoken in Nigeria as well as in parts of Equatorial Guinea, Cameroon and Ghana. The other major dialects of Afro-Caribbean English Lexifier Creole include Cameroonian Pidgin, Sierra Leonian Krio, Jamaican Creole and the English Lexifier Creoles spoken in the Lesser Antilles, and along the coasts of South and Central America. Afro-Caribbean English Lexifier Creole possibly also includes Liberian English, Ghanaian English, Bahamian Creole, Gullah and African-American Vernacular English. Well over half of the 140 million inhabitants of Nigeria are now fluent speakers of the language, making NigP the most widely spoken language in Nigeria, as well as the indigenous African language with the largest number of speakers. Given the rapid spread of NigP among younger Nigerians, this proportion should increase to over seventy or eighty percent by the time the present generation of children reaches adulthood. There is no Creole language worldwide with nearly as many speakers as NigP.

In its basilectal varieties, NigP is still undergoing pidginization, with substrate languages continuing to exert an important influence. In its mesolectal varieties, NigP can be considered to be functionally a creole, given the fact that it is used by a great number of people as their principal means of communication in all of their daily activities. In its acrolectal varieties, NigP is decreolizing under the influence of English. There is a substantial and rapidly growing number of people who speak NigP as their first language or as one of their first languages. The NigP substrate languages at present include the 400 languages of Nigeria, a number of which had developed pidginized varieties for interethnic contact and trade before the colonial period.

The features and constructions identified in this chapter as typical of NigP are those found in the speech of mesolectal speakers of the language in Port Harcourt, Rivers State. The database used comes from transcripts of tape recordings of at least one hour of spontaneous speech from each member of a sample group of 30 speakers. Sample group members belonged to a network of friends, family members and associates, who were chosen on the basis of ethnolinguistic background, sex, age, amount of formal education, whether NigP was learned as a first or second language, and the extent to which NigP was used by each speaker in day to day interactions, so that the samples would represent a rough cross section of the NigP speaking community in Port Harcourt. A systematic comparison of NigP features with those of its substrate languages was also conducted as part of this study, and the results appear in Faraclas (1990) and (1998). Numerous studies of NigP exist as well as a comprehensive grammar (Faraclas 1996). A detailed list is given in the CD-ROM accompanying the text.

The following abbreviations are used in the examples in the text: ANT = Anterior Sequence Auxiliary; +C = Completive Aspect Auxiliary; -C = Incompletive Aspect Auxiliary; COMP = Complementizer; COP = Copular Verb; HL = Highlighter; ID = Identity; LOC = Locative; NEG = Negative; PFUT = Proximal Future Auxiliary; +R = Realis Modality Auxiliary; -R = Irrealis Modality Auxiliary; REL = Relative Pronoun; SBJV = Subjunctive Marker; SRPRO = Subject Referencing Pronoun.

2.   Unmarked verbs

2.1.   Stative verbs with non-past reference

(1)   *A **sabi** yu.*
       I   know you
       'I know you.'

In NigP, verbs do not take inflectional affixes to show tense, aspect or modality. As in most NigP substrate languages, stative verbs are assumed to be non-past, unless marked otherwise by an auxiliary, an adverbial or by context.

2.2.   Stative verbs with past reference

(2)   *A **sabi** yu **bifo** yu kɔm wɔk fɔr Pitakwa.*
       I   know you before you come work LOC Port Harcourt
       'I knew you before you came to work in Port Harcourt.'

As in most NigP substrate languages, stative verbs can be interpreted as past tense, if accompanied by the appropriate contextual cues.

2.3.   Non-stative verbs with past reference

(3)   *A **bay** egusi   fɔr   makɛt.*
       I   get   pumpkin seed paste LOC   market
       'I bought egusi at the market.'

As in most NigP substrate languages, non-stative verbs are assumed to refer to events which occurred in the past, unless marked otherwise by an auxiliary, an adverbial, or by context.

2.4.   Non-stative verbs with non-past reference

(4)   A: *Dis   taym   yu   **chɔp**   wɛting?*
                   this   time   you   eat   what?
          A: What are you eating now?'
          B: *Dis   taym   a   **chɔp**   lɔylɔy.*
                   this   time   I   eat   cassava fufu
          B: 'I'm eating cassava fufu.'

As in most NigP substrate languages, non-stative verbs can be non-past for tense if accompanied by the appropriate contextual cues.

3.   Anterior tense/sequentiality

3.1.   Stative verbs with past reference

(5)   *A **bin**   sabi   yu.*
          I   ANT   know   you
          'I knew you.'

While anterior sequence is usually signalled or inferred by contextual cues, adverbials or by the use of unmarked non-stative verbs, the anterior preverbal auxiliary *bin* may also be used for this purpose.

3.2.   Non-stative verbs with (past-before-) past reference

(6)   *Di taim yu   (bin)   rich   ma ples,   a **(bin)   (dɔn) go** tawn.*
          the time you   (ANT)   reach   my place   I   (ANT)   (+C)   go town
          'When you arrived at my village, I had (already) gone to town.'

As in the case of past tense, the pluperfect is usually signalled or inferred by contextual cues, adverbials, or the use of unmarked non-stative verbs. Again, the anterior auxiliary *bin* with or without the completive aspect markers *dɔn* and/or *finish* may be used as well.

3.3.   Anterior = counterfactual

(7)   a.   ***If** a go tawn a go bay gari.*
If   I   go   town   I   -R   buy   gari
'If I go to town, I will buy gari.'

   b.   ***If** a **bin**   go tawn a fɔr   (dɔn) bay gari.*
If   I   ANT   go   town   I   should   (+C)   buy   gari
'If I had gone to town, I would have bought gari.'

As shown in (7a) the conditional is usually expressed by the construction: *if* +
rest of protasis + *go* + rest of apodosis. For past conditional constructions such
as (7b), the anterior auxiliary *bin* is usually inserted into the *if*-clause. Additionally, the modal auxiliary *fɔr* 'should', optionally followed by the completive aspect marker *dɔn*, is used in the matrix clause.

3.4.   Anterior with an adjectival verb

(8)   *(**Yestade**)   di   sɔn   (**bin**)   **hot**   welwel.*
(yesterday)   the   sun   (ANT)   hot   thoroughly
'The sun was very hot yesterday.'

The category adjective is a weak one in NigP and most of its substrate languages. Most of what are considered to be adjectives in languages like English are
expressed by adjectival verbs in NigP. Adjectival verbs can take the full range
of auxiliaries that normally occur with other verbs in the language. As noted
above, past tense can be marked or inferred in a number of ways, including: (a)
by context (in which case all of the optional elements in 8 could be eliminated),
(b) by the use of an adverbial such as *yestade*, or (c) by the use of the anterior
auxiliary *bin*.

3.5.   Anterior with locative

(9)   *Im   (**bin**)   **de**   (fɔr)   haws   (yestade).*
s/he   (ANT)   COP   (LOC)   house   (yesterday)
'S/he was at the house yesterday.'

The copula *de* can be used with a locative or an existential meaning. *De* can be
used with any of the tense/aspect/modality markers that normally occur with
NigP verbs. As noted above, past tense can be marked or inferred by context,
through the use of an adverbial such as *yestade* or by using the auxiliary *bin*.

Nicholas Faraclas

4. Incompletive aspect

4.1. Indicating the incompletive aspect

(10) a.   *A   sabi   se   yu   (de)   waka.*
         I   know   that   you   (-C)   walk
         'I know that you are walking.'

Incompletive aspect can be signalled or inferred by contextual cues, adverbials, or by the use of unmarked stative verbs. Other ways to mark the incompletive aspect include the incompletive preverbal auxiliary *de* (as in the NigP substrates, the incompletive marker is related to the locative/existential copula *de*). In (10a) the verb *sabi* is stative, and therefore has incompletive aspect unless otherwise marked, while the verb *waka* is non-stative and is therefore more likely to take the incompletive marker *de*.

4.2. Incompletive to indicate the future

(10) b.   *A   de   kɔm.*
         I   -C   come
         'I am coming.' or 'I will come.'

In the isolated case in (10), the incompletive can be used to indicate future meaning.

4.3. Anterior plus incompletive

(11)   *Taym   a   rich,   im   (bin)   (de)   ple.*
       time   I   reach   s/he   (ANT)   (-C)   play
       'When I came, s/he was playing.'

In a clause containing the incompletive marker *de*, anterior sequentiality can be marked or inferred in a number of ways, including (a) by context, (b) through the use of an adverbial and (c) by using the auxiliary *bin*.

4.4. Incompletive with adjectival verb = inchoative

(12)   *Im   de   yɛlo.*
       it   -C   be yellow
       'It is getting yellow.'

The incompletive marker *de* may be used with some adjectival verbs to indicate the inchoative.

5. Habitual aspect

5.1. Zero marker for the habitual aspect

Habitual aspect cannot normally be expressed by zero marking in NigP.

5.2. Incompletive marker for the habitual aspect

(13) *A **de** chɔp fɔr makɛt.*
I -C eat LOC market
'I (habitually) eat in the market.'

Habitual aspect can be expressed by the incompletive marker *de* in NigP.

5.3. Marker for the habitual aspect only

There is no marker in NigP whose sole function is to signal habitual aspect.

5.4. Anterior plus habitual

(14) *Di pikin dem **(bin)** **de** kray evritaym.*
the child them (ANT) -C cry often
'The children used to cry all the time.'

In a clause containing the incompletive auxiliary *de*, anterior sequentiality can be marked or inferred in a number of ways, including (a) by context, (b) through the use of an adverbial or (c) by using the auxiliary *bin*. When used as a habitual auxiliary, *de* can also be used in the same clause with the irrealis marker *go*. Habitual *de* is not normally found in the same verb phrase with any of the other auxiliaries.

6. Completive aspect

6.1. Completive only before verb

(15) *A **don** sabi **finish** se yu kɔm.*
I +C know +C say you come
'I already know/knew that you came.'

Completive aspect can be signalled or inferred by contextual cues, adverbials, or by the use of unmarked non-stative verbs. The completive aspect may also be marked by the auxiliary *dɔn* which precedes the verb and/or by the post-verbal auxiliary *finish*, which is related to the verb *finish* 'to finish' (as in most NigP substrate languages). In (15) the verb *kɔm* is non-stative, and therefore completive unless otherwise marked, while the verb *sabi* is non-stative and is therefore more likely to take the completive markers *dɔn* and/or *finish*.

6.2.   Completive with adjectival verb

(16)   a.   *Im **dɔn** yɛlo   finish.*
              it   +C   be yellow   +C
              'It is completely yellow.'

(16)   b.   *A **dɔn** taya   finish.*
              I   +C   be tired   +C
              'I'm completely exhausted.'

Either one or both of the completive markers *dɔn* and *finish* may be used with adjectival verbs to indicate achieved as opposed to inceptive states. *Finish* can also be used to emphasise the high degree to which the state of affairs expressed by the verb has been accomplished.

6.3.   Anterior (or other verbal markers) plus completive

(17)   a.   Anterior plus completive (*dɔn* and/or *finish* possible here)
              *Bifo   im   kɔm rich,   a **bin**   **dɔn**   chɔp **finish**.*
              Before s/he +R   reach I ANT   COMP   eat   +C
              'Before s/he arrived, I had already eaten.'

        b.   Irrealis plus completive (*dɔn* and/or *finish* possible here)
              *Di taym we   yu   go rich,   a go **dɔn** chɔp **finish**.*
              the time that   you   -R   reach I -R +C   eat   +C
              'When you arrive, I will have already eaten.'

        c.   Realis (narrative) plus completive (*finish* only possible here)
              *Im   kɔm   rich   **finish**.*
              s/he +R   arrive   +C
              '(It came to pass that) s/he arrived.'

7. Irrealis mode

7.1. Future

(18) a. *A **go** waka.*
I -R walk
'I will walk.'

b. *A **wan** waka.*
I PFUT walk
'I am about to walk.'

Verbs are assumed to be realis, unless otherwise marked. In narratives, the truth value of a statement can be emphasised by using the preverbal realis auxiliary *kɔm*, which is related to the verb *kɔm* 'to come' (see [17c] above). Irrealis modality is sometimes signalled or inferred by contextual cues and/or adverbials, but in most cases irrealis is marked by the use of the preverbal irrealis marker *go* (see [17b] above) or the preverbal proximal future auxiliary *wan* (which is related to the verb *wan* 'to want/desire', see [18b] above). As in most of the NigP substrate languages, the irrealis marker is normally used to mark the future tense.

7.2. Anterior plus irrealis = conditional

(19) *A **(bin)** **wan** rich, bɔt di rot dɔn spoil.*
I (ANT) PFUT reach but the road +C be spoiled
'I would have made it, but the road was no good.'

In a clause containing the irrealis marker *go* or the proximal future auxiliary *wan*, anterior/past tense can be marked or inferred by context or through the use of an adverbial. The meaning conveyed by such sentences has a conditional flavour, to the extent that it expresses an event that almost occurred. While the anterior/past auxiliary *bin* may occur in the same clause with the proximal future auxiliary *wan*, it does not normally occur with the irrealis marker *go*.

7.3. Anterior plus irrealis = future in the past

Combinations of *bin* and *wan* discussed in section 7.2. above could be considered to convey future in the past meanings as well as conditional meanings.

7.4.   Anterior plus irrealis = past in the future (future perfect)

Constructions containing the irrealis marker *go* and the completive auxiliary *finish* are utilised to express the future perfect in NigP (see [17b] above).

8.   Other combinations of verbal markers

8.1.   Irrealis plus incompletive

(20)   *A   go   de   wet.*
    I -R -C wait
    'I will be waiting.'

8.2.   Proximal future plus irrealis plus incompletive

(21)   *A **go de wan** wɔk, bot a no   go fit.*
    I -R -C PFUT work but I NEG -R be fit
    'I will be about to work, but I won't be able to.'

8.3.   Other auxiliary-like elements

Preverbal modality markers include *fit* 'be able, be fit', *wan* 'desire, wish', *mɔs* 'must', *fɔr* 'should' and *trai* 'try'.

9.   Complementizers

9.1.   No infinitive marker

(22)   *A   go   (fɔr)   baf.*
    I go (COMP) bathe
    'I went to bathe.'

In some constructions and with some verbs, complementizers are optional.

9.2.   *Fɔr* (general adposition) as infinitive marker

(23)   *A   de   redi   fɔr   go.*
    I -C ready LOC go
    'I am ready to go.'

(24)   a.   *Im   go   (fɔr)   baf,   bɔt   im   no   fit.*
        s/he go (LOC) bathe but s/he NEG be able
        'She went to bathe but she wasn't able to.'

b. *Im   go   (fɔr)   baf,   and   im   kɔm   riton.*
    s/he go   (LOC)   bathe and   s/he +R   return
    'He went to bathe and she came back (from washing).'

The general adposition *for* in NigP, which is found in a number of Atlantic and Pacific pidgins and creoles, is commonly used as a complementizer (see 20.1 below). The use of *for* and other complementizers in NigP does not depend on whether the events referred to by the verbs in the clauses that they introduce are actually completed or not.

9.3.   *Fɔr* as a quasi-modal

Fɔr can have a modal or quasi-modal function in NigP (see section 3.3. above):

(25) *Dɛm fɔr   fray di   planten.*
      They should fry   the plantain
      'They should fry/should have fried the plantain.'

9.4.   *Fɔr* introducing a tensed clause

Fɔr is not normally used to introduce an overtly tensed clause in NigP.

9.5.   Subordinator from superstrate *that*

There is no subordinator in NigP that can be readily recognised as being derived from *that* in its lexifier language English.

9.6.   Distinct subordinator after verbs of speaking/thinking

(26) *Dɛm tel mi (se)   dɛm no   si   yu.*
      they tell me COMP   they NEG see yu
      'They told me that they didn't see you.'

The complementizer *se*, which is derived from the verb *se* 'to say' is utilized rather than other subordinators such as *wɛ* after verbs of communication and cognition. The use of *se* is often optional.

9.7. No subordinator

(27) *A tink (se)   im redi   fɔr   kɔm.*
      I think (COMP) s/he be ready COMP   come
      'I think that she is ready to come.'

As noted in sections 9.1. and 9.6. above, subordinate constructions with no overtly marked subordinator are very common in NigP.

10.   Dependent clauses

10.1.   Subordinate clauses (non-embedded)

(28) a. *If yu   rich makɛt, mek   yu   bay kokonyam.*
          If you reach market SBJV you buy Singapore taro
          'If you go to the market, buy Singapore taro.'

      b. *Mek yu   bay kokonyam   if yu   rich makɛt.*
          SBJV you buy Singapore taro if you reach market
          'If you go to the market, buy Singapore taro.'

A non-embedded subordinate clause introduced by an adverbial like *(di) taym* 'when' or *if* 'if' may either precede or follow its main clause.

10.2.   Subordinate clauses (embedded)

(29) *A hapi   se   yu fit   kɔm.*
      I be happy COMP you be able come
      'I'm happy that you were able to come.'

Subordinate clauses introduced by *se* can function as objects of adjectival verbs and as objects of verbs of communication and cognition (see section 9.6. above).

10.3.   Relative clauses (relative pronoun = subject)

(30) *Di   pikin wɛ (i)   sik   (im) go haws.*
      woman DEM REL (SRPRO) be ill s/he go house
      'The child who has a cold went home.'

The relative pronoun *wɛ* may serve as the subject of a subordinate clause, in which case it may be optionally followed by the subject referencing pronoun that corresponds to the subject of the main clause. If *wɛ* is deleted, the subject referencing pronoun must be included.

10.4.   Relative clauses (relative pronoun = direct object)

(31)   Di   *pikin (wɛ)   yu   bin   bit(-am)*   *(im)   dɔn go haws.*
the   child   (REL)   you   ANT   beat(-him/her)   (s/he)   +C   go house
'The child whom you beat went home.'

The relative pronoun *wɛ* may refer to the object of a subordinate clause. In such cases, an anaphoric object pronoun optionally follows the verb in the relative clause and the use of *wɛ* is optional.

10.5.   Relative clauses (relative pronoun = object of an adposition)

(32)   *Di moto   (wɛ)   injin   no   de   for-am de   for   yad.*
the vehicle (REL)   engine   NEG   LOCCOP   LOC-it COP   LOC   yard
'The vehicle which has no engine in it is in the yard.'

The relative pronoun *wɛ* may refer to the adpositional object of a subordinate clause. In such cases, an anaphoric object pronoun must follow the adposition in the relative clause and the use of *wɛ* is optional.

10.6.   Relative clauses (no relative pronoun)

As shown in sections 10.3., 10.4., and 10.5. above, the inclusion of relative markers in relative clauses is optional, except in relative clauses where the relative marker has the subject role and no other subject marker is present. In relative clauses whose adpositional objects are coreferent to main clause nouns, object pronouns obligatorily follow the adposition.

11.   Negation

11.1.   Single negation (verbal)

(33)   A: *Yu   no   go maket?*
you   NEG   go market?
A: 'Didn't you go to the market?'

B: *Yɛs. A bin   wan   go, bɛt a nɛva rich.*
no   I ANT   want   go   but I NEG reach
B: 'No. I wanted to go, but I couldn't.'

The verbal negative marker *no* occurs before the verb, following the subject, the subject referencing pronoun and preceding all preverbal tense aspect modality markers, except the completive auxiliary *dɔn*, with which it combines to form the completive negative marker *nɛva*. Other constituents are also negated by the marker *no*. Responses to negative questions are logical, as in the NigP substrate languages. Note that discontinuous double negation constructions do not exist in NigP. Furthermore, there is no evidence for negative concord in NigP.

12.   Passive

12.1.   Passive construction

There is no passive construction in NigP. There are, however, a few idiomatic constructions using the role reversal verbs *kach* 'catch' and *du* 'do' that convey meanings similar to the passive in English:

(34)   *Hɔngri kach mi.* or *Hɔngri du mi.*
        hunger catch me   hunger do me
        'I'm famished.'

12.2.   Passive equivalents

(35)   *Chɔp dɔn finish.*
        food +C finish
        'The food is finished.'

(36)   **Dɛm** *kɔm kɔl yɔ   nem.*
        they +R call your name
        'Your name has been called.'

Constructions that approximate the semantics of agentless passives include the passive use of verbs such as *finish* 'finish' and the generic use of the third person plural pronoun *dɛm*.

13.   Adjectives = verbs

13.1.   Tense/aspect/modality markers with adjectival verbs

(37)   *A go hot   di wota sote im go dɔn hɔt finish.*
        I -R be hot the water until it -R +C hot +C
        'I will heat up the water until it is completely hot.'

As in the NigP substrate languages, adjectival verbs normally occur with any tense/aspect/modality marker. In some cases, adjectival verbs can take objects as well. Adjectival verbs can be used as nouns without any additional marking. See also sections 3.4. (anterior), 4.4. (progressive), 6.3. (completive) and 14.3.

13.2.   Tense/aspect/modality markers with nouns

(38)   *A   neva   sabi   se   im   dɔn kɔm ticha   finish.*
       I   NEG+C   know   that   s/he +C +R   teacher   +C
       'I never knew that you were already a teacher.'

In some constructions, nouns may occur with a number of tense/aspect/modality markers. See also section 14.1.

13.3.   Tense/aspect/modality markers with locatives

(39)   a.   *A go de   (fɔr)   haws.*
            I -R COP   (LOC)   house
            'I will be at home.'

       b.   *Moni   go de   mi fɔr   hand.*
            money -R COP me LOC   house
            'I will have money.'

The locative copula *de* can occur with most tense/aspect/modality markers. In some cases the locative copula can take objects as well. See also 3.5.

13.4.   Predicate clefting (adjectives or adjectival verbs)

(40)   *Na   taya   (wɛ)   a dɔn taya.*
       HL   be tired (REL)   I +C be tired
       'It's tiredness that tires me.'

The highlighter *na* obligatorily precedes a fronted constituent in a cleft construction, while relative markers follow optionally.

13.5.   Predicate clefting (other verbs)

(41)   *Na   chɔp (wɛ)   a dɔn chɔp.*
       HL   eat (REL)   I +C eat
       'It's eating that I ate.'

The highlighter *na* obligatorily precedes a fronted constituent in a cleft construction, while relative markers follow optionally.

13.6.   Comparison with 'pass'

(42)   a.   *Ma haws fayn   pas.*   or   *A waka pas.*
             My house be fine pass   I   walk   pass
             'My house is better/best.'   or   'I walked more/most.'

        b.   *Ma haws fayn   pas   yɔ   on.*   or   *A waka pas   yu.*
             My house be fine pass your own   I   walk   pass   you
             'My house is better than yours.'   or 'I walked more than you.'

        c.   *Ma haws fayn   pas   ol.*   or   *A waka pas   ol.*
             My house be fine pass all   I walk   pass   all
             'My house is the best.'   or 'I walked most.'

Comparative and superlative constructions usually include the verb *pas* 'surpass' in a serialized verb construction (see section 15.5.). Without an object, *pas* conveys either a comparative or superlative meaning. With the object *ol* 'all,' *pas* expresses the superlative, while it signifies the comparative with any other object.

13.7.   Comparison as in the superstrate

(43)   a.   *Na bɛta   nyam bi   dat.*
             HL better yam COP that
             'That's better (high quality) yam.'

(43)   b.   *Im   go   yɛlo   moa.*
             S/he -R be pale more
             'S/he will get even more pale.'

While no superstrate-like comparative construction exists in NigP, some items from superstrate comparative constructions such as *bɛta* 'better' and *moa* 'more' are occasionally used in related constructions.

14.   Copula

14.1.   Equative copula (before NP)

(44)   *Uche bi   ticha.*   or   *Uche na   ticha.*
        Uche COP teacher   Uche HL teacher
        'Uche is a teacher.'

Either the identity copula *bi* or the highlighter *na* may be used in equative constructions. In a restricted set of equative constructions, tense/aspect/modality markers can be used with nouns without a copular verb (see section 13.2. above).

14.2.   Locative copula (before expressions of place)

(45)   A: *Uche   de   wɛ?*
             Uche COP   where
             'Where is Uche?'

        B: *Uche   de   (fɔr)   haws.*
             Uche COP   (LOC)   house
             'Uche is at home.'

The locative copula *de* can be used with a locative or an existential meaning (see section 14.3. below). *De* can be used with any of the tense/aspect/modality markers that normally occur with NigP verbs (see section 3.5. above). In some cases, *de* can take an object (see section 13.3. above).

14.3.   Copula before 'adjectives' (see section 12.1.)

(46)   a.   A: *Haw   yu   de?*
               how   you   COP
               'How are you?'

       b.   B: *A   hapi.*   or   *A   de   hapi.*
               I   be happy   I   COP   happiness
               'I am happy.'

       c.   C: *A   de   layk   a   no   de.*
               I   COP   like   I   NEG   COP
               'I exist as if I weren't existing.' or 'I am on the edge of existence.'

As in most NigP substrate languages, adjectives usually function as verbs and therefore are not normally preceded by copulas. Nominalized adjectival verbs may, however, be found in zero equative copular constructions (see example [46b] above).

14.4.   Highlighter with question words

(47)   *Na hu   tek   solt kɔm spoil di   styu?*
HL who take salt +R   spoil the stew
'Who is it who put too much salt in the stew?'

The highlighter *na* may sometimes be used before question words. See also sections 13.4. and 14.5.

14.5.   Highlighter with other structures

(48)   *Na Halima dɛm mek-am, no   bi   mi o.*
HL Halima they do-it   NEG IDCOP me +R
'It was Halima and her people who did it, it wasn't me.'

The highlighter *na* can be used to introduce a wide range of fronted topicalized constituents. See also sections 13.4. and 13.5.

14.6.   Existential ('have' = 'there is')

(49)   *I   gɛt   tu   moto   fɔr   rod.*
SRPRO have   two   vehicle LOC road
'There are two vehicles on the road.'

In the affirmative, the verb *gɛt* 'have' is normally preceded by a dummy subject to express existential 'there is.' In the negative, the use of the dummy subject with *gɛt* is optional.

15.   Serial verbs

15.1.   Directional with 'go'

(50)   *Kari buk   go.*
take book go
'Take the book away.'

As in most NigP substrate languages, *go* 'go' is commonly used in serialized verb constructions to indicate motion away from the speaker.

15.2.   Directional with 'come'

(51)   *Kari buk kɔm.*
       take book come
       'Bring the book.'

As in most NigP substrate languages, *kɔm* 'come' is commonly used in serial-ized verb constructions to indicate motion toward the speaker.

15.3.   Serial 'give' meaning 'to, for'

(52)   *Kari buk giv mi.*
       take book give me
       'Give the book to me.'

As in many NigP substrate languages, *giv* 'give' can be used in serialized verb constructions to introduce indirect objects.

15.4.   Serial 'say' meaning 'that'

As in many NigP substrate languages, *se* 'say' can be used in a serialized verb construction as a complementizer after verbs of communication or cognition (see sections 9.6. and 10.2. above).

15.5.   Serial 'pass' meaning 'more than'

As shown in 13.6 above, the verb *pas* 'to surpass' is used in serialized verb constructions to express the comparative in NigP.

15.6.   Three serial-verb construction

(53)   *Kari buk kɔm giv mi.*
       take book come give me
       'Bring the book to me.'

As in most NigP substrate languages, serialized verb constructions containing three verbs are not uncommon in NigP.

15.7.   Four or more serial-verb construction

(54)   *Im   bay   nyam   kari-am   go   rich   haws   kuk-am   chɔp.*
s/he buy yam   take-it go reach house cook-it eat
'She bought yams and took them home and cooked and ate them.'

Four or more verbs may occur in the same serial verb construction in NigP.

16.   Noun phrases

16.1.   Bare nouns

(55)   *Im   kari buk   kɔm.*
S/he take book come
'S/he brought a/the book.'

Bare nouns are normally interpreted as definite or indefinite by the context, without the use of articles.

16.2.   Indefinite article

(56)   a.   *Wɔn man de slip.*
one   man -C sleep
'A man is sleeping.'

       b.   *Sɔm   man   de   slip.*
some man -C sleep
'Some men are sleeping.'

Wɔn 'one' marks indefinite nouns in the singular (as in most NigP substrate languages), while *sɔm* 'some' marks indefinite nouns in the plural.

16.3.   Definite article

(57)   *Di man de slip.*
the man -C sleep
'The man is sleeping.'

The definite article *di* 'the' is used to mark the definiteness of nouns.

16.4.   Plural marker = 'they'

(58)   *Di man dɛm de slip.*
       the man they -C sleep
       'The men are sleeping.'

As in most NigP substrate languages, *dɛm* 'they' is used both as the third person plural pronoun and as the plural marker for nouns, in which case it follows the noun that it modifies.

16.5.   Personal noun plus plural marker

(59)   *Shehu dɛm de slip.*
       Shehu they -C sleep
       'Shehu and his people are sleeping.'

As in most NigP substrate languages, *dɛm*, which is both the third person plural pronoun and the plural marker for nouns, may follow a personal noun to refer to people associated with the person whose name is mentioned.

16.6.   Demonstratives

(60)   a.   *Dis man de slip.*
            this man -C sleep
            'This man is sleeping.'

       b.   *Dat man de slip.*
            that man -C sleep
            'That man is sleeping.'

In NigP, the proximal demonstrative is *dis* 'this,' while the distal demonstrative is *dat* 'that.'

16.7.   Demonstrative plus definite or plural

(61)   a.   *Dis man dɛm de slip.*
            this man they -C sleep
            'These men are sleeping.'

       b.   *Dat man dɛm de slip.*
            that man they -C sleep
            'Those men are sleeping.'

The plural marker *dɛm* may be used with the demonstratives *dis* 'this' or *dat* 'that' to express the plural 'these' and 'those' respectively. Demonstratives cannot be used with the definite article *di*.

16.8.   Relative clauses plus definite or plural marker

(62)   *Di man (dɛm) (wɛ)   (dɛm) de slip   (dɛm) nɛva   chɔp.*
        the man (they) (REL) (they) -C sleep (they) NEG+C eat
        'The men who are sleeping have not eaten.'

Neither the definite article nor the demonstratives have a relativizing function in NigP. No conclusive arguments have as yet been put forward as to whether *dɛm* functions as a plural marker or as a pronoun when it is found at the head of a relative clause.

16.9.   Prenominal adjective

(63)   *Di yɛlo wɛ   di   yɛlo   man de yɛlo   go yɛlo   moa.*
        The palor REL the pallid man -C be pale -R be pale more
        'The paleness that the pallid man is pale by will be even more pale.'
        or 'The pallid man will be getting a lot paler.'

As explained in section 13.1. above, adjectival verbs can be used as nouns without any additional marking. Nominalised adjectival verbs are placed before nouns in a possessive construction (see section 17.1. below) when they are used as prenominal 'adjectives'.

16.10. Postnominal adjective

(64)   *Adeola sik.*
        s/he   be sick
        'Adeola is sick.'

Adjectival verbs normally occur after the subject to which they refer.

16.11. Gender agreement

As in most of its substrates and superstrates, there is no gender agreement within noun phrases in NigP.

17.   Possession

17.1.   Unmarked noun plus noun constructions

(65)   *di   pikin   plet*
        the   child   plate
        'the child's plate'

When nouns are juxtaposed without any overt markers indicating the relationship between them, the usual order in NigP is modifier noun + head noun:
Nayjirya wuman 'a Nigerian woman.' The same pattern applies to unmarked
possessives in NigP as well, where the noun which refers to the possessor precedes the noun that refers to the possessed entity: possessor + possessed.

17.2.   Noun plus noun constructions containing adpositions

(66)   *nayf   fɔr   Chinyere*
        knife   LOC   Chinyere
        'Chinyere's knife'

A marginal noun + noun construction containing the adposition *fɔr* exists in
some lects of NigP. In this construction, the usual order is head noun + *fɔr* +
modifier noun *tebol fɔr rayt* 'writing table' or possessed + *fɔr* + possessor.

17.3.   Noun plus noun constructions containing possessive adjectives

As shown in 17.4. below, possessive adjectives are normally placed between
two nouns in NigP possessive constructions, yielding the following structure:
possessor + possessive adjective + possessed entity.

17.4.   Possessive adjectives

(67)   a.   *Chinyere   im   nayf*
             Chinyere   her   knife
             'Chinyere's knife'

Possessive adjectives precede the nouns that they modify. The possessive adjectives in NigP include the following:

         b.   *ma* 'my'
             yɔ 'your (singular)'
             im 'his/her/its'

awa 'our'
una 'your (plural)'
dɛm 'their'

17.5.   Possessive pronouns

(68)   *Ma   on   fayn   pas   yɔ   on.*
My   own   be fine pass your own
'Mine is better than yours.'

Possessive pronouns are formed by using the particle *on* 'own' after a possessive adjective (see section 13.6. above).

17.6.   Possessive pronouns as emphatic possessive adjectives

(69)   *Ma   on   haws   fayn   pas   yɔ   on.*
My   own   house be fine pass your own
'My (emphasis on my) house is better than yours.'

In some lects of NigP possessive pronouns may be used as emphatic possessive adjectives.

18.   Pronouns

18.1.   Personal pronouns: first person singular

(70)   *mi* (high tone)   'I (emphatic)'
a (low tone)   'I (SRPRO)'
mi   'me'

The emphatic first person singular subject pronoun *mi* carries a high tone, while the subject referencing first person singular subject pronoun *a* carries a low tone. The first person singular object pronoun is *mi*. See also sections 17.4. and 17.5. above.

18.2.   Personal pronouns: second person singular

(71)   yu (high tone)   'you (singular, subject, emphatic)'
yu (low tone)   'you (singular, subject, SRPRO)'
yu   'you (singular, object)'

The emphatic second person singular subject pronoun *yu* carries a high tone, while the subject referencing second person singular subject pronoun *yu* carries a low tone. The second person singular object pronoun is *yu*.

18.3.   Personal pronouns: third person singular

(72)   *im* (high tone)   'he/she/it (emphatic)'
       im~i (low tone)   'he/she/it (SRPRO)'
       -am   'him/her/it (object)'

The emphatic third person singular subject pronoun *im* carries a high tone, while the subject referencing third person singular subject pronoun *im* (which may be shortened to *i*) carries a low tone. The third person singular object pronoun is the clitic *-am*.

18.4.   Personal pronouns: first person nonsingular

(73)   *wi* (high tone)   'we (emphatic)'
       wi (low tone)   'we (SRPRO)'
       ɔs   'us'

The emphatic first person plural subject pronoun *wi* carries a high tone, while the subject referencing first person plural subject pronoun *wi* carries a low tone. The first person plural object pronoun is *ɔs*.

18.5.   Personal pronouns: second person nonsingular

(74)   *una* (low-low tone) 'you (plural, subject, emphatic)'
       una (low-low tone) 'you (plural, subject, SRPRO)'
       una   'you (plural, object)'

Both the emphatic second person plural subject pronoun *una* and the subject referencing second person plural subject pronoun *una* carry a low-low tone sequence. The second person plural object pronoun is *una* as well.

18.6.   Personal pronouns: third person nonsingular

(75)   *dɛm* (high tone)   'they (emphatic)'
       dɛm (low tone)   'they (SRPRO)'
       dɛm   'them'

The emphatic third person plural subject pronoun *dɛm* carries a high tone, while the subject referencing third person plural subject pronoun *dɛm* carries a low tone. The third person plural object pronoun is *dɛm* as well.

18.7.   Reflexive pronouns

(76)   a.   *A si   ma sɛf   for   glas.*
I   see   my   self   LOC   glass
'I saw myself in the mirror.'

   b.   *A si   (ma)   bɔdi   for   glas.*
I   see   (my)   body   LOC   glass
'I saw myself in the mirror.'

Reflexive pronouns are formed by using the words *sɛf* 'self' or *bɔdi* 'body' after a possessive adjective. *Bɔdi* may be used as a reflexive pronoun alone without the possessive adjective as well.

18.8.   Interrogative pronouns and other question words
(see also section 14.4. above)

wating, wɛting	'what, which'
hu, huspɛsin	'who, whom'
haw mɔch, haw mɛni	'how much, how many'
haw, wichwe	'how'
way, wɛting mek	'why'
wɛ, wɛples	'where'
wichtaim, hustaim	'when'
abi, no bi so	'*yes-no* question tag'

18.9.   Relative pronouns (see also section 10.3. above)

(77)   *wɛ* 'what, which'

19.   Coordinating conjunctions

19.1.   Clause coordination

(78)   *A go go makɛt   and yu   go go haws.*
I   -R   go   market   and   you   -R   go   house
'I'll go to the market and you'll go home.'

The conjunctions *and* 'and', *ɔ* 'or' and *bɔt* 'but' are used to join full sentences.

19.2.   Constituent coordination

(79)   *Mi and yu   go go makɛt.*
       me and you -R go market
       'I and you will go to the market.'

And 'and' and *ɔ* 'or' may be used to join a wide variety of constituents.

20.   Adpositions

20.1.   General locative preposition

(80)   *A kɔm fɔr   haws witi yu   and Okon.*
       I come LOC house with you and Okon
       'I came home with you and Okon.'

Following a pattern typical of both the NigP substrates and the Atlantic creoles, *fɔr* 'at, in on, to, etc.' is the general adposition in NigP. *Fɔr* may be followed by locational nouns to further specify its function, *fɔr insayd* 'inside of', or it may be used as a subordinator or as a modal (see sections 9.2. and 9.3. above). A few other secondary prepositions occur in NigP, including *of* 'of,' *wit(i)* 'with' and *sote* 'until.'

20.2.   Zero preposition between motion verb and destination

(81)   *A go makɛt   witi yu   and Okon.*
       I go market with you and Okon
       'I went to market with you and Okon.'

It is not always necessary to include *fɔr* before the destination of a verb of motion.

21.   Miscellaneous

21.1.   Word order: questions

(82)   *Yu   chop wɛting?* or *(Na) wɛting yu   chop?*
       you eat   what?   (HL) what?   you eat
       'What did you eat?'

In questions, interrogative words (see section 18.8. above) normally occupy the position of the constituent they question. There is no special inversion process or other obligatory word order modification in interrogative constructions. All interrogative words, however, may be fronted, in which case the highlighter *na* (see section 14.4. above) may be used with all except the *yes-no* question tags *abi* and *no bi so*, which may occur either immediately before or after the constituent or construction that they question.

21.2. Sentence-final *o*

(83)   *A nɛva   ring yu   o.   Sori   o.*
        I NEG+C ring you +R sorry +R
        'I didn't get a chance to call you. Sorry.'

As in most of its substrate languages, the sentence-final realis modality particle *o* is used with a range of meanings in NigP, from solidarity and empathy to stressing the realis (truth value) of the entire proposition.

21.3. Ideophones

(84)   *A go slap yu   zaway!*
        I -R slap you ideophone
        'I'm going to slap you so that it really hurts!'

As in most of its substrate languages, an open and productive class of onomatopoetic words called ideophones may be used at the end of NigP utterances (and sometimes elsewhere in a sentence) to punctuate or dramatize the event expressed by a verb.

Exercises and study questions

1. What is the difference between an anterior marker (*bin*) and a completive marker (*don*)?

2. What is meant by irrealis marking? What are the two irrealis auxiliaries in NigP?

3. Compare the responses to negative questions in NigE and NigP.

4. Discuss the form and function of *pas* in a sentence like *A waka pas you* ('I walked more than you').

5. What is a serial verb construction? Give three examples from NigP.

Selected references

Please consult the General references for titles mentioned in the text but not included in the references below. For a full bibliography see the accompanying CD-ROM.

Faraclas, Nicholas
  1988   Nigerian Pidgin and the languages of southern Nigeria. *Journal of Pidgin and Creole Languages* 3: 77–97.
  1990   From Old Guinea to Papua New Guinea: a comparative study of Nigerian Pidgin and Tok Pisin. In: John Verhaar (ed.), *Melanesian Pidgin and Tok Pisin*, 91–169. Amsterdam/Philadelphia: Benjamins.
  1996   *Nigerian Pidgin*. London: Routledge.

Ghanaian English: morphology and syntax

Magnus Huber and Kari Dako

1. Introduction

As in the field of phonology, the morphological and syntactical differences between Ghanaian English (GhE) and British English (BrE) are variable rather than categorical. They are more strongly present in spoken varieties than in the written mode and also depend on the degree of formality, with conversational GhE showing more Ghanaianisms than more formal styles.

Tingley (1981) investigated the English of Ghanaian newspapers in the period between 1976 and 1977 and found significant deviances (Tingley 1981: 40) in the domain of (a) articles (omission, insertion and diverging use), (b) prepositions (omission, insertion and substitution), (c) phrasal verbs (omission, insertion, substitution), (d) mass nouns (used as count nouns), (e) concord (verbs, nouns, personal pronouns), (f) modal auxiliaries (use of past tense forms where BrE has present tense forms, substitution), (g) infinite verb forms (infinitive for *-ing* form and vice versa), (h) intransitive uses of transitive verbs, (i) omission of the coordinator *and*, (j) change in the sequence of premodifiers, and (k) adjective forms used adverbially.

In spite of this variety of differences, the overall syntax of GhE is rather close to BrE and intelligibility for the native speaker is generally maintained. Note also that many of these characteristics are not specific to GhE but can be found in many English as a Second Language (L2) varieties of English around the world.

2. Verb phrase

In the domain of phrasal verbs three basic patterns of substitution, insertion and omission of the particle can be observed. Particle substitution is illustrated in (1)–(3):

(1)   ***Put off*** *the gas before you leave.*

(2)   *The audience is invited to **cheer** their favourite team **up.***

(3)   *He was **charged for** stealing a goat.*

A sentence like (3) may even be used by senior judges and professors of law. In some verbs a particle is inserted, as in (4) and (5):

(4)   *They requested **for** higher pay.*

(5)   *We were encouraged to voice **out** our opinion.*

In other cases the particle is omitted, as in (6):

(6)   *The man they arrested answers ∅ the description of the armed robber.*

The intransitive use of some transitive verbs and the transitive use of intransitive verbs is relatively common. The verb *reply*, for instance, is consistently used in the same structure as *answer*, that is, as a transitive verb, as in example (7) taken from a newspaper:

(7)   *The counsel ... will today **reply an argument** ... by the Acting Attorney-General.*

On the other hand, *afford* is often used intransitively:

(8)   *Few people go to hospitals at all. They cannot just **afford**.*

Award is often used for *reward* or *award with/reward for*:

(9)   *So this man was **awarded**. But nobody in the whole town liked him.*

Stative verbs are often used progressively, as in (10)–(12):

(10)   *She **is having** a child with a certain man from Ho.*

(11)   *I **am having** a book.*

(12)   *The rural areas **are not having** access to higher education.*

The *to*-infinitive and the *-ing* form are often used interchangeably, as in (13) and (14):

(13)   *He **considered to leave** before sunrise.*

(14)   *The government **wishes eradicating** poverty.*

2.1.   Tense-aspect-modality

There is a certain tendency to substitute the past perfect for the present perfect and to use the present perfect with reference to a completed action. Examples are given in (15) and (16):

(15)   *The Government will have to take sterner measures than it **had**
        hitherto **done**.*

(16)   *It **has been established** hundreds of years ago.*

Especially in spoken GhE, *be coming to* and *be going to* are used interchangeably to encode (proximate) future or ingressiveness:

(17)   *I **am coming to** cook your meal.*
        'I am about to cook your meal'.

This appears to be a calque on the equivalent Akan structure: in the Twi dialect,
for example, ingressive constructions are formed with the prefixes *be-* or *ko-*,
derived from the verbs meaning 'come' and 'go' as in (18):

(18)   *ǫ-   kǫ-/bɛ-   fá   n'   adé.*
        he-   go-/come- take this thing
        'He is about to take his property'.

There is also a proximate ingressive in Twi, where these prefixes combine with
the progressive marker *re-* as in (19):

(19)   *ǫ-re-   kǫ-/bɛ-   fá   n'   adé.*
        he-PROG- go-/come- take this thing
        'He is (just) about to take his property'.

At times, *never* expresses negative completive aspect:

(20)   *I **never** knew you were in town.*
        'I didn't know you were in town'.

2.2.   Auxiliaries

Would commonly expresses definite future, as in (21). A similar trend, albeit on
a lesser scale, can be observed in *could* for *can*, as in (22):

(21)   *We hereby wish to inform you that the meeting **would** take place on
        Thursday.*

(22)   *We are hoping that he **could** finish it by tomorrow.*

A much lower rate of the politer modal forms than in BrE can be observed.
Polite requests such as *could I/you, might I, would it be possible* and others
are relatively rare. What is viewed as a polite request in Ghana is often what
a native speaker of Standard British English (StBrE) would consider an order
with the addition of *please*. (23), addressed to a lecturer in his office, illustrates
this use:

(23)   *I want to borrow your book, please.*

Tagging is relatively rare in GhE. If it is used at all, it tends to be added in the invariant form *isn't it?* as in (24) and (25):

(24)   *He lives in Kumasi, isn't it?*

(25)   *Kwadwo left early for work, isn't it?*

2.3.   Negation

A constant source of confusion for the overseas visitor is the fact that Ghanaians (like other West Africans) answer to the form, not the contents of *yes-no* questions. This can create serious misunderstandings as far as negative questions are concerned:

(26)   Q: *Isn't your mother at home?*
       A: *Yes.*
            '(What you say is true,) she is **not** at home'; or
            She is there.
            'She is at home'

Tagging is hardly used in responses:

(27)   Q: *You didn't find the book, did you?*
       A: *Yes.*
            'I didn't'. (*Yes, I did* is rare); or
            I found it.
            'I did'

The distribution of the indefinite pronouns *some/none/any* and their compounds is sometimes different from that in BrE, in that they appear to be in free variation. Compare (28) and (29) taken from the recording accompanying this text:

(28)   *He is not supposed to mention **nobody's** name.*

(29)   *You are not supposed to mention **somebody's** name.*

In negative sentences, the indefinite adverb *either* is at times replaced by *too*, as in (30):

(30)   *You didn't have enough rest **too**.*

Please collocates with *no* or *not* to indicate polite negative sentences and denials:

(31)   Q: *Have you seen my red pen?*
        A: ***Please, no.***

(32)   ***Please**, I cannot come to class tomorrow.*

Please is a general politeness marker, also used in sentences with positive polarity:

(33)   Q: *Did you drop Seedu in Madina?*
        A: *Yes, **please**.*

3.   Relativization and complementation

Relative clause formation closely follows StBrE, both in the choice of the relativizer (*who, which, that*) and the syntax of the subordinated clause (postnominal, no inversion of word order). However, particularly in conversational varieties of GhE, there is a tendency for the underlying nominal of the relative clause to surface as a resumptive pronoun, especially in non-subject positions, as in (34) and (35):

(34)   *The book that I read **it**.*

(35)   *The old woman who I gave **her** the money.*

For a discussion of the complementizer *that* see section 2.3. on suprasegmentals in the companion chapter on GhE phonology (this volume).

4.   Adverbial subordination

Especially in the more informal range of conversational GhE, some adverbial subordinators show slight difference in usage. For example, *if* tends to be replaced by *suppose(ing)*:

(36)   ***Suppose** I put the wire this way it won't be a problem.*

There is a preference for relating events in the order that they actually occurred. The resulting iconic syntax requires subordinators that are different from the ones used in StBrE, as illustrated by (37):

(37)   *The man came there, **before** one of the Muslims went there.*

StBrE would have something like (38):

(38)   *One of the Muslims went there **after** the man had come.*

The tendency towards syntactic iconicity also results in constructions like the one in (39):

(39)   ***Unless** you speak loud **before** he can understand.*
'He can (only) hear you if you speak loud'.

Probably on the basis of such uses, *unless* frequently signals a state or an action that is perceived to precede another either temporally or logically, as in (40):

(40)   A: *I want some tea*
        B: ***Unless** I boil some water first.*
            'Let me boil some water for you'.

5.   Agreement

With a few minor exceptions, Ghanaian languages do not morphologically encode gender. Therefore the pronominal distinctions present in BrE sometimes break down in GhE, even among the most highly educated users as in (41) and (42):

(41)   ***He** is called **Mary**.*

(42)   *When **he** wanted to marry him **she** said he would wait till **he** had finished **her** education.*

However, variation is not completely random, since there appears to be a tendency for the pronominal determiner to select the gender of the noun it modifies:

(43)   *He was looking for **her aunt**.*

(44)   *She thought **his husband** had travelled.*

Such variation can also be observed with biological gender in nominals: *Master* is often found in free variation with *Madam* (the deferential address for a female boss), or *nephew* with *niece*, regardless of the sex of the referent.

Many GhE speakers do not maintain the distinction between *this* and *these*, realizing both as [ðis/dis]. The result is that there seems to be no agreement between the proximate demonstrative and a plural noun. To a native speaker of BrE, GhE [dis bɔis] sounds like *this boys*. Note that this erosion of the number distinction may possibly have its explanation in phonology rather than morphology: GhE neutralizes the length and quality distinctions of BrE [iː – ɪ] to [i] and tends to devoice final obstruents, yielding [-s] for BrE [-z], which results in [ðis/dis] for both demonstratives.

Notional subject-verb concord accounts for examples like (45):

(45)   *The burial of dead bodies **are** becoming expensive.* (Gyasi 1991: 30)

6.   Noun phrase structure

One of the most frequent differences between BrE and GhE concerns the use of definite and indefinite articles. GhE omits articles that are required in BrE, inserts articles where there are none in BrE, and also ignores distinctions of definiteness that are made in BrE.

The omission of the definite article in the names of national and international bodies is very common:

(46)   *She just arrived from ∅ United States of America.*

(47)   *The representative of ∅ World Health Organisation visited the facility.*

However, if the noun is the name of a commercial establishment or public facility, the article is often inserted:

(48)   *He was appointed sales representative at **the** Nestlé, Ghana Ltd.*

(49)   *They are supposed to arrive at **the** Kotoka International Airport this evening.*

The definite article also tends to be deleted where the head of the NP is post-modified with an *of*-phrase, as in:

(50)   *He called for ∅ abolition of the death penalty.*

(51)   *...when ∅ remuneration of health workers needs to be addressed.*

Even the most highly educated speakers of GhE sometimes omit the indefinite article, as in (52):

(52)   *I want to buy ∅ car.*

Often, this happens by analogy with similar collocations, as in (53):

(53)   *My sister became ∅ teacher in Achimota.*
        (analogous to StBrE *My sister became chairperson*).

This can also be observed with the definite article:

(54)   *She was on her way to Ø bank.*
       (analogous to StBrE *She was on her way to church*).

(55)   *When we talk of the freedom of Ø press.*
       (analogous to StBrE *When we talk of the freedom of speech*).

The omission of an article in *majority (of)/minority (of)* can be described as default usage in Ghana. These forms are used extensively in the printed press, in news broadcasts and in official speeches:

(56)   **Majority of** *Ghanaians live in rural areas.*

(57)   **Minority of** *those present voted for him.*

(58)   *The ruling party hoped for **majority** when the House voted.*

Analogy also accounts for the levelling of the definiteness distinctions to be found in BrE. GhE has

(59)   *He started at **an** early age of 15.*
       (analogous to StBrE *He started work at an early age*).

(60)   *I had **a** shock of my life yesterday.*
       (analogous to StBrE *I had a shock yesterday*).

Few/a few are often used interchangeably, as illustrated by (61), spoken with some variations on the weather forecast every evening:

(61)   *There will be Ø **few** scattered showers over the country.*

The use of the prenominal *a certain* for *some* or *a* generally indicates that the modified element is not to be named, as in the following examples from newspaper articles:

(62)   **A "certain** *somebody" – as we say in these parts – intimated that it was unnecessary to stage a peaceful demonstration.*

(63)   *This landfill project serves as ample evidence of the failure of **certain** people, and institutions.*

In addition to article usage, the treatment of non-count nouns as count nouns is another salient feature of GhE (and of other Englishes around the world). A number of non-count nouns are persistently used as count nouns in Ghana. These include *accommodation, advice, correspondence, equipment, furniture, luggage* and *work.*

(64)   *We see the students looking for **an accommodation** anywhere they can find.*

(65)   *She gave me **many advices** before she left.*

(66)   *I have to do **the correspondences** before I leave.*

(67)   *The firm donated **equipments** worth 5 mill. cedis to the university.*

(68)   *You should have seen **the furnitures**!*

(69)   ***Five luggages** were left unclaimed at the State Transport.*

(70)   *Congratulations for **a good work** done!*

Conversely, count nouns are sometimes treated as mass nouns, as in (71):

(71)   ***This spaghetti is** thicker small.*
        'These spaghetti are a little thicker'.

The use of prepositions constitutes another area of common divergence between BrE and GhE. Written and spoken varieties of GhE are characterized by the replacement, omission and insertion of prepositions vis-à-vis BrE. Apart from the area of phrasal verbs mentioned above, substitution can be observed in combinations of noun + preposition (e.g. *insistence at, contender to*), of adverb + preposition (e.g. *unworthy for, conducive for*) and of preposition of place + noun (*at the boiler room, on the stadium*). In addition, we find *of*-deletion in partitive constructions (*five bags rice, six bottles Schnapps*), while *of*-insertion occurs in phrases like *many of such cases* or *one of such organisations*. Structures of the form *in Ghana here* 'here in Ghana' appear to be calqued on Akan *wo Ghana ho*.

7.   Topicalization and focus constructions

Spoken GhE in particular has a strong tendency towards left-dislocation, realized through topicalization and focus constructions as in (72) and (73):

(72)   *After church I'll come.*

(73)   *That teacher in Achimota, is he your uncle?*

Left-dislocation is also achieved through pronominal apposition, that is the insertion of a copy pronoun of the noun phrase:

(74)   *That woman **she** cheated me.*

Constructions like these are very common, but restricted to the first person singular if the copied noun phrase is a pronoun:

(75)   *Me **I** cannot come.*

The rather frequent topicalizing construction *as for...*, for example *As for me, I won't like it,* can also be interpreted as an instance of left-dislocation and possibly constitutes the source of the pronominal apposition of the *Me I...* type (through deletion of *As for*). Cleft and pseudo-cleft constructions are also much more common than in BrE. See (76)–(78):

(76)   *It is here that I live.*

(77)   *It was then that she came.*

(78)   *Is it me you are looking for?*

Spoken GhE is also marked by the frequent presence of topicalizers, most of which are borrowed from local Ghanaian languages. The most common are *aː, diɛ, kɔraː, nɔ, paː, waː* and *tu* (the latter derives from English *too*).

(79)   *But the rumour **too** in town is that...*

(80)   *So she decided **nɔ** to report him.*

(81)   *As for me **diɛ** me I don't understand.*

Note the triple topicalization in the last sentence: *As for me* + *diɛ* + pronominal apposition *me I*.

Sentence coordination is often achieved by *and then* in informal spoken GhE, especially where there is a perceived temporal order or causal relationship between the coordinated sentences:

(82)   *I woke up **and then** found that the television was still on.*

By analogy, the use of *and then* is sometimes extended to constructions where there is no obvious temporal or causal relationship between the coordinated sentences or constituents, as in (83):

(83)   *You take beans **and then** plantains.*

Alternatively, NPs can also be conjoined by the coordinator *plus*:

(84)   *Rice **plus** beans.*

8.   Lexicon

Dako (2001; 2003) has documented some 3,000 borrowings in constant use in
GhE writing. The number is considerably higher in spoken discourse, but includes a less fixed vocabulary. About 60 percent of these Ghanaianisms derive
from English and have undergone semantic change. Most conspicuous among
these are the items *fool(ish)*, *mad*, *insane*, *silly*, *stupid* and *nonsense*, which are
considered translations of local taboo words and are highly insulting.

The same processes that other varieties of English undergo in their word-formation processes can be discerned in GhE, including semantic extension (for
example *musical* 'musical interlude on the radio'), restriction (*chock* 'heavy
wooden wedge used as brake for older lorries'), shift (*mineral* 'soft drink'),
pejoration (*silly* '[taboo] stupid'), and amelioration (*trinkets* 'gold jewellery').
Sorry is an expression of commiseration and thus the response to mishaps,
caused by the speaker or not:

(85)   *I am sorry to tell you that the slaves were kept in these dungeons*
        (a guide on a tour of a trading station).

Some frequent idiomatic expressions are:

(86)   *I am coming* or *I am going to come.*
        'I will be back.' (said when leaving)

(87)   *I met your absence.*
        'You were not there.'

(88)   *I am taking the lead.*
        'I'll go ahead (and you will follow later).'

The following word-formation categories can be observed:

– Functional shift (e.g. *to outdoor* 'the bringing out of doors of a new-born
  after seven days, or of a child after puberty rites')
– Compounding of English items (*blowman* 'hero in film, strong man')
– Compounding of English item + local item (*jollof rice* 'West African risotto'
  < Wolof + English)
– Compounding of local item x + local item y (*koko sakora* 'porridge without
  milk' < Akan + Hausa)
– Reduplication (*red-red* 'fried plantains and bean-stew')
– Affixation (*confusionist* 'someone causing confusion')
– Clipping (*colo* 'old, old fashioned, from the colonial period' < *colonial*)
– Blending (*shoogle* 'shake' < *shook* + *wriggle*)

- Neologism (*akatamansonian* 'supporter of the National Democratic Congress party' < Akan + English affixation)
- Coinage (*kalabule* 'black market business/prices' < ?Hausa *kere kabure* 'keep it quiet')
- Idiomatic expressions (*item thirteen* 'refreshment', i.e. item not on the agenda)

Borrowings from local languages can be classified semantically according to the following categories

- abstract concepts (e.g. *Kofe Ne/and Amma* 'day-name collection in church')
- references/appellations for persons (*magajia* 'woman, wife' < Hausa)
- food and drink (*kokonte/nkonkonte* 'fufu made from cassava flour' < Akan)
- interjections/exclamations (*tsoo boii/tsooboi/chooboi* [battle cry] < Ga)
- cultural concepts (*adowa* [Akan dance] < Akan)
- religion and beliefs (*Asaman* 'land of the dead' < Akan)
- clothes and ornaments (*fugu* 'northern smock' < Moore)
- gadgets/tools/implements (*g(a)rawa* 'kerosene tin container, capacity measure' < Hausa)

Culture-specific borrowings in particular retain their original phonological contour. Thus, the tones of *nananom* 'chiefs' are always LLH. A similar tendency can be observed in grammatical adaptations. Borrowed nouns usually maintain their original plural markers, for example singular *okyame* 'chief's spokesman' (< Akan) – plural *akyame* and singular *togbe* 'grandfather (and appellation for chief in Ewe)' – plural *togbuiwo*. While the plural is not encoded by English *-s* alone (**okyames*, **togbes*), a combination of the Akan plural marker *a-* and English *-s* is possible (*akyames*).

Since at times replaces *on* + definite time as in (89), at times *for* as in (90) and at times *in* as in (91):

(89)   *It was deposited **since** February 6, 1989.*

(90)   *We have been friends **since** three years.*

(91)   *The opposition alliance which he started championing **since** 1989.*

Last + time reference is used as time reference + *ago* as in (92), while *next* + time reference means *in* + time reference as in (93):

(92)   ***Last two days** I met my sister on campus.*
         'Two days ago...'

(93)   *I expect him **next two weeks**.*
        '...in two weeks'.

Whiles for *while/whilst* is very common. Some newspapers use only this form:

(94)   *A train and a car used by him **whiles** alive.*

Exercises and study questions

1. Supply an example of 'notional subject-verb concord' similar to sentence (45).

2. Give an example of "syntactic iconicity" from Standard English in connection with the discussion around sentence (139).

3. How would the non-count nouns in bold in sentences (64) to (69) be expressed in Standard English?

4. Review the example of *too* as a topicalizer in sentence (79). How would this nuance be expressed in Standard English?

5. What reasons can you propose for the replacement of *if* by *suppose* in sentences like (36)?

Selected references

Please consult the General references for titles mentioned in the text but not included in the references below. For a full bibliography see the accompanying CD-ROM.

Dako, Kari
    2001   Ghanaianisms: towards a semantic and formal classification. *English World-Wide* 22: 23–53.
    2003   *Ghanaianisms – a Glossary*. Accra: Ghana University Press.
    (forth-   Some thoughts about the use of dental fricatives by students at the University
    coming) of Ghana. *Exploration: Journal of the Department of English* 1.
Gyasi, Ibrahim K.
    1991   Aspects of English in Ghana. *English Today* 26: 26–31.
Tingley, Christopher
    1981   Deviance in the English of Ghanaian newspapers. *English World-Wide* 2: 39–62.

Ghanaian Pidgin English: morphology and syntax

Magnus Huber

1.   Introduction

Ghanaian Pidgin English (GhP) is part of the West African Pidgin (WAP) continuum, which includes the varieties spoken in Sierra Leone (Krio), Ghana, Nigeria, and Cameroon. There are many similarities between the restructured Englishes spoken in these countries, which can to a large part be explained by the fact that the pidgins spoken in Ghana, Nigeria, and Cameroon are offshoots of Krio (see Huber 1999: 75–134 for details). For this reason, the following sections will place special emphasis on those aspects where GhP differs from the other WAPs, in particular Nigerian Pidgin (NigP). Readers are therefore advised to consult the articles by Elugbe and Faraclas (this volume) to get a full contrastive view of NigP and GhP.

Abbreviations used in this chapter are as follows: ABIL = ability (mood); CAUS = causative; COMPL = completive aspect; COP = copula; COMP = complementizer; DEF = definite article; DEM = demonstrative; EMPH = emphasizer; FOC = focus marker; INCOMPL = incompletive aspect (progressive, habitual); INDEF = indefinite article; INT = intentionalis; IRR = irrealis mood (future, conditional); NEG = negator; PLF = plural free subject pronoun; PLB = plural bound subject pronoun; PL = nominal plural; PLOB = plural bound object pronoun; SGB = singular free subject pronoun; SB = singular bound pronoun; SEQ = sequential tense; SGOB = singular bound object pronoun; SGPOSS = singular possessive pronoun; SGREFL = singular reflexive pronoun; TOP = topicalizer.

2.   Syntax and morphology

In comparison to other WAPs, GhP is notable for its lack of some of the more central grammatical morphemes and in some areas of grammar it looks like a simplified version of e.g. NigP. Nevertheless, the structure of GhP is still complex enough for it to be called a creole, even though it is not used as a mother tongue. The following will place special emphasis on GhP's major divergences from NigP.

2.1.   Verb phrase

GhP, like the rest of the WAPs, is characterized by preverbal markers that express modal and aspectual meanings. Bickerton (1980: 5–6) outlined the following prototypical Creole TMA system, which he claimed to be universal in Creole languages:

(a) the zero form marks simple past for action verbs and non-past for state verbs.
(b) a marker of anterior aspect [sic] indicates past-before-past for action verbs and simple past for state verbs.
(c) a marker of irrealis aspect [sic] indicates 'unreal time' (= futures, conditionals, subjunctives, etc.) for all verbs.
(d) a marker of non-punctual aspect indicates durative or iterative aspect for action verbs.

The following table is a contrastive overview of these Bickertonian tense-mood-aspect markers in NigP and GhP (grave accent = low tone):

Table 1.   The NigP and GhP core TMA systems

Tense		Mood		Aspect	
NigP	**GhP**	**NigP**	**GhP**	**NigP**	**GhP**
bìn anterior	Ø	*gò* irrealis	*gò* irrealis	*dè* incompletive	*dè* incompletive

2.1.1.   Tense

GhP lacks the marker for anterior tense (*contra* Turchetta 1996: 124). Therefore, relative tense (past for stative verbs and past-before-past for action verbs) can only be inferred from the context or from time adverbials. Also, since there is no formal way of marking anteriority, the Bickertonian default tense allocation for active and stative verbs (point [a] above) plays a less prominent role in GhP. In fact, unmarked verbs, stative or active, are equally open to a non-past, past, or past-before-past reading in GhP.

Although GhP shares the incompletive (= nonpunctual) aspect marker with other WAPs, another central aspectual auxiliary is absent from its TMA inventory: in NigP the completive marker is preverbal *dɔn*, and its negative counterpart is *nɛva*. *Dɔn* is unknown in GhP (*contra* Amoako 1992: 73). However, GhP shares with other WAPs an alternative strategy to encode completion: serialized *finiʃ*, which follows the verb marked for completiveness:

(1)   à   baf **finiʃ**,   à   dè   kom ma   hɛ o.
      1SGB bathe COMPL 1SGB INCOMP comb 1SGPOSS hair TOP
      'I had finished my bath and was combing my hair'.

Other TMA markers that are shared by NigP and GhP will only illustrated here
by one example each:

(2)   afta skul à   tek hɛ   as ɛ gɛlfrɛn   bifɔ   wì
      after school 1SGB take 3SGOB as a girlfriend before 1PLB

      kam bɔn.   (*kam* – sequential tense)
      SEQ give-birth
      'She became my girlfriend after school and then we got a child'.

2.1.2. Mood

(3)   jù   no   **gò   fit**   slip.   (*gò* – irrealis, *fit* – ability)
      2SGB NEG IRR ABIL sleep
      'You won't be able to sleep'.

(4)   wì   fɔ   giv   àm   tʃans.   (*fɔ* – deontic mood)
      1PLB DEO give 3SGOB chance
      'We should/have to give her/him a chance'.

(5)   dɛ   fait   ì   **wan** tʃɔp-tʃɔp a: frɔm dat   ples   tu
      DEF fight 3SGB INT eat(x2)   TOP from DEM place to

      aʃanti   ridʒɛn   o.   (*wan* – proximate future)
      Ashanti region   TOP
      'The fighting was about to spread from that place to the Ashanti
      Region'.

The NigP infinitive marker *fɔ* is not attested in GhP.

2.1.3. Aspect

(6)   dɛ   tin   ì   no   **dè**   go fɔwad. (*dè* – incompletive)
      DEF thing 3SGB NEG INCOMP go forward
      'The thing was not moving forward'.

2.1.4. Copula verbs

GhP does not have the positive equative copula/highlighter *na*, common in
other WAPs. Instead, GhP makes use of *bì* (7), which is also used in cleft sentences (8). In both cases, NigP, CamP, and Krio use *na*.

(7)   wì   tiŋk   se   ì   **bì**   bad tiŋ.
       1PLB   think   COMP   3SGB   COP   bad thing
       'We thought it was something bad'.

(8)   ì   **bì**   so fɛs   ŋkruma   wan   mek   àm.
       3SGB   COP   so first   Nkrumah   INT   make   3SGOB
       'That's how Nkrumah wanted to do it first'.

Although existential *get* 'there is' is attested in GhP, it is not used in the impersonal *i get* (3sg *get*) construction as in NigP. Rather, speakers of GhP prefer
wì get:

(9)   **wì**   **gɛt**   sɔm   lokal   lamp.
       1PLB   get   INDEF   local   lamp
       'There are local lamps'.

2.1.5. Comparison

Comparison is usually achieved by serialized *pas*. In other WAPs, the omission of the object of comparison in such constructions conveys a comparative
or superlative meaning. In GhP, however, deletion of the object (bold in the
following example) is not possible.

(10)   ì   luk   fain sɛf   pas   **dis**   **aua**   **ɛria**   sɛf.
       3SGB   look   fine FOC   pass   DEM   1PP   area   FOC
       'It even looks nicer than our area'.

2.2.   Noun Phrase

2.2.1. Articles

Non-specific (generic) nouns, both countables and uncountables, are not accompanied by an article:

(11)   nɔmali   wì   dè   bai   Ø ʃip   kil   àm.
       normally   1PLB   INCOMP   buy   sheep   kill   3SGOB
       'Normally, we buy a sheep and kill it'.

Specific singular and plural nouns can be marked by the invariant definite article *dɛ*, corresponding to NigP *di*:

(12) jù   gò   fit   stan   ɛn   luk   insai   **dɛ**   sinɛma   sɛf.
     2SGB   IRR   ABIL   stand   and   look   inside   DEF   cinema   FOC
     'You would have been able to stand (on a heap) and look into the cinema'.

(13) **dɛ**   traib   we   à   kɔl   fɔ   jù   ì   bì   dɛm.
     DEF   tribe   COMP   1SGB   call for 2SGOB 3SGB   COP   3PLF

     dɛa   tʃifs   de
     3SGPOSS   chiefs   COP
     'The chiefs of the tribes that I enumerated are around'.

The GhP indefinite articles are different from those of NigP. In GhP, *sɔm* is usually used in the singular (PL in NigP):

(14) wì   gɛt   **sɔm**   ɛria   dè   dè   kɔl   àm   kaokodi.
     1PLB   get   INDEF   area   3PLB   IRR   call 3SGOB   Kaokodi
     'There is an area that is called Kaokodi'.

Only occasionally does *sɔm* occur in plural contexts, its common environment in NigP:

(15) à   si   **sɔm**   smɔ-smɔ   pikins.
     1SGB   see   INDEF   small(x2)   child-PL
     'I saw small children'.

Note that in these cases, plurality of the noun is always also indicated by other means such as reduplication of an attributive adjective and/or an *-s* suffix. In more acrolectal varieties, *sɔm* varies with the StGhE *ɛ* in the singular:

(16) à   de   as   ɛ   batʃɛla   ap   til   nau.
     1SGB   COP   as   INDEF   bachelor   up   till   now
     'I have been living as a bachelor until now'.

In the singular, *sɔm* is occasionally replaced by *wan*, the NigP indefinite singular article:

(17) àm   draivin   **wan**   alahadʒi.
     I'm   driving   INDEF   Hadji
     'I'm driving a Hadji'.

Article + noun + article structures occur in the student variety (i.e. an informal, spontaneous spoken but nevertheless educated subset of English in Ghana) and are calqued on the respective structure in Akan (i.e. one of the major languages of Ghana). (18) illustrates the postposed Akan specifier *bi*:

(18) *a   dʒas de   insai sɔm   smɔl ʃɔts   **bi.***
1SGB just COP   inside some small shorts [Akan specifier]
'I was only wearing shorts'.

Note that the use of all overt articles is optional if the context provides sufficient information concerning the definiteness of the noun.

Table 2.   The GhP article system

		Non-specific	Specific Indefinite	definite
Countables	**singular**	Ø	sɔm, ɛ, (wan), Ø	dɛ, Ø
	plural	Ø	(sɔm), Ø	dɛ, Ø
Uncountables		Ø	sɔm, Ø	dɛ, Ø

2.2.2. Number

GhP does not have the postposed plural marker *dɛm* found in Krio, CamP, and NigP. However, there are several ways to indicate nominal plurality. First, plural nouns may remain unmarked, so that number has to be inferred from the context. In the following example, the plurality of *wumã* can be deduced from the fact that the resumptive pronoun in the relative clause is third person plural:

(19) *wì   gɛt   sɔm   **wumã** we   **dè**   dè   kuk.*
1PLB get   INDEF woman   COMP 3PLB INCOMP cook
'There were women who cooked (for us)'.

By far the most common plural marker in GhP is the *-s* suffix, as in StGhE. The *-s* may occur on its own or combine with other pluralization strategies, such as reduplication (21):

(20) *dis **tʃifs**   ì   bì   dɛm   gɛt   nima.*
DEM chief-PL 3SGB COP   3PLF get   Nima
'It is these chiefs who rule Nima'.

(21) *ʃuʃain-ʃuʃain **bɔis***
shoe-shine(x2) boy-PL
'Shoe-shiner boys'

For the expression of plurality through reduplication of nouns see 2.4.1. below.

2.2.3. *Personal pronouns*

GhP has two sets of pronouns: free and bound. Free pronouns bear a high tone (marked with an acute accent) and cannot directly precede a verb. They occur in emphatic or contrastive contexts, e.g. in the focussed position of cleft constructions, while the low-toned bound pronouns (glossed B) always precede the verb slot. In (22) the focussed 3SG pronoun occurs in the free form *in*, whereas the one in the following relative clause is the bound form:

(22) ì   bì   **in**   [*we*   ì   *mek   gɔvanmɛnt   no   put*
      3SGB COP 3SG [COMP 3SGB CAUS government NEG put

      mɔ   prɛʃa   fɔ   wi].
      more   pressure for 1PLF]
      'That is what prevents the government from using more pressure on us'.

Free subject pronouns cannot directly precede the verb but must be separated from it by an intervening bound pronoun:

(23) **mi**   **à**   *no   gò   fit   bai   àm.*
      1SG   1SGB   NEG   IRR   ABIL buy   3SGOB
      'I won't be able to buy it'.

Tables 3 and 4 give an overview of the GhP subject and object pronouns:

Table 3. GhP subject pronouns

| | **Subject pronouns (free)** | | | | **Subject pronouns (bound)** | |
	sg	*pl*			*sg*	*pl*
1	mi	wi		1	à	wì
2	ju	ju		2	jù	jù
3	in	dɛm		3	ì	dè, dèm

Table 4. GhP object pronouns

| | **Object pronouns (free)** | | | | **Object pronouns (bound)** | |
	sg	*pl*			*sg*	*pl*
1	mi	wi, ɔs, ɛs, as		1	mì	wì, ɔ̀s, ɛ̀s, às
2	ju	ju		2	jù	jù
3	am	dɛm		3	àm	dèm

Like in other WAPs, there is variation in the first person plural between basilectal *wi* and the successively more acrolectal forms *ɔs, ɛs, as*.

The major characteristic that distinguishes the GhP pronominal system from that of the other WAP dialects is the absence of the second person plural form *una*. Instead, GhP has *ju*, a form identical with the StGhE pronoun. Further, the educated variety of GhP has two possessive pronouns that to my knowledge do not occur anywhere else in West Africa: *wana* 'our' and *dema* 'their'.

2.2.4. Noun + bound pronoun constructions

A construction that is similar to the free + bound pronoun sequence mentioned in the previous section can be found with nouns in subject position. In principle, all nouns can directly be followed by a verb (24) or may optionally be separated from it by a bound pronoun (25):

(24)   **wɔta   kari   dὲm   ɔl   insai   dε   gɔta.**
      water   carry   3PLOB   all   inside   DEF   gutter
      'The flood washed them all into the drain'.

(25)   *mà   sɔfa   ì   plenti   hiε.*
      1SGPOSS   suffer   3SGB   be-plenty   here
      'My suffering is a lot here'.

However, noun + bound pronoun constructions are especially frequent in emphatic environments, e.g. in focus or emphasis through *sεf*, or topicalization through e.g. *diε* or *nɔ*:

(26a)   *fɔrenε   sεf   ì   dè   wɔka̧.*
       foreigner   FOC   3SGB   INCOMP   walk
       'Even foreigners walk around'.

(26b)   *smɔl   **bebi   diε**   ì   plenti.*
       small   baby   TOP   3SGB   be-many
       'There are many small babies'.

Abstracting from these examples, any separation of the subject noun from the verb through intervening material favours the insertion of a bound pronoun. For example, relative clauses modifying a subject head are in almost all cases followed by a bound pronoun.

(27)   *dε*   **bɔs**   [*we*   *ì*   *de*   *dε*]   *ì*   *bì*   *mà*
DEF   boss   [COMP   3SGB   COP   there]   3SGB   COP   1SGPOSS

ɔŋkεl.
uncle
'The boss there is my uncle'.

2.2.5. Prepositions

Fɔ is the main general locative/directional preposition in GhP. As in NigP, locative *fɔ* can be followed by *insai* or *autsai* (< *inside, outside*) to express location in or outside the point of reference. The *insai/autsai* + noun construction following the preposition resembles a possessive noun phrase – 'the inside of Accra' in (28). The uneducated variety prefers constructions where *insai* and *autsai* precede the possessed. The preposition may be omitted:

(28)   *jù*   *de*   *go*   [*fɔ*   [*insai*   *akra*]].
2SGB   INCOMP   go   for   inside   Accra
'You go to the centre of Accra'.

In student pidgin, an informal variety spoken in a more or less educated context, *insai* and *autsai* follow the reference point:

(29)   *dè*   *go*   *tek*   *kɔva*   [*fɔ*   [*buʃ*   *insai*]].
3PLB   go   take   cover   for   bush   inside
'They went and took cover in the bush'.

Another characteristic of the student variety is the use of *plas* 'with':

(30)   *ì*   *kam*   **plas**   *sɔm*   *big*   *taim*   *raid.*
3SGB   come   plus   INDEF   big   time   ride
'He came with a flashy car'.

2.3.   Conjunctions

Dεn 'and' is used in the educated variety to conjoin words and phrases, as in:

(31a)   *mi*   **dεn**   *dε*   *tʃik*   *gò*   *tɔk*   *smɔ*   *nɔ.*
1SG   and   DEF   chick   IRR   talk   small   TOP
'The chick and I will talk a little'.

(31b)   *à*   *fɔ*   *trai*   **dεn**   *tɔk*   *sɔm*   *dʒeman.*
1SGB   DEO   try   and   talk   INDEF   German
'I should try to speak some German'.

Very occasionally *plas* 'and, with' is heard in the uneducated variety:

(32) *dɛ   mɔni   we   ì   tek   bì   ĩ   õ   **plas** dɛ*
      DEF money COMP 3SGB   take COP 3SGPOSS   own and   DEF

      bɛt.
      bet
      'The money that he took was his own and the bet'.

2.4.   Reduplication

Reduplication is very frequent in GhP. It affects verbs, nouns, attributive adjectives (predicative forms are verbs in GhP), time and manner adverbials, adverbs, and numerals. The prototypical function of reduplication is the expression of plurality (verbs, nouns, numerals) or intensity (adjectives, adverbials). As to the formal characteristics of the process: GhP reduplicates the whole word stem without changing its phonological or tonemic form. For a more exhaustive treatment of reduplication in GhP, see Huber (2003).

2.4.1.   Reduplication of nouns

Apart from *-s* suffixation, reduplication of nouns is another strategy to indicate the plural. Noun reduplications carry with them a dispersive ('here and there, all over the place') or sometimes an iterative ('again and again, i.e. nothing but') meaning, as exemplified in (33):

(33a) *wì   no   dè   si   sɔm   **lait-lait-lait-lait-lait-lait***
       1PLB NEG   INCOMP   see   some light(x6)   (dispersive).
       'We did not see any lights (here and there)'.

(33b) *fɛs   jù   dè   tʃɔp   ɔiɛl-ɔiɛl* (iterative).
       first 2SGB INCOMP   [eat]   oil(x2)
       'First, you eat oil (again and again, i.e. nothing but nice food)'.

Plurality of the noun can also be expressed by reduplicating an attributive adjective (34). This is often accompanied by an *-s* suffix on the noun (35):

(34) *ì   kari   **smɔl-smɔl**   bebi.*
      3SGB   carry   small(x2)   baby
      'It carried small babies away'.

(35) *dè   dè   giv   ɔs   sɔm   **smɔ-smɔ-smɔ**   tablɛs.*
      3PLB   INCOMP   give   1PLOB   INDEF   small(x3)   tablet-PL
      'They gave us small tablets'.

Since reduplicated adjectives can also signal intensity – see (38)–(39) below
– the first example in (34) has two potential meanings: (a) simple plural – 'small
babies', and (b) intensive – 'very small babies'.

Reduplication as a word-formation strategy appears to be restricted to the
derivation of deverbal nouns. As a rule, GhP verbs can be used as nouns without reduplicating them – as in e.g. *dɛ sɔfa de* (DEF suffer COP) 'there is suffering around'. What reduplication adds is a dispersive/iterative meaning, e.g.
'recurring births here and there, in different families' (36a) or 'poverty everywhere you look' in example (36b).

(36a) *dɛ*   **bɔn-bɔn**   *ì*   *plɛnti* (verb → noun).
     DEF   give-birth(x2)   3SGB   be-plenty
     'The births are many'.

(36b) *ì*   *bì*   **puɔ-puɔ** *dè*   *mek* *jù* *dè*
     3SGB COP   poor(x2) INCOMP CAUS 2SGB INCOMP

     go   *bus* (adjective → noun).
     go   booze
     'It is poverty that makes you go and drink'.

2.4.2. *Reduplication of adjectives and adverbials*

Reduplicated time and manner adverbials express precision (37) or intensification (38):

(37) *ì*   *bì*   **nau-nau-nau** *if* *jù*   *go* *ritʃ* *dɛa...*
    3SGB COP   now(x3)   if   2SGB go   reach there...
    'Even at this very moment, if you go there...'

(38) *à*   *tɔk* *tu* *dɛm*   **wɛl-wɛl**.
    1SGB talk to   3PLOB well(x2)
    'I talked to them very sensibly'.

The function of adjective reduplication is also intensification:

(39) *à*   *go* *tek* *jù*   **dip-dip-dip-dip-dip-dip** *plesis*
    1SGB IRR take 2SGOB deep(x6)   place-PL

     we *ju* *jɔsɛf* *gò* *dè*   *si.*
     COMP 2SG 2SGREFL IRR INCOMP see
     'I'll take you to very remote places where you will see with your own
     eyes'.

2.4.3. Reduplication of verbs

Reduplication of verbs expresses plurality of action. This can either be iterative/habitual (repeated or regularly recurring actions) or dispersive (several actions performed by one or more individuals, affecting several objects or different locations). One of the principal differences between iterative and dispersive aspect is whether or not the actions are performed at recurring intervals or more or less synchronically.

(a)   Iterative or habitual
In GhP, the iterative aspect of the reduplicated verb is often emphasized by the non-punctual (habitual or progressive) marker *dè*. An example of iteration is given in (40):

(40)   *ì   bì   biko we   ì   de   dɛ   we   ì*
       3SGB COP Biko COMP 3SGB COP there COMP 3SGB

      dè   **vɔmit-vɔmit** *dɛn* **ʃɪt-ʃɪt**.
      INCOMP   vomit(x2)   and   shit(x2)
      'It was Biko who (was there and) kept on vomiting and shitting'.

(b)   Dispersive
Examples are (41) with a singular subject and (42) with a plural subject:

(41)   *mà   tao   ì   **tia-tia**.*
       1SGPOSS towel 3SGB tear(x2)
       'My towel is all torn (i.e. torn here and there)'.

(42)   *dos   pipu   **dè**   de   insai dè   **haid-haid** dɛmsɛf.*
       DEM people 3PLB COP inside 3PLB hide(x2)   3PR
       'Those people who were inside hid themselves (i.e. individually in different places)'.

2.5.   Focus

Sentence constituents can be focussed through the insertion of emphatic particles after the focussed element. The most common focus particle is *sɛf* 'even', which not only focalizes individual nouns, verbs, or adverbs, but also entire noun phrases, verb phrases, or adverbial phrases:

(43a) *nau   à   **ʃɪt**   **wɔka** sɛf   kã   ʃɪt.*
       now   1SGB ABIL walk FOC come shit
       'Now I am even able to walk (here) to ease myself'.

(43b) _{NP}[*dɛ* *rum* [*we* *mi* *à* *de* *insai*]] *sɛf* *kɔlapst.*
        DEF room COMP 1SG 1SGB COP inside FOC collapsed
        'Even the room in which I lived collapsed'.

2.6. Topicalization and emphasis

The two major topicalization strategies in GhP are the use of particles after the topicalized element and left-dislocation. The most common topic particles are *aː*, *diɛ*, *kɔraː*, *nɔ*, *paː*, *tu*, and *nau*. Topicalization will be illustrated with sentences containing the two most common particles, *nɔ* and *diɛ*:

(44) [[*dat* *big* *gɔta*] **nɔ** *we* *wì* *gɛt* *àm* *hiɛ*] **nɔ.**
      DEF big gutter TOP COMP 1PLB get 3SGOB here TOP
      'That big drain that we get here' (topicalization of NP and sentence).

(45) [*dɛ* *tin* [*we* *wì* *dè* *tʃɔp* *nau*]] **diɛ,** *ì*
      DEF thing COMP 1PLB INCOMP [eat] now TOP 3SGB

      no *gò* *fit.*
      NEG IRR ABIL
      'She will not be able (to eat) what we eat now' (complex NP).

The particle *o* is found in sentence-final position and adds emphasis to the whole sentence. It signals emotional involvement on the part of the speaker or appeals for hearer empathy:

(46) *mà* *frɛn,* *jù* *gò* *pe* *fɔ* *dis* *wan* **o.**
      1SGPOSS friend, 2SGB IRR pay for DEM one EMPH
      'My friend, you will (have to) pay for this one!'

The other major topicalization strategy is left-dislocation. This moves the topicalized element to the beginning of the sentence and fills the element's original position with an anaphoric pronoun. Left-dislocated elements may optionally be introduced by *fɔ* 'as for':

(47) **(*fɔ*)** **kliniks**, *wɪ* *gɛt* **àm** *nau.*
      for clinic-PL 1PLB get 3SGB now
      'As for clinics, we now have them'.

Exercises and study questions

1. Review the use of the focus marker [sEf] in sentences (10), (12), (26) and (43). How would this nuance be expressed in Standard English?

2. What similarities are there between verb and noun reduplication in sections 2.4.1 and 2.4.3?

3. What are the pragmatic functions of the particle *o* in sentence (46)?

4. How does 'serialised *finish*' (2.1.1) function?

5. How does incompletive *de* function semantically?

Selected references

Please consult the General references for titles mentioned in the text but not included in the references below. For a full bibliography see the accompanying CD-ROM.

Amoako, Joe K.Y.B.
    1992   Ghanaian Pidgin English: in search of synchronic, diachronic, and sociolin-
            guistic evidence. Ph.D. dissertation, University of Florida at Gainsville.
Bickerton, Derek
    (1974) Creolization, linguistic universals, natural semantax and the brain. In: Richard
    1980   R. Day (ed.), *Issues in English Creoles. Papers from the 1975 Hawaii
            Conference*, 1–18. Heidelberg: Groos.
Huber, Magnus
    1999   *Ghanaian Pidgin English in its West African Context. A Sociohistorical
            and Structural Analysis*. Amsterdam/Philadephia: Benjamins.
    2003   Verbal reduplication in Ghanaian Pidgin English. Origins, forms, and func-
            tions. In: Silvia Kouwenberg (ed.), *Twice as Meaningful. Reduplication
            in Pidgins, Creoles and Other Contact Languages*, 139–154. London:
            Battlebridge.
Turchetta, Barbara
    1996   *Lingua e Diversità. Multilinguismo e Lingue Veicolari in Africa Occiden-
            tale*. Milano: FrancoAngeli.

Liberian Settler English: morphology and syntax[*]

John Victor Singler

1.   Introduction

The Liberian Settlers of today are the descendants of the 16,000 African Americans who immigrated to Liberia in the years from 1821 to 1872, with the largest numbers immigrating in the period from 1848 to 1854. The present examination of the syntax of Liberian Settler English (LibSE) focuses on the speech of the Settlers of Sinoe County, specifically on the speech of elders who lived in the upriver settlements above Greenville, the county seat (see chapter on LibSE phonology, this volume). Several factors point to the LibSE of Sinoe as especially likely to provide information about the history of African American Vernacular English (AAVE). To begin with, most of the immigrants to Sinoe came from the Lower South, primarily Georgia and Mississippi, but also South Carolina, Louisiana, and Alabama. Further, factors that might have pushed the Settlers' language towards standard English, e.g. government support of education or the presence of missionaries, were virtually non-existent in Sinoe before the middle part of the twentieth century. At the same time, chronic hostility between the Sinoe Settlers and the indigenous people of Sinoe likely served to limit local influence upon the Sinoe Settlers' LibSE.

The discussion that follows is divided into seven sections. First, the following aspects of LibSE grammar are addressed in sections 2. – 5.: the verb phrase, adjectives, the noun phrase, and relativization and complementation. Then, the position of LibSE within the African American Diaspora is considered, with reference not only to its status as a modern descendant of the speech of agricultural workers in the lower South of the US around 1850 (section 6.), but also to its status as a Liberian speech variety and the possible influence upon it of contact with other Liberian speech varieties (section 7.). The final section 8. assesses the future of LibSE.

2.   The verb phrase

2.1.   Tense – aspect

2.1.1. Completive, perfective, and perfect aspect and the past tense

There is an extensive overlap in function among verb suffixes and preverbal auxiliaries in LibSE. Accordingly, while one can provide a characterization of a given form, that characterization will not necessarily be discrete and is not necessarily part of a simple opposition to some other form or forms.

The treatment of the completive – perfective – perfect range is a case in point. Definitions of the three concepts can make them sound distinct, but the reality is that there is often extensive overlap among them. The distinction between the concepts of completive and perfective with reference to actions illustrates this. Completive focuses on the completion of an action, while perfective presents the action as an unanalyzed whole. Since ordinarily one cannot present an action as an unanalyzed whole until after its completion, completive and perfective are hard to distinguish (cf. Singler 1984). The LibSE auxiliaries *feni* (< *finish*) and *done* would seem, on the surface, to focus on the endpoint of an action or state. Yet they can be used with reference to actions where the endpoint – as opposed to the action as an complete entity – is trivial or irrelevant. This is the case in (1).

(1)   *Now I got a son, that my first child, a son till he **done born** child now.*
       Now I have a son–he's my first child–a son who's big enough that he
       has now fathered a child.'

Similarly, there are contexts when an action is of extremely short duration and its internal constituency irrelevant. In such cases, it is the complete action – rather than the act of completing it – that is temporally relevant. In (2), for example, the emphasis is on the act of telling, not on the endpoint of the act of telling.

(2)   *In that time, the old people, if you go, when you get to they place, time you get there, "What you ma send you for?" You better tell 'em quick. And when you **feni telling** them, [they say,] "All right, come on, go home."*

The markers in question can function to signal the perfect aspect as well, as in (3):

(3)   *I **done forget** the year I born.*

The choices open to speakers include the auxiliaries *done, feni, na,* and *have/had* as well as the verb suffix *-ed. Done* is the single most salient affective marker of Settler identity. Non-Settlers do not use it, and Settlers and non-Settlers alike identify it as signalling Settlerhood. Within the Sinoe Settler corpus, there is a three-way social distinction that consistently signals linguistic difference, namely whether an individual held a government job as a teacher, held some other government job (such as a justice of the peace or janitor), or never worked for the government at all. A part of the significance of this division is that those who never held a government job are the ones most likely to display vernacular LibSE features in the course of sociolinguistic interviews, with teachers the least likely to do so. The distribution of the use of *done* is a case in point. The speakers in the corpus who never held a government job use the auxiliary *done* quite frequently, while teachers use it rarely if at all. The middle group – those who held government jobs other than teacher – pattern in the middle, using *done* occasionally but not frequently.

In contrast (as discussed in Section 7. below), *feni* has entered LibSE from Vernacular Liberian English (VLE), the pidginized variety that most non-Settler speakers of English use. Here, too, the distribution is tied to questions of contact: Settlers who lived or worked as adults in Greenville, the more integrated county seat, use *feni* while other Sinoe Settlers do not.

The third option, the auxiliary *na*, illustrated in (4) and (5), is used less frequently, and its provenance is not so straightforward.

(4)   *I swear, Sarah, they **na** stay long o.*
       '… they've been gone a long time.'

(5)   *Like we sitting down here talking, me and my children and my wife,*
       we sitting down talking, the moment we see a friend coming to me
       and my wife, as that man or that woman reach in the house and speak,
       "Yall, hello," before we feni greeting them when, to say, "Take seat,"
       *those children **na get** up long time and gone.*
       'The way we're sitting down here talking now, if it were me and my
       children and my wife and we were sitting down talking, the moment
       we saw a friend coming to me and my wife, when the man or that
       woman entered inside the house and spoke, "Yall, hello," by the time
       we had greeted them and told them to have a seat, those children
       would have gotten up a long time ago and left the room.'

Na is an auxiliary in VLE as well as in LibSE. Singler (1987) presents various scenarios for its origin, arguing ultimately that it represents a phonological adaptation of *done* (the Kru languages along the coast not making a distinction between

/dṼ/ and /nV/). The Sinoe Settlers do not use *na* a lot, but they perceive it as theirs rather than as a recent borrowing like *feni*. (On the basis of homophony, Liberians analyze it as deriving from the temporal adverb *now*.) The auxiliaries *feni* and *done* can co-occur (as in [6]), as can *na* and *feni* (as in [7]), and any of the three can co-occur with a form of *have*. However, *na* and *done* cannot co-occur. This would seem to constitute evidence that *na* does come from *done*.

(6)   *We two, we get to sewing them, we **feni done sew** it, then I join it up.*
       'The two of us, we get to sewing quilt pieces, and when we finish, then I join the pieces up.'

(7)   *We **na feni** do the work.*
       'We've done the work.'

Forms of *have* are also used frequently, serving to signal present perfect and past perfect. The form of the auxiliary is very often *ha*, with the final consonant absent on the surface. In those cases it is not always clear whether the intended form is *have*, *had* or *has*.

The addition of the *-ed* suffix is variable. Its principal semantic function is to signal past tense, with perfective aspect often but not always inferable. Whether or not speakers use the *-ed* suffix is sensitive to semantic factors and phonological constraints. In the course of sociolinguistic interviews with elders, a lot of questions arise as to how things used to be. When LibSE speakers respond with non-specific examples or how things used to be or describe past procedures that no longer obtain, they do not use the past-tense suffix. (8) illustrates this:

(8)   JVS: *When you were a young boy, did you use to fight with the*
                  other boys?
       Ishmael: *Oh, when I wa young boy?*
       JVS: *Yes.*
       Ishmael: *Well, yeah. Because ... sometime we goes to play ... and*
                  *fuss **come** there. You **pick** fuss at me, I **pick** fuss, we **fight**.*
                  [laughs] That's all.

On the other hand, a LibSE speaker who is describing an actual event or state is likely to use the past-tense suffix if the verb is perfective, somewhat less likely if it is imperfective. Moreover, speakers are most likely to mark past tense overtly if a strong verb is involved, e.g. *took* for *take*, and quite likely to do so if the verb, while weak, takes a syllabic ending, e.g. *reported* for *report*. They are far less likely to mark the past tense overtly if the verb takes a non-syllabic weak ending, especially if the stem ends with a consonant. In such a case, the addition of the suffix creates a coda cluster, and these are disfavored in LibSE (see the article on LibSE phonology, this volume).

2.1.2. Imperfective aspect

While the past-tense suffix is reasonably robust and will ordinarily be present if the semantic and phonological conditions are right (see 2.1.1. above), the same does not hold for the third person singular -*s*. A crucial difference between -*ed* and the third person singular -*s* is that there are a number of irregular verbs, so that the existence of past tense marking does not depend solely on the saliency of a coda consonant. One might make the same point about plural marking (discussed below in 4.1.). Here, too, there are commonly occurring irregular forms. In contrast, there is nothing like that for the third person singular -*s*. The copula aside, the only stem change that accompanies the addition of third person singular -*s* is the vowel change that occurs in the shift from *do* to *does*, from *have* to *has*, and from *say* to *says*. Speakers of LibSE rarely use the third person singular -*s*. When they use it at all, it is likely to be to mark habitual occurrence, to be with the verb *go*, and/or to be with reference to religion. The example in (9) illustrates all three of these.

(9)   *Every Sunday we **goes** to church.*

Even when these favouring conditions hold, the use of the third person singular -*s* is infrequent.

Progressive aspect is routinely signalled by the -*ing* suffix (pronounced [ẽ]). In standard English, the appropriate tensed form of *be* co-occurs with V-*ing*, e.g. *it's raining* and *I was just leaving*. In LibSE, on the other hand, it is relatively rare for a tensed form of *be* to co-occur with V-*ing* in a non-past environment. A tensed form of *be* does co-occur with V-*ing* when the verb has specific reference (as opposed to a hypothetical example or non-specific instantiation, as discussed in 2.1.1.). An exception to this characterization of *be* involves *when* clauses; invariant *be* often co-occurs with V-*ing* in them, like in (10):

(10)   *Even much, my little son, I was teaching him how to make quilt but this young generation, they like to laugh at the children **when** they **be turning** toward these thing.*

Habitual and iterative actions can be marked by zero, by the third person singular -*s*, by *də*, by *de*, or by *useta*. *Də*, discussed below in Sections 5. and 6., is illustrated in (11), and *de* in (12). Each of them is tenseless and occurs in non-past and past environments alike.

(11)   *Every time I see someone from America I **də ask** them say, "Yall hear talk of any Walkers?"*

(12)   *Cash bag, I **de tote** the cash bag on my head, to carry it from the pay ground, to, to the waterside.*
        'The bag containing the payroll, I used to carry it on my head from the pay ground to waterside.'

The tenselessness may follow from the strong tendency in LibSE for overt past-tense marking to be largely restricted to specific events rather than the habitual, non-specific ones that *də* and *de* characteristically mark. *Də* ordinarily is restricted in distribution to habituals; moreover, it occurs with the bare verb. In contrast, *de* can occur with states, too (13), and it can occur either with the bare verb or with V-*ing* (14).

(13)   *I went and sat for the examination because I **de want** to be a travelling elder.*

(14)   *He **de try/trying** to find a job.*

As noted in Section 6. below, while virtually all LibSE speakers use *də*, it is used most by the people who live in the upriver settlements, the speakers of what appears to be the most conservative variety of LibSE. In contrast, *de* is used primarily by speakers with extensive formal education. In the phonology chapter on LibSE (this volume), the point was made that formal education serves an integrative function in Liberia. *De* is an imperfective auxiliary in VLE (and in the English pidgins of West Africa more generally). Within VLE, *de* is a basilectal feature, indeed a stigmatized basilectal feature. It is ironic, then, that the Sinoe settlers who use it are the ones with more education, not less.

LibSE also makes use of the past habitual AUX *useta*, which can mark past states as well. It is subject to phonological reduction, occurring as *stə* and even as *sə*. In Standard English (StE), *used to* alternates with *would*, with *used to* marking the first of a series of past habitual events, and *would* marking the rest of them. While that alternation also occurs in LibSE, it does not happen often. Instead, *useta* is used repeatedly, as in (15).

(15)   *We **useta go** to dances, we **useta play** music box, and guitar. We **useta come**, when we come, see us dancing, man. We **useta dance**. When we finish dancing, then we go home.*

2.2. Mood

The future is expressed both by *will* ([we]) and *gan*. (16) illustrates the use of *gan*.

(16)   *How he **gan** come back home today?*

Would and a range of English modals do crop up in LibSE, but only *can* and *must* occur with any frequency. *Must*, frequently pronounced [mə], has a wider semantic range in LibSE than it does in American vernaculars. One common use of it is in questions like the one in (17).

(17)   Q: *And how they can dance that one there?*
       A: *I **must** dance it?*
            'Should I dance it?"

2.3. The copula

A great deal of attention has been directed toward the copula in AAVE and in diaspora varieties, including LibSE (Singler 1991a). In his classic study of the copula, William Labov (1969) argued that AAVE was like other American vernaculars in having an underlying full copula and an optional rule of contraction that acted upon the copula in non-past contexts. He claimed that AAVE departed from the other vernaculars in having an additional rule of deletion that acted upon the output of the contraction rule. Romaine (1982) argued for a different relationship for the three surface variants. Like Labov, Romaine posited an underlying full copula. However, she posited an optional rule of deletion; then, for full forms that had not undergone the deletion rule, she posited an optional rule of contraction.

The LibSE of Sinoe is crucially different from the other varieties under consideration and is indeed different from other varieties of LibSE. In the LibSE of Sinoe, the choice is binary, between a zero variant and a surface variant. When one organizes the data by subject type, there is no category for which a three-way division exists. Instead, the surface forms are the following:

subject	copula
I	*'m*
he, she, it, that, what	*'s*
here, there, where, this	*is*
Singular full NP	*is*
these, those, they, we, you, yall	*are*
Plural full NP	*are*

Singler (1993) proposes to account for the variation with a rule of insertion rather than deletion. There is one exception to the assertion that no three-way division exists. While ordinarily the choice for *he/she* is either *'s* or zero, *he* (or *He*) *is* and *she is* do occur when the topic is God or religion.

Labov (1969) asserts that deletion of the AAVE copula is restricted to non-past copulas (and not even to all of those, in that *I'm* and *it's/that's/what's* are categorical in AAVE). However, in LibSE zero copulas sometimes show up in past-tense environments, as in the lower clause of the second sentence in (18). The person being described in (18) is the elderly speaker's grandfather, dead for more than sixty years at the time of the interview.

(18)   *So they came out now, and he drew about 61 acres of land in*
        Bluntsville. There where he at.
        'So they came out to Liberia now, and he was given about 61 acres in Bluntsville. That's where he was.'

Another copula worthy of mention is *sə*, discussed in Section 6. and illustrated in (19) and (20).

(19)   *But still we sə hard up.*
        'But still we're hard up.'

(20)   JVS: *And only boys would play [the game]? Or boys and girls?*
        Claudius: *Sə only boy. Only boy play Bantu. The girls got they own*
        play to play.

2.4.   Negation

As noted in Section 6. below, the use of *ain't* in place of *didn't* is a common occurrence in LibSE. *Ain't* can occur with past preterits (as in [21]), as well as with verbs that are arguably present perfect (as in [22]):

(21)   *I telling you what the old people told me now. Because that one I **ain't***
        ***see** with my own eye.*

(22)   *Sister Rose **ain't come** yet o.*

The negative auxiliary, whether *ain't*, *didn't*, or *don't*, is subject to extreme reduction. In the examples in (21) and (22), taken from sociolinguistic interviews, *ain't* is pronounced with a full vowel, i.e. as [ẽ]. At other times, speakers use the full forms *didn't* (pronounced [dẽ]) or *don't* [dõ]. However, the usual pronunciation of the negative auxiliary consists simply of a high-toned nasalized copy of the vowel preceding it, like in (23) – (25):

(23) ***He n't** [hı̃ı̃] tell me that.*

(24) *Slipper self, **I n't** [áǎ] use to wear.*
      'I didn't even use to wear slippers.'

(25) ***It n't** [eě] been paying me from that time.*
      'It hasn't been paying me since that time.'

Negative concord is a regular feature of LibSE, as illustrated in (26) and (27).

(26) *Churchy and myself, **I n't never** do **nothing** to him.*

(27) Q: *What happen you be walking and the night catch you, catches
          you on the road? What yall do?*
      A: *I **n't** gan **never** tamper to go long distance, I know night gan
          catch me on on the road, I **n't** gan get to **no** house.*
          'I would never attempt to go a long distance if I knew darkness
          was going to catch me on the road and I wouldn't be able to get
          to a house.'

In AAVE and other American dialects that have double negation, the usual site
for additional markers of negation is an indefinite NP. While LibSE can place
no in front of an indefinite noun, it also permits the emphatic use of negation in
front of adjectives (28) and definite nouns (29).

(28) *When I look at it, they say these is modern day, the thing better, but I
      n't see **no better**, I see worse.*

(29) *Oh, and my heart **don't** tell me to go to **no Monrovia**.*

In StE, when the subject phrase of a sentence is negative, the verb is not. LibSE
speakers vary as to whether they place negation in the verb phrase in such
cases, as illustrated in (30) and (31).

(30) ***No** organization in the church **can't** do without me.*

(31) *At that time **no** doctor was here.*

In general, LibSE speakers tend to use the pattern in (31), i.e. confining negation to the subject phrase, rather than that in (30). They perceive the sentence
in (30) as more formal, hence more appropriate with outsiders than in in-group
conversation (The Rev. Hosea Ellis, p.c.).

3.   Adjectives

3.1.   The status of adjectives

While there are Niger-Congo languages for which adjectives are syntactically a type of verb and while there has been an ongoing controversy in creole studies regarding the status of adjectives in particular creoles, there is no doubt that LibSE has true adjectives. At the same time, it is still the case that there are times when LibSE speakers treat adjectives like verbs. Specifically, speakers place preverbal auxiliaries immediately before adjectives, as in (32) – (34).

(32)   *Next morning, the soap **done hard**.*
        'By the next morning, the soap will have hardened completely.'

(33)   *But now, everybody **na kwi**.*
        'But now, everybody has become westernized.'

(34)   *So he said this S.A. Ross, he **də friendly** with the Dutch agent.*
        'So he said this S.A. Ross used to be friendly with the Dutch agent.'

3.2.   Comparatives and superlatives

It was noted above that preverbal auxiliary *done* is the linguistic badge of Settler identity par excellence. A further signal of Settler identity is the use of doubly marked comparatives (and superlatives), as in (35) and (36):

(35)   *But they are **more wiser** than what we are.*

(36)   *I would like it **more better** if I could see more change.*

In the case of double comparatives, the association of the construction with Settlers is reinforced by a fixed phrase used by Liberians generally. In the exchange of greetings, a jocular way of saying that things are going badly is to say:

(37)   *Congo man say "**worser**."*
        'As Settlers say, "The situation is worser."'

(The use of *Congo* to refer to Settlers is discussed in the chapter on LibSE phonology.)

4.   The noun phrase

4.1.   Plural marking

If a noun is semantically plural and morphologically irregular, it will be marked for the plural. In contrast, semantically plural *regular* nouns are variably marked, with overt marking occurring less than half the time. Whether or not a regular noun will be overtly marked is sensitive to a number of factors, including the final segment of the noun. If it is a sibilant and therefore the plural suffix is syllabic, overt marking is highly likely. In contrast, if the final segment is a non-sibilant consonant and therefore the plural suffix will create a coda cluster, then overt marking is far less likely. Particular semantic categories pattern in surprising ways, with units of time likely to be overtly marked while plants, crops, and units of money are extremely unlikely to take an overt suffix. More general syntactic-semantic categories fall in between. Generic plurals are also unlikely to receive plural marking (since they are not truly plurals). As with many other elements of the grammar, the likelihood that a form will appear is sensitive to a speaker's background. Thus, among the Sinoe Settlers, there is much less likelihood of overt plural marking if the speaker comes from an upriver settlement and/or has never held a government job. The relevance of a government job is that the speakers who are the most insularly Settler in their language tend to be those who never held government employment; the correlation between job status and frequency of overt plural forms suggests that wide scale marking of the plural is not a traditional feature of vernacular LibSE.

In the VLE basilect, as in West African pidgins more generally, the plural can be marked by placing *them* (pronounced [dɛ̃]) after the head noun. Settlers don't use *them* to mark the simple plural. They do, however, use it to signal the associative plural, as illustrated in (38) and (39).

(38)   ***David Mitchell them*** *use to draw their music box.*
'David Mitchell and his group used to play their concertinas.'

(39)   *So with that **my old lady them** reared plenty boys and girls to learn the Christian way of living.*
'So in that way, my mother and her generation trained many boys and girls in the Christian way of living.'

406 John Victor Singler

4.2. Possession: pronoun choice

Possession is ordinarily expressed by word order, with the possessor preceding the possessed, e.g. *his aunty husband; the people cows.* Among the speakers in the Sinoe Settler corpus, those who are teachers sometimes insert possessive *'s*, e.g. *my father's mother,* but other speakers do not. The possessive adjectives are the following:

my	*our* (or, infrequently, *we*)
you	*yall*
his, *her*	*they*

As the table suggests, *we* sometimes appears rather than *our*, as in (40):

(40)   *When we done make **we farm**, we n't know nothing about sell, we keep it, to have to eat.*
'After we made our farm, we didn't think at all about selling [the produce]; we kept it so that we would have something to eat.'

The modern distribution of *we* within the Sinoe community suggests that it is a feature of long standing within LibSE; what is not clear is whether the Sinoe Settlers brought *we* with them from the US or only adopted it after arriving in Liberia. The same uncertainty regarding provenance within LibSE applies to *we* as an object pronoun, as in (41):

(41)   *Our people didn't learn **we** how to swim.*

4.3. Prenominal elements: demonstratives

The usual plural demonstratives are *these* and *those* (pronounced [di(z)] and [do(z)]). In addition, some upriver speakers use preposed *them* in place of *those*, as in (42) and (43):

(42)   *But all **them big meats and thing**, they gone.*

(43)   ***Them** days we had plenty rice.*

At least among younger speakers in Greenville, preposed *them* marks one as being upriver and, therefore, "country".

5.   Relativization and complementation

5.1.   Relativization

LibSE uses the restrictive relative pronouns *who*, *what*, and infrequently *that*. *What* may be used with either human or non-human nouns. Examples of its use with human nouns are given in (44) and (45).

(44)   *They were the first immigrant **what** come out in Liberia.*

(45)   *Those Morris children **what** in Monrovia now and myself we grow together.*

For nonrestrictive relatives, LibSE uses *who*, *what* and infrequently *which*. While the use of *who* is confined to human nouns, *what* and *which* can be used with either human or non-human nouns.

5.2.   Complementation

The usual complementizer is *that*:

(46)   *But our mother told us **that** he say **that** he want to come to Liberia to find his people.*

With verbs of speaking and communication, *say* is also used, as in (47) – (50).

(47)   a. *So I went to the ... hospital and I **told** the people **say**, "Well, two months I n't get my check, and I still working."*
        b. *So I went to the ... hospital and I **told** the people **I say**, "Well, two months I n't get my check, and I still working."*

(48)   *He went to Samuel Ross and Samuel Ross **promise** him **say**, "O.K, I will take you to the Dutch agent."*

(49)   *They went, they **də write** to the people **say**, "... "*

(50)   *If you see the eggplant and pepper in Louisiana, Bluntsville, and Lexington, you will **swear say** that in the country.*
        '... you will swear that you are in the country.'

Arguably *swear say* has been both lexicalized and frozen. Thus, it seems unlikely that a speaker would use *swear* without *say*, e.g. *you will swear that in the country*, or would inflect *swear*, e.g. *You swore say that you were in the country*. Sometimes, speakers insert a subject pronoun before *say*, as in (47b). The structure of (47b) represents a step towards standard English and may occur more often in formal contexts.

Speakers can use *say* to signal a direct quotation, even when the preceding verb is not a verb of saying and when *say* does not itself have an overt subject, as in (51) and (52):

(51)   *They all got there, and they all **sit** down now **say**, "Let's put idea together now."*

(52)   *If you playing in the road and a older person **meet** you **say**, "What you doing down here? You better go to you ma," we fool to retaliate say, "What you got to do with me"?*
       '... would we be foolish enough to retaliate and say, "what do you have to do with me?"'

It is possible to use *say* to signal a direct quotation even when it is not attached to a higher sentence, as in (53) and (54):

(53)   *In the process of time they got dissatisfy. **Say**, "Well, our denomination, we can't let it down."*

(54)   *They come inside, they beg the people. Beg all the civilize people. **Say**, "We beg yall, we grant arm."*

6.   Liberian Settler English in the African American diaspora

In considering the history of African American English, scholars have turned in recent years to examining the language of communities whose founders were African Americans who left the United States in the period between the American Revolution (1775–1781) and the American Civil War (1861–1865). Such studies attempt to extrapolate an earlier stage of African American English, especially AAVE, from the current grammar of the transplanted community. Thus, Poplack and Tagliamonte's *African American English in the diaspora* (2001) represents the culmination of more than a decade's study of the language of the Samaná community in the Dominican Republic and two Afro-Nova Scotian communities in Canada.

Poplack and Tagliamonte (2001) and other authors working with them find the language of these varieties to be more similar to white vernaculars than is modern AAVE, leading them to argue both that core features of African American English come from British regional dialects (theirs is a re-invigoration of the anglicist position advocated by McDavid and McDavid [1951]) and also that modern AAVE features that differ from white vernaculars represent a recent divergence. However, others who have studied Samaná English, notably DeBose (1996) and Hannah (1997), do not reach the same conclusion as Poplack and Tagliamonte.

The data from the LibSE of Sinoe also push towards a different conclusion, indicating instead that many of the prominently unique features of AAVE are actually features of long standing. Myhill (1995) presented eight features of modern AAVE as putative post-Civil War, i.e. relatively recent, innovations in AAVE: omission of verbal -*s*; omission of possessive -*s*; copula absence, specifically *is* deletion; the use of *ain't* for *didn't*; the use of *be done*; the semi-auxiliary *come*; the auxiliary *steady*; and stressed *been*.

However, Singler (1998b) was able to draw on evidence from LibSE and elsewhere to show that seven of them are not innovations but are instead features that were part of AAVE well before the American Civil War. The following examples illustrate the non-standard features in the list (as opposed to instances where the innovation was the absence of a standard feature):

The use of *ain't* for *didn't*:

(55)   *I telling you what the old people told me now. Because that one I* ***ain't see*** *with my own eye.*

The use of *be done*:

(56)   *You* ***be done crack*** *you palm nut, palm kernel, everything, then you make you palm butter and set it down.*
       '(By that time) you would have cracked all your palm kernels, and then you would make your palm butter [a stew made from palm nut pulp] and set it down.'

The semi-auxiliary *come* (to signal disapproval):

(57)   *We talking about ending the war, and you* ***come talking*** *about Sinoe Defense Force. You not serious.*

The auxiliary *steady*:

(58)   *When I go to school, when the teacher beat me, I run, man, I* ***(be) steady*** *halling all the way home.*
       'When I went to school, if the teacher beat me, I would run, man, I would be hollering non-stop all the way home.'

The only one of the features on Myhill's list that Singler (1998b) was not able to locate in LibSE was stressed *been*. However, subsequent research has shown that the feature is a part of LibSE grammar. There as in AAVE stressed *been* is used to express temporal remoteness (and extent of duration) or, less frequently, intensity. The use of *BÍN* (stressed *been* in Rickford's [1975] notation) to focus upon a state's duration can be illustrated with the following set of sentences involving the adjective *greedy*. In the unmarked case in LibSE, being *greedy* refers specifically to food. One who is *greedy* eats too much and, crucially, does not readily share food with others. The interpretations of the sentence were provided by the Rev. Hosea Ellis.

(59)   a. *He been greedy.*
       'Many people know about his greediness.'
    b. *He BÍN greedy.*
       'He has long been known for greed. It's not just now he started being greedy. Since people got to know him, he has been like that.'
    c. *He been GREEDY.*
       'He is excessively greedy.'

While (59b) can also emphasize the extent of the subject's greediness, an intensive sense is more likely to be expressed by (59c). Thus, all eight of the features on Myhill's list are features of LibSE.

In discussing the eight features on Myhill's list, it is appropriate to separate the positive features, i.e. those that involve a non-standard form, from the negative features, those that involve the absence of a standard form. With the exception of the highly infrequent use of *ain't* in place of *didn't*, none of the positive features obtain in modern Samaná English (Shana Poplack, p.c.). Inasmuch as the positive features occur in LibSE and AAVE but do not occur in Samaná English, the more parsimonious account is that they are old and Samaná English has either lost them or never had them.

Singler (1998a) proposes that the differences between Samaná English and LibSE in their relationship to modern AAVE are to be accounted for in part by differences in provenance between the original settlers of the respective communities, with those who settled in Samaná coming in large part from in and near Philadelphia at a time when Philadelphia was the most important city in the US for free people of color. As noted, the Sinoe Settlers came overwhelmingly from the Lower South of the US. Poplack (2000: 27n) and Poplack and Tagliamonte (2001) disagree with Singler (1998a), but their accounts of the provenance of the Samaná settlers contradict each other.

Poplack and Sankoff (1987) appear to have had it right the first time: as the title of their article asserts, the story of Samaná is *The Philadelphia Story in the Spanish Caribbean*. Certainly, after 175 years it is not provenance of original inhabitants alone that distinguishes the people of Samaná from those of Sinoe. In the case of Samaná there was a British and Jamaican missionary presence that has no analogue in Sinoe; further, extensive intermarriage between the Samaná folk and Methodists from Turks Island and settlement in the late nineteenth century by people from elsewhere in the anglophone Caribbean have also shaped the current character of the community's language, as Samaná phonology attests. Post-settlement influence in Sinoe is addressed in Section 7.

For each of the negative features on Myhill's list, there is – in addition to the LibSE evidence – North American historical evidence that establishes it as a longstanding AAVE feature. It is noteworthy that the LibSE frequency of these features is measurably greater than the AAVE frequency. This would seem to reflect the fact that, compared with AAVE, LibSE has had far less contact with white vernaculars and with StE over the past 150 years.

For the positive features, in every case except the use of *ain't* rather than *didn't*, the feature has undergone an expansion – either of semantic range, syntactic domain, or simple frequency – in AAVE that has not occurred in LibSE. In sum, the features are quite old, but the extended range of their usage within AAVE reflects their ongoing evolution within that variety.

There are grammatical elements that persist in LibSE but no longer obtain in AAVE. The copula *sə* – illustrated in (19) and (20) above – and the habitual auxiliary *də* are two such features. The creation of *sə* appears to be the result of recutting, whereby *'s a* in a string like *he's a newcomer* gets re-analyzed as *he sə newcomer*. Comparable strings are to be found in Gullah and in the Ex-Slave Recordings (cf. Singler 1991b). A Gullah example is given in (60):

(60)   *Your daughter-in-law say say you's **a** woman.*

(Gullah; Cunningham 1970: 167)

As discussed in 2.1.2. above, the auxiliary *də* marks habitual aspect, as in (61) and (62):

(61)   *They went, they **də** write to the people say, ...*
       'They used to go and write to people and tell them ...'

(62)   *Some country people **də** eat it [snake]. But civilize people don't.*

As the example in (62) illustrates, *də* can only occur in the affirmative.

7.   Local influences on LibSE

The post-settlement forces that have affected the LibSE of Sinoe would all seem to involve English itself. This is obvious in terms of forces that might move LibSE closer to StE, but it is also true with reference to those that might pull it away from the standard. Of the forces that might push the LibSE of Sinoe closer to StE, three stand out: the church, the school, and Liberian Settlers from elsewhere. The absence of missionaries in Sinoe has been noted, but even settler clergy were likely to be a force for StE, if not in the vernacular at least in the language used in formal settings such as church services themselves. The influence of schooling is equally evident. Many of the elderly Sinoe Settlers whose speech provided the corpus on which this article is based had had very little formal schooling, some none at all; nonetheless, the importance of education in the Settler community is clear. Finally, Settlers from elsewhere – especially Monrovia – have traditionally possessed greater standing than Sinoenians. Overall, the difference between the LibSE of Sinoe and the LibSE of other Settler communities appears to be quantitative more than qualitative. That is, with few exceptions, the Sinoenians do not use non-standard features that other Settlers do not also use; rather, they use the same non-standard features as other Settlers but they use them far more often.

As for the factors and forces that might have moved LibSE further away not only from StE but also AAVE, the primary influence would have been VLE, with influence from Niger-Congo languages much more likely to be transmitted through VLE than to affect LibSE directly.

A crucial point about the relationship of VLE to LibSE is that, in cases where the two varieties share a feature, it is rarely difficult to determine where the feature originated. (The use of *we* as a pronominal adjective and an object pronoun, as discussed in 3.2., is an exception.) Establishing a feature's provenance can be done on the basis of evidence internal to the VLE and LibSE communities as well as by evidence external to Liberia. The auxiliaries *də* and *feni* make the point.

Among the settlers in Sinoe, while *də* is used by virtually all speakers, it is used more by speakers in the upriver settlements, i.e. more by the hard-core settlers. The opposite holds true for *feni*; its use in Sinoe is virtually confined to settlers who either live or work in Greenville, the county headquarters, i.e. the settlers with the most contact with VLE speakers. In contrast, a study of VLE speakers in Monrovia shows the use of *də* among older speakers to be confined to individuals whose ethnic group has historically had extensive contact with the settlers. The VLE speakers in Monrovia showed no comparable distributional restrictions in the use of *feni*. Thus, the evidence inside Liberia points to settler provenance for *də* and VLE provenance for *feni*. The external evidence external to Liberia corroborates the evidence internal to it.

There are Western Hemisphere varieties which use *də* (or a form very close to it in shape) to mark imperfective aspect, among them Gullah (Hopkins 1994) and Anguillian English (Williams 2003). However, no Western Hemisphere varieties of which I am aware have a completive auxiliary based on *finish*. In contrast, there are no West African varieties outside of Liberia that have an auxiliary that is both phonologically and semantically similar to *dɔ*, and clause-final *finish* occurs in both Kru Pidgin English (Singler 1990) and Nigerian Pidgin English (Faraclas, this volume).

I have argued that, for the features that LibSE and VLE share, one can determine which of the two varieties had the feature first. At the same time, I acknowledge that my discussion of sources of influence upon LibSE has not taken into account the potential consequences of internal change for the variety.

8. The future of Liberian Settler English

The civil war that began in Liberia in 1989 has yet to be resolved. Until it is, the future of LibSE remains uncertain. Still, given the central role of ethnicity in defining a Liberian's identity, the distinctiveness of the Settler ethnic group (relative to Liberia's indigenous ethnic groups), and the role of language in reinforcing that distinctiveness, there seems little reason to predict that Settler speech will be absorbed into a homogeneous Liberian English. LibSE seems likely to continue to exist for time indefinite.

Less certain, however, is the fate of LibSE at its most highly distinctive and conservative, e.g. the variety spoken by elderly Settlers in the upriver settlements of Sinoe County. In the late 1980's it was still the case that Settler children living in an upriver settlement like Louisiana and attending elementary school there were acquiring the conservative dialect. Since then, however, civil war has devastated the region. If isolated Settler enclaves like the upriver settlements of Sinoe County cease to exist, then the survival of unassimilated varieties of LibSE is likely to be threatened.

* A National Science Foundation grant and a National Endowment for the Humanities summer stipend made possible my research on the LibSE of Sinoe. I am grateful to the Rev. D. Hosea Ellis for his assistance throughout. I wish to thank the older heads of the Settler community in Sinoe County for allowing Hosea and me to carry out sociolinguistic interviews with them. I am grateful to the late Missouri Montgomery for her friendship, her generosity, and her wisdom. I count myself fortunate to have the ongoing advice of the Rev. Charles Bailey, Nora Jones, and the Rev. Emmanuel Hodges. Peter Roberts Toe and Comfort Swen Toe facilitated my research in Sinoe. Samson Tiklo, John Mason, David Peewee, Dubel Nyankun, Tinisi Saytue, Boakai Zoludua, Tamba Mayson, and many others have assisted me in my work on Liberian English more generally.

Exercises and study questions

1. Discuss two ways in which the copula in LSE differs from that of AAVE.

2. In what ways do sentences (32) to (34) show adjectives being treated like verbs?

3. Review the five features retained in LSE that suggest that they are old features shared with AAVE.

4. What is the function of *o* in sentences (4) and (22)?

5. Discuss the semantics of auxiliary *de* in sentences (12) to (14).

Selected references

Please consult the General references for titles mentioned in the text but not included in the references below. For a full bibliography see the accompanying CD-ROM.

Cunningham, Irma A. E.
    1970   A syntactic analysis of Sea Island Creole ("Gullah"). Ph.D. dissertation, University of Michigan, Dearborn.
DeBose, Charles E.
    1996   Question formation in Samaná English. Paper presented at NWAVE 25, the University of Nevada, Las Vegas.
Hannah, Dawn
    1997   Copula absence in Samaná English: implications for research on the linguistic history of African-American Vernacular English. *American Speech* 72: 339–372.
Hopkins, Tometro
    1994   Variation in the use of the auxiliary verb *da* in contemporary Gullah. In: Michael Montgomery (ed.), *The crucible of Carolina: Essays in the development of Gullah language and culture*, 60–86. Athens: University of Georgia Press
Labov, William
    1969   Contraction, deletion, and inherent variability of the English copula. *Language* 45: 714–62.
McDavid, Raven I. and Virginia G. McDavid
    1951   The relationship of the speech of American Negroes to the speech of whites. *American Speech* 26: 3–17.
Myhill, John
    1995   The use of features of present-day AAVE in the ex-slave recordings. *American Speech* 70: 115–147.

Poplack, Shana and Sankoff, David
  1987   The Philadelphia story in the Spanish Caribbean. *American Speech* 62:
             291–314.
Poplack, Shana and Sali Tagliamonte
  2001   *African American English in the diaspora.* Malden, Massachusetts:
             Blackwell.
Poplack, Shana (ed.)
  2000   *The English History of African American English.* Malden, Massachusetts:
             Blackwell.
Rickford, John R.
  1975   Carrying the new wave into syntax: the case of Black English *been.* In:
             Ralph W. Fasold and Roger W. Shuy (eds.), *Analyzing Variation in the
             Form and Use of Language*, 162–183. Washington: Georgetown University
             Press.
Romaine, Suzanne
  1982   *Socio-historical Linguistics: Its Status and Methodology.* Cambridge:
             Cambridge University Press.
Singler, John Victor
  1984   Variation in tense-aspect-modality in Liberian English. Ph.D. dissertation,
             University of California, Los Angeles.
  1987   Where did Liberian English *na* come from? *English World-Wide* 8: 69–
             95.
  1990   The impact of decreolization upon TMA: tenselessness, mood, and as-
             pect in Kru Pidgin English. In: John Victor Singler (ed.), *Pidgin and cre-
             ole tense-mood-aspect systems*, 203–230. (Creole Language Library, 6.)
             Amsterdam/Philadelphia: Benjamins.
  1991a   Copula variation in Liberian Settler English and American Black English.
             In: Walter F. Edwards and Donald Winford (eds.), 129–164.
  1991b   Liberian Settler English and the ex-slave recordings. In: Guy Bailey,
             Natalie Maynor, and Patricia Cukor-Avila (eds.), 249–274.
  1993   The Liberian Settler English copula revisited. Paper presented at NWAVE
             23, University of Ottawa.
  1998a   The African-American diaspora: who were the dispersed? Paper presented
             at the NWAVE 28, University of Georgia
  1998b   What's not new in AAVE. *American Speech* 73: 227–256.
Williams, Jeffrey P.
  2003   The establishment and perpetuation of anglophone white enclave commu-
             nities in the Eastern Caribbean: the case of Island Harbour, Anguilla. In:
             Michael Aceto and Jeffrey P. William (eds.), *Anglophone Varieties of the
             Eastern Caribbean*, 95–119. Amsterdam/Philadelphia: Benjamins.

Cameroon English: morphology and syntax

Paul Mbangwana

1.   Introduction

As English changes in time and space among native speakers, it also takes many twists and turns in the countries that have adopted it as a second or foreign language. Sala (2003: 66) describes how fossilized errors are recycled and given a wider spread from generation to generation in Cameroon English (CamE). While purists view this process in terms of falling standards, most linguists regard it as an indigenization process according to which "adopted" English is being "adapted" to suit the expressive needs of its users. All users of English, especially those in the English as a second language (SL) or English as a foreign language (FL) situation, seek to build a convenient medium of communication that is simple and economical. When English is transplanted, it acculturates to the new environment in all aspects (lexis, semantics, syntax, etc). In this process it acquires multicultural identities. This study of CamE will focus on the ways in which English has become indigenised syntactically.

The data used in this overview come from previous published research work, literary production, and jottings by myself from a body of live speeches and conversations. Sala (2003: 341) suggests that there are two varieties of CamE: (a) the imposed (exonormative) variety which hardly goes out of the classroom setting that engenders and regulates it, and (b) the innovative (indigenised) variety which is acquired in the greater English-using community showing a great deal of creativity and acculturation to local norms. This innovative variety is the more significant site of research for CamE.

Since syntax relates grammar to meaning by its particular arrangement of words, it is of interest to examine how British English (BrE) and CamE contrast. The adaptation of English in SL and FL situations is usually toward simpler forms. This study examines the various processes and strategies which render CamE convenient, simpler and practically economical in terms of structural levelling-out. Though CamE users have learnt how to build sentences using the rule-governed patterns of clause formation in formal situations, they are still observed to be less competent in actual use.

However, even their innovative performance can be shown to be relatively systematic and amenable to close syntactic analysis. For example, as I will discuss in section 3.5., CamE shows a predilection for sentences replete with subordinate clause structures that avoid prepositions in post-movement positions. It also favours patterns that may be considered redundant in Standard English (StE). Sala (2003) reminds us that

> speakers of CamE should not be considered to be learners of BrE but speakers of a particular brand of English. They learnt the English language and in the course of doing so, they put their emblem on it, that is, they moulded it to fit their needs and ways. (Sala 2003: 338)

CamE has been studied by Todd (1982), Mbangwana (1992; 2002), Simo Bobda (1994) and Sala (2003), amongst others. These studies have identified how certain structures depart from the BrE prototype. Some of these studies point to the low status of the innovations in CamE. However, Sala (2003: 112) takes a more descriptive approach by examining CamE syntax with the aim of understanding the rules and processes involved in structural simplification. These processes are robust, productive and predictable; hence they give evidence of a certain degree of competence underlying their users' creativity.

2.   Idioms in CamE creative writing

Sala (2003) identifies many instances of usage which might appear redundant as writers attempt to recreate the idiom of the Cameroonian mother tongues. Examples include *cry a loud cry, smile a dry smile, walk on foot, seeing with one's eyes, eat with ones's mouth, laugh a terrible laughter, die a good death.* Further examples from creative writers include the following:

(1)   *You (Achiebefuo) have failed me and so I do not have the **ears to listen** to you at all.*
       'Achiebefuo, you have failed me and so I cannot listen to you at all.'
       (Asong, *The Crown of Thorns* [1995: 14])

(2)   *Mbamu stopped suddenly where two paths crossed and **sniffed the air**.*
       'Mbamu stopped suddenly where two paths crossed, and sniffed.'
       (Eba Nsanda, *The Good Foot* [1984: 7])

(3)   *Women were to supply **potatoes and food** for **the men who carried the luggage** of the White Man of God. How can a man lie to the **mother of his children**, and to his children and himself?*
       'Women were to supply food to the carriers of the White Man of God. How can a man lie to his wife, his children and to himself?' (Jumbam, *The White Man of God* [1980: 30])

(4)   *With his **two fingers of the right hand, the thumb and the finger next to it,*** *he squeezed the hot peppers.*
       'With his two right hand fingers, the thumb and forefinger, he squeezed the hot peppers.' (Ngongwikuo, *Taboo Love* [1980: 5])

3.   Syntax

3.1.   Elliptical *but*

Sala (2003: 17) reports elliptical instances of *but* used in CamE:

(5)   *I am going to eat but bread.*
       'I am rather going to eat bread than take in that mess of yours.'

(6)   *We are leaving but tomorrow.*
       'We are leaving tomorrow rather than wait for the weekend.'

Ellipsis in these CamE sentences involves two elements: (a) an equivalent of English *rather* and (b) what is actually rejected as expressed by a *than* clause. Sala (2003: 200) concludes that in such situations CamE favours preference-focusing and leaves unstated what is rejected.

3.2.   *Like this* and *like that* as elliptical comparative markers

Like this and *like that* tend to function clause-finally in a rather elliptical fashion when an immediate shared context between the speaker and interlocutor occurs, making the ellipted elements recoverable from the context. In BrE such structures are possible in concrete circumstances, such as the following:

(7)   *A house like this [house] is quite convenient*

(8)   *A day like that [one we had last week] is always very refreshing.*

But in CamE those phrases are used in broader contexts, largely associated with the intention of the utterer:

(9)   *I am cooking food like this.*
       'I am cooking food to carry to the death celebration.'

(10)   *I was just coming from Bamenda like that.*
       'I was just coming from Bamenda like that to see you.'

Sala (2003: 210) concludes that such ellipsis requires the effective presence of interlocutors for their content to be recovered either from ocular evidence or from some other context, near or remote. The shared context makes it unnecessary to state the obvious.

3.3. *Like this* and *like that* used as concessive clauses

(11) *Though you are strong like that, I can beat you.*

(12) *Though I am old like this, I can run.*

(13) *You think that I am small like this that I cannot fight you?*

Here the comparative phrases (*like this/that*) are equivalent to the standard English pre-modifier *so*. They occur under the influence of pidgin English and Cameroonian mother tongues.

3.4. Innovations in word order

Dangling modifiers and avoidance of self-embedding are notable in CamE. Since non-restrictive relative clauses and non-finite clauses are not attested in the home languages or pidgin English, dangling modifiers become the typical structure which is freely used. Sentences (14) and (15) are speech forms noted on CRTV (Radio Cameroon):

(14) *Doing the day's assignment, his mother who was cooking asked her son to stop reading.*
'As her son was doing the day's assignment, his mother who was cooking asked him to stop reading.'

(15) *The technician stepped on the dog's tail when he was bitten.*
'The technician was bitten when he stepped on the dog's tail.'

3.5. Preposition 'chopping' in relative clauses

Whereas many varieties of English increasingly favour preposition stranding with relative clauses, CamE tends to delete such prepositions:

(16) *He is being followed by an old man which the name is not given Ø.*
'He is being followed by an old man whose name is not given.'

(17) *There is a certain girl that we were in Bamenda together Ø.*
'There is a certain girl together with whom we were in Bamenda.'

(18) *We have produced an album which we want you to buy a copy Ø.*
'We have produced an album which we want you to buy a copy of.'

3.6.   Avoidance of self-embedding

Self-embedding is another difficulty in structuring in CamE. Subordinating elements in CamE tend not to embed elements:

(19)   *CRTV is an institution which people will come and go and it will remain.*
'CRTV is an institution which, though people will come and go, will remain.'

(20)   *He ate the beans which Peter bought bread to eat with it.*
'He ate the beans which Peter had bought bread to eat with.' – i.e. Peter had been expecting to eat beans with his bread, but they had already been eaten.

4.   *That*-complement clauses

In BrE, *that*-clauses are strategies to mark embedding, i.e. they embed one clause into another one. The set of verbs that take *that* and the range of contexts surrounding its use are extended in CamE.

4.1.   *That*-clauses

Sala (2003: 136) cites a number of sentences to show how *that*-clauses in CamE are extended to a wider set of verbs than in StE.

(21)   *He **phoned me that** he is coming.*
'He phoned me to say that he is coming.'

(22)   *He **insulted me that** I am a thief.*
'He insulted me saying that I am a thief.'

(23)   *He **mocked me that** I failed my exams.*
'He mocked me because I failed my exams.'

These verbs have been recategorised to take a direct object and a *that* + sentence complement. *That*-complement clauses may clearly stand as sui generis clauses in CamE, as in Ngongwikuo's *Taboo Love* (1980: 65):

(24)   *That Kwifon has asked me to greet all the young mothers and to give to him. That Kwifon has asked me to greet all the old and sick and to give to him.*
'I wish to inform you that Kwifon has asked me to greet all the young mothers and all the old and sick, on his behalf.'

4.2.   *That*-adverbial clauses

That-clauses in CamE also occupy syntactic slots which are usually occupied by adverbial clauses of reason in BrE. Sala (2003: 147–149) provides the following examples:

(25)   *He is crying **that** I have eaten his food.*
        'He is crying because I have eaten his food.'

(26)   *His boss bears a grudge against him **that** he is always late.*
        'His boss bears a grudge against him because he is always late.'

(27)   *He refused the food **that** it was too small.*
        'He refused the food because it was too small.'

4.3.   *That*-adverbial clause with *what* in situ

(28)   *He is crying that I have eaten **what**?*
        'What have I eaten that he is crying about?'

(29)   *He bears a grudge against me that **what**?*
        'What does he bear a grudge against me for?'

(30)   *You have eaten all the food that I should eat **what**?*
        'What am I going to eat now that you have eaten all the food?'

(31)   *You reported me to the principal that he should do **what**?*
        'What do you want the principal to do now that you have reported me to him?'

These novel examples of "long distance" *what* in combination with *that* clearly do not translate easily into StE. Nor have they been reported in varieties of English elsewhere. Further research has to be done to understand them fully. See also section 5.1.

5.   *Wh*-word and constituent questions

Sala (2003: 196) shows how *wh*-movement does not occur in CamE. Questions are generated at the base, that is in situ. Their intonation contour is similar to that of normal declarative sentences. Such a *wh*- in situ rule for questioning is structurally simple:

5.1.   *Wh-* in root clauses

(32)   *You are going **where**?*
'Where are you going?'

(33)   *He is eating **what**?*
'What is he eating?'

(34)   *He has sent the letter to **who**?*
'Who has he sent the letter to?'

5.2.   *Wh-*word in subordinate clauses

Since the *wh-*word remains at the base, constituent questions can occur in subordinate clauses contrary to the way they function in BrE:

(35)   *He wants that I should do **what**?*
'What does he want me to do?'

(36)   *He told you that he was going **where**?*
'Where did he tell you he was going?'

(37)   *You are expecting that **who** will come?*
'Who are you expecting to come?'

Similar to the structures in section 5.1., these sentences taken from my data base are examples of syntactic economy: they require a minimum of movement, eschewing both *wh-*movement, auxiliary shift and *do-*support.

5.3.   Echo questions

Echo questions are used as a reaction to a statement or a declarative sentence, usually expressing disbelief or incredulity in StE. In CamE, echo questions are frequently preceded by the complementiser *that*.

(38)   ***That** you are going where?*
'You are going **where**?'

(39)   ***That** Thomas is coming when?*
'Thomas is coming **when**?'

(40)   ***That** Thomas ate what?*
'Thomas ate **what**?'

5.4.   *Yes/no* questions

Yes/no questions show the same word order as ordinary statements and are used for greetings, for phatic communion (41–43) or deference (44).

(41)   *You are breaking your fast?*
'Are you breaking your fast?'

(42)   *The children are studying?*
'Are the children studying?'

(43)   *The day is getting dawn?*
'Is the day dawning?'

(44)   *The Fon is in the meeting?*
'Is the Fon in the meeting?'

These questions are realised as statements with a rising tone.

5.5.   Tag questions

The normal form of the tag question in CamE is *isn't it*, a generalised form of the range of possibilities that occur in StE:

(45)   *Ekindi will be coming, **isn't it**?*
'Ekindi will be coming, won't he?'

(46)   *Ngwana didn't do the work, **isn't it**?*
'Ngwana didn't do the work, did he?'

(47)   Q: *We're expecting visitors to night, **isn't it**?*
A: *Yes.*
Q: 'We're expecting visitors tonight, aren't we?'
A: 'We are.'

The CamE pattern of tag questions is a clear case of simplification, since it does not require pronoun copying, auxiliary copying, *do*-support or negative polarity. Occasionally, other forms of tag questions are used interchangeably: *na, not so, ein, is that, right* and *okay.*

(48)   a. *I told you she will come, **na**?*
b. *You will pay the debt, **na**?*

(49)   a. *You will be around, **not so**?*
b. *She said it, **not so**?*

(50)   a. *Jane will not eat, **ein**?*
       b. *We should stop it, **ein**?*

(51)   a. *She's married, **is that**?*
       b. *Yaya finished the work, **is that**?*

(52)   a. *You'll wait for me outside the courtyard, **right**?*
       b. *Carry this log of wood over there, **right**?*

(53)   a. *Mati will be on time, **okay**?*
       b. *Mazo has finally arrived, **okay**?*

6.   Dummy subject *they* in quasi-passives

Sala (2003: 217) provides three examples from CamE where no NP-movement is involved:

(54)   ***They** have published results.*
       'Results have been published [by the principal].'

(55)   ***They** are paying salaries.*
       'Salaries are being paid [by the bank].'

(56)   ***They** have soiled the toilet.*
       'The toilet has been soiled [by a tenant].'

In CamE the pronoun *they* has no antecedent and is therefore non-referential in this sense: it is neither anaphoric nor cataphoric because it cannot be linked to an NP that is explicitly stated. If *they* has no antecedent, then it is only a slot filler like other dummy pronouns such as *it* and *there* in BrE. Passivisation in CamE thus makes use of active verbs and *they* in dummy subject position. The following chain of events is likely:

(a) There is no overt (content) agentive NP.
(b) Hence there is no NP-movement with potential passives.
(c) The subject position is therefore potentially empty.
(d) It is therefore filled by expletive (or dummy) *they*.

7. Resumptive, copy and other pronouns

7.1. Left dislocation

As is common in many varieties of African English, left dislocation is a regular feature of CamE, involving the identification of a topic NP followed by a copy pronoun like *she* in (57) below:

(57)   *Martina's aunt **she** works in the Ministry of Public Health.*
       'Martina's aunt works in the Ministry of Public Health.'

7.2. Resumptive pronouns

These are also copy pronouns which fill in categories often left empty in StE subordinate clauses. They are most common in CamE relative clauses, including ones with indefinite heads, such as (58):

(58)   *There are some students whom I am teaching **them** to write.*
       'There are some students whom I am teaching to write.'

(59)   *The other teacher that we were teaching English with **her** went away.*
       'The other teacher with whom we taught went away.'

(60)   *What men can do, women can do **it** better.*
       'What men can do, women can do better.'

(61)   *The area where we find the capital **there today** is Yaounde.*
       'The area where we find the capital is Yaounde.'

7.3. Dative of obligation

There are some examples in which copy pronouns (usually *me* or *us*) express a sense of obligation.

(62)   *I am going **me** away.*
       'I must go away.'

(63)   *We are sitting **us** down.*
       'We have to sit down.'

It is not possible to say whether the pronouns are in the accusative or the dative case. However, because of constructions like the dative of advantage in varieties of English in the U.S. and elsewhere (*I'm gonna get me a gun*), and because obligation is expressed by the dative in many case-bearing languages, it seems appropriate to label the construction as a dative of obligation.

Finally, in connection with pronouns it is noteworthy that anaphoric nouns are avoided in certain CamE sentences where they are preferred in BrE:

(64)   *We have **names** like Nathana, Clara and Joel which are familiar*
        ***names**.*
        'We have names like Nathana, Clara, and Joel which are familiar.'

(65)   *You have bought **clothing items** like shirts, trousers, hats, and gloves*
        *which are common **clothings**.*
        'You have bought clothing items like shirts, trousers, hats, and gloves which are common.'

8.   Conclusion

CamE has a wealth of syntactic constructions which challenge our traditional notions about the structure of English. There is a general avoidance of movement rules with interesting syntactic consequences. One of these is the frequent similarity in form between direct and indirect questions. Secondly, there is the frequent appearance of *wh*-words in situ, of resumptive pronouns and of the complementiser *that* in root clauses. Thirdly, there is the possibility of using *there* as a dummy subject in quasi-passives. It therefore seems justified to regard the grammar of CamE as a cognitive, non-deficient system, rather than as a substandard version of BrE.

Exercises and study questions

1. Try and provide another example similar to (6) and (7) in connection with elliptical *but* (section 3.1).

2. In connection with section 7, make up some examples to show the difference between a copy pronoun (in sentences with left dislocation) and a resumptive pronoun (in a relative clause).

3. Now make up a sentence having both a resumptive pronoun and a copy pronoun (in left dislocation).

4. Outline four differences between example (29) *He bears a grudge against me that what?* and its equivalent in Standard English.

5. How are echo questions of colloquial StE like *John ate what?* expressed in CamE (see 5.3)?

Selected references

Please consult the General references for titles mentioned in the text but not included in the references below. For a full bibliography see the accompanying CD-ROM.

Asong, Linus
  1995   *The Crown of Thorns.* Bamenda: Patron Publishing.
Eba Nsanda, Peter
  1984   *The Good Foot.* Bamenda: Unique Press.
Jumbam, Kenjo
  1980   *The White Man of God.* London: Heinemann.
Mbangwana, Paul
  1992   Some grammatical sign-posts in Cameroon Standard English. In: Josef Schmied (ed.), *English in East and Central Africa 2*, 93–102. (Bayreuth African Studies 24.) Bayreuth: Bayreuth University Press.
  2002   *English Patterns of Usage and Meaning.* Yaounde: Presses Universitaires de Yaounde.
Ngongwikuo, Joseph
  1980   *Taboo Love.* New York: Hicksville.
Sala, Bonaventure
  2003   Aspects of the Cameroon English sentence. Ph.D. dissertation, University of Yaounde.
Simo Bobda, Augustin
  1994   *Watch Your English: A Collection of Remedial Lessons of English Usage.* Yaounde: AMA.
Todd, Loreto
  1982   *Cameroon.* (Varieties of English Around the World: Text Series 1.) Heidelberg: Groos.

Cameroon Pidgin English (Kamtok): morphology and syntax[*]

Miriam Ayafor

1. Introduction

Kamtok, the name that is used today to designate the English-based Pidgin spoken in Cameroon, is believed to have evolved as far back as the 15th century, with the arrival of the Portuguese on the West African coast. By the 17th century, many other European and African ethnic groups had begun to use it in their contacts and transactions with each other, and had contributed to its development. Cameroon is known to have a wide variety of ethnic languages: "the number of languages listed for Cameroon is 286. Of those, 279 are living languages, 3 are second languages without mother tongue speakers, and 4 are extinct. Diversity index 0.97." (Ethnologue.com: 1)

Today, Kamtok is the major lingua franca in the country and, in terms of geographical spread, is rivaled by no other national language. In terms of number of speakers, Fulfulde, one of the Cameroonian ethnic languages, ranks first, but is localised to a particular region. The fact that Kamtok is now "a fully-fledged language learned by children from their mothers" (Mackenzie 2002: 1) cannot be over-emphasized. Kamtok has developed its own phonological, lexical, and grammatical structures.

2. Sources of Kamtok lexis

2.1. From borrowing

Even though Kamtok is an English-based Pidgin, its lexicon has drawn from other European languages as well, notably Portuguese, Dutch, German and French. Some West African languages have contributed to Kamtok as well, including, of course, Cameroon national languages. Table 1 below gives some examples.

Table 1.   Examples of Kamtok borrowings

Origin	Original word	Kamtok word	English equivalent
Portuguese	piqueno	*pikin*	child
	dache	*dash*	gift/tribute
	saber	*sabi*	know
	palaba	*palaba/palava*	conference/discussion
French	beaucoup	*boku*	many/much/plenty of
	stade	*stad*	stadium
	bonbons	*bonbon*	sweets
	manger	*dameh*	eat
Yoruba (Nigeria)	wahala	*wahala*	trouble/hassle/confusion
	akara	*makara*	bean cake
	egusi	*egusi*	pumpkin seeds
Igbo (Nigeria)	okro	*okro*	the vegetable okra
Kikongo	nkanda	*nkanda*	hide/skin
Twi	pima	*pima*	vagina
Duala (Cameroon)	ngondele	*ngondere*	young woman/girl
	munyu	*moyo*	in-law
	nayo	*nayo-nayo*	carefully
	mukala	*mukala*	white man/albino
Fula (Cameroon)	chuk	*chuk*	pierce/prick
Mungaka (Cameroon)	Ni	*ni* (a polite manner of addressing a senior male)	(none)
	Ma	*ma* (a polite manner of addressing a senior female)	(none)
	nkang	*nkang/corn beer*	maize drink
	sanjap	*sanja/rapa*	loin-cloth
Bakweri (Cameroon)	mbanjah	*banja*	ribs/waist
Mandankwe (Cameroon)	ngumsi	*mengwin*	locusts
Lamsoh (Cameroon)	mboh	*mboh*	groundnut paste

Some of the Kamtok words that are assumed to be English-derived may have come from German or Dutch since the three languages are all Germanic, and since the Germans occupied Cameroon for some time. Also, both Dutch missionary and Peace Corps volunteers were present in the country for some time. It is worthy of note that most Cameroonian dishes have Kamtok names derived from the languages of the ethnic regions where these various foodstuffs come from, e.g. *achu, ndole, eru, ekwang, miondo, kwa-koko, mbanga, kum-kum, mbongo-chobi,* and *bobolo.*

2.2. Normal processes of word-formation

2.2.1. Compounding

In order to express some ideas or thoughts, Kamtok uses compounding productively. Examples are *bon-haus* 'birth + house' (ceremony to recognize and celebrate the birth of a child), *folo-bak* 'follow + behind' (younger brother/sister), *las-bon* 'last + deliver' (last child of a family), *mimbo-haus* 'wine + house' (bar), *chop-haus* 'eat + house' (restaurant), *chopchia* 'eat + chair' (successor), and *hayop* 'high + up' (pride/ to be proud).

2.2.2. Inversion

In some cases, Kamtok inverts the position of English compound words or phrasal nouns to create new words like *koshot* 'cut + short' from *shortcut* ('path'), *tronhet* 'strong + head' from *headstrong, taihet* 'tie + head' from *head tie/scarf,* and *fufu-con* 'flour + corn' from *corn flour. Reme* 'mother' and *repe* 'father' are from the French words *mere* and *pere* that have been inverted phonologically.

2.2.3. Truncating or clipping

Some borrowed words are shortened and may seems neologisms. Examples are *clando* from *clandestine* ('illegal transportation'), *mbut* from *mbutuku* (word from local language for 'a worthless and stupid person'), *nga* from *girlfriend, asso* from *associé* (French word for 'an accomplice', used in Kamtok to mean 'my good friend'), and *pang* from *pantalons* (French word for a pair of trousers).

2.2.4. Reduplication

Reduplication resulting in a meaning different from that of the original lexical item is another strategy of word formation in Kamtok. Hence there is the reduplication of the conjunction *so* to create an adverb *soso* in sentences like *Da pikin di soso kray* 'That child is always crying'. The adjective *kain* 'kind/type' has been reduplicated but with less change of meaning than is the case with *so*. *Kainkain* has a plural quality *kain* is missing. Compare *Mi an ma sista get wan kain klos* 'My sister and I have the same kind of dress' with *Kainkain klos dem dey fo maket* 'There are various kinds of dresses in the market'.

2.2.5. Neologisms

As noted by several commentators, Cameroonian youths are becoming very innovative in their speech. Examples of Kamtok coinages created from no known source and used and understood by many youths and a few adults include *chaka* 'shoes', *buka* 'to play cards', *yang* 'to buy', *tum* 'to sell' and *nyama* 'to eat' (probably from the Bantu word for 'meat').

3. An overview of Kamtok lexis

For reasons of space I limit myself to examples of words from different domains of family, social, and professional life.

3.1. Members of the family

Table 2. Kamtok words from the domain of the family

Kamtok word	English equivalent
Papa	'Father'
Mami	'Mother'
Pikin	'child'
Bik-papa	'grandfather'
Bik-mami	'grandmother'
Bik broda/sista	'elder brother/sister'
Smol broda/sista	'younger brother/sister'
Folo-bak	'immediate younger brother/sister'
Fes-bon	'first child of the family'

Table 2. (continued)   Kamtok words from the domain of the family

Kamtok word	English equivalent
Las-bon	'last child of the family'
Mbanya	'co-wife' (in polygamous marriages)
Moyo	'in-law'
Njumba	'concubine/girlfriend'
Kwakanda	'old bachelor/old maid'

3.2.   Social life

Table 3.   Kamtok words from the domain of social life

Kamtok word	English equivalent
mimbo-haus	'bar'
chop-haus	'restaurant'
njangi	'a kind of Credit Union'
bon-haus	'a ceremony to recognise and celebrate birth'
krai-day	'a funeral/mourning ceremony'
juju	'secret society/a masquerade'
Fon	'traditional head of a clan'
Chif	'traditional head of a village'
ninga	'slave'
kombi	'friend'
sevis	'waiter/waitress

3.3.   Professional life

Table 4.   Kamtok words from the domain of professional life

Kamtok word	English equivalent
ticha	'teacher'
hedmassa	'headmaster/head teacher'
polis	'policeman'
kapinta	'carpenter'
brikleya	'bricklayer/mason'
washnait	'night watch'

Table 4. (continued)   Kamtok words from the domain of professional life

Kamtok word	English equivalent
darekto	'Director'
bikman	'important personality'
bikman fo wok	'boss'
bikman fo jandam	'Gendarmerie Commander'
bayam-sellam	'foodstuff retailer/petty trader'
noss	'nurse'
dokta	'doctor'
kombi fo wok	'colleague'

3.4.   Some Kamtok idiomatic expressions

Table 5.   Kamtok idiomatic expressions

Kamtok expression	English equivalent
Fo nak skin	'To trouble oneself/to be bothered unnecessarily'
Du weti du weti	'No matter what happens'
Man no run!	'Don't give up or abandon at the last minute!'
Fo show man pepe	'To deal severely with some one'
Fo kot man yi fut	'To undercut someone'
Du mi a du yu	'Tit for tat'
Woman rapa	'A male flirt'
Fo put san-san fo man yi gari	'Sabotage'

3.5.   Some Kamtok proverbs

Trobu no di ring bel.
'It never rains but it pours'

Bele no get Sonday.
'The stomach never rests'

Wuman weh yi di kuk wowo chop no laik trenja.
'A poor cook doesn't like to receive guests'

Smol pikin kotlas di shap fo monintaim.
'Time will eliminate the inexperienced, giving way to the experienced to become famous'

Kombi wey yi nia pas broda wey yi fawe.
'A close friend is better than a distant brother'

Tori bi fain sote tifman laf fo banda.
'A cheerful attitude can win over enemies'

Wan han no fit tay bondul.
'Many hands make light work'

Tok fo mop no bi kago fo hed.
'What you claim you can do is not what you actually can do'

Pesin wey yi get mop no fit mis rod.
'He who asks questions never goes astray'

Wan bangul no fit hala.
'Working together/cooperation brings about efficiency and success'

4.   Parts of speech

4.1.   Nouns

Unlike in English, Kamtok nouns do not take plural forms through inflexions. Plurals are always expressed in the noun phrase through the addition of the plural marker *dem.* Even when there is a numeral in the phrase indicating plurality, the plural marker is still used, contrary to the observation made by Mackenzie (2002: 1–2). Hence, singular *man* becomes plural *man dem*, *wan buk* becomes *tu buk dem* or *plenty buk dem*, and so forth. Abstract nouns are expressed by explanatory noun phrases or relative clauses, e.g. 'imagination' would be *weti wey man de tink,* literally 'what one thinks'.

Synonyms do exist in Kamtok. Some examples are given in Table 6 below:

Table 6.   Kamtok synonyms

Kamtok word	Synonym	English
Tek taim	*lukot*	'be careful'
Kassingo	*ken*	'cane'
Kotrot	*koshot*	'shortcut'
Kwa	*poket, hanbag*	'pocket/handbag'
Nyongo	*famlah*	'secret society that practises witchcraft/witchcraft'
Mimba	*chek/tink*	'to think'

There are some homophones in Kamtok: *aks* meaning 'to ask' and 'an axe', *taya* meaning 'a motor tyre' and 'to be tired'. Since these involve different parts of speech (nouns and verbs), the homophony/homonymy is tolerated.

Gender is expressed by adding the prefix *man-* and *woman-* to the noun in question. Hence *man-pikin* 'male child' and *woman-pikin* 'female child', *man-dog* 'dog' and *woman-dog* 'bitch'.

Some nouns in Kamtok are reduplicated. When this happens they either maintain their functions as nouns or become adjectives. Examples are *san-san* 'sand', *bia-bia* 'hair', *koro-koro* 'scabies', *pala-pala* 'wrestling', *pof-pof*, 'dough nuts', *chuku-chuku* 'thorns' and *kenen-kenen* 'a slimy vegetable'. Used as adjectives, one can have *san-san boy* 'irresponsible fellow' or 'rascal', *bia-bia ches* 'hairy chest', *koro-koro fut* 'scabies-infected leg', *chuku-chuku bif* 'thorny animal' (e.g., porcupine), and *kenen-kenen rot* 'slippery road'.

4.2. Pronouns

Personal pronouns in subject function are *A* 'I', *yu* 'you', *I* 'he/she/it', *wi* 'we', *wuna*, 'you' (plural), and *deh* 'they'. Object personal pronouns are *mi* 'me', *yu* 'you', *yi* 'him/her', *am* 'it', *wi* 'us', *wuna* 'you' (plural) and *dem* 'them'. The following sentences illustrate these different functions.

(1) a. *A laik fo wok.*
'I love to work.'

b. *I laik fo wok.*
'He/she/it likes to work.'

c. *Wuna laik fo wok.*
'You (plural) love to wok.'

(2) a. *Gif wi de wok.*
'Give us the job.'

b. *Gif de wok fo wi.*
'Give the job to us.'

c. *Gif am de bif.*
'Give it the meat.'

The relative pronoun in Kamtok is expressed by the words *weh* and *se*. *Weh* is used to link two propositions. The equivalent of *weh* in English is expressed by the words *what, who, whose, whom* and *that*. The context of use differentiates these meanings. In the following examples two sentences are given in each case and then linked with the relative pronoun *weh*. Note that the subject of the second clause is not omitted.

Weh as 'who'
(3) a. *A di tok fo Lum.*
b. *I di silip fo trenja rum.*
c. *A di tok fo Lum **weh** I di silip fo trenja rum.*
'I am talking to Lum who sleeps in the guest room.'

Weh as 'whose'
(4)   a.   *Nji don si da kapinta.*
      b.   *Yi wok tin dem don los.*
      c.   *Nji don si da kapinta **weh** yi wok tin dem don los.*
           'Nji has seen the carpenter whose tools are missing.'

Weh as 'whom'
(5)   a.   *Na Massa Paul dat.*
      b.   *Yu bi gif tu bak simen fo yi.*
      c.   *Na Massa Paul dat **weh** yu bi gif tu bak simen fo yi.*
           'That is Mr. Paul to whom you gave two bags of cement.'

Weh as 'which'
(6)   a.   *Wi don put ol pent fo haus.*
      b.   *Yu bi bay am yeseday.*
      c.   *Wi don put ol pent **weh** yu bi bay am yeseday fo haus.*
           'We have used all the paint which you bought yesterday on the house.'

Weh as 'that'
(7)   a.   *Mike no go drin wata.*
      b.   *Da wata komot fo wel.*
      c.   *Mike no go drin wata **weh** yi komot fo wel.*
           'Mike will not drink water that comes from the well.'

Note that *weh* meaning 'that' or 'which' can be used interchangeably. The other relative pronoun, *se*, which can be translated as 'that' in English, is usually used with verbs expressing an opinion or attitude.

(8)   a.   *Wi mimba **se** Piskops dem get plenty moni.*
           'We think that Peace Corps are very rich.'
      b.   *Wi sabi **se** tumoro na bik dey.*
           'We know that tomorrow is a public holiday'.
      c.   *A bi di fia **se** ma pikin don mis rot.*
           'I was afraid that my child had lost the way'.

In Kamtok the word *on* is added to possessive adjectives in order to form possessive pronouns. Possessive adjectives in the language are *ma* 'my', *ya* 'your', *yi* 'his/her/its', *wi* 'our', *wuna* 'your' (plural) and *dia* 'their'. They precede the nouns they determine, for example *ya moto* 'your vehicle', *dia haus* 'their house'. Possessive pronouns, therefore, are *ma on* 'mine', *ya on* 'yours', *yi on* 'his/hers/its', *wi on* 'ours', *wuna on* 'yours' (plural) and *dia on* 'theirs'. Ownership can also be expressed by the use of *get am* or simply by *get* preceded by an object pronoun.

(9) a. *Dis pusi na **ma on**.*
     'This cat is mine.'
  b. *Dis pusi na mi **get am**.*
     'I am the owner of this cat.'
  c. *Na mi **get** this pusi.*
     'I am the owner of this cat.'

A reflexive pronoun is used in a statement when the agent and patient of an action are identical, that is, when the subject and the object of the sentence refer to the same person. In Kamtok, the reflexive is formed by adding the expression *sef-sef* to the object pronoun in question.

(10) a. *Yu **sef-sef** yu go go fo hospitel.*
     'You'll go to the hospital by yourself.'
  b. *Yu bi kuk de chop yu **sef-sef**.*
     'You cooked the food yourself.'
  c. *Yi **sef-sef** bi wash de klos dem.*
     'He/she did the laundry him-/herself.'

Note that unlike in English, where the reflexive pronoun can only occur in clause-final position, in Kamtok it can occur after initial subjects or in final position. When a reflexive pronoun does occur in initial position, the subject pronoun can still be used in the same clause, as in example (10a) above. In example (10c), the subject pronoun *yi* has been omitted to portray the flexibility of usage of reflexives in Kamtok. Reflexive pronouns can also be used for emphasis. In (11a) and (11b) they stress the subject of the sentence:

(11) a. *Peter yi **sef-sef** bi kol mi fo chop-haus.*
     'Peter himself invited me to the restaurant.'
  b. *Darekto yi **sef-sef** tek wi go pati.*
     'The Director himself took us to the party.'

To make the emphasis even stronger, a preceding particle *na* is added to the noun phrase:

(12) a. *Na Peter yi **sef-sef** bi kol mi fo chop-haus.*
  b. *Na Darekto yi **sef-sef** tek wi go pati.*

A related form involves the object personal pronoun to focus on the VP:

(13) a. *A di **go mi** fo mimbo haus.*
     'I am going [me] to the drink parlour/bar.' (i.e. I *really* want to go to the bar)

b.   *I di **chop** yi.*
'He/she is eating [him/her].' (i.e. he/she is actually eating, despite all)
c.   *Deh di **vex** dem.*
'They are angry [them].'

The negative marker *no* does not change the position of the emphatic pronoun, as illustrated in (14):

(14)   *A no di go mi fo mimbo haus.*
'I am not going [me] to the bar.'

4.3.   Verbs

4.3.1.   The verb fo bi *'to be'*

This verb has four forms: *bi, na, di* and *dey*. *Bi* is often used with subject pronouns, as equational copula. *Na* is often used to identify people and places (identificative copula). They function as copular verbs in the simple present.

(15)   a.   *Yu **bi** big man.*
'You are an important personality.'
b.   *Wuna **bi** sikul pikin dem.*
'You are school children.'
c.   *Ma papa **na** ticha.*
'My father is a teacher.'
d.   *Bamenda **na** big taun fo Cameroon.*
'Bamenda is a big town in Cameroon.'

Di is used as an auxiliary verb denoting progressive aspect:

(16)   a.   *A **di** shidon witi ma anty.*
'I'm living with my aunt.'
b.   *Deh **di** tok kontre tok fo klas.*
'They're speaking vernacular languages in class.'

Dey is used as a locative copula:

(17)   a.   *Ma mami **dey** fo maket.*
'My mother is in the market.'
b.   *Wuna famili dem **dey** fo Nigeria.*
'Your families are in Nigeria.'
c.   *Moni no **dey** fo ma broda yi kwa.*
'There is no money in my brother's pocket.'

4.3.2. The verbs get 'be', laik 'like' and sabi 'know'

These verbs do not use the auxiliary *di* in the present tense, as they are statives rather than action verbs. Examples:

(18)   a.   *Ma kombi get sikin.*
              'My friend is fat.'
       b.   *A laik ma pikin.*
              'I love my child.'
       c.   *Yu sabi yi papa.*
              'You know his/her father.'

4.3.3. The verbs fit and wan

These are auxiliary verbs and can be used in different ways. Firstly, *fit* can be used as a polite way of making requests. Secondly, it can be used to indicate the ability and the will to do something, as illustrated in (19a)–(19d). *Wan* is used to express an intention, a desire, or a wish, as in (19e).

(19)   a.   *Wi **fit** go sinima dis nait?*
              'Could we go to the movies this night?'
       b.   *Yu **fit** gif mi mimbo?*
              'Could you give me a drink?'
       c.   *A **fit** kuk rais.*
              'I can cook rice.'
       d.   *Ndikum no **fit** draif moto.*
              'Ndikum cannot drive a car.'
       e.   *Pasto **wan** preya fo yu.*
              'The Pastor would like to pray for you.'

4.3.4. Verb reduplication for intensity

In the following sentences the reduplicated words are used as verbs only. They often signify or emphasize a continual occurrence of a phenomenon. Note that the sentences would still be correct Kamtok sentences if the words were not repeated. However, their implications and meaning would be different. Compare (20a) and (20b) with (20c) and (20d) below:

(20)   a.   *Ren di **fol fol**.*
              'It is raining all the time.'

b. *Fo shap monin, wuman dem di **hori hori** fo go fam.*
    'Early in the morning, women are always in a mad rush to go to
    the farm.'

c. *Ren di **fol**.*
    'It is raining.'

d. *Fo shap monin, wuman dem di **hori** fo go fam.*
    'Early in the morning, women hurry to go to the farm.'

4.3.5   Repeated verbs with the object pronoun am

This construction is used to emphasize a contrast, as in (21):

(21)   a.   Q: *Yu bi trowe da sup?*
                 'Did you throw away that soup?'
            A: *No-oh, A no bi **trowe am** fo **trowe am**; A bi **drink am** fo **drink
                 am**.*
                 'No, I didn't throw it away; I drank it instead.'

Sometimes the resulting sentence structure from these repeated verbs expresses
the passive voice, which otherwise would be considered absent in Kamtok. The
third person plural subject personal pronoun *deh* must be used in this case:

       b.   Q: *Deh di kuk soya, no bi so?*
                 'Soya is boiled, isn't it?'
            A: *No-oh, **deh** no di **kuk am** fo **kuk am**; **deh** di **bon am** fo **bon
                 am**.*
                 'No, it is not boiled; it is roasted.'

       c.   *Deh no di **pawn** fufu fo **pawn am**; deh di **ton am** fo **ton am**.*
            'Fufu is not pounded; it is stirred.'

Note that in Kamtok the verb *kuk* is used to mean boiling or steaming only.
Other methods of cooking like grilling, roasting and baking are called *bon*
'burning'. Cooking in hot oil is called *frai* 'fry'. When food is cooked and ready,
the Kamtok word is *don* and not *kukt* 'cooked', e.g. *De planti don don* 'The
plantain is cooked/ready'.

4.3.6.   The verb get fo *'must/have to'*

Get fo is used when giving directives. It expresses obligation. The use of *get
fo* in giving orders is more polite than its synonyms *mos* and/or *mostu*. These
have the same function as *get fo* but appear to be rather impolite.

(22)   a.   *Yu **get fo** rid ya buk.*
          'You have to study.'
      b.   *Beri **mostu** maret dis man.*
          'Beri must get married to this man.'

4.4.   Verb tense and aspect

4.4.1.   The past

The past simple is formed by using the auxiliary *bi* + Verb.

(23)   a.   *Yesedey A **bi go** fo maket.*
          'Yesterday I went to the market.'
      b.   *Ma sista no **bi go** fo maket.*
          'My sister did not go to the maket.'

The recent past or present perfect and the unspecified past are marked by the auxiliary *don* + Verb. As unspecified past, it is used to ask whether one has ever done something or not. Sometimes the word *bifo* 'before' is added at the end of the question. The negative of *don* is *noba*.

(24)   a.   *I **don** si dokta.*
          'He/she has seen the doctor.'
      b.   *Paul **don** sik plenty.*
          'Paul has been very sick.'
      c.   *Yi bele **don** poch bifo?*
          'Has he ever had diarrhoea?'
      d.   *I **noba** si dokta.*
          'He hasn't seen the doctor.'

Adding the auxiliary *bi* to the recent past marker *don* and the main verb forms the past perfect: *bi* + *don* + Verb.

(25)   a.   *Ren **bi don fol** bifo wi komot.*
          'Rain had fallen before we went out.'
      b.   *Kao no **bi don chop** ol kon fo fam taim weh de pikin dem bi kam.*
          'The cow had not eaten all the corn in the farm when the children came.'

The imperfect *be* + *di* + Verb is used to indicate actions begun in the past but not necessarily completed as in (26a), for habitual actions as in (26b), and for two past actions taking place at the same time as in (26c):

(26)   a.   *Tif pipol dem **bi di run** foseka se polis bi kam.*
'The thieves were running because the police came.'
b.   *San-san boi dem **bi di hambok** woman dem plenty.*
'The rascals were disturbing women a lot.'
c.   *Tif pipol dem **bi di brok** yi haus taim weh yi bi di slip.*
'Thieves were breaking into his house when he was sleeping.'

4.4.2.   The future

The simple future tense in Kamtok is formed by adding the auxiliary *go* to the main verb: *go* + Verb.

(27)   *Ngwing **go go** holide fo Limbe nex wik.*
'Ngwing will go on vacation to Limbe next week.'

The progressive aspect of the future is obtained by adding the auxiliary *di* to the future marker *go*: *go* + *di* + Verb.

(28)   a.   *Taim weh a go inta Njangi, a **go di chop** kola.*
'When I join the "Njangi" group, I will be eating kola nuts.'
b.   *Pipol dem no **go di kam** fo ma haus fosika se a no get moni.*
'People will not be coming to my house because I have no money.'

4.4.3.   Dropping tense markers

In narrations, once the time of the story has been established, tense markers can be dropped. It is not necessary in Kamtok to use auxiliary verbs throughout a narrative. Compare the two texts below and observe the absence of auxiliaries in the second.

(29)   a.   *Yesede, Manka **bi** go fo Mankon Maket. Taim weh yi **bi** rich fo maket, yi **bi** bay plenty tin dem. Afta, yi **bi** go chop-haus an yi **bi** chop achu an yi **bi** drin top.*
b.   *Yesede, Manka **bi** go fo Mankon Maket. Taim weh yi Ø rich fo maket, yi Ø bay plenty tin dem. Afta, yi Ø go chop-haus an yi Ø chop achu an yi Ø drin top.*
'Yesterday Manka went to Mankon Market. When she arrived at the market she bought many things. After that, she went to a restaurant and ate achu and drank a soft drink.'

Some verbs such as *wan*, *get fo*, *fit*, and *sabi* may not need tense-markers or auxiliaries when they are used in the present tense. However, they may need tense-markers when they are used in other tenses.

(30)   a.   *Joseph **wan** join Kwifo.*
            'Joseph wants to become a member of Kwifo.'
       b.   *Yi **get** fo bay kotlas an spia.*
            'He has to buy a cutlass and a spear.'
       c.   *Trenja no **fit** inta juju.*
            'A foreigner cannot become a member of a secret society.'
       d.   *Fon sabi ol kontri fashon fo vilej.*
            'The chief knows all the traditional rites of the village.'

4.5.   Adjectives

The position of adjectives in Kamtok sentences is the same as in English, that is, they can be used both attributive as in (31a) and predicative as in (31b):

(31)   a.   *Ma kombi get **bik** fut dem.*
            'My friend has big feet.'
       b.   *Ma kombi yi fut dem **bik**.*
            'My friend's feet are big.'

Possessive adjectives are: *ma* 'my', *ya* 'your', *yi* 'his/her/its', *wuna* 'your' (plural), *wi* 'our', and *dia* 'their'. They precede the nouns they determine, e.g., *ma papa* 'my father', *wuna moyo* 'your father-in-law'.
    Certain reduplicated forms are used as adjectives and adverbs, and can modify both nouns and verbs depending on the context of the sentence.

(32)   a.   *Pipol dem for kontre get **fain fain** fashon.*
            'Villagers are well behaved.'
       b.   *Da Pa di **wok fain fain.***
            'That elderly man works well/hard.'
       c.   *Shu get **nyu nyu** kombi dem.*
            'Shu has new friends.'
       d.   *Shu don jos **kam nyu nyu.***
            'Shu has just recently come.'

4.6.   Adverbs

Adverbs in Kamtok include *simol-simol* 'slowly/softly/gradually', *sofli-sofli* 'slowly/steadily/calmly', *popo* 'really', *kwik-kwik* 'quickly' and *ova* 'very/too much'. Unlike in English, *ova* can both precede and follow the verb it is modifying. All other adverbs, however, are post-modifying only.

(33)   a.   *Ma bik broda di chop **ova**.*
              'My elder brother eats too much.'
        b.   *Ma bik broda di **ova** chop.*
              'My elder brother eats too much.'
        d.   *Wuna di waka **sofli-sofli**.*
              'You are walking slowly.'
        e.   **Wuna di **sofli-sofli waka**.*

4.7.   Prepositions

The most common preposition *fo* can take the Standard English (StE) meaning of 'to', 'at', 'in', 'on', 'about', and 'from'. The meaning depends on the context of use. The following sentences illustrate this fact.

(34)   a.   *A di go **fo** ma wok.*
              'I'm going **to** my place of work.'
        b.   *Pikin dem di pley futbol **fo** stad.*
              'The children are playing football **at** the stadium.'
        c.   *Piskops don wok **fo** Cameroon fo long taim.*
              'The Peace Corps have worked **in** Cameroon for long.'
        d.   *Ha fo ya wok witi fama dem?*
              'What **about** your work with farmers?'
        e.   *De kapinta yi wok tin dem dey **fo** tebul.*
              'The carpenter's tools are **on** the table.'
        f.   *Wuna komot **fo** England?*
              'Do you come **from** England?'

When *fo* is functioning as 'to', it can be omitted from a sentence without causing any change of meaning, e.g. *A wan go Ø taun* is exactly the same as *A wan go fo taun* 'I want to go to the town'.

Although *fo* functions as a preposition in its own right, it can also be attached to other prepositional words to indicate location of places and things. Thus we have *fo kona* 'close to/near', *fo midul* 'in the middle of/between', *fo ontop* 'on top of/on', *fo onda* 'under', *fo bak* 'behind' *fo bifo/fo fron* 'in front of', *fo wu-*

man han 'to the left', *fo man han* 'to the right', *fo oposit* 'opposite/across', *fo insai* 'inside', and *fo opsai* 'outside'.

4.8. Conjunctions and interjections

Kamtok conjunctions are the same as in English but for the difference in spelling and pronunciation. One exception is Kamtok *an* 'and' which is omitted in a combination of *kam* or *go* with another action verb:

(35) a. **Kam ∅ helep** *mi wash dis klos dem.*
        'Come and help me wash these clothes.'
    b. **Go ∅ gif** *dis basket fo bik-mami.*
        'Go and give this basket to grandmother.'
    c. *Onana don* **go ∅ bit** *yi wuman fo mimbo haus.*
        'Onana has gone and beaten his wife in the drink parlour.'
    d. *Ticha bi* **kam ∅ tok** *fo Pa se a di wok fain fo sikul.*
        'The teacher came and told Papa that I do well in school.'

The most common interjections in Kamtok are *Massa! Ma mamy ey!* and *A sey eh!* The latter is also used as an introduction to questions.

5.   Sentence structure

5.1.   The simple sentence

As in English, simple declaratives in Kamtok follow an SVO pattern:

(36) a. *Pikin di kray.*
        'The child is crying.'

Unlike in English, where the negative *not* or *n't* occurs after the first auxiliary, in Kamtok the negative marker *no* is placed in front of the verb phrase.

    b. *Pikin no di kray.*
        *'The child not is crying.'

Similarly, with interrogatives there is no subject-operator inversion in Kamtok. In speech, only the rising intonation differentiates the question from the statement, while in writing, only the question mark does the same.

    c. *Pikin di kray?*
        'Is the child crying?'

Wh-words, however, are also used to ask questions. For a selection of Kamtok *wh*-words, see Table 7 below:

Table 7. Kamtok *wh*-words

Kamtok	English	Question
Weti	'what'	*Weti yu di do?* 'What are you doing?'
Wusay	'where'	*Wusay yu di go?* 'Where are you going?
Wishtaim	'when'	*Wishtaim sikul di klos?* 'When are schools closing?'
Way	'why'	*Way da boi di ron?* 'Why is that boy running?'
Ha	'how'	*Ha yu dey?* 'How are you?'

The particle *na* can sometimes be used alongside *wh*-words, for example *Na weti dis?* 'What is this?' or *Na wusay yu komot?* 'Where are you coming from?'

Question tags do not vary according to the tense of the verb in the preceding statement. There is just one question tag for all statements, *no bi so*:

(37) a. *Yu laik fo chop wata-fufu an eru, **no bi so**?*
          'You like to eat wata-fufu and eru, don't you?'
      b. *Da wuman dem bi mami-pikin dem, **no bi so**?*
          'Those women are nursing mothers, aren't they?'
      c. *Wuna go bay moto smol taim, **no bi so**.*
          'You will soon buy a car, won't you?'

As far as the imperative is concerned, a distinction occurs between the singular and the plural subject. In the singular, the direct command takes no subject pronoun, while it does in the plural.

(38) a. Ø *Wukop!*   c. Ø *Kam dong!*
          'Wake up!' (sg.)   'Descend!' (sg.)
      b. ***Wuna** wukop!*   d. ***Wuna** kam dong!*
          'Wake up!' (pl.)   'Descend!' (pl.)

Indirect commands are expressed using the word *mek*. Unlike with direct commands, the speaker using the indirect command has no authority over the addressee. It is rather a polite way of giving instructions. The indirect command can be used with all subject pronouns.

(39) a. *Mek **A** komot fo moto.*
          'Let me get out of the vehicle.'
      b. *Mek **wuna** push moto.*
          'Please push the vehicle.'
      c. *Mek **dem** shidon fo bak.*
          'Let them sit at the back.'
      d. *Mek **wi** jek kago.*
          'Let us lift the luggage.'

5.2.   Comparison

Words used to express comparison in Kamtok are *pas* (< pass), *laik*, *rich* (< reach), and *no rich*.

With nouns:
(40) a. *A get klos dem **pas** yu.*
          'I have more clothes than you.'
      b. *Mofor get trosa dem **laik** Anye.*
          'Mofor has as many trousers as Anye.'
      c. *Massa Ndikum no get moni **rich** Massa Nde.*
          'Mr. Ndikum doesn't have as much money as Mr. Nde.'

With adjectives:
(41) a. *Ma sista yi rapa fain **pas** ma mami yi on.*
          'My sister's loin-cloth is nicer than my mother's.'
      b. *John yi fut dem bik **rich** Peter yi on dem.*
          'John's feet are as big as Peter's.'
      c. *Dis rod **no** long **rich** da ada wan.*
          'This road is not as long as the other one.'

With verbs:
(42) a. *Susana di bay nyanga tin dem **pas** Mary.*
          'Susan buys beauty products more than Mary.'
      b. *Ngwe sabi ayon klos **pas** yi big sista.*
          'Ngwe does ironing better than her elder sister.'

c.   *Lum no di gif moni fo yi mami **pas** Siri.*
     'Lum doesn't give more money to her mother than Siri does.'

With adverbs:

(43) a.   *Yu di soh kwik-kwik **laik** mi.*
           'You sew as fast as I do.'
      b.   *Dis pikin di tok sofli-sofli **pas** yi papa.*
           'This child speaks more slowly than his father.'
      c.   *Wuna no fit wok tron-tron **rich** wi.*
           'You cannot work as hard as we do.'

Superlatives exist in two forms relating to superiority and inferiority. The former is marked by the expressions *pas ol*, *taim no dey*, and *pas mak*, the later by *atol-atol* and *no smol*. They express the highest degree of comparison.

(44) a.   *Sikam rapa fain. Nangeria wax fain pas sikam. Bot Holan wax*
           *fain **pas mak** / Holan wax fain **pas ol**/Holan wax fain **taim no dey**.*
           'But Holland Wax is the best.'
      b.   *Da telo no sabi mak klos **no smol**/Da telo no sabi mak klos*
           ***atol-atol**.*
           'That tailor doesn't know how to embroider at all/not the least.'

6.   Conclusion

Much of the published research that has been carried out on Kamtok has been of a sociolinguistic nature. Very little has been done in the field of linguistic description. There is a debate among Cameroonian linguists as to whether Kamtok has reached a status fit enough to be given official recognition by the government of the country. It could then be treated like any other Cameroonian national language, possibly even as a medium of instruction in the first few years of primary education in the regions of the country where Kamtok is highly respected. It is hoped that a scientific study of the language like the one done here will shed more light on its nature and quality, rendering it more prestigious in the eyes of those who have so far thought it was not, and consequently enhance and improve the quality of the debate.

*   I am deeply indebted to Joseph Wabo, a former teacher of Cameroon Pidgin to American Peace Corps volunteers, who permitted me to photocopy the Trainers' Manual that he and other Peace Corps trainers compiled and used for their teaching. Many of the examples are modified versions of exercises from this manual. Unfortunately, the document is not a published book and is neither dated nor authored.

Exercises and study questions

1. Write questions for these answers:

   a. *Ma papa di wok fo fam.*
   b. *A dey fain.*
   c. *Wuna moyo dey fo Gabona.*
   d. *Dem mami don go fo maket.*
   e. *Wi anti di kuk wi chop.*

2. Change the following sentences into the negative:

   a. *Wuna bi pipol dem fo Yaounde.*
   b. *Nintai na kuk.*
   c. *Yesedey ma papa bi go fo fam.*
   d. *Yu don bay nyu rapa.*
   e. *Paul go go Bamenda nex mun.*

3. Join the following sentences using the relative pronoun *weh*:

   a. *Da wata dey fo tebul. Da wata komot fo don hil.*
   b. *Wi di go bay simen. Yi dey fo maket.*
   c. *A don go kapinta. Yi wok fain pas mak.*
   d. *Ted bi chenj lok. Yi bi dey fo yi dooh.*
   e. *Ma lanlod di kam. Yi pikin dey fo ma haus.*

4. Change the sentences into the simple past or past perfect as appropriate:

   a. *Patrick sabi ple futbol.*
   b. *Son di shain plenty.*
   c. *Wi di chapia fam taim weh wi di chop.*
   d. *Win di pas an sun di shayn.*
   e. *Bush don katch faya, wata ren don quentch'am.*

5. Translate the following sentences into Kamtok using repeated words as nouns, adjectives, verbs or adverbs.

   a. *That elderly man talks all the time about his tribe.*
   b. *A daily walk is good for you.*
   c. *Do you eat the kola nut one at a time?*
   d. *If you hurry, you will not catch the monkey.*
   e. *During the ceremony, people were dancing again and again.*

Selected references

Please consult the General references for titles mentioned in the text but not included in the references below. For a full bibliography see the accompanying CD-ROM.

< www.ethnologue.com/show_country.asp?name=Cameroon >
Mackenzie, J. Lachlan
    2002   Cameroonian Pidgin English: a grammatical sketch. http://cursus.let.vu.nl/
            engels/Kamtok.htm

East African English (Kenya, Uganda, Tanzania): morphology and syntax

Josef Schmied

1. Introduction

An outline of grammatical features of East African English (EAfE) is even more difficult to produce than that of its phonology, because deviations in grammar occur in much lower frequencies. One reason for this lower frequency is perhaps that grammatical deviations are more stigmatised. Thus, an independent EAfE grammar is even less distinguishable than an independent phonology or lexicon.

East African tendencies in morphology and syntax can often also be found in other parts of Africa and even beyond, in so-called New Englishes (cf. Hickey 2003), and even in some First Language (L1) varieties in Britain, America or Australia. Partly at least, English varieties all seem to develop in similar directions in some respects, as for instance in terms of simplification and regularisation. Frequency, consistency, systematicity and the developmental, regional and social distribution over various spoken and written text types are a matter for further research as well as the discovery of implicational hierarchies in frequency and acceptability.

2. Morphology

In this section the grammatical description of EAfE will therefore be presented in broad categories of word class type, independent of any specific syntax or interpretation according to language learning theories. This sometimes leads to overlaps of explanations with underlying semantic structures, such as the 'count – non-count' distinction, which has repercussions for plural formation as well as the use of articles, although with different frequencies. The pluralisation *advices*, for instance, seems to be less frequent than *an advice*. What are called grammatical features do not occur consistently each time a construction is used and are very often related to sub-rules of more general rules, which are not affected.

2.1.   Verb phrase

As far as the verb phrase is concerned, the following tendencies have been noted.

Inflectional endings are not always added to the verb, but the general, regular or unmarked forms are used instead:
This applies to the regular endings of the 3rd sg. present tense and of the past tense as well as to irregular verb forms. Since such deviations from the (British) norm are stigmatised, educated East Africans only use them in special cases. This may happen when they are supported by the pronunciation (e.g. alveolar fricatives/plosives for marking past and plural, respectively, are added to alveolar fricatives/plosives). The phenomenon can also be seen when verb forms like *ran* and *run* are not clearly distinguished, especially when it seems redundant (e.g. after time adverbials). Some cases, like (1) for example, seem a simple expansion of the British norm, where a unit can be seen as a whole or as several pieces:

(1)   *K.shs. 33,500/-* **was** (StE *were) raised during our pre-wedding.*
       (ICE-EA: S1BCE05K)

Complex tenses tend to be avoided:
This tendency occurs particularly with the past perfect and conditionals (*It would have been much better if this was done*) and is also common in less formal native-speaker usage today. It affects mainly the sequence of tenses taught in school grammar, particularly in the case of subordinate clauses in past contexts and when certain types of modality (especially irrealis) are expressed. Past tense forms are rarely used to express modality as in Standard English (StE) *I had better* or *If I went*; this is considered pedantic and typically British. Constructions with *will* are used instead.

Extended forms (BE + VERB + -*ing* construction) are used frequently and do not necessarily imply StE (progressive) meanings:
This affects the distinction between the non-stative and the stative use of verbs. It applies particularly to some verbs that are used with -ing forms only in marked, specific meanings. The prime example is *have*, which is used with the semantics of 'temporariness' but also 'habitual', as in (2).

(2)   *Some of us may think that women always* **are having** *a lot of things to do.* (ICE-EA: S1BINT13T)

(3)   *It is really very toxic to the user because it produces a lot of smoke heavy smoke and it* **is smelling**. (ICE-EA: S1BINT13T)

Patterns and particles of phrasal/prepositional verbs vary:
Phrasal and prepositional verbs are particularly important in English word formation. Adding particles or prepositions after the English verb is a style-spe-
cific alternative to prefixation, especially with Germanic stems, for example *go
about* 'begin', *go ahead* 'proceed', *go back* 'return', *go down* 'decrease', *go
on* 'continue' and *go up* 'increase'). This alternative and special phrasal/prepo-
sitional usage is unknown in African languages. Especially for phrasal verbs,
the corresponding preposition is not easily accessible for non-native speakers,
since the meanings are figurative.

Selection criteria may be extensions from semantically similar phrasal verbs
or from etymologically related nouns in English, like *talk about* > *discuss
about* or *discussion about* > *discuss about*. Whether a phrase should be considered tautologous is not easy to decide. In the end, the difference between
British English (BrE) and EAfE is often a matter of frequency: *discuss about*,
for example, occurs relatively three times as often on web pages in the Kenyan
domain (*.ke*) as on the corresponding UK pages (*co.uk*).

In formal descriptive categories, of course, prepositions may be omitted (the
well-known *I will pick you* [StE *up*] *at eight, crop* [StE *up*], *provide* [*with*]),
substituted (e.g. *attach **with*** [StE *to*], *concentrate **with*** [StE *on*], *congratulate
for* [StE *on*], *participate **with*** [StE *in*], *result **into/to*** [StE *in*]), or added, which
seems to be the most frequent case (e.g. *advocate **for**, attend **to**, mention **about**,
join **with***). Particles are omitted when they appear "obvious", as in *protest* (StE
against).

The substituted particles are often consistent with the prefix morpheme (e.g.
*deprive **from*** instead of *deprive of*) or closely related in meaning (e.g. *out* and
off, as in *switch **out*** [StE *off*] *the light, put **off*** [StE *out*] *the fire*). The additional
particles are often logically possible, but considered redundant with the verb
according to StE norms. They are, however, used after the corresponding noun
(e.g. *emphasise **on*** < *emphasis*$_N$ *on*; similarly, *demand for, request for, stress
on*). Besides analogy, interference from African languages is possible, since
their prepositional system is relatively simple and thus polysemous. For instance, one basic locative proposition in Kiswahili, *mwituni,* can be translated
as *at, to,* i*n/inside, by/near/next to* and *from the forest.*

Verb complementation (especially infinitives and gerunds) varies freely:
As verb complementation is usually a matter of individual lexemes rather than
rules, this feature would have to be listed or taught with the individual verb lexemes. This also determines how stigmatised the expression is. Again, speakers
of EAfE often try to solve apparent irregularities by applying semantic criteria,
thus *allow him go* is analogous to *let him go* and *made him to do* parallel to

forced him to do. These are equivalent structures, but they do not correspond to British norms. Sometimes two similar constructions are confused (as *decide to* + infinitive and *decide on* + *-ing*). The subtle distinctions between infinitive and gerund constructions (e.g. between *tried to walk* and *tried walking*) tend to be neglected and the choice seems random, as can be seen in (4) and (5):

(4)   *Would you mind **to** tell us uh a brief background about ICAC and uh what uh are you going to discuss in Arusha.* (ICE-EA: S1B041T)

(5)   *He has indicated to want to stop **to** deliver what he has.* (ICE-EA: S1B031T)

2.2.   Noun phrase

The construction of noun phrases in EAfE is the same as in StE, although a few simplifying tendencies have been observed.

Noun phrases are not always marked for number and case (by inflectional endings):
Although English nominal inflections are simple compared to Bantu languages, which have complex nominal classes marked by prefixes, the systems cannot be compared. Further simplification of the English system is therefore possible in EAfE. This applies to certain plural endings (especially when they are redundant after numerals) as well as to genitives (especially when they are redundant in noun modifications that can be interpreted as compounds). It also applies to relative pronouns, where the inflected forms *whom* and *whose* are occasionally avoided in favour of invariable *which* constructions:

(6)   *Adult education **which** its main purpose is to help adults to learn how to read and write faces many problems.*

The use of *-s* plural markers is overgeneralised:
This tendency is quite common in New Englishes and in most cases semantically motivated: although they can also be seen as a collective unit, several individual pieces can be distinguished, for example with *luggages, furnitures, firewoods* or *grasses.* Sometimes this tendency conflates more or less subtle semantic differentiations in StE, such as between *food – foods, people – peoples,* sometimes it merely regularises (historical) morphological StE irregularities, as in *fishes.*

   East African usage basically ignores the grammatical distinction of count vs. non-count nouns, which does not always correspond to the semantic one. In StE, plural *-s* is not added to nouns that are considered abstract or collective/

mass and thus non-count, as for example *discontent* or *informations*. But even in StE, some of the non-countables may occur in the plural in special meanings (*works*) or in stressed contexts (*experiences*). Thus, differences are often a question of interpretation and frequency.

(7)   *These **advices** are coming because they've already studied all of us.* (ICE-EA: S1BINT12T)

Articles and other determiners tend to be omitted:
This tendency may partly be an overgeneralization of British usage (*I am going to church/school/*post office*). Often, subrules of StE grammar are neglected, e.g. the rule that a definite article is used when nouns are postmodified by *of*-genitives or defining relative clauses, as in (8). The basic function of the definite article is of course to refer back to something mentioned earlier in the discourse. Thus, *the others* is clearly cataphoric and specific and different from *others* referring generally to "other people", but such distinctions are not always maintained in New Englishes.

(8)   *Standing hay, though of poor quality, offers animals nutrients required for Ø maintenance of their body condition.* (ICE-EA: W2B033K)

(9)   *There is Ø need for development of small, hand-driven machines.* (ICE-EA: W2B033K)

In contrast to the system in StE, some linguists (e.g. Platt, Ho and Weber 1984: 52–59) even see a completely different system of articles in New Englishes. They argue that StE uses the definite/indefinite system (known vs not known) as the basic distinction, while the New Englishes prefer to use the specific vs non-specific (particular vs not particular) system, as in the StE determiner pair *a certain – any*. In this system, non-specific reference is expressed by the absence of an article (as in *Give me beer*, which gives the typical impression of EAfE "rude style") and specific by the use of the article *the*. The tendency of omitting determiners also expands to indefinite, possessive and demonstrative pronouns.

2.3.   Pronouns

Pronouns may be redundant, especially in pronoun appositions:
A pronoun apposition occurs after the noun it refers to, that is, it does not have the usual anaphoric function of linking sentences but that of "repeating" a noun (phrase) in the same sentence. This usage is a particular discourse strategy in which the theme of a sentence is fronted with the pronoun as a placeholder for

the noun phrase which was extracted by the fronting process. In StE, pronoun apposition is perfectly accepted when the previous noun phrase is introduced by *as for* NP or *as far as* NP *is concerned*, as illustrated in (10) and (11). When speakers seem to hesitate or have lost their thread, copying a pronoun may help the listener to process the message.

(10)   *As for the calcium in bone, it plays two important roles.* (ICE-EA: W2B030K)

(11)   *As for me and my house, we declared war on poverty.* (ICE-EA: W2F002K)

EAfE seems to be more liberal as far as these rules are concerned, at least in speech. Pronoun copying occurs especially in oral English after long and complex subjects, because of prepositional constructions as in (12), infinitives or relative clauses, as in (13):

(12)   *So human being in the first time of his existence **he** found that he was <-/subjected> to the work.* (ICE-EA: S1B004T)

(13)   *there is our glue which we are getting **them** near.* (ICE-EA: S1B047I)

Redundant pronouns can be found within relatives when personal pronouns take up the head of a relative construction, as in (6) above, and when possessive pronouns premodify the head of a relative construction (i.e. the possessive pronoun and the relative clause subject refer to the same person, as in ***my** book that I read*).

Pronouns are not always distinguished by gender:
The three possibilities of third person singular pronouns, *he, she* and *it* in subject roles and *his, her* and *its* in possessive roles, are often used indiscriminately, especially when their pronunciation is only distinguished by one consonant, as in the case of *he* and *she*. This can be accounted for as simplification or as interference from African mother tongues that do not have sex distinctions in pronouns (e.g. languages that have only one class for animate or human beings in general).

Prepositions are underdifferentiated:
English prepositions are among the most polysemous and most idiomatic. Because of its lack of inflectional morphology, prepositions are particularly important in English. StE is peculiar in that the use of prepositions is often fixed and either dependent on the preceding verb, noun, adjective or adverb or the following noun. The choice of the idiomatic preposition may follow semantic, morphological or even traditional Latin rules. The matching of prepositions

to verbs, nouns, adjectives or adverbs is therefore neither easy nor logical to a second-language user.

Generally, the most frequent English prepositions *of* and *in* (at the expense of the more special *into*) occur significantly more frequently in EAfE than in BrE (cf. Mwangi 2003). This may be explained as a "safety strategy". More specific simple prepositions (like *off* or *across*) are used less often. This is sometimes seen as underdifferentiation in EAfE, e.g. disregarding the distinction between restricted position and extended position.

Thus, a phrase like *at Nairobi* is used regularly in Kenya, even when it does not suggest a point in a global perspective, but an extended place for which *in Nairobi* is clearly preferred in StE. Since the prepositional systems in English are much more complex than in African languages, standard prepositions tend to be chosen (e.g. *in* for *into*) and analogy plays an important role. Rare prepositions (like *underneath*, spatial *past*, or *down*) are used even less in EAfE. Another case of simplification is the neglected distinction between locative *beside* and contrastive *besides*.

Similarly, frequent complex prepositions (like *because of, according to* and *due to*) occur more often, less frequent and more complex ones (like *in front of, in favour of, by means of, in the light of*) less often in spoken EAfE.

(14)   *What is the main reason **of** (StE for) the decrease of production.*
        (ICE-EA: S1B041T)

(15)   *...many people are just coming **in** (to) the country.* (ICE-EA:
        S1A018T)

2.4.   Adjectives

Adjective forms tend to be used as adverbs. The unmarked adverbial form is correct in very few cases in StE (*hard, first, high* in certain contexts or sayings like *take it easy*, etc.; but not in *Do it proper*). Unmarked adverbials occur not only in African but also in some American and British English varieties.

2.5.   Question tags

Question tags tend to occur in invariant form. Tag questions are vital in discourse, but unusually complex in StE morphology. Their form depends on the main clause verb, the gender of the subject and its affirmative or negative character. They tend to be generalised in African varieties of English as in others, e.g. Welsh English. This means that the tag is neither adapted to the verb form nor to the subject of the main clause. *Is* and *it* occur with all verbs and subjects and are repeated consistently to make sure the listeners are still listening. Example (16) is an extreme case of a coherent speech excerpt with three (out of five) non-standard *isn't it* cases in half a minute.

Often the tag is used indiscriminately in the negative form, after affirmative as well as after negative clauses; thus subtle StE distinctions in speaker assumption between positive and negated tags (*is it?* and *isn't it?* with raising and falling intonation, respectively) disappear. Occasionally, non-verbal particles with the same functions are added. *Not so* in (17) has an equivalent in many African languages, e.g. *sivyo* in Kiswahili, but there is also the common *init* in non-standard urban mother-tongue English.

(16)   *We have <-/haa> and then or this time,* **isn't it?** *,cause it's an existential quantifier or* **isn't it?** *the other side we get it – and then or. There we are,* **isn't it?** *We come again all right uh uh right. That's our statement,* **isn't it.** *Okay. And take note that in that statement now we have two different quantifiers,* **isn't it?** *universal and existential.* (ICE-EA: S2B057K)

(17)   *The price in the display is a very good idea because ...* **Not so?** *uh okay?* (ICE-EA:S1B010K)

2.6   Responses to *yes/no* questions

Negative *yes/no* questions are confirmed by responding to the form of the question and not to the absolute "inner logic". Those who are used to the StE system of answering direct questions *Yes, it is* or *No, it isn't* may receive a "confusing" mixture of *Yes, he isn't* or *No, he is.* This can be particularly confusing when the tags are omitted and only the particles *no* or *yes* are used. This occasional habit derives from a different frame of reference: EAfE speakers perceive that the negatively stated question queries the accuracy of the statement and thus assert ('Yes, what you say is true') or deny the basic statement ('No, what you say is wrong'). In StE, the particle is chosen in accordance with the answer and in EAfE in accordance with the question. The tag, however, is the same.

(18)   Q: *These problems are uh not biological?*
        A: **Yes,** *they're not biological factor.* (ICE-EA: S1B047K)

3.   Word order

In general, word order in EAfE is much more flexible and can be used to express emphasis and focus more readily than in StE (in this respect it can be seen as being closer to colloquial spoken English).

The basic interrogative word order is maintained in indirect speech and questions:
Indirect speech using the word order of direct speech could be interpreted as correct in spoken English where one cannot distinguish between the direct and indirect versions – if it is marked by a different intonation and a break marking a question mark. That may be the reason why this feature occurs also in non-standard native-speaker English.

(19)   *I would like to know as to where and when **are you going** to have your celebrations and who will be the guest of honour.* (ICE-EA: S1BINT13T)

(20)   *Are there any other activities you're going to show in this week or **you'll be only informing** the public about the two international conferences in Arusha.* (ICE-EA: S1B041T)

Maintaining the *question word – verb – subject* word order seems to contradict another tendency, i.e. to retain the most normal *subject – verb – object* order wherever possible, but it must be interpreted as a simplification or regularisation of the formation rules for all types of questions, direct and indirect.

The strict English word order rules for adverb positions are weakened:
Some adverbs tend to come as an afterthought, often without a break at the end of the clause or sentence, as for example *unfortunately* in (21). Others can be found at the very beginning, as *already* in (22).

(21)   *... thinking that he would not understand **unfortunately**.* (ICE-EA: W1A016T)

(22)   ***Already** appeals have been sent out to individuals, foundations, and other organisations to help contribute.* (ICE-EA: W2B009K)

4.   Discourse

4.1.   Information processing and presentation

More than in other areas of grammar, emphasis is difficult to judge right or wrong vis-à-vis StE norms, and is considered inappropriate only in few cases since the presentation of information remains flexible to a large extent. Often, however, the question whether an unusual construction implies special emphasis or contrast is difficult to decide.

In contrast to other New Englishes, emphatic pronouns and simple repetitions do not seem to imply emphasis. But related processes occur for instance when the stressed reflexive pronoun is placed in front and repeated as a personal pronoun afterwards, as in (23).

(23)   *Uh **myself** uh I am I started working at Muhimbili in nineteen eighty-seven.* (ICE-EA: S1B046T)

Topicalisation through fronting and corresponding intonation is rare in StE, but common in many English varieties (e.g. Irish English). StE has developed special forms like cleft and pseudo-cleft constructions instead, which are again too complex for second-language speakers.

Similarly, in StE *never* refers to a longer period or adds special emphasis, but occasionally it may simply be used to avoid a complex *to-do* construction required before *not*, as in (24):

(24)   *Most Kenyans **never** hesitate to give generously to help build hospitals, schools, dispensaries...* (ICE-EA: W2E018K)

Generally, the presentation of information varies considerably and the perception whether something is marked in discourse or the natural flow varies accordingly, since the optimal choice of a phrase may depend on many factors.

4.2.   Culture-specific discourse

In African societies that maintain more links with oral tradition than European ones, it is not surprising that some discourse features are culture-specific in the sense that they are customarily used and not really marked for the insider, but are clearly unusual for the European outsider. Many such culture-specific discourse features are linked to traditional African social values involving the extended family, the ethnic group, their environment and their habits.

East Africans tend to greet each other elaborately. If visitors wish to make a good impression they should follow the standard patterns of asking *How is the family, the health, the journey/safari* or so on (straightforward translations from the Kiswahili *Habari ya watoto, ... ya afia, ... ya safari*, etc), before launching into a direct request. This is considered polite and more appropriate than toning down direct questions with *I'm terribly sorry to bother you* or *Would you mind telling me*, which are considered affected in ordinary conversation and are not used by East Africans. Furthermore, some code-mixing is possible with handy little words like *sawa* for 'okay' or *asante* (or intensified *asante sana*) for 'thank you', or exclamations like *kumbe* and *kweli* for surprise.

Another East African politeness strategy is to express one's sympathy with some misfortune or unlucky event – e.g. when someone is obviously tired or ill, by inserting *pole* (or intensified *pole sana*) at the beginning, middle or end of a conversation (not to be confused with *pole pole*, which means 'slowly'). This is often translated as *I am sorry*. However, the expression is untranslatable when someone stumbles, because it often implies some fault on the part of the speaker in StE, which is clearly not intended in EAfE.

Other cultural practices have indirect consequences on English word-meanings. Thus the day and the time starts at 6 o'clock in East Africa and in the Swahili counting of hours. Thus *6 o'clock* is actually in Western terms '12 noon' and not '6 p.m.', which would be *12 in the evening* if it is taken over directly from African languages.

Finally, even non-verbal communication patterns contribute to the East African flavour of a conversation, such as frequent nodding supported by a long and reassuring *eehee* shows the speaker that the listener is still following him attentively.

5.   Lexis

The lexicon of EAfE (cf. also Schmied forthcoming) comprises the core lexicon of StE and specific East Africanisms, which would not be interpreted easily or equally by the non-initiated user, for example readers/listeners not familiar with English usage in East Africa. Despite some cultural, especially sociopolitical, differences between Kenya, Uganda and Tanzania, the use of (Kiswahili) loans, the semantic extension of StE lexemes and the idiomatic flexibility are common features.

5.1.   Loanwords from African languages

In this short section, it will suffice to cover three specific and interesting aspects: the range of the Africanisms, the areas of life in which Africanisms occur and the origin of Africanisms: from external sources, i.e. from other African languages, or from internal material, i.e. through English word formation processes.

The first issue deals with the question of how far Africanisms are used and understood in the English-speaking world. Lexical East Africanisms consist of several layers: old Africanisms that developed during colonial days and remained in use in East Africa (not only in international films, like *daktari*), post-independence Africanisms (mainly in politics, like *ujamaa*) and recent Africanisms (like *mitumba* for 'used/second-hand clothes', but sometimes transferred to 'second-hand' in general, as in *mitumba cars* or even *mitumba mentality*).

Very old borrowings, such as *askari, baobab, bwana* or *safari*, mainly in the environmental field, have already been incorporated into general English and are thus codified in general large dictionaries of World English, the *Oxford English Dictionary* with its supplements, for instance. Their range transcends African English by far, and some have even been integrated into other European languages. They are, however, restricted to African contexts and thus have a more specific meaning in general English than in the particular regional English. A well-known example is the Kiswahili word *safari*. In East Africa it denotes any 'journey' (*journey* is hardly ever used, possibly because of pronunciation difficulties). For European tourists it always refers to a small 'expedition' to see and shoot game (in colonial days with a gun, nowadays usually with a camera), normally in national parks. Interestingly enough, *safari* in StE can also refer to the group of people setting out on such a safari, a semantic expansion which is not possible in Kiswahili. Very few Africanisms have such a secure existence in general English, most of them being marginal and only used to render meanings in an African context.

This becomes understandable when one examines the areas of life or domains in which most East Africanisms occur. Schmied (1991: 80–81) shows a few examples mainly from Kiswahili, grouped in the major domains of Africanisms. As can be expected, the African environment is inadequately reflected in the StE lexicon and is supplemented by African names for characteristic landscapes, plants or animals. African loans cluster around "African domains" just as English loans cluster around "European domains". It is interesting to see that the semantic expansion of StE lexemes may create problems of distinction as in the case of *potatoes*, where Africans often have to specify *Irish/European potatoes* or *sweet potatoes*. In general, the preferred staple food dish is hardly ever translated: Kenya's and Tanzania's *ugali* is Uganda's *posho* (from the colonial English *portion*, which was allocated to workers), the traditional maize dish (a little like *polenta* in Italy).

The field of food is probably culture-specific everywhere, but in many African countries there is a marked contrast between European and African food (and eating habits) because Europeans in East Africa have tended not to adopt African food, in contrast to the British in India. Some dishes are also marked by ethnicity or region, like *githeri* for a Gikuyu bean dish or *vitumbua* for a coastal rice-cake. Some are of course clearly imported from Asia like *bajia* (an Indian potato dish) and *chai* (usually black tea).

Interestingly, many African words for kin relations in the intimate family and beyond are retained, especially when used as a form of address (like *Babu* for 'grandfather'). Where African clothing is still worn it is, of course, referred to by African names. Other African customs, which have to be rendered in African words, are concerned with traditional customs or pastimes, like *lobola* 'bride-price', or with rules of politeness (see section 5.3.2.).

An important domain of Africanisms today is politics. African languages have often played a major role in mobilising the masses, even before *uhuru* 'independence' was reached, and before *harambee* 'pulling together' and *nyayo* (ex-President Moi's following in the 'footsteps' of Kenyatta) were national slogans in Kenya and *Ujamaa* 'familyhood' and *Kujigetemea* 'self-reliance' in Tanzania. It is clear that most of these terms have to be seen in their socio-political context, otherwise they may conjure up the wrong connotations. Many politicians wish to demonstrate their local roots by including African vocabulary in their speeches even when using English.

A more comprehensive dictionary entry would have to add typical collocations and sample sentences (in some cases only a picture may explain matters to the non-initiated). Thus a dictionary entry for the famous East Africanism *matatu* (including inflections and denotative and connotative meanings, etymology and collocates) could be as follows:

matatu pl ~s N 'collective taxi' in EAfr., especially Kenya
usu. licensed for fixed routes of public transport, but flexible, they leave when 'full';
infamous for reckless driving and overcrowding;
etym. <Swahili "three", orig. 3 shillings fare;
collocates: N driver, tout, operator, passenger; LOC. park, stand, stage, stop; PREP in, on board a ~; VERB enter, board

These examples also illustrate that many lexemes cannot be translated in a single term or even a few words satisfactorily (cf. *pole* in section 4.2.). This is why many explanations start with *a type of*, indicating a hypernym or a term with a similar function or form from a different culture (like *polenta* above).

Of course, isolated words have to be seen in their cotext, and phrases and collocates may occur like *bahati mbaya* ('bad luck'). Then the borderline between code-mixing and loan words can be blurred when for instance the Kiswahili locative or directive particle *–ni* is added to a word, as when an *officer* is *porini* (i.e. 'in the bush', 'up-country', 'away from the capital or administrative head-quarters').

5.2.   Semantic change of StE lexemes

Even if the words used in African English retain the traditional English form, their meanings may be quite different. Although word usage may depend on the specific linguistic and extralinguistic context and although individual words may show many different deviations, some tendencies may be summarised in a categorisation based on the StE correspondence of meaning and form.

This correspondence may be changed in the particular East African environ-ment or context, for instance when a particular meaning is expressed more than once in the same context (redundancy), when in the fixed correspondence between form and meaning the former is changed, usually on the morphologi-cal level, (idiomaticity), when words extend (shift or occasionally restrict) their meanings in some contexts (reference expansion), when they are confused or when the context of an English lexeme is different, either in terms of colloca-tions or in terms of connotations usually associated with a certain lexeme.

The level of semantic redundancy tends to be higher:
Examples of redundancy can be found on many levels. The repetition of se-mantic elements may occur in connection with word formation. For example, the suffix *-able* expresses the same as the modal auxiliary *can*, so the two do not co-occur, thus *something is traceable to* or *something can be traced to*. Redundancy can also be found with modifying elements like adjectives or adverbs. For example, one defining element of a *ballot* in StE is that it is held secretly, thus a *secret ballot* is considered a tautology. Similarly, *perhaps* is redundant in the cotext of the modal *may*.

Sometimes a (Latin) prefix corresponds to a Germanic particle, and when both are used (as in ***return back** home*) this is considered tautological in StE. Other meaning elements may be reinforced because they seem to have lost part of their meaning, as the feature [+DURATION] immanent in *during* (less so in *in*), which is emphasised a second time by *the course of*. Other subtle cases of redundancy would be *include* in connection with *and so on*, which both convey the idea of an incomplete list, and *reason* in connection with *because* (as in *the reason why he came is because*). However, such cases can also be found in British or American style guides or rules of rhetoric.

Idiomatic expressions are used in a slightly different morphological form:
Idiomatic expressions usually have a very fixed form as the idiomatic meaning consists of more than that of the single word elements involved. Thus, variation in form is not common in StE, for instance, in terms of pluralisation (as in *just pulling your legs*). Sometimes idiomatic expressions are mixed with similar ones (*with regards to* for instance combines *with regard to* and *as regards*). There is also a tendency to make idioms more transparent and/or use more common synonyms, as in *silence **means** (StE gives) consent.*

English word forms are used in other reference contexts (usually expanded):
In African English, word forms occur in slightly different contexts than in British Standard English (BrStE), thus usually expanding their referential meaning. The most striking examples of this are kinship terms. Even the most casual visitor to Africa notices that Africans seem to have very many brothers and sisters or even fathers; this can not only be attributed to the birth rate and the extended family structure. Kinship terms are expanded as reference and address terms, because they go far beyond the British core meanings related to the biological features of consanguinity, generation and sex, and are related to the social features of seniority (age), solidarity, affection and role-relations. Thus, all the mother's co-wives or sisters may be addressed as *mother*, many elderly men as *father* and people from the same village without direct blood relations as *brothers and sisters*. As it is very important to show respect to older people in general, even older sisters may be ascribed the higher status of *auntie*. This is supported by different kinship categorisations in African languages, where seniority is most important.

Another culture-based term that even the casual tourist notices is *hoteli*, which in Kiswahili refers to a restaurant, so if a stranger or foreigner asks for a *hotel* they may be shown a place to eat. This change of meaning of English loans in African languages including African English is of course the reverse side of the loans from African languages mentioned (in section 5.1. above).

The use of the English discourse particle *sorry* was mentioned in section 4.2. Many visitors to Africa have noticed that their African friends seem to apologise frequently. When Africans say *sorry*, however, they merely use the appropriate African form of expressing solidarity or sympathy, because it is customary to express sympathy when someone has an unfortunate experience. Thus, the word which expresses apology in StE, *sorry*, has expanded its meaning to sympathy in African English, because a gap in the vocabulary seems to have been felt by African users. Other semantic incongruencies can be detected when the usage of expressions of gratitude (*thank you*) and politeness (*please*), in replies corresponding to American *You are welcome*, are examined carefully.

English word forms are confused with similar ones:
In lexical fields, word meanings overlap so that expansions of one lexeme affect the others in the same field. Common "confusables" clash, for instance, the cases when *to book* is used like StE *to hire*, *to forget* like *to lose*, *to refuse* like *to deny*, *to convince* like *to persuade*, *to see* like *to look*, *to reach* like *to arrive*, *arm* like *hand*, *guest* like *stranger*, *strange* like *foreign* and so on. In most of these cases, either the meanings have been expanded or more specific features (selection restrictions) have been dropped. *To escort*, for instance, originally implies a special guard or act of courtesy, but by Africans it may be used in the more general sense of *to accompany*, without the narrower restrictions.

Occasionally, meanings are restricted, as in *move with* in the sense of 'go out with friends or a boy-/girlfriend'. Sometimes the semantic overlap between items accounts for the "confusion". For example, *exchange information* has certainly a close relationship with *compare*, but when British students *exchange notes* this implies that sheets of paper are swapped and not merely that *notes are compared*, as with African students. Again, some problem cases can also be found in StE style guides. *Clarify* usually means 'an effort by somebody who holds information and is in a position to make things clearer'. Thus *I should clarify that point from the principal* refers to an authority from whom one can seek clearance or permission.

English word forms are used in other contexts: collocations and connotations:
Collocations occur when certain words go together particularly well or frequently and are associated with each other because they co-occur with unusual frequency. They may be less fixed than idioms, because their particular meaning occurs not only in the idiomatic context; but collocates still "expect" each other to some extent. If similar words are used, the combination is less fixed or differs from what is expected in the context, as in *smooth* (StE *plain*) *sailing*. Often fairly general terms are used instead of more specific collocates: *an election is done* (StE *conducted/held*) or *to commit an action* (StE *crime*). It is not always the case that collocations are stronger, or lexemes used more specifically, in BrStE, because African English has developed its own specific forms, as in *I (dropped, got out/down, alighted) from the car near the hospital*.

Most of the connotations of English lexemes in an African context can lead to intercultural problems in discourse. It seems too obvious to mention that *rich* may conjure up very different ideas in a rural African context, but this may also apply to *travelling* and *holiday*, even *Sunday* and *game*, where associative African values and preferences may differ considerably from European traditions.

5.3.   Idiomaticity

It has been mentioned that second-language English is usually less idiomatic than first-language English, which may make communication more difficult for Africans listening to European English speakers than the other way round. But EAfE has developed some idiomatic meanings, which may not be obvious at first sight. Thus, if an unsuspecting traveller needed *to make a short call* he might be shown the way to a toilet (or place used for that purpose). Of course, extreme cases are rare and the few exceptions prove the rule.

However, as has been mentioned above, contexts and style choices constituting idiomaticity form a complex interplay and this special flavour can only be studied in larger sections of authentic texts. This is why a few examples of typical verb usage in the spoken part of the Corpus of EAfE may suffice:

(25)   *I am a matatu driver **operating** route No. 44.* (ICE-EA: S1B065K)

(26)   *It is the City Inspectorate who **assigns** the City Askari.* (ICE-EA: S1B066K)

(27)   *But he never saw anybody himself; nor anybody **alighting** from the police m/v go to the house.* (S1BCE07K)

Whether EAfE is really more explicit (*according to me* 'in my view'), more flexible (*to drag someone through the mud* 'to drag someone through the mire') and more illustrative (as in *big with child*), can only be decided on the basis of large-scale comparative surveys or informant interviews and elicitation tests (cf. Skandera 2003).

6.   Research issues

6.1.   Research data

The problem of insufficient research data has been mentioned in various parts of this article. Although the internet, with East African newspapers and even radio broadcasts (cf. the accompanying CD), has made new data more accessible to the European arm-chair researcher, fieldwork is still essential, partly to evaluate and scrutinise the data available and partly to complement them with other text-types, situations and speakers. Data from the media tend to mirror public oral and written production and clearly have an urban and elitist bias.

The only broad and stratified collection of EAfE is the East African part of the *International Corpus of English* (ICE-EA, freely available complete with handbook from the internet). It was collected between 1990 and 1996 and is compatible with the other ICE-copora, an effort to record true English usage in its first and second-language varieties (principally each with 1 million words in 500 text types, half written and half spoken). The computerised collection from Kenya and Tanzania allows comparisons with the first-language varieties of Britain and Australia, but also with the second-language varieties of India and the Philippines, for instance.

Thus general processes of second-language development can be distinguished from specifically East African features. The size of the corpus (about 1,5 million words with only about half a million words of spoken English) makes it a convenient source for analyses of grammar and frequent lexemes, especially as far as stylistic or text-type-specific differences are concerned. It is, however, not really sufficient for lexical and collocational research, where a much larger corpus is necessary.

For such quantitative comparisons and sample retrievals the *www* with the domains *.ug*, *.ke* and *.tz* can be used. Such a procedure using modern web browsers provides examples of rare cases much more easily now. However, the texts have to be evaluated critically, that is, the question has to be considered whether they can really be seen as "educated EAfE". By using the *www*, country-specific patterns can be distinguished. For example, Kiswahili address forms like *ndugu* or *mzee* have higher hits in Tanzania than in Kenya, *duka* and *fundi* are less frequent in Uganda, but *sodas* occurs in all three East African countries in contrast to South African *minerals*.

Finally, again a plea to look at the data carefully: *soda* as well as *minerals* of course also belong to general English, but in other contexts – baking and mining, for instance. Even *mitumba* occurs on *.uk* web sites as well, but usually with an explicit explanation in the form of premodifiers or appositions (*the second-hand mitumba* or *mitumba, second-hand clothes*). In South Africa, it is often used with explicit reference to East Africa.

Table 1.   EAfE lexemes on the *www*

		ndugu	mzee	duka	fundi	mitumba	matatu
	absolute:	220	292	431	954	25	279
	relative:	0.003 %	0.004 %	0.007 %	0.015 %	0 %	0.004 %
uk	intrasite share:	10 %	13.3 %	19.6 %	43.3 %	1.1 %	12.7 %
6,510,000	intrasite factor:	8.8	11.68	17.24	38.16	1	11.16
	intraphrase share:	0.2 %	0.1 %	0.8 %	0.9 %	0.1 %	0.1 %
	intraphrase factor:	1	1	1	1	1	1

Table 1. (continued) EAfE lexemes on the *www*

		ndugu	**mzee**	**duka**	**fundi**	**mitumba**	**matatu**
ke 8,180	absolute:	7	45	4	89	6	185
	relative:	0.086 %	0.55 %	0.049 %	1.088 %	0.073 %	2.262 %
	intrasite share:	2.1 %	13.4 %	1.2 %	26.5 %	1.8 %	55.1 %
	intrasite factor:	1.75	11.25	1	22.25	1.5	46.25
	intraphrase share:	4 %	17.7 %	5.6 %	63.8 %	21.2 %	74.8 %
	intraphrase factor:	25.32	122.65	7.39	74.25	191	527.71
tz 5,140	absolute:	105	131	42	31	14	39
	relative:	2.043 %	2.549 %	0.817 %	0.603 %	0.272 %	0.759 %
	intrasite share:	29 %	36.2 %	11.6 %	8.6 %	3.9 %	10.8 %
	intrasite factor:	7.5	9.36	3	2.21	1	2.79
	intraphrase share:	95.8 %	82.1 %	93.6 %	35.4 %	78.7 %	25.1 %
	intraphrase factor:	604.48	568.21	123.42	41.16	709.26	177.04

6.2. Practical language issues

The most pressing problem in East Africa is related to the functions of English in education. Teaching English properly within the limited means in the socio-cultural contexts of Africa has been a burning issue for many years. Although these problems are tackled in many development projects, the scientific basis is usually limited, partly because ideological convictions tend to interfere and partly because the teaching materials are only moderately adapted to the local linguistic needs. On this basis, the study of English for academic and specific purposes, especially for science and technology, would help to make learning in English easier, especially on higher levels of education. Thus, studies in educational linguistics are the major desideratum in East Africa.

Other linguistic subdisciplines can support them: more studies on attitude and actual usage could use larger corpora to help draw the borderline between general usage and learner English, which would be useful for the testing specialists in national testing centres and the local writers of adapted teaching materials and text-books. Only much later can questions of national norm be addressed on this scientific basis.

6.3. Intercultural problems

The adoption of some English words into African usage can also give rise to connotational problems. Forms like *blackmail* or *black market* are stigmatised because the word *black* is used to characterise activities beyond what is permitted by law. The long European tradition of equating *black* with *bad* and *white* with *good* can also be seen in *black* versus *white magic*, which is difficult to compare with equivalent complex African concepts anyway. It is therefore not surprising that many language-conscious Africans object to these terms and replace them.

This is why Africanisms for *black market* occur almost as frequently all over Africa as the phenomenon itself, e.g. *magendo* in Tanzania and *kibanda* in Uganda. However, such unofficial parts of the economy tend to change expressions rapidly; thus *kitu kidogo* (literally 'something small') and *chai* ('tea') are well-known in Kenya as euphemistic expressions for a bribe and tend to be replaced already in the inner circle of users.

The connotation "African style" occurs in many areas of the informal sector or petty trade, from the infamous parking boys, who force car owners to pay them for "looking after their cars" to the *jua kali* artisans, who follow their craft in the "hot sun" and not in a shop or garage in Kenya. Similarly, the StE expressions *second-hand* or *used clothes* do not have the same connotations as *mitumba* in Kenya. These examples illustrate that it is necessary to pay attention to denotative but also to connotative meanings.

6.4. Outlook

Since their independence over forty years ago, East Africans have developed an interesting trifocal language system: English, widespread throughout Africa, is rivalled by Kiswahili in high language functions in the region (and through the Organisation of African Unity even on the continent) and by a local vernacular language having low functions. Although other African languages play a role in subnational communication and influence English pronunciation, East Africa is unique among the English-speaking areas of the world because of this dichotomy. Interestingly enough, Kiswhahili does not threaten English in the area since its losses in national functions have by far been compensated by the many international functions of English that have been important for East Africans since their integration into world-wide communication networks over 100 years ago.

EAfE shares many features, especially in grammar, with other New Englishes, which also have comparable tendencies in lexical development. Thus

EAfE can be seen in a larger framework (e.g. as in ICE above). In the long tradition of African multilingualism, English has a promising future in the area. The knowledge and appreciation of national and regional features will develop and make English in East Africa interesting for casual global users and specialised researchers alike.

Exercises and study questions

1. "The tendency to overgeneralise -*s* plural noun markers is semantically motivated" (see 2.2). Discuss and illustrate.

2. Discuss three major syntactic similarities between an EAfE and a WAfE variety like that of Ghana or Nigeria.

3. Discuss three syntactic differences between EAfE and the variety you chose in 2.

4. Discuss the pragmatics of the interjection *sorry* in EAfE.

5. Negative *yes/no* questions are confirmed by responding to the form of the question and not to the absolute "inner logic". Discuss and compare with this analysis for EAfE the same phenomenon in BlSAfE.

Selected references

Please consult the General references for titles mentioned in the text but not included in the references below. For a full bibliography see the accompanying CD-ROM.

International Corpus of English, East African Component (ICE-EA)
        < http://www.tu-chemnitz.de/phil/english/real/eafrica/ >
Mwangi, Serah
  2003   *Prepositions in Kenyan English: a corpus-based study in lexical-grammatical variation.* Aachen: Shaker.
Schmied, Josef
  forthcoming East Africa. In: Allan Davis (ed.). *Handbook of Lexicography.* Berlin/New York: Mouton de Gruyter.
Skandera, Paul
  2003   *Drawing a Map of Africa: Idiom in Kenyan English.* Tübingen: Narr.

White South African English: morphology and syntax

Sean Bowerman

1. Introduction

White South African English (WhSAfE) differs little superficially from other first language varieties of English, and Cultivated WhSAfE approximates reasonably closely to southern British standards and even to RP norms. There are, however, some distinctly South African features in its morphosyntax, and particularly its vocabulary, the latter reflecting the range of languages with which WhSAfE has been in contact. Morphological and phonological features which are distinctive of WhSAfE have often been put down to Afrikaans influence. However, Lass and Wright (1986) and Mesthrie and West (1995) caution against this approach, pointing out that many of these features may be survivals from Settler English.

2. The verb phrase

2.1. Deletion of verbal complements

In context, the complement(s) of transitive and ditransitive verbs may be omitted or ellipsed. In the case of ditransitive verbs, either one or both of the complements may be omitted, as in (1a) – (1e).

(1)   a. *Oh good, you've got ∅.*
       b. *Did you bring ∅?*
       c. *Did you give ∅ ∅?*
       d. *He's already given the money ∅.*
       e. *You can put ∅ in the fridge.*

Complement ellipsis can occur in a context quite far outside the immediate situation. For example, if you promise somebody that you will bring something to them, they might well say next time they see you: *Did you bring?* Deleting verb complements is a common feature of General and Broad WhSAfE, but is perhaps more associated with Broad.

2.2. *Busy* + progressive

The verb *busy* followed by a present participle is a prominent feature of Wh-SAfE. It is frequently used with non-active (or non-busy) and seemingly anomalous verbal complements.

(2)   a. *I'm busy relaxing.*
       b. *I was busy losing my house.*
       c. *When I got to the car, he was busy dying* (Lass 2002: 123).

There seems to be little difference between this construction and the ordinary progressive; though Lass and Wright (1986: 213–214) suggest that it may be emphatic, excluding the suggestion of any endpoint to state or activity expressed by the verb. *Busy* in this construction is certainly not to be analysed as a lexical verb; rather, it is a grammatical item, more exactly an aspectual marker. For example, *I'm busy relaxing* would most likely be a jocular response to *Are you busy?* By the same token, the question *Are you busy sleeping?* would be meant in all seriousness.

It is possible that this construction has arisen as a translation of a similar construction in Afrikaans, where *besig* 'busy' is used in exactly the same way. However, Lass and Wright (1986: 217) point out that a similar construction was also available well beyond the Early Modern English period, and could be a development from the English of the 19th century British settlers.

2.3. Past *do* + uninflected verb

Perfective aspect is frequently indicated in WhSAfE by the use of the past tense form of DO, with an uninflected verb complement. It occurs in the immediate situation, where the present rather than past tense is normative, and usually takes the place of present tense *have* + past participle. Thus:

(3)   a. *Did you bring my books?*
         'Have you brought my books?'
       b. *Did you have lunch yet?*
         'Have you had lunch yet?'

This construction is often stigmatised as Broad or Afrikaans English, but in my experience it is quite common in General WhSAfE. For some speakers, the only time that the *have* + past participle construction occurs is with the possessive verb *got*, when perfective aspect is not intended to be marked. It is interesting that, for these speakers, auxiliary *have* only occurs with possessive *got*. This is probably because *get* would indicate obtaining, rather than possessing, thus ruling out the DO + uninflected verb construction.

(4)   a. *Have you got a watch?*
            'Do you have a watch?'
        b. *Did you get a watch?*
            'Have you obtained a watch?'

Have you got occurs more frequently (in Broad and General) than *Do you have*, and the use of past DO + past participle is stigmatised as an Afrikaans English construction, hence the classic parody of the Afrikaans traffic officer: *Did you got a licence?* 'Have you got/Do you have a licence?'. *Gotten* as the past participle form of *got* is rare in WhSAfE, but is becoming noticeable among younger speakers, probably as a result of American influence.

The use of DO + uninflected verb for the perfective could well stem from Afrikaans, which does not distinguish simple past and present perfect. Both 'Did you bring it?' and 'Have you brought it?' would be realised in Afrikaans as:

(5)   *Het   jy   dit   gebring?*
        Have   you   it   brought?
        'Did you bring it? / Have you brought it?'

In other words, Afrikaans uses *have* + past participle for both constructions.

2.4.   Adjective + infinitive

The use of a range of adjectives with infinitive clauses is a feature of Broad WhSAfE:

(6)   a. *This container is capable to withstand heat.* (Lass 2002: 123)
        b. *I am lazy to acquire the skills.* (Branford 1987 in Mesthrie and West 1995: 115)
        c. *Bob is reticent to talk about that day.* (Branford 1987 in Mesthrie and West 1995: 115).

Mesthrie and West (1995: 116) show that this is a common feature of Settler English. Indeed, in contemporary English, many adjectives show this same pattern normatively:

(7)   a. *She's crazy to go there.*
        b. *He is able to climb very tall trees.*

Moreover, any adjective can take an infinitive complement if it is qualified with the intensifying adverb *too*, though the meaning changes somewhat:

(8)   a. **She's sleepy to do her homework / She's too sleepy to do her homework.*
        b. *I'm too lazy to acquire the skills.*

Thus, the construction could once again be a generalisation or overgeneralisation of a process that operated in Settler English, or an analogical innovation.

2.5.   *Is*-inversion

This occurs in constructions with a topicalised locative determiner. The determiner is topicalised, and the verb, always *be*, is cliticised to it. It, too, is a somewhat stigmatised construction, but I have heard it in General speakers.

(9)   a. *Here's it!*
            'Here it is! < It is here!'
       b. *There's your father, on the roof!*
            'Your father is there, on the roof!'

I have heard constructions like (9b) in other varieties of English; however, *here's it / there's it* seems to be uniquely South African, and has a parallel in Afrikaans: *Daar's hy* 'There he/it is!' – also with *be* cliticised to the topic.

3.   Prepositions and the prepositional phrase

3.1.   Preposition complement ellipsis

The complement of a preposition is sometimes ellipsed in contexts where the preposition is not a phrasal verb particle; this frequently affects the preposition *with*:

(10)   *Are they coming with Ø?*

This is probably another influence from Afrikaans, where *saam* 'together' has been misinterpreted as 'with' (see also Mesthrie and West 1995: 117):

(11)   *Hulle   kom   saam   met   ons.*
        They   come   together   with   us
        'They are coming with us.'

(12)   *Hulle   kom   saam.*
        They   come   together
        'They are coming along' misanalysed as 'They are coming with.'

The preposition *met* 'with' cannot be stranded in Afrikaans:

(13)   **Hulle   kom   saam   met.*
        'They   come   together   with'
        'They're coming with'.

3.2.   Semantic range of prepositions

The preposition *by*, as in Afrikaans, covers a wide semantic range in WhSAfE. Mesthrie and West (1995: 117) show that Settler English had a similar range for *by*:

(14)   a. *I live by the station.* ('near')
         b. *I left it by my friend's house.* ('at')
         c. *He stays by his parents.* ('with')

This is a feature of SAfE in general, except for the cultivated variety. Children are taught at school to avoid this usage.

By is frequently used, especially in Broad WhSAfE, with heavily stressed locative *there*:

(15)   a. *It's there by the couch.*
         b. *I was standing there by the shop...*

3.3.   Other prepositions

Even more stigmatised than the non-standard use of *by* is the substitution of *for* for *of* – again, most likely an Afrikaans influence:

(16)   *She's scared for spiders.*

This feature is unlikely to be found in General, and definitely not in Conservative WhSAfE. The substitution of *for* for *of* is more associated with the second language Afrikaans English variety.

3.4.   'Throw me with a stone'

In Broad and some General WhSAfE, the verb THROW...AT may be substituted with THROW WITH, in which case the DP complements are reversed. For example:

(17)   *He threw me with a stone.*
         'He threw a stone at me.'

This is a highly stigmatised construction, associated with Afrikaans English, and is indeed a direct translation of the Afrikaans equivalent:

(18)   *Hy   het   my   met   ,n   klip   gegooi.*
         He   has   me   with   a   stone   thrown
         'He threw a stone at me.'

However, there are also many parallels in English, provided one accepts a wider semantic range for *throw* than that of standard English:

(19)   a.   *He shot me with a pellet.*
        b.   *He hit me with a stone.*

Mesthrie and West (1995: 119) cite Pettman's (1913) example of this construction:

(20)   *He threw me over the hedge with a stone*
        'He threw a stone at me over the hedge.'

4.   Modals and modality

There are two features of modality that are distinctively WhSAfE.

4.1.   Illocutionary force of *must*

The strong obligative modal *must* has much less social impact in WhSAfE than in other varieties of English, and often substitutes for polite *should / shall*. This comes as a surprise to many foreigners asking for directions!

(21)   a.   *You must turn left at the robots…*
        b.   *You must just knock on my door when you get here…*
        c.   *Must I make you some tea?*

4.2.   *Won't* as a directive "softener"

The use of *won't* to soften a request (though it might not always achieve this effect) is a feature of General and Broad WhSAfE. It uses two directive softeners: the voluntative modal *will* and the negative *won't*.

(22)   a.   *Won't you pass me the salt?*
        b.   *Won't you do me a favour?*

Won't is usually pronounced with a sharply rising intonation and strong emphasis, and may have the force of a command. The intonation and emphasis makes this construction sound very different to ordinary question intonation that one would find in *Will you do me a favour?*

5.   Present markers as proximal future markers

5.1.   Present tense + *now*

The present tense construction and the adverb *now* are both normative markers of the present in WhSAfE, but are frequently used to indicate the proximal future. Thus, (23) below could have the normative present tense meaning, indicating that the speaker is on his/her way at the time of utterance:

(23)   *I'm on my way now.*

But it is equally likely to mean that the speaker intends to be on his/her way in the near future. Similarly (24):

(24)   A: *Do you want to come over?*
        B: *No, I'm sleeping now.*

In the use of the present tense + *now*, the speaker indicates that he/she intends to sleep soon. The present tense + *now* construction can also be used to indicate a delay to the proximal future:

(25)   A: *Supper's ready.*
        B: *I'm coming now.*

I'm coming now in this context probably does not mean that the speaker is underway, or that s/he is coming immediately; rather, s/he will be coming soon. Afrikaans has the same construction, with the same meaning.

5.2.   Reduplicative *now-now* and *just now*

The reduplication *now-now* is used to mean 'very soon' rather than 'immediately':

(26)   *I'll do it now-now.*

This usually means that the speaker intends to finish what s/he is already doing before embarking on another activity.

Unlike the U.S. usage, indicating immediacy, *just now* is used in WhSAfE to put something off into the further, but still proximate future:

(27)   *I'll be there just now.*

Just now means 'not immediately, but soon'; 'later than' would be indicated by *now-now*. A similar construction, *now-now-now* expresses the sense of immediacy lacking in *now-now*.

The British English sense of recent past in *just now* (as in *She left just now*) is less common in WhSAfE than the collocation with the near future. *Now-now* and *just now* are often stigmatised (particularly by non-SAfE speakers) as being procrastination devices that put matters off into the indeterminate future. It is likely that both *now-now* and *just now* are calqued from the similar Afrikaans expressions *nou-nou* and *net nou* respectively.

6. Negatives

6.1. Non-negative *no*

While *no* is a normative negative marker in WhSAfE, Broad and General speakers frequently employ it in a non-negative sense to introduce an affirmative clause:

(28)   A: *How are you?*
       B: *No, I'm fine.*

(29)   A: *Isn't your car ready yet?*
       B: *No, it is.*

In these cases, following Trudgill and Hannah (1994: 32), the function of *no* may be to offset any negative assumptions made by the interlocutor. However, I have also heard things like:

(30)   A: *She's getting big, hey?*
       B: *No, she is!*

Here, the *no* may indicate surprise, or the negation of the speaker's assumptions. It is qualitatively different to, for example, the simple agreement *Yes, she is!*.

6.2. *Never*

Never is often used in WhSAfE to indicate only one negative instance. It is not confined to the normative sense of *not ever*, and can be used in the place of *do not*:

(31)   A: *Did you see him on Tuesday?*
       B: *No, he never arrived on Tuesday, but he was there on*
            Wednesday.

In (32), *never* again has scope over only one point in time:

(32)   *I made you a cake, but I never brought it with.*

In both (31) and (32), *never* scopes over only one instance, and (31) shows that it does not prevent the verb from happening at all. *Never* is also used for emphatic denial:

(33)   A: *Did you take my jersey?*
        B: *No, I never.*

Afrikaans has some similarity, in that an Afrikaans response to (33) could be *nooit* 'never'; however, Mesthrie and West (1995: 119) show that *never = do + not* existed in Settler English, and probably antedates contact with Afrikaans / Dutch.

7.   Adjective comparison

The use of both the periphrastic and inflexional comparative in the same construction is largely a second language English feature; however, it occurs in Broad and even General varieties from time to time:

(34)   a.   *That's the most easiest course I've ever done!* (General WhSAfE student)
        b.   *My fez is much more funkier than yours!* (spoken by a General WhSAfE television presenter).

The provenance of this is uncertain: there is no similar construction in Afrikaans. The construction most likely stems from the lack of clarity, even in prescriptive English grammars, as to when *more/most* and *-er/-est* should be used.

8.   Agreement features

While English has very little agreement, Afrikaans has almost none, and it is possible that Afrikaans influence is responsible for some of the relatively uncommon, non-normative agreement patterns in Broad WhSAfE. However, Settler English displayed inconsistent agreement too, which might have influenced Broad WhSAfE. Inconsistent or non-normative agreement is a highly stigmatised feature, frequently used to satirise Afrikaans English.

8.1.   3rd person singular agreement in the present tense

The normative 3rd person singular agreement marker is the inflexion *-s* on the verb or auxiliary. Common agreement errors involve omitting or overgeneralisation, so that both (35a) and (35b) occur:

(35)   a. *Does you go to school?*
        b. *He like to read.*

This is very rare (I think) in native speakers; but especially (35a) occurs fairly frequently in Afrikaans English.

8.2.   Singular demonstrative with plural noun complement

A much more common lack of agreement occurs between the demonstrative determiner (*this*, *that*) and its noun complement. This is also a stigmatised feature, but I believe it is making its way into General WhSAfE:

(36)   a. *I'd better go and pick up this bags.*
        b. *It's because of that birds.*

The agreement "error" apparently always assigns a singular demonstrative to a plural noun. I have never heard, or heard of, a plural demonstrative being used with a singular noun. Once more, this has a parallel in Afrikaans, which does not distinguish a singular and plural demonstrative.

8.3.   *Is it?*

This phrase, in the superficial form of a question, is generally a response to a statement. It is widespread through General and Broad WhSAfE. Depending upon the intonation with which it is uttered, it can express anything from keen interest to total disinterest, and is roughly equal to replies like *Really, Has he?*. The form is always *is it*—it never agrees in person or number with what has gone before.

(37)   A: *The kittens ran away.*
        B: *Is it?* ('Did they?')

(38)   A: *I'm going overseas*
        B: *Is it?* ('Are you?')

9.   Greetings, tags and expletives

9.1.   *Howzit!*

This is the quintessential SAfE salutation, and probably started as a marker of solidarity among white males. Now, however, it is a solidarity marker among South Africans generally, and is more or less restricted by gender and ethnicity. Derived from *How is it?* rather than *How are you?*, it is not really intended as a question, and is closer in meaning to *Hello* than *How are you?*. The usual response is *Howzit*, and it is not at all unusual for *How are you?* to follow an exchange of *Howzits*.

9.2.   *Ag*, *Man* and *Hey*

Ag and *man* are two very common tags in WhSAfE; the former is more closely associated with Broad and Afrikaans English, but occurs quite frequently in General, too. Both are usually exclamations of annoyance, but *man* can also express pleasure or delight. *Ag* precedes a sentence; *Man* generally follows a sentence but can also precede it; and the two together can constitute an expletive of annoyance.

(39)   a.   *Ag, the Stormers lost again.*
      b.   *Get out of my way, man.*
      c.   *Man, it's beautiful!*

Ag appears to be an Afrikaans expletive, while *man* as an exclamation is very common in both Afrikaans and many varieties of English, including British English.

Another very common tag in WhSAfE is *hey*, which is roughly equivalent to 'isn't it' or 'not so' in other varieties. With strong emphasis and a sharp fall in intonation, it invites agreement:

(40)   a.   *Wow, it's big, hey.*
      b.   *We're going to Durban, hey Dad.* ('aren't we')

10.   One as non-specific determiner

One is frequently used to pick out one of a set, without specifying exactly:

(41)   a.   *My one cat is sick.*
           'One of my cats is sick.'

b. *He's broken his one leg.*
'One of his legs / a leg is broken.'

(41b) is stigmatised as it is closely associated with Afrikaans English. However, the usage is not confined to Afrikaans English or even to Broad WhSAfE. (41a) is common in General SAfE.

11. Lexis

The vocabulary of WhSAfE has been influenced and enriched by a variety of languages. Afrikaans and the indigenous languages have naturally had the most input; but there are also vocabulary items from Malay, Portuguese, Indian languages and eastern European languages. Many African language expressions have found their way into WhSAfE, sometimes via Afrikaans. Globalisation and increased exposure to British and American English are likely to have a significant influence on the lexicon too. Most of the lexis exemplified in this section is in general use among South Africans, and will at least be generally understood by most English-speaking South Africans.

11.1. English South Africanisms

Most vocabulary items that differentiate WhSAfE from other international Englishes are drawn from the languages with which English has been in contact in South Africa. There are few uniquely South African English expressions:

- *Turn left at the **robot*** ('traffic light')
- *They live in a **township*** ('town or suburb, usually poor, formerly reserved for Black people'; also 'location')
- *Let's go to the **bioscope** on Saturday* ('cinema'; common among older WhSAfE speakers).

WhSAfE usually follows British rather than North American vocabulary, where these differences are salient: e.g. *torch* rather than *flashlight*; *jug* rather than *pitcher*; *jersey* rather than *sweater*.

11.2.   Vocabulary items borrowed from other languages

Term	Gloss / explanation	Source language
PEOPLE AND FAMILY		
sangoma	traditional healer, often a.k.a. 'witchdoctor'	Zulu
imbongi	traditional praise singer	Xhosa, Zulu
gogo	'grandmother' (term of address); polite term of reference for older woman	Xhosa, Zulu
oupa / ouma	'grandfather / grandmother'; polite terms of reference for older people	Afrikaans
tannie	'aunt, auntie'; polite form of address or term of reference. Sometimes used derogatorily, especially outside of the Afrikaner community.	Afrikaans
boetie	'brother / little brother'; term of reference for one younger than oneself; not always polite.	Afrikaans
buti / sisi	'brother / sister'; polite form of address / term of reference for one the same age as oneself.	Xhosa, Zulu
bra	informal term of address to an equal.	slang, from English *brother*.
boer	'farmer'; sometimes extends to 'Afrikaner', when it can be derogatory.	Afrikaans.
kugel	a wealthy Jewish woman, usually derogatory.	Yiddish, 'ball'
ubuntu	spirit of fellowship, humanity and compassion	Xhosa, Zulu
FAUNA AND FLORA		
mamba	a very poisonous snake	Bantu *imamba* 'snake'
brommer	large fly or buzzing insect	Afrikaans *brom* 'buzz'
duiweltjie	small, three-pointed burr	Afrikaans *little devil*
witgatboom	'white-barked tree'	Afrikaans *wit* = 'white' + *gat* = 'hole' + *boom* = 'tree'

Term	Gloss / explanation	Source language
FOOD AND DRINK		
mielie	'maize'	Afrikaans
pap	'maize porridge'; can be crumbly or stiff	Afrikaans 'porridge'
braai	fire for cooking esp. meat, barbecue	Afrikaans
potjiekos	food cooked over an open fire in a round, cast iron pot	Afrikaans 'potfood'
bobotie	curried mince baked with a savoury custard topping	Afrikaans < Malay
bredie	meat stewed with vegetables	Afrikaans < Portuguese
mampoer	strong distilled spirit	Pedi
rooibos	locally made herbal tea	Afrikaans 'red bush'
witblits	strong distilled spirit	Afrikaans 'white lightning'
mqombothi	sorghum beer	Xhosa
PLACES AND THINGS		
lapa	enclosed outside entertainment area / sunroom	Sotho
kraal	traditional African village	Dutch < Portuguese
imbizo	'meeting / workshop'	Zulu
indaba	'meeting / discussion'; also 'news'	Xhosa, Zulu 'business'
bosberaad	'summit meeting' / meeting held outside of the workplace	Afrikaans 'bush conference'
stoep	porch or veranda	Afrikaans
DEEDS AND ACTIONS		
vuka	'wake up, get up, hurry up, move quickly'	Zulu
suka	'go away'	Zulu
dikbek	'cross, sulky, taciturn'	Afrikaans 'thick mouth'
deurmekaar	'untidy, messed up, confused'	Afrikaans
weggooi	'disposable'	Afrikaans

12.   Conclusion

This article has listed some of the salient morphosyntactic features of WhSAfE. There is not much deviation from other standard Englishes in its morphology and syntax: WhSAfE is primarily distinguished by its accent and its borrowed vocabulary. However, it must be pointed out that the morphosyntax of Wh-SAfE has not been well or consistently studied. Moreover, it is likely to be influenced by the expansion of the variety, particularly in education, to other (ethnic) groupings which had been largely excluded from joining white peer groups, and some change is bound to result from this.

The influence of Afrikaans on both the phonology and morphosyntax of Wh-SAfE is an important feature. However, Lass and Wright's (1986) proposal that many features previously accepted as being Afrikaans influence may be Settler input survivals, may indicate that Afrikaans has not had as much impact on the variety as previously thought.

Exercises and study questions

1. Review the examples in 2.4 of 'adjective with infinitive' constructions. Give the equivalents of sentences (6a) to (6c) in StE.

2. Review the response *is it?* to certain statements (see 8.3). In what ways is this usage different from the generalised tag *isn't it* common in other varieties in South Africa, EAfE (see section 2.5) and WAfE (see section 3 on Nigerian English)?

3. In what ways is the use of *busy* special in WhSAfE? Are the examples in 2.2 found in other varieties of English that you are familiar with?

4. Review the discussion of *just now* in 5.2. Is this usage similar to other varieties you are familiar with?

5. How would the following sentence of SAfE be rendered in StE?: *She threw me with a stick.*

Selected references

Please consult the General references for titles mentioned in the text but not included in the references below. For a full bibliography see the accompanying CD-ROM.

Branford, Jean
    1987   *A Dictionary of South African English*. Cape Town: Oxford University Press.
Lass, Roger
    2002   South African English. In: Rajend Mesthrie (ed.), 104–126.
Lass, Roger and Susan Wright
    1986   Endogeny vs Contact: "Afrikaans influence" on South African English. *English World-Wide* 7: 201–223.
Mesthrie, Rajend and Paula West
    1995   Towards a grammar of Proto-South African English. *English World-Wide* 16: 105–133.
Pettman, Charles
    1913   *Africanderisms*. London: Longmans, Green and Co.

Black South African English: morphology and syntax

Rajend Mesthrie

1. Introduction

This article provides an overview of the main syntactic features of Black South African English (BlSAfE), as used by fluent L2 speakers. Some black South Africans now speak English as a first language, especially children who are being brought up in middle-class suburbs where English is a dominant L1. Since these numbers are relatively small, and since children form part of neighbourhood and school peer groups, whose norms are essentially those of General or "Cultivated" South African English, there is currently little to be gained by considering these to be speakers of BlSAfE. BlSAfE differs from other varieties of English in South Africa more in terms of its phonetics and discourse organisation than its grammar. It shares many syntactic features with other varieties of Sub-Saharan L2 English (see Schmied in this volume and 1991), perhaps more so with East Africa than West Africa. Part of the reason for this is that Pidgin English is an influence over West African L2 English, but no Pidgin English exists in Southern or East Africa.

Except where otherwise indicated, examples for this study are drawn from part of my database of sociolinguistic interviews involving university undergraduates and graduates, coming mainly from the Eastern Cape, Western Cape and Gauteng areas. This chapter exemplifies mesolectal varieties of BlSAfE, i.e. the variety of speakers who speak English fluently, but with phonetic and grammatical norms that are clearly different from "Cultivated" SAfE.

2. Tense – aspect – modality systems

2.1. Tense

The broad present – past – future tense distinction of StE is unaltered in BlSAfE; where variation exists it is usually in combinations of tense and aspect. The third person singular present tense –*s* is variable for some speakers.

2.2. Aspect

2.2.1. Be + -ing *occurs in a range of contexts that do not always coincide with those of StE*

Stative verbs that do not generally permit *be + -ing* in formal StE, allow it as a frequent option:

(1)   *Because most of the people are hailing from Malawi ...*
      '...hail from...'
(2)   *People who are having time for their children ...*
      '...who have time for ...'
(3)   *Even racism is still existing ...*
      '... still exists ...' (De Klerk and Gough 2002: 362)

Whereas the equivalents of (1)–(3) above would not allow *be + -ing* at all in the Standard, there are some examples of verbs in StE where *be + -ing* is allowed in one sense, but not another. BlSAfE generally allows *be + -ing* in both. Thus *He is speaking Navajo* is admissible as present progressive in the Standard, but not as stative, where *He speaks Navajo* is the grammatical form. BlSAfE, however, does not always make this distinction, or, at least, allows *be + -ing* as an option with the stative:

(4)   *There were quite a few people who were speaking Shangaan.*
      ' ... who speak Shangaan.'

Similarly the distinction between *I'm having (tea)* and *I have (a job)* is frequently overridden in BlSAfE:

(5)   *The one I'm having presently is a temporary post.*
      'The job I have presently is a temporary one.'

2.2.2. *Past* be + -ing *for habitual*

(6)   *The essays here are different from the essays we were writing in Vista.*
      ' ... from the essays we used to write at Vista (University).'

(7)   *When my mother was here, she was here for a month, my father was phoning almost everyday.*
      '... used to phone ...'

2.2.3. *Rarity of* have + -en

In certain contexts (e.g. a subordinate clause preceded by a main clause with past tense verbs) the simple past corresponds to the past perfect of StE:

(8)   *She said she came looking for me.*
       'She said she had come looking for me.'

2.2.4. -s *in past tense contexts*

De Klerk and Gough (2002) give examples of the use of the third person singular present tense *–s* in past tense contexts:

(9)   *In 1980 the boycott starts.*

However, it is not clear if this is from spoken or written data. Such examples are non-existent in my database of spoken university students' English.

2.3.   Modality

Some differences in the syntax and semantics of BlSAfE from other varieties in South Africa can be discerned. The most noticeable of these is the phrase *can be able*, also found in other parts of Africa:

(10)   ... *how am I going to construct a good sentence so as this person can be able to hear me clearly.*
       ' ... so that this person can understand me clearly.'

The negative *can't be able* is also attested. It is unclear whether 'can be able' and 'can' are synonymous, though that is my first impression. A likely explanation is a non-semantic one – analogy with the other modals (*shall, must, may, might, will, would, should*), which all allow collocations with *be able* (see sentence [11] from StE).

(11)   *She might be able to work.*

There are some overlaps between the modals. The present forms *can* and *will* are occasionally used where StE prefers the past forms *could* and *would* in irrealis contexts:

(12)   *I wish that people in the world will get educated.*
       (De Klerk and Gough 2002: 362)

(13)   *Maybe it can be in Computer Science.*
       'Perhaps it could have been in the field of Computer Science.'

Can occasionally has the (irrealis) semantics of *might*:

(14)   *I said, "No, they can be wild, but they're human beings."*
       ' … they might be wild…'

It also co-occurs with *know*, violating a StE collocation:

(15)   *I could know …*
       'I knew/was able to tell …'

May sometimes occurs as a polite form of (irrealis) *could*:

(16)   *May you please lend me a pen.*
       'Could you please …'

This may well be a hypercorrection, based on the belief promulgated in class-rooms that *may* is preferable to *can* (cf. the schoolteacher's *You can go to the toilet, but you may not*).

As in Indian South African English (IndSAfE), *wouldn't* is a polite form for *don't* in the phrase *I wouldn't know.*

2.4.   Other auxiliaries

Apart from discussions of modals in Section 2.3., auxiliaries appear to be more or less standard. For instance, no studies have suggested any special forms of *be* or *have* or rules like copula deletion (see Undeletions in 5.1.).

In indirect questions auxiliaries tend to be inverted with the subject, thus generalising the main clause rule for direct questions:

(17)   *A Catholic bishop who asked me what would I do if he could pay for my studies.*

(18)   *I didn't know what were they saying …*

Likewise *do*-support occurs in indirect questions:

(19)   *I don't know what did he say.*
       'I don't know what he said.'

The verb *be* is involved in two idiomatic constructions. In the first, auxiliary *be* stands for *be* + verb of motion:

(20)   *I'm from his room.*
       'I've just come from his room.'

In the second, copula *be* is used in PRO + *be* + NUMERICAL constructions corresponding to the StE construction *there* + *be* + NUMERICAL:

(21)   Q: *Have you got a full squad today?*
        A: *We are ten.*
        'There are ten of us.'

This construction, which always involves a partitive genitive sense 'ten of us', 'three of them' etc., does not occur in other varieties of SAfE.

3.   Negation

Verb phrase negation has not been remarked upon in any overview of BISAfE speech. One phenomenon that has been studied concerns responses to *yes/no*-questions couched in the negative.

In positive *yes/no*-questions, BISAfE is no different from StE. Thus:

(22)   Q: *Is he arriving tomorrow?*
        A: *Yes (he is); or No (he isn't).*

That is, in both BISAfE and StE *yes* implies 'yes he is', and *no* implies 'no, he isn't'.

The rules in these two varieties are different if the questions are initiated in the negative:

(23)   a.   Q: *Isn't he arriving tomorrow?*
              A: *Yes (he is).*   (StE)
                    Yes (he isn't).   (BISAfE)
                    No (he isn't).   (StE)
                    No (he is).   (BISAfE)

That is, the answer *yes* implies 'he is' according to the conventions of the one variety, and 'he isn't' in the other. The same holds for the answer *no* in isolation.

The logic underlying the examples is consistent with Bantu and West African languages, and the construction has been reported in other parts of Africa (see Schmied, this volume and Schmied (1991: 73) for East Africa; Huber, this volume for Ghana). I propose that there is one rule underlying the BISAfE examples, even though *yes* implies 'he is' in one set and 'he isn't' in another. Furthermore, I propose that the rule for BISAfE is different from StE even in the positive, where they appear to coincide.

In order to decide upon this we need to examine the answers *yes* and *no* in their full dialogic context. If the forms of the verb *be* in the answer (whether overtly stated or not) matches that of the question, the answer is always *yes*. If there is no match, the answer is *no*. Thus (23b) shows the single rule for StE:

(23)   b.   Q: *Is he arriving tomorrow?*

              A: *Yes (he is);* or *No (he isn't).*

              Q: *Isn't he arriving tomorrow?*

              A: *Yes (he is);* or *No (he isn't).*

Sentences (24a) and (24b) show a single rule for BlSAfE:

(24)   a.   Q: *Is he arriving tomorrow?*

              A: *Yes (he is).*

              Q: *Isn't he arriving tomorrow?*

              A: *Yes (he isn't).*

        b.   Q: *Is he arriving tomorrow?*

              A: *No (he isn't).*

              Q: *Isn't he arriving tomorrow?*

              A: *No (he is).*

In each dialect there is one underlying agreement rule for both questions. Agreement in BlSAfE holds not laterally, but vertically between question and answer. If this analysis is correct, it would show that dialects may be different in areas of grammar that on the surface appear to be the same. That is, the agreement rule for questions posed *positively* is actually different in the two dialects, even though the surface output is the same.

4.   Relativisation

There is little to report here, apart from the occasional use of resumptive pronouns.

(25)   *Students discovered that the kind of education that these people are*
        *trying to give **it** to us...*
        '...that these people are trying to give to us...'

5.   Complementation

BlSAfE has a preference for the overt expression of complementisers like *that* and *to*, and for occurrences of *to be* that are implicit in StE, but rarely expressed.

5.1.   "Undeletions"

I use this term to denote retentions in BlSAfE for elements which are typically deleted (or unexpressed) in StE.

In expository style, speakers use *that* rather than Ø in expressions like the following ([26] and [27] are from a teacher dispensing advice on television):

(26)   *As it can be seen **that** there is a problem here.*
        'As can be seen, there is a problem here.'

(27)   *As it has been said **that** history repeats itself.*
        'As has been said, history repeats itself.'

The surfacing of *that* might well be on analogy of main clauses like 'It has been said that X'. The surfacing of dummy *it* is probably due to analogy with 'It has been said'.

Likewise, where *to* is deleted in some contexts after causative main verbs like *let* and *make* in StE, it proves more tenacious in BlSAfE:

(28)   *Can you tell me what made you to decide **to** come and study?*

(29)   *Even my friends were asking me, "Why do you let your son **to** speak Zulu?"*

To be also remains in "small clauses" of BlSAfE, in contrast to their StE counterparts.

(30)   *...treat a person as a person, and maybe pointing out things that can make that person to be a character that he is.*
        '... can make that person the character that he is.'

(31)   *...and it challenges me or makes me to be challenged.*

5.2.   Variation in the form of complementisers

De Klerk and Gough (2002: 362) report occasional variants like the following:

(32)   *I went to secondary school for doing my Standard 6.*
       '… to do Standard 6.'

(33)   *I tried that I might see her.*
       'I tried to see her.'

(34)   *He went there in order that he sees her.*
       'He went there in order to see her.'

5.3.   Comparatives

As in other varieties of English in Africa, comparative constructions are occasionally simplified. In (35) *than* is preferred to *rather than* while in (36) the superlative form *most* is left unstated.

(35)   *… if you are not in a hurry, you can take it today – now – than Thursday.*
       '…today, rather than Thursday.'

(36)   *… my school was one of the radical schools that you can ever find.*
       '…one of the most radical schools…'

6.   Other subordination and coordination phenomena

6.1.   Double conjunctions

Adversative constructions involving conjunctions like *although, but, even, so* etc. mark each clause separately:

(37)   **But** *I don't know it well,* **but** *I like it.*

(38)   **So** *we (= each family) had about two rooms each,* **so** *we stayed.*

(39)   **Although** *I'm not that shy,* **but** *it's hard for me to make friends.*

Such constructions are especially prevalent in lower sociolects and/or unplanned extended discourse.

6.2.   *Other … other* constructions

Corresponding to a similar form in languages like Zulu and Sotho, many BlSAfE speakers use *other … other* in place of StE *one…the other* or *some … other* (Buthelezi 1995: 248):

(40)   *Others are for the proposal, others are against it.*
        'Some … others…'

(41)   *The other side is that… you make friends; and on the other side*
        enemies are created again.
        'On the one hand you might make friends; on the other hand you
        might make enemies.'

(42)   *The other one was smart, but the other one was not clever.*
        'One was smart, but the other one was not.'

The StE idiom *this, that and the other* is sometimes replaced by *this and this
and that* or *this and that and that.*

6.3.   Innovations in the form of conjunctions

These innovations include *if at all,* which is a variant of *if; supposing* for *suppose* or *if; because-why* for *because.*

7.   Agreement

There is very little to report here. Subject-verb concord for third person singular is variable between –*s* and Ø, especially in lower sociolects. Whereas *it*
and *they/them* are distinct as referential pronouns, there is some syncretism in
anaphoric contexts:

(43)   *Both things I have to do it.*
        'I have to do both things.'

There is some variability in pronoun gender, with *he* and *she* occurring interchangeably in lower sociolects especially. This also applies to the case-marked
forms *his* and *her* and to *him* and *her.*

8.   Noun phrase structure

8.1.   Articles

There is some variability between the use of Ø, *a,* and *the.* Most noticeably, *a*
often replaces zero articles of StE:

(44)   *I was on a maternity leave.*

(45)   *You're going to have a trouble.*

(46) *You might create a chaos.*

(47) *If we talk of...migrant labour system.*

8.2. Adjectives

A striking characteristic is the use of adjectives as nouns. In this function they may take an article (usually *the*) and may take a plural *–s*. The noun that they are understood to quantify is deleted:

primary	'primary school'
tertiary	'tertiary education'
religious	'religious studies'
the rurals	'rural places'
the remote	'remote places' etc.

(48) *People who come from the rurals have a hard time...*
       '...from the rural areas'

(49) *I'm taking Religious.*
       '...Religious Studies'

Adjectives also show variability in degrees of comparison. *Too* or *very much* are treated as equivalents of *very*:

(50) *It is too difficult.*
       '... very difficult'

(51) *Hatred is very much common.* (De Klerk and Gough 2002: 363)

The phrase *the most thing* may be used for 'the thing I [verb] most':

(52) *The most thing I like is apples.* (De Klerk and Gough 2002: 363)

8.3. Nouns

Non-count nouns are frequently treated as if they are count nouns: hence *staffs, a luggage, a transport, machineries* etc. Occasionally the plural *–s* ending on regular nouns is absent:

(53) *We did all our subject in English.* (De Klerk and Gough 2002: 362)

9.   Pronominal systems

As gender differences are not marked in pronouns in Bantu languages, some variability shows up in BlSAfE, even amongst fluent speakers. In particular *he* and *she* may be substituted for each other, or subject to self-correction, suggesting that the distinction does not always come automatically to some speakers. Likewise *his* and *her* are not always differentiated:

(54)   *He's working in a factory.*
        (Graduate student referring to her mother)

The opposite, *he* for *she*, occurs as well.
        In lower sociolects the possessive pronoun sometimes follows the noun it qualifies e.g. *father of me* for *my father*. The substitution of *We* + *be* + NUMERAL for *There* + *be* + NUMERAL + *of us* is discussed in section 2.4. above:

(55)   *We were nine.*
        'There were nine of us.'

Occasionally second person plural pronoun forms like *you people* (genitive *your peoples'*). occur. The demonstrative pronouns *this* and *that* are sometimes substituted (strengthened) by the forms *this one* and *that one*:

(56)   A: (Cracks a joke)
        B: *I like that one.*
        'That's a good one/that's a good joke.'

10.   Word order

10.1.   Topicalisation and focussing

BlSAfE makes high use of topicalisation phenomena like left dislocation, fronting and focus-movement. Mesthrie (1997: 127) gives a percentage of 5.6 in his corpus of 8,200 sentences, in contrast to a white L1 control group's 1.8 percent (of 1,080 sentences).
    Left dislocation involves the leftward movement of an NP, with an appositional (or copy) pronoun in the main or subordinate clause:

(57)   *Today's children, they are so lazy.*

Fronting puts old or given information first, and does not involve a copy pronoun:

(58) Q: *I think you did your degree in three years?*
A: *Three years, and then the fourth year I did BEd.*

Focus movement shows a different intonational contour from fronting, and puts new information first:

(59) Q: *And how long did you live in East London?*
A: *For my life I'm there.*

Whilst these three constructions are found in most varieties of English, there are some aspects of their use in BlSAfE that are noteworthy. For left dislocation, the most common pragmatic function is the same as in other varieties – for contrastive effect, especially when speakers go through lists and make comments about individual NPs in the list:

(60) *Oh, Haroun, he was the co-ordinator. Farouk, that's my economics teacher.*

As in other varieties, left dislocation may also serve the discourse function of reintroducing given information that has not been talked about in the two previous sentence. Some other functions appear to be more common in BlSAfE than other varieties – left dislocation with partitive genitives (61), and relative clauses (62). For statistics and further details see Mesthrie (1997: 130–134).

(61) *Some of them, they'll use Afrikaans.*

(62) *The people who are essentially born in Soweto, they can speak Tsotsi.*

There is a large residue (of about 10 percent of all left dislocations in my database) which does not appear to have any pragmatic function, and are therefore labelled neutral predicates. Particularly noticeable is the use of left dislocation with the subject NP *the people*:

(63) *The people, they got nothing to eat.*

Mesthrie (1997: 129–130) reports that the other two constructions, focus movement and fronting, do not appear to differ in their pragmatics or syntax from other varieties of English.

Exercises and study questions

1. Examine sentence (21) again and the discussion surrounding it. Do you agree with the judgement that although *We are ten* is an acceptable sentence in StE, in the sense intended 'There are ten of us', it is not a feature of StE?

2. In connection with differences outlined in section 3 on negation, discuss what is presupposed in each of the following StE questions:
(a) *Is she your aunt?*
(b) *Isn't she your aunt?*

In other words, what answer are you predisposed to give to (a) and (b): *yes* and *no* or no predisposition (either *yes* or *no*).

3. Define the term *undeletion* as used in this chapter. Can you think of other examples of elements that are deleted in StE but might not be in BlSAfE?

4. What reasons can you give to motivate the form *can be able* (which is equivalent to *can*)?

5. Review the arguments for assuming there to be one rule underlying all *yes/no* questions in BlSAfE, rather than separate rules for positive and negative *yes/no* questions.

Selected references

Please consult the General references for titles mentioned in the text but not included in the references below. For a full bibliography see the accompanying CD-ROM.

Buthelezi, Qedusizi
    1995   South African Black English: lexical and syntactic characteristics. In: Mesthrie (ed.), 242–50.
De Klerk, Vivian and David Gough
    2002   Black South African English. In: Mesthrie (ed.), 356–78.
Mesthrie, Rajend
    1997   A sociolinguistic study of topicalisation phenomena in South African Black English. In: Schneider (ed.), Volume 2, 119–40.

Indian South African English: morphology and syntax

Rajend Mesthrie

1. Introduction

The description of Indian South African English (IndSAfE) syntax in this chapter is based on my fieldwork in the mid-1980s, when I interviewed 150 speakers in KwaZulu-Natal (Mesthrie 1992). IndSAfE offers an almost inexhaustible treasure trove of syntactic innovations as the variety moved from being a Second Language (L2) to being a First Language (L1) in the 1960s, within a century of its inception in South Africa. The variety clearly shares many features with its antecedent in India, but also shows a variety of features due to Natal colonial English, other L2 varieties of English in South Africa, processes of second-language acquisition and influence from the substrate languages (mainly Tamil and Bhojpuri).

2. Tense – aspect – modality

2.1. Tense

A broad present – past – future tense distinction forms the backbone of the IndSAfE system, though not without considerable alteration involving aspectual and modal distinctions. A few verbs have non-standard forms in lower sociolects:

seen	'saw'
been	'have been'
done	'did' (as full verb)

The third person singular present tense -*s* is variable in lower sociolects and in informal speech generally.

2.2.   Aspect

2.2.1   *BE* + -ing

BE + -*ing* occurs in a number of contexts beyond (and in addition to) the usual progressive in StE.

Historic present of narration
As a stylistic device to create a vivid and immediate effect, the present tense form of BE, instead of the standard past tense form *was*, combines with -*ing*:

(1)   *I'm suffering here now and the pain is getting worse.*
        'I was suffering and the pain was getting worse.'

A related usage uses historic present *be* + -*ing* to replace the preterite with verbs like *tell*, *say*, and others.

(2)   *Hawa, she's telling she cooks an' all.*
        'Don't you remember, she said she (still) cooks and so forth.' (*hawa* < 'here you are').

Perfect / Perfect progressive
In sentences with an adverbial phrase of time, some speakers use *be* + -*ing* instead of the standard *have* + PP:

(3)   *I'm staying this house seven years.*
        'I've been staying in this house for seven years.'

Habitual
Be + -*ing* is extended to habitual senses, usually expressed in StdE by the present tense:

(4)   *She's working by Foschini's.*
        'She works at Foschini's.'

Stative
Be + -*ing* is generalised in lower sociolects to co-occur with stative verbs:

(5)   *We thinking now why we can't get eddication.*
        'We now think back/regret why we didn't get an education.'

2.2.2   Have + -en

By contrast, *have* + -*en* occurs rarely in lower sociolects, where it may be replaced by markers like *finish* or *already* or by the simple past:

(6)   *I **finish** eat.*
'I've finished eating.'

(7)   *You **finish** eat?*
'Have you eaten? / Have you finished eating?'

This is subject to occasional hypercorrection in informal acrolect or upper mesolect to forms like the following:

(8)   *You finish eat**ing**?*

(9)   *You finish**ed** eat?*

2.2.3. Past habitual

There is a striking use of *should* for 'used to' in most sociolects of IndSAfE:

(10) *We **should** fright!*
'We used to be afraid.'

(11) *We **shouldn't** go to the cinema.*
'We never used to go to the cinema.'

This is probably based on the form *would*, though phonetic similarities between *should* and *used to* in fast speech may have played a role as well.

2.2.4. Leave / stay

The verbs *leave* and *stay* are used to convey aspectual distinctions in the constructions *and stay* and *and left her/him/it*. The former signals a habitual sense,
the latter is a completive marker:

(12) *We'll fright **an' stay**.*
'We used to be afraid (for a long time).'

(13) *We whacked him **an' left him**.*
'We beat him up thoroughly.'

2.3. Modality

Shall is rare in IndSAfE. In declaratives it is replaced by *will* (most commonly
the reduced form *'ll*), In questions it is used in formal acrolectal use (*Shall I
bring it?*). More commonly one hears the following in casual speech:

(14) Ø *I bring it?*
'Shall I bring it?'

(15)   *I must bring it?*
        'Shall/should/must I bring it?'

The negative form *shan't* is not part of everyday use and surfaces in formal or literary contexts. It is replaced by *won't* in casual speech.

The past tense form *should* (negative : *shouldn't*) is used as an equivalent to 'used to' – see sentences (10) and (11). In addition to this habitual sense, it is used as a replacement of the irrealis form *would*:

(16)   *Imagine if the other dog was here, how jealous he **should** get, ey!*
        '...how jealous he would get/would have got.'

Whereas *will* occurs with more or less standard semantics, *would* is rare in lower sociolects. *Would* and its reduced form *'d* are usually replaced by *will* or its reduced form *'ll*:

(17)   *He said he'll do it.*
        'He said he'd do it.'

The form *wouldn't* occurs as an idiomatic softener in place of *don't*:

(18)   Q: *So why are people so cruel today?*
        A: *I **wouldn't** know.*
        'I don't know/can't say.'

May in polite, permissive questions or commands is rare. (19) and (20) are examples of informal basilect equivalents of StE *May I go now?* or *You may go*:

(19)   *I can go now?/Can I go now?*

(20)   *You can go./Go!*

In addition to the standard permission or ability semantics, *can* can also be used to signify emphasis, 'can really'. Whereas in StdE this has a positive reading (*Mary can act* 'Mary can really act well'), in IndSAfE negative readings are also possible:

(21)   *Miriam can irritate you!*
        'Miriam can really irritate you!'

3.   Auxiliaries

3.1.   Have + *-en*

Have + *-en* is rare in lower sociolects – see section 2.2.2. above.

3.2.   BE + -*ing*

Be + -*ing*, on the other hand, is used in a range of functions – see section 2.2.1. above. Copula *be* is subject to variable deletion. A large measure of the deletion is phonological in nature, the segment most affected in this non-rhotic dialect being [ə]. Thus, *we're sick* may surface as [wi: sɪk] (with phonological deletion) or [wɪə: sɪk], but not [wɪər sɪk]. Cluster simplification appears to lead to deletion of *'s*:

(22)   *Harry Ø not here.*
          'Harry's not here.'

(23)   *What Ø Dan's age?*
          'What's Dan's age?'

With focus movement involving *that*, the copula is usually absent:

(24)   *My brother that!*
          'That's my brother.'

(25)   *From Sezela that people.*
          'Those people are from Sezela.'

On the other hand, the copula is mandatory in the following contexts:

(26)   *He's my brother. (*He my brother.)*

(27)   *She's sick. (*She sick.)*

(28)   *I'm (very) sick. (* I (very) sick.)*

3.3.   Habitual *be*

Invariant habitual *be* is a feature of IndSAfE, albeit not a frequent one.

(29)   *Spar's tomatoes be nice.*
          'Tomatoes from Spar (a supermarket) are usually nice.'

(30)   *Every time I go there she be all dressed up.*
          'Whenever I go there she's (usually) all dressed up.'

3.4.   *Do*-deletion

Do-support occurs in negative declaratives and negative questions, but is rarely used in their positive counterparts:

(31)   *Ø you saw my new hat?*
        'Did you see my new hat?'

(32)   *Ø you like this new programme?*
        'Do you like this new programme?'

(33)   *How often Ø she goes to her mother's place.*
        'How often does she go to her mother's place?'

3.5.   Auxiliary inversion

The use of auxiliary inversion is mainly reserved for formal contexts. Most speakers keep auxiliaries in situ in informal speech, both in *yes/no* questions and in *wh-* questions:

(34)   *What I must do? If my father say I must go an' plough today what I can do?*

(35)   *Must I put some more milk in it? ...Now you haven't...you didn't go back to eating meat?*

(36)   *So whereabout in India she's? How many years she's there now?*

Paradoxically, in subordinate clauses, as in the English of India, an inversion might occur:

(37)   *I wonder what will she think?*

Similarly, even though *do* is absent in positive questions in main clauses, it sometimes surfaces in subordinate clauses:

(38)   *I wonder where **does** it go in winter.*

3.6.   Auxiliary attraction to *wh-*

The auxiliary BE is frequently contracted in indirect questions and attracted to *wh-* words:

(39)   *Do you know when's the plane going to land?*

(40)   *Do you know what's roti?*
        '...unleavened bread...')

4. Negation

In most respects the IndSAfE system is that of StE. However, the use of *never* as an equivalent of *didn't* or *haven't* is widespread in lower sociolects. Basilectal speakers tend to use the unmarked verb after *never*:

(41) *I **never** go there to find out ...*
      'I didn't go there to find out (what was happening).'

(42) *They **never** play with those crooks.*
      'They didn't play with those crooks.' (i.e. they beat them up)

(43) *We **never** write yet.*
      'We haven't written (our exams) yet.'

Sometimes the standard semantics of 'not ever' apply:

(44) *He **never** finish his matric.*
      'He never finished matric.'

Mesolectal speakers tend to use the past tense of the verb after *never*, with similarities to basilectal semantics:

(45) *But I **never** made it to the end.*
      'But I didn't make it to the end.'

StdE offers two options of contraction when *not* combines with present *be*:

(46) a. *It **isn't** my cat.* (Negative contraction with attraction to copula)
      b. *It's not my cat.* (Copula contraction with attraction to pronoun)

(47) a. *You **aren't** my friend anymore.*
      b. *You're not my friend anymore.*

Only the forms in (b), involving copula contraction and attraction to pronouns, occur in informal IndSAfE. The forms in (a)may occur as rare stylistically marked alternatives in higher sociolects. With the auxiliary *have* the preference is reversed:

(48) a. *It **hasn't** rained for months.*
      b. *It's not rained for months.*

(49) a. *You **haven't** tried very hard.*
      b. *You've not tried very hard.*

This time, the (a) sentences are idiomatic in informal IndSAfE while the (b) forms are rare and stylistically marked. Some speakers even avoid the

(a) sentences with their perfective HAVE + -en forms, using *never* + unmarked verb or *didn't* + verb instead.

5.   Relativisation

Variation in relative clause (RC) formation is a vast topic that takes up a whole chapter (Chapter 3) in Mesthrie (1992). A brief outline of the four types of RCs identified there will be given: standard RCs, almost standard RCs, substrate-influenced RCs and discourse-governed RCs.

5.1.   Standard RCs

These are post-nominal and introduced by an appropriate relative pronoun like *that*, *which*, *who* or Ø. *Whom* is not a colloquial form in IndSAfE and *that* may be used with human as well as non-human nouns.

(50)   *People **who** come an' visit without phoning first make her cross.*

5.2.   Almost-standard RCs

One set of "almost-standard" RCs keeps the structure of the standard RC, but differs in the choice of relative pronoun, like *what*, *which one* and occasionally *which* for human NPs:

(51)   *But the kind of boodle **what** I'm earning is grand man, man.*
       '…that I'm earning…'

(52)   *That's the maid **which one** was here...*
       'That's the maid who was here...'

The other set is the "contact relative" which relativises a subject NP without an overt relative pronoun:

(53)   *We talking about my friend Ø lives down there.*
       'We're talking about my friend who lives down there.'

5.3.   Substrate-influenced RCs

Correlatives occur in the speech of older speakers, especially those with an Indic (North Indian) background:

(54)   *Which-car they supposed to give us, someone else got it.*
'Someone else got the car they were supposed to give us.'

(55)   *Which-one I put in the jar, that-one is good.*
'The ones (i.e. pickles) that I put in the jar are the best.'

These correlatives have the following characteristics:

– The RC is pre-nominal (i.e. it precedes the head noun)
– It is introduced by a *wh-* relative pronoun
– The *wh-* relative has an anaphoric counterpart in the main clause (usually a pronoun or a demonstrative like *that-one*)
– The full NP usually occurs in the preceding subordinate clause, compare *which-car* in (54). There are exceptions when the full NP may occur in both clauses, or when it may occur as *wh-* + pronoun in both clauses as in (55)

A second substrate-influenced type follows the Dravidian (South Indian) proto-type. In (56) the relevant RC has been bracketed for ease of identification:

(56)   *People who got (working here for them) sons,...*
'People who've got sons who are working here (for the company)...'

(57)   *That's all (we had) trouble.*
'That's all the trouble we had.'

Sentence (56) has a standard post-nominal relative with *who* (*People who've got ...*) followed by the substrate-influenced one *(working here for them) sons.* This RC and the one in (57) have the following characteristics:

– They are pre-nominal.
– They do not use a relative pronoun.
– There is a single occurrence of the domain noun.

Such prenominal external constructions are quite rare, but identifiably part of the dialect.
    A third substrate-influenced type is the past participle strategy:

(58)   *You can't beat Vijay's-planted tomatoes.*
'You can't beat the tomatoes planted by Vijay/that Vijay planted.'

(59)   *That Neela's-knitted jersey is gone white.*
'That jersey knitted by Neela/that Neela knitted is gone white.'

This RC, which follows from a detail of Bhojpuri syntax, shares its characteristics with the pronominal external RC above and has two additional characteristics:

- It is pre-nominal
- It involves agentive nouns in the RC, marked by the genitive *'s* (*Vijay's, Neela's*)
- It involves a single occurrence of the domain noun
- It does not use a relative pronoun
- The verb in the RC is in the past passive participle form

For further details on all of these, see Mesthrie (1992: 73–76).

The fourth class involves several sub-types which are intermediate between 'pragmatic' and 'syntactic' RCs.

5.4.   "Near relatives"

Sometimes clauses are linked together via intonation patterns, rather than overt syntactic marking. These are paratactic rather than fully fledged relatives:

(60)   *I'm a man, I don't go church an' all.*
'I'm a man who doesn't go to church, and so forth.'

(61)   *I put a* litee *from Renishaw, I don't even know him, in the goals.*
'I put a youngster, whom I don't even know, as goalkeeper.'

Topicalisation strategy
In this sub-type, a topicalised NP is relativised, with a copy (or appositional) pronoun in the "comment clause":

(62)   *One chap who used to stay here, he was a builder – Arjun.*

(63)   *Thing that is coming to you from the government, man, you should be appreciated with that thing.*
'You should be appreciative of a thing that comes to you from the government.'

Preposition-chopping strategy
In some cases the PP of the relative clause occurs in a reduced form with the preposition deleted:

(64)   *That's the place I retired Ø, you know.* (*to* > Ø)

(65)   *...like a big yard that you do gardening Ø an' all.* (*in* > Ø)

Paratactic RCs with possessives
The StdE constraint against relativising NPs involved in possessive constructions is lifted in informal IndSAfE:

(66)   *You like my shirt I bought?*
'Do you like my shirt, which I bought?'

(67)   *Remember Mr. Vahed's coat, he used to wear?*
         'Do you remember the coat that Mr. Vahed used to wear?'

These relatives have an "afterthought" feel about them.

6.   Complementation

6.1.   Parataxis

In upper mesolectal and acrolectal speech there is very little to report under complementation. Basilectal speakers, on the other hand, have developed complementation strategies that exhibit striking differences from StdE. Parataxis (loosely arranged clauses, each retaining main clause syntax) is favoured over hypotaxis (the use of clearly marked subordinate clauses):

(68)   *They told I must come and stay that side.*
         'They asked me to come and live there.'

(69)   *I like children must learn our mother tongue.*
         'I'd like our children to learn our mother tongue.'

This pattern also applies to modal-like or adverbial modifiers:

(70)   *Lucky, they never come.*
         'We were lucky that they didn't come.'

(71)   *Must be, they coming now.*
         'Perhaps they're coming now/It must be that they're coming now.'

For further details see Mesthrie (1992: 194–197).

6.2.   *Oh* as subordinator

Oh is occasionally used as an element that has COMP-like status:

(72)   *It's not that you'll be scared **oh** you're going to die there.*
         'It's not as if you're scared that you'll die there.'

In this construction, *oh* seems to signal direct speech with the semantics of disapproval. That is the speaker signals a slight criticism of the assertion or presupposition made in the direct or indirect quotation introduced by *oh*.

6.3.   Conditional clauses

In the basilect non-marking of the conditional is common:

(73)   Ø *we gonna keep servant, we must pay the servant.*
'If we want to hire a servant, we will have to pay them well.'

The conditional nature of the sentence is understood by the context and by the iconic nature of the arrangement (supposition first, consequence second). When conditionality is marked, a host of alternatives are possible. An intriguing one is the use of *too* at the end of the first clause:

(74)   *It can be a terrible house **too**, you have to stay in a terrible house.*
'Even if it's a terrible house, you have to live in it.'

In Section 10. other word-order principles, deriving in part from the OV substrates, are outlined; other functions of *too* are discussed in 10.1. and 10.2. (see example [112]).

7.   Agreement

There is little to report here. Subject-verb concord for third person singular verbs is variable between *-s* and Ø. The use of the demonstrative adjective *this* with both singular and plural nouns is very common:

(75)   ***This** people drive me crazy.*

Whereas *it* and *they/them* are clearly differentiated as referential pronouns, there is some syncretism in anaphoric contexts:

(76)   A: *I was looking for those shoes all over.*
B: *And did you find it?*

8.   Noun phrase structure

8.1.   Articles

One is an alternative form for the indefinite article *a*:

(77)   *I was feeling thirsty, so I bought **one** soda water.* (Unstressed, asserted, specific)

In elliptical, casual style the definite article may be deleted if it is presupposed and specific:

(78)   *Ø food is lovely.* (*The* understood in context)

Non-specific uses of a noun also allow variable deletion of the indefinite article:

(79)   *Because if they give us Ø chance...*
        '...give us a chance...'

8.2.   Adjectives

Adjectives may be reduplicated to signal plurality (80) or indicate distribution (81):

(80)   *You're doing **wrong-wrong** things.*
        '... many wrong things.'

(81)   ***One-one** time you see a blue lizard.*
        'Occasionally you see a blue lizard.'

Adjectives do not reduplicate with singular nouns in other contexts: *wrong-wrong thing. The irregular adjective *bad* has comparative forms like *more worse* for 'worse' and *worst* for 'worse' or 'worst'. Some speakers of Dravidian background occasionally use adjectives as substantives, preceded by an article, as in (82):

(82)   *I'm **a strong**, but now I'm gone **a thin**.*

8.3.   Nouns

Irregular nouns of StdE are sometimes made regular: *oxens, childrens, bucks, sheeps.* On the other hand, plural nouns may be used without an ending if clear in context, though not very frequently. Mesthrie (1992: 130) reports a deletion rate of 5% for *-s* plurals in his corpus of 2,530 nouns not preceded by quantifiers. With quantifiers the deletion rate was 7.3%.

An associative plural marker *them* occurs with human nouns:

(83)   ***Johnny-them** going 'way tomorrow.*
        'Johnny and family are moving tomorrow.'

(84)   *I saw **Saras-them's** cat by the road.*
        'I saw the cat belonging to Saras's family on the roadside.'

The form *and-them* may be preferred in higher sociolects, and coincides with the general South African English (SAfE) form.

In lower sociolects, *all* may be used as an emphatic plural form or as an associative plural marker with human and non-human nouns:

(85)   *After he died his **books-all** was at home.*
        '...all his books...' or possibly 'his books and other effects.'

(86)   *How's **mother-all**?*
        'How's your mother and the others at home?'

8.4.   Noun phrase reduction

Very commonly complex noun phrases made up of NP + PP are reduced to ADJ + N or to compound nouns:

cold-touch	'touch of cold'
top-house	'house at the top'
like-his shirt	'shirt like his'
my-house wedding	'wedding at my house'

9.   Pronominal systems

The most notable characteristic of IndSAfE is the regular use of *y'all* (< *you all*) for second person plural pronouns. It has a genitive form *yall's*:

(87)   *Is that **yall's** car?*
        'Is that your (pl.) car?'

A less common equivalent is *you people* with the genitive form *your people's.*

(88)   *Is that **your people's** car?*

In lower sociolects an alternative form for *he* is *daffale* (< *that fellow*).

(89)   ***Daffale** said I must come today.*

10.   Word order

10.1.   OV influence in VO dialect

Although the basic word order in IndSAfE is clearly SVO, the variety has a greater tolerance than most varieties of English for constructions typically associated with OV languages, due to the SOV nature of both the Indic and Dravidian substrates in IndSAfE. Sentences with the actual order SOV are not characteristic of IndSAfE, even though a few were produced by speakers who were "pre-basilectal". The following OV features were common in informal IndSAfE:

10.1.1. Quasi-postpositions

Although prepositions are widespread, some uses of *side*, *time*, *part* and *way* approach that of prepositions:

(90) *I'm going **Fountain Head-side** tomorrow.*
      'I'm going towards Fountain Head tomorrow.'

(91) ***Afternoon-part** gets too hot.*
      'It gets too hot in the afternoon.'

(92) *We have our lunch **twelve o'clock-time**.*
      'We have our lunch at/at about twelve o'clock.'

10.1.2. Co-ordination

Some speakers use co-ordinative constructions which are reminiscent of OV structures, since ellipsis is rare and a marker like *too* occurs in final position in both clauses:

(93) *I made rice **too**, I made roti **too**.*
      'I made both rice and roti.'

A second type involves a survival of a pattern from Indic and Dravidian, in which preference is given to subordinating "conjunctive" constructions over co-ordination:

(94) *He bring and sells mango.*
      'He brings mangoes and sells them.'

This is reminiscent of substrate influence since the phrase *bring an' sell* is intonationally one unit, with the first verb in stem form.

10.1.3. Kinship titles

OV languages prefer the order proper noun before common noun. This pattern survives especially well in IndSAfE, since it is associated with respectful kinship titles, in which an Indian kinship term survives: *Virend maama* '(maternal) uncle Virend', *Rani akka* 'sister Rani', etc. In informal speech the pattern is retained even if an English kinship term is used: *Johnny-uncle* 'Uncle Johnny', *Daisy aunty* 'Aunt Daisy'. It also applies to terms of address: *Somera Doctor* 'Doctor Somera', *Johnny Police* 'Policeman Johnny', *Naicker teacher* 'teacher Naicker'.

10.1.4. Question-final particles

For emphasis, question words (especially *what*) are occasionally used in final position as interrogative markers:

(95)   *You din' hear me, **what?***
       'Didn't you hear me?' (emphatic)

10.1.5. Clause-final conjunctions

But is used at the end of clauses with affective meaning, roughly equivalent to 'really, though, truly':

(96)   *She donno Tamil? She can talk English, **but!***

(97)   *I was unconscious, **but.***

Too occurs at the end of clauses, as an equivalent of the clause-initial standard conjunction *even if*, as in (74).

Other manifestations of OV influence include rank-reduction (see section 8.4.) and substrate-influenced RCs (see section 5.3.).

10.2.   Topicalisation and focussing

IndSAfE has a predilection for an array of processes that can be loosely characterised as topicalisation. The two main processes involved are fronting (98) and left dislocation (99):

(98)   *Change I haven't got.*
       'I don't have change.'

(99)   *Tommy – he was a builder.*

Both occur in informal StdE. Fronting puts old or given information first and frequently involves a contrastive effect. Left dislocation is similar in its pragmatics but not in its syntactic form, since the fronted NP is represented by a pronoun trace in the main clause, for example the pronoun *he* in (99).

Many factors make topicalisation a prominent feature of IndSAfE syntax and discourse organisation. Firstly, it enables the verb to come last, a position that is compatible with the OV structure of the substrates:

(100)   *Alone you came?*
        'Did you come alone?'

Secondly, a process like fronting is not always controlled by discourse organisation. It may occur initially in a stretch of discourse, without any apparent recourse to givenness or contrast:

(101)   *Your tablet, you took?* (No previous discussion of medication or illness)

Thirdly, fronting and left dislocation occur with a range of semantic roles: temporal, locative (102), genitive, comitative, instrument, goal, beneficiary, source and others.

(102)   *Near to Margate that is.*
        'That place is near to Margate.'

(103)   *My grandfather, I talk with him.*
        'I speak (in Gujarati) with my grandfather.'

Fourthly, topics occur in a wide array of main clauses involving *yes/no* questions, *wh-* questions (105), negatives (104) and comparatives (106):

(104)   *I'm here 14 years, not with one neighbour I had problems...*

(105)   *Your car – where you parked?*
        'Where did you park your car?'

(106)   *Like a wild animal you are!*

Fifthly, topics may be "extracted" out of embedded clauses:

(107)   *Indians, I donno why they like that!*
        'I don't know why Indians are like that!'

(108)   *Beans-price, I told is high because nobody has got it.*
        'I've said that price of beans is high because nobody has got them to sell.'

Sixthly, "stacking" of topics is possible within a sentence:

(109)   *Therefore, I mean, I feel, Phoenix, living like this, I don't like it.*
        'Therefore, I don't like living like this in Phoenix.'

For further examples of more complex stacking, see Mesthrie (1992: 113–114).

Seventhly (and finally), topicalisation seems so strong that sometimes, even when speakers begin with an SVO structure, they round it off by recapitulating the pronoun subject and the verb:

(110)   *We stayed in the Finn Barracks **we stayed**.*

There is less to say about focussing in IndSAfE. Focussing of the sort found in other varieties involving a special intonation is possible:

(111)   ***Twenty years** I've been living here!*

Here the rise-fall intonation on *twenty years* serves a highlighting function. An alternative strategy is for speakers to use *too* as a highlighter after the NP:

(112)   *This weather **too**, it's terrible.* (No other terrible thing mentioned).

Too may also highlight an entire sentence, roughly equal to standard 'even':

(113)   *Can't give one slice of bread **too**.* 'You can't even give me a slice of bread.'

11.   Selected paradigms

There is little to report in respect of BE, HAVE and DO apart from some variability in third person singular forms. Whereas the present tense paradigm for BE is standard for most speakers, the past tense shows considerable variation between *was* and *were*. Some speakers use *was* throughout the paradigm, and forms like *you was*, *we was* or *they was* are unremarked upon in the lower sociolects.

In these sociolects, *been* replaces *have been* in phrases like *I been there*, (but not as an auxiliary as in **I been playing*). For these speakers the present paradigm for DO may also be regularised, with *do* occurring throughout, e.g. *he do*. The verb HAVE is more interesting, admitting fewer non-standard forms, if only because it is a rare form itself in lower sociolects. Perfective *have* is frequently replaced by markers like *finish*, whilst possessive *have* is typically replaced by the regular form *got*. In lower sociolects the paradigm is *I got/you got/he got* etc. for *I've got/you've got/she's got* etc.

Fairly similar observations hold for negative forms of BE/HAVE/DO. Forms like *he don't, he wasn't, you wasn't* and *they wasn't* are possible for some speakers. The negatives of *I got/you got/he got* are *I haven' got/you haven' got/he haven' got*.

The negative *ain't* is not a feature of IndSAfE. See section 3.2. for interaction between pronouns, the verb *be* and negative contraction. The negative of *used to* is either *never used to* or *shouldn't* (see section 2.3.). The forms *didn't use(d) to* and *used not to* are not a feature of IndSAfE.

In contrast to the immense variation in auxiliary forms relating to aspect and modality already discussed, there is little variation in the form of lexical verbs relating to tense or strong/weak distinctions, where the StBrE forms generally apply.

The prepositional verb *look after* and the compound *by-heart* are treated as one lexical item:

(114)　*He **look-afters** the baby.*
　　　'…looks after…'

(115)　*They **look-aftered** me when I was sick.*
　　　'…looked after…'

(116)　*I'm tired of **look-aftering** the baby.*
　　　'…looking after…'

(117)　*The teacher told us not to **by-heart** our work.*
　　　'…to learn off by heart…'

(118)　***By-hearting** your work doesn't mean you understand it.*
　　　'…learning by heart…'

12.　Current research

Not much new work has been undertaken in IndSAfE syntax. In Mesthrie (2003) I examine the choices being made by younger speakers who are faced with an immense variety of morphosyntactic choices. The younger (fifth) generation of children do not seem to innovate much; rather they are selecting features from the pool of variants available to them. However, they are not jettisoning all of the more divergent structures in their parent's speech. Some OV constructions remain and carry a degree of covert prestige. Speakers are increasingly polystylistic, depending on dimensions of formality, as well as on the identity of the interlocutor, the nature of the interaction and other factors. Since the publication of Mesthrie (1992), IndSAfE-speaking children are effectively, for the first time in South African history, able to attend desegregated schools, including private schools, at which the prestige varieties of (white) SAfE prevail. The give-and-take between ethnolect and prestige variety has still to be studied.

Exercises and study questions

1. Use the maps on the CD Rom to ascertain if the following InSAfE forms discussed in this section exist anywhere else in the world:
   (a) *y'all*   (b) *yall's*   (c) *should* = 'used to'
   (d) habitual *be*   (e) *more worse* or *worst* for 'worst'

2. Compare the features of InSAfE with those described for IndE (i.e. the English of India).

3. "InSAfE has a far greater number of non-standard grammatical forms than other varieties of English in South Africa." Read through the other chapters on English in South Africa to verify or disprove this assertion. If the assertion is true, why do you think this should be so?

4. Outline the three non-standard functions of *too* described in this chapter.

5. Discuss the correlatives of InSAfE.

Selected references

Please consult the General references for titles mentioned in the text but not included in the references below. For a full bibliography see the accompanying CD-ROM.

Mesthrie, Rajend
   1992   *English in Language Shift – The History, Structure and Sociolinguistics of South African Indian English.* Cambridge: Cambridge University Press.
   2003   Children in language shift – the syntax of fifth-generation Indian South African English speakers. *South African Journal of Linguistics and Applied Language Studies* 21: 119–126.

Cape Flats English: morphology and syntax

Kay McCormick

1. Introduction

As indicated in the introduction to the phonology of Cape Flats English (CFE) chapter (this volume), the English spoken by coloured people in Cape Town is not homogeneous. Variation reflects regional and class differences, and also level of schooling and whether schooling took place in predominantly coloured schools or in schools with a more mixed intake, and – in the case of the latter – whether the school was formerly a white state school, or one of the prestigious private schools. Until recently, it was only linguists who asserted that CFE could be viewed as a dialect. It was more commonly regarded, by its speakers and by outsiders alike, as "broken English", English that had been inadequately learned.

It did not have a name, unlike the local dialect of Afrikaans, which is called *Kaaps* 'Cape, Cape Speech' or *kombuistaal* 'kitchen language'. This is not surprising, given that for decades the situation in many homes, schools and neighbourhoods has mitigated against clearly distinguishing between L1 and L2 speakers of English. Even within families siblings who are close in age may identify themselves differently from one another, as "English-speaking" or "Afrikaans-speaking". Also to be taken into account is the very common parental practice of speaking Afrikaans to one another at home, while speaking only English to children of school and pre-school age.

Speakers of CFE who have had ten or more years of schooling are usually also able to speak and write standard South African English (SAfE). (Depending on where and how they learned it, they may or may not have a distinctive accent associated with coloured Capetonians – see chapter by Finn, this volume.) Since, in their communities, coloured people's command of standard SAfE has commonly been associated with aspirations of upward mobility or with assimilation into a white world, people who can speak both dialects choose the contexts in which they use them carefully.

Those who speak the standard dialect at home may well not use it in casual conversation with friends and acquaintances who speak CFE at home, since to do so would suggest social distance. Conversely, people who have mastered the standard dialect but do not speak it at home, would reserve its use for formal occasions or for contexts in which they wished to indicate to interlocutors that they were educated or authoritative. Most Capetonians who have CFE in their linguistic repertoire also speak a non-standard dialect of Afrikaans and are likely to switch between Afrikaans and CFE, even within the same conversation.

The ability to use the non-standard dialect of Afrikaans and to switch appropriately between it and CFE is a powerful indicator of solidarity, of recognition of roots in Cape Town's working-class coloured communities. For more detail, see McCormick (2002). In sum, attitudes towards English are ambivalent. It is seen as a powerful means of upward mobility and as a sign of urban sophistication, but also as a sign of snobbery and the abandoning of roots. CFE does not attract the strongly positive or the strongly negative versions of these attitudes. It seems to be perceived as a code which shows that its speakers are educated but still rooted in their communities. More research needs to be done to test this tentative claim.

Published research on CFE includes Malan (1996), McCormick (2002), Mesthrie (1999) and Mesthrie and West (1995). There is also a growing body of as yet unpublished dissertations on CFE, for example Malan (2000) and Wood (1987). Recordings of interviews held in Oral History archives at the University of the Western Cape, the University of Cape Town, and the District Six Museum in Cape Town are rich sources of linguistic data. Because of their subject matter, these interviews also provide contextually relevant information about the speakers and their communities.

For this paper I have drawn on the published and unpublished sociolinguistic work mentioned above, on Field (2001) (a book about forced removals in Cape Town which is based on local oral histories), on my own corpus of audio-recordings, and on transcripts of recordings made by the Centre for Popular Memory at the University of Cape Town and held in that university's archives.

2.   Morphology and syntax

While the standard form is an option in CFE for all of the constructions identified below, many of the non-standard variants are the ones that are more commonly heard, especially in informal speech. As yet there has been no systematic, quantitative study of the comparative prevalence of the variables.

2.1.   Tense – aspect – modality systems

2.1.1. *Non-standard use of auxiliaries*

Unstressed *did* is very commonly used in past tense utterances, especially by children. It is stigmatised and is the target of corrective exercises in grammar lessons at school. Nonetheless, it remains a fairly commonly used optional form in the speech of adults.

(1)   *He **did** work for Taylor and Horn, that time.*
       'He worked for Taylor and Horn then.'

(2)   *We **did** move here a week already.*
       'We had moved here a week previously.'

The perfective may be avoided, its function being served by an alternative form, as in (3):

(3)   ***Were** you there already?*
       'Have you been there before?'

(4)   *This is the first time in my life I **heard** it.*
       'This is the first time in my life I have heard it.'

Must commonly replaces *has/have/had to*, *should* and *ought to*:

(5)   *We **must** have respect for each and every one.*

(6)   *We **must** still wait.*

Will commonly replaces *would* in hypothetical, iterative and habitual constructions:

(7)   *How **will** it be if I put this two milks together?*

(8)   *If I answer the door, that person **will** say something first.*

2.1.2. *Contraction and deletion of auxiliary verbs*

Are can be contracted and deleted. Speakers are not always consistent, even when instances of *are* occur in a similar phonological environment, as in example (9). Since SAfE is non-rhotic, the deletion of contracted *are* is probably phonologically motivated. If it were part of a morpho-syntactic process, one would expect that *is* would also be both contractable and deletable, but no instances of *is* deletion have been reported in the literature so far.

(9)   *You ∅ educated. They're all uneducated.*

(10)   *They ∅ going to say "Ja, ('yes') what's wrong with you?"*

As tense auxiliaries and the past tense morpheme *-ed* may be deleted, the unmarked form of the verb may be left to express the past tense:

(11)   *We **stay** now here for twenty-four years.*

(12)   *Sometimes also when you **enter** those rooms there everybody was making a big noise singing Afrikaans liedjies* ('songs').

Will and *would* as well as *has* and *have* can be contracted and deleted:

(13)   *When it gets too much for her, she Ø even phone the police.*
        (Context indicates that the speaker is referring to a pattern of behaviour in the past.)

(14)   *I said "Let's get together this evening and we Ø talk about things."*

(15)   *I said to him, "You Ø finish working."*
        (Context indicates past.)

(16)   *Ja, because we Ø grown up in Africa.*

2.2.   Deletion of adverbial suffix

The suffix *-ly* may be deleted from adverbs giving them the same form as the related adjectives.

(17)   *We must move **quick**.*

(18)   *People would look at him **strange**, you know.*

2.3.   Complementation

The *that* complementizer may be omitted:

(19)   *So my granny said Ø he was 21 years old.*

(20)   *Well, I knew Ø they went to church there.*

2.4.   Agreement

2.4.1.   *The verb* to be *as copula and auxiliary*

The verb *to be* commonly has the same form for third person singular and plural, namely the singular form. This is more likely to occur when the subject is a noun than when it is a pronoun. It happens in both present and past tense utterances:

(21)   *The parents **is** paying.*

(22)   *The people **was** saying he is laying there.*

(23)   *We **was** very forceful.*

In rare instances speakers use the contracted form of the auxiliary for the third person singular after a second person singular subject:

(24)   *You try when you's talking to a Boere.*

2.4.2. Subject-verb agreement in other verbs

The modal construction *would have (had) to* in which *would* has been deleted may allow the plural form after a singular subject:

(25)   *Otherwise she Ø have to phone the neighbours.*

The verb *to do* in a third person singular negative construction is usually rendered in its Standard English (StE) plural form *don't:*

(26)   *He **don't** allow her inside the door.*

(27)   *My husband **don't** like this district.*

Other verbs may reverse the StE concord rules by taking a word-final *-s* with a plural subject and omitting it with a singular subject. However, this reversal is not an absolute rule. There are more instances of singular verbs without an *-s* than of plural verbs with one. As examples (29) and (30) suggest, the concord pattern is unstable.

(28)   *If somebody **chop** it then it **fall** down.*

(29)   *They **drink** and they **makes** a lot of noise.*

(30)   *Then she **goes** and **visit** this one and that one.*

2.4.3. Agreement between noun, demonstrative adjective and demonstrative pronoun

The singular form of the demonstrative adjective tends to be used with both singular and plural nouns.

(31)   *He must take from **that** reserves.*

(32)   *I've watched **this** children.*

The demonstrative pronoun is usually used in its singular form, whether the referent is singular or plural:

(33)   **That** *is other people's constitutions.*

(34)   **That's** *sandwiches.*

2.4.4. Agreement between determiner and noun

Singular nouns ending in *-s* such as *jeans* or *pants* may lose the *-s* as in *a jean* or *a pant*. Alternatively, they may keep the *-s* but lose the preceding *pair of* which is obligatory in StE if the phrase starts with an indefinite article. Hence *a pants, a jeans* and *a shorts* are also heard.

2.5.   Noun plural formation

Them may be added to a noun to form an associative plural, with or without an intervening *and*, as in (35) and (36). This construction can then be used in the possessive form, as in (37):

(35)   *Maybe because of Joy-**them**, but I knew there was a difference.*

(36)   *We were by Marlene-**them** yesterday.*

(37)   *Marlene-**them's** car was stolen.*

2.6.   Phatic question concord

Is it? and *ne?* (from Afrikaans) may be used as phatic questions to express interest or sympathy. They keep these forms regardless of person, number or positive/negative polarity in the statement to which they respond:

(38)   A: *"No, they don't come visit no more."*
        B: *"Is it?"*

(39)   A: *"He is so rich!"*
        B: *"Ne?"*

2.7.   Phrase structure

2.7.1. Noun phrases

The determiner may be omitted in noun phrases where it would be included in StE. However, as the first example indicates, this is not consistent.

(40)   *I was **an** altar boy. I was ∅ altar boy then.*

(41)   *When they come for ∅ holiday, we go to the beach.*

2.7.2.   *Prepositional phrases*

The initial preposition may be absent, particularly when the prepositional phrase in question is temporal:

(42)   *After she finished her work ∅ the day, she...* '*...for the day*'

(43)   *If only Mandela lived ∅ that time, we would have stayed.* '*...at that time...*'

(44)   *Zelda died ∅ the Friday.* '*...on the Friday*'

(45)   *Two o'clock ∅ the morning, I'm walking down the street.* '*...in the morning...*'

2.7.3.   *Serial verbs*

Serial markers *and* and *to* may be deleted, creating serial verb constructions that are not common in standard SAfE. They may involve up to three verbs, as in (49).

(46)   *He go ∅ learn there by CAP.*

(47)   *You run and go ∅ watch the Brigade.*
       (Context indicates repeated action.)

(48)   *I'll come ∅ fetch you one day.*

(49)   *Yesterday I went ∅ go ∅ buy fruit.*

2.8.   Word order

Temporal adverbials commonly precede locational adverbials, as they do in Afrikaans:

(50)   *I'll go **now** on the bed.*

(51)   *You come **in the morning** there.*

The direct object may follow the indirect object if the latter consists of a preposition and a pronoun. This is the normal word order in Afrikaans:

(52)   *I was speaking **to her** English.*

(53)   *He explained **to me** a lot of things.*

2.9.   Pronominal systems

The accusative form of a pronoun may be used in subject position when the subject includes another person. This is an optional construction for adults and is commonly used by children. It is also found in other dialects of SAfE.

(54)   *Now **me and Elizabeth** speaks English.*

(55)   ***Me and my first baby** were here.*

The dative of advantage (benefactive) is sometimes found. In my data the main examples of this construction are in the first person singular or plural:

(56)   *I'm going to buy **me** biscuits and chocolates.*

(57)   *We all take **us** down to Hout Bay for the day.*

A related construction occurs in the idiom *keep you / us / him etc.* The phrase means 'regard or present oneself as …', especially as "high and mighty". Interestingly, the suspicion that one is keeping oneself high and mighty is often triggered by using English instead of the bilingual vernacular in an informal environment:

(58)   *We don't **keep us** high and mighty.*

Pronominal apposition may occur in topic-comment structures:

(59)   *Those children **they** had to leave school at standard three already.*

It may be used instead of *there* in existential verb phrases, as in (60):

(60)   ***It** must have been two or three families sharing a room.*

The second person pronoun may be avoided when directly addressing a person of higher rank, or through a wish to be formal and polite. In such cases the addressee's title is used instead of *you*. This follows the Afrikaans pattern. Many bilingual speakers of CFE are not comfortable using *you* to address someone of higher rank, even within the family, being accustomed to having the option – in Afrikaans – of choosing the polite form of the second-person pronoun, an option not available in English.

(61)   *Good morning Doctor. Would **Doctor** like some tea?*

2.10.   Negation

Double negation is common. It is particularly likely to occur when the utterance has a slot for *any, anything* or *anyone* as in (62)–(64). *Never* may be used instead of *did not / didn't*, as in (65).

(62)   *He **didn't** have **no** respect for his mother.*

(63)   *It's **not** nice neighbours **no** more, here.*
         (StdE for *no more* would be *any longer*)

(64)   *Here they **don't** worry with **nobody**.*

(65)   *I **never** saw the goose again.*
         'I didn't see the goose again'

3.   **Lexicon**

The lexicon is largely the same as that of standard SAfE. Differences can be located in the absorption of loanwords, special usage of some English words, and calques.

3.1.   Loanwords

The most commonly used loanwords come from Afrikaans. The ones most frequently heard are not nouns, as might be expected, but discourse markers: particles that contribute to the informal conversational tone of the utterance, as they would in Afrikaans. They have no satisfactory English equivalent, and the standard translations of the words do not capture their effects as discourse markers. Indispensable items are *mos* 'indeed, of course', *sommer* 'just, merely', *maar* 'but', and *ne*. The latter is not used only as a phatic question, as it is in (36), but also functions as a tag question.

(66)   *I wasn't **mos** so well.*

(67)   *I rather **maar** go sleep.*

(68)   *It was like a family before, **ne**?*

(69)   *Sometimes when I get the moer in I **sommer** hit from A to Z.*
         (*To get the moer in* is 'to become angry or fed up', but it is a mild obscenity.)

The obscenity in example (69) is one of several that are used in English. Given the nature of the data bases used for this article, obscenities are few and far between. However, in interviews bilingual respondents indicated that Afrikaans is the language for swearing or expressing anger, and observation confirms this.

In the speech of Muslims and those who frequently associate with Muslims there are loanwords from Arabic such as the greeting *Salaam Aleikum*, and words relating to religious practices, such as *Haj*. Afrikaans is the source of a few items, such as the title for a Muslim male peer, *Boeta*. From Malay CFE has absorbed words pertaining to religious practices like *labarang* 'the festival of Eid', to food like *bobotie* 'curried mince dish with fruit and savouries', and titles of respect like *Oetie* 'title of respect for an older woman'.

3.2.   Usage of English words

3.2.1.   Adverbs

Instead of *always*, CFE speakers often use *every time*. Instead of *again*, *any longer* or *no longer*, CFE speakers may use *no more*:

(70)   *What is the purpose of you doing this **every time** here?*

(71)   *She didn't want to go **no more** there, mos.*

(72)   *There's **no more** terminus there.*

3.2.2.   Prepositions

The choice of prepositions is frequently different from that in contemporary StE. The prepositions used in English sentences are often direct translations of those that would appear in the equivalent Afrikaans sentence.

(73)   *She did take photos **from** us.* '...of us...'

(74)   *They phoned me **with** my birthday.* '...for...'

(75)   ***On** school he was in Afrikaans class.* '...at...'

(76)   *You see, they were very scared **for** the police.* '...of...'

(77)   *We didn't ask to come **in** this world.* '...into...'

Other non-standard usage of prepositions is not directly attributable to Afrikaans influence, for example the *in* in (78):

(78)   *Everyday she is **in** work.*

In CFE *by* is used in many environments where alternatives would be used in StE. It occurs, for example, where StE would use *at, near, with, next to, in,* or *to.* Mesthrie and West (1995) argue that some of these uses could be traces of settler dialects. They show that several of the usages typical of CFE were present in texts written by 19th century British immigrants (Mesthrie and West 1995: 140).

(79)   *I was living **by** my granny that time.*

(80)   *I'm telling you, **by** him you must do things right.*

(81)   *I went to go fetch my grandchild here **by** the school.*

As in some other dialects of SAfE, the preposition *with* does not have to be followed by a noun, as in (82):

(82)   *As they grew older then the next lot goes **with**.*

3.2.3. Redundancies

The following redundancies are fairly common, as they are in some other dialects of SAfE: *my utmost best, I'd rather prefer, more happier, more superior.*

3.2.4. Particles

Now is often used as a discourse marker having nothing to do with present time. It may, as in the first two examples below, indicate a regular occurrence, but it does not always serve that purpose, as is shown by (85) which refers to a one-off occasion.

(83)   *If her mother's **now** angry, she will **now** speak English.*

(84)   *If somebody **now** passed away or dies, everybody is there.*

(85)   *I had to **now** maar wear it.*

Here may be used as a discourse marker that has nothing to do with place. It doesn't always have the same meaning or function. In (86) below it seems to function as a filler while the speaker thinks about his age, while in (87) its function may be to point out the contrast.

(86)   *That time I was **here** twenty three, twenty four.*
       'At that time I was twenty three or twenty four.'

(87)   *I'm always claiming that we started Afrikaans, and **here** I don't want to speak it anymore.*

3.2.5.   Conjunctions

Very common in children's speech but also found among adults is the use of *so* to mean 'and' or 'and then' in utterances where it is clear from the context that it doesn't suggest consequence:

(88)   *They came from that terrace, **so** they move in here.*

(89)   ***So** I took the ball after the ref indicated where the mark is, **so** I tapped the ball.*

The phrase *because why* may be used instead of *because*. It has a rising intonation but is not followed by a pause:

(90)   *So I don't know nothing **because why** I haven't seen them for years.*

(91)   *Yes, **because why** the reason is that whenever I file anything...*

3.2.6.   Archaism

The word *thrice* is found even in informal usage.

(92)   *She came back **thrice**.*

(93)   *I asked him twice, **thrice**, and still he didn't reply.*

3.2.7.   Euphemism

As other varieties of SAfE, CFE makes predicative use of *late*, meaning 'deceased':

(94)   *Then there's my sister, Mary, who is **late**.*

(95)   *My aunt is **late** now about fifteen years.*

3.3.   Calques

Calques occur frequently in the speech of children who are being brought up in English by parents whose first language is Afrikaans and who do not speak StE. However, they also occur in adult speech, as in (96)–(99):

(96)   *He sommer used to **throw** his mother **with big, big stones** when he is drunk.*

(97)   *...and a **long** teacher, Mr Abbas...*

(98)   *They had **promised for** the elders that we would be put together.*

(99)   *We grew up **in front of them**.*

The calque in (96) *throw with y* is a word-for-word translation of the Afrikaans construction *gooi x met y*. It is used where *y* is an inanimate instrument, and *x* is an animate patient. In (97) *long* is calqued from Afrikaans *lang*, which means both 'long' and 'tall'. In (98), *promised for* is calqued from the construction in Afrikaans, in which the verb for 'to promise' is followed by *vir*, meaning 'for'. Finally, (99) involves a literal translation of the phrase used to denote growing up knowing someone well.

4.   Recent research on Cape Flats English

Recent research on CFE has been on (a) aspects of the history of some of its features (Mesthrie 1999; McCormick 2002), (b) the implications of dialect differences for the testing of CFE-speaking children's language development (Southwood 1996), (c) the development of children's oral narratives in CFE (Malan 2000) and (d) on the development and use of CFE in the context of social-economic, political, linguistic and discourse facets of the language contact situation between English and Afrikaans in Cape Town (McCormick 2002).

Exercises and study questions

1. Study the section on auxiliaries (2.1.1.). Then refer to the other articles on English in South Africa. List one auxiliary feature that appears to be unique to CFE. List one that is shared by other varieties of SAfE.

2. Review the section on Pronominal Systems (2.9). List one pronominal feature not generally found in other varieties of SAfE. List one pronominal feature CFE shares with other varieties of SAfE.

3. Comment on the following examples and compare with other varieties of English in South Africa:
   (a) *The people was saying he is laying there.*
   (b) *He don't allow her inside the door.*
   (c) *They drink and they makes a lot of noise.*
   (d) *I've watched this children.*
   (e) *That's sandwiches.*

4. Although the dative of advantage (2.9) at first sight appears to resemble the equivalent of a reflexive of StE, the two are quite different. Can you think of ways of differentiating them?

5. In what ways is unstressed *do* of CFE different from stressed *do* of StE?

Selected references

Please consult the General references for titles mentioned in the text but not included in the references below. For a full bibliography see the accompanying CD-ROM.

Field, Sean (ed.)
  2001   *Lost Communities, Living Memories: Remembering Forced Removals in Cape Town.* Cape Town: David Philip.
Malan, Karen
  1996   Cape Flats English. In Vivian de Klerk (ed.), 125–148.
  2000   Oral narratives of personal experience – a developmental sociolinguistic study of Cape Flats children. PhD dissertation, University of Cape Town.
McCormick, Kay
  2002   *Language in Cape Town's District Six.* Oxford: Oxford University Press.
Mesthrie, Rajend
  1999   Fifty ways to say "I do": tracing the origins of unstressed *do* in Cape Flats English. *South African Journal of Linguistics* 17: 58–71.
Mesthrie, Rajend and Paula West
  1995   Towards a grammar of Proto South African English. *English World-Wide* 16: 103–133.
Southwood, Frenette
  1996   The clinical evaluation of the expressive syntax of bilingual English pre-schoolers in the greater Cape Town area: suggested modifications to the 1981 LARSP profile. *Stellenbosch Papers in Linguistics (SPIL) Plus* 29: 360–371.
Wood, Tahir M.
  1987   Perceptions of, and attitudes towards, varieties of English in the Cape Peninsula, with particular reference to the 'Coloured Community'. M.A. thesis, Rhodes University, Grahamstown.

St. Helena English: morphology and syntax

Sheila Wilson and Rajend Mesthrie

1.   Introduction

St. Helena English, as Hancock (1991: 17) wrote, is significant for many reasons: "firstly because of the many similarities with island dialects elsewhere, and secondly because of its implications for the study of nautical English, and its relationship to creolised forms of that language." The syntax of St Helena English (StHE) does indeed show intriguing features which support Hancock's assertions. The following account is based principally on fieldwork that Sheila Wilson undertook on the island in 1998. It also draws upon the features outlined by Hancock (1991), who prepared a questionnaire that was administered by a 'Saint' (St. Helenan resident). He also drew on the unpublished material on dialect place names by Dr Vivienne Dickson, a former resident on the island.

We argue that present-day St Helena English is the result of the contact between regional varieties of Southern British English, many of them 'non-standard', and the rudimentary pidginised English ('slave fort English') that some slaves must have brought with them to the island. While StHE no doubt has developed into a unique variety of English, it bears evidence of retained archaisms due to its relatively stable and isolated population. Lexical items such as *a twelve month*, *yonder* and *saucy* are commonly used, although semantic shifts have occurred: *yonder* may apply to even a short distance, such as across a room, and *saucy* is used in reference to vicious dogs.

2.   Tense – aspect – modality systems

2.1.   Tense and aspect

While some past tense forms in StHE comply with those of Standard English, like *died*, *brought*, *left*, *said*, in general StHE does show a massive restructuring of the English tense and aspect system. Some speakers give evidence of a system in which aspect is the underlying foundation, with tense distinctions being 'reconstituted' or, at best, an overlay.

In certain speakers a frequent lack of past tense inflections can be seen in examples like the following:

(1)   *And we look after those children like we look after our own.*
       '...looked after...'

(2)   *Because he was thirteen years old when his mama die.*
       '...died...'

(3)   *She work after she left school.*
       '...worked...'

Done is used to mark completive aspect:

(4)   *He done see Black Beauty?*
       'Did he see Black Beauty?'

(5)   *Us done finish the introduction.*

(6)   *I done bathed the baby.*

(7)   *I done bath the baby.*

Done is an invariant form used with all pronouns. Whereas *done* focuses on the completion of an action, unstressed *did* appears not to have this primary function. It signifies 'past tense' with perhaps a 'highlighting' function:

(8)   *They did cheat the woman, see?*

(9)   *But yet I was so pleased that he did got something with it.*

(10) *Then after my daughter died, I did feel lonely inside the house.*

Equivalents of unstressed *do* in the present tense are rare, and may well be recessive. One example in our corpus (compiled by Sheila Wilson during her field trip to St. Helena in 1998) signals habitual, as is still common in southwestern BrE dialects:

(11) *She always do put my name on it.*
       '...always puts my name...'

Furthermore, (12) below is an example of the main verb *(be) done* having passive, completive, and possibly irrealis, semantics, in conjunction with *don't* as simple present negator:

(12) *No, I don't be done yet!*
       'No, I'm not done yet'

Bin does not appear as a completive marker in our data. However, one such form (*have ben seen it*) is given in Hancock's data (1991: 22):

(13)   *I have ben seen it round the [wireless station] when Mrs E.T. ben dere.*

Hancock provides two examples of past locative copula *ben*. One of these is given in (13) above; the other in (14) below is intermediate between past locative copula and verb of motion ('go to'):

(14)   *You ben town lately?*
       'Have you been to town lately?'

Hancock (1991: 22) also provides an example of *bin* (also spelt *ben*) as a past equational copula:

(15)   *Great Grandpa, he was bin a doctor.*

An -*s* inflection occasionally occurs with first person present tense verbs:

(16)   *Yes, I does.*

(17)   *And we goes along and we spread out.*

Far more prominent is the use of *is* (or its reduced form '*s*) or *was* with un-marked main verbs:

(18)   *So people is always ask me if I feel lonely.*

(19)   *What you's do in your spare time?*

(20)   *You's go up to K.J.'s?*

(21)   *But he's only have a little bit of ground.*

(22)   *I's be very lucky.*

(23)   *The hops is be quite boring.*

(24)   *'Cos that is be nice.*

(25)   *But that little bit of money was mean lot to us.*

Examples (18) to (25) suggest a subsystem with main verbs in invariant form, unmarked for tense or aspect. Tense and aspect are marked by pre-verbal particles, of which *done* and *did* have been noted already. Here, *is* marks non-past tense and *was* past tense. These appear to be invariant; certainly from our data *is* occurs as *I's, you's, he's, us is, the hops is, the people is*, etc. There appear to be no occurrences of *be* on its own (as opposed to occasional forms of *bin* on its own noted above in (13) and (14). *Be* is always preceded by *is*, as in examples (22) to (24). However, *is* may occasionally occur on its own:

(26)   *Who dat is?*

(27)   *Us is round there.*
        'We are there/were there'

(28)   *I is eighty-three now.*

From these examples it would appear that *is be* has stative meaning, with *be* as the habitual and *is* as the tense marker. No examples of *was be* occur in our data base, but this is presumably an acceptable past stative form. This appears to be confirmed by Hancock's example of *was bin* in (15) above. In (26) to (28) *is* on its own is predicative or identificational, rather than stative – see especially (28) where the adverb *now* precludes a habitual reading.

How does one reconcile the non-use of invariant copula *be* in favour of *is* in (26) to (28) with the frequent *is be* forms? One can conjecture that this is de-creolisation in action. That is, one might speculate whether an earlier system had zero copula, except in habitual contexts where invariant *be* was used. The effects of the StE system also spoken and promulgated on the island was to introduce tensed forms like *is* or *was*. Zero copula was then replaced by *is/was*, while habitual *be* was replaced by *is/was be*. From Sheila Wilson's data there are occasional glimpses of such a hypothesised earlier stage, with zero copula in non-habitual contexts:

(29)   *But her husband dead now.*

(30)   *She busy.*

Hancock (1991: 22) supplies further examples of zero copula:

(31)   *He family yours?*
        'Is he family of yours?'

(32)   *Us firs' cousins.*
        'We're first cousins.'

(33)   *I alright.*
        'I'm alright.'

Turning now to BE + -ING progressives, there is noticeable occurrence of -ING without BE as in (34) to (36):

(34)   *They shouting to one another.*
        '…were shouting…'

(35)   *So now I cooking my dinner.*
       '...am/was cooking...' (narrative tense)

(36)   *Shut it, because she talking to that boy again.*
       '...is talking...'

-ING may also co-occur with BE as in (37) and (38):

(37)   *I's going town.*
       'I am/will be going to town.'

(38)   *I's telling him.*
       'I told him/was telling him.'

In contrast to the form *I's* in (37) and (38), Hancock's data contains a form with StE *I'm*:

(39) *I'm going now to Sandy Bay.*

2.2.   Modality

As far as future time marking is concerned, Hancock (1991: 22) notes that the small corpus he used contained only two future tense constructions, one with *will* and one with *go*.

(40)   *I'll quit here.*

(41)   *Us go look.*

Hancock (1991: 24) glosses *have to* as (deontic) *must* in sentences like (41):

(42)   *You don't have to do that.*
       'You musn't do that'.

The following example with *would* appears in our corpus:

(43)   *He say he would write a letter.*

Hancock (1991: 22) notes alternate Ø-forms of *would*:

(44)   *Yes, I like to go to England, I like to see somewhere.*

Future tense may be represented by *'s*, as in (45). This striking use of *'s* for StE modal *will* suggests an earlier zero form now being filled by competing forms (*'s; 'll; go*).

(45)   *Us's come pick you up later.*

The modal *mussee* is probably a contraction of *must be*, though it might be related to the Creole Portuguese form *maski* used to indicate uncertainty about the action of the predicate. It is a recessive form, judging from speakers' comments and the fact that it occurs rarely in our data base and only with older speakers.

(46)   *They mussee fight with the British.*
        '... must have fought with...'

3.   Auxiliaries

Most of the areas of interest have already been covered, in considering forms of *be* and the modals. *Have* may be deleted, as in (47) from Hancock (1991: 22):

(47)   *You ben town lately?*

Auxiliaries are not generally inverted in questions, even amongst younger speakers. Sentences (48) to (50) were uttered by schoolchildren interviewing senior citizens for the radio station:

(48)   *So how old you was when you first start workin'?*

(49)   *What religion you is, ma'am?*

(50)   *So what the roads was like when you used to go school?*

Similarly, for the same speakers *do*-support is frequently absent in *wh*-questions:

(51)   *What ship he come in?*

(52)   *Why she ask him?*

(53)   *Which way he went?* (Hancock 1991: 22)

4.   Negation

The form *ain't* is present in our data base, and is described by Hancock (1991: 23) as a 'general negator' in the dialect:

(54)   *Ain't nothing to do, sir!*

Double negation is common. This may occur within the same clause verb and object NP being negated:

(55) *I say he's not done nothin'.*

Sometimes subjects like *everybody* may be negated, together with the following verb:

(56) *And not everybody don't go hop.*

The two negatives may occur across clauses as in (57), which involves raising of the embedded subject:

(57) *...but she wouldn't even let none of the children come.*

5. Relativisation

What occurs quite frequently as a relative marker:

(58) *I still got the copy in there now what he send up by his messenger.*

(59) *You know, money what made on the island can be tax, right?*

However, it alternates with forms like *who* or Ø:

(60) *And his auntie who brought him up because he was thirteen days old when his mama die.*

(61) *So at that time we did have problems in the house we was living.*

6. Complementation

The system of complementation appears to be standard insofar as *that* or Ø are the usual complementisers and *to* (rather than *for*) in infinitival complements:

(62) *...when she hear the bobbins stop she know that he was out there, you know.*

(63) *...an' I say he's not done nothing.*

(64) *She had to wait until he bring fish in to sell it.*

Hancock (1991: 21) notes that the infinitival marker is generally *to*, but also supplies one example with *for*:

(65) *[I'm] most too tired for eat.*

7.   Agreement

There is a tendency towards using *is* as the invariant form of the present tense for (*am/is/are*):

(66)   *They is.*

(67)   *Us is round there.*

(68)   *I's telling him.*

(69)   *I is eighty-three now.*

(70)   *What religion you is, ma'am?*

Likewise, *was* is not limited to first and third singular subjects:

(71)   *'Cos they was asking too much.*

(72)   *Because he was thirteen days old when his mama die.*

(73)   *So how old you was when you first start workin'?*

(74)   *When us was the youngest children going hop.*

However, there are occasional attestations of *were*, paradoxically in non-standard positions:

(75)   *She were working Missus Humphrey.*

As we have noted, most verbs occur in stem form with pre-verbal auxiliaries like *'s, done, did* conveying aspectual information (*habitual, completive* and [*salient*] *past* respectively). There is a slight tendency for verbs in subordinate clauses to occur in stem form:

(76)   *Because he was thirteen days old when his mama die.*

(77)   *I still got the copy in there now what he send up by his messenger.*

(78)   *She had to wait until he bring fish in to sell it.*

However, past forms like *was* are also common in subordinate clauses; as well as occasional past forms like *died, left* and *used to*.
    As noted in section 3, occasional forms of *-s* with first person or other pronouns occur:

(79)   *And then we goes along and we spread out.*

Further work needs to be done to ascertain whether *goes* is a variant of *go* or whether *-s* fulfills a narrative function here.

8.   Noun phrase

With verbs of motion the preposition *to* is frequently dropped, leaving a bare NP:

(80)   *I's goin' town.*

(81)   *Before she go school.*

(82)   *He's go seaside.*
       'He has gone to the seaside/wharf.'

9.   Pronouns

The most striking characteristic with regard to pronouns is the use of *us* as subject:

(83)   *Us done finish the introduction.*

(84)   *When us was the youngest children goin' hop.*

(85)   *Us's come pick you up.*

The alternative form *we* is also in use. The second person genitive form is *you* or *your*:

(86)   *Because you getting you pay very early in December.*

Although *you's* [ju:z] is a form commonly heard, it is a cliticised form of *you* + *is*, and not a form of *youse* with which it might be confused. In this regard it is not clear whether Hancock's statement that there is a second person plural pronoun *youse* is correct. The dummy (or pleonastic) pronoun *it* often replaces *there* in '*there is/are*' constructions:

(87)   *I suppose it was cancer inside, but **it** was nothing wrong outside.*
       '...there was nothing wrong on the outside'

(88)   *...because we used to have bit of litter, it wasn't no great beer tins and that.*
       '...there weren't many beer tins etc.'

10.   A St. Helena vocabulary

As a short illustration of the characteristic vocabulary of StHE, we present a glossary of terms beginning with <b>:

- before days: adv., in the old days, could mean just a few years previous.
- belong to (*who you belong to?*): who are/what are the names of your parents?
- bite: spicyness of food, usually fishcakes or tomato paste, ref. to the amount of chilli in recipe;
  pred. adj. – *Are those bite?*
  attrib. adj. – *Don't want no bite ones*
  noun – *Got bite?* – i.e. 'have those (fishcakes) got chilli in them?'
- black tea: Ceylon-style tea, ref. to colour of dry tea leaves, contrasted with 'red tea'
- bold: adj./adv., of a person – jocular or derogatory, not in standard sense of 'brave' or 'decisive' e.g. *'e gettin' on quite bold wid 'iself* – i.e. he is overconfident, getting above himself
- boojies: headlice
- bread 'n dance: [breed'ndahns] sandwiches with cold tomato paste filling (a traditional St Helenian dish, originally brought to or served at various community dances). Recipe includes chopped tomatoes simmered with onion, chilli and egg, and can include pieces of bacon or grated cheese.

11.   Conclusion

St Helena English raises several challenges for future research. One of these is the extent to which it has incorporated fossilised forms of Early Modern English into a local 'colloquial standard'. Another is the contribution of West African and other languages in re-shaping the variety. This influence is particularly felt in the restructuring of the verb system. It is our impression that StHE shows a blend of two systems: one, a superstratal variety of English (made up of a koiné of mainly non-standard dialects) and the other, a pidginised variety of English originating in the slave population. Present-day StHE vernacular shows the outcome of this blend, whilst more formal situations require adjustments in the direction of Standard English. The closest analogue to this situation that we know is the account of the development of Afrikaans in South Africa from a similar blend of acrolectal Cape Dutch and a Dutch-based pidgin developed by the indigenous Khoe-Khoen. However, whilst the Cape Dutch communities eventually jettisoned Standard Dutch in favour of Afrikaans, the prestige of StE is very much an ideological and educational force in St. Helena.

Exercises and study questions

1. Review the difference between unstressed *did* and *done* in 2.1.

2. Can you find a way of accounting for the form *was mean* in sentence (25) (*But that little bit of money was mean lot to us*) in terms of the discussion in section 2.1?

3. What is a dummy (or pleonastic) pronoun – see the discussion around sentences (87) and (88)? Give an example of non-dummy/pleonastic pronoun usage from StE.

4. What is 'deontic modality' (2.2)? How is deontic *must* of StE rendered in StHE?

5. Go through all the illustrative sentences in the chapter to calculate the proportion of subject pronoun *us* versus *we*.

Selected reference

Hancock, Ian
    1991   St. Helena English. In: Francis Byrne and Thom Huebner (eds.), *Development and Structures of Creole Languages*, 17–28. Amsterdam/ Philadelphia: Benjamins.

Indian English: syntax

Rakesh M. Bhatt

1.   Introduction

This chapter presents descriptive generalizations about the syntax of Indian English (IndE), drawing mainly from the theoretical model that takes socio-linguistic-syntactic variation as the proper empirical domain of linguistic inquiry. There are, at least, two grammars of English that educated members of the Indian speech community control: Vernacular IndE and Standard Indian English (StIndE) (Bhatt 2000). The latter, StIndE, is essentially similar in its core syntax to Standard British English (StBrE), but differs largely in aspects of phonetics.

Vernacular IndE, on the other hand, shows strong identification with local ideologies: it shows structural influence of the local languages of India, it is not codified or standardized, it does not have official status, and is used in relatively 'Low' functions. Assuming that vernacular IndE is just as systematic and logical as StIndE, this chapter presents the syntax of both varieties, focusing more, however, on aspects of the vernacular since they represent the Indianness of English.

This focus is necessitated by the important and systematic ways in which the vernacular variety differs from the local (Indian), regional (South Asian), and supra-regional (Asian, European and American etc.) standard varieties. For example, the subject-auxiliary rule in vernacular IndE is the mirror opposite of StIndE: the movement of the auxiliary verb (to Comp) is forbidden in matrix questions but permitted in embedded questions. Further, both referential and expletive arguments are allowed to drop, contrary to the standard expectation, that is, the expectation that the syntax of vernacular IndE must be like other standard varieties, like BrE or AmE.

This lack of recognition of syntactic variation as systematic and rule-governed has misled many prominent English grammarians to posit the "deviation from the norm" hypothesis (for example Quirk 1990) to account for vernacular IndE. As the discussion of the syntax of vernacular IndE will show, such deviation hypotheses are untenable, and the evidence supporting them is tenuous.

The discussion of the syntax of English in India will focus specifically on the behavior of (i) questions, direct and indirect *wh*-questions and tag questions,

(ii) topicalization (iii) the focus particle *only* and (iv) null subjects and objects, the phenomena known as *pro*-drop and expletive subjects. In a final section, I will list other features cited in the literature. These aspects of the syntax of English in India demonstrate the underlying patterns of English language use in different contexts of situation.

In other words, whether a subject will be dropped or not depends on, among other things, the formality of the context: in less formal contexts the probability of subject-drop is high, close to 100 percent, whereas in formal, and especially in the written mode, the probability of subject-drop is very low, close to zero. Although eventually a restrictive theory of language use is obligated to declare the precise nature of the context of situation, which presumably yields observed realization of linguistic expressions of a certain communicative act, such an attempt is beyond the scope of this chapter.

As a very brief, yet bold, speculation I suggest that some adaptations of Ferguson's theory of diglossia – where certain High/Low forms are indexed to certain High/Low functional domains – may account for the observed choices among the competing candidates of linguistic expressions. The syntactic description of English that follows is based on the methodological premise that a descriptively adequate grammar must address the relationship between the forms that a language manifests and its speakers' perception of reality and the nature of their cultural institutions. This premise yields an interpretation of language use constrained by the grammar of culture.

This is particularly true of English in India: the particular form taken by the grammatical systems of IndE is closely related to the social and personal needs that language is required to serve – issues of language identity, and historical and political patterns of its contact, that is, issues of language ideology. Before discussing the syntax of English in India, I briefly present the socio-historical context of the development of English in India to properly situate the discussion of its grammatical aspects.

1.1.   English in India: a brief socio-historical contextualization

English was introduced to India around 1600 via the establishment of the East India Company. Although initially severely limited in the numbers of its speakers, English bilingualism increased with various strategies of trade and proselytizing, especially from the early 17th century up to the 18th century. The proselytizing strategy was chiefly instrumental in introducing English bilingualism to the Indian subcontinent. After 1765, when the East India Company established political control in India, and especially in the early 19th century, the spread of English was aided and abetted by support from prominent Indians who preferred English to Indian languages for academic, scientific and other intellectual inquiry. This local demand for English, coupled with Thomas B. Macaulay's *Minute* of 1835 (see Kachru 1983: 68–69), led to the use of English in all official and educational domains.

Although English instruction created bilinguals, the models for learning and teaching were not native speakers. As Kachru (1996: 907) notes:

> Whatever the assumptions, in reality the teaching of English was primarily in the hands of the locals, and not with the native speakers of the language. [...] It was, therefore, not unusual to find teachers with Irish, Welsh, or Scottish backgrounds overseeing the local teachers and educators involved in the teaching of English, who provided the models for the teachers, both in class and outside it.

Moreover, as the use and users of English increased, so did its acculturation to non-Western sociolinguistic contexts.

By the time India got its independence from Britain in 1947, English was firmly established as a medium of instruction and administration. With respect to the role of English in post-colonial India, little has changed. English still enjoys the status of associate official language and continues to be the language of the legal system and Parliament. It is one of the three mandatory languages introduced in schools. English newspapers are published in twenty-seven of the twenty-nine states and union territories, and they command the highest circulation in terms of the total reading public. The percentage of books published in English is higher than the percentage of books published in any other language. Finally, in 1971, 74 percent of India's scientific journals and 83 percent of its nonscientific journals were published in English (Kachru 1986: 36). Presently, India is the third largest English-using nation (60 million) after the USA and the UK.

This chapter is based on three kinds of data collected in New Delhi: (a) recordings of spontaneous speech (b) data from published sources and (c) introspective judgments. Altogether nine speakers (five men and four women) participated in the conversations. All belonged to educated middle-class families and spoke, in addition to English, fluent Hindi. Their permission to use the recorded material in an anonymous fashion was obtained. The main topics discussed were: neighborhood disputes, weddings in the family, a recent summer vacation and pollution levels in New Delhi. The conversations vary in length from approximately 10 to 20 minutes, representing approximately 7 hours of collected material. Furthermore, where recordings were not possible, notes were taken of what was said, and in what context. Finally, the data were collated and a catalogue of the following syntactic properties was drawn up:

(a)   inversion/adjunction in *wh*-questions
(b)   invariance in tag questions
(c)   topicalization
(d)   focus constituents
(e)   null arguments (subject/object *pro*-drop)
(f)   null expletive subjects ("silent" *it*)

The second kind of data comes from published sources. These sources were consulted, where possible, for comparison with the spontaneous speech data. Finally, judgments on crucial data (inversion in indirect questions, and subject and object NP drop), unavailable in the published sources, were elicited from 27 speakers of IndE, which included, among others, high school English teachers, professionals (three doctors, two engineers) and two linguists. I have drawn comparisons of introspective data with spontaneous speech data to minimize the risk of hypo- and hyper-correction.

Although this article uses (sparingly) the terminology and conceptual approach of modern theoretical syntax, every effort has been made to render it accessible to scholars outside the field. That is, non-specialists may choose to ignore certain technical terms, usually provided in brackets or conventions involving traces (*t*) and the like.

2.   Direct and indirect questions

In StIndE, direct (root) questions are formed by moving the *wh*-phrase to the left-edge of the clause (Spec-CP) followed by the auxiliary verb (in Comp), in those questions where the *wh*-phrase is not a subject, as in (1) below:

(1)   *What are you doing?*

Further examples from StIndE are given in (2) below. I first furnish the example and then in square brackets show the peculiarities of movement, using current syntactic conventions. Here *t* is the original position from which the *wh*-phrase (t_i) and the auxiliary verb (t_j) move in interrogative constructions. The subscripts show the proper indexing.

(2)   a.   *What has he eaten?*
           [What$_i$ has$_j$ he t_j eaten t_i?]
      b.   *Where has he gone now?*
           [Where$_i$ has$_j$ he t_j gone t_i now?]
      c.   *How long ago was that?*
           [How long ago]$_i$ was$_j$ that t_j t_i ?]

    d.   *When are you coming home?*
        [When$_i$ are$_j$ you t$_j$ coming home t$_i$?]

Embedded indirect questions in StIndE also involve movement of the *wh*-phrase to the left-periphery (Spec-CP) of the embedded clause, without, however, any auxiliary verb following it (in Comp). Some examples are given in (3) below:

(3)   a.   *They know who Vijay has invited tonight.*
           [They know who$_i$ Vijay has invited t$_i$ tonight.]
      b.   *I wonder where he works.*
           [I wonder where$_i$ he works t$_i$.]
      c.   *I asked him what he ate for breakfast.*
           [I asked him what$_i$ he ate t$_i$ for breakfast.]
      d.   *Do you know where he is going?*
           [Do you know where$_i$ he is going t$_i$?]

The well-known empirical generalization about example such as those (2) and (3) is that the rule of subject-auxiliary inversion is restricted to matrix sentences and does not apply in embedded contexts.

    In vernacular IndE, on the other hand, direct questions are also formed by moving the *wh*-phrase to the left-periphery (Spec-CP) of the clause. However, there is no auxiliary (in Comp) following the left-moved *wh*-phrase. Some illustrative examples are given in (4) below:

(4)   a.   *What he has eaten?*
           [What$_i$ he has eaten t$_i$?]
      b.   *Where he has gone now?*
           [Where$_i$ he has gone t$_i$ now?]
      c.   *How long ago that was?*
           [How long ago]$_i$ that was t$_i$?]
      d.   *When you are coming home?*
           [When$_i$ you are coming home t$_i$?]

Embedded (indirect) questions in vernacular IndE involve *wh*-movement to the left-periphery (Spec-CP) of the embedded clause. The *wh*-phrase, surprisingly, is followed by the auxiliary verb, i.e., *wh*-movement in embedded contexts is accompanied by auxiliary verb movement (inversion) to, presumably, (Comp). The relevant examples are given in (5) below:

(5)   a.   *They know who has Vijay invited tonight.*
           [They know who$_i$ has$_j$ Vijay t$_j$ invited t$_i$ tonight.]

b. *I wonder where does he work.*
   [I wonder where$_i$ does he work t$_i$.]

c. *I asked Ramesh what did he eat for breakfast.*
   [I asked Ramesh what$_i$ did he eat t$_i$ for breakfast.]

d. *Do you know where is he going?*
   [Do you know where$_i$ is$_i$ he t$_j$ going t$_i$?]

The simple empirical generalization that emerges from the data in (4) and (5) is that in vernacular IndE inversion is restricted to embedded questions; it does not apply in matrix questions. The question formation strategy in vernacular IndE is the mirror image of that of StIndE, where inversion is restricted to matrix contexts.

The fact that direct *wh*-questions in IndE do not invert is not mysterious; StdInd/Br/AmE questions with the question phrase *how come*, as in (6) below, do not involve inversion either:

(6) *How come this is grammatical?*

Multiple questions provide another context where the syntax of vernacular IndE differs from StIndE in systematic ways. There is a curious property exhibited by the syntax of *wh*-questions in vernacular IndE: its lack of a superiority effect. Superiority effects refer to the constraint on multiple *wh*-questions in English that disallows the order where the object question word precedes the subject question word. However, in vernacular IndE, matrix questions with multiple *wh*-phrases with object-subject order in (7a) and with subject-object order in (7b) are often both judged as grammatical.

(7) a. *What who has eaten?*
     b. *Who has eaten what?*

In other words, the *wh*-phrases in matrix questions can occur in any order. However, this is not possible for embedded questions with multiple *wh*-phrases: subject-object order, as in (8a), is preferred to the object-subject order as in (8b). Thus, superiority effects reappear in embedded contexts in vernacular IndE.

(8) a. *I asked Ramesh who ate what for breakfast.*
     b. **I asked Ramesh what did who eat for breakfast.*

3.   Tag questions

In StIndE, tag questions are formed by a rule that inserts a pronominal copy of the subject after an appropriate modal auxiliary. A typical example is given in (9) below.

(9)   *John said he'll work today, didn't he?*

Tags have also been analyzed as expressing certain attitudes of the speaker toward what is being said in the main clause; and in terms of speech acts and/or performatives. Functionally, tags in English behave like epistemic adverbials, such as *probably* or presumably as shown in (10) below.

(10)   a.   *It's still dark outside, isn't it?*
        b.   *It's probably dark outside.*

Kachru (1983: 79) and Trudgill and Hannah (1985: 111) discuss the use of undifferentiated tag questions as one of the linguistic exponents of vernacular IndE. Their examples of the undifferentiated tags are given below:

(11)   a.   *You are going home soon, isn't it?*
        b.   *You have taken my book, isn't it?*

This description, however, leaves out the important pragmatic role played by these undifferentiated tags. In most cases, the meaning of the tag is not the one appended to the meaning of the main proposition; rather the tag signals important social meaning. In fact, tags in vernacular IndE are a fascinating example of how linguistic form is constrained by cultural requirements of politeness. More specifically, these undifferentiated tags are governed by the politeness principle of non-imposition. They serve positive politeness functions, signaling deference and acquiescence. Notice, for example, the contrast between examples from vernacular IndE (12) and from StIndE (13):

Unassertive/Mitigated (vernacular IndE):

(12)   a.   *You said you'll do the job, **isn't it**?*
        b.   *They said they will be here, **isn't it**?*

Assertive/Intensified (StIndE):

(13)   a.   *You said you'll do the job, didn't you?*
        b.   *They said they will be here, didn't they?*

In contrast to (13a) and (13b) above, IndE speakers find examples such as (12a) and (12b) non-impositional and mitigating. Their intuition is more clearly established when an adverb of intensification/assertion is used in conjunction with the undifferentiated tag. The result is, predictably, unacceptable to the speakers of IndE (* indicates an unacceptable utterance within the variety concerned).

(14) a. *Of course you said you'll do the job, isn't it?*
      b. *Of course they said they'll be here, isn't it?*

In a culture where the verbal behavior is constrained, to a large extent, by politeness regulations and where non-imposition is the essence of polite behavior, it is not surprising that the grammar of the variety spoken, that is vernacular IndE, permits the use of undifferentiated tags.

Undifferentiated tags are not exclusive instances in the grammar of vernacular IndE where one finds the linguistic form constrained by the grammar of culture. Such influence can be seen elsewhere in the use of the modal auxiliary *may*. *May* in vernacular IndE is used to express obligation politely, as shown below in (15). The examples in (15) (taken from Trudgill and Hannah 1985: 109) contrast systematically with the examples in (16), the option in StIndE:

(15) vernacular IndE
      a. *This furniture **may** be removed tomorrow.*
      b. *These mistakes **may** please be corrected.*

(16) StIndE
      a. *This furniture is to be removed tomorrow.*
      b. *These mistakes should be corrected.*

4. Topicalization

Topicalization is a syntactic operation that places linguistic elements representing old (given) information, the topic, at the beginning of the sentence, which is followed by new information, the comment. These topic-comment structures are widespread in vernacular varieties of English, replacing the use of the canonical subject-predicate structures of StE. As the examples in (17) show, any constituent of the clause can be topicalized in vernacular IndE. The most frequently topicalized element is the object noun phrase (17a)–(17c), but adverbials of place (17d) and time (17e) are also not uncommon:

(17) a. *Those people, I telephoned yesterday only*
          [Those people$_i$, I telephoned t$_i$ yesterday only.]
      b. *Only fashionable girls, these boys like.*
          [Only fashionable girls$_i$, these boys like t$_i$.]

    c.   *All of these languages, we speak at home.*
        [All of these languages$_i$, we speak t$_i$ at home.]

    d.   *At Ansal Plaza, it happened.*
        [At Ansal Plaza$_i$, it happened t$_i$.]

    e.   *Any minute, he will come.*
        [Any minute$_i$, he will come t$_i$.]

However, the more surprising aspect of the syntax of topicalization in vernacular IndE is that it is fairly widespread even in embedded contexts as shown in (18): both the object noun phrase, (18a) and (18b), and the adverbial prepositional phrase, as in (18c), can be topicalized.

(18)   a.   *His friends know that her parents, he doesn't like at all.*
         [His friends know that her parents$_i$, he doesn't like t$_i$ at all.]

      b.   *Papa-ji only told us that their money, he will not touch.*
         [Papa-ji only told us that their money$_i$ he will not touch t$_i$.]

      c.   *My brother warned me that young boys, I should say no to.*
         [My brother warned me that young boys$_i$, I should say no to t$_i$.]

5.   The syntax of focus particle *only*

As noted in the previous section, *wh*-phrases, which are inherently focused, move to the left-edge of the clause. Other focused elements, however, appear on the right edge of the clause. The evidence of right-edge focus can be demonstrated by the use of adverbs such as *only* which are sensitive to any focused constituent within their scope, and always require one in order to be interpreted. In (19) below, *only* can be interpreted with contrastively focused constituents: with the NP and the PP in (19a) and with the PP in (19b). The awkwardness of (19c), indicated by the use of a question mark "?", results from the fact that the underlined constituent associated with *only* is not at the right-edge of the clause. (19d) is well-formed only with an audible pause (indicated by the dash) preceding the PP, suggesting that the unfocused PP is right-dislocated.

(19)   a.   *Raj **only** gave **a book to Sita**.*
      b.   *Raj **only** gave a book **to Sita**.*
      c.   *?Raj **only** gave **a book** to Sita.*
      d.   *Raj **only** gave **a book** – to Sita.*

The right-edge focus position is also evidenced in the presentationally focused constituents. The presentational focus-marking strategy is most visibly available in vernacular IndE, as shown in (20) below. The contrastive focus reading, on the other hand, as in (20a') and (20b'), is unavailable with NP + *only* use. What is of critical importance is the fact that the grammatical utterances in vernacular IndE, (20a) and (20b) below, do not require, contra StIndE, for the verb to be followed immediately by its complement. In both of the instances, an adverb intervenes between the verb and its direct complement, which would be ungrammatical in StIndE.

(20)   a.   *These women wear everyday **expensive clothes only**.*
             [Presentational]
      a'.   **These women wear everyday **expensive clothes only.***
             (not jewelry) [Contrastive]
    b.   *He will buy over there **tickets only**.*
             [Presentational]
      b'.   **He will buy over there **tickets only**.*
             (not candy) [Contrastive]

The unavailability of contrastive readings of (20a') and (20b') suggests that the use of NP + *only* marks a non-quantificational (referred to here as 'presentational') focus, which is widespread in all varieties of vernacular IndE (Bhatt 1995, 2000; Kidwai 1997). In the absence of a nuclear stress rule that marks sentential focus, the NP + *only* presentational-focus configuration is an innovation in vernacular IndE representing the presupposition-assertion structure of an utterance. The semantics/pragmatics of NP + *only* is one of indexical assertion, drawing the attention of the hearer to a particular part of the speaker's utterance.

There is another interesting contrast in our vernacular IndE data, as shown in (21), which suggests that there is perhaps only one post-verbal focus position.

(21)   a.   *And then, for the first time, he kissed very softly **the forehead of his brand new bride**.*
    b.   *We watched **last night only** // songs from his old hit movies.*

The heavy object NP (21a) is focused (cf. Culicover and Rochemont 1990), and appears predictably on the right-edge of the clause. In (21b), however, the temporal adverb is focused, and the heavy NP is right dislocated, which is evidenced by the fact that this constituent was preceded by an audible intonational fall and a pause, indicated by //. The dislocated heavy object NP in (21b) is not interpreted as focused.

The correlation between right-edge and focus in vernacular IndE, as illustrated in (20) and (21), can be summarized in terms of the following generalizations:

(a) New information is focused and constituents bearing focus appear at the right edge of the clause.
(b) Old information, when presentationally focus-marked, appears at the right-edge of the clause.
(c) Focused object noun phrases do not always appear in canonical (adjacent to verb) positions.
(d) There is one post-verbal focus position per clause.

Finally, presentationally-focused subject noun phrases do not appear at the right-edge of the clause, as shown in (22), but in the canonical subject position.

(22) a. ***Her mother only*** *is doing this to her.*
           (Response to: *What did her mother do?*)
       b. ***These buggers only*** *are responsible for this mess.*
           [*buggers* is a reference to Indian politicians]
       c. ***She only*** *told us to write Ø like this.*
           (Response to: *Why didn't you ask your teacher to show you how to write an essay.* [Ø = 'essays'])

What we observe in (22) is that subject noun phrases violate the focus constraint noted above, that is, that focused-marked noun phrases appear post-verbally. In contrast to the generalizations noted above, there is another important generalization, given below:

(e) A subject noun phrase appears in the canonical subject position, even if it is presentationally focus-marked.

6.   Null subjects and objects: pro-drop

The generalization in languages that exhibit pro-drop (e.g. Spanish and Italian) is that a pronoun is allowed to drop only if its reference can be recovered from the agreement marking on the finite verb. The agreement marking in pro-drop languages is presumably "rich" enough to recover important aspects (person, number and/or gender) of the reference of the missing subject and/or object. In StE pro-drop is prohibited, because the agreement marking is too meager to sufficiently determine the reference of the missing subject.

With respect to argument pro-drop, StIndE works like other regional standard British and American varieties. That is, finite clauses without subject are not allowed, as shown in (23a) and (23b) below (in the following two sections, *pro* can be taken as an underlying pronoun that is not overtly expressed):

(23) a. **pro likes bananas.*
b. **He said that **pro** would come tomorrow.*

Pro-drop in vernacular IndE is very interesting: Vernacular IndE allows *pro* both in subject and object position, as shown in (24a)–(24e). The null subjects and objects in the sentences under (24) are analyzed as empty pronominals.

(24) a. *It is simple: take a dollar bill, and insert **pro** in the machine, face up, and you get four quarters.*
b. *I really wanted to read your book. Girish got **pro** from somewhere but he won't let me borrow **pro**.*
c. *A: He played cricket all day today – and now **pro** does not want to work on his homework!*
*B: Our Sanjay does that too: **pro** plays all day long, and then **pro** just comes in and demands food.*
d. *A: Is he in his office?*
*B: Sorry, **pro** left just now only.*
e. *A: You got tickets?*
*B: No, **pro** sold **pro** already.*

Other varieties of English show a very similar phenomenon, as observed in Platt, Weber and Ho (1984: 155, 92, 77) They discuss similar data of subject and object drop for Singaporean English (25a, c), and Philippine English (25b) as shown below:

(25) a. *Dis Australians, you see dem hold hand hold hand, honey here, honey there, darling here, darling dere, next moment **pro** separated already.* (Platt, Weber and Ho 1984: 155)
b. *If you don't like **pro**,* yaya ('nursemaid') *will give you water.* (Platt, Weber and Ho 1984: 92)
c. *In Australia, people never carry umbrella – so if you carry **pro** they will laugh at you.* (Platt, Weber and Ho 1984: 77)

The IndE examples in (24) pose two empirical problems for accounts that rely on the correlation of pro-drop and rich agreement. The first problem is that like StIndE, vernacular IndE is morphologically impoverished (morphologically non-uniform paradigms), and therefore should not license pro-drop; it does, however. The second problem is that vernacular IndE does behave like Spanish and Italian in that it does not require semantically empty subjects like *it* and *there*.

Although the pro-drop facts in vernacular IndE do not follow standard explanations of syntactic recoverability, on closer examination we notice that the absence of an overt argument in vernacular IndE becomes an option only when that argument is coindexed with an antecedent with topic status (cf. Grimshaw and Samek-Lodovici 1995; Huang 1984). The distribution of pro-drop in vernacular IndE is thus similar to Italian, as argued in Grimshaw and Samek-Lodovici (1995). Consider, again, the vernacular IndE examples in (26a) and (26b):

(26)   a.   A: *Is he in his office?*
            B: *Sorry, **pro** left just now only.*
       b.   A: *Gautam was there with his wife shopping.*
            B: *Doesn't his wife work now somewhere?*
            A: *Yes, **pro** teaches at a school here locally.*

In vernacular IndE, as the examples in (26a) and (26b) show, the subject argument is dropped when it has an antecedent with topic status. The generalization, then, for vernacular IndE is that pro-drop is available for only those arguments (subject/objects) that are topic-connected. Thus, vernacular IndE and Italian behave uniformly with respect to the phenomenon of topic-connected argument drop. The examples in (27) further confirm the claim that the grammar of vernacular IndE forces topic-connected arguments to be unrealized.

(27)   a.   A: *Isn't his brother in California, doing engineering?*
            B: *Yes, but these days **pro** is here looking for a KP* ['Kashmiri Pundit'] *bride.*
       b.   A: *Didn't Amitabh win the Filmfare award this year?*
            B: *No. No. No. Shah Rukh did.*
            A: *I think Amitabh wanted to win this year. And I read somewhere **pro** even gave money to buy some fellows off.*
            B: ***pro** wanted to win, but didn't.*
       c.   A: *Nancy's father-in-law may go to U.S.*
            B: *Why's that? Why not mother-in-law also?*
            C: *Two tickets get very expensive, so father-in-law only must go.*
            B: *Must? Why? What's wrong with him?*
            C: ***pro** needs special care, with his heart condition and all, old age. Last year **pro** had two heart attacks within two to three months.*

7.   Null expletive (*it*) subjects

Turning now to null expletive subjects, StIndE requires the subject position to be filled in finite clauses, even if that means using a dummy pronoun there: (28a) is unacceptable to speakers of StIndE. Vernacular IndE, on the other hand, does not require dummy subjects in finite clauses, as shown in (29a)–(29c).

(28)   a. ***pro** is clear that he will not come.*
       b. *It is clear that he will not come.*

(29)   a. *During monsoon we get lot of rain and then **pro** gets very soggy and sultry.*
       b. ***pro** rained yesterday only.*
       c. *Here **pro** is not safe to wait.*

The grammaticality of (29a)–(29c) suggests that the absence of nonreferential subjects is indeed licensed in vernacular IndE, which is consistent with other empirical observations of pro-drop in this dialect.

8.   Other miscellaneous features

For the sake of completeness, and to enable comparison with other varieties of English, I draw attention to further salient features of IndE that have been reported in other studies. For reasons of space I must refer the reader to the references cited.

- Article variability: Kachru (1983: 78) and references therein; Agnihotri (1992).
- Plural -*s* with non-count nouns: Kachru (1983: 186) for discussion of examples like *deadwoods, furnitures, apparels*.
- Progressive with stative verbs: Dasgupta (1993: 129–131) for discussion of examples like *You must be knowing him*; Sharma (2002: 367) for the use of the progressive form with the future; Trudgill and Hannah (1985: 110) for related functions like the use of progressive with habitual action and completed action.
- Present *be* for perfective *have* and *been*: Trudgill and Hannah (1985: 109) for examples like *I am here since 2 o'clock*.
- Auxiliary variation: Trudgill and Hannah (1985: 108) for examples like *could* and *would* as tentative, polite forms instead of *can* and *will*; *may* as a polite form for 'should'.

– Responses to *yes-no* questions couched in the negative: Kachru (1983: 1–13) for examples like Q: *Didn't I see you yesterday in college?* A: *Yes, you didn't see me yesterday in college.*
– Reduplication of adjectives and verbs: Kachru (1983: 78–79) for examples like *different-different things.*
– Variation in *to* complements: Trudgill and Hannah (1985: 111) for examples like *We are involved to collect poems.*
– Use of post-verbal adverbial *there* in place of dummy *there*: Trudgill and Hannah (1985: 109) for examples like *Bread is there* 'There is bread'.

9.   Conclusion

The two varieties discussed in this paper – Standard and vernacular varieties of IndE – show systematic differences in their syntax, which frequently correspond to a difference in the socio-pragmatic and ideological meanings. Sharma's (2002: 343) claim that vernacular uses of English in India introduce new pragmatic meanings deriving from ambiguity in the native system and reinforcement from substrate languages is relevant here. Aspects of the syntax of English in India demonstrate an underlying unity of pattern among different users and uses.

Focus on the vernacular variety reveals the Indian-ness of English and that this variety is most deeply entrenched in the local cultural ethos of the country. Evidence for this entrenchment comes from substrate influence in its syntax. Dasgupta (1993: 130–133), for example, relates the absence of reflexive verbs ('hurt oneself') in vernacular IndE to a general syntactic property of India's indigenous languages: the absence of combinations of verb plus pronominal noun phrase without regular theta-role. Similarly, the systematic omission of subjects and objects in vernacular IndE can be traced to substrate influence: most Indian languages require noun phrases that are topic-connected to be omitted. Bhatt (2000) has argued that non-inversion in matrix questions in vernacular IndE is an instance of a stabilized covert transfer effect from Hindi.

To summarise: some properties of IndE are shared by other varieties of English around the world; other properties are unique to the varieties of English in India. This chapter described in detail mainly those syntactic properties of English that can be identified with local practices – Indian local practices.

Exercises and study questions

1. Review the pragmatic difference between undifferentiated tags (*isn't it*) and differentiated tags (*didn't you, doesn't she*) in section 3.

2. What are the main pragmatic functions of *only* in IndE? How would sentence (22a) *Her mother only is doing this to her* be expressed in StE?

3. Under what discourse conditions does pro-drop occur in IndE?

4. Does the condition you outline in 3 hold for null expletive subjects where StE favours *it* (see section 7)?

5. In the light of question 4, comment on the IndE sentence *Bread is there* ('There's bread'), where *there* is not stressed.

Selected references

Please consult the General references for titles mentioned in the text but not included in the references below. For a full bibliography see the accompanying CD-ROM.

Agnihotri, Rama Kant
    1992   Acquisition of articles in learning English as a second language: a cross-cultural study. In: Omkar N. Koul (ed.), *English in India – Theoretical Applied Issues*, 179–192. New Delhi: Creative.

Bhatt, Rakesh M.
    1995   Prescriptivism, creativity, and world Englishes. *World Englishes* 14: 247–260.

Bhatt, Rakesh M.
    2000   Optimal expressions in Indian English. *English Language and Linguistics* 4: 69–95.

Culicover, Peter and M. Rochemont
    1990   *English Focus Constructions and the Theory of Grammar.* Cambridge: Cambridge University Press.

Dasgupta, Probal
    1993   *The Otherness of English: India's Auntie Tongue Syndrome.* New Delhi: Sage Publications.

Ferguson, Charles A.
    1959   Diglossia. *Word* 15: 325–340.

Grimshaw, Jane and Vieri Samek-Lodovici
    1995   Optimal subjects. *University of Massachusetts Occasional Papers in Linguistics* 18: 589–606.

562   *Rakesh M. Bhatt*

Huang, James C.-T.
    1984   On the distribution and reference of empty pronouns. *Linguistic Inquiry* 15: 531–574.
Kachru, Braj B.
    1986   *The Alchemy of English.* Oxford: Pergamon Press.
    1996   English as lingua franca. In: Hans Goebl, Peter Nelde and Zdenek Stary (eds.), *Contact linguistics,* 906–913. Berlin/New York: Mouton de Gruyter.
Kidwai, Ayesha
    1997   *Only* in IndE only. *Paper presented at the 18th South Asian Language Analysis Round Table, January 8th, New Delhi, India.*
Quirk, Randolph
    1990   Language varieties and standard language. *English Today* 21: 3–10.
Sharma, Devyani
    2002   The pluperfect in native and non-native English: a comparative corpus study. *Language Variation and Change* 13: 343–373.

Butler English: morphology and syntax

Priya Hosali

1. Introduction

Indian English (IndE) is a well-known example of ESL that has been extensively studied. However, side-by-side in some parts of India, a Pidgin English
also arose, out of contact between the first British colonists and the local population. Schuchardt (1980: 38 [1891]) identified five subtypes of this pidgin:
Butler English (ButlE) in Madras, Pidgin English in Bombay, Boxwallah English in Upper India, Cheechee English and Baboo English. Yule and Burnell
(1996 [1886]) observed that ButlE is

> the broken English spoken by native servants in the Madras Presidency; which is not
> very much better than the *Pigeon-English* of China [...]. The oddest characteristic
> about this jargon is (or was) that masters used it in speaking to their servants as well
> as servants to their masters. (Yule and Burnell 1996: 133–134)

An article in *The Times* of London (11/04/1882) describes the English of the
Bombay servants, who are generally half-caste Portuguese, as Pidgin English.
The same article cites Boxwallah English as the curious patois, hardly more
intelligible than the Pidgin English of servants in Bombay and Madras, that is
affected by the itinerant hawkers or box-wallahs (Hindustani *bakas* 'box' + *vālā*
'man') in Upper India. Cheechee English is the variety spoken by Eurasians or
people of mixed European and Asian descent. Cheechee is a disparaging term
applied to half-castes or Eurasians and also to their manner of speech. The
word is said to be taken from *chi*, a common native (South Indian) interjection
of remonstrance or reproof, supposed to be much used by the class in question.
The term is, however, perhaps also a kind of onomatopoeia, indicating the
mincing pronunciation which often characterizes them.

Baboo English is spoken in Bengal and elsewhere. Baboo (Hindustani *bābū*) is a
title, similar to English *Master, Mr., Esquire*. Yule and Burnell (1996) describe
the variety, whose peculiarities are not in the grammar but in the style, as follows:

> [...] among Anglo-Indians, it is often used with a slight savour of disparagement, as
> characterizing a superficially cultivated, but too often effeminate, Bengali. And from

the extensive employment of the class, to which the term was applied as a title, in the capacity of clerks in English offices, the word has come often to signify 'a native clerk who writes English'. (Yule and Burnell 1996: 44)

Despite its name, ButlE is not restricted to any occupation or region, though it is restricted to a certain class. It seems that the co-existence of interdependent but distinct hierarchically arranged social groups is a characteristic of all situations which have given rise to European-based pidgins. It should be remembered that ButlE is never spoken among butlers: it has its roots only in the hierarchical relation of the dominant and the dominated. The label pidgin for it has been questioned on this ground. Verma (p. c., 1981) labels it a semi-pidgin while Mühlhäusler (1978: 15) refers to ButlE as a "minimal pidgin". That is, the issue whether we are dealing with a pidgin or an early fossilised interlanguage is a complex one.

ButlE is spoken by generally uneducated bilinguals knowing some English, such as (a) guides showing foreign visitors around, (b) market women selling wares to foreigners frequenting Indian markets, (c) domestic staff of hotels, catering to tourists and upper-class Indians, (d) domestic staff of prestigious clubs and other recreation centres, and (e) domestic staff employed in racially mixed or westernised Indian households.

ButlE is spoken in a very restricted set of domains: the domestic work-sphere domain, fixed locales like those of hotels, clubs and households, during fixed working hours to indicate the role-relationship of master and servant and to discuss limited topics. Kachru (1969) notes that

In South Asia, it is very common to come across users of English who have acquired some control of restricted items of English, but cannot use the language in any serious sense. Some such varieties have been labelled Baboo English, Butler English, Bearer English, Kitchen English. (Kachru 1969: 637)

This would put most ButlE speakers close to the zero point on Kachru's cline of bilingualism (pertaining to fluency in ESL and in an Indian L1). Some butlers, however, through a measure of education and exposure to better models of English, may occur somewhere along Kachru's mid-point.

Schuchardt (1980: 47) gives a sample of ButlE from the 19th century as quoted in *The Times* (11/04/1882: 8c) with the following comment: "The 'Pidgin-English' of the Madras and Bombay [...] servants is chiefly remarkable for its extremely scanty vocabulary and grammar, for its love of the present participle active, and for its use of quasi-impersonal forms."

Discovery has been made of a butler stealing large quantities of his master's milk and purchasing the silence of the subordinate servants by giving them a share of the loot; and this is how the ayah (nurse) explains the transaction: *Butler's yevery day taking*

one ollock for own-self, and giving servants all half half ollock; when I am telling
that shame for him, he is telling, Master's strictly order all servants for the little milk
give it – what can I say, mam, I poor ayah woman?

Schuchardt (1877: 542) further cites *The Anglo-Indian Tongue*:

In Madras the native domestics speak English of a purity and idiom which rival in
eccentricity the famous 'pidgin' English of the treaty ports in China; and the masters
mechanically adopt the language of their servants. Thus an Englishman wishing to
assure himself that an order has been duly executed, asks, *Is that done gone finished,*
Appoo? and Appoo replies, in the same elegant phraseology, *Yes, sare, all done gone*
finished whole [...].

Schuchardt (1980: 48) observed that, as further samples were hard to come
by, ButlE was likely to have been on the wane. However, the samples quoted
from the (1882) and (1877) newspapers, when compared with excerpts from
my (1980–1982) data, show that the variety is very much alive, and that though
the samples are separated by a century, they have many features in common.
Additional recordings of ButlE (1992–2002) endorse my earlier findings. The
implication is that the socio-cultural and linguistic setting in which this pidgin
developed, has not been wholly wiped out.

Reading through interviews I undertook with 20 butlers, I find references
to various types of workers in the domestic service: the head-barman, assis-
tant-barman, and bar-steward; the head-cook, the soup-cook or the travelling-
cook; the plate-washer and glass-washer being variously termed glass-cleaner,
glass-bearer, glass-*meti* or *meti*-worker. Other household chores are handled
by the butler, bearer or boy, second-boy, house-boy, verandah-boy, room-boy,
room-service-boy and dressing-boy. Domestic service is thus far from being a
dying profession and ButlE has been stable enough to allow it to be described
linguistically. Two samples from my data, gathered between 1980-1982, are
given below:

(1)   *Dressing-boy master keep it the clothes and everythings and shoes*
       and folding socks – dinner-suit – will go the cuff – clothes I'll keep
       ready. Is tennis coming tennis I keep it. Will go hunt hunt clothes
       I'll keep it ready. Look after it...looking their rooms all linen-ginen
       everythings.
       (Krishnaswamy, reported age 56, outlines what his work as a dressing-
       boy entails.)

(2)   *All right. I can tell. Cut nicely brinjal. Little little piece. Ginger, garlic,*
       hm chilly – red chilly, mustard, and eh jira – all want it, grind it in the
       vinegar. No water. After put the hoil – then put it all the masala, little

little slowly fry it – nice smells coming – then you can put the brinjal.
Not less oil. Then after is cooking in the hoil make it cold – put it in
the bottle.
(Mary, reported age 60, tells us how to make brinjal pickle.)

The data discussed in this chapter is based on Hosali (1997; 2000). It draws
on the recorded speech of sixty domestics. The corpus comprises 275 foolscap
typed pages of text containing 4,205 utterances recorded in natural settings
over a three-month period.

2.   Reduction

ButlE generally shows retention of content words with a more frequent omission of grammatical words. Sometimes content words are absent as well. The
following are examples of reduction of form:

2.1.   Omission of pronoun

(3)   *Dining-hall just serve the soup.*
       'In the dining-hall I just serve the soup.'

(4)   *...Waiter I got I telling.*
       '...I've got a waiter's job, I'm telling you.'

2.2.   Omission of article

(5)   *...Because ball is going nearly 200/250 yards.*
       '...Because the ball is going (goes) nearly 200 to 250 yards.'

(6)   *...That is fore-carry.*
       '...That is a fore-caddy's job.'

2.3.   Omission of preposition

(7)   *Now I am barbecue section...*
       'Now I am in the barbecue section...'

2.4.   Omission of auxiliary

The ellipsis of the auxiliary, especially of a form of the verb 'to be' when followed by the present participle, is prominent.

(8)   *… Members hitting ball I watching that ball...*
        '…When members are hitting (hit) the ball I am watching (watch) that ball…'

2.5.   Omission of conjunction

When and *as* were the conjunctions most frequently omitted.

(9)   *...gents also come in the dressing-room...*
        '…when gents come to the dressing-room…'

(10)   *Room-boy we do some works...*
        'As a room-boy we do some work…'

2.6.   Omission of content words

Some examples of extreme reduction are:

(11)   *Waiter service.*
        'As a waiter I had to serve.'

(12)   *Bearer's room...*
        'As a bearer I looked after the room…'

3.   Simplification

Reduction refers to the omission of words, whereas simplification refers to the non-realisation of morphological markings. At the level of morphology, ButlE rarely uses inflectional suffixes.

3.1.   Noun morphology

Plurals and possessives are rarely used.

(13)   *...then two spoon coffee...*
        '…then put two spoons of coffee…'

(14)   ... – *that that eh master friends also like for my food...*
        '... – that that eh master's friends also like my food...'

3.2.   Omission of verb agreement

There is no agreement or concord between subject and predicate. Usually the form adapted from English is the base or unmarked form: singular for nouns/ pronouns and the imperative for verbs.

(15)   *Yes. Master like it.*
        'Yes. Master likes it.'

3.3.   Pronouns

The StE pronoun system has undergone a simplification, the possessive adjective *my* being used for the personal pronoun *I* and vice versa.

(16)   *My not eh English madam speaking.*
        'I am not eh speaking (do not eh speak) English (very well) madam.'

(17)   *Because I story...*
        'Because my story...'

The use of the object form *me* for the personal pronoun *I* was also noted.

(18)   *Me not drinking madam.*
        'I am not drinking (do not drink) madam.'

Gender distinctions in pronouns are also simplified or eliminated. In (19) *ayah* is the word used for 'female servant'.

(19)   *A.   When will the next ayah come?*
        B.   When you like it he will come.
        A.   So when will she come?
        B.   He won't come today.

(20)   *Hm first daughter is now that master master madam baby's get married in Madras. But I forgot his name – baby – we are calling baby.*

3.4.   Verb morphology

The verb phrase, in particular, is much simpler in ButlE than in StE.

3.4.1. The present participle

According to Schuchardt (1980: 49) the most characteristic feature of ButlE is the use of the present participle or gerund. This is used primarily for the present and probably only secondarily for the future. Yule and Burnell in *Hobson-Jobson* report that the present participle is used, for example, for the future indicative. Thus: *I telling* 'I will tell' (Yule and Burnell 1996: 133–134). The use of the present participle was the most prominent feature in the speech of the butlers interviewed. The present participle is used not just for the present and the future but for many StE tense and aspect forms: the present continuous, the past continuous, the simple past, the present and past perfect and the past habitual. A selection of these functions is exemplified below. Distinctions relating to time and continuity of action are understood either from the context or are indicated by adverbials.

(21)   *...and putting masala and some spices...boiling when you coming ghee on top – is ready.*
'...and I put some masala and some spices...I boil it. When the ghee comes on top it is ready.' (Present tense)

(22)   *...after Fridays not eating biryani is meat. Wednesday not eating meat.*
'...On Fridays they do not eat biryani because it is meat. On Wednesday they do not eat meat.' (Present tense negative)

(23)   *...suppose you're also being in sin – going to straightly Hell.*
'...supposing you're also steeped in sin – you will go straight to Hell.' (Future tense)

(24)   *...My voice not coming nicely no?*
'...My voice is not coming nicely is it?' (Present continuous negative)

(25)   *...When small I working to the British.*
'...When I was small I was working for the British.' (Past continuous tense)

(26)   *I know ma'am before coming.... Yes before coming father here.*
'I know you ma'am – before you used to come...yes before you used to come with father here.' (Past habitual)

The *to be* + present participle construction is also used for the different tense forms listed.

3.4.2. Auxiliary is

Many butlers tended to use *is* without an overt pronoun like *I*.

(27)   *...but is can't get work.*
'...but I can't get work.'

The use of the contracted form of *is* with the personal pronoun *I* by analogy:

(28)   *...Every day also I's going madam.*
'...Every day also I'm going madam.'

3.4.3. Omission of copula

Whereas StE does not allow copula deletion, some Indian languages permit copula deletion in equational clauses. I therefore examined Tamil, Hindi and Marathi to determine under what conditions the copula could occur. Both Dravidian and Indo-Aryan languages have copulative verbs. However, in equational sentences which identify one noun phrase with another, it is common in Dravidian languages like Tamil to have no copula. Such sentences normally have a copula in Indo-Aryan languages like Hindi, but in Marathi the copula is optional, and perhaps only occurs when emphasis is intended. In negative sentences, Tamil again has no copula unlike Hindi and Marathi. When the verb is in the past tense, a copula is obligatory in all three languages, except in certain constructions in Tamil.

All the butlers interviewed, however, tended to use copula-less clauses in English regardless of the other language(s) they spoke. One can infer that the butler simplifies the language by omitting the copula – which in English inflects for subject-verb agreement, person, number and tense.

(29)–(39) are examples of copula-less clauses from ButlE.

(29)   *That the garden.*
'That is the garden.'

(30)   *...I don't know – say I twenty-two years first.*
'...I don't know – say I was twenty-two years old.'

(31)   *...I Pattison ayah...*
'...I am Pattison's ayah...'

(32)   *Now children all gone.*
'Now the children are all gone.'

(33)   *I born in 1904.*
       'I was born in 1904.'

(34)   *– and all the children married.*
       '– and all the children are married.'

(35)   *My mother only alive.*
       'My mother only is alive.'

(36)   *They all British officers.*
       'They were all British officers.'

In all the copula-less clauses listed, the subject is expressed. In clauses where there is no expressed subject, a copula marker (generally *is*) is used. Clauses lacking both subject and verb rarely occur. When they do, we have phrases which lend themselves to varied interpretations. Usually the context helps to resolve ambiguity, as in (37).

(37)   *When service-bearer, then drink.*
       'When I am the service-bearer then *I serve* drinks.'

In ButlE *got* serves an existential or locative function 'there is / are':

(38)   *– why what you got for me no – what is what you got snacks.*
       '… What is there for me, you know – what snacks are there.'
Invariant *be* occasionally occurs with habitual meaning:

(39)   *...Suppose you be here some years...Suppose you be in sin...Otherwise you be going to Good Way.*

In contrast to copula deletion, one or two speakers produced occasional double copulas:

(40)   *...like that we are be grown, ma...*

3.4.4. Lack of preterite indicative formed by done

One of the features of 19th century ButlE, namely the preterite indicative being formed by *done* (Yule and Burnell 1996: 133–134), seems to have died out. Forms like *I done tell* 'I have told' or *done come* 'arrived' do not occur in my database. This function is more usually expressed by the present participle (V + *-ing*).

4.   Syntax

4.1.   Sentence negators

In StE the negator normally occurs between the auxiliary and the main verb. A sentence like *I have done this* can be negated in the following way: *I have not done this.* ButlE negates sentences differently with the negator being placed between the subject and the verb phrase. The auxiliary which is obligatory in StE is frequently absent in the utterances of the butlers, as in (41) and (42).

(41)   *I no go Jesus.*
        'I won't go to Jesus.'

(42)   *...then I not worry.*
        '...then I do not worry.'

The negator can also initiate a negative imperative sentence, as in (43):

(43)   *...No water add. No oil also, not necessary.*
        '...Do not add any water. Do not add any oil either – it is not necessary.'

It may be noted that the negator used in the examples is variable: no distinction is made between *no* and *not*. Further characteristics of ButlE negation are the occasional lack of a subject and dummy *do* in simplified utterances as in (44) and (45), and the occurrence of double negation as illustrated by (46) and (47).

(44)   *No listen to...*
        'I do not want to listen to it...'

(45)   *Not work.*
        'She does not work.'

(46)   *No. I didn't got no son.*
        'No. I haven't got any sons.'

(47)   *He's not made nothing madam.*
        'He's not made anything madam.'

4.2.   Question formation

In ButlE interrogation is usually signalled by intonation or intonation + the structure of a statement, whereas in StE there is normally a change in word order: the first constituent of the auxiliary inverts with the subject.

(48)   *...What parents I've got?*
       '...What parents have I got?'

(49)   *What I can tell, ma – another story?*
       'What can I tell, ma – another story?' (*ma* = respectful form for older female)

In many examples the auxiliary is omitted producing a question form like the following:

(50)   *...What I do?*
       '...What can I do?'

ButlE does not use dummy *do* in questions and negatives.

(51)   *You know Mr. Basalat Jah?*
       'Do you know Mr. Basalat Jah?'

In ButlE, word order in indirect questions is similar to that of the direct question form:

(52)   *I tell you how can you put table – how can you serve?*
       '(Shall I tell you) how you can lay the table – how you can serve?'

Thus, in some aspects ButlE accords with the rules of (educated) IndE, rather than Standard British English (StBrE).

4.3.   Question-tags

StE has a complex system of rules to generate question-tags. ButlE has reduced this complex system to one simple rule – the use of an invariant monomorphemic (and monosyllabic) tag, most commonly *no*. However, forms like *na* and *eh* may also be found. The tendency in IndE is to use *isn't it* as a universal question-tag and *no* as one of its variant forms (Verma 1978: 8).

(53)   *English-speak sahib is all gone no?*
       'The English-speaking sahibs are all gone, aren't they?'

(54)   *She is now gone to dos properly na?*
       'She is now going to do things properly, isn't she?'

(55)   *He's nice eh?*
       'He's nice isn't he?'

(56)   *It's all right ha?*
       'It's all right isn't it?'

These question-tags are also used for confirmation:

(57)   *Oh Hosali master is my Pattison master ko so friends eh. Best friend eh hm.*
'Oh Master Hosali is my Master Pattison's very good friend you know. Best friend you know, hm.'
(*Ko* is a Hindi form, here specifying possession.)

(58)   *You mix it, eh?*
'Mix it, all right.'

4.4.   Left dislocation and right dislocation

A prominent feature of the syntax of ButlE is the iteration of the subject by an anaphoric or cataphoric pronoun. The rule of left dislocation leaves a pronominal copy in the position previously occupied by the dislocated noun phrase. The pronominal copy agrees in gender and number with the dislocated noun phrase. Similarly, right dislocation copies a constituent. This feature has also been referred to as the left topic shift and the right topic shift.

The iteration of the subject by the anaphoric and cataphoric pronoun *it* are illustrated by (59) and (60) respectively:

(59)   *Cold jellies – all make it boiled and the chicken and...chicken all boiled it and keep it separate...eh and the radish – all boiled it.*
'Boil the cold jellies; boil the chicken, and keep it separate; boil the radish.'

(60)   *And make it the carrot and beans, turnips, eh and the radish – keep it piece.*
'Prepare the carrots, beans and turnips and radish, chop it up.'

Other pronouns which perform the iterative function are *he/she/they*.

(61)   *Hosali sahib he know.*

(62)   *Eve, she go this side.*

(63)   *There she is working, my daughter.*

(64)   *But British people, they are paying him eh good salary.*

4.5.   The imperative

In ButlE the imperative is of two types. The first accords with StE in being subjectless, as in (65). The second type of indirect imperative retains the pronoun *you*, as in (66). Sometimes the imperative is expressed by V + -ing as in (67) and (68):

(65)   *Boil the hot water and...boil...just pour it. Throw the water, then put the tea-leaves.*

(66)   *You first grind the chicken. Then you wipe with cloth...you mix. After that you fry the chicken...you keep this cut onion...and you cut about three onions – and this you cut – you cut cut bacon first.*

(67)   *Coffee eh making a filter coffee.*
        'Make filter coffee.'

(68)   *You putting some hot water.*
        'Put some hot water.'

A pattern that occurrs frequently in recipes is (*You*) + *can* + verb, possibly as a polite form of the imperative:

(69)   *...and separate milk and sugar – can take.*

(70)   *...you can put vegetable also.*

4.6.   The conditional

Conditional clauses are hardly ever marked overtly but have to be inferred from the context.

(71)   *After that they want something to drink, or they want some breakfast.*
        'After that if they want something to drink or if they want some breakfast.'

4.7.   Direct and indirect speech

ButlE shows a marked preference for direct speech. In direct speech the words of the speaker are incorporated within the reporting sentence, and retain the status of an independent clause.

(72)   *He coming "you come myself, you can see any Calcutta". I'm telling "I got no money I'm not coming. I poor boy". He asking "you don't worry money. I will pay and taking you".*

5.   Conclusion

This analysis of ButlE would not be complete without some reference to the occasional use of more or less standard forms. StE equivalents for all categories listed occur throughout in ButlE, raising the question whether one is dealing with one variable system or several co-existent systems. Le Page (p. c., 1981) suggests:

> [users of ButlE] may have a knowledge of or a repertoire of two systems: one of these may be a fairly stable pidgin, which does not make use of inflections nor of copular constructions, while the other one is more like StE. It may be that informants are more at home in the pidgin variety but have some partial knowledge of a more standard system and, therefore, add some of these features to their pidgin from time to time when for some reason they wish to sound more like StE speakers.

Though ButlE is a minimal pidgin, it is a rule-governed system with specific properties. There are many rules operating upon the raw material of English grammar in a distinctive way, leading to a set of differences which are persistent and well-established. It is unlikely that this pidgin will ever achieve status as a norm in its own right. ButlE will always be measured against the contemporary version of the native speaker model to which standard IndE is closest, namely StBrE. If it were to become extinct, it would not be because of any intrinsic linguistic inadequacy but because it could not compete against the overwhelming pressures of StE or StIndE.

Exercises and study questions

1. Look at the extracts given as (1) and (2). Find examples in them of the following: (a) reduplication; (b) *it* as a transitive verb marker; (c) deletion of subjects; (d) absence of expletive or dummy *it* and *there*.

2. List three syntactic features of Butler English that are also reported as features of vernacular Indian English (in the chapter on Indian English Syntax).

3. Discuss some uses of -*ing* in Butler English that differ from those of StE.

4. Review the examples of negation in Butler English. How can the great variety of forms be explained?

5. Comment on the word order of sentence (4) *Waiter I got I telling.*

Selected references

Please consult the General references for titles mentioned in the text but not included in the references below. For a full bibliography see the accompanying CD-ROM.

Hosali, Priya
  1997   *Nuances of English in India: What the Butler Really Said.* Pune: Indus Education Foundation.
  2000   *Butler English: Form and Function.* New Delhi: B. R. Publishing Corporation.
Kachru, Braj B.
  1969   English in South Asia. In: Thomas A. Sebeok (ed.), *Current trends in Linguistics, Volume 5: South Asia,* 627–678. The Hague: Mouton.
Mühlhäusler, Peter
  1978   *Pidginization and Simplification of Language.* Canberra: Australian National University.
Schuchardt, Hugo
  1980 [1891]   Indo-English. In: Glenn G. Gilbert (ed.), *Pidgin and Creole Languages: Selected Essays by H. Schuchardt,* 38–64. Cambridge: Cambridge University Press.
Schuchardt, Hugo
  1877   The Anglo-Indian tongue. *Blackwood's Edinburgh Magazine* 121: 739.541–551.
Verma, Shivendra K.
  1978   Swadeshi English: form and function. *Paper from the Tenth International Congress of Anthropological and Ethnological Sciences.* New Delhi.
Yule, Henry and Arthur C. Burnell
  1996 [1886]   *Hobson-Jobson: the Anglo-Indian Dictionary.* Hertfordshire: Wordsworth Editions Limited.

Pakistani English: morphology and syntax

Ahmar Mahboob

1.   Introduction

Pakistani English (PakE) is one of the less well–researched varieties of English. The largest body of research on PakE focuses on its historical and political status. This research is summarised in the companion piece on Pakistani English phonology (this volume). The next most commonly studied aspect of PakE is its lexis. Some studies on lexis also discuss creative processes in PakE morphology. There are fewer studies concerned with PakE syntax and even fewer dealing with phonology, discourse and pragmatics. Key research done on PakE, with year of publication and focus, is given on the CD-ROM accompanying this Handbook.

Existing studies of the variety focus on its features *vis-à-vis* Standard British (StBrE) or American English (AmE), rather than investigating the grammar of PakE in itself. For example, Talaat's (1993) study of lexical variation in PakE looks at semantic shift in certain lexical items as a shift from their original StBrE usage to a so-called Urduized meaning. Similarly, Baumgardner's (1996: 258 [1987]) discussion of PakE complementation is based on "manifest differences in PakE from Standard British and American" Englishes. Thus, the literature on PakE is based on a comparison of PakE with exonormative models of English. Non-comparative and in-depth studies of PakE grammar are greatly needed. As a prelude to such studies I present an overview of PakE syntax, morphology, and lexis as they have been discussed in the existing literature.

The examples in this paper are primarily taken from the collection of papers edited by Baumgardner (1993a) and a study of acceptability of linguistic features by Baumgardner (1995). Baumgardner's (1995) work is based on questionnaires that measured the acceptability of certain grammatical features of PakE by Pakistani teachers and journalists. He drew on 150 respondents for one of his linguistic questionnaires and 165 respondents for the second. He also had 320 respondents fill out an attitudinal survey, which is of less relevance here. Linguistic features that are acceptable to Pakistanis but are not attested in other varieties of English, especially British and American varieties, may be part of an acceptable model of local grammar and usage.

Baumgardner's (1995) discussion of the acceptability of various syntactic, lexical and morphological innovations in PakE is the only large-scale study of its kind. The scope and aims of his study did not extend to the investigation of sociolinguistic variation in PakE. Rahman (1990) attempts to do this. However, his generalizations are based on only 10 informants, and, at times, he presents examples based on his intuition rather than actual language use. As a result of the limited reliability of research on sociolinguistic variation within PakE, it will not be discussed in this paper. A study of the range and distribution of the acceptability and presence of these features needs to be conducted.

2.   Syntax

Syntactically, PakE differs from British English (BrE) at both the sentential and clausal levels. At the sentence level, a number of word-order changes can be observed. At the clausal level, complementation rules of PakE are found to deviate from BrE. In addition to these, the use of certain tenses is also different. Examples of these are presented in this section.

2.1.   Progressive aspect

PakE permits the use of the progressive aspect with the habitual and the perfective:

(1)   *I am **doing** it all the time.* (Rahman 1990: 43)

(2)   *Where are you **coming** from?*
       'Where do you come from?' (Rahman 1990: 43)

Rahman also gives examples of the use of the progressive aspect with stative verbs:

(3)   a. *I am **seeing** the sky from here.* (Rahman 1990: 54)
       b. *They were **having** a horse.* (Rahman 1990: 54)

2.2.   Perfective aspect

There is a preference for the perfective aspect over the simple past in sentences which contain a past adverbial:

(4)   *I **have seen** him yesterday.* (Rahman 1990. 58)

2.3.   Reduced relative phrases

PakE prefers preposed phrasal compounds as the equivalent of postposed attributive relative clauses. Baumgardner (1990: 47) provides the following examples:

(5)   a. *detrimental to health medicines*
            'medicines which are detrimental to the health'
        b. *public-dealing office*
            'an office which deals with the public'
        c. *under construction bridge*
            'a bridge which is under construction'

2.4.   Complementation

The main focus of work on PakE syntax has been on complementation. Baumgardner (1993c) based his discussion of PakE complementation on examples from newspapers. Rahman (1990) and Saleemi (1993) use his work and borrow/adapt his examples in their own work. Most of the examples in the following sub-sections are therefore taken from Baumgardner (1993b).

2.4.1. Adjective complementation

Two types of StBrE adjective complementation, *-ing* and *to*-infinitive, vary in PakE. In the first case adjectives in PakE are frequently followed by a *to*-infinitive instead of a preposition and participle clause as in BrE. The following set of examples taken from Baumgardner (1993b: 258–259) show the StBrE and PakE variants:

(6)   *He is **interested in learning** Urdu.* (StBrE)

(7)   *They were not at all interested in democracy...and were only **interested to grab** power at any cost.* (PakE)

(8)   *They are **capable of doing** anything.* (StBrE)

(9)   *He should be well-versed with the latest developments in the accounting profession and fully **capable to enforce** financial and budgetary controls.* (PakE)

Other adjectives in this category include *firm, insecure, committed, responsible, successful,* etc. (Baumgardner 1993c: 273).

    The difference between PakE and StBrE adjective complementation involves the use of a preposition followed by an *-ing* participle where users of

StBrE would use the *to*-infinitive. The following examples from Baumgardner (1993b: 259) illustrate this point.

(10)   *They are not **eligible to enter** the contest.* (StBrE)

(11)   *Students who are likely to be admitted by the end of January 1987 are also **eligible for appearing** in the qualifying examinations.* (PakE)

(12)   *His is not **prepared to repay** the money.* (StBrE)

(13)   *It is believed that PIA is **prepared for filing** an insurance claim.* (PakE)

2.4.2. *Verb complementation*

In addition to adjective complementation, PakE differs from StBrE in mono-transitive and ditransitive verb complementation. Within monotransitive verb complementation, Baumgardner (1993c: 259) lists three subcategories and provides examples to show how they differ in StBrE and PakE.

(a) Monotransitive verb complementation by a noun phrase as prepositional object
   In this type of complementation, the *to*-infinitive of BrE may be substituted by a prepositional verb plus *–ing* clause.

(14)   *I am **looking forward** to going to Lahore.* (StBrE)

(15)   *Javed...was **looking forward to become** a millionaire.* (PakE)

Other verbs that follow this pattern include *aim, refrain, resort, think* and others.

(b) Monotransitive verb complementation by a finite clause
   In BrE, a finite clause that complements a monotransitive verb consists of a transitive verb that has a *that*-clause as its object. PakE may replace the *that*-clause complement with a *to*-infinitive complement.

(16)   *They **announced that** there would be another drawing soon.* (StBrE)

(17)   *The Baluchistan Clerks Association has **announced to take out** a procession.* (PakE)

Other verbs that follow this pattern include *assure, demand, reiterate* and *urge.*

(c) Monotransitive verb complementation by a nonfinite clause
   This type of verb complementation is further divided into four sub-types, three of which show differences between PakE and StBrE. Firstly, in PakE, the -*ing* participle of StBrE may be replaced by a *to*-infinitive, as illustrated in (19):

(18)   *He **avoided seeing** her.* (StBrE)

(19)   *Meanwhile, the police are **avoiding to enter** the campus where the culprits are stated to be hiding.* (PakE)

Other examples of such verbs given in Baumgardner (1993c: 273) are *consider, discuss, require, suggest etc.*

   Secondly, PakE speakers may substitute the StBrE main verb plus *to*-infinitive with a main verb plus *that*-clause.

(20)   *He **wants to go**.* (StBrE)

(21)   *I **want that** I should get leave.* (PakE) (Baumgardner 1993c: 261)

Other verbs in this category include *hesitate, fail, refrain, resort, think, aim* etc. (Baumgardner 1993c: 273).

   Thirdly, the StBrE *to*-infinitive with a (raised) subject may be replaced by either a *that*-clause or an -*ing* participle clause, depending on the verb. Verbs such as *want* and *like* may be complemented with a *that*-clause in PakE.

(22)   *He **wants her to go**.* (StBrE)

(23)   *She said that her party **wanted that** we should not be intervening in internal affairs of Afghanistan.* (PakE) (Baumgardner 1993c: 262)

Verbs such as *forbid* and *beseech* may be complemented with an –*ing* participle clause in PakE.

(24)   *She forbade me to pursue...* (StBrE)

(25)   *She forbade me from pursuing the story.* (PakE) (Baumgardner 1993c: 262)

The fourth type of monotransitive verb complementation, involving the participle -*ing* with a subject, is shared by StBrE and PakE.

   In addition to the differences in monotransitive verb complementation, PakE and StBrE show differences in ditransitive complementation as well. Baumgardner (1993b: 263) lists three differences in ditransitive complementation.

(d) The StBrE prepositional object of a ditransitive verb may be replaced by a *to*-infinitive.

(26)   They **banned the film from being distributed.** (StBrE)

(27)   *The resolution banning **Americans to enter** the University campus is still in force.* (PakE) (Baumgardner 1993c: 263)

Other verbs in this category include *prevent, discourage*, etc. (Baumgardner 1993c: 263)

(e) The indirect object in ditransitive verb complementation with indirect object plus *that*-clause object may be deleted in PakE.

(28)   He **reminded the students that** *it was time for a break.* (StBrE)

(29)   *The Sind Minister **reminded Ø that** the public memory was not so short as to forget the capture of a large quantity of lethal weapons by the army on the Baluchistan border.* (PakE) (Baumgardner 1993c: 264)

Other verbs in this category include *inform, tell, assure, reassure* and others (Baumgardner 1993c: 263–264). In addition to the indirect object, a direct object may also be deleted after certain verbs like *deplore* and *rectify*. The following example is cited in Baumgardner (1993c: 264).

(30)   He **has deplored the fact that...** (StBrE)

(31)   *He has **deplored Ø that** the nation has been divided into more than 50 political units.* (PakE)

(f) The combination of *in* + gerund after certain nouns (e.g. *interest*) may be replaced by a *to*-infinitive in PakE.

(32)   He **showed no interest in studying.** (StBrE)

(33)   *The Prime Minster of Sri Lanka has **shown keen interest to send** his agricultural scientists to interact with Pakistani scientists.* (StBrE) (Baumgardner 1993c: 264)

Other verbs in this category include *play (a role)* or *save (time)* (Baumgardner 1993c: 273).

2.4.3. Noun complementation

As with adjective complementation, PakE differs from StBrE in noun complementation. Thus, a preposition plus *–ing* participle in StBrE may become a *to*-infinitive in PakE:

(34)   *Pakistan has no **influence in controlling…** (StBrE)*

(35)   *Pakistan has no **influence to control** affairs inside Afghanistan.*
        (PakE) (Baumgardner 1993c: 265)

Other nouns that follow this pattern include *insistence, inefficiency, intention, sincerity, tendency, satisfaction* and others. (Baumgardner 1993c: 265)

Similarly, a *to*-infinitive in StBrE may become a preposition plus *-ing* participle in PakE:

(36)   *The Minister said that any **decision to take**… (StBrE)*

(37)   *The Minister said that any **decision for changing** uniform from current shalwar-qamis to coat-trousers would be after an agreement with the parents and teachers.* (PakE) (Baumgardner 1993c: 265)

Other nouns that follow this pattern include *desire, curiosity, endeavors* and *tendency.* (Baumgardner 1993c: 265)

2.5.   Tag questions

Rahman (1990: 55) provides the following example of the invariant tag question *isn't it?* in PakE.

(38)   *You are ill, **isn't it?***

This use of a single tag with invariable singular verb and an invariant pronoun suggests that in PakE the whole proposition in the main clause is taken as the antecedent of the tag question, rather than the subject and the verb as separate elements. Further work needs to be done to verify such an observation.

2.6.   Word order

2.6.1.   Lack of inversion in wh-*questions*

Lack of subject-auxiliary inversion is acceptable in PakE, as illustrated by (39)–(41):

(39)   ***What this is** made of?* (Rahman 1990: 56)

(40)   ***Why a step-motherly treatment is** being meted out to the poor peons, naib qasids, chowkidars and malis* (different types of workers) *of the Education Department?* (Baumgardner 1993b: 48)

(41)   ***Why so many** are being killed?* (Baumgardner 1995: 268)

Conversely, while there is no inversion in direct questions, subject-auxiliary verb inversion is observed in some indirect questions:

(42)   *I asked him **where is he?*** (Rahman 1990: 56)

2.6.2. Lack of inversion in sentences with subject-initial adverbials

Similar to a lack of inversion in *wh*-questions, a lack of inversion in subject-initial adverbials is also acceptable in PakE:

(43)   *Wali Khan pointed out **that at no stage it was** demanded that agreements of provincial branches should be discussed in the central working committee...* (Baumgardner 1993b: 48)

That is, in PakE the common Germanic verb-second feature is not respected.

2.7.   Syntax and Morphology

Differences in the use of articles and prepositions and the omission of certain auxiliary verbs are the most commonly cited features of PakE morphology. These and other key morphological features discussed in the literature are summarized in this section.

2.7.1. Omission of auxiliary do, did and does

Rahman (1990: 57) reports that in casual speech, some Pakistani speakers may not utilize *do* support. He gives the following example:

(44)   *How you got here?*
        'How did you get there?' (Rahman 1990: 57)

Other syntactic and morphological processes which influence the lexis of PakE are examined in section 3.

2.7.2. Articles

At present there are no in-depth studies of the article system in PakE. However, Rahman (1990: 42) cites a number of examples suggesting differences from StBrE. An article may exist where it wouldn't in StBrE, as in (45). A definite article may be absent where it would be present in StBrE, as in (46). An indefinite article may be omitted, as in (47):

(45)   ***The*** *England is* ∅ / *a* / *the good place.*

(46)   *He said that* ∅ *Education Ministry is reorganizing English syllabus.*

(47)   *My father is* ∅ *lecturer.*

2.7.3.   Prepositions

PakE has a different distribution of prepositions as compared to BrE. Rahman (1990: 51) cites three forms of deviations: (a) PakE may omit prepositions where BrE has them – see (48); (b) It may add prepositions where BrE does not have them – see (49): and, (c) It may use a different preposition – see (50).

(48)   *To dispense...*

(49)   *To combat **against** poverty*

(50)   *What is the time **in** your watch*

3.   Lexis

As stated earlier, the largest body of linguistic work on PakE focuses on lexis. Researchers have pointed out that PakE lexis has evolved rapidly. One of the key processes that has resulted in an enrichment of PakE vocabulary is borrowing from Urdu and other languages. Such borrowed words show adaptation to the English grammatical system. A number of other word formation processes have also been reported in PakE. Conversion of words from one part of speech to another and semantic shift are two of these. In addition there is the retention of words that have become obsolete in BrE. In this section, I will list and present examples of some of these processes.

3.1.   Borrowing

Baumgardner, Kennedy and Shamim (1993) list 54 categories in which words are borrowed from local languages into English. A few of these categories, along with examples for these categories, are given below.

(51)   *At some time they again came to the **haleem*** (a thick soup) *shop on motorcycles and threw his two **daigs*** ('cauldrons').
        (Edibles)

(52)   *I may be a devout believer of the **purdah*** ('segregation') *system but...*
        (Religion)

(53)   *Jewelers observe **hartal** ('strike').*
       (Law and order)

(54)   *Why can't our **shaadies** ('wedding') be something like, 'O.K. bring
       in the **dulha** ('groom') and **dulhan** ('bride'), their close friends and
       relatives: dance, eat, have fun, and that's it'?*
       (Wedding)

(55)   *According to the prosecution...two proclaimed offenders...armed with
       klashnikovs demanded Rs. 5,000/- as **goonda tax** ('extortion') from
       Ghulam Akbar.* (Kennedy 1993b: 208)
       (Terms of gratification)

3.2.   Grammatical adaptations

Words from local languages, once borrowed, may be used with English grammatical morphemes. For example, the plural of *chowkidar* 'watchman' in the
following example is constructed by adding the English plural suffix -*s*.

(56)   *But the **chowkidars** working in the Technical Education Department
       are getting only a monthly dress allowance and not the washing
       allowance.* (Baumgardner, Kennedy and Shamim 1993: 152*)*

Another example of adding the plural suffix to Urdu words is given below.

(57)   *Agitational politics, **jalsas** ('rallies') and **jallooses** ('protestors') have
       become the preoccupation of political party workers in Pakistan.*
       (Baumgardner, Kennedy and Shamim 1993: 129)

3.3.   Affixation

Affixation is productively used to construct new words in PakE. The affixes
used for this purpose may be from English, Urdu, or any other local language.

3.3.1.   Urdu-based affixes

Affixes from Urdu are borrowed into PakE and retain their affix status. They
are also used productively to form new words. One of the most productive of
these morphemes is –*wala / wali* ('masculine/feminine'). Depending on the
context, these morphemes may mean 'person with / owner of / seller of' and
so forth.

(58)   *This donkey belonging to a **Gadhagari-wala** ('person who owns a donkey cart') was borrowed, cart and all, by a cop...living in the neighbourhood.*

(59)   *As soon as the **churi-wali** ('a woman who sells bangles') entered a home all young girls surround her, delving in her basket.* (Baumgardner, Kennedy and Shamim 1993: 139)

This Urdu morpheme may also be attached to words of English origin:

(60)   *But Hamza stood up to talk against the **Sugar-wali** ('person who owns sugar / sugar mill') – hinting at the Sakrand Sugar Mills alleged to be owned by Benazir Bhutto's in-laws.* (Baumgardner, Kennedy and Shamim 1993: 139)

3.3.2. *English-based affixes*

A number of English affixes are also used productively in new collocations in PakE. These suffixes may be attached to either English or Urdu words (or of words from other local languages). Examples of affixes *d-*, *-lifter* and *–ism* are given below:

(61)   *List of telephone numbers F-1 to be converted into other numbers due to **de-loading** ('decreasing the load') of F-1 exchange.* (Baumgardner 1993b: 43)

(62)   *A **motorcycle-lifter** was arrested by CIA following recovery of six stolen motorcycles at his pointation on Sunday.* (Kennedy 1993a: 72)

(63)   *...a policy of **ad-hocism** and **stop-gapism** has been followed with respect to Azad Kashmir...* (Baumgardner 1993b: 42)

3.4.   Compounding

Some new compounds have a particularly vivid effect in PakE. Consider the following examples from Baumgardner (1993b: 51): *flying coach* 'a fast bus'; *cent percent* '100 percent'.

3.5.   Hybridization

In addition to compounding involving two native English morphemes, Urdu words may also be joined with English words to form new hybrid compounds. This process of hybridization is used productively in PakE. Examples are *dou-*

ble-roti 'bread' (Baumgardner 1993b: 45) and *goonda-tax* 'extortion' (Kennedy 1993b: 208).

3.6. Conversion

Words of English and local origin which are borrowed into PakE may show a shift from one part of speech to another. (64) illustrates a shift from adjective to noun while (65) and (66) show a shift from noun to verb.

(64)   *Another **Gora** ('white, white man') telling us what we are...*
        (Baumgardner, Kennedy and Shamim 1993: 93)

(65)   *Are all the traffic sergeants there only to **challan** ('ticket') the*
        innocent? (Baumgardner, Kennedy and Shamim 1993: 90)

(66)   *Plans **to aircraft** the ailing Khan Adul Ghaffar Khan, from New Delhi*
        to Peshawar tomorrow have been deferred... (Baumgardner 1993b:
        45)

3.7. Preposed phrases

Similar to the use of preposed attributive relative clauses, certain prepositional phrases may also be preposed. For example, *jam or jelly bottle* is used to mean 'a bottle of jam or jelly' in the following example.

(67)   *Shezan has also increased the prices of some of its products...A **jam***
        ***or jelly bottle** can be purchased at Rs. 16 per bottle whereas it was*
        available at Rs. 14 per bottle. (Baumgardner 1993b:47)

Other examples provided by Baumgardner (1993b: 47) include: *milk bottle* 'a bottle of milk', *wheat bag* 'a bag of wheat' and *toast piece* 'a piece of toast'.

3.8. Archaisms

A few words that have become obsolete in British or American English may still be used productively in PakE. Marckwardt (1980) called this colonial lag. Görlach (1991), however, argued that generally such examples are so few that the term is a misnomer. An example of such a colonial lag is the use of *tantamount* in (68):

(68)   *We cannot support the demand of a confederation as it tantamounts to*
        the dismemberment of the country. (Baumgardner 1993b: 47)

The use of *tantamount* as a verb was possible in BrE, but is now obsolete. The predicative form *is tantamount to* also survives in PakE.

3.9.   Semantic shift/extension

A number of words are noted that reflect a shift in meaning from their StBrE usage. The following examples are cited in the literature.

(69)   *He ordered for necessary **patchwork** ('repair') on the roads to be carried out.* (Baumgardner 1993b: 47)

(70)   *They also as a matter of routine overload the front seat and do not care for women waiting for **conveyance** ('transport').* (Talaat 1993: 59)
(*conveyance* is cited as an example of colonial lag in Baumgardner 1993b: 47)

(71)   *Police have booked...Zaman and three others on the charge of allegedly **teasing** ('harassing') a college girl and snatching her wrist watch and books.* (Talaat 1993: 61)

4.   Concluding remarks

This paper outlines some key features of PakE grammar and lexis. The features and examples presented in this paper clearly demonstrate that PakE has unique features. Unfortunately, no reliable studies of the distribution or range of these features exist. There are also no studies that describe PakE grammar on its own, systematically rather than via comparisons with BrE and AmE. It is hoped that this summary will generate sufficient interest in PakE to encourage new studies of this variety of English.

Exercises and study questions

1. Review the examples of reduced relative phrases in 2.3. Why do you think this phenomenon occurs in PakE?

2. Compare the rules for inversion in *wh-* questions in PakE (section 2.6) with that of IndE.

3. Discuss the difference in subcategorisation of the following verbs in StE and PakE:
(a) *want*; (b) *announce*; (c) *remind*; (d) *ban*.

4. What does the suffix *-wala* (3.3.1) denote in PakE?

5. Compare the phrase *milk bottle* (with preposed noun *milk*) for 'bottle of milk' in PakE with the reduced relatives of 2.3.

Selected references

Please consult the General references for titles mentioned in the text but not included in the references below. For a full bibliography see the accompanying CD-ROM.

Baumgardner, Robert J.
  1990   The indigenization of English in Pakistan. *English Today* 6: 59–65.
  1993a   *The English Language in Pakistan*. Karachi: Oxford University Press.
  1993b   The indigenization of English in Pakistan. In: Robert J. Baumgardner (ed.), *The English Language in Pakistan*, 41–54. Karachi: Oxford University Press.
Baumgardner, Robert J.
  1993c   Utilizing Pakistani newspaper English to teach grammar. In: Robert J. Baumgardner (ed.), *The English Language in Pakistan*, 255–273. Karachi: Oxford University Press.
  1995   Pakistani English: acceptability and the norm. *World Englishes* 14: 261–271.
Baumgardner, Robert J., Audrey E. H. Kennedy and Fauzia Shamim
  1993   The Urduization of English in Pakistan. In: Robert J. Baumgardner (ed.), *The English Language in Pakistan*, 83–203. Karachi: Oxford University Press.
Görlach, Manfred
  1991   *Englishes: Studies in varieties of English, 1984–1988*. Amsterdam/ Philadelphia: Benjamins.
Kennedy, Audrey E. H.
  1993   Of dacoits and desperados: crime reporting in Pakistani English. In: Robert J. Baumgardner (ed.), *The English Language in Pakistan*, 69–79. Karachi: Oxford University Press.
Marckwardt, Albert
  1980   *American English*. New York: Oxford University Press. First published 1958.

Rahman, Tariq
  1990   *Pakistani English: The Linguistic Description of a Non-Native Variety of English*. Islamabad: National Institute of Pakistan Studies Quaid-i-Azam University.
Saleemi, Anjum P.
  1993   Native and nonnative grammars of English. In Robert J. Baumgardner (ed.), *The English Language in Pakistan*, 33–40. Karachi: Oxford University Press.
Talaat, Mubina
  1993   Lexical variation in Pakistani English. In: Robert J. Baumgardner (ed.), *The English Language in Pakistan*, 55–62. Karachi: Oxford University Press.

Singapore English: morphology and syntax

Lionel Wee

1. Introduction

It may be useful to divide the discussion of Colloquial Singapore English
(CollSgE) morphology and syntax into five parts:

(a) Features relating to the verb and verb phrase. Here, we focus on
     aspect, the absence of number agreement, copular *be* and the use of
     got.

(b) Features relating to nouns and the noun phrase. Within the noun
     phrase, CollSgE tends not to make use of articles. It treats non-count
     nouns as count nouns, and its relative clauses are ordered rather
     differently than their counterparts in more standard varieties of
     English.

(c) Features relating to the clause. These include pro-drop, object-
     preposing, question formation, and the passive voice.

(d) In addition to these three features, CollSgE makes productive use
     of reduplication, which cuts across various lexical categories. It is
     therefore important that we devote a specific section to the discussion
     of reduplication.

(e) Finally, CollSgE is also widely recognized as having a large inventory
     of particles, which serve various discourse-pragmatic functions. These
     discourse particles, too, need to be discussed separately in order to
     better appreciate the grammar of CollSgE.

2. Features relating to the verb and verb phrase

2.1. Aspect

We begin by noting that the verb generally appears in an uninflected form. As
shown below, the verb *eat* is not marked for tense or number. Because the
verbs are uninflected, time and aspectual information are conveyed lexically
(using words like *yesterday* or *already*). The lack of inflectional marking on the

verb also means that there is no subject-verb agreement in CollSgE, and even in question formation, there is a tendency to use invariant tags.

(1)   a.   *He eat here yesterday.*
        b.   *He not yet eat lunch.*
        c.   *They eat already.*

Aspect is marked via forms like *always, already* or *still*. Thus, *always* is used to mark habituality:

(2)   a.   *She always borrow money from me.*
        b.   *The bus always late!*

Already is used for both the perfective (1a) as well as inchoative aspect. Thus, (3) can be used to indicate that the speaker's son is just beginning to learn how to ride the bicycle.

(3)   *My son ride bicycle already.*
        'My son has just started riding the bicycle.'

The progressive aspect is marked by *still*.

(4)   a.   *Late already, you still eat.*
           'It's late already and you are still eating.'
        b.   *The baby still cry because you never feed it.*
           'The baby is still crying because you haven't fed it.'

Additionally, the progressive is the only aspect that is marked inflectionally. However, only the suffix *–ing* is used; the auxiliary *be* is not. As (5b) indicates, both *still* and the *–ing* suffix can be used together to convey the progressive.

(5)   a.   *The baby crying a lot.*
        b.   *The students still writing.*

2.2.   Number agreement

As mentioned, CollSgE lacks number agreement, indicated by the fact that there is no subject verb agreement in main clauses.

(6)   a.   *The teacher shout a lot.*
        b.   *The teachers shout a lot.*

In more standard varieties of English, the nature of the tag in tag questions varies according to the subject and the auxiliaries present in the clause to which the tag is being attached.

(7)   a.   *He is watching television, isn't he?*
       b.   *He isn't watching television, is he?*
       c.   *They have been watching television, haven't they?*
       d.   *They haven't been watching television, have they?*

As the CollSgE verb phrase is comparatively simpler in structure – lacking verb inflections and a complex auxiliary system – there is no such variation of the tag. Instead, CollSgE uses an invariant tag *is it*. This tag is neutral in that it carries no expectation by the speaker as to what the answer to the question might be. It can also be used when the clause being tagged contains a negative (9).

(8)   a.   *He watching television, is it?*
       b.   *They watching television, is it?*

(9)   a.   *He not watching television, is it?*
       b.   *They not watching television, is it?*

The tag can also be used in the negative form, *isn't it*, in which case the speaker conveys the assumption that the proposition described by the clause being tagged is correct.

(10)   a.   *The tea very hot, is it?*
       b.   *The tea very hot, isn't it?*

While (10a) can be considered a neutral question, in (10b) the speaker is assuming that the tea is indeed very hot. Thus, *isn't it* often has the pragmatic effect of eliciting agreement from the addressee.

2.3.   *Be* and *got*

Platt and Weber (1980) note that CollSgE clauses that are attributive or equative tend not to use the verb *be*.

(11)   a.   *The house very nice.*
           'The house is very nice.'
       b.   *That girl my neighbour.*
           'That girl is my neighbour.'

The verb *got* is used variously in CollSgE as a perfective, a possessive, and an existential marker.

(12)   a.   *He got go to Japan.*
           'He has been to Japan.'

    b.   *You got buy lottery?*
       'Did you buy a lottery ticket?'
    c.   *You got nice shirt.*
       'You have a nice shirt.'
    d.   *Here got very many people.*
       'There are many people here.'

3.   Features relating to the noun and noun phrase

3.1.   Articles

A number of researchers have commented on the general absence of articles in the noun phrase. Thus Platt and Weber (1980: 70) observe that "[i]t is noticeable that a definite or indefinite article does not always occur in [CollSgE] in positions where it is obligatory in [StBrE]". The examples in (13) come from Platt and Weber (1980: 70–71), the ones in (14) from Alsagoff and Ho (1998: 144).

(13)   a.   *I don't have ticket.*
      b.   *Maybe you better have microphone a bit closer.*

(14)   a.   *She got car or not?*
          'Does she have a car?'
      b.   *She buy dress for what?*
          'Why is she buying a dress?'

As discussed below, Alsagoff and Ho (1998: 144) make the interesting suggestion that the lack of articles in CollSgE could be due to the fact that CollSgE tends to treat nouns like *ticket* or *car* as non-count.

3.2.   Count/non-count

There is a tendency in CollSgE to treat non-count nouns as count nouns, giving rise to forms such as *luggages, equipments, staffs* and *furnitures*. Alsagoff and Ho (1998: 143) point out that in some cases the plural marker is absent where Standard English (StE) requires one. Thus, they note that in the CollSgE version (15a), *ticket* is not marked for plural though it is so marked in the StE version (15b).

(15)   a.   *She queue up very long to buy ticket for us.*
      b.   *She queued up for a very long time to buy tickets for us.*

They suggest that (15a) should not be analyzed as a lack of the plural marker; instead *ticket* in (15a) is being used as a non-count noun. Their reason for this suggestion (1998: 144) is that "when *ticket* is used with a quantifier, e.g. *four, many*, it is always inflected; where it is uninflected, it always appears alone, without premodification."

Thus, they conclude that "Most nouns that are, in StE, only classified and used as count, can in CollSgE be used both as count and non-count" (1998: 144).

3.3.   The relative clause

Consider the examples in (16) and (17), adapted from Alsagoff (1995: 85). The CollSgE relative clause in (16) is fairly similar to that found in StE. Except for the fact that the verb is not inflected for tense, the construction is regular, the relative pronouns *who* and *that* precede the modifying clauses *pinch my sister* and *John buy* respectively.

(16)   a.   *That boy who pinch my sister very naughty.*
                  'That boy who pinched my sister is very naughty.'
          b.   *The cake that John buy always very nice to eat.*
                  'The cake that John buys is always very delicious.'

(17), however, shows another kind of CollSgE relative clause, one that is much more different from the StE version. Here, the relative pronoun *one* is invariant, appearing consistently as *one*, and follows the modifying clause.

(17)   a.   *That boy pinch my sister one very naughty.*
                  'That boy who pinched my sister is very naughty.'
          b.   *The cake John buy one always very nice to eat.*
                  'The cake that John buys is always very delicious.'

(18) shows that the other relative pronouns (*that, who*) cannot be used after the modifying clause, and conversely, *one* cannot be used before the modifying clause.

(18)   a.   **That boy pinch my sister who very naughty.*
          b.   **That boy one pinch my sister very naughty.*

Thus, CollSgE appears to have two kinds of relative clauses. The first one resembles the StE relative clause: it uses the same kinds of relative pronouns and has the same word order with the pronoun preceding the modifying clause. The second one is clearly more different: it uses *one* as the relative pronoun and has a different order where *one* follows the modifying clause.

4.   Features relating to the clause

4.1.   Pro-drop

CollSgE has been described as being a pro-drop language (Gupta 1994; Platt and Weber 1980) in that the subject and/or object are often left unexpressed, particularly when the identities of the pro-dropped elements can be recovered from the context.

(19)   a.   *Always late!*
                  'You are always late!'
          b.   *Must buy for him, otherwise he not happy.*
                  'We must buy a present for him, otherwise he won't be happy.'

4.2.   Object-preposing

Though the canonical word order in CollSgE is SVO, the object (direct or indirect) is commonly preposed, giving rise to examples like the following (Platt and Weber 1980: 73).

(20)   a.   *Certain medicine we don't stock in our dispensary.*
          b.   *To my sister sometime I speak English.*

There is some disagreement over the relationship between object-preposing and information structure, specifically, over whether the fronted element is being focused or topicalized. The difference between focus and topic lies in whether the fronted object conveys old information (topic) or new information (focus). Platt and Weber (1980) treat fronting as a case of focussing while Alsagoff and Ho (1998: 148) claim that it involves topicalization.

With regard to this debate, it may be relevant to consider CollSgE constructions where doubt is being expressed. As shown below, object-preposing and the pro-drop feature often come together in utterances expressing doubt. What is relevant to the focus/topic debate is that it appears to be old or established information that is being fronted. In (21a–b), for example, the speaker and the addressee presumably already have shared knowledge about which movie or car is being discussed. Such cases suggest that object-preposing involves a topic rather than a focus.

(21)   a.   *The movie don't know whether good or not.*
                  'I don't know if the movie is good or not.'
          b.   *The car don't know whether expensive.*
                  'I don't know whether the car is expensive.'

c.   **The movie know whether good or not.*
      'I know whether the movie is good or not.'

The examples in (21) are expressions of doubt on the part of the speaker, but the preposed object and the unexpressed subject can give the impression that a lack of knowledge (*don't know*) is being attributed to an inanimate entity (*the movie, the car*). As (21c) indicates, the construction cannot be used to assert knowledge on the part of the speaker, since without the negative marker, the construction is unacceptable.

4.3.   Question formation

In *wh*-interrogatives, the interrogative pronoun typically remains in situ:

(22)   a.   *You buy what*
             'What did you buy?'
        b.   *This bus go where?*
             'Where is this bus going?'
c.   *You go home for what?*
      'Why are you going home?'

With yes/no questions, CollSgE makes use of the invariant tag *is it* (discussed above). CollSgE also has another tag *or not*.

(23)   a.   *The food good or not?*
             'Is the food delicious?'
        b.   *You busy or not?*
             'Are you busy?'

The *or not* tag often appears with the modal *can* in questions concerning permission or possibility.

(24)   a.   *Can go home or not?*
             'Can I go home?'
        b.   *Can answer the question or not?*
             'Do you know the answer to the question?'

This has led to the emergence of the tag *can or not* (25). *Can or not* can also constitute a separate conversational turn, a possibility not open to *or not* (26).

(25)   a.   *I want to go home, can or not?*
             'Can I go home?'
        b.   *Answer the question, can or not?*
             'Do you know the answer to the question?'

(26)   A: *I want to go home.*
        B: [no response]
        A: *Can or not? *Or not?*

4.4.   The passive

CollSgE has two passive constructions, the *kena* passive and the *give* passive. (27a) and (27b) below are examples of the *kena* passive, the agentive *by* phrase being optional. Although the lexical verb is sometimes inflected, this need not always be the case.

(27)   a.   *John kena scold (by his boss).*
             'John was scolded by his boss.'
        b.   *The thief kena caught (by the police).*
             'The thief was caught by the police.'

The *kena* passive has an adversative reading so that while *scold* easily allows passivization, *praise* and *like* do not.

(28)   a.   **John kena praise by his boss.*
             'John was praised by his boss.'
        b.   **Mary kena like by her tennis partner.*
             'Mary was liked by her tennis partner.'

The *give* passive, like the *kena* passive, also has an adversative reading. Thus, the examples in (30) are not acceptable compared to the ones in (29).

(29)   a.   *John give his boss scold.*
             'John was scolded by his boss.'
        b.   *The dog give the boy kick.*
             'The dog was kicked by the boy.'

(30)   a.   **John give his boss praise.*
             'John was praised by his boss.'
        b.   **The dog give the boy stroke.*
             'The dog was stroked by the boy.'

There is a slight difference in the adversative readings associated with the two passives. With the *give* passive, there is an implication that the subject contributed in some way towards its own misfortune; this reading is absent in the *kena* passive. Thus, in (29a) John, perhaps through his own incompetence, provided his boss with a reason to scold him. Likewise, in (29b), if the dog had been faster or more aggressive, it might not have gotten kicked by the boy.

There are two further differences between the passives. Unlike the *kena* passive, the *give* passive requires that the agent be present:

(31)   a.   *John give scold.*
       b.   *The dog give kick.*

Secondly, unlike the *kena* passive, the lexical verb in the *give* passive must always appear uninflected.

(32)   a.   *John give his boss scolded.*
       b.   *The dog give the boy kicked.*

5.   Reduplication

5.1.   Nominal reduplication

In CollSgE nominal reduplication occurs primarily with names of close friends or family members, or with common nouns that, when reduplicated, refer to someone who can be considered an intimate.

(33)   a.   *Where is your boy-boy* (boyfriend/son)?
       b.   *We buddy-buddy* (close male friends). *You don't play me out, OK?*
       c.   *Say who told you my mummy-mummy* (mother) *is a graduate?*
            She study more than you, she knows better than you.

In (33), the nominal bases (*boy*, *buddy* and *mummy*) undergo reduplication. The resulting forms are still nominal. The difference here is that the reduplicated forms mark affection or intimacy. Thus, when *boy* reduplicates, we get the meaning 'boyfriend' or 'son'. Likewise, when *buddy* and *mummy* reduplicate, *buddy-buddy* and *mummy-mummy* both draw attention to the close relationship that exists between the male friends, and between parent and child respectively.

Names, too, can reduplicate when they refer to close friends of the speaker. In (34a)–(34b) names of individuals, such as *Henry* and *Choon Yeoh*, are shortened to a single syllable. The resulting monosyllabic form is the basis for reduplication. This shortening is crucial since the base forms cannot reduplicate otherwise, as shown in (34c)–(34d). However, the requirement of a monosyllabic base seems to apply mainly to names. As (33b)–(33c) show, disyllabic common nouns can be reduplicated.

(34)   a.   *I'm looking for Ry-Ry* (Henry)
       b.   *Have you seen Yeoh-Yeoh* (Choon Yeoh)?
       c.   **Henry-Henry*
       d.   **Choon Yeoh-Choon Yeoh*

5.2.   Adjectival reduplication

Adjectival reduplication in CollSgE intensifies the meaning of the base adjective.

(35)   a.   *Don't always eat sweet-sweet* (very sweet) *things.*
   b.   *Why the vege got bitter-bitter* (very bitter) *taste?*
   c.   *I like hot-hot* (very hot) *curries.*

The adjectives in (35) are semantically simple in the sense that they do not indicate either the comparative or superlative meanings. These semantically simple adjectives can reduplicate. (36) suggests that comparatives are able to reduplicate (36a)–(36b) as well, while superlatives are unable to do so (36c)–(36d).

(36)   a.   *That one! That greener-greener one.*
   b.   *Make it smaller-smaller.*
   c.   *That one! That *greenest-greenest one.*
   d.   *Make it *smallest-smallest.*

We can explain why superlatives are unable to reduplicate if we think of adjectives as coding properties on a scale, and intensification as moving the properties higher up along the scale. Comparatives and the simple adjectives are not located at the end-point of the scale, and can move further up along the scale via reduplication. But if the adjective is coding a property that is already at the end-point of the scale, which is what a superlative does, then it will be unable to move up any further. We would therefore expect superlatives not to reduplicate.

5.3.   Verb reduplication

With verb reduplication, we need to distinguish two different sub-types. The first type, similar to nominal and adjectival reduplication, results in only a single copy of the base. The second, however, results in two copies of the base. There are associated meaning differences. With only a single copy in the resulting form, the meaning is that of attenuation. With two copies, the meaning is that of continuity.

 In attenuative verb reduplication, the action described by the base verb is understood to take place over a relatively short time period. In (37a), for example, reduplication of *walk* results in the meaning 'stroll', where the activity now covers a shorter time period. In the rest of the examples, the reduplication is accompanied by adverbials such as *a while* or *a bit* to indicate that the activity is less sustained.

(37)   a.   *Don't always stay in the house. Go outside walk-walk* (stroll).
        b.   *No traffic police ... stop-stop* (make a short stop) *a while.*

Verbs can also be reduplicated to indicate that the action is continuous or on-going, and in comparison with attenuative reduplication, the action is now understood to take place over a longer period of time. Compared with the examples in (37), the examples below involve two copies of the base.

(38)   a.   *I walk-walk-walk* (was walking) *then I fall down.*
        b.   *Take bus no good, always stop-stop-stop* (keeps on stopping).

The difference between the two sub-types of verb reduplication becomes clearer when we compare (39a) with (39b).

(39)   a.   *Ya, I was sick but really, nothing serious. Cough-cough a bit then no more already* (Minor coughing).
        b.   *Why you cough-cough-cough whole day long?* (keep coughing).

The examples in (39) involve reduplication of the verb base *cough*. In (39a), with a single copy, the act of coughing is given an attenuative interpretation, thus conveying that the coughing was minor or not serious. On the other hand, in (39b), with two copies of the base resulting, the act of coughing is given an interpretation of continuity, thus conveying that it was an activity that kept on recurring.

Rajendra Singh (p.c.) suggests that the two types of verb reduplication are possibly related. Since they differ primarily in terms of the length of time involved, that is, the second sub-type differs from the first by increasing the duration over which the action is performed, this suggests that instead of positing a separate and independent process, the second sub-type is better derived from the first, effectively giving it the nested structure shown below. (The use of '//' simply indicates that we have no current evidence for assuming that CollSgE reduplication is either suffixing or prefixing.)

> Attenuation: Verb base // Copy
> Continuity: [Verb base // Copy] // Copy

This also captures the iconic relationship between the two sub-types since it is the longer form that is used to convey a longer time period.

6.   Particles

CollSgE has a large number of particles that typically occur in clause-final position. Although they are optional syntactically, it is widely recognized that they perform various discourse-pragmatic functions. The most common of these particles is *lah*. Other particles include *ma, hah, meh, leh, lor, hor* and *wat*. This last particle is apparently based on the English word *what*.

. Below is a brief summary of the various properties of the CollSgE particles. Three particles, *ma, wat* and *lor*, indicate that a piece of information is obvious. However, there are differences between them. The particle *ma* is perhaps the most neutral in that other than indicating obviousness, it does little else. The other two, *wat* and *lor*, in addition to obviousness, also convey, respectively, a challenge to some earlier proposition and a sense of resignation.

lah	indicates speaker's mood/attitude and appeals to the addressee to accommodate this mood/attitude
ma	indicates information as obvious
wat	indicates information as obvious and contradictory
meh	indicates scepticism
leh	marks a tentative suggestion or request
lor	indicates obviousness or a sense of resignation
hor	asserts and elicits support for a proposition
hah	question marker

In the following discussion, we focus only on a few selected particles: *lah, lor* and *wat.*

6.1.   *Lah*

The Internet edition of the *Oxford English Dictionary* (2000) describes *lah* as 'a particle used with various kinds of pitch to convey the mood and attitude of the speaker', giving examples like *Come with us lah* to indicate persuasion, *Wrong lah* to show annoyance, and *No lah* to demonstrate strong objection. This attributes to the particle a maximally general characterization – it is simply used to convey a certain mood or attitude of the speaker. Exactly what mood or attitude is being conveyed will depend on specific contextual factors, from which the addressee will have to infer.

On the other hand, for CollSgE speakers, an objection like *No* without the particle would be perceived as being much ruder than one with the particle present. Similarly, *Come with us* and *Wrong* are respectively requests and assertions that are made more polite by the presence of *lah*. This has led to claims that the particle is a marker of solidarity, functioning to mitigate face-threatening speech acts. Expressions of annoyance and objections both threaten the addressee's positive face while attempts at persuasion threaten the addressee's negative face. The presence of *lah* as a solidarity marker is often used to soften the force of a speech act.

One way to reconcile these different accounts is to combine them and to treat the particle as having a two-part function. The particle draws the addressee's attention to some mood or attitude of the speaker and, in doing so, also appeals to the addressee to act in such a way as to accommodate this mood or attitude. The first part of this characterization treats *lah* as a highly general particle, while the second part, by appealing to the addressee, is consistent with the impression that *lah* is a solidarity marker.

6.2. *Wat*

This particle presents a piece of information as being obvious. Importantly, it also carries the force of a contradiction to something that has previously been asserted. For example, in (40), C's suggestion to buy sandals with buckles is rejected by B and A. In particular, A's use of *wat* (< *what*) both indicates that it should be obvious to C that salt will cause rusting, and that this very fact makes C's suggestion untenable. C's failure to see the relationship between salt and the buckles leads A to repeat the utterance, using the particle yet again, and to also elaborate further by pointing out that salt is present in sweat.

(40)   (A, B and C are talking about buying sandals)
     C: *Then buy a buckle type lah!*
     B: *Buckle will break because it rusts.*
     A: *Salt **wat**!*
     C: *Ah?*
     A: *Salt **wat**! ... Your sweat got salt, you see. Salt will make it corrode even faster.*

6.3. *Lor*

The *lor* particle can indicate that a piece of information should be obvious to the addressee, and also convey a sense of resignation. The following shows *lor* marking obviousness. A is asking about the kinds of things that need to be bought, and B's answer takes the form of a list. Here, B is indicating that A should already know what needs to be bought.

(41)   A: *What do I have to buy at the market?*
        B: *Fish **lor**, vegetables **lor**, curry powder **lor**.*

By attaching *lor* to an utterance, the speaker can also indicate that the situation described by the utterance is one over which nothing can be done (i.e. the situation can't be helped). And because nothing can be done, one has to simply accept the situation or its implied consequences. In (42), both A and B recognize that having children might require them to stop working. B's initial use of *lor* suggests that she can't bring herself to stop working, and her subsequent uses suggest that she is willing to accept the consequences of working, which are to not marry and to not have children.

(42)   A: *But, um, I might stop working for a while if I need to, if I need to lah, especially for looking after kids.*
        B: *But for me, I won't stop working **lor**. The most I won't give birth to kids **lor**. For the most I don't marry **lor**. (Laughing)*

7.   Conclusion

Perhaps the most fundamental issue in research on CollSgE concerns its status as an autonomous linguistic system. We saw in the companion article on SgE phonology (this volume) that an early controversy over whether or not CollSgE should be understood in terms of a post-creole continuum or diglossia was essentially a debate over whether or not CollSgE can be treated as a self-contained system that can be analyzed without reference to other, more standard varieties of English. But such debates need to consider local perspectives on and attitudes toward CollSgE. And in this regard, one must consider the possibility that government policies aimed at enforcing "good English" may lead to the eventual elimination of reduplication as a productive morphological process. The issue is not the wholesale death of CollSgE as a variety since colloquial varieties, as a matter of sociolinguistic necessity, will prevail. Rather, the question concerns the long-term stability of specific grammatical features as these become affected by language ideologies. Research into how particular properties of CollSgE are influenced by, and in turn, perhaps, influence local perceptions and values would be of interest not only to scholars interested in the status of CollSgE, but also to those with a more general interest in the study of language ideology.

Another area of research that has gained momentum in recent years is the description of intonation that takes into account the ethnically heterogeneous nature of Singapore's population. Until about a decade ago, most work concentrated on establishing differences between patterns of intonation in Singapore with that in Britain. In the last few years, however, there has been greater focus on the intonation patterns that characterize the different ethnic groups in Singapore, such as the differences in pitch range and tempo, and in the alignment of pitch peaks with syllables. For example, initial evidence suggests that Chinese speakers of Singapore English use loudness and length as cues for stressed syllables, while Malay speakers use pitch, loudness and duration, while Indian speakers uses pitch and loudness (Lim 2001). The robustness of these claims, and the extent to which they are traceable to influence from other languages such as the speakers' ethnic mother tongues, need to be further investigated.

Finally, another issue of interest concerns the discourse particles. Research on the particles has tended to follow two directions: a micro-analytic approach focusing on individual particles and attempting to provide, as far as possible, a unified account of their various properties, and a macro-analytic approach concerned with developing a broad-based classification of the particles. An example of the former is Wong's (1994) attempt to describe the "invariant meanings" of specific particles within the framework of Wierzbickan semantics. An example of the latter comes from Gupta's (1992) attempt to group the particles into three main categories (contradictory, assertive, and tentative) that cluster along a scale marking degrees of assertiveness. Individual particles, then, are said to convey different degrees of speaker commitment towards a proposition. Though there are problems with Gupta's specific proposal, there is little doubt that a large-scale attempt to explicate the paradigmatic relationships among the particles is crucial. Reconciling both the micro- and macro-analytic approaches so that descriptions of individual particles are placed within the context of a larger system would be an invaluable contribution to our understanding of CollSgE grammar.

Exercises and study questions

1. Recall the Singapore government's definition of a mother tongue and its position that English is not acceptable as a mother tongue (see the section English And The Official Mother Tongues). The Singapore government has recently emphasized the need to attract 'foreign talent' (i.e. highly skilled professionals from overseas) to work in Singapore, and perhaps to also take up Singapore citizenship. Do you think this might have any impact on Singapore's racial composition, and if so, whether this might also require any change(s) to the government's language policy?

2. Refer to the discussion of *lah* in the article (see the section on Particles) and compare it with the uses of the particle in the recordings. You'll find that among the three speakers, it is Speaker 2 who uses *lah* the most. Do you think the description of *lah* in the article can be improved or needs modification, given the data from Speaker 2?

3. The article points out that the verb generally appears in an uninflected form, particularly where tense and number are concerned (see the section on Aspect). Try to identify instances of pro-drop in the recordings. (Hint: You might find some cases of object pro-drop in the speech of Speaker 2, and cases of subject pro-drop in the speech of Speaker 3).

4. In what ways is the tag question system of SgE different from that of (a) StE and (b) IndE?

5. Review the difference between *kena* and *give* passives of SgE.

Selected references

Please consult the General references for titles mentioned in the text but not included in the references below. For a full bibliography see the accompanying CD-ROM.

Alsagoff, Lubna
    1995   Colloquial Singapore English: the relative clause construction. In: Teng Su Ching and Ho Mian Lian (eds.), *The English Language in Singapore: Implications for Teaching*, 77–87. Singapore: Singapore Association for Applied Linguistics.
Alsagoff, Lubna and Ho Chee Lick
    1998   The grammar of Singapore English. In: Joe Foley, Thiru Kandiah, Bao Zhiming, Anthea F. Gupta, Lubna Alsagoff, Ho Chee Lick, Lionel Wee, Ismail S. Talib and Wendy Bokhorst-Heng, *English in New Cultural Contexts: Reflections from Singapore*, 127–151. Singapore Institute of Management/ Oxford University Press: Singapore.
Gupta, Anthea F.
    1992   The pragmatic particles of Singapore Colloquial English. *Journal of Pragmatics* 18: 31–57.
Gupta, Anthea F.
    1994   *The Step-tongue: Children's English in Singapore*. Clevedon: Multilingual Matters.

Lim, Lisa
    2001   Everything you wanted to know about how stressed Singaporean Englishes
            are. *Paper presented at the Eleventh Annual Meeting of the Southeast
            Asian Linguistics Society*, Mahidol University, Bangkok.
Oxford English Dictionary
    2000   http://dictionary.oed.com.
Platt, John and Heidi Weber
    1980   *English in Singapore and Malaysia: Status, Features, Functions*. Kuala
            Lumpur: Oxford University Press.
Wong, Jock Onn
    1994   A Wierzbickan approach to Singlish particles. MA thesis, Department of
            English Language and Literature, National University of Singapore.

Malaysian English: morphology and syntax

Loga Baskaran

1.   Introduction

In describing some of the aspects of syntactic difference between Standard British English (StBrE) and Malaysian English (henceforth MalE) in this chapter, some emphasis will be placed on the possibility of influence from the substrate languages. The main language used here is Bahasa Malaysia. This is based on two criteria mainly:

- The population ratio is in the order: Malays (55%), Chinese (30%), Indians (10%), Others (5%). Based on these figures alone, the influence from Bahasa Malaysia could be substantial, although actual quantitative studies have not been done to prove this yet.
- Even among the Chinese and Indians (as well as the 'others'), Bahasa Malaysia is more in use by these speakers than their own mother-tongue. Thus the subsequent influence of Bahasa Malaysia on the English spoken by the non-Malays can at times be considered even more substantial than that exerted by Chinese or Tamil.

In this chapter interlingual influence from Bahasa Malaysia and Tamil will be considered. The influence of Chinese on MalE has yet to be researched. Of course some aspects of variation discussed in this chapter could well be from Chinese. The absence of the copula in certain syntactic environments in Chinese, for example, could be additionally contributive (along with the same situation in Bahasa Malaysia and Tamil) to the absence of such a copula in MalE. Then again, as Tay (1977) confirms, it could be postulated that the grammatical particle *la* in MalE has its source from the Hokkien dialect of Chinese, although Bahasa Malaysia also has a suffix of equally significant import and function.

All in all, one can say that the substrate languages have their influencing role on the syntax of MalE in various permutations and combinations. But as Platt and Weber (1980) suggest, it would be wrong to trace all characteristics of MalE/SgE to the local background languages as every interlanguage and every emerging new variety develops its own system, which is to some extent independent of the background languages.

This study, therefore, describes MalE in terms of structural differences in comparison with StBrE. The latter is used as a norm of comparison purely because it is still the grammar of this standard variety (though not the phonology) that is aimed at on the acrolectal level in Malaysia (namely programmed instruction, official media, locally organised international conferences and the like).

The results and findings in this study are culled from various types of sources, of which the primary ones are:

- Written and spoken language observations of students who are postgraduate in-service English Language teachers, undergraduate students, or secondary school pupils.
- Entry and diagnostic test sheets of in-service (postgraduate) English language teachers.
- Official statements, newspapers, radio and TV.
- Formal and informal speech of professionals and lay people.

2. Noun phrase structure

Three characteristic elements in the noun phrase of Malaysian English show that there is a specific system underlying the variety, rather than random simplificatory processes.

2.1. Article ellipsis

Article ellipsis does not just occur before any nouns as such, but abstract nouns in particular. Furthermore, ellipsis applies, only to those abstract nouns that are modified:

(1)   *Did you get **mileage-claim** for that trip?*

(2)   *Finance companies effected **drastic increase** in interest rates this year.*

(3)   ***Main reason** for their performance...*

The only other exception to this rule is the concrete noun when it is used as an institutionalised or generic noun in predicate position, as seen in the following examples:

(4)   *She is Ø **trend-setter** of the class.*

(5)   *He was Ø **most popular prefect** last year.*

(6)   *He is Ø **drug addict**.*

Such article ellipsis before modified abstract nouns could be a carryover from Malay, where there is no article system. Numeral quantification of concrete nouns is by cardinal determiners with classifiers:

(7)   Malay: *Apakah   **keadaan**   tentang   perkara   itu?*
        What (INT.)   situation   regarding   topic   that?
        'What is the situation regarding that?'

(8)   Malay: ***Penghasilan*** *motokar   sekarang   diberi   keutamaan.*
        Production   motor-cars   now   given   priority.
        'The production of motor-cars is now given priority.'

2.2.   Pronoun concord

As far as pronominal concord is concerned, there is a singular/plural distinction for animate nouns, but no number distinction for inanimate nouns. The following MalE examples are representative:

(9)   ***Those books*** *are very informative. **It** can be obtained at Dillon's.*

(10)   ***The houses*** *on Travers Road are UDA houses. **It** caters for the Division 'B' employees of the Malayan Railways.*

(11)   *Rahman bought **three ball-pens** from the Co-op, but forgot and left **it** on the cash desk.*

The partial influence from Malay can be postulated on the basis of examples like the following. In (12) to (14) *ia* is used as an invariant pronoun for inanimate as well as animate non-human nouns:

(12)   Malay: ***Surat-surat*** *itu   baru sampai – mungkin **ia** dari   ayah*
        Letters   those just   arrived – must be   *it* from   father
        saya.
        my.
        'Those letters have just arrived – they must be from my father.'

(13)   Malay: ***Baju***   *siapa   semua   itu?   **Ia**   sangat cantik.*
        Clothes whose all   those? *It*   very   pretty.
        'Whose clothes are those? They are very pretty.'

(14)   Malay: *Ada   dua   ekor   **kucing** di dalam longkang itu – ia*
        Are   two   (CLAS.) kittens   in   drain   that – *it*
        semua   berwarna   putih.
        all   coloured   white.
        'There are two kittens in that drain – they are all coloured white'.

2.3. Individuation

It is noticeable how frequently mass nouns (like *staff*) are treated as count nouns in MalE. This may be due to bilingual usage, based on familiarity with the Malay system of classifiers. The classifiers are not carried over into MalE, but the noun itself is treated as if it were indeed countable (or governed by a classifier):

(15)   *How many **staffs** are on medical leave?*

(16)   *She bought three **lingeries** at Mark's today.*

(17)   *There are not many **stationeries** in the room.*

There is also some random pluralising of such mass nouns:

(18)   *She cleared all her **paraphernalias** out of the way.*

(19)   *There were no suitable **accommodations** for them.*

Some element of analogy within English itself can be postulated where such examples like *jewellery* (*jewelleries* – MalE) and *stationery* (*stationeries* – MalE) are pluralised in a way similar to *grocery/groceries* in BrE.

   Pluralisation also occurs when a noun occurs as a hypernym or composite term. Thus MalE has *furnitures* – from 'tables, chairs, beds etc.'; *fruits* – from 'apples, pears, bananas etc.'; *offsprings* – from 'sons, daughters'. On the other hand *children* is not pluralised.

3.   Verb phrase structure

3.1.   Tense and temporal distance

Tense in MalE is determined by temporal distance from the deictic centre. The concepts of anteriority, simultaneity and posteriority are relevant to this conceptual framework:

–   Past events are considered anterior to the deictic centre, with three degrees of remoteness. These are immediate past (*I **ate/was eating** rice this morning*); recent past *(I **have eaten/have been eating** rice yesterday*); remote past (*I **had eaten/had been eating** rice last month*).
–   Present events are considered simultaneous to the deictic centre – thus with no degree of remoteness involved, as in 'I **eat (am eating)** rice now'.
–   Future events are considered posterior to the deictic centre – with two degrees of remoteness. These are immediate future (*I **will eat/will be eating** rice tonight*); remote/distant future (*I **would eat/would be eating** rice tomorrow*).

This system seems to be independent of any influence from Malay, where no deictic tense marking is involved although there is differentiation of temporal orientation in terms of anteriority, simultaneity and posteriority (in its aspectual verbs). Further, there is no tense marking in its lexical verbs either, as can be seen in the following examples:

(20)	Malay:	*Saya*	***makan***	*nasi*	*pagi*	*tadi.*	
		I	ate	rice	this	morning.	

(21)	Malay:	*Saya*	***sudah***	***makan***	*nasi*	*semalam.*	
		I	have	eaten	rice	yesterday.	

(22)	Malay:	*Saya*	***sudah***	***makan***	*nasi*	*bulan*	*lalu.*
		I	had	eaten	rice	last	month.

(23)	Malay:	*Saya*	***makan***	*nasi*	*sekarang.*	
		I	eat	rice	now.	

(24)	Malay:	*Saya*	***akan***	***makan***	*nasi*	*malam ini.*	
		I	will	eat	rice	tonight.	

(25)	Malay:	*Saya*	***akan***	***makan***	*nasi*	*esok.*	
		I	would	eat	rice	tomorrow.	

3.2.   Modals

As for the modals in MalE, the simplified system can be summarised as follows:

can	–	permission, ability
would	–	past tense of the above meanings
may	–	possibility
will	–	immediate futurity (± volition)
would	–	distant/remote futurity (± volition)
should	–	obligation, necessity
must	–	obligation, necessity

Such a system may be considered similar to the narrow-ranged modal system in Malay:

hendak, mahu, ingin	–	volition
enggan	–	weak/negative volition
harus, wajib, mesti	–	compulsion
perlu	–	obligation, necessity
boleh, dapat	–	ability, permission
mungkin	–	possibility, probability

It could, however, also be viewed as a simplification of the system, so that there is no ambivalence of meaning.

3.3. Stative verbs in the progressive

The third characteristic feature in the verb phrase is the occurrence of some of the stative verbs in the progressive, contrary to (written) StE usage. These are the relation verbs and verbs of inert perception and cognition:

(26) *That bottle **is containing** sulphuric acid.*
      '...contains...'

(27) *I **am smelling** curry in this room.*
      '...smell...'

(28) *She **is owning** two luxury apartments.*
      '...owns...'

Within BrE itself there is a possible source of over-generalisation, e.g. the verbs of bodily sensation that can occur in the progressive (as in 'My back *is aching*' or 'My foot *is hurting*'). Furthermore, there might well be reinforcement from Malay relational verbs like *contain* and *own* which can occur optionally with the equivalent V-*ing* form (although this is not a common phenomenon).

4. Clause structure variation

4.1. Lack of inversion in *wh*-questions

Noticeable in main clause *wh*-questions in MalE is a lack of auxiliary inversion with the subject NP:

(29) *What we have here?*

(30) *Where they are going?*

(31) *How they will come home?*

On the other hand, in indirect *wh*-questions inversion does occur in MalE, contrary to the rules of StE:

(32) *I wonder where is she?*

The *wh*-element in the MalE interrogative can also occur in sentence-final position:

(33)   *They are going where?*

(34)   *She is doing what?*

The use of *wh-* in situ could be transfer from Malay:

(35)   Malay: *Mereka   pergi   ke mana?*
               They   go   where
               'Where are they going?'

(36)   Malay: *Dia   menangis kenapa?*
               She   cry   why?
               'Why is she crying?'

4.2.   Tagged *yes-no* interrogatives

Another interesting feature of MalE interrogative clauses is the *yes or not?* and *or not?* tags used to mark *Yes-no* interrogatives. Thus the two variant tags are used as seen below:

(37)   a. *She can sing or not?*
               'Can she sing?'
       b. *She can sing, yes or not?*
               'Can she sing?'

(38)   a. *You are hungry, or not?*
               'Are you hungry?'
       b. *You are hungry, yes or not?*
               'Are you hungry?'

A likely source of influence for these tags is the Malay interrogative construction:

(39)   Malay: *Dia   makan   atau   tidak?*
               He   (eat)   or   not?
               'Did he eat?'

(40)   Malay: *Dia   makan   ya   `tak?*
               He   ate   yes   or not?
               'He ate, didn't he?'

4.3.   Invariant interrogative tags

Another interrogative tag that is often used in MalE is the phrase *can or not?*
It has several functions: seeking permission (41), confirming ability (42) or
assessing volition (43):

(41)   *I want to come, can or not?*
       'Can I come?'

(42)   *They must submit the forms tomorrow, **can or not**?*
       'Can they submit the forms tomorrow?'

(43)   *You carry this for me, **can or not**?*
       'Will you carry this for me?'

The only interrogative tags used for polarity-based tag interrogatives are *is it*
and *isn't it?* They serve the function of BrE reversed polarity tags, as well as
constant polarity tags:

(44)   *They are coming, **isn't it**?*
       'They are coming, aren't they?'

(45)   *He can play the piano, **is it**?*
       'He can play the piano, can he?'

4.4.   *Yes-no* questions without inversion

These use rising intonation rather than auxiliary inversion:

(46)   *They were fat or thin?*
       'Were they fat or thin?'

(47)   *He likes red or white wine?*
       'Does he like red or white wine?'

(48)   *They eat rice or noodles?*
       'Did they eat rice or noodles?'

As examples (46) to (48) suggest, this rising intonation question form frequently involves alternatives between NPs.

4.5.   Lack of verb inversion in adverbial initial sentences

In sentences with an initially-negated declarative or adverbially-fronted declarative there is no auxiliary inversion:

(49)   *Never he was so delighted.*
        'Never was he so delighted.'

(50)   *Scarcely ever he has come here.*
        'Scarcely ever has he come here.'

5.   Other syntactic variational features

Other mesolectal features in the syntax of MalE that have still to be researched in greater depth are listed here for the sake of completeness:

Pronoun-copying:

(51)   *My brother, he is an engineer.*

Further research needs to be undertaken to ascertain whether this is 'normal' left dislocation, with a contrastive, pragmatic effect, or whether – as reported in some varieties like SAfBlE – it is becoming grammaticalised in some lects.

Pronoun-ellipsis:

(52)   *She wrote the letter but forgot to post Ø.*

Adverbial positioning:

(53)   *They must admit immediately to the offence.*

Ellipsis of expletive *it/there* + *be*:

(54)   *No point pursuing the matter further.*

Whilst (54) is part of casual StE, the stylistic restriction does not appear to apply in MalE.

Substitution of *there* and *be* with existential/locative *got*:

(55)   *Got no food in the fridge.*
        '…There is…'

Grammatical particles:
There are typically MalE particles which replace the various functions represented by intonational variation and grammatical structures in BrE. These include *what* (56), *man* (57), *one* (58) and *lah* (59):

(56)   *I told, **what**, the other day.*
        'Don't you remember/Aren't you convinced that I told you?'

(57)   *He isn't the Captain, **man**, he's just a prefect.*
       'Don't talk nonsense, he's not the captain, just a prefect!'

(58)   *She is real lazy, **one**.*
       'She sure is a typical lazy thing!'

(59)   *Please, **lah**, come home early.*
       'For heaven's sake, come home early.'

Such epithets serve a grammatical and pragmatic function, usually expressing disapproval. Example (57) with *man* exists, of course, in BrE and other varieties worldwide, and is listed here for comparative purposes.

6.   Lexis

Any discussions of Malaysian English would be incomplete without mentioning features of lexical indigenisation. The main focus will be on substrate language referents (use of substrate lexicon in MalE) and on StE lexicalisation (English lexemes with MalE usage).

6.1.   Substrate language referents

Local terms can be considered from the following vantage points: institutionalised concepts; emotional and cultural loading; semantic restriction; cultural/culinary terms; hyponymous collocations; campus/student coinages.

Institutional concepts:
Some local words pertaining to particular institutions that have been borrowed into MalE have no equivalent in StE. Some examples are terms like *bumiputra* 'son of the soil, patriot' and *khalwat* 'proximity, intimacy'.

Emotional and cultural loading:
Some examples of words with local cultural and emotional association are *kampong* 'village', *dusun* 'orchard', *bomoh* 'medicine-man', *penghulu* 'village-chief' and *pantang* 'taboo'.

Semantic restriction:
These are local words with a possible English translation but used in a semantically restricted field. For example *dadah* 'drugs' does not mean drugs in general but drugs used illicitly. Other lexemes with such a semantic restriction are those like *haj* (pilgrimage, especially of Muslims to Mecca), *toddy* (fermented

coconut-water – different from fresh coconut water sold as an iced refreshment), and *silat* (the Malay art of self-defence). Thus we read of *silat*-groups and *toddy*-shops. The word *padi* (*paddy* in BrE) also has such semantic restriction – meaning 'rice-grown in the fields' – i.e. 'unhusked rice'. Hence, there is an overlap but also an opposition between the pairs *dadah* – *drugs*; *haj* – *pilgrimage*; *toddy* – *coconut water*; *silat* – *self-defence* and *padi* – *rice*. In fact the first item of each pair is a sub-type of the second item.

Cultural and culinary terms:
These are local culinary and domestic referents specifically akin to a characteristic of local origin and ecology. Some such lexemes are *durian* (a thorny fruit) and *sambal* 'condiment' paste. Such words, similar to the Indian *sari* and Japanese *kimono* are now slowly being transported to at least the South East Asian region, e.g. the words *durian* and *sambal* in Sri Lanka.

Hyponymous collocations:
The presence of local words collocated with an English term is yet another type of lexical indigenisation. A hyponymous relationship is exhibited with the English equivalent as the superordinate and the local word as the subordinate referent. Some examples are words such as *meranti* 'wood', *orang asli* 'people', *batik* 'cloth', *syariah* 'court', *nobat* 'drums', *bersanding* 'ceremony' and *path dab bhog* 'ceremony'.

Campus/student coinages:
These are a few words that have recently come into currency – being transported from Malay due to the change in medium of instruction in education and the subsequent strong influence of this language. Thus students in schools and at campuses use these local referents. Some examples are *lecheh* 'troublesome, inconvenient'; *teruk* 'serious, in bad shape'; *doongu* 'silly, dumb, stupid, foolish'. Whether these code-switched, slangy items will prove durable is hard to say.

6.2.   Standard English lexicalisation

The speaker of Malaysian English also has a tendency to use some of the StE lexemes in novel ways. The following processes will be briefly exemplified: polysemic variation; semantic restriction; informalisation; formalisation; directional reversal; college colloquialisms.

Polysemic variation:
Some StE lexemes keep their original meaning whilst taking on an extended semantic range. Examples are *cut* and *open*. In addition to its usual sense, *cut*

has the following meanings in MalE: 'to overtake' (60), 'to beat' (61) and 'to reduce' (62):

(60)   *I tried to **cut** him but he was driving too fast.*

(61)   *Rahman **cut** me by only two marks to become the first boy in class.*

(62)   *The shopkeeper **cut** twenty cents for that breakage when he gave back the change.*

Likewise *open* has an extended range of meanings taking the following direct objects: *blinds, curtains,* (StE 'draw'); *light, electrical appliances* (StE 'switch on'); *shoes, socks* (StE 'remove'); *tap* (StE 'turn on'); *clothes* (StE 'take off', 'undress'); *zip, buttons, hooks* (StE 'unfasten', 'undo').

Semantic restriction:
Some of the lexemes in MalE are used in a narrower sense, confined to specific referents only. Some noteworthy examples are the lexemes *windy, heaty* and *cooling* as applied to foods and drinks. Another example of restricted reference is the lexeme *tuck-shop* – referring specifically to the canteen or refectory of schools. Likewise *coffee-shop, five-foot, one kind* – meaning 'weird or peculiar' as in (63):

(63)   *She is **one kind** really – won't even smile at you although she knows you.*

Informalisation:
Many of the lexemes used by the MalE speaker tend to be informal (collo-quial) substitutions of StE words. As has been stated earlier, MalE in its most representative state is of widest currency among the mesolectal speakers. Thus it is not surprising to find a profusion of lexemes indicating a more informal style and register – words like *kids* (for 'children') or *hubby* (for '*husband*') appearing in headlines style in the StE local dailies, as in *Eight kids burnt to death as fire guts Kampung Jawa* and *Amok woman stabs hubby*. Other such examples are:

flick	-	'steal'
line	-	'profession'
fellow	-	'person' (male or female)
sleep	-	'go to bed'
spoilt	-	'out of order'
follow	-	'accompany'
spend	-	'give a treat'

Formalisation:
On the other hand, there are occasions, when the MalE speaker has a tendency to use more formal words in an informal context. Sey (1973: 38) termed this 'preciosity' in connection with Ghanaian English, while Goffin (1934: 14) described this as the "Latinity" of Indian English. It is not rare, therefore, to read letters of a personal nature asking a friend to *furnish* him with the details regarding a group tour (instead of *providing* or *sending him*) Likewise a friend may ask *Did you **witness** the accident last night along Jalan Bangsar?* (instead of *see*).

Directional reversal:
There are certain lexemes, especially verbs, that MalE speakers tend to use in reverse direction. This is a frequent phenomenon with converse pairs like *go/come*, *bring/send*, *fetch/take* and *borrow/lend*. This could be attributed to the absence of two separate lexemes in the local language for such a meaning. In Bahasa Malaysia, the concepts of 'borrow' and 'lend', for example, are subsumed under one lexeme *pinjam*, although the difference between the meaning of 'borrow' and 'lend' is shown by the benefactive suffix *kan*:

(61)   *She **borrowed** me her camera.*
        '...lent...'

(62)   *He always likes to **lend** my books.*
        '...borrow...'

(63)   *We'll **go** over to your house to-night.*
        '...come...'

(64)   *Can you **send** me home first?*
        '...take...'

(65)   *I **take** my daughter here everyday.*
        '...bring...'

MalE usage seems to indicate the reverse in directional terms.

College colloquialism:
The student population being a major group of MalE usage, it is inevitable that certain StE lexemes have been localised for informal use especially among students in school (secondary), at colleges (tertiary), and universities. Such words relate to studies, examinations and youth, for example:

mugger (or *book-worm*)	-	'an extremely studious person'
frus	-	'frustrated'
fantab	-	a blend of *fantastic* and *fabulous*
worst type	-	a friendly term for criticising a colleague

Exercises and study questions

1. Compare the key features of MalE syntax with that of SgE. Are there any differences between the two varieties?

2. Review the use of the tags *can or not* and *isn't it/is it* (Section 4.3). How are these constructions different – i.e. does there appear to be a main clause structure which favours one or the other?

3. Go through all the illustrative sentences to see if you can find an example of a question with auxiliary inversion.

4. In which other construction does lack of inversion occur in MalE?

5. Under what conditions does *it* occur in place of StE *they*? (Compare sentences (9) to (11) with (42), (44) and (46).

Selected references

Please consult the General references for titles mentioned in the text but not included in the references below. For a full bibliography see the accompanying CD-ROM.

Baskaran, Loga
  1987   Aspects of Malaysian English syntax. Unpublished Ph.D. thesis, University of London.
  1994   The Malaysian English mosaic. *English Today* 37: 27–32.
Goffin, Robert C.
  1934   Some notes on Indian English. *Society for Pure English* 41: 14–16.
Platt, John and Heidi Weber
  1980   *English in Singapore and Malaysia: Status, Features, Functions.* Kuala Lumpur: Oxford University Press.
Sey, Kofi A.
  1973   *Ghanaian English – an Exploratory Survey.* London: Macmillan.
Tay, Mary
  1977   The 'la' particle in Singapore English. In: William Crewe (ed.), *The English Language in Singapore*, 141–156. Singapore: Eastern Universities Press.

Synopsis: morphological and syntactic variation in Africa and South and Southeast Asia

Rajend Mesthrie

1. Introduction

The chapters describing the morphology and syntax of varieties of English from Africa and south and southeast Asia (henceforth *Africa-Asia*) show a high degree of similarity. This similarity particularly pertains to the L2 varieties of English spawned by British colonialism in Africa-Asia. In fact the main linguistic divisions discernible amongst varieties described in this section of the volume are not so much by individual country *per se*, but according to the following dimensions:

(a) L1 English (South Africa and St. Helena)
(b) L2 Englishes (Africa and Asia)
(c) Pidgins and Creoles (Africa).

This trichotomy is nonetheless a fuzzy one for many reasons. Within South Africa language shift has caused some former L2s to turn into L1s (CFE, InSAfE), with linguistic characteristics that overlap between (a) and (b) above. Whilst StHE is grouped here as an L1 it also shares many features with group (c), owing largely to the influence of the linguistic practices of slaves upon BrE settler dialects. Within west Africa, L2 English has been influenced by the rapidly spreading West African Pidgin (WAP), and *vice versa*. In India there is some overlap between the features of ButlE and certain sociolects within vernacular IndE. ButlE has always been a difficult variety to classify within contact studies (see further below) and a comparison of the relevant chapters in this volume shows that it does not really share much in common with WAP. This stands in contrast to the immense similarities amongst L2 Englishes in Africa-Asia. Recent Pidgin and Creole Linguistics has debated the status of Pidgins and Creoles (henceforth *P & Cs*) as a natural class that contrasts with other categories like L1 regional dialects of the superstrate or L2 versions of the superstrate. The chapters in this volume, however, appear to uphold the traditional division, showing clearcut differences between L1, L2 and P & Cs. However, it must be conceded that intermediate varieties between this threefold distinction do exist, showing a blend of L1 and pidgin (StHE), or characteristics akin to both

L2 formation and a degree of creolisation (InSAfE and to a lesser extent SgE). Finally ButlE looks like an L2 arrested at an early stage of development (i.e. it seems intermediate between fossilised L2 and pidgin).

It is also interesting to chart the relations of the Africa-Asia varieties with varieties of English in other continents. WhSAfE has much in common with other Southern Hemisphere Englishes, especially its Antipodean cousins in Australia and New Zealand. A link between the African and Asian varieties is provided by InSAfE, which is influenced by its position in Africa, whilst sharing a great deal with IndE (and L2 Asian Englishes generally). Likewise LibSE forms a link between African American English and P & Cs of west Africa. The only other variety in Africa-Asia which has American, rather than British roots is PhlE. StHE also has affinities with varieties outside the territory and will no doubt make a useful point of comparison with Caribbean, Pacific and Atlantic Englishes.

A few cautionary notes are in order before launching into a synopsis of the features to be found in Africa-Asia. The difficulty of compressing information from nineteen chapters into one inevitably leads to a degree of idealisation that does not always do justice to the specifics of a construction in a particular territory. Furthermore the comparability of data gathered under different circumstances by different researchers at different times brings its own challenges. For sociolinguistics this is the general methodological challenge between fidelity to an *emic* orientation and the demands of a broad comparative perspective.

In the sections that follow the main focus will fall on the L2 varieties. The P & Cs are better treated as a group on their own, as are the L1 varieties. For an account of the most important parallels and differences in the morphology and syntax within and across these three groups of varieties compare the Global Synopsis by Kortmann and Szmrecsanyi (2004). For easier reference, the number code of the morphosyntactic features investigated there will be specified in square brackets below.

2.   Tense, aspect and modality

2.1   Tense and aspect

The broad PRESENT – PAST – FUTURE tense distinction using StE morphemes is largely unaltered in L1 and L2 Englishes of Africa-Asia, in contrast to the P & Cs. Where variation occurs in the L1 and L2 varieties it is especially in the combination of tense with aspect. Unmarked verbs for the simple past [40] are noted in SgE (frequently) and NigE and CFE (occasionally). Conversely doubly marked forms (with *did* + *-ED)* are reported in NigE and EAfE (rarely in both varieties). The use of perfect forms with *HAVE* in place of the simple past

[25] (completive aspect) is noted for GhE, IndE and PakE. Conversely the use of the past for perfect occurs in (at least) CFE and BlSAfE. The past perfect for present perfect is reported for GhE. Complex tenses (involving combinations of progressive and perfective aspect and tense) tend to be avoided in at least EAfE. Few innovations in tense are reported: one such is the use of *would* for the remote distant future in contrast to *will* for the immediate future in MalE.

The P & Cs show a major restructuring of the English tense and aspect system, with pre-verbal particles used to mark tense, aspect and modality that differ not just structurally, but semantically from the English tense and aspect system. Some of these particles in WAP are: zero for simple past [40]; *go* for future and irrealis; *bi* or *bin* for anterior [29]; *de* for incompletive, *don* for completive [28] etc. There are differences within WAP as well, e.g. GhP uses zero rather than *bin* for anterior marking. In LibSE the future particle is *gan* or *will*; the incompletive, *de* (and others); and the completive, *don*. StHE does not have a system of pre-verbal particles, but does make use of *don* for completive and *is* before other verbs in stem form.

The use of present *BE* for 'have been' (*I'm here for twenty years*) is reported in InSAfE and SAfE generally. StHE occasionally uses *is* for *will*.

A striking and almost universal characteristic among L2 varieties in Africa-Asia is the extension of *BE + -ING* to stative contexts [21]. It is reported as a frequent characteristic of NigE, GhE, EAfE, BlSAfE, IndE, PakE, MalE, and as an occasional feature of InSAfE. It also occurs in SgE, though perhaps not as commonly because *be* tends to be deleted [57] in this variety. In ButlE the suffix *-ing* is overgeneralised as a verb ending for a variety of tenses and *BE* is frequently deleted. Nevertheless the basic principle stands: there is frequently no distinction between stative and non-stative verbs. This feature does not occur in the L1 varieties of WhSAfE and StHE. For WAP the very different system of pre-verbal particles makes this feature inapplicable. Noteworthy forms of semi-auxilaries that perform aspectual work are *steady* for continuous and *come* for expressing disapproval in LibSE; *busy* for 'in the process of' in all varieties of SAfE; *an' stay* for habitual and *an' leave* for completive in InSAfE; and *kena* and *give* for adversative passives in SgE.

2.2.   Modality

The semantics of the modal auxiliaries is subject to much variability in the L2 Englishes. *Will* for 'would' and *can* for 'could' in certain contexts is reported in BlSAfE, InSAfE, CFE, GhE, NigE and MalE. Similarly *shall* for 'should' occurs in NigE. Other substitutions include *can* for 'might' in BlSAfE and *may* for 'might' in NigE.

Politeness effects are also responsible for some variation in modal usage. *May* is used for polite obligation with passives in IndE; it occurs with the 2nd person pronoun in BlSAfE (*May you please give me a chance*). *Wouldn't* is used as a softener in place of *don't* in InSAfE (*I wouldn't know*). *Would* for 'will' and *could* for 'can' are reported as polite forms in IndE, in contrast to the reversal noted for other varieties in the previous paragraph. *Won't* is a directive softener in WhSAfE: *Won't you do this?* instead of 'Please do this', though it can be taken to be presumptious if overused. Conversely, in some varieties *must* does not generally carry the semantics of obligation or 'bossiness' understood in StE. Thus *must* for 'have to, ought to, should' is reported for SAfE generally and for NigE where the form is often *must have to*.

Should in SAfE has the unique semantics of 'used to' (even in upper mesolectal speech) with a negative equivalent *shouldn't*. Stressed *can* in this dialect means 'really can' (with overtones of disapproval).

3.   Verb morphology and syntax: Auxiliaries, agreement and verb forms and serialization

Not surprisingly in view of its instability in BrE dialects, the third person singular *-s* ending is quite frequently absent [53] in L2 varieties: NigE, EAfE, BlSAfE, CFE, InSAfE, SgE. It is generally absent in WAP, LibSE and ButlE; and occasionally absent in StHE. Conversely an *-s* ending may be used with first person pronouns in StHE, LibSE and CFE, though not with any great frequency. In the same vein the distinction between singular and plural for forms of *BE, DO* and *HAVE* may not always be made. *Was* for 'were' [59] is reported in StHE, EAfE, CFE, InSAfE; *is* for 'are' in StHE and CFE; *don't* for 'doesn't' [48] in at least CFE and InSAfE, and *was* for conditional 'were' in EAfE and InSAfE.

Copula deletion [57] is not very commonly reported in L2 varieties in Africa. It does occur in SgE as a grammatical deletion and in CFE and InSAfE as a phonological rule. It is common in ButlE, LibSE and StHE. A special locative copula (*de, dey*) occurs in WAP, but is not reported in any other L1 or L2 variety. Habitual (invariant) *be* is used in StHE and InSAfE. Addition of *is* to forms of habitual *be* [22] is common in StHE, making a kind of 'double *be*' construction; in ButlE an occasional feature is the addition of *is* to modals like *can*.

Absence of dummy *do* is reported in IndE, PakE and InSAfE. The survival of unstressed *do* is reported in StHE and CFE. Completive *done* [28] occurs in WAP, LibE and StHE. An irrealis *be done* construction occurs in LibSE and

StHE. *Did* in place of 'have' (*Did you bring my books?*) occurs in SAfE varieties; whilst *done* for full verb 'did' (and *seen* for 'saw' and *been* for 'have been') occur in 'lower' InSAfE sociolects.

Got as auxiliary in place of existential *be* is reported for SgE, MalE, InSAfE, WAP.

Phrasal and prepositional verbs are subject to immense variation in L2 Englishes. In some cases the preposition may be deleted, as in the type *pick* for 'pick up'. This type (not necessarily the exact token) is reported in EAfE, GhE and NigE. The converse (addition of an 'underlying' preposition) in the type *discuss* for 'discuss about' is more common and reported for EAfE, GhE, NigE, BlSAfE, IndE and InSAfE. Variation in the exact preposition used as in the type *congratulate for* (= 'congratulate on') is reported for EAfE, GhE, NigE, BlSAfE, IndE and InSAfE.

Verb serialization [72] is a salient characteristic of WAP, but is not really common in the non-P & C varieties. CFE has a small measure of them, mostly limited to sequences of two verbs. In particular the use of a serial verb with prepositional function is unknown in the L2 varieties.

4.   Negation

The only variety showing multiple negation (or 'negative spread') [44] is LibE. Double negation is more widespread, being reported as rare in BlSAfE and InSAfE, and common in StHE, GhE and ButlE. It is explicitly mentioned as not occurring in NigE and WAP. Another form common in non-standard varieties of English around the world, *ain't* [45, 46, 47], is conspicuous by its absence in Asia-Africa, except in StHE and LibE. *Never* in place of 'didn't' [49] is reported for InSAfE, CFE and WSAE.

The different system underlying the responses *yes* and *no* to questions couched in the negative (explained in Mesthrie's account of BlSAfE morphology and syntax) is widespread, being reported for BlSAfE, NigE, GhE, EAfE, and IndE.

The Pidgins and Creoles are different in their system of negation, usually having an invariant negator rather than clitics on auxiliaries: *no* or *neva* in WAP; *no* or *not* in ButlE [50].

5.   Subordination: relativization and complementation

5.1   Relative Clauses

Resumptive pronouns [67] are in common use, being reported in BlSAfE, EAfE, NigE, GhE, CamE and InSAfE. *What* [61] as a relativizer is reported in LibSE, StHE, NigE and InSAfE. Preposition chopping, i.e. the deletion of a preposition in a relative clause (e.g. *... like a big yard that you do gardening an' all*, with the preposition *in* deleted), is reported for CamE, GhE and InSAfE. PakE, IndE and InSAfE use reduced relative phrases that precede rather than follow the head noun (*detrimental-to-health medicines*). Related compound relatives and other preposed types occur in InSAfE. In SgE a local variant of the standard relative clause involves the use of *one* at the end of the relative clause as its sole marker, and the verb within the relative clause in stem form.

The dichotomy between L2 English and P & C is upheld with WAP using *where* as the relative marker in place of the full range of *who, which* etc. ButlE, being a minimal pidgin, does not appear to have a relative clause strategy.

5.2   Complementation

The *to* infinitive is subject to a fair amount of variation. In some varieties (EAfE, NigE, GhE, IndE and PakE) it replaces a gerundial form in *-ing* (*Instead of him to travel home...*). In these varieties it may also replace a preposition + gerundial form (*... forbade me to do it*). Conversely *to* may be replaced by *that* + *S* in PakE and IndE (*I wanted that I should get leave*). In EAfE and NigE *to* may be variably deleted (*Allow him [ ] go*). In BlSAfE frequently and NigE occasionally, *to* may be added in phrases like *He let me to go*. In GhE the use of V + *-ing* and *to* + V are sometimes interchangeable.

Complementiser *that* also occurs in novel ways in some varieties. As discussed above it may replace the *to* infinitive construction. In some varieties verb subcategorization restrictions are different, so that V + NP + *that* is replaced by V + *that* (hence *He has deplored that...* in PakE). *That* is overgeneralised in CamE in two ways: firstly, as a replacement for 'saying that' (*She mocked me that I failed my exam*); and, secondly, as a substitute for *because* (*He is crying that I left him behind*). The complementiser *say* [68] occurs in WAP in place of *that;* in LibSE both forms occur, with *say* limited to verbs of communication.

5.3   Questions

Several varieties (CamE, InSAfE, IndE, PakE, MalE, ButlE) do not apply
the rule of auxiliary inversion mandatorily in *yes/no* questions [74] and *wh-*
questions [73] (hence *What you would like?*). In SgE there is little room for
inversion as subject pronouns are frequently deleted anyway. The space and
function of inversion is somewhat usurped by the *can or not* tag. In indirect
questions where StE mandatorily disallows auxiliary inversion, many varieties allow it: BlSAfE, InSAfE, EAfE, SgE, PakE, IndE, MalE. In addition
some varieties do not require *do*-support in *yes-no* and *wh-* questions: StHE,
InSAfE, IndE (*What he wants?*). And again, in contrast to StE, many varieties
(e.g. NigE, IndE, InSAfE) allow *do*-support in indirect questions (*I asked him
what did he want*).

Some varieties do not use *wh-* movement mandatorily, frequently leaving
the *wh-* word or phrase *in situ* (CamE, SgE, NigP). IndE allows COMP to be
doubly filled with *wh-* (*What who has eaten?* as one rare but permitted way of
expressing 'Who has eaten what?')

The use of invariant tag questions [52] emerges as another overwhelming
rule in L2 Englishes: BlSAfE, NigE, EAfE, CamE, CFE, InSAfE, IndE, SgE,
MalE and ButlE. This tag is frequently *isn't it,* though other forms may also
be in use: *is it* in SgE and MalE; *isn't* in InSAfE; *né* in CFE and a host of other
forms in CamE. Responses to *yes/no* questions couched in the negative were
discussed above in section 4. Variation in the form of *wh-* words is discussed
under pronouns (section 7).

6.   Noun phrase structure

Articles are another area where New Englishes are united in their differences
from StE. Occasional absence of the article [17], whether definite or indefinite,
is noted in all the L2 varieties represented and in the P & Cs. By contrast, article absence is not a feature of L1 WhSAfE, which is the only variety that has
a relatively clear unilinear descent from BrE. In InSAfE (also largely an L1)
article absence does occur, but at a relatively infrequent level. This is also the
case with CFE. The article *one* as a variant of the indefinite *a* is reported in
StHE, InSAfE and WAP. The use of an article where StE favours zero [17] is
reported in BlSAfE, NigE, GhE, PakE, IndE and in special idioms like *a pant*
for 'a pair of trousers, pants' in CFE. Occasional substitution of *the* for *a* is
reported in NigE, GhE and IndE.

Equally widespread is the use of plural *-s* for what are non-count nouns in
StE: all the L2 Englishes studied have this as a prominent feature. Again, there

is an 'isogloss' between L2 and L1 varieties, with no attestations in WhSAfE. InSAfE falls on the L2 side of the boundary this time; there is no information on CFE. There is no data from the P & Cs, possibly because in the case of a rudimentary pidgin like ButlE the words concerned (*staff, machinery, luggage*) belong to a more advanced vocabulary set not typical of the variety. There is also some regularization of the plural, with at least InSAfE having forms like *childrens* and *oxens*.

For demonstratives the use of a single form *this* for both singular and plural is reported for CFE and WhSAfE and *that* for both singular and plural is reported in WhSAfE and InSAfE.

There is some variation in the form of adjectives, especially in, but not limited to, the comparative forms of irregular ones. Thus *worst* for 'worse' in NigE and InSAfE; *more worse* [19], also in InSAfE; and *worser* in LibSE. There are occasional forms like *biggerer* and *betterer* in lower sociolects of CFE; *most easiest* in WhSAfE; *more wiser* and *more better* in LibSE. *Too* may be used in place of 'very' as an adjectival qualifier in BlSAfE, InSAfE and NigE. An adjective may stand alone for 'Adj + Noun' combinations in BlSAfE (*rurals* for 'rural people'); or it may be preceded by an article (*He's a British*) in InSAfE and NigE. In some varieties like BlSAfE and NigE the basic adjective form is used rather than the superlative, when the comparative marker *than* makes the relation clear (*He is one of the radical students that you can ever find*). In these varieties *than* may replace *more than* in similar comparisons (*He loves his car than his children*). As far as the P & Cs are concerned there are clearcut differences, with predicative adjectives of WAP and LibSE capable of functioning as verbs, insofar as they take preverbal particles. WAP is also strikingly different in its use of a form of the verb *pass* as comparative form (*A waka pas* 'I walked most').

Zero possessive forms (*the people cows*) occur in LibSE and WAP. In the latter *for* is an alternative to zero [18] (*knife for John*); this pattern also occurs in lower sociolects of BlSAfE.

7.   Pronouns

Pronouns admit of some variability in all the varieties. *Us* for 'we' occurs in StHE [13]; *we* as a variant of 'our' in LibSE; *me* for 'I' [13] and *im* for 'he/she/it' in WAP. Special second person plural pronouns [3] filling a gap in StE can be found regularly in LibSE and InSAfE; in the latter the form is *yall* or *you-all*, with genitive *yall's*. The equivalent form *youse* is used occasionally by some speakers of WhSAfE and CFE. This is matched in IndE in the plural interrogative pronoun *who-all*; in InSAfE the plural interrogative is the reduplicated form *who-who*, with the semantics of 'individuated' rather than 'group' plural. The associative plural form *them* is affixed to a definite human noun, prototypically a name or family relation (*Roy-them; my grand-father-them*) in LibSE and InSAfE. The related form *and them* occurs in all varieties of SAfE. The genitive form in InSAfE is *them's* or *and them's*. *Them* is also a demonstrative in LibSE (*them days*). *Dem* is the object pronoun in WAP (for 'them') and a low tone equivalent is the subject form. It does not appear to function as an associative plural marker in this variety. The fluctuation between *he* and *she* is reported for BlSAfE, NigE and GhE, motivated by the absence of sex as a grammaticalised category in the substrate languages. The use of singular *it* for plural *them* is reported for BlSAfE, InSAfE and MalE. The indefinite use of *they* for some unspecified person(s) understood as agents of a passive construction is common in NigE and CamE. The WAP pronoun system is more intricate than that of StE; with tonal distinctions being largely responsible for a three-way differentiation between an emphatic form on the one hand and a subject and an object form on the other. WAP also has bimorphemic *wh-* question words; these are not generally found in the other varieties reported on, except in InSAfE which has some such forms in the basilect.

Pro-drop, the non-use of pronouns in certain contexts, is reported to be much more widespread in IndE, InSAfE, SgE, MalE, ButlE and WAP than in StE. In WhSAfE it is common with object rather than subject pronouns. Similarly dummy *it* (as in *It's clear that…*) may be dropped in IndE and in certain sociolects of BlSAfE. In IndE dummy existential *there* (as in *There is food*) occurs in predicate position (*Food is there*).

In NigE possessives coupled with a demonstrative or adjective admit of variable order, e.g. *teacher our new* for 'our new teacher'.

8.   Adverbs, conjunctions and prepositions

In EAfE, at least, adverbial forms are frequently the same as adjectival ones, without *–ly* [42]. Adverbials like *already*, *now* and *only* are relatively free in their placement in EAfE, CFE and MalE compared to StE. *Already* is a perfective marker in CFE and MalE. In the latter a double use of *already* - one local, one standard - might occur: *She's already gone already*. In addition to occasional standard usage, *only* and *too* are focus markers in IndE and InSAfE.

Prepositions are underdifferentiated in all the (L1 and L2) varieties reported on. In WAP the form *for* is particularly wide in its functioning. In IndE, PakE and InSAfE prepositional phrases may be reduced by deleting the preposition and preposing them to the head noun in a compound construction: a *cold-touch* for 'a touch of cold'. With verbs of motion directional prepositions may be deleted (*She went town*) in StHE and InSAfE.

Amongst conjunctions InSAfE uses clause-final *but,* equivalent in semantics to 'though' (*It's nice and quiet here, but*). Elliptical *but* in CamE in a sentence like *I am going to eat but bread*, leaves unstated a whole proposition regarding the worse alternatives. Some varieties use double conjunctions like *suppose if* for 'if' (NigE, BlSAfE, InSAfE). Double conjunctions in another sense occur across clauses where StE uses a conjunction only once; this is the case in BlSAfE, InSAfE, IndE, NigE (e.g. *Although you are smart, but you are not appreciated*). BlSAfE has a construction that replaces '*some… other*' in parallel contrastive clauses by '*other… other*' (e.g. *Other people are nice, other people are not so nice*).

9.   Word order and discourse organisation

Major perturbations to English word order are reported in InSAfE, in matters of relative clauses, placement of conjunctions and kinship syntax (*George uncle* is respectful, *uncle George* is formal). Likewise CamE in its avoidance of movement rules for *wh*-questions [73] and the like is also a major disrupter of StE word-order conventions. In addition every variety studied is reported to have a notably higher degree of topicalisation phenomena, especially involving left dislocation, than StE. Although the amount of left dislocation in ordinary colloquial L1 English should not be underestimated, it does seem to be the case from the data and ensuing discussions that InSAfE, BlSAfE, IndE and all other varieties might well favour a 'pragmatic' word order more than a strict 'syntactic' SVO order. Inversion of subject and auxiliary in the Germanic 'V2' construction does not occur in PakE and MalE (*Never I have seen such waste*).

10.   Other miscellaneous constructions

The passive is rare in several varieties (e.g. WAP) and replaced by an active construction with indefinite focus in NigE and CamE. In SgE an innovation using the Malay verb *kena* for 'adversative' passives occurs. This remarkable use of an indigenous lexicon-grammatical item for a major grammatical function in an L2 English is worthy of future monitoring. An alternative in SgE is to use *give* as a passive marker.

The dative of advantage (*I'm gonna buy me a car*) survives in CFE, and a dative of obligation appears to be an innovation in CamE (*I am going me away* for 'I must go away').

Reduplication is widespread in almost all the varieties researched in Africa-Asia. Almost all varieties (NigE, BlSAfE, CFE, InSAfE, IndE, SgE, WAP, SAfE) reduplicate adverbs. Adjectives are reduplicated in many of these (NigE, InSAfE, IndE, SgE, WAP); verbs in InSAfE, IndE, SgE, WAP; and nouns in InSAfE, SgE and WAP. In WAP the reflexive *sef* may also be reduplicated.

Clefting of the sort *It's tiredness that tires me* is a striking characteristic of WAP but is not found elsewhere in Africa-Asia.

11.   Conclusion: from description to explanation

The morphology and syntax of new varieties of English has long been the Cinderella within SLA studies, contact linguistics, typology, sociolinguistics and other branches of linguistics. The chapters in this volume show, on the contrary, that many exciting challenges await the analyst in this area. In particular, the large number of similarities across L2 Englishes (cf. also Kortmann and Szmrecsanyi, 2004) needs to be explained more carefully than in the past, where the default assumption has often been interference from the substrates. Since there are over a thousand of these substrate languages in Africa-Asia, the explanation of interference has to be considerably fine-tuned. It is *prima facie* implausible, areal linguistics notwithstanding, that over a thousand languages should induce the very same (or very similar) influences. This would be tantamount to claiming that all the languages of Africa-Asia are the same in structure, united in their differences from English. Such an explanation may at a pinch apply for articles and invariant tags, but does not have a great deal of merit in other areas of grammar. We await more sophisticated work on the psycholinguistics of second-language processing of a cognitive system like English, on the precise role of the classroom, and on the contributions made by early providers of input outside the classroom. It is time Cinderella found her slipper.

Exercises and study questions

1. There appears to be a broad dichotomy in the Africa-Asia region between L1 English, L2 English and Pidgin/Creole English.
   a. Discuss in relation to patterns of negation.
   b. Discuss in relation to the copula.
   c. Discuss in relation to relative clause characteristics.
   d. Discuss in relation to the treatment of progressive be + -*ing*.

2. 'Articles are an area where New Englishes of Africa and Asia are united in their differences form standard English'. Discuss in relation to L2 varieties of Africa and Asia. Why do you think these differences exist?

3. Outline the neologisms in pronoun forms in the L2 varieties of English in Africa and Asia.

4. Review the use of double conjunctions across clauses in L2 varieties of English in Africa and Asia. How can this phenomenon be accounted for?

5. Review the two neologisms in passive marking in SgE. In what ways is the *kena* passive unique in New English studies?

Index of subjects

A

accent (for specific accents see also *Index of varieties and languages*) 2, 3, 24, 26, 38–40, 48–49, 51, 64, 73, 78, 87, 89–90, 116, 119, 125, 131, 137, 155, 166, 177, 190, 194, 197, 204, 240–241, 256, 267–268, 273, 293, 307, 382, 387, 486, 521
  dynamic accent 49
  tonal accent 49
  ("tonal") 49, 89, 315, 632
accommodation 108, 202, 332, 375, 376
acoustic 50–51, 109, 179, 181
acquisition 190, 219, 323, 501
acrolect 3, 25–26, 81, 83, 85, 88, 94, 99, 112, 118, 121, 124, 178–179, 181–186, 225, 252, 265, 281, 294–304, 307, 340, 385, 388, 503, 511, 544, 611
acronym 73
address 5, 55, 109, 304, 333, 373, 447, 465, 468, 484, 516, 528, 547, 595, 598, 604–605
  forms of 463, 484
adjective 49, 117, 281, 303, 330, 332, 336, 343, 352–353, 355, 360–362, 364, 368, 385, 390–391, 395, 403–404, 406, 410, 412, 414, 431, 435–436, 443, 447, 449, 456–457, 464, 474, 480, 486, 497, 513, 524, 560, 568, 580–581, 583, 589, 602, 631–632, 634
  comparative (see *comparison*)
  demonstrative (see also *demonstrative* and *pronoun, demonstrative*) 512, 525
  possessive 361–362, 364, 406, 436, 443, 568
  superlative (see *comparison*)
adposition 348–349, 351, 361, 365
  postposition 515

preposition 26, 60, 241, 289, 299, 324, 335, 365, 368, 376, 389, 417, 419, 444, 453, 456–457, 475–476, 510, 515, 527, 530–531, 543, 566, 580, 583–586, 628–629, 632–633
  preposition stranding 419
adverb 158, 336, 371, 376, 390, 392, 398, 431, 443–444, 448–449, 456–457, 459, 464, 474, 478, 524, 530, 538, 552, 554–555, 632, 634
  without –*ly* 632
adverbial clause (see *subordination*)
adverbials 342, 344–345, 347, 382, 390–391, 452, 457, 527, 552–553, 569, 585, 602, 632
affix 587
  prefix 130, 435, 453, 464
  suffix 110, 126, 229, 271, 316, 385–386, 390, 397–399, 405, 464, 524, 587, 594, 610, 622, 626
affixation 378–379, 587
affricate 57, 141, 267, 315
agreement 5, 68, 129, 331, 373, 479–482, 493, 496, 512, 524–526, 542, 556–568, 584, 593–595, 627
  agreement marker 481
  gender agreement 360
  invariant form(s) 327, 371, 457, 536–537, 542
  lack of 481
  number agreement 594
  subject-verb agreement 374, 380, 496, 512, 525, 570, 594
  third person singular -*s* absence 325, 331, 399, 496, 501, 512
ain't (see *negation*)
aktionsart
  durative 382
  ingressive 370
  stative (see *verb*)

allophone 42, 62, 85, 87, 180–182, 300
alveolar 57, 80, 85, 111, 125, 140–141, 157, 184, 195–196, 212, 229, 237–238, 252–254, 267, 286, 300, 452
    palato- 141
    post- 267
amplitude 255, 256
animate 456, 533, 612
anterior (see *tense*)
anymore 50, 507, 531
apocope 116
apposition 455, 468
    pronominal 376–377, 528
approximant 57–58, 62, 87, 99, 185, 196, 228, 238, 254, 315
archaism 226, 532
article
    definite 81, 254, 331, 358, 360, 374, 381, 385, 455, 512, 585
    indefinite 81, 254, 289, 331, 358, 374, 381, 385, 512–513, 526, 585, 596
    omission of 331, 566
    relative particle (see *subordination, relative clause*)
aspect 5, 35, 39, 41, 63, 100, 127, 142–143, 161, 178, 182, 185–186, 189, 232, 262, 264, 266, 278, 280, 323, 325, 331, 341–345, 351–353, 355, 370, 381–383, 392, 395–396, 398–399, 411–412, 416, 438, 441–442, 473, 488–489, 501–502, 519, 523, 533, 535–537, 546–547, 569, 573, 578–579, 593–594, 625–626
    completive 341–343, 345–346, 348, 352–353, 366, 370, 381–382, 396, 412, 503, 536–537, 542, 626, 627
        done 342-343, 345–346, 352–353, 382, 396, 536, 627
    continuous (see *aspect, progressive*)
    habitual 345, 381, 392, 399–400, 411, 441, 452, 489, 502–505, 520, 523, 536, 538, 542, 559, 569, 571, 579, 626–627
        be 502, 505, 520, 539, 627
    imperfective 398–400, 412

    incompletive 341, 344–345, 348, 381–383, 394, 626
    invariant *be* 399, 538, 571
    iterative 382, 390–392, 399, 523, 574
    perfective 396, 398, 473–474, 508, 518, 523, 559, 579, 594–595, 626, 632
    present perfect (see *present perfect*)
    progressive [continuous] 49, 122, 325–326, 353, 370, 381, 392, 399, 438, 442, 452, 473, 489, 502, 559, 569, 579, 594, 603, 615, 626, 635
aspiration 184, 195, 197, 198, 212, 255, 267, 299
    de- 212, 216, 218
    non- 198, 237, 267
    not pre-aspirated 239
assimilation 78– 80, 118, 123, 125, 184, 300, 521
auxiliary 326–327, 491, 506
    absence 442, 567
    contraction 523
    deletion 523
    modal (see *modal verb*)
    semi-auxiliary 409

B

back vowel (see *vowel*)
backing 4, 207, 208, 217, 219
basilect 25, 178, 265, 281, 294–304, 405, 504, 512, 632
BATH 42–43, 108, 118, 124, 169, 171, 191, 205, 207, 216, 218, 225, 235, 251, 267, 283, 296, 310–311
be
    habitual (see *aspect*)
    invariant (see *aspect*)
    be all 505
    be like 546
been
    anterior (see *tense*)
bilabial (see also *labial*) 80, 110, 140–141, 229, 254
bilingualism 29, 259, 262–263, 292, 323, 547, 564

borrowing 73, 135, 150, 398, 428, 586
breaking 207, 301, 423, 442
burr 484

C

Canadian Raising (see *raising*)
case 425, 454, 496
   accusative 425, 528
   dative 425, 528, 534, 634
      of advantage 425, 528, 534, 634
centering (see *glide*)
centering diphthong (see *diphthong*)
central *vowel* 76, 160, 170, 178–182, 250
centralization 192, 207, 216, 218
chain shift (see also Northern Cities Shift/
   Northern Cities Chain Shift) 174, 175,
   308
CHOICE 42, 44, 108–109, 120, 123, 169,
   171, 191, 194, 205, 209, 216, 218, 225,
   228, 236, 267, 283, 296, 298, 312
clause
   adverbial (see *subordination*)
   embedded (see *subordination*)
   if 343
   main [matrix] 327, 330, 343, 350–351,
      457, 490–491, 494, 506, 509, 511,
      516–517, 552, 584, 594, 615, 623
   relative (see *subordination*)
clear /l/ (see /l/)
cleft sentence [clefting] 384, 634
   predicate clefting 353
   reverse 87, 194, 465, 525, 622
clipping 219, 378, 430
cliticization 363
closing (see *diphthong*)
CLOTH 42–43, 108, 118–119, 124, 191,
   205, 207, 225, 235, 250–251, 267, 283,
   296, 297
coda 47, 84, 110–111, 113, 126, 185–186,
   268–269, 399, 405
   cluster 111, 399, 405
colloquial variety 259–260, 263, 265
colonial lag 589–590

commA 44, 108, 123–124, 191, 194, 205,
   211, 237, 250, 267, 283, 296–297, 314
comparison 447–448, 480, 497
   comparative (construction) 121–122,
      132, 185, 330, 332, 354, 357, 384,
      404, 418–419, 480, 495, 513, 602,
      631
   double comparative 404
   superlative 332, 354, 384, 404, 448,
      495, 602, 631
competition 67, 329
complement clause (see *subordination*)
complementary distribution (see *distribution*)
complementizer (see *subordination, complement clause*)
completive (see *aspect*)
compound 274, 303, 378, 430, 514, 519,
   588, 629, 633
concessive clause (see *subordination, adverbial clause*)
concord 324, 368, 525–526, 568, 612
   negative (see *negation, multiple*)
   subject-verb (see *agreement*)
conditioned 77, 80, 118, 123, 160
conditioning 118
consonant
   cluster 47–48, 52, 58–59, 88, 99, 126,
      130, 142, 146, 161, 178, 185–186,
      214, 216, 218, 229, 238, 239, 254,
      255, 285, 290, 301, 305
   deletion (see *deletion*)
   deletion/reduction/simplification/disso-
      lution etc. (see also *coda cluster*)
   devoicing (see *devoicing*)
   final 146, 162
   substitution 125, 287
constraints 3, 4, 6, 185, 269, 398
contact
   between dialects 230
   between language 30, 51, 202, 533
   contact clause (see *subordination, zero
      relative*)
   continuous (see *aspect, progressive*)

continuum 3, 25, 38, 40, 51, 73, 94, 99, 153, 160, 178–179, 225, 259, 265, 282, 317, 381, 606
  lectal 179, 259, 265–266, 282, 294, 296
  post-creole 606
contraction 108, 401, 507, 519, 523, 540
coordination 364–365, 377, 495
  coordinating conjunction 364
copula 343–344, 353–355, 381, 384, 399, 401–402, 409, 411, 414, 438, 491, 505, 507, 524, 537, 538, 570–571, 610, 627, 635
  (deletion) 491, 570–571, 627
  absence 409
corpus [corpora] 4, 27, 41, 90, 107, 110, 112, 150, 180–181, 186, 245, 397, 406, 412, 467–468, 469, 498, 513, 522, 536, 539, 566
covert prestige (see *prestige*)
creole (see *variety*)
creolization (see also *decreolization*) 625
CURE 42, 44, 108, 118, 122, 124, 169, 172, 191, 194, 205, 211, 216, 225, 236, 251, 266, 283, 285, 296, 298, 313

D

dark /l/ (see /l/)
dative (see *case*)
declarative 421, 422, 617
decreolization (see also *creolization*) 538
deletion
  consonant 146, 269, 270–272
  /h/ 196, 238
  jod/yod 88, 125–126, 317
  of auxiliary 523
demonstrative (see also *adjective, demonstrative* and *pronoun, demonstrative*) 334, 359–360, 373, 381, 406, 455, 481, 498, 509, 512, 525, 526, 631, 632
dental 85, 141, 157, 173, 184, 195, 212, 216, 218, 229, 238, 252, 267, 286

  inter- 110, 229, 267, 300, 315
  labio- 140–141, 228, 238, 254
dentalization 252
deontic [root] (see *modality*)
determiner 373, 455, 475, 481–482, 526, 612
devoicing 47, 86, 88, 110, 125–127, 145, 184, 211–212, 216–218, 229–230, 270–271, 286, 300, 317
  consonant 145–146, 269, 271
diagnostic 290, 611
dialect
  boundary 3, 28, 52, 86, 88, 125, 127, 239, 631
  contact (see *contact*)
  ethnic 2, 3, 38–39, 73, 77, 79, 94, 102, 106, 115, 151–152, 159, 161, 168, 175, 244, 259, 260–262, 278–279, 292, 295, 412–413, 428, 430, 460, 486, 607
  intensification 391, 552, 602
  leveling 26, 375
  rural 35, 70, 72–73, 136, 466
  social 2, 24, 35, 36, 40, 95, 153–154, 164–166, 188, 196, 265, 287, 324, 397, 431–432, 451, 477, 521, 547, 552, 564
  traditional 73, 94, 97, 151, 256, 263–264, 405, 426, 432, 443, 456, 460, 462–464, 484–485, 544, 624
  urban 37, 70, 72–73, 93, 96–97, 136–137, 189, 458, 467, 522
diffusion (geolinguistic) 4, 80, 198
diphthong 4, 41, 58–60, 65, 75, 81–82, 91, 109, 121–122, 124, 139, 143–145, 148, 160, 163, 171–172, 175, 179, 181–182, 186, 193–194, 198, 207–208, 210, 218–221, 226–228, 236, 242, 248–251, 257, 267–268, 284–285, 291, 296–298, 311, 318
  centering 59, 82, 144, 160, 181–182, 231
  closing 81, 160, 200, 219, 251, 446
diphthongization 81

directives 440, 464, 477, 627
  marker 531
  organization 488, 517, 633
  particle 465
dislocation 499, 633
  left 334, 339, 376–377, 393, 425–426, 498, 499, 516–517, 574, 618, 633
  right 574
dissimilation 196
distribution 4–5, 41, 72, 79, 81, 85, 87, 99, 138, 142, 145, 180, 184, 207–208, 246, 251–253, 255, 268, 371, 397, 400, 406, 451, 513, 558, 579, 586, 590
  complementary 116, 139
disyllabic 288, 601
divergence 376, 408
done
  completive (see *aspect*)
double comparative (see *comparison*)
double modal (see *modal verb*)
double object construction (see *object*)
double superlative (see *comparison*)
DRESS 42, 108, 116–117, 119, 123, 169–170, 191, 204, 206, 216, 218, 225–226, 234, 266, 283, 295, 297, 308–309
dropping 45, 111, 116, 162, 239, 317, 329, 442
  /h/ (see *deletion, /h/*)
  /j/ (see *deletion, jod/yod*)
  /r/ (see */r/, postvocalic*)
dual (see *pronoun* and *number*)
durative (see *aktionsart*)

E

ecology 27, 264, 620
elicitation 467
  tests 467
elision 88, 212, 214, 217–218
ellipsis 83, 336, 418, 472, 475, 515, 567, 611–612, 618
embedded clause (see *subordination*)
enclave 413
enclitic (see *cliticization*)

endonormativity 40, 324
epenthesis 146, 254, 301
epistemic (see *modality*)
ethnicity 28, 39, 78–79, 200, 413, 463, 482
ethnolect 519
exaptation [remorphologization]
existentials [presentationals] 343–344, 355–356, 384, 458, 528, 554–555, 571, 595, 618, 628, 632
expletives 424, 482, 546–547, 549, 559, 561, 576, 618

F

FACE 43, 108, 115, 117, 119–120, 122–124, 169, 171, 191, 193, 205, 207–209, 216–220, 225, 227, 236, 251, 266, 283, 295, 298, 311
fall(ing) (see *intonation*)
fall-rise (see *intonation*)
feature
  distinctive 79, 108
  grammatical 30, 294, 451, 578, 606
  interlanguage 219–220
  morphosyntactic 4, 486, 629
  pervasive 206
  phonetic 294–295, 304
  phonological 28–30, 74–75, 138, 178, 216, 253, 294, 472
  prosodic 5, 39, 138, 147, 240, 255, 272, 282
  segmental 204, 255
  suprasegmental 4, 28, 127, 161, 163, 179, 180, 185, 214, 287, 290
fieldwork 191, 467, 501, 535
filler 424, 531
first language (see *L1*)
flap(ping) 87, 99
FLEECE 42–43, 108, 115, 119, 124, 169–170, 191–192, 205, 207, 216–217, 225, 227, 234–235, 266, 283, 295, 297, 310
FOOT 42–43, 108, 118, 120, 124, 169–170, 191, 192, 205, 207, 208, 217–218,

225–226, 235, 251, 266, 283, 296–297, 309–310

FORCE 44, 108, 117, 119–120, 122, 124, 191, 193, 205, 210, 235, 266, 283, 295, 297–298

frequency 4, 78, 111, 124, 127, 138, 162, 180, 183, 211, 255–256, 289, 401, 405, 411, 451, 453, 455, 466, 627

fricative (see also *glottal fricative*) 45, 57, 85, 110–111, 125, 140–141, 157, 173, 185, 196, 213, 217, 219, 229, 238, 254, 267, 315, 319

front vowel raising (see *raising*)

fronted 86, 180, 192–193, 209, 312, 353–354, 356, 366, 455, 516, 598

fronting 4, 456, 460, 498, 499, 516, 517, 598

function
    grammatical 634

future, (see *tense*)

G

geminates 239

gender 360, 373, 435, 456–457, 482, 496, 498, 556, 568, 574
    agreement (see *agreement*)
    pronominal (see *pronoun, gendered*)

General American 293, 307

genitive (see *case, possessive*)

gerund 158, 330, 453–454, 569, 583
    gerund-participle 580–584

Glide Formation Rule 120

glide/gliding (see also *diphthong*) 45, 119–120, 122, 124, 126, 141, 144, 160, 174–175, 185, 193–194, 207–210, 214, 228, 236, 267, 284, 299–300, 312, 317
    off- 81, 171–172, 216, 218
    up- 109

glottal 45, 57, 83–84, 111, 141, 174, 185, 191, 196, 214, 225, 228–229, 238, 267, 271–272, 287, 299, 309
    fricative 141, 238
    onset 214

reinforcement 83
    stop 45, 84, 111, 174, 229, 271–272, 287, 299
    word-initial 84, 169, 197, 214, 228, 239, 300

glottalization 84, 98, 229, 269, 271–272, 275, 287

GOAL 74, 120, 124, 205, 251

GOAT 43, 108, 120, 124, 169, 172, 191, 193, 205, 207–208, 216–220, 225, 227, 236, 251, 266, 283, 295, 298, 312

GOOSE 42–43, 108, 120, 124, 169, 171, 191, 192, 205, 208, 217–218, 225, 227, 235, 266, 283, 296–297, 310

greeting 333, 397, 404, 423, 482, 530

H

/h/ deletion (see *deletion*)

habitual (see *aspect*)

happY 44, 74, 98, 108, 123–124, 161, 179, 182, 191, 194, 205, 211, 216, 218, 234, 237, 267, 283, 296, 313

hiatus 173, 208–210, 214, 217

historical present 502

homophony 75, 159, 398, 435

horsES 44, 74, 98, 116, 161, 179, 182, 191, 194, 205, 211, 234, 237, 250, 267, 314

hybridized English 100

I

iconicity 373, 380

identity 2, 36, 94, 158, 200, 244, 261–262, 275, 293, 333, 341, 355, 397, 404, 413, 416, 519, 547, 598

ideophone 366

idiom 324, 335, 337–338, 417, 465–466, 496, 528, 565, 630

imperative 446, 568, 572, 575

imperfective (see *aspect*)

implicational 451
    hierarchy 451

inanimate 533, 599, 612
indicative (see *mood*)
indigenization 40, 337, 416, 619–620
individuation 613
infinitive 158, 326, 329, 348, 368, 383, 453–454, 456, 474, 486, 629
ingressive (see *aktionsart*)
innovation 29–31, 104, 174, 330, 332, 337, 409, 417, 419, 475, 496, 501, 555, 579, 626, 633–634
interdental (see *dental*)
interference 26, 94, 98, 145, 157, 160, 177, 294, 323–324, 453, 456, 634
interjection 379, 445, 471, 563
interrogative 325, 364–366, 445, 459, 516, 549, 599, 615–617, 632
direct question 458, 461, 491, 550, 573, 585
indirect question (see *subordination, embedded clause*)
tag (see *tag*)
WH-question 584–585, 590, 595, 615
yes/no question 327–328, 339, 423, 458, 471, 492, 500, 506, 517, 599, 630
intonation 5, 39, 50–51, 63–65, 88, 161, 177–178, 215, 232, 240–242, 275, 282, 289, 304, 317–319, 421, 459–460, 477, 481–482, 510, 518, 572, 606
falling 241, 458
fall-rise 51, 289
rise-fall 51, 289, 518
rising 215, 241, 304, 317, 445, 477, 532, 617
invariant form 327, 371, 457, 536–537, 542
inversion 365, 372, 430, 445, 506, 549–551, 584–585, 590, 615, 617, 623, 630, 633
subject-verb [subject-auxiliary] 374, 380, 496, 506, 512, 525, 546, 550, 570, 584–585, 594, 615, 617, 623, 630
IPA 197
invariant (see *tag*)

isochrony 50
isogloss 631

J

jod/yod 125, 126
dropping (see *deletion, jod/yod*)

K

KIT (see also *dropping, final KIT*) 42–43, 108, 115–116, 123, 169, 191, 204, 206, 216, 218, 225, 230, 233–234, 266, 283, 295, 297, 309–310
split (see also *split*) 116, 175, 191, 204, 206, 216, 218, 225, 230
koiné 544

L

/l/
clear/palatal/light 174, 196, 238, 353
dark/velarised 213, 218, 238
vocalization (see also *coda /l/*) 87
L1 24–25, 72–74, 76–77, 79, 85–86, 89, 98, 132, 164–165, 167–168, 170, 174, 188–190, 192, 203–204, 206–207, 209–210, 212–213, 215–217, 220, 239, 252, 255, 280, 285, 307, 319, 451, 488, 498, 501, 521, 564, 624–627, 630–631, 633, 635
L2 23–25, 28–29, 41, 72, 74, 168, 173, 177, 188, 202–204, 206–207, 211, 213, 220, 295, 299, 307, 309–310, 318–319, 329, 368, 488, 501, 521, 624–630, 633, 634–635
labial 57, 79, 180, 267
labiodental (see *dental*)
language
acquisition 25–26, 157–158, 198
change 219–220
contact (see *contact*)
shift 24, 30, 189, 219, 624
youth (see *youth*)

lateral (see also /l/ *vocalization*) 57–58, 62, 110, 180, 254, 269, 299–300

lax 109, 178–180, 182, 227, 250–251, 268

left dislocation (see *dislocation*)

lengthening 180, 186, 212, 288

lenis 211

lettER 44, 108, 123, 191, 194, 205, 211, 218, 237, 250, 267, 283, 296, 314

levelling 26, 165, 375

lexical set 4–5, 52, 108, 115, 118, 123–124, 131, 169, 204–205, 233–234, 248, 266–267, 283, 285, 295–296, 308

lexicon 23, 48, 74, 100, 161, 190, 294, 378, 428, 451, 461–462, 483, 529, 619

lexifier 65, 99, 340, 349

liaison 173, 272, 280, 290

light /l/ (see /l/)

lingua franca 23–24, 35, 72, 94–95, 137, 150–154, 167, 189, 201, 260–261, 292, 428

linking 85, 87, 125, 173, 196, 213, 272, 290, 316, 455

liquid 79, 110, 141, 185, 238, 267, 299–300

loan word 46, 464

locatives 353

long (see also *vowel, length*)

half- 172

vowel 160, 172, 181, 197, 283, 297

LOT 42–43, 108, 117, 119, 122–124, 169–170, 191–193, 204, 206–207, 218, 225–226, 233–234, 237, 250, 266, 283, 295, 308–310

lowering 77, 89, 186, 193, 206, 208

M

merger 77, 143, 159, 220, 308

mesolect 25–26, 85, 94, 99, 118, 161, 178, 179–186, 191, 197–198, 252, 265, 281, 294–304, 307, 340, 488, 503, 507, 511, 618, 621, 627

metathesis 47, 269, 272, 276

minimal pair 63, 75, 139, 159, 194, 197–198

modal verb 326, 343, 349, 365, 368, 370, 382, 364, 477, 501, 511, 539, 540, 552–553, 599, 614, 626–627

quasi-modal 349

modality 5, 325–326, 341, 343, 347–348, 352–353, 355, 366, 452, 477, 488, 490, 501, 503, 519, 523, 535, 539, 545, 625–626

deontic [root] 28, 36, 82, 202, 244, 288, 383, 422, 426, 463, 522, 539, 545, 549, 564, 625

epistemic 552

monophthongization 4, 75, 172, 194, 216, 251, 285, 319

mood 381–383, 401, 604–605

indicative 569, 571

irrealis 341, 345–348, 366, 381–383, 452, 490–491, 504, 536, 626–627

realis 341, 346–347, 366

subjunctive 341

mora 52

morphology

inflectional 127, 331, 341, 452, 454, 456–567, 593

motion verb (see *verb*)

MOUTH 44, 108, 120, 123, 169, 171, 191, 194, 205, 208–210, 216–220, 225, 228, 236, 267, 283, 296, 298, 312

multilingualism 189, 471

N

nasal 45, 57–59, 61–62, 65, 80, 83–84, 88, 109–111, 119, 126, 130, 140, 142, 159, 173, 185, 192, 195, 212, 214, 226, 237, 267, 269–270, 293, 299, 300, 316

nasalization 45, 61–62, 83–84, 111, 214

national language 151, 154, 247, 261, 279, 292, 428, 448

nativization 244, 280

NEAR 42, 44, 108–109, 117, 121–124, 169, 172, 191, 194, 205, 210, 216, 225, 228, 236, 251, 266, 283, 295, 298, 313 negation 5, 351–352, 371, 402–403, 479, 492, 500, 507, 529, 540–541, 572, 576, 628, 635

ain't 519, 402, 409–411, 540, 628

double (see also *negation, multiple*) 58–59, 90, 160, 180, 325, 328, 330, 352, 403–404, 495, 529, 541, 571, 572, 627–628, 632–633, 635

multiple [negative concord] 352, 403, 628

quantifier 458, 513, 597

negative concord (see *negation, multiple*)

neutralization 178, 184, 268

non-reduction (see *vowels, unreduced/ nonreduced*)

NORTH 42, 44, 108, 122, 124, 191, 193, 205, 210, 216–217, 227, 235, 266, 283, 295, 298

Northern Subject Rule (see *agreement*]

noun

count 118, 323, 332, 368, 375–376, 413, 451, 454, 497, 593, 596–597, 613

mass 39, 137, 154, 293–295, 332, 368, 376, 455, 613

noun phrase 5, 331, 358, 360, 374, 376–377, 384, 389, 392, 395, 405, 434, 437, 454, 456, 496, 512, 514, 526, 543, 553–554, 556, 560, 570, 574, 581, 593, 596, 611, 630

nucleus 49, 58, 79, 109, 184, 207, 269, 289, 311

number

absence of 593

agreement (see *agreement*)

associative plural 405, 513–514, 526, 632

distinction 373, 612, 624–626

plural form 332–333, 388, 405

plural noun 373, 385–386, 471, 512–513, 525

plural pronoun 333, 352, 359, 498, 574, 543, 631

third person plural 352, 359, 364, 386, 440

plural (marking) 111, 359–360, 379, 386, 399, 405, 434, 454, 596–597, 632

NURSE 42–43, 52, 108–109, 118, 122, 124, 169–170, 191–192, 194, 205, 207, 216–217, 219, 225, 227, 235, 250, 267, 283, 296–298, 310, 318

O

object

direct 338, 351, 420, 527, 583, 621

indirect 357, 527, 583

prepositional 581–582

obstruent 48, 84, 86, 110–111, 113, 127, 130, 180, 185, 196, 211, 213, 216, 218, 269–270, 317, 374

offglide (see *glide/gliding*)

onset (see also *glottal onset*) 47, 110, 126, 171–172, 180, 185, 207–208, 216, 218, 220, 227, 268

cluster 110, 185

oral 59, 111, 158, 203, 214, 247, 279, 456, 460, 467, 522, 533

orthography 46, 79–80, 153, 255, 290

P

palatal 140–141, 162, 170, 184, 267

/l/ (see /l/)

pre-, 141

palatalization 126–127

PALM 42–43, 108, 119, 124, 191, 193, 205, 207, 216, 218, 225, 227, 235, 237, 266, 283, 295, 297

participle 80, 474, 510, 569, 580, 582–583, 584

gerund-participle 580–584

past 473–474, 509

present 473, 564, 567, 569, 571

particle 266, 289, 362, 366, 368–369, 392–394, 437, 446, 453, 458, 464–465, 475, 516, 529, 531, 537, 547, 554, 593, 604–605, 607–608, 610, 618, 626, 631 partitive 376, 492, 499

passive 31, 95, 334, 336, 352, 424, 440, 510, 536, 593, 600–601, 608, 626–627, 632–633, 635

past tense (see *tense*)

perfect

    future 326, 348

    past [pluperfect] 342, 369, 398, 441, 449, 452, 490, 569, 626

    present (see *present perfect*)

perfective (see *aspect*)

phoneme 5, 39, 45, 56, 76, 80, 86–87, 98, 139–141, 159, 161, 173, 180–185, 211, 220, 268, 296–300

phonotactic 5, 161, 220, 268, 289, 290

pidgin (see *variety*)

pitch 49, 51–52, 62–65, 89, 147–148, 186, 196, 215, 255–256, 272–273, 275, 289, 318, 604, 607

plosive 57, 79, 88, 173, 184–185, 212, 267

plural (see *number*)

polysyllabic 83, 89, 147, 194, 215, 240, 288, 297, 301

post-creole 606

postposition (see *adposition*)

postvocalic 173, 193, 235, 238, 252, 313–314

pragmatics 26, 339, 471, 499, 516, 555, 578

prefix (see *affix*)

preposition (see *adposition*)

present perfect 369, 398, 402, 441, 474, 626

presentationals (see *existentials*)

prestige 2, 38–39, 95, 97, 155, 189, 193–194, 206, 260, 307, 324, 519, 545

    covert 97, 519

preverbal marker 382

PRICE 42–43, 108–109, 120, 124, 169, 171, 191, 193, 205, 209–210, 216–220, 225, 227, 230, 236, 267, 283, 296, 298, 311

pro-drop 547, 549, 556–559, 561, 593, 598, 608, 632

progressive (see *aspect*)

pronominal system (see *pronoun*)

pronoun

    copying (see *subordination, relative clause*)

    demonstrative (see also *demonstrative* and *adjective, demonstrative*) 334, 455, 498, 525–526

    gendered 456, 496, 498, 568, 574

    generic 333, 352

    indefinite 333, 371

    interrogative 364, 599, 632

    personal 362–363, 368, 387, 435, 437, 440, 456, 460, 568, 570

    possessive 334, 362, 381, 388, 436, 456, 498

    pronominal gender (see *pronoun, gendered*)

    pronominal system 5, 388, 498, 514, 528, 533

    reflexive 333, 364, 381, 437, 460, 534, 560, 634

    relative (see *subordination, relative clause*)

    resumptive [shadow] 328–329, 339, 372, 386, 425–426, 493, 629

    second person plural 363, 388, 498, 514, 543, 631

prosody 48, 112–113

Q

quantitative studies 610

    tag question (see *tag*)

question (see *interrogative*)

questionnaire 121, 535, 578

quotative 89

R

/r/ (see also *rhoticity*)

    intrusive 87, 159, 173, 196, 272, 290

    linking 85, 87, 125, 173, 196, 213, 272, 290, 316, 455

postvocalic 173, 193, 235, 238, 252, 313–314
raising 109, 175, 228
  Canadian Raising 207–211, 217, 219, 221
Received Pronunciation [RP] 75–90, 116–117, 119, 122–127, 130–131, 160–165, 170–172, 174, 192–195, 197, 198, 204, 206, 212, 215, 226–227, 229, 231–232, 236, 238–241, 242, 248–257, 266–275, 284–285, 287–290, 307, 317–318, 472
  Mainstream 145, 204, 232
redundancy 464, 531
reduplication 266, 336, 378, 385–386, 390–392, 394, 431, 439, 478, 560, 576, 593, 601–603, 606, 634
referent 333, 373, 526, 619–621
  animate 456, 533, 612
  inanimate 533, 599, 612
regularization 325, 332, 459, 631
relative clause (see *subordination, relative clause*)
relative particle (see *subordination, relative clause*)
relativizer (see *subordination, relative clause*)
relexification 134
resonant 213
restructuring 117, 121, 124, 131, 142–143, 145, 535, 544, 626
retraction 191, 206
retroflex 87, 173, 195, 252, 299–300, 316
rhotic(ity) 87, 185, 211, 250, 252, 298, 310, 316
  non- 45, 81, 87, 159, 173, 196, 213, 227, 237, 310, 505, 523
rhythm 5, 39, 50–51, 65, 124, 150, 161–163, 186, 197, 241, 255–256, 272–273, 288, 301
right dislocation (see dislocation)
rise-fall (see *intonation*)
rising (see *intonation*)
rounding 170, 192–193, 207–208, 227
rural 35, 70, 72–73, 122, 126, 136, 166, 369, 375, 466, 497, 631

S
schwa 81, 88, 124, 132, 178, 180, 182, 192, 194–195, 206, 228, 250, 254, 269, 284, 290, 297, 308, 317–318
second language (see *L2*)
segmental features 204, 255
selection 3, 5, 25, 231, 337, 446, 453, 466, 569
semilingualism 292
shortening 193, 197, 210, 283, 601
simple past (see *tense, past*)
simplification 4, 23, 30, 47, 60, 75, 111, 126, 146, 157, 178, 185, 229, 281, 417, 423, 451, 454, 456–457, 459, 505, 567, 568, 615
slang 94, 484
smoothing 81
sociolect 287, 295, 326, 329, 332, 335–336, 495–496, 498, 501, 503–504, 507, 513–514, 518, 524, 528, 531–532
sonorant 239
speaker
  educated 23, 48, 85, 88, 89, 120, 158, 178, 231, 290, 325, 331–332, 334, 374
  female 192
  male 180
  middle-class 191, 194, 204, 212–213, 215
  working-class 213
speech
  casual 148, 503–504, 585
  connected 125, 148, 229, 250, 254, 289–290, 317
  direct 459, 511, 575
  indirect [reported] 459, 575
  informal 288–289, 501, 506, 513, 522, 611
  rapid 297
  spontaneous 49, 51, 185, 297, 340, 548–549
spelling pronunciation 46, 52, 79–81, 84, 87–88, 119, 158, 161, 238, 254
split 116, 118, 122–123, 145, 162, 169–170, 226–227, 230, 300, 309

CURE 42, 44, 108, 118, 122, 124, 169, 172, 191, 194, 205, 211, 216, 225, 236, 251, 266, 283, 285, 296, 298, 313

DRESS 42, 108, 116–117, 119, 123, 169–170, 191, 204, 206, 216, 218, 225–226, 234, 266, 283, 295, 297, 308–309

KIT 42–43, 108, 115–116, 123, 169, 191, 204, 206, 216, 218, 225, 230, 233–234, 266, 283, 295, 297, 309–310

NURSE 42–43, 52, 108–109, 118, 122, 124, 169–170, 191–192, 194, 205, 207, 216–217, 219, 225, 227, 235, 250, 267, 283, 296–298, 310, 318

PRICE 42–43, 108–109, 120, 124, 169, 171, 191, 193, 205, 209–210, 216–220, 225, 227, 230, 236, 267, 283, 296, 298, 311

TRAP 42, 77, 108, 117–119, 122–123, 169–170, 191–192, 204, 206, 225–226, 234, 266, 283, 295, 297, 308–309

SQUARE 42, 44, 108–109, 121, 124, 169, 172, 191, 194, 205, 210, 216, 225, 228, 236, 251, 266, 283, 295, 298, 312, 318

standard (see *variety*)

standardization 153

START 42, 44, 108, 119, 122, 124, 191, 193, 205, 210, 225, 227, 235, 266, 283, 295, 298

stop (see *plosive, glottal stop*)

stress 5, 28, 44, 48–52, 63–65, 80, 89, 110, 126–127, 129–130, 132, 138, 142, 144, 147–148, 160–163, 169, 172–173, 178, 180, 185–186, 197, 207–210, 214–215, 228–229, 234, 240–242, 250, 254–256, 262, 266, 272–274, 276, 282, 287–289, 297, 299, 301–304, 317–319, 331, 409, 437, 453, 455, 460, 476, 512, 523, 534, 536, 545, 555, 561, 607, 627

STRUT 42, 108, 117, 124, 169–170, 191–192, 204, 207, 225–226, 234, 266, 283, 295, 297, 308–309

subject
dummy 356, 424, 426, 494, 543, 545, 559–560, 572–573, 576, 627, 632
-verb concord (see *agreement*)

subjunctive (see *mood*)

subordination 5, 330, 372, 495, 629
adverbial clause 421
complementizer 89, 341, 349, 357, 372, 381, 407, 524
of comparison 404
of concession 419
of condition 512, 575
complement clause 5, 158, 329, 372, 395, 407, 453, 494, 511, 524, 541, 578–583, 629
embedded clause 420, 517, 550
embedded question 426, 491, 506, 546, 549, 550–551, 573, 585, 630
indirect question 426, 491, 506, 549, 550, 573, 585, 630
relative clause 5, 31, 328–329, 339, 350–351, 360, 372, 386–388, 395, 407, 419, 425–426, 434, 455–456, 493, 499, 508, 510, 541, 580, 589, 593, 597, 629, 633, 635
non-restrictive [non-defining] 329, 339, 419
pronoun copying 423, 456
relative particle
that 372, 407, 597, 629
what 329, 364, 407, 508, 541, 629
relative pronoun 52, 329, 341, 350–351, 364, 372, 407, 435–436, 449, 454, 508–510, 597, 629
restrictive 52, 107, 189, 209, 217, 269, 407, 413, 455, 464, 547

subphonemic level 159

substrate 2, 26, 31, 65, 99, 157, 190, 219, 271, 282, 287, 291, 295, 305, 324, 340–344, 346–347, 352–353, 355–360, 365–366, 501, 512, 514–515, 517, 560, 610, 619, 632, 634

suffix (see *affix*)

superlative (see *comparison*)

superstrate 2, 3, 63, 265, 349, 354, 624
supraphonemic level 159
suprasegmental 4, 28, 127, 161, 163, 17–180, 185, 214, 287, 290
svarabhakti 239
syllabic 47, 58, 87, 229, 239, 269, 290, 301, 317, 398, 405
/l/, 87, 269
consonant 47, 239, 301, 317
nasal 58, 290
syllable structure 47, 51, 58, 100, 111, 161, 185, 268, 290, 301
syllable timing 256, 317–318
syncope 116

T

tag 30, 51, 241–242, 304, 327–328, 423, 446, 457–458, 482, 486, 529, 546, 549, 552–553, 573, 584, 594–595, 599, 608, 617, 630
interrogative 617
invariant 30, 327, 584, 594–595, 599, 630, 634
tag question 30, 51, 241–242, 304, 364, 366, 423, 446, 457, 529, 546, 549, 552, 584, 594, 608
tap 117, 213, 271, 300, 621
tense
anterior 342, 347, 382
anterior *been* 342–347, 382, 626
future 147, 326, 347, 442, 488, 501, 539, 569, 625
past 116, 271, 325, 341–343, 368, 382, 396, 398, 399, 449, 452, 473–474, 490, 502, 504, 507, 518, 523–524, 535–537, 569–570, 579, 614, 625–626
perfect (see *perfect*)
present 325, 368, 439, 443, 452, 473, 478, 481, 488, 490, 501–502, 518, 536–537, 542, 569
historical present 502
sequence of tenses 452
tense marker 442, 538

tensing 116–117, 119, 121, 125
TH 125, 212
stopping 212, 217–218
THOUGHT 42–43, 108, 117, 119, 122, 124, 169, 171, 191, 193, 205, 208, 216–217, 225, 227, 235, 237, 266, 283, 295, 297, 310
time reference 379
tone 28, 49–52, 62–65, 81, 89, 129, 138, 147–148, 186, 238, 317–318, 362–364, 382, 387, 423, 529, 632
lexical 63
topicalization 376–377, 380–381, 388, 393, 460, 498, 510, 516–518, 547, 549, 553–554, 598, 633
transitivity (see *verb*)
TRAP 42, 77, 108, 117–119, 122–123, 169–170, 191–192, 204, 206, 225–226, 234, 266, 283, 295, 297, 308–309
trill 99, 141, 193, 213
triphthong 144, 236

U

unaspirated (see *aspiration*)
of New Englishes 29, 154
vernacular 24, 96, 102, 104, 107, 152, 174, 189, 192–193, 195, 197, 203–204, 217, 279, 340, 395, 397, 405, 412, 438, 470, 528, 544, 546, 550–555, 557–560, 576, 624
unreleased 211, 271, 272
unrounding 192, 226
upgliding (see *gliding*)
urban 37, 70, 72–73, 93, 96–97, 136–137, 189, 458, 467, 522
uvular 173, 213

V

variability 5, 41, 52, 78, 82–83, 86–87, 180, 182, 197, 207–208, 211, 331, 496–498, 518, 559, 626, 631
variant 4, 26, 40, 76, 81, 83, 85–86, 97, 180, 182–183, 185, 192–195, 209–210,

213, 219, 227, 236–238, 247, 251, 309–
311, 313–315, 318, 324, 401, 494, 496,
519, 522, 543, 573, 580, 616, 629–631
variation 2, 4, 6–7, 40, 49, 51, 63, 74, 77,
80–84, 109, 115–116, 120, 137–138,
153–154, 157, 160, 164, 168–170, 182,
184–185, 190–191, 195, 197, 212–213,
224, 226–227, 231–232, 234–236, 238,
242, 246, 248–253, 255–257, 259, 265,
275, 282, 287, 290–291, 296–297, 307,
310, 313, 335, 373, 375, 388, 402, 465,
488, 494, 508, 518–519, 521, 546, 559,
560, 578–579, 595, 610, 615, 618, 620,
625, 627–631
  cross-dialectal 4
  cross-linguistic 4
  free 42, 78, 99, 147, 296–298, 300, 309,
    310, 371, 373
  morphosyntactic 3
  patterns of 1, 4, 5, 48–49, 52, 124, 127–
    130, 150, 161, 163, 195, 197–198,
    215, 232, 240–242, 255, 273, 288–
    289, 303–304, 319, 326, 368, 416–
    417, 453, 460–461, 468, 480, 510,
    547, 607, 635
  syntactic 190, 546, 618, 624
variety (see also *Index of varieties and
  languages*)
  colloquial 259–260, 263, 265, 334, 606
  contact 2, 3, 190, 260
  creole 23, 25, 55, 103, 201, 224, 340,
    381–382, 404, 540, 624, 635
    continuum 103
    English-based 29
  L1 132
  L2 41, 203, 627
  non-standard (see also *vernacular*) 2,
    27, 95, 628
  pidgin 576
  regional 29, 55, 232, 242, 535
  standard 2, 39, 98, 113, 225, 229, 263–
    264, 266, 294, 324, 546, 593–594,
    606, 611

vernacular (see also *non-standard*) 546,
  553, 560
velar 45, 57, 80, 110, 140–141, 162, 170,
  173, 191, 206, 225, 237, 267, 309, 315
velarization (see also */l/ velarized*) 185
verb
  intransitive 336, 369
  irregular 399, 452
  modal (see *modal verb*)
  motion 365
  regularization of verbal paradigm 325
  serial verb 356, 358, 366, 527–628
  stative 325, 341–342, 344, 369, 382,
    489, 502, 559, 579, 615
  transitive 368–369, 576, 581
verb form 240–241, 325, 328, 331, 335–
  336, 368, 441, 452, 457, 627
  invariant 536–539, 571
verb phrase 30, 345, 368, 382, 392, 395–
  396, 403, 445, 452, 472, 492, 528, 568,
  572, 593, 595, 613, 615
vernacular universals (see *universals*)
vocalization (see also */l/, /r/*) 87
voicing 46, 86, 89, 125–126, 184, 254,
  286, 300
  voiced 79, 85, 86, 109–110, 140–141,
    169, 172–173, 184–185, 196–197,
    212, 237, 238, 254–255, 269, 270,
    312, 315
  voiceless 85, 89, 110–111, 140–141,
    145, 169, 172–173, 184–185, 197,
    211–212, 237–239, 254–255, 267–
    270, 299, 312
vowel
  back 76, 80, 84–85, 139, 161, 185, 192–
    193, 198, 226, 235, 238, 250–251,
    283
  central 76, 160, 170, 178–180, 181,
    182, 250
  epenthetic 47, 88, 246, 301
  front 76, 80, 84–86, 109, 139, 160–161,
    173–175, 180, 183, 216, 218, 221,
    228, 251, 308

harmony 38, 82–83, 91, 162, 301
length (see also *long*) 38, 41, 51, 75, 89, 160, 180–181, 268, 274, 283, 297, 305, 310
reduction 51, 88, 112, 115, 121–125, 131, 254–255, 284, 301, 317
retraction 206, 216, 218
unreduced/nonreduced 144, 284
untensed 239

W

word order 5, 26, 334, 365–366, 372, 406, 419, 423, 459, 498, 514, 527, 572–573, 576, 584, 597–598, 633

word-final 45, 47, 59, 81, 84–85, 120, 162, 173, 208–213, 220, 239, 267, 269, 270, 272, 300, 525
word-initial 84, 169, 197, 214, 239, 300

Y

yod (see *jod*)
youth 138, 622
    culture 72, 78, 137, 200, 224, 323, 463, 547, 553

Z

zero marker 345

Index of varieties and languages

A

African American Vernacular English [AAVE, African American English, AAE] 28, 30, 104, 111–112, 230, 307, 395, 401–403, 408–412

African English 29–30, 77, 150, 157, 161, 163, 178, 281, 328, 425, 462, 464–466

African Nova Scotian English [Nova Scotian] 228

Afrikaans 28, 30, 164, 166–168, 170, 172–174, 190, 201–204, 206, 213–214, 216–217, 219, 472–476, 478–486, 499, 521–522, 524, 526–533, 544

Afrikaans English [AfkE] 164, 166, 168, 170, 172–173, 204, 206, 213, 216, 473–474, 476, 480–483

Akan (see also *Igbo, Mandankwe*) 69–70, 72–73, 75–77, 82, 84–87, 89, 91, 93, 95, 98–99, 370, 376, 378–379, 385–386

American English [AmE] 38, 46, 48, 87, 109, 112, 162, 181, 191–192, 256, 293–294, 299, 323, 338, 483, 546, 551, 578, 589–590

Anglo-Indian (see *Indian English*)

Anglo-Saxon 106

Anglo-Welsh (see *Welsh English*)

Arabic 35, 152, 189, 202–203, 530

Australian English [AusE] 175

B

Baba Malay 260

Bahamian Creole [BahC] 340

Bahasa Malaysia 278–280, 283, 290, 610, 622

Bakweri 429

Balochi 246, 247

Bantu (see also *Twi*) 105, 150, 159–160, 177, 184–186, 200, 334, 402, 431, 454, 484, 492, 498

Bazaar Malay 260

Bengali 188, 255, 279, 315, 563

Bhojpuri 188, 501, 509

Black South African English [BlSAfE] 29–30, 163, 168, 177–186, 308–317, 328, 471, 488–490, 492–495, 498–500, 626–634

British English [BrE] 2, 26, 29–30, 38–41, 47, 49, 51–52, 73, 75, 81, 83–85, 87–90, 98–99, 123, 162–163, 174, 193, 202, 215, 217–218, 220, 230, 237, 239, 265, 281, 305, 323, 326, 338, 368, 370–371, 373–377, 416–418, 420–422, 424, 426, 453, 457, 479, 482, 535–536, 546, 579–581, 586, 590, 613, 615, 617–620, 624, 627, 630

Butler English (India) [ButlE] 29–30, 563–576, 624, 626–632

C

Cameroon English [CamE] 28, 30, 115–132, 142, 186, 308–317, 416–427, 629–630, 632–634

Cameroon Pidgin [CamP, Cameroon Pidgin English, Kamtok] 28, 115, 118, 133–149, 384, 386, 428–450

Canadian English [CanE] 294

Cantonese 260, 278

Cape Flats English [CFE] 26, 29–30, 168, 200, 202, 204–217, 219–221, 307–317, 521–522, 528, 530–534, 624–628, 630–632, 634

Caribbean English [CarE] 215, 230

Cockney 40

Colloquial Singapore(an) English [Coll-SgE] 259–260, 263, 266–275, 593–604, 606–607
Creole (see also *Pidgin and Creole*) 25, 55, 201, 340, 382, 540

D

Dravidian languages 189–190, 244, 570
Duala 429
Dutch 133–134, 164–167, 200–201, 428, 430, 480, 485, 544

E

Early Modern English [EModE] 473, 544
East African English [EAfE] 30, 150–163, 451, 453–459, 461, 467–471, 486, 625–630, 632
Edoid 55, 63
Emai 35
English as Foreign Language [EFL] 23–24, 27
English as Native language [ENL] 23, 28
English as Second Language [ESL] 23–28, 30, 325, 563–564
English in Singapore and Malaysia [ESM], 282
European English 157, 467

F

Fante 72, 77–78, 84
First Language [L1] variety 132
French 35, 37, 51, 67 135–138, 170, 428–430
Fula 429
Fulfulde 428

G

Ga 72, 76, 79, 94, 99, 379
General American 293, 307
German 49, 389, 428, 430

Germanic 162, 430, 453–464, 585, 633
Ghanaian English [GhE] 26, 28–29, 67–92, 97–100, 163, 308–318, 340, 368–380, 622, 626, 628–630, 632
Ghanaian Pidgin English [GhPE, Kru English] 30, 90, 93–101, 381–394
Ghotuo 63
Gujarati 155, 189–190, 279, 517
Gullah 228, 340, 411–412
Gur 70, 72, 86–87, 99

H

Hausa 28, 35–36, 38, 41–45, 47, 52, 56, 72, 75, 78–79, 94-95, 98–99, 327, 337–379
Hausa English 38, 41–45, 47, 78
Hebrew 202–203
Hindi 24, 189, 238, 244, 255–256, 548, 560, 570, 574
Hokkien 260, 278, 610

I

Iban 278–279
Igbo (see also *Akan, Mandankwe*) 28, 35, 42, 46, 52, 55–56, 327, 337, 429
Igbo English 38, 40–45
Indian English [AngloIndian, IndE] 27, 29, 30–31, 189–190, 192, 195–196, 198, 231–243, 256–257, 276, 307, 309–317, 520, 546–562, 573, 576, 590, 608, 624–634
Indian South African English [InSAfE] 24, 29–30, 188–198, 307, 309–317, 491, 501, 520, 624–634
Irish English [IrE] 24, 202, 460
Italian 51, 556–558

J

Jamaican Creole [JamC] (see also *Patwa*) 340
Japanese 620

K

Kamtok (see *Cameroon Pidgin*)
Konkani 189, 190
Krio [Sierra Leone Krio] 28, 93, 110, 340,
381, 384, 386
Kru Pidgin English [KPE, Kru English]
93, 103, 413
Kwa [Kwa languages] (see also *Wolof*)
70, 72, 86–87, 434

L

L1 variety (see *First Language variety*)
L2 variety (see *Second Language variety*)
Latin 152 456, 464
Liberian English [LibE] 77, 340, 413,
627–628
Liberian Settler English [LibSE] 28, 30,
102–114, 307, 309–317, 395–415, 625–
627, 629, 631
Liberian Vernacular English [LibVE, Vernacular Liberian English, VLE] 102–
103, 109–112, 397, 400, 405, 412–413

M

Malay (see also *Bahasa Malaysia, Bazaar
Malay*) 24, 31, 201–203, 223, 260–261,
263–264, 271, 278–279, 287, 316, 483,
485, 530, 607, 612–616, 620, 633
Malayalam 188, 279
Malaysian English [MalE] 29, 31, 278–
291, 307, 309–318, 610–623, 626, 628,
630, 632–633
Mandankwe (see also *Akan, Igbo*) 429
Mandarin 261–263, 278–279
Mande 70, 86, 111
Marathi English 232
Moore 379
Mungaka 429

N

New Zealand English [NZE] 175
Nigerian English [NigE] 28–29, 35–54,
59, 65, 78, 80, 307, 309–318, 323–339,
366, 486, 625–634

Nigerian languages 35–36, 38, 51, 55, 65,
77, 325, 327, 334
Nigerian Pidgin [NigP] 24, 29–30, 36,
55–65, 148, 308–314, 317–318, 340–
367, 381–386, 389, 413, 630
Northern English dialect 215
Norwegian 49
Nova Scotian (see *African Nova Scotian
English*)

P

Pakistani English [PakE] 29, 31, 244–
257, 307, 309–317, 578–591, 626–627,
629–630, 633
Panjabi 155, 246–247, 254, 315
Pashtu 246–247
Patwa [Patois] (see also *Jamaican Creole*)
282, 290
Philippine English [PhlE] 292–306, 307,
309–317, 557, 625
Pidgin (see also *Pidgin and Creole*) 23–
24, 28, 36, 55, 93–97, 99–100, 133–135,
340, 381, 428, 488, 563, 624, 635
Pidgin and Creole (see also *Pidgin* and
Creole) 624
Portuguese 428–429, 483, 485, 540, 563
Portuguese Pidgin 55, 93, 133–134, 201
Pushto 253, 255

R

Received Pronunciation [RP] (see *Index
of subjects*)
Romance 162
Russian 202

S

Sanskrit 189, 279
Scots 157
Scottish English [ScE, Scots] 157, 215
Sea Island Creole (see *Gullah*)

Second Language [L2] variety 41, 203, 627

Sindhi 190, 244, 246–247

Singapore English 259–277, 593–609

Siraiki 246–247

Sotho 202, 485, 495

South African English [SAfE] 164, 167–168, 173, 175, 180–186, 189–197, 204, 206, 208–209, 214–217, 313, 316–317, 472, 476, 482–483, 486, 488, 491–492, 501, 513, 519, 521, 523, 527–529, 531–533, 626–628, 632, 634

South Asian English [SAsE] 240, 244–245, 252–253, 255–256

Spanish 51, 292, 556–557

St. Helena English [StHE] 30, 223–230, 307, 309–317, 535–545, 624–631, 633

Standard British English [StBrE] 26, 38, 59, 225, 323, 370, 372, 374–375, 519, 546, 573, 576, 578, 580–585, 590, 596, 610–611

Standard English [StE] 2, 26, 30, 38–39, 90, 97, 154, 156–157, 160, 162, 264, 324, 326–333, 335, 339, 380, 394, 400, 403, 411–412, 417, 420–423, 425–426, 444, 452–462, 464–466, 470, 486, 488–492, 494–496, 499–500, 502, 504, 507, 525–526, 530–532, 534–535, 538–539, 544–545, 553, 556, 561, 568–570, 572–573, 575–576, 591, 596–597, 608, 615, 618–623, 625, 627, 630–633

non-standard English 40

Standard Ghanaian English [StGhE] 94–96, 98, 385–386, 388

Standard Indian English [StIndE] 546, 549–553, 555–557, 559, 576

Standard Philippine English 293–294

Swahili [Kiswahili, Kiswaheli] 24, 150–156, 453, 458, 461–465, 468, 470

T

Tamil 31, 188, 190, 196, 198, 232, 234–236, 255, 260–261, 263, 279–280, 287, 315, 501, 516, 570, 610

Tanzanian English [TanE] 156

Telugu 188, 190

Temiar 278

Twi 69, 72, 79, 95, 370, 429

U

Urdu 189–190, 192, 244–247, 250–251, 253–256, 279, 580, 586–588

W

Welsh 457, 548

Welsh English [WelE] 457

West African English [WAfE] 30, 75–77, 88, 103, 186, 334, 471, 486

West African languages 51, 76, 428, 492

West African Pidgin (English) [WAfPE, WAP] 30, 93, 133, 381, 388, 624, 626–634

White South African English [WhSAfE] 30, 164, 168–173, 198, 221, 472–474, 476–483, 486, 625–627, 630–632

Wolof (see also *Kwa*) 378

X

Xhosa 202, 484–485

Y

Yiddish 202–203, 484

Yoruba 28, 35–36, 38, 41–46, 50, 52, 62, 78, 316, 336–337, 429

Yoruba English 38, 41–45, 52

Z

Zulu 189–190, 202, 484–485, 494–495